HANDBOOK
OF
POSTTRAUMATIC GROWTH

Titles of Related Interest

Posttrautmatic Growth: Positive Changes in the Aftermath of Crisis, edited by Richard Tedeschi, Crystal Park, and Lawrence Calhoun

Facilitating Posttraumatic Growth: A Clinician's Guide, edited by Lawrence Calhoun and Richard Tedeschi

Handbook of Culture, Therapy, and Healing, edited by Uwe Gielen, Jefferson Fish, and Juris Draguns

The Handbook of Chicana/o Psychology and Mental Health, edited by Roberto Velasquez, Leticia Arellano, and Brian McNeill

Cognitive Vulnerability to Emotional Disorders, edited by Lauren Alloy and John Riskind

The Mind in Therapy: Cognitive Science for Practice by Katherine Arbuthnott, Dennis Arbuthnott, and Valerie Thompson

Psychopathology: Foundations for a Contemporary Understanding, edited by James Maddux and Barbara Winstead

Counseling Psychology and Optimal Human Functioning, edited by W. Bruce Walsh

Well-Being: Positive Development Across the Life Course, edited by Marc Bornstein, Lucy Davidson, Corey Keyes, and Kristin Moore

Handbook
of
Posttraumatic Growth
Research and Practice

Edited by

Lawrence G. Calhoun
and
Richard G. Tedeschi
The University of North Carolina at Charlotte

Routledge
Taylor & Francis Group

www.routledgementalhealth.com

First Published by Lawrence Erlbaum Associates, Inc., Publishers
10 Industrial Avenue
Mahwah, New Jersey 07430

Reprinted 2009 by Psychology Press

Library of Congress Cataloging-in-Publication Data

The handbook of posttraumatic growth : research and practice / edited by
  Lawrence G. Calhoun and Richard G. Tedeschi.
    p. ; cm.
    Includes bibliographical references and indexes.
    ISBN 0-8058-5196-8 (cloth : alk. paper) – ISBN 0-8058-5767-2 (pbk. : alk. paper)
    1. Post-traumatic stress disorder–Treatment.   2. Post-traumatic stress
    disorder–Patients–Rehabilitation.   I. Calhoun, Lawrence G.   II. Tedeschi, Richard G.
    [DNLM: 1. Stress Disorders, Post-Traumatic–psychology.   2. Stress Disorders,
    Post-Traumatic–rehabilitaion.   3. Life Change Events.   4. Stress, Psychological–rehabilitaion.
    5. Survivors–psychology.   WM 170 H234 2006]

    RC552.P67.H34   2005
    616.85′21—dc22

                                                                    2005029300

Printed in the United States of America
10 9 8 7 6 5 4

CONTENTS

Preface   ix

Contributors   xi

I. Posttraumatic Growth: Theory and Method

**1. The Foundations of Posttraumatic Growth:
An Expanded Framework**   **1**
Lawrence G. Calhoun and Richard G. Tedeschi

**2. Relationships Between Posttraumatic Growth
and Resilience: Recovery, Resistance,
and Reconfiguration**   **24**
Stephen Lepore and Tracey Revenson

**3. Measurement Issues in Assessing Growth Following
Stressful Life Experiences**   **47**
Crystal L. Park and Suzanne Lechner

**4. Re-Storying Loss: Fostering Growth
in the Posttraumatic Narrative**   **68**
Robert Neimeyer

5. Schema-Change Perspectives on Posttraumatic Growth   **81**
Ronnie Janoff-Bulman

6. **Posttraumatic Growth and Other Outcomes
   of Major Loss in the Context of Complex Family Lives**   100
   John Harvey, Katherine Barnett, and Stephanie Rupe

II. Posttraumatic Growth in Specific Contexts

7. **Spirituality: A Pathway to Posttraumatic Growth
   or Decline?**   121
   *Kenneth I. Pargament, Kavita M. Desai,
   and Kelly M. McConnell*

8. **Posttraumatic Growth After Cancer**   138
   Annette L. Stanton, Julianne E. Bower, and Carissa A. Low

9. **Bereavement and Posttraumatic Growth**   176
   Hansjörg Znoj

10. **Posttraumatic Growth After War**   197
    Rita Rosner and Steve Poswell

11. **Positive Changes Attributed to the Challenge
    of HIV/AIDS**   214
    Joel Milam

12. **Posttraumatic Growth in Disaster
    and Emergency Work**   225
    Douglas Paton

13. **Growing Out of Ashes: Posttraumatic Growth
    Among Holocaust Child Survivors**   248
    Rachel Lev-Wiesel and Marianne Amir

14. **Resilience and Posttraumatic Growth in Children**   264
    Ryan P. Kilmer

III. Clinical Applications of Posttraumatic Growth

15. **Expert Companions: Posttraumatic Growth
    in Clinical Practice**   291
    Lawrence G. Calhoun and Richard G. Tedeschi

16. **The Link Between Posttraumatic Growth
    and Forgiveness: An Intuitive Truth**   311
    Pamela C. Fischer

17. **Posttraumatic Growth and Psychotherapy**   **334**
     Tanja Zoellner and Andreas Maercker

18. **Resilience and Posttraumatic Growth:**
     A Constructive Narrative Perspective   **355**
     Donald Meichenbaum

     Author Index   369
     Subject Index   385

PREFACE

Posttraumatic growth is an area in which investigations are now being undertaken in many different parts of the world. The view that individuals can be changed, sometimes in radically good ways, by their struggle with trauma is ancient and widespread. The systematic focus by scholars and clinicians on the possibilities for growth from the struggle with crisis, however, is relatively recent. There are now a growing number of studies and scholarly papers on the antecedents, correlates, and consequences of posttraumatic growth, and there are also theoretical models that can help guide the research further. It is clear, however, that this phenomenon is not yet well understood.

This volume is designed with two general goals in mind. First, to provide both clinicians and researchers with a comprehensive and up-to-date view of what has been done so far. Second, to use the foundation of what has been done to provide suggestions for the next useful steps to take in understanding posttraumatic growth. It was clearly not possible to include contributions from all of the scholars in the field, but this volume offers the contributions of important and influential scholars representing a wide array of perspectives on posttraumatic growth. It is our hope that rather than providing final answers, this volume will serve as an impetus for additional work, both in the academic aspects and in the possibilities for clinical applications of posttraumatic growth.

It would not have been possible to assemble a volume such as this without the contributions of the leading international scholars who have graciously agreed to make contributions to this book and to them, we are deeply grateful. We must also thank Susan Milmoe, Kristen Depken, Victoria Forsythe, and Steve Rutter of Lawrence Erlbaum Associates, Publishers, for their guidance throughout this project. We also wish to thank our professional colleagues in this work whose expertise has added so much to our own understanding, and whose grace, wit, and breadth of knowledge make scholarly work both pleasant and enriching: Arnie Cann, Virginia Gil-Rivas, and Ryan Kilmer. We have also been fortunate to have worked with many gifted students in recent years and we wish to thank them: Jennifer Baker, Katie Bellon, Lisa Keeler, Erin Mills, Deborah Proffitt, and Debora Arnold. The staff of the academic department in which we work also deserve our gratitude and we thank Sean Barnett, Mary Olbrich, Shannon Randall, and Marti Sherrill.

Special thanks go to the chair of our department, Brian Cutler, who has always been supportive of our work.

Contributors

Marianne Amir
Ben Gurion University,
Beer Sheva

Katherine Barnett
University of Iowa

Julienne E. Bower
University of California, Los Angeles

Lawrence G. Calhoun
The University of North Carolina
at Charlotte

Kavita M. Desai
Bowling Green State University

Pamela C. Fischer
Oklahoma University Health
Sciences Center

John H. Harvey
University of Iowa

Ronnie Janoff-Bulman
University of Massachusetts, Amherst

Ryan P. Kilmer
University of North Carolina
at Charlotte

Suzanne C. Lechner
University of Miami School of Medicine

Stephen J. Lepore
Columbia University

Rachel Lev-Wiesel
Ben Gurion University,
Beer Sheva

Carissa A. Low
University of California, Los Angeles

Andreas Maercker
University of Zurich

Kelly M. McConnell
Bowling Green State University

Donald Meichenbaum
University of Waterloo

Joel Milam
University of Southern California

Robert A. Neimeyer
University of Memphis

Kenneth I. Pargament
Bowling Green State University

Crystal L. Park
University of Connecticut

Douglas Paton
University of Tasmania,
Launceston

Steve Powell
ProMENTE Organisation for Psychological
Research and Action,
Sarajevo

Tracey A. Revenson
City University of New York

Rita Rosner
Ludwig-Maximilians University,
Munich

Stephanie Rupe
Columbia University

Annette L. Stanton
University of California, Los Angeles

Richard G. Tedeschi
The University of North Carolina
at Charlotte

Hansjörg Znoj
Universität Bern

Tanja Zoellner
Dresden University of Technology

HANDBOOK
OF
POSTTRAUMATIC GROWTH

Posttraumatic Growth:
Theory and Method

1

THE FOUNDATIONS OF POSTTRAUMATIC GROWTH: AN EXPANDED FRAMEWORK

LAWRENCE G. CALHOUN AND RICHARD G. TEDESCHI, 2006
THE UNIVERSITY OF NORTH CAROLINA AT CHARLOTTE

Without a bit of sadness
A beautiful samba cannot be made.
　　　　　　—Vinicius de Morais and Baden Powell
　　　　　　　"Samba da Bençção" [translation]

The idea that difficult life struggles can lead human beings to change, sometimes in radically positive ways, is neither recent nor something that was "discovered" by social and behavioral researchers or clinicians. As we and others (Saakvitne, Tennen, & Affleck, 1998; Tedeschi & Calhoun, 1995) have indicated the assumption that, at least for some people, an encounter with trauma,[1] which may contain elements of great suffering and loss, can lead to highly positive changes in the individual is ancient and widespread.

The possibilities for growth from the struggle with suffering and crisis is a theme that is present in ancient literature and philosophy and, at least in some ways, the problem of human suffering is central to much of both ancient and contemporary religious thinking. For example, the origins of Buddhism are said to lie in the attempts by the prince Siddhartha Gautama to come to terms with human suffering and the inevitability of human mortality. Christianity, in most of its branches, regards the suffering of Jesus as a central and important event that has saving consequences for human beings. Some Islamic traditions also view suffering, at least in some circumstances, as a means for better preparing oneself for the

---

[1]As we have elsewhere (e.g., Calhoun & Tedeschi, 1999; Tedeschi & Calhoun, 2004), we use the terms *trauma, crisis, major stressor,* and related terms as essentially synonymous expressions to describe circumstances that significantly challenge or invalidate important components of the individual's assumptive world.

"journey heavenward." In a similar vein, the cathartic or transformative consequences of human suffering are themes in Greek tragedy. Literature throughout the world for a few thousand years, in all its various forms, has attempted to come to grips with the possibilities for meaning and change emerging from the struggle with tragedy, suffering, and loss. The idea that the individual's encounter and struggle with life trauma can lead to significant growth is not new.

What is of relatively recent vintage, however, is the systematic focus by scholars in the fields of psychology, counseling, psychiatry, social work, and others, on the phenomenon of posttraumatic growth (PTG), using the best tools of contemporary quantitative and qualitative research. There were clearly major pioneers who addressed the possibility of growth from the encounter with loss in the 20th century including Caplan (1964), Dohrenwend (1978), Frankl (1963), Maslow (1954), and Yalom (1980). Although there were some preliminary investigations focused on this domain (e.g., Finkel, 1975) and some findings showing the possibility for positive outcomes arising from the encounter with negative events (e.g., Cella & Tross, 1986; the work of Tennen & Affleck and colleagues beginning in the 1980s), the systematic attention to trauma-related positive change has occurred only in the past 15 to 20 years.

From our point of view, several significant elements came together at about the same time to encourage clinicians and researchers to begin to focus on growth per se. For example, Jeanne Schaefer and Rudolph Moos (1992) wrote a chapter on crisis and personal growth; Virginia O'Leary and Jeanette Ickovics (1995) published a paper on "resilience and thriving in response to challenge"; Crystal Park, Lawrence Cohen, and Renee Murch (1996) published their findings and introduced their measure of stress-related growth; and we published the first book (Tedeschi & Calhoun, 1995) looking specifically at the phenomenon of positive change arising from the encounter with trauma from the point of view of the social and behavioral sciences. We also reported on the development of our own scale, the Posttraumatic Growth Inventory (PTGI) (1996). By mid-2005, a search using the PsychInfo system of the American Psychological Association produced 92 sources on "posttraumatic growth" and 33 on "stress-related growth" (with a bit of overlap, as one would expect). Clearly, much has been done since the earlier publications that focused explicitly on the phenomenon of growth, or the perception of benefits, associated with the struggle with highly difficult life events.

Although perhaps unnecessary, it is appropriate to remember that many, perhaps most, persons who experience severe life stress tend to report a variety of negative psychological and physical troubles that have been well documented and are now widely known. The focus on the possibilities for growth in coping with trauma can provide the opportunity for the erroneous conclusion that by trying to understand the positive, investigators are ignoring the negative. They are not. Negative events tend to produce, for most persons, consequences that are negative. But, paradoxically, the data indicate that for many persons the encounter with very negative events can also produce positive psychological change. In this chapter, we will provide a general overview of PTG, discuss whether it is "useful" or not, provide a description of modifications of our model of the process of PTG, discuss the threshold for calling changes "growth," and conclude with a discussion of the future of work on posttraumatic growth.

THE EXPERIENCE OF GROWTH: A BRIEF LOOK

As Park and Lechner (this volume) clearly indicate, the statistical delineation of the factors that comprise PTG remains an area that still requires investigation. However, the suggestive quantitative data available and the accounts of persons who have experienced trauma provide a good source from which to infer the major domains of the experience of growth. We first used qualitative data to discern the broad categories of growth (Tedeschi & Calhoun, 1995) that we divided into three general domains: changes in the perception of self, changes in the experience of relationships with others, and changes in one's general philosophy of life. Subsequently (Tedeschi & Calhoun, 1996), factor analysis yielded a five-factor approach to PTG, although there can be changes beyond this common core that are quite specific to the struggle with particular stressors (e.g., healthier eating habits adopted in the aftermath of a battle with cancer). These five domains are personal strength, new possibilities, relating to others, appreciation of life, and spiritual change. We will address issues of measurement more fully later in this chapter.

Changed Perception of Self: Strength and New Possibilities

The phrase that we have used often to summarize this area of growth is *vulnerable yet stronger,* or in the complete sentence, *I am more vulnerable than I thought, but much stronger than I ever imagined.* The threat to the assumptive world presented by the major crisis can produce cognitive responses that are now well known. Typically there are also changes in self-perception reflecting a significant disruption of the assumptive world (see Janoff-Bulman, 1992, this volume). One of these common changes is the experience of one's world as more dangerous, unpredictable, a world in which one's own vulnerability becomes clear and salient. The encounter with a major life challenge can also include an increased sense that one has been tested, weighed in the balance, and found to be a person who has survived the worst, suggesting that one is indeed quite strong. As one bereaved parent has told us: *I've been through the absolute worst that I know. And no matter what happens, I'll be able to deal with it.*

Some persons also report the emergence of new possibilities in life, developing new interests, new activities, and perhaps embarking on significant new paths in life. One of the persons who talked to us about her experience with loss embarked on a career in oncology nursing as a result of the death of her own child.

Relating to Others

It is clear that times of trial in life can produce the waning, loss, and sometimes the destruction of important relationships, but the consequences of coping with trauma can also include significant changes in human relationships that the individual can experience as highly positive. One of these changes occurs in how the person who has experienced the crisis views other human beings. At least at the experiential level, respondents have often told us about how, as a result of their own experience with loss and tragedy, they feel a greater connection to other people in general, particularly an increased sense of compassion for other persons who suffer.

This sense of increased compassion may lead to an increased sense that, in John Donne's well-known phrase, they are not islands, but indeed "part of the main" of those who suffer. It remains an empirical question as to whether or not this increased experience of compassion translates into a greater degree or frequency of altruistic acts, but our qualitative data suggest that, at least for others, this may indeed be the case.

A greater sense of intimacy, closeness, and freedom to be oneself, disclosing even socially undesirable elements of oneself or one's experience are also reported by persons who have struggled with traumatic events. This increased sense is sometimes viewed as a double-edged sword—you find out who your real friends are and those that stay you get a lot closer to. Although not always, family members do report a greater sense of intimate closeness in the process of dealing with the terminal illness or with the death of a beloved family member.

Changed Philosophy of Life: Priorities, Appreciation, and Spirituality

A changed sense of what is of most importance is one of the elements of a changed philosophy of life that individuals can experience as PTG. The goal of amassing a million dollar stock portfolio, for example, may become much less important than the relationship with one's family, when the possibility of loss of one's life exists in the struggle with cancer. A common way in which the change of priorities is experienced is that what previously was viewed as a small thing, the happy giggle of a toddler, for example, may now become much more important than ever before.

A greater appreciation for life and for what one actually has and a changed sense of the priorities of the central elements of life are common experiences of persons dealing with crisis. "We [now] realize that life is precious and that we don't take each other for granted" was how one bereaved parent put it. Or as Hamilton Jordan put it (Jordan, 2000, p. 216), describing his diagnosis with multiple cancers, "Even the smallest joys in life took on a special meaning." The same kinds of goals and objectives that seemed so important before the crisis recede in importance, and others attain much greater significance. Although the specifics are different for different persons, a common theme is the articulation of greater meaning being found in intrinsically important priorities (e.g., spending time with one's children) and less importance being attached to extrinsic priorities (e.g., making lots of money).

It is in the realm of existential and, for some persons, of spiritual or religious matters that the most significant PTG may be experienced. The time frame in which the positive transformations in the existential or spiritual domain occur may vary, with some persons experiencing changes in this area much sooner in the posttraumatic period than others. Indications are that the trajectories may be quite different, even when the quality or content of the experiences are similar. The experiences that comprise this domain tend to reflect a greater sense of purpose and meaning in life, greater satisfaction, and perhaps clarity with the answers given to the fundamental existential questions. For some persons, the experience can include deeply meaningful spiritual elements. Although many persons report significant PTG in their philosophies of life, it is also true that great loss and senseless tragedy can lead others to lose faith and experience significant existential despair. This later kind of experience, however, does not predominate in the sample of persons studied in the United States (Tedeschi & Calhoun, 2004) because the reports of positive religious change are not uncommon for them.

It is not yet entirely clear the degree to which the religious dimension of PTG is relevant to countries that are significantly more secular than the United States. Hans Znoj and Andreas Maercker, for example, (personal communications, November 11, 2004 and May 24, 2003, respectively) have suggested that questions inquiring about the impact of trauma on religious elements are viewed as irrelevant, and perhaps even somewhat offensive by at least some, perhaps many, European participants.

Although a strictly religious component of this domain may not be relevant in some contexts, the more general arena of confrontation with existential questions about life's purpose appears to be important for many persons coping with major life crises, and this is a domain in which a significant number may report positive change.

WHAT GOOD IS POSTTRAUMATIC GROWTH?

The experience of persons who have struggled with crisis indicates that many of them undergo changes that they regard as highly positive. Although some report that they would not undo the crisis and return to the way things were before the event, because of the positive changes they have undergone, others, and we might assume they would be a majority, would indeed give up all of the positive changes if they could simply recover what had been lost. This view is clearly reflected in Kushner's words:

> I am a more sensitive person, a more effective pastor, a more sympathetic counselor because of Aaron's life and death than I would ever have been without it. And I would give up all of those gains in a second if I could have my son back. If I could choose.... But I cannot choose. (Quoted in Viorst, 1986, p. 295)

One of the important questions that can be usefully answered with quantitative data is what is the relationship between PTG and adjustment? As we have suggested (Calhoun & Tedeschi, 2004), the answer depends in part on the general approach that is taken to define and measure adjustment. In the United States, scholars and clinicians tend to favor a utilitarian view, one that regards a decrease in distress and an increase in psychological well-being as the desirable outcome for persons who have faced highly stressful events. As practicing clinicians ourselves, this hedonic (Ryan & Deci, 2001) goal seems desirable for persons who are experiencing psychological discomfort.

However, in understanding persons struggling with the aftermath of trauma, it may also be desirable to broaden the perspective. The satisfactory engagement with and, for many persons who have struggled with trauma, the satisfactory response to the major existential questions and to the questions about how to live one's life in the fullest way possible, may be more important than the reduction of psychological discomfort. Reducing distress and thinking deeply about how best to live are not mutually exclusive possibilities, but they are not always likely to correlate either.

The data on the relationship between distress and growth are mixed, with some studies indicating that benefit finding and PTG may have negative relationships to measures of general well-being and distress (Cadell, Regehr, & Hemsworth, 2003; Lev-Wiesel & Amir, this volume; Tomich & Helgeson, 2004). Posttraumatic growth, then, may not necessarily be "good" from a utilitarian perspective—the presence of PTG may not necessarily be accompanied by greater well-being and less distress. However, if the perspective is broadened, the data do seem to suggest that the presence of PTG is an indication that persons who experience it are living life in ways that, at least from their point of view, are fuller, richer, and perhaps more meaningful. But that richer life may come at the price of the discomfort that tragedy and loss almost always produce. As one version of Samuel Johnson's familiar quote says, "The prospect of death wonderfully clarifies things." Perhaps we could say the same, at least for some people, about major life crises. However, the "clarification of things," may not result in a decrease in psychological distress. The encounter with trauma may indeed produce growth, but it also tends to produce significant pain. If an exclusively utilitarian, hedonic view of posttraumatic adjustment is taken, the price that may be required for the newfound perspective on life may not be worth it. The experience of a traumatic set of circumstances usually produces distress, disrupts one's understanding of the world, makes salient one's vulnerabilities and lack of power and control, and may make more salient one's mortality. These disruptions and reminders tend not to be pleasant, but they may lead to richer and more purpose-filled lives. However, the experience of increased meaning may be concomitant with less psychological comfort.

After we discuss the process of PTG, we will return to this question of the usefulness of the experience and refer to some of the ideas of Ronnie Janoff-Bulman. She posits that PTG can create "psychological preparedness" that can allow trauma survivors to confront subsequent events with less anxiety. Therefore, the relationship between PTG and distress in the aftermath of trauma may be mixed because there are various kinds of outcomes that are possible, including the "sadder but wiser" and the "better prepared."

HOW DOES POSTTRAUMATIC GROWTH OCCUR?

We have already articulated our general model of the process of PTG elsewhere (Calhoun & Tedeschi, 1998; Tedeschi & Calhoun, 2004). Here, we will provide only a brief description of the general components, along with a slightly updated schematic (see Fig. 1.1). We

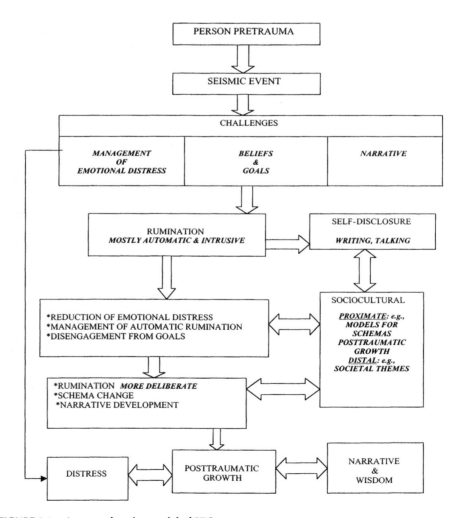

FIGURE 1.1.   A comprehensive model of PTG.

will also provide a more extensive description of some elaborations and expansions of the model that may help broaden the ways in which the process of PTG is studied and understood.

Some of the key elements of the model include the following: the characteristics of the person and of the challenging circumstances, management of emotional distress, rumination, self-disclosure, distal and proximate sociocultural influences, narrative development, and life wisdom. In the sections that follow, we will provide an elaboration of elements of the model that represent extensions of what we have done previously.

We recognize that this is a general model, and that some specific variations may be necessary to account specifically for different domains of PTG. Given that individuals often report some aspects of growth more than others, it will be necessary to be able to predict how these variations occur. However, we may be too early in the development of the field to develop such complete models.

Rumination/Cognitive Engagement

The word *rumination*, at least within the confines of social and behavioral research, has acquired quite a negative connotation in recent years, and perhaps even a clearly negative denotation. We continue to use the word in its original sense, "to turn over in the mind," *repeated thinking that is not necessarily intrusive and that includes reminiscing, problem solving, trying to make sense* (Martin & Tesser, 1996), and perhaps searching for how the struggle has changed one in positive ways. For those for whom the word *rumination* now means repeated intrusive thinking that is negatively valenced, we suggest they regard the word as synonymous with cognitive engagement.

The degree of PTG reported tends to be related to rumination about elements related to the stressful event. One strand of evidence is indirect and suggestive, but congruent with our view that PTG is more likely to occur when the circumstances are highly disruptive to the individual. Several studies have reported that greater amounts of growth are reported for persons who report higher levels of stress or threat associated with the crisis (Linley & Joseph, 2004; Stanton, Low, & Bower, this volume; Weiss, 2004; Wild & Paivio, 2003). This pattern of results suggests that for PTG to occur in response to a stressful event, the set of circumstances the individual faces must present a significant degree of threat to the preexisting assumptive world (Calhoun & Tedeschi, 1998, 2004; Janoff-Bulman, this volume; Tedeschi & Calhoun, 1995, 2004).

In fact, this emphasis on the disruption of the assumptive world is a reason that we have used the term *posttraumatic growth* as opposed to others that do not so clearly acknowledge this level of disruption to peoples' lives. A good way to judge whether an event is truly traumatic may be to consider the way it disrupts the personal narrative. If a person refers to a negative event as a watershed that divides a life into "before and after" the event, it has been traumatic and it can initiate the cognitive engagement that produces PTG. How to restructure the life narrative in a way that accommodates the unanticipated event is a part of the cognitive challenge of trauma.

However, once the minimal threshold of cognitive disruption has been reached, it is not clear the extent to which the relationship between growth and disruption is linear or nonlinear. Although additional factors need to be considered (e.g., the person's personality style and characteristics pretrauma, proximate culture), there are some results suggesting that, at least in some contexts, the relationship between strength of the traumatic "dose" and the experience of growth may be curvilinear (Fontana & Rosenheck, 1998; Linley & Joseph, 2004). Considering only the relationship between traumatic exposure and the degree of positive change experienced, it may be that although a minimal level of exposure is necessary, extremely high levels of exposure may not result in any increase in experienced growth. The reasons for this apparent curvilinear relationship include some form of "diminishing returns," and extreme doses of trauma may simply overwhelm the psychological resources of most persons. The result may be disruption of the cognitive mechanisms necessary for processing the subtleties that can be involved in constructing perceptions of PTG.

As we conceptualize it, the experience of a major life crisis leads the individual to engage in ruminative processes in the immediate aftermath, with the likelihood that, for most persons, these early processes of cognitive engagement are more intrusive than deliberate. We have distinguished this early form of automatic and intrusive processing in our model from the later, more deliberate type of processing involved in producing PTG (Calhoun & Tedeschi, 1998). Recently, researchers who have done much work on rumination have made a distinction between "brooding" and "reflective" rumination that makes a similar distinction (Nolen-Hoeksema & Davis, 2004). As others have suggested (Epstein, 1990; Janoff-Bulman, 1992, this volume), the content of this more deliberate, reflective ruminative process tends to be the repair, restructuring, or rebuilding of the individual's general way of understanding the world. Posttraumatic growth tends to be more likely when the individual ruminates, with a wide variety of content, trying to make sense out of what has happened. Following the thinking of Aronovsky, in our original model (Tedeschi & Calhoun, 1995) we emphasized that this ruminative process involved establishing "comprehensibility" first. This is the attempt by survivors to grasp that what has happened really *has* happened. When fundamental understandings of personal reality are violated, there seems to be a time lag between the event and the full appreciation that circumstances are irrevocably changed. "I can't believe he's dead." "I really do have cancer."

With the emerging comprehensibility comes a better chance at manageability, figuring out ways to cope with the changed circumstances, and reaching the conclusion that one has the resources to deal with it. These first two aspects of cognitive engagement with the trauma are akin to the primary and secondary appraisals described by Lazarus and Folkman (1984). But in the kinds of traumatic events we concern ourselves with here, these appraisals are not necessarily instantaneous, and they do not occur only in the midst of the trauma. They can take time, and it is not at all clear to many trauma survivors in the immediate aftermath what exactly has happened and if they are going to manage it. A final piece of the engagement is "meaningfulness," and this is the more reflective element that can yield PTG. This probably happens in earnest only after the person is coping successfully, or managing the aftermath of trauma well enough so that they are not constantly preoccupied with mere survival. In this reflection on their plight, they can move from the mere survival that was their original focus to recognizing some other possibilities that become PTG.

It appears that for PTG to be more likely, significant cognitive engagement with elements of the life crisis must occur. Several studies have indicated that the amount of growth reported is significantly related to cognitive activity (Linley & Joseph, 2004; Manne et al., 2004). Given the wide array of purposes and content of posttraumatic ruminative activity, the timing and degree of activity for different domains of PTG needs to be considered. The slim evidence available so far suggests that content is important, and that cognitive processing of content more directly connected to growth may be more likely to be associated with the amount of growth reported (e.g., Calhoun, Tedeschi, Fulmar & Harlan, 2000).

The Fruits of Cognitive Engagement: Preparedness and Resilience

Janoff-Bulman (this volume) postulates another aspect of PTG that she calls "preparedness," the ability of transformed assumptive worlds, or schemas, to resist subsequent traumas. This kind of preparedness appears to be similar to what has been conceptualized as "resilience," the ability to bounce back from or to resist the effects of apparently traumatic events. We have described the results of PTG (Calhoun & Tedeschi, 1998, 2004) using the metaphor of traumas as psychological earthquakes that shake the foundations of schemas that will then need to be rebuilt to standards that allow resistance to future earthquakes. Our view is that the personal strength that is acknowledged by some trauma survivors and a changed philosophy of life that can accommodate the possibility of truly traumatic events with a revised perspective on life priorities, together create this psychological preparedness that equips people to manage subsequent traumas. These stronger and wiser people embody resilience. They are able to say about subsequent traumas that they are confident they can handle these because of what they managed before. They can say that they understand better what is important in the aftermath of such events because they processed this when they went through a life crisis before. They may compare what is happening now to a previous trauma and conclude it is not as bad. Their revised assumptive worlds allow for these perspectives that allay anxieties, make it unnecessary to do much additional cognitive processing, and allow the world to remain comprehensible. Subsequent events do not set in motion the extensive cognitive processing involved in establishing comprehensibility, manageability, and meaningfulness, and do not act as major disruptions to the life narrative, the events do not meet the criteria for trauma in our model, and are not experienced as such by the individuals going through them. These events may not produce any additional PTG. That is not to say that the events have no impact. There is likely to be loss, grief, suffering, or other negative responses. But they may not be transformative of the view of self, others, and philosophy of life. This "preparedness" suggests an increase in the individual's resilience to future stressful circumstances.

Our view of the relationship between PTG and resilience is a bit complex. Our model of PTG has, from the beginning (Tedeschi & Calhoun, 1995), incorporated an acknowledgment that some successful coping or managing of the event is necessary for people to be able to begin to cognitively process what has happened into a perspective that has elements of PTG. As we hypothesized in 1995, people who have a moderate degree of coping capability would be most likely to report PTG. We postulated a curvilinear relationship whereby those with substantial psychological weakness would suffer purely negative responses to trauma, and those with the strongest capabilities would not be strongly affected. They would appear resilient in the face of the event. Furthermore, following Janoff-Bulman's formulation (this volume), and our discussions of rebuilt schemas as resistant to traumas, people who experience PTG may become psychologically better prepared for subsequent events that may otherwise be traumatic.

This kind of relationship between resilience and PTG is one reason why *it is important to maintain a clear distinction between these two concepts* rather than calling PTG a form of resilience (see Lepore and Revenson, this volume). Another reason for maintaining the disctinction is that the word *resilience* was never defined as transformation or reformulation. Dictionary definitions of the term state that resilience is "the power or ability to return to the original form or position after being bent, compressed, or stretched" or to "recover readily from illness, depression or adversity."

Cultural Context: Distal and Proximate

An individual's "culture" can be thought of in two broad categories, distal and proximate (previous discussions of similar ideas in the domain of ecological psychology have used terms such as *microsystems*, *exosystems*, and *macrosystems* to describe similar domains of focus—Brofenbrenner, 1979). Distal cultural elements represent the broad cultural themes that tend to predominate in larger societies or broad geographic areas, such as countries, and proximate culture represents the small communities and social networks of people with whom an individual interacts (Calhoun & Tedeschi, 2004). We think that it is useful to consider both of these domains when trying to understand the process of PTG.

Broad domains of culture are typically not studied by psychologists and other scholars and professionals whose primary interests lie with what happens with individuals, couples, and families. But attending to these cultural themes and more "distant" sources of social influence is desirable to understand the possibilities for growth in the struggle with crisis.

Individuals who are directly exposed to particular events are likely to consider themselves to be part of quite large social groupings that comprise such broad categories as societies and countries (e.g., Americans) and are, in some ways, more distant from the individual than the physical persons with whom they interact within the context of their proximate cultural contexts. The prevailing modes of thinking, the ways the world in general is construed within the contexts of those social and cultural entities, and the general cultural narratives that are broadly accepted and influential within those broad contexts may help shape how individuals understand what has happened to them (Goss & Klass, 2005). We have suggested in the preceding text, for example, that in the United States religious ways of understanding the trauma experience are a more important part of the larger societal themes than they are in Europe. The "American" narrative (Pals & McAdams, 2004) might be expected to influence the individual American's response to trauma by providing already existing narrative frameworks that include religious themes and perhaps themes of optimism and self-reliance. The themes that are prevalent in such distal cultural forms, and the ways in which they do or do not influence the individual's own experience of growth remain a largely unexamined area.

The individual's proximate cultural influences may provide a more direct avenue for evaluating how the process of PTG may occur. Of particular importance are the mutually influential processes of rumination, self-disclosure, and the qualities and responses of the cultural world close at hand to the individual and to that person's posttraumatic journey.

Although there are a wide variety of elements on which to focus, we will describe only the possible roles played by the following: primary reference groups and the language, concepts, and assumptions employed by primary references to make sense of trauma and its aftermath generally, and the conceptualization of PTG in particular.

Primary reference groups are those that have immediate influence over the individual. They tend to be comprised of persons with whom interactions occur on a regular basis and with whom the individual tends to share certain attitudes and assumptions. In the current colloquialism, primary reference groups are those the person "identifies with"— the people whose responses have a significant probability of affecting the individual and his or her behavior. These groups could include, for example, family and close friends, religious groups or congregations, a team, one's neighbors, a gang, or one's professional peers. Individuals usually do not experience the aftermath of crisis as socially isolated and disconnected persons, but their experience unfolds within the diverse influences of their primary reference groups. It seems reasonable to expect that the possibilities for PTG, including the degree and the characteristics of growth, will be influenced by the prevailing views and the types of responses of the individual's proximate cultures.

Three elements of the proximate social world seem to be particularly important (although there are many others). One important element is the responses of important others to disclosures related to the trauma and in particular responses to intimations about growth or direct articulation of that experience. Another important element is the degree to which a traumatized person's ruminations are congruent, in content and degree, with the kinds of thoughts significant others have about the individual's situation and response or, put in other words, the degree to which "co-ruminations"[2] (Rose, 2002—although Rose's concept is restricted to disclosure of *negative* content only and thus much more restrictive than the more general meaning of the word *rumination* as we use it here) are adaptive and the degree to which they are congruent between the persons directly affected and important others from the proximate social world. A third cultural element is the presence of models of PTG.

The responses of others to the individual's disclosure are important, but individuals will vary in the degree to which they experience distressing internal states, including unpleasant ruminations, and individuals will vary in the degree to which they wish to engage in self-disclosure related to their stressful experience, as suggested by the model summarized in Figure 1.1. It follows that PTG is likely to be influenced by the interplay of rumination characteristics, disclosure factors, and the influences of both distal and proximate cultural factors. In particular, what are some of the relationships that might be expected between characteristics of rumination, cultural factors, and PTG?

Available work on the relationships between rumination, social constraint, and psychological distress (Lepore & Helgeson, 1998; Lepore, Silver, Wortman, & Wayment, 1996) provides some suggestive indications. It is likely that individuals who have high rates of cognitive engagement with trauma-related elements, and who have a high need to self-disclose, may be particularly likely to engage in event-related disclosure, and in turn may be particularly affected by the kinds of responses received from the proximate culture. In addition, the style, manner, and content of the individual's disclosure may elicit different kinds of responses from others. The kinds of responses, in turn, would be expected to have an impact on the content of the individual's rumination about what has happened.

However, when the individual experiences social constraint about stress-related disclosure, then one might expect that the possibilities for growth would be reduced. Research on the effects of negative responses to persons in adverse circumstances indicates that there are a number of ways that people can be unsupportive to those experiencing trauma, and that the severity of the circumstances may play a role in determining what kinds of problems survivors experience with their social networks (Ingram, Betz, Mindes, Schmitt, & Smith, 2001). It might be useful to examine the effects of various supportive and unsupportive responses on the willingness to self-disclose and the effect of these responses on the production of additional ruminations about the possible reactions of others. For example, we have found in our work with bereaved parents that a substantial degree of their suffering and rumination is focused on the disappointments they have endured in the reactions of persons they have assumed would be supportive and compassionate (Tedeschi & Calhoun, 2004). Ingram et al. (2001) reported that stressor-specific unsupportive social interactions lead to problems in adjustment. We also expect that an increase in unproductive ruminations that are set in motion by unsupportive responses of others may make it

---

[2]We are grateful to Dr. Virginia Gil-Rivas for suggesting this area of inquiry.

more difficult for the individual to maintain a focus on the reflections on content that can lead to PTG.

In addition, it would seem that when the individual is able to engage in disclosures that contain themes of growth, when growth themes are part of the narratives and idioms of the proximate culture's narratives and idioms related to posttraumatic response, and when disclosures are met with accepting or affirming responses from significant others, then growth is more likely to be experienced. Clearly, what we are suggesting involves the mutual interplay of a variety of factors in differing domains, and the challenge of translating such theoretical predictions into manageable investigations is great. Nevertheless, it would seem to be a challenge worth accepting, because elements in these domains seem likely to be connected to the experience of crisis-related growth.

A simple and direct way of beginning to examine the influence of proximate cultural elements is to look at the presence of models of PTG. Weiss (2004), for example, found that husbands of women with breast cancer who answered *yes* to a question about whether or not they knew someone (other than their spouse) who had experienced "benefits from the experience" (p. 265) were somewhat ($p < .06$) more likely to experience growth than those who reported not knowing such a person. Although not conclusive, these findings clearly suggest that exposure to models of PTG is a relevant domain for additional inquiry.

Although difficult to operationalize and quantify, it seems desirable to attempt to assess the narrative themes about the process of coping with loss and tragedy that predominate in the individual's primary reference groups. And to examine the degree to which themes of resilience and growth are present within the general ideas about how people should, and how they typically do, respond to major life challenges. Going even further with this process, it seems highly desirable to examine the ways in which the experience of PTG in individuals is related to the ways in which coping with trauma is conceptualized by others (e.g., partner/spouse, friends, neighbors) who have significant influence on the person directly affected by the circumstance (e.g., the man who is the cancer patient). One expectation is that the greater the prevalence of themes related to the view that the struggle with trauma can change one for the better, then the more likely it is that individuals in those contexts will report higher levels of PTG. As a potential corollary, however, it might be expected that those persons whose experiences with the struggle with crisis do not include elements of growth, but whose cultural influences inform them that the expectation is that they *will* grow from the encounter with loss, may experience greater constraint in disclosing their experiences and may consequently experience greater levels of distress (Wortman, 2004) than persons whose experience of growth more closely reflects the themes of their proximate culture.

One variable that has been investigated in the cultural domain is general social support. This is a general element that we have previously suggested might be related to PTG (Calhoun & Tedeschi, 1998, Tedeschi & Calhoun, 1995). However, studies using general measures of social support have tended not to find reliable relationships between scores on the PTGI (Tedeschi & Calhoun, 1996) and social support (Cordova, Cunnigham, Carlson, & Andrykowski, 2001; Sheikh, 2004). But more specifically focused assessments of social factors in this domain have tended to show a relationship between growth and support (Weiss, 2004). Our current thinking about the relationship of growth to social factors is more specific, suggesting that certain types of responses, including supportive ones, to certain kinds of behaviors on the part of the person in crisis, will have a relationship with the degree of growth reported. The utilization of broad gauge, general measures of social support, however, seems a less fruitful approach to utilize than we previously anticipated.

In sum, we have expanded some of the elements of our model of PTG. In particular, the ways in which the individual's internal psychological states, particularly with reference to ruminative cognitive engagement with crisis-related elements, the interest in engaging in trauma-related disclosures, the style and content of disclosures, and the influences of sociocultural factors, both distal and proximate, represent important elements to be considered in order to more fully understand the process of PTG. We have discussed the other important elements of the model, for example, narrative development and wisdom elsewhere (Calhoun & Tedeschi, 1998, 1999, 2004; Tedeschi & Calhoun, 1995, 2004).

HOW MUCH POSITIVE CHANGE REPRESENTS "GROWTH"?

Posttraumatic growth is not a universal experience. Estimates of the "prevalence" of growth that have relied on quantitative assessments suggest that the range is from 3% to 100%, and more commonly reported percentages tend to range from sizeable minorities (e.g., 30%–40%) to majorities (e.g., 60%–80%) of persons who have struggled with trauma (Linley & Joseph, 2004). Examined in a different way, mean scores on established measures of growth, such as the Stress-Related Growth Scale (SRGS) (Park, Cohen, & Murch, 1996) and the PTGI (Tedeschi & Calhoun, 1996) tend to show some variability as well, raising the question of the appropriate "cutoff" scores to use as the criteria for growth.

Qualitative studies also offer the same kind of variability, both between persons and between different groups of persons (e.g., Calhoun & Tedeschi, 1989–1990; Salter & Stallard, 2004). Different persons report different degrees (including the absence) of growth and different kinds of growth and ascribe widely differing significance to the positive changes they have experienced.

One important concern expressed about the research on PTG (Wortman, 2004) is the accuracy of the assumption that PTG is indeed highly prevalent, and the potential negative impact of the popularization of the notion of growth on persons experiencing personal tragedies when they do not find themselves undergoing the "wonderful" growth that so many others are assumed to have experienced when they have not. *This is an important concern with which we agree* and about which we have already written extensively (Calhoun & Tedeschi, 1999; Tedeschi & Calhoun, this volume). The issue of the prevalence of growth is important and it hinges, to some degree, on the question of *how* we determine if there is a sufficient amount of positive change experienced to justify labeling the change as reflecting PTG.

We do not have an easy answer, but we do *not* think that the answer lies in trying to establish single, precise scores on growth scales, even if the cutoff scores are chosen based on sound statistical and empirical foundations. Although such processes might be useful for the understanding of aggregate data, the use of a specific score does not seem a useful avenue to pursue when trying to understand the experience of individual persons. Is it reasonable, for example, to categorize as growth both the experience of the woman who chooses to change careers and become an oncology nurse, regarding this as a way of honoring the memory of her lost child and the experience of a man who now appreciates sunsets more because he lost his vision for a few days? Is a vocational change honoring a lost loved one not more significant than an increase in aesthetic appreciation of a common natural event? Perhaps. We are not discouraging the use of cutoff scores to create groups for statistical analysis or similar uses to which such data points might be put. We are somewhat skeptical, however, of the degree to which average scores on inventories can capture the importance, quality, and centrality of the changes experienced by individuals in their struggle with trauma. As researchers further explore the degree and prevalence of growth with the assistance of quantitative measures, the answer to the question "was the change sufficiently positive to merit the label posttraumatic growth?" is one that seems most appropriately answered by the individuals affected.

FUTURE RESEARCH ON POSTTRAUMATIC GROWTH: WHAT NEXT?

Mortality Salience

The data have generally supported our view that the stressfulness of the event experienced is correlated with and tends to predict higher levels of growth reported. Our general framework for understanding this process builds on the work of Janoff-Bulman and others (e.g., Epstein, 1991; Parkes, 1971). Highly stressful events threaten or require restructuring of the assumptive world, and this process of restructuring the assumptive world results in the conscious experience and awareness of PTG. A specific area of inquiry that may have potential for understanding further the process of PTG, which many traumas include, is the role played by the increased salience of one's mortality (Cozzolino, Staples, Meyers, & Samboceti, 2004; Martin, 2003). Much of the work on PTG has been done with persons whose stressful experiences include the threat of losing or actual loss of life (e.g., cancer, combat, and bereavement). The ways and degree to which the traumatic experience makes one's own mortality salient and how this salience is related to posttraumatic growth seem to represent another area for investigation. In particular, do crisis events where mortality is made highly salient lead to *more growth* than those that do not, and is the *kind of growth* different in situations that vary in mortality salience?

Methodologies

The methodology used to study PTG is an area that future investigations need to consider. As we have previously suggested (Calhoun & Tedeschi, 1998; Tedeschi & Calhoun, 2004), it seems important to continue to investigate growth from the perspective of traditional quantitatively oriented positivistic science. These kinds of investigations provide interesting possibilities for testing specific predictions and associations, and provide useful descriptions of what characterizes the process, predictors, and consequences of the positive changes that can emerge from the struggle with crisis. Several important findings have already been reported with sophisticated quantitative approaches (e.g., Cadell, Regehr, & Hemsworth, 2003; Frazier, Ty, Margit, Michael, & Jeffrey, 2004; Sears, Stanton, & Danoff-Burg, 2003; Tomich & Helgeson, 2004). The use of longitudinal strategies is also a useful step. Because longitudinal methodologies typically require significantly greater resources than cross-sectional investigations and because there are many important variables that either have not yet been investigated or that require further investigation, we think it is *useful to continue the use of cross-sectional methods*, particularly when the questions are related to the investigation of variables or relationships that have not been previously studied. Longitudinal designs have clear advantages, particularly for identifying antecedents and predictors of growth, but cross-sectional designs would seem to have a role to play in answering questions about PTG.

Although they tend to rest on different sets of assumptions than traditional "scientific" investigations, the use of qualitative methodologies is also desirable. Qualitative methodologies can provide the rich descriptive detail and deep understanding of the experiences of individuals who have faced major life crises that are not possible with quantitative strategies that focus, appropriately so, on variables rather than persons. Perhaps, because

of our own training and professional preferences, we tend to favor qualitative methodologies that clearly specify repeatable steps in the process of analysis and that attend to
issues that quantitatively oriented investigators describe with the terms *reliability* and *validity*, and qualitative researchers tend to describe with the term *trustworthiness* (Lincoln
& Guba, 1985). Although the approaches of qualitative investigators and of scientifically
oriented quantitative researchers can be viewed as contradictory and, perhaps, mutually
exclusive (Gergen, 2001; Lincoln & Guba, 1985), we see great potential for studies that
utilize both qualitative and quantitative methods in the same investigation. In spite of their
sometimes antipathetic stances, the possibility seems to be that each approach can inform
the other, leading to greater progress in the understanding of consequences of the struggle
with trauma. Given the current *Zeitgeist* within the domain of research psychology and
other disciplines in the social and behavioral sciences, we think it is particularly important
that investigators be encouraged to employ qualitative methods that can offer an expanded
understanding of the experience of persons dealing with a wide array of major life crises.

   Within the general approaches of quantitative and of qualitative perspectives, it is
important to incorporate *multiple methodologies*, and to obtain the perspective of *multiple
sources*. For example, studies of women with breast cancer have included information
obtained from their partners (Manne et al., 2004; Weiss 2004). This allows not only a
better understanding of the person directly affected by the stressful event, but also an
understanding of how significant others are affected by what happens to persons who
are important to them. Future studies on growth that obtain the perspectives of multiple
members of the individual's proximate cultural networks are highly desirable.

Rumination and Cognitive Processing

The evaluation of the sociocultural factors that are related to growth is important, but
perhaps one of the most promising areas in which much more work needs to be done is in
the ways in which cognitive factors are connected to growth. As we interpret it, the available
data suggest that the important role accorded to rumination or cognitive engagement in our
model of growth is justified, but much more information is still required. As others have
suggested (Manne et al. 2004), it is important to begin to examine the role of cognitive
factors with a bit more precision and breadth.

   There are at least four dimensions that might profitably be considered in future studies
of the relationships between cognitive factors and PTG, as follows: (a) intrusive versus
deliberate cognitions, (b) the valence of the cognitions, (c) the content of the cognitions,
(d) and the frequency and timing of cognitions. Both deliberate and intrusive ruminations
have been found, at least in some instances, to be correlated with and predictive of PTG
(e.g., Calhoun et al., 2000; Mann et al., 2004). However, results have not been consistent,
indicating that there is still much that is not known. Future investigations of PTG might
well include assessment of both the intrusive ruminations that are typical of posttraumatic
experiences and more deliberate kinds of repetitive thinking that would include elements
such as trying to make sense or even more directly, engaging in "growth reminding"
(Tennen & Affleck, 1998, p. 84).

   The *content* of ruminations also seems to be an appropriate area for further investigation.
What individuals exposed to trauma think about may typically include unpleasant elements
related to the crisis, and the content may be primarily event related. However, cognitions
that have other content may also occur repeatedly in the aftermath of trauma and future
studies would fruitfully include a wide array of content.

Posttraumatic cognitions can vary in *valence*. Some thoughts, for example, recalling the pain and fear of experiencing a combat wound, may have strong negative valence, although other recurring thoughts may have strong positive valence, for example, recalling the selfless actions of fellow soldiers who came to the rescue and provided immediate assistance. Dohrenwend et al. (2004) considered valence and salience in a study of what they called "tertiary appraisals" of military service among Vietnam War veterans. They examined both positively and negatively valenced interpretations among veterans reporting that the military experience was highly salient for them, that is, it was a major life event and affected everyday life. Positive and negative interpretations tended to co-occur, and veterans making primarily negative appraisals tended to show high levels of alienation. The group of veterans showing positive appraisals almost always included negative appraisals as well, and showed the best adjustment, although some also had posttraumatic stress disorder (PTSD). There was almost no indication of exclusively positive appraisals or defensive denial.

Finally, the *frequency* of the posttraumatic cognitions would seem important, and it seems likely that the frequency would be differentially related to growth depending on the intrusiveness, content, and valence of the cognitions being studied. There is some indication that the timing of cognitions may be important in determining the likelihood of PTG (Tedeschi, Calhoun, & Cooper, 2000), but that the action of this variable may depend on the particular domain of PTG in question. The data available strongly indicate that cognitive elements are potentially of great importance to the understanding of PTG, but the role of different characteristics of the ruminations and other cognitive elements is not yet well understood.

As we have suggested in the preceding text, the responses of others to the disclosures related to trauma-related ruminations also seem to be an important area for further investigation. Expectations, based on our model of growth, are that growth is more likely to occur when models of growth and themes of growth are available in the proximate culture, the individual who wishes to disclose does not experience social constraint about disclosure, and others respond with social acceptance or affirmation to trauma-related disclosures that reflect themes of PTG.

Positive Emotions

Current data indicate that positive emotions can play a significant role in coping with difficult life events and, as Stanton and Low (2004) have suggested, they may have important connections to PTG, yet positive emotions are still not explicitly included in our model of PTG. We agree that they are likely to be important in the process of PTG (Fredrickson, Tugade, Waugh, & Larkin, 2003). Although temporary positive affective states may be found to be important in the process of PTG, it is more likely that more trait-like characteristics, such as "preexisting dispositional positive affectivity" (Stanton & Low, 2004, p. 78) will prove to be relevant. Extraversion is a personality characteristic that has been found to correlate with PTG (Linley & Joseph, 2004), and extraversion has a component that might well be described as dispositional positive affectivity. The appropriate place to include positive emotions in our model, then, seems to be within the category of relevant characteristics of *the person pretrauma*. For the present, it is our view that the continued presence of some form of psychological discomfort appears to be a more relevant element to study as a variable contemporaneous to PTG and that dispositions toward positive affect are more appropriately studied as characteristics of the person that antecede the trauma.

Cross-National Studies

The investigation of PTG in different countries has supported the importance of also considering distal cultural elements (e.g., Ho, Chan, & Ho, 2004; Powell, Rosner, Butollo, Tedeschi, & Calhoun, 2003; Zoellner & Maercker, this volume; Znoj, this volume). Preliminary findings suggest that the occurrence of PTG is not unique to one continent or to one society. However, findings do suggest that the ways in which growth is manifested may contain elements that are unique to certain sociocultural settings. A major question that still remains is—what elements of the PTG experience appear to be found across different societies, and which elements appear to be confined to only some kinds of sociocultural contexts? First steps have already been taken, but more cross-cultural or cross-national studies clearly are needed.

Ongoing Issues in the Quantitative Measurement of Posttraumatic Growth

One of the criticisms of the PTGI, the SRGS, and similar inventories is that they do not allow respondents to report negative aspects of trauma (Frazier, Oishi, & Steger, 2003; Park & Lechner, this volume). The assumption is that this characteristic of the scales can lead to validity problems in at least two ways: respondents may develop a "positivity response bias," leading respondents to report positive change when in fact none has occurred or, perhaps more importantly, the scale does not allow respondents to report changes about which they are not asked.

Although the identification of the problem of a possible positive response bias is reasonable, it is an empirical question. Is there evidence that the *content* and *structure* of the current scales do indeed lead to the "false positive" report of growth? We are aware of none, and what data do exist argues against this particular criticism of available scales. For example, the PTGI is not correlated with measures of social desirability (e.g., Wild & Paivio, 2003); respondents may actually underreport growth on growth scales (Smith & Cook, 2004); respondents report PTG along with highly negative psychological states (Park, 1998; Tedeschi & Calhoun, 2004); and self-reported growth tends to be corroborated by others (McMillen & Cook, 2003; Park, Cohen, & Murch, 1996). General self-protective cognitive biases may affect self-reports generally and reports about growth in particular (McFarland & Alvaro, 2000; Tedeschi & Calhoun, 1995), but the majority who report positive changes appear not to be engaging in some form of defensive denial (Dohrenwend et al., 2004).

We have previously addressed the possibilities that PTG may involve some self-enhancing bias in some persons (Calhoun & Tedeschi, 2004; Tedeschi & Calhoun, 1995). Our current view is that there may be variability in research samples, so that a few persons in such samples might demonstrate this tendency, or a tendency toward denial of the negative aspects of traumatic experience. However, as Dohrenwend et al. (2004) reported, this may be a very small proportion of research participants. We have also suggested another way the self-enhancing aspect of growth may operate (Calhoun & Tedeschi, 2004). An initial phase characterized by a somewhat distorted positive view of the traumatic event or a determination to produce a positive response to the event might generate positive responses by others that result in clear, observable positive outcomes in the long term. In other circumstances, initial growth perspectives may not produce desirable results, leading to a fading of this perspective over time. For example, Milam (2004) reported in a longitudinal study that there were identifiable groups in his sample that showed trajectories of stable growth, increasing growth, and decreasing growth.

A second problem that has been identified with current measures is that they do not allow respondents to report negative changes. Clearly, studies that include measures of psychological distress and problems in adjustment along with measures of growth already have done that. The core issue, however, seems to be the interest in the examination of negative changes in the domains of PTG, that is, changed relationships, new priorities, changed philosophy of life, and so forth. More information about a particular phenomenon is always desirable. Constructing new inventories that include "negative growth" (a concept that seems somewhat illogical) will certainly provide more information, and it may well have some degree of utility that goes beyond what can be found with the hundreds (thousands?) of measures of distressing psychological responses generally, and distressing posttraumatic responses in particular, that are already available. Individuals exposed to major life crises do indeed typically experience negative changes, sometimes in the very domain in which they experience growth (Calhoun & Tedeschi, 1999; Tedeschi & Calhoun, 1995). But if the interest is in the *positive changes* that individuals experience as a result of their struggle with traumatic events, what do we learn about growth when we obtain information about negative changes? We learn more, but do we learn anything more about growth?

There are at least two strategies that can solve the alleged problems of the available inventories: using bipolar items or allowing the respondent to make a judgment as to whether a particular change is positive or negative (Park & Lechner, this volume). Both of these suggestions, however, seem to have unavoidable limitations—they are based on the assumption that the changes individuals experience in the aftermath of a major life crisis are *either* positive *or* negative. The available data on the experience of persons struggling with the aftermath of trauma indicate that the experience is mixed, that there is good intermingled with the bad (Dohrenwend et al., 2004). There appear to be insurmountable problems with measurement strategies that rely on bipolar items or that ask respondents to characterize a particular change as *either* positive or negative. Both of these strategies will lead to greater problems of interpretation, and greater loss of data, than is the case with the currently available measures. Particular measures can always be improved. But the changes argued for and the changes made need to be based on solid empirical foundations. They need to improve, and perhaps expand, the available measures of PTG rather than simply to produce changes without improvements.

How might the interest in measuring negative changes, on the same dimensions in which growth tends to reported, be undertaken if bipolar items and post hoc judgments have inherent and from, our view, insurmountable limitations? One solution is simple, and has already been undertaken by many researchers—to include established measures of negative posttraumatic responses along with measures of growth. A second and "more valid" solution (Tomich & Helgeson, 2004, p. 22), which is more challenging, is one with which we have been experimenting—the construction of a scale with items that are both positive and negatively worded, that allows respondents to report *both* positive and negative changes in the same area. This approach has its own challenges, but it avoids the clear pitfalls of bipolar ratings and of categorical dichotomous judgments. Preliminary work on the kind of scale suggested by Tomich and Helgeson (2004) indicates that individuals do report positive and negative changes in the same domains, that they tend to report more positive than negative changes in those domains, and that the mix of positive and negative items may create significant problems for interpreting scores (Baker, 2005).

But is such a scale, which also includes measures of "negative" growth, *really necessary?* If the content and format of current measures of stress-related growth are not contaminated by social desirability, if responses tend to be corroborated by others, if there is no evidence that inquiring about positive changes on these scales leads to a "positive response bias," and if there are a very wide array of measures of the negative aftermath of crisis, what is gained by creating a new scale? This seems to be a question worth pondering.

REFERENCES

Affleck, G., Tennen, H., & Gershman, K. (1985). Cognitive adaptations to high-risk infants: The search for mastery, meaning, and protection from future harm. *American Journal of Mental Deficiency, 89,* 653–656.

Baker, J. M. (2005). An investigation of the impact of response format on the Posttraumatic Growth Inventory. Unpublished master's thesis, The University of North Carolina at Charlotte.

Brofenbrenner, U. (1979). *The ecology of human development: Experiments by nature and design.* Cambridge, MA: Harvard University Press.

Cadell, S., Regehr, C., & Hemsworth, D. (2003). Factors contributing to posttraumatic growth: A proposed structural equation model. *American Journal of Orthopsychiatry, 73,* 279–287.

Calhoun, L. G., & Tedeschi, R. G. (1989–1990). Positive aspects of critical life problems: Recollections of grief. *Omega, 20,* 265–272.

Calhoun, L. G., & Tedeschi, R. G. (1998). Posttraumatic growth: Future directions. In R. G. Tedeschi, C. L. Park, & L. G. Calhoun (Eds.), *Posttraumatic growth: Positive change in the aftermath of crisis* (pp. 215–238). Mahwah, NJ: Lawrence Erlbaum Associates.

Calhoun, L. G., & Tedeschi, R. G. (1999). *Facilitating posttraumatic growth: A clinician's guide.* Mahwah, NJ: Lawrence Erlbaum Associates.

Calhoun, L. G., & Tedeschi, R. G. (2004). The foundations of posttraumatic growth: New considerations. *Psychological Inquiry, 15,* 93–102.

Calhoun, L.G., Tedeschi, R.G., Fulmer, D., & Harlan, D. (2000, August). *Parental bereavement, rumination, and posttraumatic growth.* Poster presented at the meeting of the American Psychological Association, Washington, DC.

Caplan, G. (1964). *Principles of preventive psychiatry.* New York: Basic Books.

Cella, D. F., & Tross, S. (1986). Psychological adjustment to survival from Hodgkin's disease. *Journal of Consulting and Clinical Psychology, 54,* 616–622.

Cordova, M. J., Cunningham, L. L. C., Carlson, C. R., & Andrykowski, M. A. (2001). Posttraumatic growth following breast cancer: A controlled comparison study. *Health Psychology, 20,* 176–185.

Cozzolino, P. J., Staples, A. D., Meyers, L. S., & Samboceti, J. (2004). Greed, death, and values: From terror management to transcendence management theory. *Personality and Social Psychology Bulletin, 30,* 278–292.

Dohrenwend, B. S. (1978). Social stress and community psychology. *American Journal of Community Psychology, 6,* 1–15.

Dohrenwend, B. P., Neria, Y., Turner, J. B., Turse, N., Marshall, R., Lewis-Fernandez, R. et al. (2004). Positive tertiary appraisals and posttraumatic stress disorder in U.S. male veterans of the war in Vietnam: The roles of positive affirmation, positive reformulation, and defensive denial. *Journal of Consulting & Clinical Psychology, 72,* 417–433.

Epstein, S. (1991). The self-concept, the traumatic neurosis, and the structure of personality. In D. J. Ozer, J. M. Healy, and A. J. Stewar (Eds.), *Perspectives in personality, Vol 3* (pp. 63–98). London: Jessica Kingsley.

Finkel, N. J. (1975). Strens, traumas and trauma resolution. *American Journal of Community Psychology, 3,* 173–178.

Fontana, A., & Rosenheck, R. (1998). Focus on women: Duty-related and sexual stress in the etiology of PTSD among women veterans who seek treatment. *Psychiatric Services, 49,* 658–662.

Frankl, V. E. (1963). *Man's search for meaning.* New York: Pocket Books.

Frazier, P., Oishi, S., & Steger, M. (2003). Assessing optimal human functioning. In W. B. Walsh (Ed.), *Counseling psychology and optimal human functioning* (pp. 251–278). Mahwah, NJ: Lawrence Erlbaum Associates.

Frazier, P., Ty, T., Berman, M., Steger, M., & Long J. (2004). Correlates of levels and patterns of positive life change following sexual assault. *Journal of Consulting and Clinical Psychology, 72,* 19–30.

Fredrickson, B., Tugade, M., Waugh, C., & Larkin, G. R. (2003). What good are positive emotions in crisis? A prospective study of resilience and emotions following the terrorist attacks on the United States on September 11th, 2001. *Journal of Personality and Social Psychology, 84,* 365–376.

Gergen, K. J. (2001). Psychological science in a postmodern context. *American Psychologist, 56,* 803–813.

Goss, R. E., & Klass, D. (2005). *Dead but not lost—Grief narratives in religious tradition.* Lanham, MD: Altamira Press.

Ho, S. M. Y., Chan, C. L. W., & Ho, R. T. H. (2004). Posttraumatic growth in Chinese cancer survivors. *Psycho-oncology, 13,* 377–389.

Ingram, K. M., Betz, N. E., Mindes, E. J., Schmitt, M. M., & Smith, N. J. (2001). Unsupportive responses from others concerning a stressful life event: Development of the unsupportive social interactions inventory. *Journal of Social and Clinical Psychology, 20,* 173–207.

Janoff-Bulman, R. (1992). *Shattered assumptions.* New York: The Free Press.

Jordan, H. (2000). *No such thing as a bad day.* Atlanta: Longstreet Press.

Lazarus, R. S., & Folkman, S. (1984). *Stress, appraisal, and coping.* New York: Springer.

Lepore S. J., & Helgeson, V. S. (1998). Social constraints, intrusive thoughts, and mental health after prostate cancer. *Journal of Social and Clinical Psychology, 17,* 89–106.

Lepore, S. J., Silver, R. C., Wortman, C. B., & Waymaent, H. A. (1996). Social constraints, intrusive thoughts, and depressive symptoms among bereaved mothers. *Journal of Personality and Social Psychology, 70,* 271–282.

Lincoln, Y. S., & Guba, E. G. (1985). *Naturalistic inquiry.* Beverly Hills, CA: Sage Publications.

Linley, P. A., & Joseph, S. (2004). Positive change following trauma and adversity: A review. *Journal of Traumatic Stress, 17,* 11–21.

Manne, S. (2003). Coping and social support. In A. Nezu, C. Nezu, & P. Geller (Eds.), *Handbook of health psychology, Vol. 9* (pp. 51–74). New York: Wiley.

Manne, S., Ostroff, J., Winkel, G., Goldstein, L., Fox, K., & Grana, G. (2004). Posttraumatic growth following breast cancer: Patient, partner and couple perspectives. *Psychosomatic Medicine, 66,* 442–454.

Martin, L. L. (2003, November). Letting go: Finding yourself through mortality acknowledgement. In L. L. Martin (Chair), *When good comes from bad: Pulling one's self together vs. letting one's self go.* Symposium conducted at the annual meeting of the Society of Southeastern Social Psychologists, Greensboro, NC.

Martin, L. L., & Tesser, A. (1996). Clarifying our thoughts. In R. S. Wyer (Ed.), *Ruminative thought: Advances in social cognition, Vol. 9* (pp. 189–209). Mahwah, NJ: Lawrence Erlbaum Associates.

Maslow, A. H. (1954). *Motivation and personality.* New York: Harper.

McFarland, C., & Alvaro, C. (2000). The impact of motivation on temporal comparisons: Coping with traumatic events by perceiving personal growth. *Journal of Personality and Social Psychology, 79,* 327–343.

McMillen, J. C., & Cook, C. L. (2003). The positive by-products of spinal cord injury and their correlates. *Rehabilitation Psychology, 48,* 77–85.

Milam, J. E. (2004). Posttraumatic growth among HIV/AIDS patients. *Journal of Applied Social Psychology, 34,* 2353–2376.

Nolan-Hoeksema, S., & Davis, C. G. (2004). Theoretical and methodological issues in the assessment and interpretation of posttraumatic growth. *Psychological Inquiry, 15,* 60–64.

O'Leary, V. E., & Ickovics, J. R. (1995). Resilience and thriving in response to challenge: An opportunity for a paradigm shift in women's health. *Women's Health: Research on Gender, Behavior, and Policy, 1,* 121–142.

Pals, J. L., & McAdams, D. P. (2004). The transformed self: A narrative understanding of posttraumatic growth. *Psychological Inquiry, 15,* 65–69.

Park, C. L. (1998). Implication of posttraumatic growth for individuals. In R. G. Tedeschi, C. L. Park, & L. G. Calhoun (Eds.), *Posttraumatic growth: Positive change in the aftermath of crisis* (pp. 153–177). Mahwah, NJ: Lawrence Erlbaum Associates.

Park, C. L., Cohen, L., & Murch, R. (1996). Assessment and prediction of stress- related growth. *Journal of Personality, 64,* 645–658.

Parkes, C, M. (1971). Psycho-social transitions: A field for study. *Social Science and Medicine, 5,* 101–115.

Powell, S., Rosner, R., Butollo, W., Tedeschi, R. G., & Calhoun, L. G. (2003). Posttraumatic growth after war: A study with former refugees and displaced people in Sarajevo. *Journal of Clinical Psychology, 59,* 71–83.

Rose, A. J. (2002). Co-rumination in the friendship of girls and boys. *Child Development, 73,* 1830–1843.

Ryan, R. M., & Deci, E. L. (2001). On happiness and human potentials: A review of research on hedoni and eudaimonic well-being. *Annual Review of Psychology, 52,* 141–166.

Saakvitne, K., Tennen, H., & Affleck, G. (1998). Exploring thriving in the context of clinical trauma theory: Constructivist self-development theory. *Journal of Social Issues, 54,* 279–299.

Salter, E., & Stallard, P. (2004) Posttraumatic growth in child survivors of a road traffic accident. *Journal of Traumatic Stress, 17,* 335–340.

Schaefer, J. A., & Moos, R. H. (1992). Life crisis and personal growth. In B. N. Carpenter (Ed.), *Personal coping: Theory, research, and application* (pp. 149–170). New York: Praeger.

Sears, S. R., Stanton, A. L., & Danoff-Burg, S. (2003). The yellow brick road and the emerald city: Benefit-finding, positive reappraisal coping, and posttraumatic growth in women with early-stage breast cancer. *Health Psychology, 22,* 487–497.

Sheikh, J. I. (2004). Central type benzodiazepine receptors in Gulf War veterans with posttraumatic stress disorder. *Biological Psychiatry, 56,* 95–100.

Smith, S. G., & Cook, S. L. (2004). Are reports of posttraumatic growth positively biased? *Journal of Traumatic Stress, 17,* 353–358.

Stanton, A. L., & Low, C. A. (2004). Toward understanding posttraumatic growth: Commentary on Tedeschi and Calhoun, *Psychological Inquiry, 15,* 76–80.

Tedeschi, R. G., & Calhoun, L. G. (1995). *Trauma and transformation: Growing in the aftermath of suffering.* Thousand Oaks, CA: Sage.

Tedeschi, R. G., & Calhoun, L. G. (1996). The posttraumatic growth inventory: Measuring the positive legacy of trauma. *Journal of Traumatic Stress, 9,* 455–471.

Tedeschi, R. G., & Calhoun, L. G. (2004). The foundations of posttraumatic growth: New considerations. *Psychological Inquiry, 15,* 1–18.

Tedeschi, R. G., Calhoun, L.G., & Cooper, L. (2000, August). *Rumination and posttraumatic growth in older adults.* Paper presented at the meeting of the American Psychological Association, Washington, DC.

Tennen, H., & Affleck, G. (1998). Personality and transformation in the face of adversity. In R. Tedeschi & L. Calhoun (Eds.), *Posttraumatic growth: Positive changes in the aftermath of crisis* (pp. 65–98). Mahwah, NJ: Lawrence Erlbaum Associates.

Tomich, P. L., & Helgeson, V. S. (2004). Is finding something good in the bad always good? Benefit finding among women with breast cancer. *Health Psychology, 23,* 16–23.

Viorst, J. (1986). *Necessary losses.* New York: Fawcett.

Weiss, T. (2004). Correlates of posttraumatic growth in husbands of breast cancer survivors. *Psycho-oncology, 13,* 260–268.

Wild, N., & Paivio, S. (2003). Psychological adjustment, coping, and emotion regulation as predictors of posttraumatic growth. *Journal of Aggression, Maltreatment and Trauma, 8,* 97–122.

Wortman, C. B. (2004). Posttraumatic growth: Progress and problems. *Psychological Inquiry, 15,* 81–90.

Yalom, I. (1980). *Existential therapy.* New York: Basic Books.

2

RESILIENCE AND POSTTRAUMATIC GROWTH: RECOVERY, RESISTANCE, AND RECONFIGURATION

STEPHEN J. LEPORE

TEACHERS COLLEGE, COLUMBIA UNIVERSITY

TRACEY A. REVENSON

THE GRADUATE CENTER OF THE CITY UNIVERSITY OF NEW YORK

INTRODUCTION

Life is inevitably stressful, and there is tremendous variability in how people respond to and manage life's stressors. This chapter strives to explain the diversity of human responses to stressful life events, particularly traumatic events, which we ordinarily expect to overwhelm people's coping resources. That is, we are concerned with understanding human resilience and a particular form of resilience, posttraumatic growth (PTG), in the face of adversity. We will review some of the personal and environmental concomitants of resilience and examine how people might develop a capacity for resilience in the face of extreme stressors. We also consider the relation of resilience to transformative experiences, particularly growth, in the aftermath of stress.

RESILIENCE: RECOVERY, RESISTANCE, AND RECONFIGURATION

We have identified three related, but distinct uses of the term *resilience* in the literature on stress and trauma. The three usages reflect different dimensions of resilience, as no single definition fully captures this construct. Resilience has been conceptualized as an outcome, such as when it is viewed as an endpoint of stress and coping processes. It also has been viewed as a process, possibly involving dynamic interactions between risk and protective factors internal (e.g., biology, personality) and external (e.g., social support) to a person at various life stages (Bonanno, 2004; Luthar, Cicchetti, & Becker, 2000; Masten et al., 1995; Rutter, 1985, 1999). The different usages of the term *resilience* can lead to confusion, but as long as we are clear about which usage we are considering at any given time, we can avoid undue complexity. It may be especially important that we avoid using the terms *resilience* and *PTG* to describe both processes and outcomes in a single study, and that we be clear in our research about whether our measures reflect outcomes or processes.

Recovery

To introduce the three facets of resilience, we will use the analogy of a tree blowing in the wind. Ordinarily, when a strong wind blows a tree, the tree will bend to accommodate the wind or else it will break. When the wind stops, the tree resumes its original upright state. This elasticity is an important aspect of resilience: A stressor disrupts a person's normal state of functioning, but when the stressor passes, the person eventually resumes his or her normal or prestressor level of functioning. Psychologists also refer to this as a "normative" adaptation pattern. It finds its roots in the early stress literature (Selye, 1956), which depicts optimal adaptation as a process of homeostasis, or a return to some prestressor state. Bonanno (2004) maintains that this process is "recovery," not resilience. Yet others have argued that people who cannot rebound in the ways we have described are not resilient (Garmezy, 1991; Lazarus, 1993; Masten & Reed, 2002). The debate appears to revolve around how quickly individuals must return to normal (or better-than-normal) functioning to qualify for the label resilient. For Bonanno, the criterion appears to be immediate recovery or, possibly, even no negative reactions whatsoever in the aftermath of a stressful event. In contrast, we would argue that even persons who are slow to resume normal functioning are resilient relative to persons who never recover. We return to this point later in the chapter.

Resistance

Resistance is a second form of resilience. Returning to our metaphor, this form of resilience would be evident when a tree stands still, undisturbed, in the face of a howling wind. Bonanno (2004) captures this dimension of resilience in his conceptualization, which maintains that people who exhibit normal functioning before, during, and after a stressor— even long after a stressor—are exhibiting resilience. This conceptualization of resilience is somewhat controversial among psychologists. As Wortman and Silver (1989) noted in their classic paper on the "myths of coping," because this type of human response to stressors does not square with prevailing psychological theories or cultural expectations, it provokes suspicion. As a result, there has been a tendency to "pathologize" this type of response to stressors, although it may be normal and healthy (Bonanno, 2004; Wortman & Silver, 1989).

According to Wortman and Silver (1989), the tendency to pathologize resilience may stem from expectations, or "myths," among mental health professionals and laypersons about what constitutes normal grief following a major loss. Prevalent myths include the following: a) distress is inevitable following a major loss, b) failure to experience distress is pathological, c) it is important to psychologically work through a loss, d) distress will eventually subside, and e) individuals will reach a state of resolution. Despite the widespread acceptance of these assumptions, the evidence supporting them is weak and contradictory. For example, in a rare study that included data on bereaved individuals both before and after suffering a loss, Bonanno and his colleagues (2004) identified different patterns of responses to bereavement, including a relative absence of grief among some bereaved individuals that was quite stable over time. Using prospective data beginning before the death and continuing through 18 months of bereavement, Bonanno and his colleagues showed that the most frequent pattern was not the so-called normal pattern of elevated depression that gradually subsides (10.2%), but a pattern of stable and low depression (45.9%). Further, there was virtually no evidence for a delayed grief pattern, raising questions about the inevitability and abnormality of low distress responses following loss.

There are potentially unfortunate consequences of these myths of coping with loss. For example, mental health professionals may be routinely prescribing therapy and interventions to people who do not need them, and some methods of intervention may be doing more harm than good. After major traumatic events, counselors—the so-called grief brigade—are often dispatched to the scene (Labi, 1999). These counselors apply psychological debriefing techniques, such as critical incident stress management, to trauma survivors. Debriefing aims to keep survivors mentally engaged in thinking about a traumatic experience in order to "accept the reality of it" and confront negative emotions. There is no solid evidence that this form of intervention is helpful (Suzanna, Jonathan, & Simon, 2002), and some studies have suggested a possible worsening of stress-related symptoms in individuals receiving this type of therapy (Bledsoe, 2003). In some cases, it may be unhelpful to get people to remember and talk about their emotional reactions to trauma if it only leads to rumination and not to true cognitive resolution.

Another problem with labeling a resilient response to stress as maladaptive is that it has led psychologists to develop interventions that emphasize breaking down defense mechanisms, as opposed to building resources for resilience (e.g., developing cognitive strategies for reappraising stressors, developing positive social ties, and engaging in uplifting activities). For example, the technique of expressive writing, in which people write about traumatic life experiences, has been gaining increasing popularity as a therapeutic tool (Lepore & Smyth, 2002). This technique appears to result in long-term improvements in health, but also increases short-term negative affect. An early and still popular theory is that expressive writing is beneficial to trauma survivors because it gets them to confront rather than suppress and avoid trauma-related thoughts and feelings (Pennebaker, 1989). However, mounting evidence suggests that disinhibition does not account for the observed benefits of expressive writing (Greenberg & Lepore, 2004; Lepore & Smyth, 2002). For example, writing about noninhibited thoughts and feelings, or even writing about positive aspects of traumatic events, can facilitate adjustment (Greenberg & Lepore, 2004; King, 2002; Lepore, Greenberg, Bruno, & Smyth, 2002). In his recent writings, Pennebaker suggests that there may be multiple pathways through which individuals benefit from writing about stressful life events (Pennebaker, 2002).

Reconfiguration

Reconfiguration is a third form of resilience. To apply our metaphor, when the wind blows, the tree does not simply make a temporary accommodation and then resume its original shape; instead, it changes its shape. The reconfigured tree can accommodate prevailing winds, but it also may make the tree resistant to breaking in future wind storms. This conceptualization mirrors Walsh's description of resilience as the "capacity to rebound from adversity strengthened and more resourceful" (Walsh, 1998). The notion is also evident in evolutionary perspectives, which conceive of resilience as successful adaptation to a changing environment (Cicchetti & Cohen, 1995). Individuals may exhibit this type of resilience when they are able to reconfigure their cognitions, beliefs, and behaviors in a manner that allows them to adapt to traumatic experiences and, possibly, withstand future traumas. These processes have been described in cognitive-processing theories of trauma as assimilation (e.g., making benign appraisals of threatening events) or accommodation (e.g., revising beliefs about personal invulnerability to threatening events) (Lepore, 2001).

Reconfiguration resilience is similar to PTG in some ways. For instance, both are distinct from resistance or recovery resilience because they entail important transformations that go beyond simply maintaining or returning to normal functioning. We would argue, however, that whereas PTG refers specifically to positive elements of transformations, reconfiguration might include changes that can be both positive and negative. For example, a woman who divorces her husband because he was unfaithful in the marriage may become less trusting in her relationships with men. This newly acquired cynicism may be perceived by the woman as personal growth ("I learned from the experience," "I now understand men," "I'm no longer naive," etc.). Indeed, this attitude may serve her well in some relationships. However, the cynicism from this woman's changed world views also may have a cost if it interferes with her ability to develop intimate relationships with men.

In summary, we conceive of resilience as a multidimensional construct that encompasses a variety of adaptive processes and outcomes. Resilience is evident when individuals are able to resist and recover from stressful situations, or reconfigure their thoughts, beliefs, and behaviors to adjust to ongoing and changing demands. We view PTG as one possible outcome for individuals who go through a reconfiguration process. In the following sections, we further refine our conceptualization of resilience (What is resilience?), identify personal and environmental concomitants of resilience (Who is resilient?), and speculate on how individuals develop a capacity for resilience in the face of stressors (How does the capacity for resilience develop?). We also briefly consider the concept of resilient and resilience-promoting environments in an attempt to move the resilience concept beyond the realm of biological constitution or personality traits and, possibly, forge new directions for developing interventions and programs that help people adapt to stressful events. Along the way, we also point to some further distinctions and parallels between resilience and PTG.

WHAT IS RESILIENCE?

The bulk of research and theorizing on resilience derives from the field of childhood psychopathology. Scholars in this area define resilience as a propensity toward positive (or nonpathological) developmental outcomes under high-risk conditions. The early work in this area centered on trying to explain why many children who grow up in chaotic, neglectful, and otherwise unhealthy environments, or who possess personal vulnerabilities, such as mental and physical disabilities, develop into well-functioning, healthy adults (Garmezy, 1991, 1993; Garmezy, Masten, & Tellegen, 1984; Rutter, 1985, 1987; Werner & Smith, 1977, 1989, 1992).

The study of resilience began with investigations into the etiology of abnormal behaviors and outcomes in children. The early studies showed that risk factors, such as
low intelligence and poverty, do not necessarily lead to behavior problems (Garmezy
et al., 1984), that having a mentally ill parent does not necessarily lead a child to develop
mental illness (Rutter, Maughan, Mortimore, & Ouston, 1979), and that it is possible
to be born into an environment of abject poverty and family discord yet develop into a
competent, confident, and caring young adult (Werner & Smith, 1992). These studies are
historically significant because they signaled a paradigm shift in the field of developmental psychopathology from a focus on deficits to one that encompasses both deficits and
strengths.

The early resilience studies also showed that protective factors and risk factors are
often orthogonal—not just opposite ends of a continuum. Thus, researchers began to look
for factors that could directly promote positive developmental outcomes and, thereby,
compensate for the negative effects of risk factors. In addition to compensatory factors,
researchers sought to identify protective factors that could mitigate the negative effects of
risk factors. These two approaches drive much of the resilience research conducted today,
but the models are becoming more complex as the interrelationships between risk and
protective factors are viewed as dynamic and sometimes reciprocally related. Resilience
research also has informed individual-level psychological interventions, community-based
interventions, and school planning (e.g., health education curricula). The task of promoting
healthy development still emphasizes searching out and removing risk factors, but also
requires identification and nurturance of factors that promote healthy development in
general and resilience in the face of adversity.

For a relatively short period of time, some scholars described resilient children as
invincible or invulnerable (Anthony & Cohler, 1987; Cowen & Work, 1988; Werner &
Smith, 1989) and resilient adults as hardy (Kobasa, 1979). Today, most investigators
have abandoned these labels because they suggest that individuals are unaffected by their
circumstances, that they lack the capacity to experience distress or disorder, and that
resilience is a static, trait-like property of a person. Our conceptualization of resilience
recognizes that in some circumstances and for some outcomes, individuals may appear to
be invulnerable or, as previously described, stress resistant. This does not mean, however,
that these individuals would be resistant to all stressors or even the same stressor at
another time. The ability to resist the negative effects of stressors is a dynamic property of
individuals and their environments—a point we return to later. As a result, individuals may
exhibit disorder in response to one stressor but not another, or to a particular stressor at one
time but not at another because resilience may be cultivated and influenced by personal
and environmental factors across the life span. Luthar and her colleagues have reported
examples of these dynamic qualities of resilience. They observed that children in high-risk
situations sometimes exhibit behavioral competence at one time and distress at another
(Luthar & Zigler, 1991), and that children at high risk may exhibit some negative outcomes
(e.g., anxiety) but not others (e.g., drug use or delinquency) (Luthar, Doernberger, & Zigler,
1993; Luthar & Zigler, 1991).

The dynamic quality of resilience is also evident when one considers how long it
may take for resilience to become apparent in individuals experiencing life stressors.
As Masten and Reed (2002) have noted, resilience may be a slowly unfolding process,
evident only in retrospect and, possibly, only years after an extreme stressor has passed.
The time course of this process is difficult to predict for any individual; thus, people
who do not appear resilient in one phase of their life trajectory may appear to be quite
resilient in another phase. For example, the late actor Christopher Reeve, who was left

paralyzed after an equestrian accident, wrote that his paralysis left him severely depressed and suicidal (Reeve, 1999), but years later, he became a director and a world-renown advocate for spinal cord research. Similarly, many leaders of medical mutual-help groups first join the group to receive help and work though their problems, but later they assume leadership roles and become advocates for their cause (Revenson & Cassel, 1991). Thus, over time it is possible to observe resilience when it initially appears that an individual is not resilient. These observations support our notion that the capacity to rehabilitate or recover functioning over time is one manifestation of resilience.

Some scholars have conceptualized resilience as the ability to transform traumatic experiences into positive personal growth experiences. For example, Polk writes: "The ability to transform disaster into a growth experience and move forward defines the concept of resilience" (Polk, 1997, p. 1). We believe that resilient people may experience growth, generative experiences, and positive emotions (Bonanno, Papa, & O'Neill, 2001; Tugade & Fredrickson, 2004), as opposed to simply being resistant to developing pathology. However, individuals also may experience distress and problems of adjustment during this transformative process, and do not necessarily experience growth as a result of changes in cognitions and beliefs about the self or the world (Janoff-Bulman, 2004; Wortman, 2004). Reconfiguration may facilitate adjustment to stressors without necessarily reaping benefits. Further, like recovery, reconfiguration may be a slowly unfolding process.

Not all scholars subscribe to the notion that reconfiguration, or transformation, is part of resilience. Tedeschi and Calhoun (2004) have suggested that PTG is distinct from resilience, arguing that PTG is transformative, whereas resilience is not. In another paper, Tedeschi and Calhoun (1995) suggested that individuals who are resilient may be the least likely to experience transformation, particularly PTG, because the traumatic experience may be less challenging to such individuals. For example, individuals who are resilient may resist threats to self- or world-views that often accompany traumatic events, thereby mitigating the impact of the event and simultaneously bypassing any opportunities to grow or learn something from the trauma. This perspective appears to equate resilience with a trait-like capacity to resist stressors. However, in other writings, Tedeschi and Calhoun (1996) introduce the idea that PTG has multiple components, including a factor of "personal strength." This, in some ways, acknowledges that resilience to future stressors may develop from transformations that occur while individuals are struggling with a stressor or that occurred earlier in life during previous struggles. This perspective is more consistent with the view we espouse in this chapter. However, we maintain that resilience also may occur through reconfiguration of knowledge and beliefs that does *not* lead to growth. Thus, we believe that PTG is one form of reconfiguration and, hence, one form of resilience.

In sum, resilience, in the broadest sense, refers to dynamic processes that lead to adaptive outcomes in the face of adversity. Resilience is not a static property of individuals, nor is it immutable: Individuals may experience good outcomes in the face of some adverse events but not others, may experience both good and bad outcomes in response to the same adversity, or may experience a bad outcome in the face of an adverse event at one time but not at another time. In addition to describing resistance to stressors, we are using the term *resilience* to describe a capacity to recover from stressors over time, as well as the capacity to change one's self to adapt to a stressor. To the extent that resilience emerges from transformative processes (i.e., reconfiguration), it may manifest in PTG, but not necessarily. Depending on one's focus, resilience may be examined as an outcome or a process. The view of resilience as a process is apparent in the developmental literature, but in the adult literature, it is often an outcome. The importance of the concept of resilience is that it broadens our thinking about human adaptation to stressful life events by forcing us not just to look for (unexpected) positive or nonpathological outcomes, but to search for compensatory and mitigating factors that explain and promote adaptation.

WHO IS RESILIENT?

Returning to our tree metaphor, we can ask what kinds of trees bend with or resist the wind, or what predicts how long it takes different kinds of trees to recover after bending in the wind. Obviously, there is the composition of the tree—is it soft and pliable like a willow, or hard and rigid like an oak? In humans, analogous factors include biology and personality. In the literature on adults coping with trauma, there is a strong tendency to associate resilience with personality traits, such as optimism (Farber, Schwartz, Schaper, Moonen, & McDaniel, 2000), hardiness (Kobasa, 1979), ego strength (Farber et al., 2000), and sense of mastery (Hobfoll et al., 2002).

In addition to the tree's composition, characteristics of the tree's environment influence its response to the elements, including availability of water, nutrients, composition of the soil, presence of other trees that might buffer the wind, and so on. In humans, we consider characteristics of an individual's environment, both past and present, which may influence resilience. In the developmental literature, great attention has been given to the association between environment factors, particularly social support, and resilience (Hardy, Concato, & Gill, 2004; Werner & Smith, 1992). We feel that it is time for research to adopt a social-ecological perspective to understand the multiple processes of resilience. A social-ecological perspective recognizes that resilience is not the product of a single underlying factor, but is the result of the interplay of multiple personal and environmental factors (Bronfenbrenner, 1977; Revenson, 1990).

Researchers have only begun to identify the factors associated with optimal functioning in individuals exposed to major stressors. Historically, research on adjustment to stressors has focused on predictors of pathology. Nonetheless, scholars have proposed a number of models of predictors of resilience—including nonpathological or even positive changes—in response to adversity (O'Leary, Alday, & Ickovics, 1998). Some of these models resemble classic models of psychological adaptation to stress (Stanton & Revenson, in press). These models include both social and environmental resources as distal predictors of resilience, but tend to focus on the individual's cognitive appraisals of stressors and individual-level coping strategies as more proximal, mediational processes. Although demographic variables have been conceptualized as personal resources in these models, they really are proxies for unspecified (and unmeasured) variables and processes and, thus, they are not reviewed in this chapter. Similarly, although some developmental models of resilience emphasize temperament as a personal resource—even a biologically determined one—we will not emphasize it in this chapter, as there has been scant research on it. Finally, because few studies operationalize resilience directly, we draw on literature that examines outcomes such as mental health, psychological adjustment to stress, PTG, and benefit finding.

Personality

Personality factors, including a sense of coherence (Antonovsky, 1979), hardiness (Kobasa, 1979), and dispositional optimism (Scheier & Carver, 1985) have garnered a good deal of attention as correlates of resilience. Because the personality characteristic of dispositional optimism has received the most research attention, it will be used here as an exemplar. Dispositional optimism is the stable, generalized expectancy or belief that one will experience good things in life and that future outcomes will be positive. There is evidence of an association between optimism and positive outcomes across a number of adverse conditions, including bereavement (Davis, Nolen-Hoeksema, & Larson, 1998) and illnesses, such as cancer (Carver et al., 1993), heart disease (Scheier et al., 1989), rheumatologic and orthopedic disorders (Chamberlain, Petrie, & Azariah, 1992), and HIV (Taylor et al., 1992).

Optimism may influence resilience through various pathways. First, optimists may try harder. They may use more coping efforts, particularly approach-oriented, problem-focused strategies. In a study of women with breast cancer, investigators found that optimists took more active steps to do whatever there was to do (Carver et al., 1993). Second, optimists may reframe negative experiences in a more positive way and adopt a more positive focus toward negative events. Positive reframing is an attempt to change one's appraisal of the experience or to impose meaning on it. This reframing may help individuals to integrate their experience into their worldview or see it in a more positive light (Collins, Taylor, & Skokan, 1990; Taylor, 1983). Research has shown that optimists were more likely to use positive reframing as a coping strategy before and after breast cancer surgery, and that use of reframing at one point predicted better outcomes at the next (Carver et al., 1993).

Optimists also have a greater tendency to anticipate finding benefits in adversity (Affleck, Tennen, Croog, & Levine, 1987) and to find benefits after experiencing a trauma (Tennen, Affleck, Urrows, Higgins, & Mendola, 1992). Benefit finding has been linked to other indicators of adaptation, whether studied prospectively or retrospectively (Tennen & Affleck, 1999). Optimists do not simply report greater benefits from adversity, but actively remind themselves of the benefits they have found. Tennen and Affleck (1999) have labeled this *benefit reminding* (in contrast to *benefit finding*) and view it as a coping strategy and not an outcome. In a study of women with fibromyalgia, greater benefit reminding was associated with more pleasant mood (Affleck et al., 1987).

Another reason why optimists may be more resilient is that they may know when to disengage from certain (unachievable) goals and to engage in others (Aspinwall, Richter, & Hoffman, 2001). Three decades ago, a similar concept—homeostatic flexibility or the ability to accept alternative roles—was identified as a component of resilience (Antonovsky, 1974). Self-regulatory theory (Scheier & Carver, 2003) suggests that weakening one's commitment to improbable or unattainable goals enables one to shift to more practical, attainable goals. In a study of women with breast cancer, optimists used the coping strategy of acceptance more than pessimists, and showed less distress and better outcomes at several points after surgery (Carver et al., 1993). Optimists may accept the reality of an extreme stressor more easily than pessimists may, without denying the pain and distress that has occurred. Perhaps, optimists are more confident of an eventual positive outcome or, perhaps, they are more willing to discard a worldview that is no longer valid. The idea of being able to shift attention from maladaptive to adaptive thought processes resonates with other work, which suggests the importance of disengaging or not ruminating on unproductive thoughts.

Finally, optimists may have better quality social relationships and, thus, greater social resources to draw upon. Optimists may signal to others that they have positive expectancies about recovering from stressors, so others may feel that any efforts they take to help an optimist are likely to be fruitful. In one experimental study, individuals listening to people who presumably had a serious illness responded better to patients who presented themselves as struggling but fairly positive in their expectations than to individuals who presented themselves either as "supercopers" or not coping well (Silver, Wortman, & Crofton, 1990). In a study of women being treated for early stage breast or colon cancer, optimists perceived lower social constraints (i.e., they felt better able to express their emotions to others), which, in turn, was associated with lower negative affect and higher positive affect (Lepore & Ituarte, 1999).

Although the literature links personality factors, such as optimism, to resilience and other positive outcomes through various plausible mechanisms, it is not without its critics. Tennen and Affleck (1999) have questioned whether personality characteristics, such as optimism, are not unique predictors of positive outcomes, such as benefit-finding, but outcomes themselves of coping with adversity. Because so many of the studies in the area of personality, stress, coping, and adaptation are cross-sectional and nonexperimental, causal inference is severely limited and seldom addressed. A growing number of studies are looking longitudinally at adaptation to stressors, and finding that adults have different trajectories of resilience (Frazier, Tashiro, Berman, Steger, & Long, 2004; Helgeson, Snyder, & Seltman, 2004).

Resilience-Promoting Environments

In addition to personality traits, environmental factors contribute to resilience. Our primary emphasis in this chapter is on the social environment, although we acknowledge that aspects of the natural and built environment may lead to resilience. Returning to our earlier metaphor, a tree that by its nature is brittle and not resistant to wind may exhibit resilience if it is planted among other trees that block the wind or is planted in a climate zone that makes its branches moist and pliable. Sometimes, staking a new sapling is called for, for example, when planting on a windy slope. Similarly, people coping with trauma are often embedded in a supportive social context and it is important for those resources to be there when needed.

What are the qualities of environments that promote resilience? We suggest three global dimensions: a) environments that promote physical and mental health; b) environments that promote normative development; and c) environments that promote social cohesion and the development of social capital. Within the developmental literature, we know that cognitively enriching environments, close relationships with caregiving adults, and ties to community organizations enhance human development (Evans, 2004; Masten & Reed, 2002). Similarly, greater social support, access to more resources and people, and neighborhoods with greater social capital should lead to resilience, even among populations facing adversity (Saegert, Thompson, & Warren, 2001).

Moving the focus away from individuals to the settings they inhabit avoids the trap of "blaming the victim" for negative circumstances or poor adaptation (Wortman, 2004) and may point to more fundamental, "upstream" social-environmental factors that create negative outcomes (Link & Phelan, 1995). For example, poverty is a fundamental cause of multiple risk factors and disease outcomes. A recent review of the effects of poverty on children's health and well-being points to both physical and social environmental mechanisms that link poverty to poor health outcomes, including substandard housing, crowding, and chaotic and impoverished schools (Evans, 2004). Mirroring the notion of risky situations (Price, 1980), we propose thinking about resilience-promoting environments, in which individuals can thrive. Thus, we take the responsibility of "being resilient" off individuals and place it on situations or settings or, more accurately, on the interaction between persons and their environments.

Safe Social Environments Facilitate Coping

A growing body of research suggests that individuals who are able to disclose in confidence to others are more resilient. Disclosure and receipt of social support may lead to resilience through a number of mechanisms. Helpful, pleasant interactions with others provide opportunities to express feelings and concerns (emotional disclosure), and help individuals to more fully process traumatic events and come to a better understanding of the issues involved. Supportive transactions may provide specific suggestions for coping and validation of worth. Through these mechanisms, social support can facilitate coping and reduce emotional distress. Dozens of studies have linked social support to better mental and physical health (Cohen, 1988). Experimental research suggests that social support influences biological variables that could be relevant to health outcomes (Lepore, 1998; Uchino, Cacioppo, & Kiecolt-Glaser, 1996). Aspects of social support also have been implicated in the development of PTG. For example, through disclosure of emotional experiences and the exchange of social support, individuals may perceive increased closeness in their relationships with others (Tedeschi & Calhoun, 2004). In some studies (Park, Cohen, & Murch, 1996; Weiss, 2004), social support has been associated with stress-related growth. In one study, the perception of social constraints—the perception of network members as unreceptive to emotional disclosure (Lepore, 2001)—was associated with lower well-being and greater depression among women with breast cancer (Cordova, Cunningham, Carlson, & Andrykowski, 2001).

Recent empirical evidence suggests that the benefits of disclosure are enhanced when individuals have opportunities for safe emotional expression (Lepore, 2001; Stanton et al., 2000). If cognitive processing of trauma-related stimuli occurs in a supportive social context, associations between the traumatic stimuli and negative emotional responses may be weakened, and even supplanted by positive emotional responses (Lepore, 1997). Disclosure of stressful experiences may regulate emotion by changing the focus of attention, increasing habituation to negative emotions, and facilitating positive cognitive reappraisals of threats (Lepore et al., 2002).

A number of empirical studies provide evidence for these processes. Being able to safely confide in significant others about cancer-related thoughts and concerns has reduced the negative effects of intrusive thoughts on depressive and somatic symptoms in studies of cancer patients (Cordova et al., 2001; Devine, Parker, Fouladi, & Cohen, 2003; Lepore, 2001; Lepore & Helgeson, 1998), people suffering a significant loss (Lepore, Silver, Wortman, & Wayment, 1996; Major & Gramzow, 1999), and children exposed to violence (Kliewer, Lepore, Oskin, & Johnson, 1998). For example, in a cross-sectional study of prostate cancer survivors, Lepore and Helgeson (1998) found that men who reported constraints in talking with their significant others about their cancer, reported more cancer-related intrusive thoughts and were more likely to avoid thinking and talking about their cancer, compared with men who had few constraints. Moreover, there was a stronger negative association between intrusive thoughts and mental health in men who had high constraints in talking with their spouse or family and friends than in men who had few constraints. And in a study of women with early stage breast cancer, Stanton and her colleagues (2000) found that for women who reported high social receptivity (equivalent to low social constraints), emotional expression was related to an improved quality of life.

Social Capital

A number of environments or institutional structures have been described as promoting psychosocial resilience: effective schools, cohesive neighborhoods, religious institutions, and available health care and social services (Masten & Reed, 2002). Similarly, "health-promoting environments" have been described as those that are safe and nonpathogenic, have a moderate amount of control, predictability, and stimulation, include symbolic and spiritual elements, are flexible and stable, and contain a variety of social networks (Stokols, 1992).

One way that these settings may promote resilience is through providing social support and the opportunities to process a trauma socially, as previously described. A second mechanism is that these settings incorporate a high degree of social capital. *Social capital* is defined as the resources inherent in social relationships, including mutual trust, reciprocity, and community participation (Saegert et al., 2001). Thus, an additional process through which environments may promote resilience is by mobilizing agency and effective coping through social connections and a synchronization of resources. For example, for an adolescent coping with a parent's death, having a community-based recreation center may provide the opportunity to participate in health-promoting and engaging sports activities, thus encouraging the development of physical skills, social networks, and a sense of community. A Big Brother/Big Sister program may provide resources for reengaging in life and disclosing emotional concerns. Participation in a religious institution may provide a sense of belonging and community, as well as "proxy" parenting. In these ways, community settings may provide resources that promote the development of resilience.

The Physical Environment

We also need to focus on features of the physical environment that may promote resilience. Environmental design can help to promote health and well-being (Stokols, 1992). For example, incorporating spaces in hospitals where families of surgical patients can comfortably spend the night may promote patient health by increasing familial support. Natural environments have long been suggested as restorative (Hartig, Book, Garvill, Olsson, & Garling, 1996) and, thus, might be good candidates for their resilience-promoting potential. "Healing gardens" may provide a restorative environment within medical settings. Healing gardens provide a sense of control, facilitate interpersonal interactions, offer positive distraction from the traumas that have been experienced, and allow more focused attention; thus, having the potential to reduce stress (Ulrich, 1999). By providing an environment that counters the directed attention fatigue experienced by seriously ill people, healing gardens can provide a safe environment for both disclosure to others and intrapsychic processing of the experience. At this point, however, no studies that link natural, healing environments with resilience or particular coping mechanisms have been conducted; this is a new path for resilience research.

A Few Caveats

Although we have broad evidence that social environments affect resilience, we want to raise a few caveats. First, we tangled with the distinction between resilience-promoting environments versus environments that are resilient. This distinction lies in the level of analysis—whether what is resilient is an individual, or group of individuals, or a social structure (church, school, community). For example, a close-knit family may be a resilience-promoting environment, as it provides resources and stability that family members can draw on in times of extreme stress. However, major stressors may affect the entire family, either because they happen to all members (e.g., the death of a family member or moving to a new home) or because one member's adversity affects all family members (e.g., unemployment). Researchers have shown that community-wide disasters, such as floods, can deteriorate social support resources (Kaniasty & Norris, 1993), as can the chronic stress of living in a crowded residence (Lepore, Evans, & Schneider, 1991) or raising a child with a disability (Quittner, Glueckauf, & Jackson, 1990). However, a resilient environment is one that can weather the storm as a unit; for example, being flexible enough to maintain social roles or changing them if appropriate, and preserving a coherent collective identity. In a study of families coping with a child's juvenile rheumatoid arthritis, families that coped with the illness and its daily demands in a team fashion and by seeking meaning in the illness reported greater quality of life (Degotardi, 2000).

Second, maintaining a resilient environment may extract a cost for inhabitants of that environment. For example, relationship-focused coping involves attending to other persons' emotional needs while maintaining the integrity of the relationship, and managing one's own stress without upsetting or creating problems for others. Engaging in relationship-focused coping (Coyne & Fiske, 1992; O'Brien & DeLongis, 1997) may be good for marital quality, but have negative consequences if it is not congruent with each partner's individual-level coping efforts. In studies of couples coping with heart disease, wives' coping efforts to shield husbands from stress in the postinfarction period (a coping strategy described as *protective buffering*) contributed to their own distress (Coyne, Ellard, & Smith, 1990), as did husbands' efforts to protect their wives (Suls, Green, Rose, Lounsbury, & Gordon, 1997). Perhaps this happens because the partner using protective buffering feels constrained to express negative emotions or worries to the other person.

Third, requesting social support or receiving unwanted support has its costs (Revenson, Schiaffino, Majerovitz, & Gibofsky, 1991). An underlying assumption of the social support literature is that people need support at times of crisis and that any support is better than none (Lanza, Cameron, & Revenson, 1995). However, the efficacy of social support seems to depend on a number of contextual factors, including the timing of the support, the type of support that is needed, and the source of the support (Cutrona & Russell, 1990). For example, in studies of patients with cancer (Dakof & Taylor, 1990) and rheumatoid arthritis (Dakof & Taylor, 1990; Lanza et al., 1995), emotional support was rated as most helpful when it was provided by family members, whereas informational support was rated as most helpful when it was provided by medical professionals. Returning to our gardening analogy, although securing a newly planted tree with guy wires seems to make sense in a windy climate, allowing the tree to move a bit is necessary for cell and root growth. Translating our gardening analogy back to people, too much support can be restricting and can hinder individuals from learning to cope on their own. Studies of families with a schizophrenic member showed that more enmeshed or highly critical family interactions were associated with increases in patients' symptoms (Leff, 1976). Help may be counterproductive if it threatens autonomy or self-worth or if in immobilizes coping efforts (Coyne et al., 1990).

Fourth, we caution against overplaying the influence of the social environment, particularly as a stress buffer. Despite the presence of social support, some people may still be vulnerable to stressors. Furthermore, personality can interact with the social environment.

Socially competent persons, who are more resistant to the negative effects of stressors, also are more likely to have highly developed social networks (Heller, 1979). Research suggests that people with a positive, trusting social orientation, rather than a cynical one, may derive more benefit from supportive people. In an experimental study (Lepore, 1995a), college students gave a speech either alone or in the presence of a supportive confederate. Low cynicism participants who received support had smaller increases in blood pressure during the speech than low cynicism participants without support and high cynicism participants with or without support. Thus, a trusting social attitude allowed some students to experience reduced stress because of social support, whereas a cynical attitude appeared to eliminate any stress buffering effects of support. In another study, investigators found that having a ruminative coping style was associated with seeking more support, but receiving less compared with people with a less ruminative coping style (Nolen-Hoeksema & Davis, 1999). These studies suggest that the fit between individuals and their social environment may be a critical determinant of resilient outcomes.

It also must be acknowledged that particularly stressful experiences can affect social environments as a whole. Trauma can be channeled into attempts at social change by affected individuals, or widespread effects of trauma can produce changes in cultural perspectives that result in important social developments (Bloom, 1998; Tedeschi, Park, & Calhoun, 1998). This social change can be seen as an outcome of resilience and PTG on both the individual and community level.

In conclusion, the interplay between individual-level and environmental-level factors in promoting resilience and PTG should not be underestimated. Discussing stressful events with others may help people to maintain or re-establish a positive self-concept and make sense of the events. Although there is evidence that individual difference factors relate to resilience, a more potent mix includes aspects of the social environment. For example, we have fairly strong evidence from studies of people facing different traumatic events that disclosure of emotions surrounding traumatic events to a receptive audience leads to less avoidant coping and fewer stress-related intrusive thoughts, both of which have been linked to mental health outcomes. Similarly, environments that are full of the resources that social capital brings afford a greater opportunity to cope with trauma in an effective manner.

HOW DOES THE CAPACITY FOR RESILIENCE DEVELOP?

A critical question in this field is, "Where does resilience come from?" To address this question, we must consider the origins of both personal and contextual resources for resilience. Life context is shaped by many social, economic, political, familial, and institutional factors that are too varied to discuss in this chapter. Thus, we will limit our comments to the origins of personal resilience resources, a topic that has received some attention by psychologists.

Bonanno and colleagues' (2002) findings on the relation between "world views" and responses to bereavement suggest that early childhood experiences, particularly parent-child relations, may be critical antecedents to resilience. Children who grow up in an environment that is loving and responsive to their basic needs are likely to form a positive self-image, a general sense of trust in others, and positive expectations about the future (Ahmann, 2002; Masten & Coatsworth, 1998). Perhaps the most often cited evidence of the importance of the early-childhood social environment on resilience in adulthood comes from the Kauai longitudinal study by Werner and Smith (1992). The investigators followed a large birth cohort of high-risk children from before the age of two to the age of

18. A subgroup of children was identified that could be considered resilient because they had normal levels of functioning on multiple developmental and mental health markers. A variety of early childhood factors distinguished the resilient from the not-so-resilient group, including: more social support from family and friends, better quality of care in infancy, and a higher sense of self-worth and intellectual functioning.

Unfortunately, as Masten and Reed (2002) note, our ability to draw strong inferences about the role of the social environment on the development of resilience from the Kauai data is limited for two reasons. First, the analysis actually suggests that relative to non-resilient children, the resilient children may have had relatively lower cumulative risk factors (especially with respect to the quality of their family environment). Second, none of the children in the Kauai study was without risk factors. Thus, it is not clear whether the correlates of good outcomes are predictive of good outcomes in all children, or if they are especially beneficial to children at high risk. In an effort to examine these questions, Masten and her colleagues (1999) identified children who possessed variable levels of risk (low to high) and variable levels of success (low to high) on important developmental outcomes (academic achievement, social behavior, and social competence). The results suggested that resilient youth (high risk, positive developmental outcomes) had much in common with competent youth (low risk, positive developmental outcomes) in terms of intellectual skills and effective parents. However, both resilient and competent youth differed markedly from their maladaptive peers (poor developmental outcomes in either high- or low-risk situations) on personal and social resources.

The findings from Masten and her colleagues (1999) suggest that social and individual traits may be important antecedents to good developmental outcomes in general, as well as in the context of adversity. What we still do not know, however, is specifically how social environments, or even individual traits, translate into resilience. Most of the studies on predictors of resilience examine associations in a static snapshot (e.g., with cross-sectional, correlational studies) or with several static snapshots taken within decades of one another. We need a more fine-grained analysis of what develops in early childhood experiences that translates into successful adaptation to stressors (e.g., exploring what resilient and not-so-resilient individuals think and do during and after stressful events that differentiates their outcomes).

While the early social environment is a modest predictor of adult functioning, the proximal social environment also can influence resilience. We presented some evidence for this statement in previous sections of this chapter. Here, we point to evidence that some interpersonal experiences can promote positive social attitudes, which, in turn, may enable individuals to withstand major life stressors. Recent longitudinal studies have shown that behaviors such as sacrificing or accommodating to a partner in a close relationship provide important diagnostic information about the partner's commitment to the relationship (Wieselquist, Rusbult, Foster, & Agnew, 1999). These commitment-inspired acts promote a cycle of mutual growth and increased interdependence in a couple: commitment promotes pro-relationship acts (e.g., personal sacrifice, accommodation), pro-relationship acts are perceived by the partner and increase feelings of trust, and the increased trust enhances the partner's willingness to become dependent on the relationship, which further cycles back to increase commitment. In committed relationships, individuals can count on their partners to be there when times are tough. As Lepore (1995a) observed, individuals who are trusting of others appear better able to take advantage of social resources during times of stress. There has been relatively little research on how the quality of relationships, such as degree of interdependence and commitment, influences adjustment to life stressors.

This topic would appear to be an obvious direction for future research and intervention (e.g., couple therapy to promote resilience).

Interestingly, a number of theorists have pointed to the role of prior stress exposure as an important determinant of resilience. More than 20 years ago, Garmezy (1983) noted that children who develop into healthy and well-adjusted adults despite their exposure to risk factors—such as poverty, divorce, or racial discrimination—often share the characteristic of having successfully negotiated aversive environmental stimuli early in life. More recently, Dienstbier (1989) made similar observations about the relation between stress exposure and resilience and generated the "toughening hypothesis." This hypothesis maintains that people who have early, repeated exposure to stressors become physiologically toughened or inoculated by the experience. The process that Dienstbier described could be likened to the conditioning of an athlete who, with repeated training, flexing of the muscles, acceleration of the heart, and so forth, is able to endure physical challenges with greater ease than before his or her conditioning began.

The inoculation and toughening hypotheses are striking because they appear to be at direct odds with both contemporary and very early models of stress, which maintain that chronic or repeated stress is likely to be the worst kind (Lepore, 1995; McEwen, 1998; Seeman, Singer, Rowe, Horwitz, & McEwen, 1997). Lepore and Evans (1996) conducted a review of the literature on multiple stressors to evaluate the evidence that repeated exposure to stress contributes to resilience. They found that exposure to multiple stressors precipitates *greater* vulnerability to subsequent stressors, rather than less.

For example, investigators have found that workers in chronically demanding occupations tended to have higher resting levels of diastolic blood pressure, lower cardiovascular responsivity to acute challenges, and delayed cardiovascular recovery following acute challenges—suggesting pathophysiological effects of chronic stress (Schaubroeck & Ganster, 1993). Similarly, others have found that college students with high levels of chronic life stress have exhibited exaggerated blood pressure reactivity to an acute laboratory challenge (e.g., mental arithmetic, giving a speech) (Lepore, Miles, & Levy, 1997). Another study determined that neuroendocrine stress reactivity (i.e., increases in plasma adrenocorticotropin and cortisol responses to acute laboratory stressors) was positively related to having a history of childhood abuse, the number of separate abuse events, and the number of adulthood traumas (Heim et al., 2002). Finally, investigators have shown that trauma-specific stress reactions (intrusive thoughts and avoidance) tended to decrease or resolve within the first 12 months after a single exposure to a life-threatening event, but tended to increase over the first 12 months in individuals with multiple exposures to life-threatening events (Johnsen, Eid, Laberg, & Thayer, 2002). These studies suggest that both early life and recent stress experiences may sensitize rather than inoculate individuals to subsequent stressors, reminding us not to blithely accept romanticized notions that exposure to stress is a good thing—that it will "toughen" us up.

Despite evidence of sensitization responses, it is theoretically possible that experiences of mastery over stressors will confer some protection or inoculation against subsequent stressors. For example, investigators have found that paratrooper trainees have dramatic decreases in physiological reactivity as their training progresses (Ursin, 1978). It has been hypothesized that inoculation is most likely to happen in the following circumstances: in the face of intermittent rather than continuous stressors (Lepore & Evans, 1996; McEwen, 1998); when there is an opportunity to apply effective coping strategies or resources (Rutter, 1987); and when the experience of coping with the stressor leaves a person with a generalized sense of control or self-efficacy (Rutter, 1987). Although these ideas have been around for some time, compelling empirical evidence is lacking. The major challenge, of course, is to determine what kind and amount of stress will stimulate individuals to stretch and improve their coping skills versus become overwhelmed.

CONCLUDING REMARKS

Our reflections on resilience revealed a wide variety of definitions, models, and even myths. We have proposed a broad conceptualization of resilience for this relatively young, but promising field of study. This conceptualization includes three facets of resilience: recovery, resistance, and reconfiguration (including PTG). Our examination of each of these facets suggests that resilience is often the product of dynamic interactions between a range of risk and protective factors internal and external to a person at various stages of a person's life. Importantly, the evidence suggests that resilience, as well as PTG, should not be conceived of as static properties of an individual, but as qualities that are variable over time, stressors, and outcomes. Our analysis also suggests that PTG is one possible outcome of reconfiguration processes: whereas reconfiguration resilience may include both positive and negative outcomes, PTG just includes positive outcomes.

Several important take-home messages arise from our review. One is that for those interested in improving mental and physical health outcomes for high-risk populations, it is at least as important to build resources for resilience as it is to remove risk factors. Some of the resources we identified involve positive social environments and coping skills, including cognitive strategies for reappraising stressors. It also may be important at times not to encourage people to dwell on traumatic events (see, e.g., Lepore, Fernandez-Berrocal, Ragan, & Ramos, 2004), but, perhaps, to encourage involvement in life-affirming and uplifting activities that enable people to develop a sense of purpose and meaning in life and allow them to forget about their troubles for awhile.

A second message is that individuals respond to traumatic events in a wide variety of ways, and we must be cautious about imposing one set of standards on others. Most importantly, we should recognize that an absence of pathology does not necessarily mean that unhealthy denial processes or other aberrant psychological processes are at work. Offering individuals unnecessary aid, or encouraging individuals to ruminate about traumatic events or question their responses to such events, may cause more harm than good.

Just as we should not look for pathology after every trauma, we should not romanticize notions of resilience. In particular, we must be cautious not to overly prescribe tonics associated with resilience, such as optimism, disclosure, and positive social exchanges. If individuals are not feeling particularly optimistic, talkative, or social, they may feel that they are failing to live up to others' expectations. Inhibiting one's true feelings can create a sense of alienation and may give others the wrong impression that social support or help is not needed. Worse is the possibility that presenting a positive face or finding benefits in adversity may become so automatic and socially desirable that one falls prey to the notion that any distress or negative thinking contributes to physical disease. Among individuals afflicted with diseases, such as cancer, there is often a social expectation to be strong.

Consider, for example, the success of the Lance Armstrong Foundation's "Live Strong" campaign. Armstrong was a world-class cyclist when he was diagnosed with metastatic cancer at age 25. Not only did he overcome long odds at beating his cancer, he went on to win the Tour de France several more times. Armstrong then established a foundation to increase money for cancer research. To raise funds, the foundation created yellow rubber wristbands with the motto "Wear Yellow, Live Strong." The suggestion is that if people with cancer apply the same fight and determination as Lance Armstrong, they can beat their cancer. It is clear that people literally buy this message, as over 22 million wristbands have been sold to date and an average of 150,000 are sold daily by the Lance Armstrong Foundation (LAF, 2004). Holland and Lewis (2000) caution against creating such a "tyranny of positive thinking," as it may not bode well for patients.

A third message is that exposure to stress is seldom good and is an unlikely source of resilience. Stress exposure often increases rather than decreases individuals' resistance to future stressors. The factors that seem most critical to promoting resilience are the positive qualities of individuals' early and current social and physical environments, as well as certain positive individual qualities, such as optimism and intelligence. Some theorists have argued that exposure to stressors can lead to resilience, much like exercise can strengthen muscles and make their work easier (Rutter, 1987), whereas others (Collins, Taylor, & Skokan, 1990; Taylor, 1983; Tedeschi & Calhoun, 2004) have argued that traumatic events that challenge individuals' basic assumptions about themselves and the world can open them up to growth experiences. Data are quite limited on these theories, and more work in this area is needed because most of the current theorizing about resilience is based on coarse, cross-sectional, or correlational data. Another implication of our review is that resilience is unlikely in the face of multiple stressors, which one commonly finds in poor and socially disadvantaged populations. In the face of chronic or multiple stressors, people may survive, but their body, mind, and social relations are likely to be adversely affected. Individuals do adapt to chronically adverse situations, but not without costs (Lepore & Evans, 1996). That said, we must also remember that the human accommodations to chronic stressors—or the form that the human body, thoughts, feelings, and social relations take under chronic stress—might be well suited for the circumstance. Just like the gnarled, wind-blown tree observed atop a windy mountain bluff, the shape might not be pretty, but it works well in context.

To conclude, we have learned that resilience takes on a variety of forms, is common, and is not pathological. We also have learned that resilience is more than just a personality trait; it is the product of the person, his or her past experiences, and current life context. By examining the pathways to resilience, and acknowledging its prevalence, we can begin to develop more accurate perceptions of trauma survivors than we currently posses and, perhaps, find ways to promote resilience.

REFERENCES

Affleck, G., Tennen, H., Croog, S., & Levine, S. (1987). Causal attribution, perceived benefits, and morbidity after a heart attack: An 8-year study. *Journal of Consulting and Clinical Psychology, 55*(1), 29–35.

Ahmann, E. (2002). Promoting positive parenting: an annotated bibliography. *Pediatric Nursing, 28*(4), 382–385, 401.

Anthony, E. J., & Cohler, B. J. (1987). *The invulnerable child.* New York: Guilford Publications.

Antonovsky, A. (1974). Conceptual and methodological problems in the study of resistance resources and stressful life events. In B. S. Dohrenwend & B. P. Dohrenwend (Eds.), *Stressful life events: Their nature and effects* (pp. 245–258). New York: Wiley.

Antonovsky, A. (1979). *Health, stress, and coping.* San Francisco: Jossey-Bass.

Aspinwall, L. G., Richter, L., & Hoffman, R. R. (2001). Understanding how optimism works: An examination of optimists' adaptive moderation of belief and behavior. In E. C. Change (Ed.), *Optimism and pessimism: Implication for theory, research, and practice* (pp. 217–238). Washington, DC: American Psychological Association.

Bledsoe, B. E. (2003). Critical incident stress management (CISM): Benefit or risk for emergency services? *Prehospital Emergency Care, 7*(2), 272–279.

Bloom, S. L. (1998). By the crowd they have been broken, by the crowd they shall be healed: The social transformation of trauma. In R. G. Tedeschi, C. L. Park, & L. G. Calhoun (Eds.), *Posttraumatic growth: Positive changes in the aftermath of crisis* (pp. 179–214). Mahwah, NJ: Lawrence Erlbaum Associates.

Bonanno, G. A. (2004). Loss, trauma, and human resilience: Have we underestimated the human capacity to thrive after extremely aversive events? *American Psychologist, 59*(1), 20–28.

Bonanno, G. A., Papa, A., & O'Neill, K. (2001). Loss and human resilience. *Applied and Preventive Psychology, 10*, 193–206.

Bonanno, G. A., Wortman, C. B., Lehman, D. R., Tweed, R. G., Haring, M., Sonnega, J., et al. (2002). Resilience to loss and chronic grief: A prospective study from preloss to 18-months postloss. *Journal of Personality and Social Psychology, 83*(5), 1150–1164.

Bronfenbrenner, U. (1977). Toward an experimental ecology of human development. *American Psychologist, 32*, 513–531.

Carver, C. S., Pozo, C., Harris, S. D., Noriega, V., Scheier, M. F., Robinson, D. S., et al. (1993). How coping mediates the effect of optimism on distress: A study of women with early stage breast cancer. *Journal of Personality and Social Psychology, 65*(2), 375–390.

Chamberlain, K., Petrie, K., & Azariah, R. (1992). The role of optimism and sense of coherence in predicting recovery following surgery. *Psychology & Health, 7*, 301–310.

Cicchetti, D., & Cohen, D. (1995). *Developmental psychopathology, Vol. 2: Risk, disorder, and adaptation.* New York: John Wiley & Sons.

Cohen, S. (1988). Psychosocial models of the role of social support in the etiology of physical disease. *Health Psychology, 7*(3), 269–297.

Collins, R. L., Taylor, S. E., & Skokan, L. A. (1990). A better world or a shattered vision? Changes in life perspectives following victimization. *Social Cognition, 30*, 263–285.

Collins, R. L., Taylor, S. E., & Skokan, L. A. (1990). A better world or shattered vision? Changes in life perspectives following victimization. *Social Cognition, 8*, 263–285.

Cordova, M. J., Cunningham, L. L., Carlson, C. R., & Andrykowski, M. A. (2001). Social constraints, cognitive processing, and adjustment to breast cancer. *Journal of Consulting and Clinical Psychology, 69*(4), 706–711.

Cowen, E. L., & Work, W. C. (1988). Resilient children, psychological wellness, and primary prevention. *American Journal of Community Psychology, 16*(4), 591–607.

Coyne, J. C., Ellard, J. H., & Smith, D. A. F. (1990). Social support, interdependence, and the dilemma of helping. In B. R. Sarason, I. G. Sarason & G. R. Pierce (Eds.), *Social support: An interactional view* (pp. 129–149). New York: John Wiley & Sons.

Coyne, J. C., & Fiske, V. (1992). Couples coping with chronic and catastrophic illness. In S. E. Hobfoll & J. Crowther (Eds.), *Family health psychology* (pp. 129–149). Washington, DC: Hemisphere.

Cutrona, C. E., & Russell, D. W. (1990). Type of social support and specific stress: Toward a theory of optimal matching. In I. G. Sarason & B. R. Sarason (Eds.), *Social support: An interactional view* (pp. 319–366). New York: John Wiley & Sons.

Dakof, G. A., & Taylor, S. E. (1990). Victims' perceptions of social support: What is helpful from whom? *Journal of Personality and Social Psychology, 58*(1), 80–89.

Davis, C. G., Nolen-Hoeksema, S., & Larson, J. (1998). Making sense of loss and benefiting from the experience: Two construals of meaning. *Journal of Personality and Social Psychology, 75*(2), 561–574.

Degotardi, P. B. (2000). *Stress, family coping and adjustment in adolescents with juvenile rheumatoid arthritis.* Unpublished dissertation, The Graduate Center of the City University of New York, New York.

Devine, D., Parker, P. A., Fouladi, R. T., & Cohen, L. (2003). The association between social support, intrusive thoughts, avoidance, and adjustment following an experimental cancer treatment. *Psychooncology, 12*(5), 453–462.

Dienstbier, R. A. (1989). Arousal and physiological toughness: Implications for mental and physical health. *Psychological Review, 96*(1), 84–100.

Evans, G. W. (2004). The environment of childhood poverty. *American Psychologist, 59*(2), 77–92.

Farber, E. W., Schwartz, J. A., Schaper, P. E., Moonen, D. J., & McDaniel, J. S. (2000). Resilience factors associated with adaptation to HIV disease. *Psychosomatics, 41*(2), 140–146.

Frazier, P., Tashiro, T., Berman, M., Steger, M., & Long, J. (2004). Correlates of levels and patterns of positive life changes following sexual assault. *Journal of Consulting and Clinical Psychology, 72*(1), 19–30.

Garmezy, N. (1983). Stressors of childhood. In N. Garmezy & M. Rutter (Eds.), *Stress, coping and development in children*. New York: McGraw-Hill Book Co.

Garmezy, N. (1991). Resilience in children's adaptation to negative life events and stressed environments. *Pediatric Annals, 20*(9), 459-460, 463–456.

Garmezy, N. (1993). Children in poverty: Resilience despite risk. *Psychiatry, 56*(1), 127–136.

Garmezy, N., Masten, A. S., & Tellegen, A. (1984). The study of stress and competence in children: A building block for developmental psychopathology. *Child Development, 55*(1), 97–111.

Greenberg, M. A., & Lepore, S. J. (2004). Theoretical mechanisms involved in disclosure: From inhibition to self-regulation. In I. Nyklicek, L. R. Temoshok, & A. J. J. M. Vingerhoets (Eds.), *Emotional expression and health: Advances in theory, assessment and clinical applications* (pp. 43–60). London: Brunner-Routledge.

Hardy, S. E., Concato, J., & Gill, T. M. (2004). Resilience of community-dwelling older persons. *Journal of the American Geriatric Society, 52*(2), 257–262.

Hartig, T., Book, A., Garvill, J., Olsson, T., & Garling, T. (1996). Environmental influences on psychological restoration. *Scandinavian Journal of Psychology, 37*(4), 378–393.

Heim, C., Newport, D. J., Wagner, D., Wilcox, M. M., Miller, A. H., & Nemeroff, C. B. (2002). The role of early adverse experience and adulthood stress in the prediction of neuroendocrine stress reactivity in women: a multiple regression analysis. *Depression and Anxiety, 15*(3), 117–125.

Helgeson, V. S., Snyder, P., & Seltman, H. (2004). Psychological and physical adjustment to breast cancer over 4 years: Identifying distinct trajectories of change. *Health Psychology, 23*(1), 3–15.

Heller, K. (1979). The effect of social support: Prevention and treatment implications. In A. P. Goldstein & F. H. Kanfer (Eds.), *Maximizing treatment gains* (pp. 353–382). New York: Academic Press.

Hobfoll, S. E., Bansal, A., Schurg, R., Young, S., Pierce, C. A., Hobfoll, I., et al. (2002). The impact of perceived child physical and sexual abuse history on Native American women's psychological well-being and AIDS risk. *Journal of Consulting and Clinical Psychology, 70*(1), 252–257.

Holland, J. C., & Lewis, S. (2000). *The human side of cancer: Living with hope, coping with uncertainty*. New York: Harper Collins.

Janoff-Bulman, R. J. (2004). Posttraumatic growth: Three explanatory models. *Psychological Inquiry, 15*, 30–34.

Johnsen, B. H., Eid, J., Laberg, J. C., & Thayer, J. F. (2002). The effect of sensitization and coping style on post-traumatic stress symptoms and quality of life: Two longitudinal studies. *Scandinavian Journal of Psychology, 43*(2), 181–188.

Kaniasty, K., & Norris, F. H. (1993). A test of the social support deterioration model in the context of natural disaster. *Journal of Personality and Social Psychology, 64*(3), 395–408.

King, L. A. (2002). Gain without pain? In S. J. Lepore & J. M. Smyth (Eds.), *The writing cure: How expressive writing promotes health and emotional well-being* (pp. 119–134). Washington, DC: American Psychological Association.

Kliewer, W., Lepore, S. J., Oskin, D., & Johnson, P. D. (1998). The role of social and cognitive processes in children's adjustment to community violence. *Journal of Consulting and Clinical Psychology, 66*(1), 199–209.

Kobasa, S. C. (1979). Stressful life events, personality, and health: An inquiry into hardiness. *Journal of Personality and Social Psychology, 37*(1), 1–11.

Labi, N. (1999). The grief brigade. *Time Magazine*.

LAF. (2004). *Lance Armstrong Foundation: 20 million people wear yellow, live strong*. Retrieved December 14, 2004, 2004, from www.laf.org/News_Events/News/pr-20041026.cfm.

Lanza, A. F., Cameron, A. E., & Revenson, T. A. (1995). Helpful and unhelpful support among individuals with rheumatic diseases. *Psychology & Health, 10*, 449–462.

Lazarus, R. S. (1993). From psychological stress to the emotions: A history of changing outlooks. *Annual Review of Psychology, 44*, 1–21.

Leff, J. P. (1976). Schizophrenia and sensitivity to the family environment. *Schizophrenia Bulletin, 2*(4), 566–574.

Lepore, S. J. (1995). Measurement of chronic stress. In S. Cohen, R. C. Kessler, & L. Gordon (Eds.), *Measuring stress: A guide for health and social scientists* (pp. 102–120). New York: Oxford University Press.

Lepore, S. J. (1995a). Cynicism, social support, and cardiovascular reactivity. *Health Psychology, 14*(3), 210–216.

Lepore, S. J. (1997). Expressive writing moderates the relation between intrusive thoughts and depressive symptoms. *Journal of Personality and Social Psychology, 73*(5), 1030–1037.

Lepore, S. J. (1998). Problems and prospects for the social support-reactivity hypothesis. *Annals of Behavioral Medicine, 20*(4), 257–269.

Lepore, S. J. (2001). A social-cognitive processing model of emotional adjustment to cancer. In A. Baum & B. Andersen (Eds.), *Psychosocial interventions for cancer*. Washington, DC: American Psychological Association.

Lepore, S. J., & Evans, G. W. (1996). Coping with multiple stressors in the environment. In M. Zeidner & N. S. Endler (Eds.), *Handbook of coping: Theory, research, and applications* (pp. 350–377). New York: Wiley.

Lepore, S. J., Evans, G. W., & Schneider, M. L. (1991). Dynamic role of social support in the link between chronic stress and psychological distress. *Journal of Personality and Social Psychology, 61*(6), 899–909.

Lepore, S. J., Fernandez-Berrocal, P., Ragan, J., & Ramos, N. (2004). It's not that bad: Social challenges to emotional disclosure enhance adjustment to stress. *Anxiety, Stress and Coping: An International Journal, 17*, 341–261.

Lepore, S. J., Greenberg, M. A., Bruno, M., & Smyth, J. M. (2002). Expressive writing and health: Self-regulation of emotion-related experience, physiology, and behavior. In S. J. Lepore & J. M. Smyth (Eds.), *The writing cure: How expressive writing influences health and well-being* (pp. 99–118). Washington, DC: American Psychological Association.

Lepore, S. J., & Helgeson, V. S. (1998). Social constraints, intrusive thoughts, and mental health after prostate cancer. *Journal of Social and Clinical Psychology, 17*, 89–106.

Lepore, S. J., & Ituarte, P. H. G. (1999). Optimism about cancer enhances mood by reducing negative social interactions. *Cancer Research, Therapy and Control, 8*, 165–174.

Lepore, S. J., Miles, H. J., & Levy, J. S. (1997). Relation of chronic and episodic stressors to psychological distress, reactivity, and health problems. *International Journal of Behavioral Medicine, 4*, 39–59.

Lepore, S. J., Silver, R. C., Wortman, C. B., & Wayment, H. A. (1996). Social constraints, intrusive thoughts, and depressive symptoms among bereaved mothers. *Journal of Personality and Social Psychology, 70*(2), 271–282.

Lepore, S. J., & Smyth, J. M. (2002). *The writing cure: How expressive writing promotes health and emotional well-being.* Washington, DC: American Psychological Association.

Link, B. G., & Phelan, J. (1995). Social conditions as fundamental causes of disease. *Journal of Health and Social Behavior, Spec No.* 80–94.

Luthar, S. S., Cicchetti, D., & Becker, B. (2000). The construct of resilience: A critical evaluation and guidelines for future work. *Child Development, 71*(3), 543–562.

Luthar, S. S., Doernberger, C. H., & Zigler, E. (1993). Resilience is not a unidimensional construct: Insights from a prospective study of inner-city adolescents. *Development and Psychopathology, 5*, 703–717.

Luthar, S. S., & Zigler, E. (1991). Vulnerability and competence: A review of research on resilience in childhood. *American Journal of Orthopsychiatry, 61*(1), 6–22.

Major, B., & Gramzow, R. H. (1999). Abortion as stigma: Cognitive and emotional implications of concealment. *Journal of Personality and Social Psychology, 77*(4), 735–745.

Masten, A. S., & Coatsworth, J. D. (1998). The development of competence in favorable and unfavorable environments. Lessons from research on successful children. *American Psychologist, 53*(2), 205–220.

Masten, A. S., Coatsworth, J. D., Neemann, J., Gest, S. D., Tellegen, A., & Garmezy, N. (1995). The structure and coherence of competence from childhood through adolescence. *Child Development, 66*(6), 1635–1659.

Masten, A. S., Hubbard, J. J., Gest, S. D., Tellegen, A., Garmezy, N., & Ramirez, M. (1999). Competence in the context of adversity: Pathways to resilience and maladaptation from childhood to late adolescence. *Developmental Psychopathology, 11*(1), 143–169.

Masten, A. S., & Reed, M. J. (2002). Resilience in development. In C. R. Synder & S. J. Lopez. (Eds.), *Handbook of positive psychology* (pp. 74–88). New York: Oxford University Press.

McEwen, B. S. (1998). Stress, adaptation, and disease. Allostasis and allostatic load. *Annals of the New York Academy of Science, 840*, 33–44.

Nolen-Hoeksema, S., & Davis, C. G. (1999). "Thanks for sharing that": Ruminators and their social support networks. *Journal of Personality and Social Psychology, 77*(4), 801–814.

O'Leary, V. E., Alday, C. S., & Ickovics, J. R. (1998). Life change and posttraumatic growth. In R. G. Tedeschi, C. R. Park, & L. G. Calhoun (Eds.), *Posttraumatic growth: Positive changes in the aftermath of crisis* (pp. 127–151). Mahwah, NJ: Lawrence Erlbaum Associates.

O'Brien, T. B., & DeLongis, A. (1997). Coping with chronic stress: An interpersonal perspective. In B. Gottlieb (Ed.), *Coping with chronic stress* (pp. 161–190). New York: Plenum.

Park, C. L., Cohen, L. H., & Murch, R. L. (1996). Assessment and prediction of stress-related growth. *Journal of Personality, 64*(1), 71–105.

Pennebaker, J. W. (1989). Confession, inhibition and disease. In L. Berkowitz (Ed.), *Advances in experimental and social psychology*: Vol. 22, pp. 211–244. Orlando, FL: Academic Press.

Pennebaker, J. W. (2002). Writing, social processes, and psychotherapy: From past to future. In S. J. Lepore & J. M. Smyth (Eds.), *The writing cure: How expressive writing promotes health and emotional well-being* (pp. 279–292). Washington, DC: American Psychological Association.

Polk, L. V. (1997). Toward a middle-range theory of resilience. *ANS Advances in Nursing Science, 19*(3), 1–13.

Price, R. H. (1980). Risky situations. In D. Magnusson (Ed.), *Toward a psychology of situations: An interactional perspective* (pp. 103–112). Hillsdale, NJ: Lawrence Erlbaum Associates.

Quittner, A. L., Glueckauf, R. L., & Jackson, D. N. (1990). Chronic parenting stress: Moderating versus mediating effects of social support. *Journal of Personality and Social Psychology, 59*(6), 1266–1278.

Reeve, C. (1999). *Still me*. New York: Ballantine Books.

Revenson, T. A. (1990). All things are not equal: An ecological perspective on the relation between personality and disease. In H. S. Friedman (Ed.), *Personality and disease* (pp. 65–94). New York: John Wiley.

Revenson, T. A., & Cassel, J. B. (1991). An exploration of leadership in a medical mutual help organization. *American Journal of Community Psychology, 19*(5), 683–698.

Revenson, T. A., Schiaffino, K. M., Majerovitz, S. D., & Gibofsky, A. (1991). Social support as a double-edged sword: The relation of positive and problematic support to depression among rheumatoid arthritis patients. *Social Science & Medicine, 33*(7), 807–813.

Rutter, M. (1985). Resilience in the face of adversity. Protective factors and resistance to psychiatric disorder. *British Journal of Psychiatry, 147*, 598–611.

Rutter, M. (1987). Psychosocial resilience and protective mechanisms. *American Journal of Orthopsychiatry, 57*(3), 316–331.

Rutter, M. (1999). Resilience concepts and findings: Implications for family therapy. *Journal of Family Therapy, 21*, 119–144.

Rutter, M., Maughan, N., Mortimore, P., & Ouston, J. (1979). *Fifteen thousand hours: Secondary schools and their effects on children*. Cambridge, MA: Harvard University Press.

Saegert, S., Thompson, J. P., & Warren, M. R. (2001). *Social capital and poor communities*. New York: Russell Sage Foundation Publications.

Schaubroeck, J., & Ganster, D. C. (1993). Chronic demands and responsivity to challenge. *Journal of Applied Psychology, 78*(1), 73–85.

Scheier, M. F., & Carver, C. S. (1985). Optimism, coping, and health: Assessment and implications of generalized outcome expectancies. *Health Psychology, 4*(3), 219–247.

Scheier, M. F., & Carver, C. S. (2003). Self-regulatory processes and responses to health threats: Effects of optimism on well-being. In J. Suls & K. Wallston (Eds.), *Social psychological foundations of health and illness* (pp. 395–428). Oxford, England: Blackwell Publishing.

Scheier, M. F., Matthews, K. A., Owens, J. F., Magovern, G. J., Sr., Lefebvre, R. C., Abbott, R. A., et al. (1989). Dispositional optimism and recovery from coronary artery bypass surgery: The beneficial effects on physical and psychological well-being. *Journal of Personality and Social Psychology, 57*(6), 1024–1040.

Seeman, T. E., Singer, B. H., Rowe, J. W., Horwitz, R. I., & McEwen, B. S. (1997). Price of adaptation—allostatic load and its health consequences. MacArthur studies of successful aging. *Archives of Internal Medicine, 157*(19), 2259–2268.

Selye, H. (1956). *The stress of life*. New York: McGraw-Hill.

Silver, R. C., Wortman, C. B., & Crofton, C. (1990). The role of coping in support provision: The self-presentational dilemma of victims of life crises. In B. R. Sarason, I. G. Sarason, & G. R. Pierce (Eds.), *Social support: An interactional view* (pp. 397–426). New York: John Wiley & Sons.

Stanton, A. L., Danoff-Burg, S., Cameron, C. L., Bishop, M., Collins, C. A., Kirk, S. B., et al. (2000). Emotionally expressive coping predicts psychological and physical adjustment to breast cancer. *Journal of Consulting and Clinical Psychology, 68*(5), 875–882.

Stanton, A. L., & Revenson, T. A. (in press). Progress and promise in research on adaptation to chronic illness. In H. S. Friedman & R. C. Silver (Eds.), *Oxford handbook of health psychology*. New York: Oxford University Press.

Stokols, D. (1992). Establishing and maintaining healthy environments. Toward a social ecology of health promotion. *American Psychologist, 47*(1), 6–22.

Suls, J., Green, P., Rose, G., Lounsbury, P., & Gordon, E. (1997). Hiding worries from one's spouse: Associations between coping via protective buffering and distress in male post-myocardial infarction patients and their wives. *Journal of Behavioral Medicine, 20*(4), 333–349.

Suzanna, R. O., Jonathan, B. I., & Simon, W. E. (2002). Psychological debriefing for preventing post traumatic stress disorder (PTSD). *Cochrane Database of Systematic Reviews* (2), CD000560.

Taylor, S. E. (1983). Adjustment to threatening events: A theory of cognitive adaptation. *American Psychologist, 38*, 1161–1173.

Taylor, S. E., Kemeny, M. E., Aspinwall, L. G., Schneider, S. G., Rodriguez, R., & Herbert, M. (1992). Optimism, coping, psychological distress, and high-risk sexual behavior among men at risk for acquired immunodeficiency syndrome (AIDS). *Journal of Personality and Social Psychology, 63*(3), 460–473.

Tedeschi, R.G., & Calhoun, L.G. (1995). *Trauma & transformation: Growing in the aftermath of suffering*. Thousand Oaks, CA: Sage.

Tedeschi, R. G., & Calhoun, L. G. (1996). The postraumatic growth inventory: Measuring the positive legacy of trauma. *Journal of Traumatic Stress, 9*, 455–471.

Tedeschi, R. G., & Calhoun, L. G. (2004). Posttraumatic growth: Conceptual foundations and empirical evidence. *Psychological Inquiry, 15*, 1–18.

Tedeschi, R. G., Park, C. L., & Calhoun, L. G. (1998). Posttraumatic growth: Conceptual issues. In R. G. Tedeschi, C. L. Park, & L. G. Calhoun (Eds.), *Posttraumatic growth: Positive changes in the aftermath of crisis* (pp. 179–214). Mahwah, NJ: Lawrence Erlbaum Associates.

Tennen, H., & Affleck, G. (1999). Finding benefits in adversity. In C. R. Snyder (Ed.), *Coping: The psychology of what works* (pp. 279–304). New York: Oxford University Press.

Tennen, H., Affleck, G., Urrows, S., Higgins, P., & Mendola, R. (1992). Perceiving control, construing benefits, and daily processes in rheumatoid arthritis. *Canadian Journal of Behavioral Science, 24*, 186–203.

Tugade, M. M., & Fredrickson, B. L. (2004). Resilient individuals use positive emotions to bounce back from negative emotional experiences. *Journal of Personality and Social Psychology, 86*(2), 320–333.

Uchino, B. N., Cacioppo, J. T., & Kiecolt-Glaser, J. K. (1996). The relationship between social support and physiological processes: A review with emphasis on underlying mechanisms and implications for health. *Psychological Bulletin, 119*(3), 488–531.

Ulrich, R. S. (1999). Effects of gardens on health outcomes: Theory and research. In C. C. Marcus & M. Barnes (Eds.), *Healinig gardens: Therapeutic benefits and design recommendations* (pp. 27–86). New York: John Wiley & Sons.

Ursin, H. (1978). Activation, coping, and psychosomatics. In H. Ursin, E. Baade & S. Levine (Eds.), *Psychobiology of stress: A study of coping in men* (pp. 201–228). New York: Academic Press.

Walsh, F. (1998). *Strengthening family resilience*. New York: Guilford Press.

Weiss, T. (2004). Correlates of posttraumatic growth in husbands of breast cancer survivors. *Psychooncology, 13*(4), 260–268.

Werner, E. E., & Smith, R. S. (1977). *Kauai's children come of age*. Honolulu, HI: University of Hawaii Press.

Werner, E. E., & Smith, R. S. (1989). *Vulnerable but invincible: A longitudinal study of resilient children and youth*. New York: Adams-Bannister-Cox.

Werner, E. E., & Smith, R. S. (1992). *Overcoming the odds: High risk children from birth to adulthood.* Ithaca, NY: Cornell University Press.

Wieselquist, J., Rusbult, C. E., Foster, C. A., & Agnew, C. R. (1999). Commitment, pro-relationship behavior, and trust in close relationships. *Journal of Personality and Social Psychology, 77*(5), 942–966.

Wortman, C. B. (2004). Posttraumatic growth: Progress and problems. *Psychological Inquiry, 15*, 81–89.

Wortman, C. B., & Silver, R. C. (1989). The myths of coping with loss. *Journal of Consulting and Clinical Psychology, 57*(3), 349–357.

3

MEASUREMENT ISSUES IN ASSESSING GROWTH FOLLOWING STRESSFUL LIFE EXPERIENCES

CRYSTAL L. PARK
UNIVERSITY OF CONNECTICUT

SUZANNE C. LECHNER
UNIVERSITY OF MIAMI SCHOOL OF MEDICINE

Measuring growth following stressful or traumatic life events is both one of the most challenging and most important tasks facing growth researchers. It is imperative that we use comprehensive and valid measurement strategies to capture this phenomenon. While we have made some advances toward this end, we have a long way to go, and some of the most difficult and exciting research endeavors lie in this direction. In this chapter, we describe the current methods of assessing growth and elucidate the strengths and weaknesses of the various methods. We then turn to a discussion of measurement issues. We address the concept of dimensionality and review notions about whether growth is a unitary or multidimensional construct, weighing the evidence for both of these possibilities.

The chapter continues with a discussion of the implications of methods of scoring of the different measures. We then speak to whether a single questionnaire or interview format is appropriate for all populations. We also examine cultural issues and speculate whether growth would be an expected outcome in people of collectivist cultures versus the predominant individualistic/Western culture in which this phenomenon was first identified. We then turn to the topic of life stage–specific issues. The section concludes with a discussion about the possibilities for response choices and item content. Specifically, we consider whether it is necessary to include negative items or assess negative change simultaneously with perceptions of positive growth. We then focus on issues related to implications related to the timing of measurement. Finally, we address validity issues related to the measurement of growth. The constructs of social desirability, cognitive bias, self-enhancement, and past self-derogation to inflate current functioning are also important.

We then describe the measurement issues related to the individual's previous experience with traumatic and stressful events. Specifically, in line with stress inoculation theory (Meichenbaum & Novaco, 1985), we posit that earlier experiences may predispose an individual to cope more effectively with new stressful events, which may lead to more growth. Finally, we address whether groups or communities can experience growth in the manner that individuals do, using the American experience of September 11, 2001 as an example. The chapter concludes with suggestions about the future directions of the measurement of growth.

QUALITATIVE METHODS

Researchers have used two main qualitative methods to ask participants about growth. Some asked participants to identify the ways in which their lives had changed as a result of their trauma (i.e., Collins, Taylor, & Skokan, 1990; Schwartzberg, 1993), whereas others explicitly queried about perceived benefits/growth and positive life changes (i.e., Affleck, Tennen, Croog, & Levine, 1987; Affleck, Tennen, & Gershman, 1985; Mendola, Tennen, Affleck, McCann, & Fitzgerald, 1990; Petrie, Buick, Weinman, & Booth, 1999; Sears, Stanton, & Danoff-Burg, 2003). One might surmise that the wording of the interview questions may create a bias in the responses of participants. However, to date, this notion has not been formally tested.

Among the qualitative methods, one study used an open question format (combat veterans: Fontana & Rosenheck, 1998). Other researchers employed a written essay (various life events: King & Miner, 2000), a life-story technique (female HIV/AIDS patients: Massey, Cameron, Ouelette, & Fine, 1998), or focus groups (chemical dependency: McMillen, Howard, Nower & Chung, 2001). Interview techniques have been used to study growth in a variety of populations, including female survivors of abuse (Poorman 2002), women with HIV/AIDS (Siegel & Schrimshaw, 2000; Updegraff, Taylor, Kemeny, & Wyatt, 2002) and women who were survivors of rape (Thompson, 2000).

An early study of positive change illustrates the use of open-ended interviews in 22 individuals in remission from various forms of advanced cancer. Reports of benefits were purely descriptive, and no statistics concerning the positive impact of cancer were presented. Patients reported that they felt they had a more positive attitude as a result of their experience. They felt more tolerant and appreciative, were less concerned about money, and were more religious than they were before the cancer diagnosis. These individuals also reported that they were living each day to its fullest (Kennedy, Tellegen, Kennedy, & Havernick, 1976).

One of the most noteworthy series of studies of growth in cancer patients was conducted by Taylor and her colleagues. All of the patients had breast cancer, the majority of whom had stage 1 or 2 tumors at the initial diagnosis prior to surgery. Subjects were interviewed between 1 and 60 months postsurgery (median length of time since surgery = 25.5 months). Subjects' prognoses at the time of the interview ranged between obvious deterioration and subsequent death to small tumors with no nodal involvement. Women were asked how their illness influenced their daily activities, plans for the future, goals, views of themselves, views of the world, and relationships with others. Coded interview data revealed that breast cancer patients felt that their lives had changed in a number of ways. Interviewees reported a new attitude toward life, self-knowledge or self-change, and a reordering of priorities from mundane and petty events to emphasis on relationships and enjoyment of life (e.g., Collins, et al. 1990; Taylor, 1983; Taylor, Lichtman, & Wood, 1984). In fact, the authors observed that between 53% (Taylor et al., 1984) and 84% (Collins et al., 1990) of respondents felt that they found meaning in the experience.

Following the interview, Taylor et al. (1984) asked subjects to fill out a number of questionnaires. Adjustment was measured by a composite score of 10 indicators of psychological adjustment, including a physician rating, self-reports of adjustment and distress, and total mood disturbance from the Profile of Mood States (POMS), among others. Taylor (1983) suggested that positive meaning may lead to better adjustment, although no statistics were provided to address this idea.

Another study using qualitative interviews with women with breast cancer revealed that 43% felt that family and spousal relationships had improved, and 66% reported either a more positive outlook on life, closer family ties, feeling cared for, increased character strength, increased empathy, or more intense feelings of spirituality (Zemore, Rinholm, Shepel, & Richards, 1989). Similarly, Belec (1992) observed that 90% of the survivors of bone marrow transplants expressed that the transplants made them better, more empathic people, with new priorities, fuller and more meaningful lives, and a renewed appreciation of life. Subjects with malignant melanoma also reported similar changes (Longman & Graham, 1986).

Relatedly, Fromm, Andrykowski, and Hunt (1996) conducted interviews with 90 bone marrow transplant (BMT) patients. The interview focused on the negative and positive effects of the BMT on family members, the patient's life, changes in personal relationships, and the patient's general outlook on life. Responses were coded and categorized into three broad categories: self, family, and other (comprised of mostly interpersonal sequelae). The most frequently reported positive aspects of cancer were a new philosophy of life (59%), a greater appreciation of life (47%), change in personal attributes (54%), more supportive family relationships (51%), emotional growth of the family (38%), improved family relationships (52%), and more support from friends (39%).

One noteworthy study of survival in male cardiac patients investigated the relationship between growth and morbidity (Affleck et al., 1987). Using an interview format, the authors found that over 58% of subjects reported that they felt that they had benefited from their experience at seven weeks after their myocardial infarction (MI) and at follow-up eight years later. Patients who did not report any benefits at the initial assessment were more likely to experience another MI, even when age, socioeconomic status, and prognosis were statistically controlled. In addition, reported positive sequelae were negatively associated with the occurrence of another MI during the study period. Again, these findings were independent of age, socioeconomic status, and prognosis. Individuals in this study who were able to perceive benefits, or find positive meaning, were more likely to survive their cardiac event and still be alive eight years later, as compared to men who did not report growth.

Another method of measuring growth was employed by Bower, Kemeny, Taylor, and Fahey (2003). As part of an expressive writing paradigm, themes of positive meaning were derived from participants' written disclosures. Participants were women who had recently lost a relative to breast cancer. Findings showed that women who reported growth had increases in natural killer cell cytotoxicity, a measure of the effectiveness of the immune system.

Details of the debate regarding the pros and cons of using qualitative versus quantitative data are beyond the scope of this chapter. However, one of the primary advantages of a qualitative approach is that quantitative questionnaires cannot capture all of the domains of growth (McMillen, 2004). Because participants provide their information without being prompted by specific items, researchers can be relatively certain that the growth responses that are given are meaningful and relevant to the participant. Such information is particularly useful in the early phases of research on a given topic, because it allows researchers to identify the content of items that can then be used in quantitative research.

Life narrative techniques have also been used in identifying positive life changes and growth. Life narratives refer to the story that individuals create about their lives and their development as a person. Analyzing life narratives may be another way to accurately measure growth. One recent study identified four themes of growth in adults' stories of life transitions (integrative, intrinsic, agentic, and communal) and found that communal growth themes were particularly strongly related to well-being (Bauer & McAdams, 2004). Pals and McAdams (2004) suggested that narrative approaches are free from some of the criticisms of quantitative measures, such as constraints on the aspects of growth that are assessed.

EVALUATION OF QUALITATIVE METHODS

It is clear that the wording of the interview questions is of extreme importance in assessing growth. Some have suggested that using different wordings of questions may produce different results. That is, asking participants whether they have experienced *any* changes, versus experiencing any *positive* changes, will likely yield different responses. For example, Wortman and her colleagues have used the phrase "Tell me what your life is like these days" as the interview question in a study of persons who had experienced traumatic loss (e.g., Lehman, Wortman, & Williams, 1987). Results indicated that most participants reported at least one positive result of the loss, but that the negative sequelae experienced by participants were highly prevalent and enduring. Contrasted with Sears et al.'s (2003) interview question "Have there been any benefits that have resulted from your experience with breast cancer?", it is clear that the wording of the question may prime a participant to discuss certain topics. This is not a criticism of the methods used per se. However, because results of qualitative studies may vary widely depending on the specifics of the methodology, caution should be taken when interpreting the results of interview-based studies.

A recently published study that compared a qualitative interview question that queried about benefits (benefit finding) and a quantitative scale (Posttraumatic Growth Inventory [PTGI]) found that there was no correlation between benefit finding and scores on the PTGI (Sears et al., 2003). Benefit finding and growth showed very different patterns of correlations with demographics and adjustment measures. While authors interpreted this result as indicating that benefit finding (conceived as a measure of the process by which growth occurs) and growth are different constructs, there are alternative explanations for the discrepancy. Perhaps the two measures are simply assessing different aspects of growth that are not well represented by the other tool.

Life narratives are a compelling and valuable way to understand a participant's experience with a challenging life event. However, they are complicated and time consuming to conduct. Moreover, there is no accepted method of comparing the data gleaned from life narratives from one individual to another in the context of measuring growth.

QUANTITATIVE QUESTIONNAIRES

One promising area of research involves the development of quantitative scales to measure growth. Researchers have created a variety of questionnaires to assess growth among individuals who have experienced various traumatic or stressful life events (Abraido-Lanza, Guier, & Colon, 1998; Aldwin, Levenson, & Spiro, 1994; Andrykowski, Brady, & Hunt, 1993; Burt & Katz, 1988; Ebersole & Flores, 1989; Fife, 1995; Frazier, Conlon, & Glaser, 2001; Hamera & Shontz, 1978; Joseph, Williams, & Yule, 1993; McMillen & Fisher, 1998; Ross, Stockdale, & Jacobs, 1978). However few of these scales have been subjected to psychometric validation procedures.

While most researchers have utilized scales that asked about various positive changes and provided a Likert format in which the participant selects one option from a number of response choices that range from "not at all" to "very much" or equivalent statements, a few researchers have opted for a structured, open-ended questionnaire (Curbow, Somerfield, Baher, Wingard, & Legro, 1993). Responses to this self-report measure were then coded for loss and recovery themes by the research team. Losses included feeling that life was interrupted by the cancer, experiencing difficulties with sexual functioning, and dealing with physical disabilities, and limitations. Recovery themes included more direction in life or redirection, greater compassion for others, spending more time engaged in pleasurable activities, and improved family relationships. Eighty-seven percent of the respondents reported at least one theme of loss (mean = 2.6) and 83% expressed recovery themes (mean = 2.4).

Three psychometrically validated measures are currently in use: the Stress-Related Growth Scale (SRGS) (Park, Cohen, & March, 1996), the PTGI (Tedeschi & Calhoun, 1996), and the Benefit Finding Scale (BFS) (Antoni et al., 2001; also Tomich & Helgeson, 2004). Each of these measures asks respondents to indicate the extent to which they have changed on a variety of items, using a Likert response scale. While these measures have been extremely useful in advancing our understanding of this phenomenon of growth, researchers and theorists have identified numerous shortcomings. It is also important to note that all of them are retrospective measures of perceived change. That is, participants are asked to compare their current functioning to their previous functioning, or to remember who they were prior to the event compared to who they are currently. This method has various shortcomings, as will be discussed in a later section.

The Stress-Related Growth Scale

The Stress-Related Growth Scale (SRGS) (Park et al., 1996), a 50-item scale, asks participants about changes in personal resources, social relationships, life philosophy, and coping skills. Response choices range from 0 (not at all) to 2 (a great deal). Sample items from the SRGS include, "You learned to be open to communicate more honestly with others" and "You learned to be a more confident person." The SRGS was developed and validated in several samples of college students dealing with a variety of stressful life experiences (e.g., death of a loved one, medical illnesses, relationship breakups). Factor analyses revealed a single unitary factor, suggesting that a total score should be used for this scale. In the validation sample, Cronbach's α was .94 and two-week test–retest reliability was .81. Examining relations with other measures, Park et al. found that the SRGS was unrelated to social desirability but was related in expected ways to variables such as optimism, religiousness, and positive reappraisal coping.

Several versions of the SRGS are available. A short form of the SRGS, comprised of the 15 highest-loading items, was also developed (Cohen, Hettler, & Pane, 1998) and has been used in a number of studies. A revised version of the SRGS was developed by Armeli, Gunthert, and Cohen (2001), in which the items and response format were revised to allow for reports of negative in addition to positive change; the authors reported good psychometrics for this new version in samples of college students and adults.

Posttraumatic Growth Inventory

The PTGI (Tedeschi & Calhoun, 1996) is a 21-item self-report inventory that measures the individual's perception of positive changes following a traumatic life experience. Subjects are asked to rate, on a scale of 0 to 6, the extent to which their views changed as a result of their crisis. Items on the PTGI include statements such as "Appreciating each day," "My priorities about what is important in life," and "A feeling of self-reliance." Like the SRGS, the PTGI was also developed and validated in a sample of college students. A principal components analysis of the validation sample, using varimax rotation, differentiated five subscales: new possibilities, relating to others, personal strength, appreciation of life, and spiritual change. Responses to the items are summed to produce a total score (highest possible score = 126). Scale intercorrelations ranged from $r = .62$ to $r = .83$, and internal consistency ranged from $\alpha = .67$ to .85. The alpha coefficient for the normative sample was $\alpha = .90$. Another study found that the PTGI total score had the highest alpha in relation to the five subscales (Sears et al., 2003). Test–retest reliability, measured two months later, was within acceptable limits ($r = .71$) for the total score, but quite low for some of the subscales (e.g., personal strength, $r = .37$).

Tedeschi and Calhoun examined relationships between the PTGI and other validated scales and individual difference variables. To ensure that reports of growth were not merely the result of subjects' wishes to present a socially desirable response, correlations between the PTGI and the Marlowe-Crowne Social Desirability Scale were reported. Analyses revealed that PTGI scores were not significantly correlated with social desirability scores. Similarly, the PTGI was found to be nonsignificantly correlated with the neuroticism subscale of the NEO scale (Costa & McCrae, 1985), suggesting that growth reports are not due to the lack of chronic negative emotionality.

The Benefit Finding Scale

The BFS (Antoni et al., 2001; Tomich & Helgeson, 2004) is a 17-item questionnaire developed to assess growth among women with breast cancer; it has since been used with prostate cancer patients and men and women with HIV/AIDS. The stem for each item is "Having cancer...", followed by a potential benefit from the experience. The scale includes items such as "has made me a more responsible person" and "led me to be more accepting of things." Items are scored on a five-point scale ranging from "a little" to "extremely." The internal consistency of the BFS is very good (Cronbach's alpha = 0.95).

Evaluation of Quantitative Methods

Quantitative measurement appears to be a necessary approach in allowing researchers to conduct larger-scale studies with a variety of populations to advance our understanding of growth following stressful life experiences. However, there are many problems with current quantitative approaches that must be addressed. First, although the three psychometrically validated measures have been used to assess growth in individuals with a variety of stressors, traumas, and chronic illnesses, none have been validated on more than one population. The PTGI and SRGS were validated on college students and the BFS was validated with breast cancer patients. It is unclear to what extent they may adequately assess, or fail to assess, dimensions of growth that are specific to certain populations. More basic psychometric work is needed on the quantitative measures that researchers employ.

Further, currently available instruments are not comprehensive with regard to item content. Qualitative research and anecdotal evidence shows that, following a challenging life event, positive change may occur in domains that are unassessed by current scales. For example, qualitative studies suggest that one of the most prevalent positive changes among individuals with HIV is the adoption of positive health behaviors (Siegel & Schrimshaw, 2000; Updegraff et al., 2002). Similarly, many people view cancer as a wake-up call and make positive changes in their health habits, such as dietary changes, increasing regular exercise, and reducing the use of nicotine or alcohol (American Cancer Society, 2004). None of current scales of growth assess the dimension of positive health habits and lifestyle change.

Additionally, the most widely used measures of growth have unipolar response scales (i.e., are positively worded) and thus do not assess whether a participant has experienced a negative change on a domain. For example, it is conceivable that a person might perceive that their family and friends are less supportive following a cancer diagnosis, but the currently available scales only ask whether the change in a particular domain occurred in the positive direction. That is, current scales only allow the participant to respond that significant others are either more supportive and helpful or that no change has occurred, but it may be that there has been change in the negative direction. Because this measurement technique limits the ability to fully report change, it should be avoided to accurately assess growth (Linley & Joseph, 2004).

In addition, because the instruments query only about positive life changes, these scales may create a positive response bias. Participants are asked to indicate how much they may have grown or benefited from their traumatic or stressful experience, and may feel that they must say something positive (Tomich & Helgeson, 2004). This bias undermines the validity of reports of growth because all people are likely to be motivated to believe that they are growing and learning as they mature (McFarland & Alvaro, 2000).

Another criticism of the current measures is that their language may be confusing to participants. For example, in the Powell, Bosner, Butollo, Tedeschi, and Calhoun (2003) study, many of the respondents had difficulties understanding PTGI items in which the aspect of change was not explicitly stated. Although this criticism was directed at the PTGI, it may be applicable to other quantitative scales.

Finally, current growth scales do not provide any information about participants' intentions when they choose the response choice of "no change." In one of our preliminary studies, a number of participants wrote in the margin of the PTGI, "I was already this way," and indicated that they were already as high on that domain as they felt they could possibly be *prior* to learning that they had cancer. Another option would be to allow respondents two possible choices for reasons why they might not have changed on a domain (e.g., "No change, because no change was needed" or "I just didn't change in this area").

A new scale that is currently in development by Park, Lechner, and colleagues is designed to address some shortcomings of the aforementioned measures. The development of the new growth scale involved a number of important preliminary steps. First, we identified the weaknesses of currently available measures. A team of experts on the topic of growth, including researchers from a variety of backgrounds, clinicians, and theorists who have worked with the growth construct in their professional work, consulted on the development of the new scale. We then compiled a list of potential items that was broader than the target construct with possibly tangential items (Clark & Watson, 1995). The language is simple and straightforward and avoids trendy expressions. Items were derived from the qualitative literature on growth, in addition to extant scales. We are currently validating this measure with individuals with various forms of cancer and in a group of students dealing with a variety of life stressors. We intend to validate the scale with a number of additional populations (e.g., HIV+ persons, diabetics) in the future and translate (and subsequently validate) the scale for use with Spanish-speaking participants.

Two other topics in measure development, use of retrospective measures of perceived change and use of test–retest reliability methods, also warrant discussion. With regard to *retrospective measures of perceived change*, there is an inherent problem with asking people to recall how they were prior to the time of the challenging life event. McFarland and Alvaro (2000) observed that the participants in their studies derogated their former selves in relation to their new selves. This is a serious threat to studies that employ a retrospective self-report format. How can we be sure that participants' reports are not simply the result of people's desire to perceive themselves as continually growing and self-actualizing? The lack of preevent information makes it difficult to evaluate the validity of self-reports.

In all validation studies, authors commonly report test–retest reliability statistics. However, some have questioned the utility of computing this statistic in a construct that is expected to change over time. An example may be drawn from a recent study of sexual assault trauma survivors (Frazier et al., 2001). In these participants, most growth occurred between two-weeks and two-months posttrauma. Growth scores then remained consistent through the first year posttrauma. However, if growth is measured during this time of dynamic changes in scores, there will be many unanswered questions about the stability of the construct. If we expect that growth scores will change, but that they might not change uniformly, what information does test–retest reliability provide about the psychometric properties of the scale in question? We cannot know whether the change in growth scores is due to test–retest instability or due to changes in the construct of interest itself.

Other Measurement Possibilities

As we will discuss in greater detail later in this chapter, many have questioned the validity of reports of growth. To address these concerns, some have suggested that other forms of measurement be employed to authenticate participants' reports. These include using reports of others, comparison groups, and behavioral measures.

Reports of Others

Can the self-reports of individuals who report growth be corroborated? One suggested method of "verifying" reports of growth is to ask informants (other people close to the traumatized person) about their perceptions of positive change in their loved one. In the Park et al. (1996) study, students completed the SRGS and also had a parent or a close friend complete the SRGS with regard to the student's change related to the identified stressor. Informants' reports of growth were significantly correlated with students' self-reported growth. Similar findings were reported by Weiss (2002) in a sample of breast cancer patients and their husbands.

In a recent study, Manne et al. (2004) examined growth reports in partnered couples (the woman of each heterosexual couple had been treated for breast cancer). Unlike previous studies, they examined vicarious growth—that is, they examined whether the partner of the breast cancer survivor felt that HE had grown as a result of his experience. Although the males partners' scores were consistently lower than the survivors' scores, they did indeed experience growth. Patient growth and partner growth correlated significantly over time (from initial to nine-months and 18-months follow-ups). This would suggest that vicarious growth is an important topic to investigate (and see Weiss, 2004, for a similar cross-sectional study). In previous reports, the authors did not control whether the informant was impacted by the event too, and we are not aware of what influence that may have had on their reports of growth in the participant. This is an intriguing idea worthy of further investigation.

Using this form of validation of self-reports of growth is problematic and complicated. Does a high degree of correlation between self-reports and other reports indicate true growth, or is it simply an artifact of participants' reports to informants about their positive changes? Might the domain of growth also influence the degree of correlation between reports? Perhaps behavior changes may be more easily observed by a significant other than internal feelings and belief systems.

Control or comparison groups. Some authors have used control or comparison groups to establish the validity of reports of growth. Cordova et al. (2001) matched a cohort of healthy women to a cohort of breast cancer survivors. Both groups rated how they had changed over the time since diagnosis (for the controls, the time frame was as long as the survivor's time since diagnosis) using the PTGI. Results showed that breast cancer survivors had significantly higher growth scores on the PTGI as compared to the healthy age- and education-matched participants. However, another study of five-year survivors of breast cancer found that they did not differ from matched controls in faith, meaningfulness in life, or perceiving positive changes in their selves or relationships. However, on a single item assessing benefits, some groups of survivors (those in an education intervention) reported greater benefits than controls (Tomich & Helgeson, 2004). In a study of college students, reports of growth from the most positive event in the past year were higher than reports of growth from the most negative event in the past year. Interestingly, general re-ports of positive change in a comparison group of students were higher than these reports of growth due to a positive or a negative event (Park et al., 1996).

Although compelling, using control groups also has its drawbacks. According to cognitive-processing models of growth, the individual must experience a truly stressful event to initiate the cognitive processing that is required to begin the process of searching for meaning (Tedeschi & Calhoun, 2004). Without a clearly stressful life event, there is no impetus to begin re-evaluating one's life and its meaning. However, matching someone with cancer to someone of the same age who did not experience cancer does not take into account all of the stressful encounters that each group may have had irrespective of the cancer. Of course, this technique provides information about the validity of reports of growth, that is, whether simply asking people to report on their growth is the same whether or not the individual has experienced a traumatic event. However, it is not useful as a technique for measuring growth per se.

Behavioral Manifestations of Reported Changes

It has been noted that not all growth can be assessed through self-report. Janoff-Bulman (2004) proposed three different aspects of growth. In addition to (1) gaining strength through suffering and learning fortitude, self-reliance and respect, and (2) existential reevaluation, which are adequately represented in current measures of growth, there is a third aspect that is not measured: psychological preparedness. Preparedness involves changes in one's assumptive world, where people are better prepared for subsequent tragedies and less traumatized. Rebuilding a viable assumptive world leads to greater psychological protection. This is not well represented in the quantitative measures of growth because it does not reflect a self-reported positive change. Preparedness is surely a potential benefit of a traumatic experience, but represents the survivor's ontological status rather than perception or self-report. Survivors reestablish generally positive, yet less absolutely positive, core assumptions. In response to the difficulties and limitations posed by self-report, a number of researchers have called for the use of behavioral measures of growth.

The main question with behavioral measures centers on whether it is important to know that a person reports that he or she feels changed, or whether there must be some discernable behavioral change in order for growth to have occurred. For example, it is enough to report feeling altruistic, or must the individual begin to do volunteer work in the community? Certainly this would be one way to measure growth. However, there are many drawbacks to this approach.

Although some have argued for the use of behavioral indicators of growth (Linley & Joseph, 2004), this is no easy feat. The main limitation of using obervational methods and behavioral indicators to measure growth is that many facets of growth do not have obvious behavioral manifestations. For example, while it is plausible to measure the behavioral manifestation of altruism in the number of hours a participant spends doing volunteer work, it is less straightforward to measure changes in a participant's feeling that life is precious. Future research may benefit from the inclusion of behavioral indices, where possible. For example, reports of improved interpersonal relations may have many interesting observable behaviors. However, the fact remains that many of the dimensions of growth that appear to be most valuable to participants, and of most interest to researchers, are unobservable experiences that do not have obvious behavioral correlates.

MEASUREMENT ISSUES

Is Growth a Unitary or Multidimensional Construct?

The notion that growth may occur in a variety of distinct domains following a life stressor is intuitively appealing. Several researchers have designed questionnaires to assess these different domains of growth. A number of authors have posited that these different domains of growth may arise through very different pathways and that, perhaps, different models should be developed for each domain (e.g., Janoff-Bulman, 2004; McMillen, 2004).

However, there is little agreement at present on which specific dimensions of growth should be assessed or whether, in fact, dimensions are essential aspects of growth. Whereas the dimensions assessed in most scales encompass changes in personal strengths and competencies, social relationships, and personal life philosophies (Schaefer & Moos, 1992), results of factor analyses of commonly used measures of growth have revealed very different sets of factors. For example, in a study of 416 adults dealing with a variety of stressors, McMillen and Fisher (1998) found eight dimensions of the Perceived Benefits Scale (lifestyle changes, material gain, self-efficacy, family closeness, community closeness, faith in people, compassion, and spirituality). Meanwhile, using a measure compiled from several sources, including the SRGS and the PTGI, identified a rather different set of six dimensions (positive social orientation, wisdom and skills, self-insight and appreciativeness, honesty and reliability, spirituality, and opportunities in life), in addition to a well-being factor in a sample of undergraduates (McFarland & Alvaro, 2000). Using a modified version of the SRGS, a study of undergraduate students and university alumni dealing with a variety of stressful encounters experienced in the past two years yielded six dimensions of growth (affect regulation, treatment of others, self-understanding, belongingness, personal strength, and optimism), along with a dimension of well-being (Armeli et al., 2001).

Although it is possible that some of the inconsistency in factors may be due to differences in measures used, factor structures have also been shown to shift across studies using the same measure. For example, in their study of undergraduates dealing with a variety of life stressors, Tedeschi and Calhoun (1996) identified five domains in the PTGI (greater appreciation of life and changed sense of priorities, warmer/more intimate relationships with others, greater sense of personal strength, recognition of new possibilities or paths for one's life, and spiritual development), but a study of Bosnian refugees found only three factors in the PTGI (changes in self/positive life attitude, philosophy of life, and relating to others), and these three factors had a significant amount of cross-loading, suggesting that the factors were not distinct (Powell et al., 2003).

This shifting factor structure also appears to be more than just a function of the stressor encountered, because even within similar groups dealing with similar stressful situations, different factor structures have been reported. Using Behr, Murphy, and Summer's (1992) scale to assess five different dimensions of growth (personal priorities, daily activities, family, worldviews, relationships) in a sample of women who had survived breast cancer, Tomich and Helgeson (2002) found only two factors (personal growth and acceptance). In a second sample of breast cancer survivors, they again identified only two factors, but found that these factors were highly correlated and had a factor structure that suggested that there was just one common dimension of growth (Tomich & Helgeson, 2004). A factor analysis of results in another study of breast cancer patients using an adaptation of Behr's scale similarly found only one underlying factor in a factor analysis (Antoni et al., 2001). These findings are similar to the original factor analysis of the SRGS scores of undergraduates reporting on growth from a recent significant life stressor that found a robust single "growth" factor (Park et al., 1996).

The idea that growth comprises a single factor is taken to the extreme by Nolen-Hoeksema and Davis (2004), who maintain that a simple score of "yes" or "no" to the question of whether any benefits have been derived from a stressful encounter is not only adequate to assess the construct of growth or benefit finding, but also, in fact argue that multiple-item measures may artificially inflate the amount of growth reported.

In sum, the evidence regarding whether people experience growth in distinct domains is inconclusive. Studies have yet to demonstrate that the major conceptual domains of positive change exist in ways that are distinct from one another. Although, in some studies, the different domains have somewhat different patterns of correlations with other variables, the domains tend to be fairly highly intercorrelated (e.g., Cordova et al., 2001; McMillen & Cook, 2003). Further, studies employing factor analysis have typically found that the first factor extracted explained a great deal more variance than subsequent factors or that most items loaded on one factor. Finally, total growth scores tend to have higher internal consistency reliability than the individual subscales in spite of comprising a variety of domains of growth (e.g., Tedeschi & Calhoun, 1996).

DO THE PREDOMINANT MULTIDIMENSIONAL SCALES TAP ALL OF THE RELEVANT DOMAINS?

The types of growth that people report experiencing depend, obviously, to some extent, on the instrument used to measure growth. Because investigators determine what comprises these scales, the dimensions measured may vary across instruments, and it appears that no particular scale captures all of the potentially important domains of growth or positive change that have been theoretically posited or identified through qualitative research. For example, in a study of people living with AIDS, Siegel and Scrimshaw (2000) found that health behavior change was one of the primary domains of growth identified. However, health behavior change items (or other concrete instrumental changes) are not included on any of the primary measures of growth currently in common use. The domain of compassion or increased empathy toward others, along with the ability to help others, is also poorly assessed in existing measures (McMillen, 2004).

Some authors have argued that one's culture, in large part, determines the types of growth that are likely or even possible. For example, changing one's priorities and finding new paths in life may imply a degree of flexibility and independence specific to modern Western societies that emphasize individuality over collectivism (Ho, Chan, & Ho, 2004; Pals & McAdams, 2004). Similarly, the emphasis on spiritual development in many studies of growth may reflect the importance of religion and personal spirituality in contemporary American life rather than being a universal positive outcome of stressful experiences (Pals & McAdams, 2004). Thus, studies of different cultural groups may yield different dimensions of growth. For example, in a study of elderly Latinas who were dealing with arthritis, patience emerged as one of the primary dimensions of growth reported; the authors speculated that the prominence of patience may be a function of this particular cultural group (Abraido-Lanza et al., 1998).

It is also possible that highly important aspects of growth cannot be tapped in simple self-report measures. For example, both McMillen (2004) and Janoff-Bulman (2004) speculated that an important aspect of growth is the changes in world assumptions, such as decreased naiveté or tempered optimism, that are protective against the effects of trauma that may subsequently be encountered. This "psychological preparedness" against future devastating expectancy disconfirmation is an important dimension of growth or gain, but one that cannot be reported directly as it exists below the person's level of awareness (Janoff-Bulman, 2004). Perhaps sophisticated research designs will allow the assessment of individuals growing from stressful encounters and then coping more effectively or experiencing less shattering of assumptions in future stressful encounters (cf., Carver, 1998).

In a thoughtful commentary, McMillen (2004) noted that the domains tapped by current measures of growth are "by no means exhaustive" (p. 51) and cautioned, "such an assertion may prematurely limit study of some of the more unusual positive by-products of adversity" (p. 51). For example, he cited increased faith in other people, material or financial gain, increased knowledge about oneself, desisting harmful alcohol or dug use, increased community closeness and cooperation among neighbors, and increased organizational preparedness for further adversities as areas that most measures of growth ignore. Further, he noted that there are idiosyncratic benefits that any standardized instrument might have trouble assessing, citing the example of a participant meeting her future husband in the context of a crisis (McMillen, 2004).

CAN A SINGLE MEASURE BE USED FOR ALL POPULATIONS?

Studying poststressor positive changes across different populations is a complex venture. First, research has examined growth in groups dealing with very different kinds of stressful events, ranging from divorce and bereavement to environmental disasters and war to cancer and diabetes. Some of these stressors are acute, others chronic; some involve a degree of control, some are brought about by the malevolence of another. It is well known that different stressful experiences can bring about different sequelae (e.g., Schnurr, Friedman, & Bernardy, 2002) and it may also be that different types of events tend to bring about different types of change. For example, health crises, such as cancer, may be more likely to bring about improvements in health behavior than would a non-health-related crisis, although this notion remains to be empirically tested. Including health behavior change may improve the sensitivity of measures, but it is always possible that some dimensions will not be particularly relevant to some types of stressors.

Another potential limitation of using the same measure is the potential for cross-cultural differences in the experience and expression of growth, as noted in the preceding text. While most of the research on growth has been conducted in the United States, there is interest in examining growth in other countries in addition to focusing more explicitly on subcultural differences within the United States (e.g., Ho et al., 2004; Powell et al., 2003). Some authors have suggested that growth may be primarily a function of the unique philosophy of the United States and "Americanized cultures" that promote the view that people gain wisdom and experience positive personality change in the aftermath of threatening encounters (McMillen, 2004; Tennen & Affleck, 2002). Indeed, some studies conducted in non-Western countries have found much lower rates of reported growth when compared to those conducted in the United States (e.g., Peltzer, 2000; see Powell et al., 2003, for a review).

There may also be issues that are specific or particularly relevant to a particular life stage that limit the appropriateness of using the same scale across samples. For example, aspects of wisdom or gerotranscendence may be particularly relevant in older adults while tempered perceptions of invulnerability may be more relevant to young adults (e.g., Aldwin & Levenson, 2004).

While some researchers have questioned whether the same instrument can or should be used across different groups, there are benefits to this approach. For example, aggregating results from different studies can allow comparison across groups (e.g., see Powell et al., 2003), and the more information that is collected regarding a specific measure, the more that researchers can understand its subtleties.

Mechanics of Measurement

In addition to the above-mentioned shortcoming regarding the limited item selection inherent in all standard measures of growth, there are several other issues regarding the mechanics of measurement that researchers have recently addressed. These include issues of directionality of change, ceiling effects, and timing.

Assessing Directionality of Change

One important issue in questionnaire design is whether all of the items assessing growth should be worded in a positive direction (e.g., "my relationships improved") or whether both positively and negatively directed changes should be included in the questionnaire, as some researchers have proposed (e.g., Tomich & Helgeson, 2004). These researchers noted that many people who experience stressful life experiences, such as cancer, report both positive and negative changes and that including both on a questionnaire allows participants to more accurately report their experiences. Further, positive and negative change items would help to minimize potential biases that may result from using uniformly positive wording, and may help to reduce the potential for a socially desirable response set (Tomich & Helgeson, 2004). Such changes in wording, however, appear to essentially be an issue of semantics rather than a substantial improvement in measurement (e.g., "my relationships got worse" is simply the opposite of the item mentioned previously).

A more elegant solution to this issue is to simply state the domain and allow the participant to report whether he or she experienced change in this dimension and, if so, whether the change was considered by the person to be positive or negative. Although none of the most widely used measures of growth currently employ this system, it has several advantages over the use of positive wording (or positive and negative wording) (see Armeli et al., 2001 and Frazier, Tashiro, Berman, Steger, & Long, 2004 for examples of this approach). First, it eliminates the inherent value judgment involved when the designer of the questionnaire, rather than the participant, determines what changes are considered "positive." Second, it allows the tracking of positive and negative changes on the same items or dimensions over time in longitudinal research.

It is important to note, however, that because people often report experiencing both positive and negative outcomes of stressful encounters, the scoring for positive changes and the scoring for negative changes should be kept separate (e.g., Frazier et al., 2001; Klauer & Filipp, 1997). Otherwise, an individual who has experienced many positive changes and many negative changes may appear to have experienced no change at all (e.g., Frazier et al., 2004). The notion that in the midst of great suffering and damage, an individual can also experience positive changes is the driving notion behind much of the research on growth. However, scores of positive change must be examined separately from negative change scores in order for these assessments to be accurate reflections of the changes in participants. It remains to be determined what the negative changes might mean, particularly in the context of positive change.

Ceiling Effects

One potential problem with growth scales is that people may feel that they are already very high on some dimensions of growth being assessed, leaving little room to show positive change (e.g., those who are self-actualized), or do not desire to change in particular dimensions, for whatever reasons. This makes interpretation of results problematic. For example, a person who was already fully actualized prior to a stressful event would score very low compared to a person who, prior to the event, was functioning poorly. While the concept of growth or positive change would still be adequately captured, its meaning would be less clear. For example, correlations with adjustment measures would be attenuated.

TIMING ISSUES IN MEASUREMENT

When is the best time to assess positive changes or growth—during a crisis? Immediately afterward? One month, six months, a year later? Theoretical conceptualizations of growth have not directly addressed the question of when growth occurs or what course it takes, although a number of researchers have suggested that early reports of growth may be a less valid reflection of true growth or be less likely to relate to psychological well-being than later reports of growth (e.g., Tomich & Helgeson, 2004) and that substantive positive changes are more likely to occur when considerable time has passed, to allow for the coping or cognitive processing that leads to growth (e.g., King & Raspin, 2004; Tedeschi & Calhoun, 2004).

However, reviewing the evidence for these contentions, Tennen and Affleck (2002) noted that there is minimal support for the view that growth occurs later in the coping process. They cited several studies that found that growth or positive changes occurred early in the process of adjusting to stressful experiences. Further, they cited several longitudinal studies that found that growth assessed early in the process of coping and assessed again later was remarkably stable. For example, their own study of heart attack patients found remarkable stability in reports of growth from the first assessment, seven weeks after the heart attack, and to the follow-up, eight years later (Affleck, Tennen, Croog, & Levine, 1987).

Practically speaking, the answer to when to assess growth depends on the specific research question being addressed, such as how soon after an event growth is manifested, whether growth lasts or dissipates over time, and how growth may change over time.

Assessment at each of the various points in time has both advantages and drawbacks. Assessing growth immediately following a stressful encounter allows the researcher to examine growth while the event is still vivid and the person may still be in the throes of coping. While some have argued that positive change may occur immediately after an event (e.g., Lechner & Zakowski, 2002; Miller & C'deBaca, 2001), others have argued that such reports may be unreliable because they are more influenced by coping efforts in addition to such artifacts as euphoria over simply having survived.

Most research has used a time frame of several months to several years, more consistent with the notion that growth comes only after a period of coping and struggle (Tedeschi & Calhoun, 2004). However, because the processes of growth are still poorly understood, the implications of delayed assessments of various lengths are not known. The varied lengths of time used in various studies make cross-study comparisons even more difficult.

As the field of growth research has matured, more researchers have employed longitudinal designs that allow for the tracking of patterns of growth over time (e.g., Frazier et al., 2004). Longitudinal approaches are still in the early stages of development and much remains to be known, such as how often and at what intervals assessments must be made to capture growth processes. Still, longitudinal research represents an advance in the area of growth. An even better approach would be prospective studies that assess people on important domains *prior* to their experiencing events and then follow up after the occurrence of a highly stressful event. Given the fact that most highly stressful events are unpredictable, prospective studies are very difficult to conduct.

Validity Issues

Perhaps the greatest challenge for researchers in the area of growth following trauma or significant life stressors is establishing whether growth actually occurs. Tennen and Affleck (2002) argued that concepts of "reality" and "gains 'actually made'" are "quaint notions" (p. 593) and suggested that the establishment of the veridicality of positive changes or growth may not only be impossible, but also not particularly important or desirable. It may be that perceptions of growth, regardless of any grounding of those perceptions in reality, are what may make a difference in psychological or even physical well-being. Still, most researchers in this area (although not all; see, e.g., Collins et al., 1990; Klauer & Filipp, 1997) express an interest in the phenomenon of "veridical transformative life changes that go beyond illusion" that are experienced as "an outcome or ongoing process" rather than a coping mechanism (Tedeschi & Calhoun, 2004, p. 4). However, one of the most difficult aspects of this research is empirically establishing the validity of growth or positive change as a construct distinct from psychological processes such as self-enhancement, illusion, or defensiveness that result in inaccurate reports of growth, or "pseudo-growth" (Lechner & Antoni, 2004).

A number of theories have been advanced to explain how people may report growth that is not factual, including both conscious and unconscious processes, such as social desirability, cognitive bias, self-enhancement, and past self-derogation to inflate current functioning (e.g., Tennen & Affleck, 2002; Wortman, 2004). For example, motivated self-enhancement involves perceiving oneself in ways that make one feel better about one's current self relative to others or to a previous self (e.g., Ross & Conway, 1986), such that the standards by which one judges oneself or one's quality of life are altered, leading to perceptions of positive change. A recent series of studies directly examined the self-enhancement motive relative to perceptions of stress-related growth (McFarland & Alvaro, 2000). Participants were asked to describe their previous and current selves under a variety of experimental conditions. Essentially, findings indicated that participants reporting on their personal changes following a stressful experience tended to shift their self-reports of their previous selves to be more negative (relative to controls), while their current ratings of themselves did not differ from controls who were not reporting on growth. The net effect of denigrating recollected previous selves was to give an impression of positive change. These results suggest that reports of positive change are, at least in part, illusory and call into question the validity of self-reports of growth. This set of studies is not conclusive, however. For example, participants were not selected because of their experiencing of a particular stressful event. Further, it is possible that asking participants to focus on a previously experienced negative event could create a marker in time by which people would be able to more accurately recollect who they were at that point. Still, researchers must take this challenge to our self-report methodology seriously and design research that can address the issue of self-enhancement tendencies.

A related problem concerns the common tendency of people to cope with stressful situations by identifying positive aspects of the situation (e.g., positive reinterpretation) (Carver, Scheier, & Weintraub, 1989). These coping strategies are often related to growth (e.g., Park & Fenster, 2004) in that individuals may cope with trauma by attempting to perceive growth from it, but this perception does not necessarily reflect genuine positive change. Instead, individuals may exaggerate self-improvement to help alleviate their distress. The motivation to identify benefits is driven by distress reduction and makes reports suspect. On the other hand, having identified positives may be an accurate report. Further, reminding oneself of these positive changes (benefit finding; Tennen & Affleck, 2002) may again be a coping strategy.

To date, researchers have attempted to demonstrate the validity of growth in several ways, including relying on informant reports of growth, examining changes in psychosocial resources across time, and examining growth in the context of adjustment. We are aware of only three studies that attempted to establish the validity of growth independent of self-report by asking informants to report on the growth experienced by the participants (i.e., McMillen & Cook, 2003; Park et al., 1996; Weiss, 2002). All of these studies found moderately strong relations between self-reports and informant reports of growth. Because much that individuals regard as growth involves private inner processes, it is encouraging that significant others would be aware of it. However, it is possible that study participants discussed many of their perceived positive changes with informants and that these results simply reflect informants' reports of participants' self-reports to them.

Some researchers have examined changes in resources across time as a reflection of growth. For example, in two longitudinal studies of college students reporting on their most stressful event in the past six months, stress-related growth was related across time to increases in positive affectivity, optimism, and social support (Park et al., 1996) and to increases in mastery and intrinsic religiousness (Park & Fenster, 2004). Another method used to examine validity is to examine how closely direct reports of growth match with more indirect reports elsewhere in the interview. Wortman (2004) noted that in their study of bereaved spouses or parents who had lost a loved one in a motor vehicle accident, reports of growth were not reflected in their responses elsewhere in the interview and were not evident when comparing their responses with those of other participants who had not reported growth or with control participants (Lehman et al., 1987).

Group and Community Growth

Several writers have observed that the positive changes that arise in the aftermath of crises may not only be of a personal nature, but may also involve benefits to families, communities, or even nations (e.g., Bloom, 1998). For example, after the 9/11 terrorist attacks, there was a brief period in the United States in which people reported that the attacks had made Americans closer and more united in purpose (e.g., Bossolo, Bergantino, Lichtenstein, & Gutman, 2002; Torabi & Seo, 2004). This community-wide growth was evidenced by outpourings of volunteerism and altruism, seen particularly in New York City. However, as time progressed, altruism and volunteerism dropped off and closely resembled pretrauma levels. In discussing the concept of social transformation, Sandra Bloom (1998) presented an eloquent overview of the many ways that personal and group trauma can be converted into community resources.

However, most empirical studies of positive changes following stressors have focused on changes perceived by individuals to have taken place internally or within their immediate social environment. It was noted previously that in some studies, measures asking participants whether they had derived any benefits from their experience and quantitative scores of growth were unrelated (e.g., Sears et al., 2003). It is possible that this is because when individuals report on benefits that have arisen from a stressful event, they refer to positive changes that have occurred outside their own personal lives rather than only the very personal changes that are tapped by current quantitative measures of growth. For example, the death of someone due to a drunk driver may shatter one family, but also serve as an example to others to not drink and drive.

SUMMARY

We urge researchers in this area to take the issues of operational definition and validity very seriously. We suggest that qualitative methods continue to be employed to fully illustrate the many ways that growth is manifested. However, sophisticated longitudinal designs will require the use of valid quantitative measures. While the first generation of these measures has provided a good start in this new area of research, the development of better measures will require future work and refinement. Serious challenges to the validity of our self-report methodologies have been posed (e.g., McFarland & Alvaro, 2000), compelling us to deal with the vexing issue of validity head-on. Only very carefully designed and sophisticated research that takes into account these challenges will advance the field by allowing us to explore the nature, character, and complexity of the positive changes that some people experience following stressful life events.

REFERENCES

Abraido-Lanza, A. F., Guier, C., & Colon, R. M. (1998). Psychological thriving among Latinas with chronic illness. *Journal of Social Issues, 54,* 405–424.

Affleck, G., Tennen, H., Croog, S., & Levine, S. (1987). Causal attribution, perceived benefits, and morbidity following a heart attack. *Journal of Consulting and Clinical Psychology, 55,* 29–35.

Affleck, G., Tennen, H., & Gershman, K. (1985). Cognitive adaptations to high-risk infants: The search for mastery, meaning, and protection from future harm. *American Journal of Mental Deficiency, 89,* 653–656.

Aldwin, C. M., & Levenson, M. R. (2004). Commentaries on posttraumatic growth: A developmental perspective. *Psychology Inquiry, 15,* 19–92.

Aldwin, C. M., Levenson, M. R., & Spiro, A., 3rd. (1994). Vulnerability and resilience to combat exposure: Can stress have lifelong effects? *Psychology and Aging, 9,* 34–44.

American Cancer Society (2004). Cancer Resource Center: Breast Cancer. (On-line). Internet Web site: http://www.cancer.org/cancerinfo.

Andrykowski, M. A., Brady, M. J., & Hunt, J. W. (1993). Positive psychosocial adjustment in potential bone marrow transplant recipients: Cancer as a psychosocial transition. *Psycho-oncology, 2,* 261–276.

Antoni, M. H., Lehman, J. M., Klibourn, K. M., Boyers, A. E., Culver, J. L., Alferi, S. M., et al. (2001). Cognitive-behavioral stress management intervention decreases the prevalence of depression and enhances benefit finding among women under treatment for early-stage breast cancer. *Health Psychology, 20,* 20–32.

Armeli, S., Gunthert, K. C., & Cohen, L. H. (2001). Stressor appraisals, coping, and post-event outcomes: The dimensionality and antecedents of stress-related growth. *Journal of Social and Clinical Psychology, 20,* 366–395.

Bauer, J. J., & McAdams, D. P. (2004). Personal growth in adults' stories of life transitions. *Journal of Personality, 72,* 573–602.

Behr, S. K., Murphy, D. L., & Summers, J. A. (1992). *User's manual: Kansas inventory of parental perceptions.* Lawrence: University of Kansas Press.

Belec, R. H. (1992). Quality of life: Perceptions of long-term survivors of bone marrow transplantation. *Oncology Nursing Forum, 19,* 31–37.

Bloom, S. (1998). In Tedeschi, R. G., Park, C. L., & Calhoun, L. (Eds.), *Posttraumatic growth: Positive changes in the aftermath of crisis* (pp. 179–214). Mahwah, NJ: Lawrence Erlbaum Associates.

Bossolo, L., Bergantino, D., Lichtenstein, B., & Gutman, M. (2002). Many Americans still feeling effects of September 11th; Are reexamining their priorities in life. At http://www.apa.org/practice/poll_911.html.

Bower, J. E., Kemeny, M. E., Taylor, S. E., & Fahey, J. L. (2003). Finding positive meaning and its association with natural killer cell cytotoxicity among participants in a bereavement-related disclosure intervention. *Annals of Behavioral Medicine, 25,* 146–155.

Burt, M. R., & Katz, B. L. (1988). Coping strategies and recovery from rape. *Annals of the New York Academy of Sciences, 528,* 345–358.

Carver, C. S. (1998). Resilience and thriving: Issues, models, and linkages. *Journal of Social Issues, 54,* 245–266.

Carver, C. S., Scheier, M. F., & Weintraub, J. K. (1989). Assessing coping strategies: A theoretically based approach. *Journal of Personality and Social Psychology, 56,* 267–283.

Clark, L. A., & Watson, D. (1995). Constructing validity: Basic issues in objective scale development. *Psychological Assessment, 7,* 309–319.

Cohen, L. H., Hettler, T. R., & Pane, N. (1998). Assessment of posttraumatic growth. In R. G. Tedeschi, C. L. Park, & L. Calhoun (Eds.), *Posttraumatic growth: Positive changes in the aftermath of crisis* (pp. 23–42). Mahwah, NJ: Lawrence Erlbaum Associates.

Collins, R. L., Taylor, S. E., & Skokan, L. A. (1990). A better world or a shattered vision? Changes in life perspectives following victimization. *Social Cognition, 8,* 263–285.

Cordova, M. J., Cunningham, L. L. C., Carlson, C. R., & Andrykowski, M. A. (2001). Posttraumatic growth following breast cancer: A controlled comparison study. *Health Psychology, 20,* 176–185.

Costa, P. T., Jr., & McCrae, R. R. (1985). *The NEO personality inventory manual.* Odessa, FL: Psychological Assessment Resources.

Crowne, D. P., & Marlowe, D. (1960). A new scale of social desirability independent of psychopathology. *Journal of Consulting Psychology, 24,* 349–354.

Curbow, B., Somerfield, M. R. Baker, F., Wingard, J. R., & Legro, M. W. (1993). Personal changes, dispositional optimism, and psychological adjustment to bone marrow transplantation. *Journal of Behavioral Medicine, 16,* 423–443.

Ebersole, P., & Flores, J. (1989). Positive impact of life crises. *Journal of Social Behavior and Personality, 4,* 463–469.

Fife, B. L. (1995). The measurement of meaning in illness. *Social Science and Medicine, 40,* 1021–1028.

Fontana, A., & Rosenheck, R., (1998). Psychological benefits and liabilities of traumatic exposure in the war zone. *Journal of Traumatic Stress, 11,* 485–503.

Frazier, P., Conlon, A., & Glaser, T. (2001). Positive and negative life changes following sexual assault. *Journal of Consulting and Clinical Psychology, 69,* 1048–1055.

Frazier, P., Tashiro, T., Berman, M., Steger, M., & Long, J. (2004). Correlates of levels and patterns of positive life changes following sexual assault. *Journal of Consulting and Clinical Psychology, 72,* 19–30.

Fromm, K., Andrykowski, M. A., & Hunt, J. (1996). Positive and negative psychosocial sequelae of bone marrow transplantation: Implications for quality of life assessment. *Journal of Behavioral Medicine, 19,* 221–240.

Hamera, E. K., & Shontz, F. C. (1978). Perceived positive and negative effects of life-threatening illness. *Journal of Psychosomatic Research, 22,* 419–424.

Ho, S. M. Y., Chan, C. L. W., & Ho, R. T. H. (2004). Posttraumatic growth in Chinese cancer survivors. *Psycho-oncology, 13,* 377–389.

Jacobs, C., Ross, R. D., Walker, I. M. & Stockdale, F. E. (1983). Behavior of cancer patients: A randomized study of the effects of education and peer support groups. *American Journal of Clinical Oncology, 6,* 347–350.

Janoff-Bulman, R. (1989). Assumptive worlds and the stress of traumatic events: Applications of the schema construct. *Social Cognition, 7,* 113–136.

Janoff-Bulman, R. (2004). Posttraumatic growth: Three explanatory models. *Psychological Inquiry, 15,* 30–34.

Joseph, S., Williams, R., & Yule, W. (1993). Changes in outlook following disaster: The preliminary development of a measure to assess positive and negative response. *Journal of Traumatic Stress, 6,* 271–279.

Kennedy, B. J., Tellegen, A., Kennedy, S., & Havernick, N. (1976). Psychological response of patients cured of advanced cancer. *Cancer, 38,* 2184–2191.

King, L. A., & Miner, K. N. (2000). Writing about the perceived benefits of traumatic events: Implications for physical health. *Personality and Social Psychology Bulletin, 26,* 220–230.

King, L. A., & Raspin, C. (2004). Lost and found possible selves, subjective well-being, and ego development in divorced women. *Journal of Personality, 72,* 603–632.

Klauer, T., & Filipp, S. (1997). Life-change perceptions in cognitive adaptation to life-threatening illness. *Revue Europiene de Psychologi Appliquee, 47,* 181–187.

Lechner, S., & Antoni, M. H. (2004). Posttraumatic growth and group-based interventions for persons dealing with cancer: What have we learned so far? *Psychological Inquiry, 15,* 35–41.

Lechner, S. C., & Zakowski, S. G. (2001). Benefit-finding changes over time in individuals with cancer. *Annals of Behavioral Medicine, 23,* S0010 (Abstract).

Lechner, S. C., Zakowski, S. G., Antoni, M. H., Greenhawt, M., Block, K., & Block, P. (2003). Do sociodemographic and disease-related variables influence benefit-finding in cancer patients? *Psycho-oncology, 12,* 491–499.

Lehman, D. R., Wortman, C. B., & Williams, A. F. (1987). Long-term effects of losing a spouse or child in a motor vehicle crash. *Journal of Personality and Social Psychology, 52,* 218–231.

Linley, P. A., & Joseph, S. (2004). Positive change following trauma and adversity: A review. *Journal of Traumatic Stress, 17,* 11–21.

Longman, A. J., & Graham, K. Y. (1986). Living with melanoma: Content analysis of interviews. *Oncology Nursing Forum, 13,* 58–64.

Manne, S., Ostroff, J., Winkel, G. Goldstein, L., Fox, K., & Grana, G. (2004). Posttraumatic growth after breast cancer: Patient, partner, and couple perspectives. *Psychosomatic Medicine, 66,* 442–454.

Massey, S., Cameron, A., Ouellette, S., & Fine, M. (1998). Qualitative approaches to the study of thriving: What can be learned?—Thriving: Broadening the Paradigm Beyond Illness to Health. *Journal of Social Issues, 54,* 373–391.

McFarland, C., & Alvaro, C. (2000). The impact of motivation on temporal comparisons: Coping with traumatic events by perceiving personal growth. *Journal of Personality and Social Psychology, 79,* 327–343.

McMillen, J. C., Howard, M. O., Nower, L., & Chung, S. (2001). Positive by-products of the struggle with chemical dependency. *Journal of Substance Abuse Treatment, 20,* 69–79.

McMillen, J. C. (2004). Posttraumatic growth: What's it all about? *Psychological Inquiry, 15,* 48–52.

McMillen, J. C., & Cook, C. L. (2003). The positive by-products of spinal cord injury and their correlates. *Rehabilitation Psychology, 48*, 77–85.

McMillen, J. C., & Fisher, R. H. (1998). The Perceived Benefit Scales: Measuring perceived positive life changes after negative events. *Social Work Research, 22*, 173–186.

McMillen, J. C., Smith, E. M., & Fisher, R. H. (1997). Perceived benefit and mental health after three types of disaster. *Journal of Consulting and Clinical Psychology, 65*, 733–739.

McMillen, C., Zuravin, S., & Rideout, G. (1995). Perceived benefit from child sexual abuse. *Journal of Consulting and Clinical Psychology, 63*, 1037–1043.

Meichenbaum, D., & Novaco, R. (1985). Stress inoculation: A preventative approach. *Issues in Mental Health Nursing, 7*, 419–435.

Mendola, R., Tennen, H., Affleck, G., McCann, L., & Fitzgerald (1990). Appraisal and adaptation among women with impaired fertility, *Cognitive Therapy and Research, 14*, 79–93.

Miller, W. R., & C'deBaca, J. (2001). *Quantum change: When epiphanies and sudden insights transform ordinary lives.* New York: Guilford.

Nolen-Hoeksema, S., & Davis, C. G. (2004). Theoretical and methodological issues in the assessment and interpretation of posttraumatic growth. *Psychological Inquiry, 15*, 60–64.

Pals, J. L., & McAdams, D. P. (2004). The transformed self: A narrative understanding of posttraumatic growth. *Psychological Inquiry, 15*, 65–69.

Parappully, J., Rosenbaum, R., van den Daele, L., & Nzewi, E. (2002). Thriving after trauma: The experience of parents of murdered children. *Journal of Humanistic Psychology, 42*, 33–70.

Park, C. L. (1998). Post-traumatic growth and adjustment. In R. Tedeschi, C. L. Park, & L. Calhoun (Eds.), *Post-traumatic growth: Theory and research on processes of change in the aftermath of crises* (pp. 153–178). Mahwah, NJ: Lawrence Erlbaum Associates.

Park, C. L., Cohen, L. H., & Murch, R. (1996). Assessment and prediction of stress related growth. *Journal of Personality, 64*, 71–105.

Park, C. L., & Fenster, J. R. (2004). Stress-related growth: Predictors of occurrence and correlates with psychological adjustment. *Journal of Social and Clinical Psychology, 23*, 195–215.

Peltzer, K. (2000). Trauma symptom correlates of criminal victimization in an urban community sample. *South Africa. Journal of Psychology in Africa, 10*, 49–62.

Petrie, K. J., Buick, D. L., Weinman, J., & Booth, R. J. (1999). Positive effects of illness reported by myocardial infarction and breast cancer patients. *Journal of Psychosomatic Research, 47*, 537–543.

Poorman, P. B. (2002). Perceptions of thriving by women who have experienced abuse or status-related oppression. *Psychology of Women Quarterly, 26*, 51–62.

Powell, S., Rosner, R., Butollo, W., Tedeschi, R. G., & Calhoun, L. G. (2003). Posttraumatic growth after war: A study with former refugees and displaced people in Sarajevo, *Journal of Clinical Psychology, 59*, 71–83.

Ross, M., & Conway, M. (1986). Remembering one's own past: The construction of personal histories. In R. M. Sorrentino & E. T. Higgins (Eds.), *The handbook of motivation and cognition: Foundations of social behavior* (pp. 122–144). New York: Guilford.

Ross, R. D., Stockdale, F. E., & Jacobs, C. (1978). Cancer patient behavior scale: Scores of cancer patients and healthy adults. *Proceedings of the American Society of Clinical Oncology, 19*, 348.

Schaefer, J. A., & Moos, R. (1992). Life crises and personal growth. In B. Carpenter (Ed.), *Personal coping: Theory, research, and application* (pp. 149–170). Westport, CT: Praeger.

Schnurr, P. P., Friedman, M. J., & Bernardy, N. C. (2002). Research on posttraumatic stress disorder: Epidemiology, pathophysiology, and assessment. *Journal of Clinical Psychology, 58*, 877–889.

Schwartzberg, S. S. (1993). Struggling for meaning: How HIV positive gay men make sense of AIDS. *Professional Psychology: Research and Practice, 24*, 483–490.

Sears, S. R., Stanton, A. L., & Danoff-Burg, S. (2003). The yellow brick road and the emerald city: Benefit-finding, positive reappraisal coping, and posttraumatic growth in women with early-stage breast cancer. *Health Psychology, 22*, 487–496.

Siegel, K., & Schrimshaw, E. W. (2000). Perceiving benefits in adversity: Stress-related growth in women living with HIV/AIDS. *Social Science and Medicine, 51* 1543–1554.

Sprangers, M. A. G., & Schwartz, C. E. (1999). Integrating response shift into health-related quality of life research: A theoretical model. *Social Science & Medicine, 48*, 1507–1515.

Torabi, M. R., & Seo, D. (2004). National study of behavioral and life changes since Septem_____ _Education and Behavior, 31_, 179–192.

Taylor, S. E. (1983). Adjustment to threatening events: A theory of cognitive adaptation. _American Psy___ _38_, 1161–1173.

Taylor, S. E., Lichtman, R. R., & Wood, J. V. (1984). Attributions, beliefs about control, and adjustment _ breast cancer. _Journal of Personality and Social Psychology, 46_, 489–502.

Tedeschi, R. G., & Calhoun, L. (1996). The Posttraumatic Growth Inventory: Measuring the positive legacy of trauma. _Journal of Traumatic Stress, 9_, 455–471.

Tedeschi, R. G., & Calhoun, L. (2004). Posttraumatic growth: Conceptual foundations and empirical evidence. _Psychological Inquiry, 15_, 1–18.

Tennen, H., & Affleck, G. (2002). Benefit-finding and benefit-reminding. In C. R. Snyder & S. J. Lopez (Eds.), _Handbook of positive psychology_ (pp. 584–597). London: Oxford University Press.

Thompson, M. (2000). Life after rape: A chance to speak? _Sexual and Relationship Therapy, 15_, 325–343.

Tomich, P. L., & Helgeson, V. S. (2002). Five years later: A cross-sectional comparison of breast cancer survivors with healthy women. _Psycho-oncology, 11_, 154–169.

Tomich, P. L., & Helgeson, V. S. (2004). Is finding something good in the bad always good? Benefit finding among women with breast cancer. _Health Psychology, 23_, 16–23.

Updegraff, J. A., Taylor, S. E., Kemeny, M. E., & Wyatt, G. E. (2002). Positive and negative effects of HIV infection in women with low socioeconomic resources. _Personality and Social Psychology Bulletin, 28_, 382–394.

Weiss, T. (2002). Posttraumatic growth in women with breast cancer and their husbands: An intersubjective validation study. _Journal of Psychosocial Oncology, 20_, 65–80.

Weiss, T. (2004). Correlates of posttraumatic growth in husbands of breast cancer survivors. _Psycho-oncology, 13_, 260–268.

Wortman, C. B. (2004). Posttraumatic growth: Progress and problems. _Psychological Inquiry, 15_, 81–90.

Zemore, R., Rinholm, J., Shepel, L. F., & Richards, M. (1989). Some social and emotional consequences of breast cancer and mastectomy: A content analysis of 87 interviews. _Journal of Psychosocial Oncology, 7_, 33–45.

CHAPTER

4

Re-Storying Loss: Fostering Growth in the Posttraumatic Narrative

Robert A. Neimeyer
University of Memphis

Reflecting on the profound personal changes he has observed in himself and in his life since the suicidal death of his son five years ago, a 58-year-old father observes:

> As a result of my son's death, I have been energized to study and learn more about depression, psychotherapy and mental illness in general. After a great deal of reading and personal reflection, I now have a better understanding of suicide and of my son's struggles with substance abuse and depression—or at least this is my interpretation. I still grieve and have feelings that I could have been more supportive of him so that he might not have taken his life, even though others suggest that there was little that I could have done. Styron's book (*Darkness Visible*) and Kay Redman's book (*An Unquiet Mind*) probably have had the most profound influence on my attempts to make sense of his death. Little has made much of a difference with respect to the feeling of loss—the void. It still aches.
>
> Despite this continuing pain, or perhaps because of it, I have noticed positive effects of this experience in my personal life and in my work. I have a new perspective regarding things that do and those that do not matter so much in the larger scheme.
>
> In terms of my sense of myself, I find that I am driven to learn more, but I am calmer and more reflective of my interactions with others. I'm not sure I am more tolerant, but I am better able to understand my own emotions and the reactions of other people. Although it seems strange to acknowledge it, I feel that I have grown in important and enduring ways as a result of this loss and my attempt to find meaning in it.

As is abundantly clear throughout this book, this father's response to a tragic loss is echoed by many whose life stories have been massively rewritten by traumatic events they could not have anticipated. As a burgeoning field of research documents, whether the challenges to the fundamental schemas of survivors' lives result from encounters with tragic bereavement, catastrophic illness, interpersonal violence, or political oppression, a great many experience growth as well as grief, being prompted by highly distressing circumstances to higher levels of posttrauma adaptation. Integrating these specific findings with the broad literatures on stress and coping, social support, and especially the cognitive processing of negative experiences, Tedeschi and Calhoun (2004) offer a comprehensive model of responses to "seismic" life events, and invite the attention of other theorists and investigators to the many unanswered questions concerning how and why intense suffering so frequently occasions profound personal development.

My intent in the present chapter is to accept this invitation, with the goal of making a modest contribution to our understanding of posttraumatic growth (PTG) as a form of *meaning reconstruction* in the wake of crisis and loss (Neimeyer, 2001a). As Tedeschi and Calhoun (2004, p. 15) note, although "the overall picture of posttraumatic growth has been sketched . . . describing the details of cognitive processing and narrative development will be much more difficult, and will demand from researchers an intimate knowledge of many literatures . . . ." By drawing, in particular, on the literature concerning constructivist and narrative models of psychotherapy (Neimeyer & Mahoney, 1995; Neimeyer & Raskin, 2000), I will attempt to tease out some heuristics for understanding the construction of life narratives and illustrate their application to PTG following loss. I hope that this effort offers some useful concepts and methods to other scholars seeking to extend and refine our understanding of positive changes resulting from the struggle with life crises, in addition to helping professionals attempting to facilitate this process in their concrete work with traumatized clients.

THE NARRATIVE NATURE OF HUMAN LIFE

Of the many literatures relevant to the phenomenon of PTG, literature concerned with the construction, deconstruction, and reconstruction of narratives may be among the richest, but also least utilized. At one level, the human penchant for meaning-making through the medium of storytelling is obvious, whether we position ourselves as the authors or audience of these accounts. On the one hand, we spend countless hours telling bedtime stories to our children and grandchildren, relating the events of our day to our partners when we return from work, writing annual holiday letters summarizing the highlights of family stories from the year that has past, and sometimes, when the accounts of our experience are too painful to share even with those we love, we seek professional counselors or therapists who we hope can hear and respond to life stories that others cannot. On the other hand, we readily offer ourselves as an audience to the narrative activity of others, whether the stories in which we immerse ourselves are told in conversation, written in books, or performed in the theater, in films, or on television (Neimeyer & Levitt, 2001).

So pervasive is this human predilection toward "storying" experience that our species might appropriately be labeled not simply *homo sapiens*, emphasizing our effort to seek knowledge, but more specifically *homo narrans*, stressing our tendency to organize such knowledge in storied form (Hermans, 2002). Indeed, a good deal of research in cognitive science suggests that the fundamental architecture of narratives, punctuating the endless flow of events and organizing them into stories having clear beginnings, middles, and ends, may provide the basic schematic structure for much of human thought (Barsalou, 1988; Mandler, 1984). Likewise, developmental psychologists have chronicled the gradual emergence of narrative capacities in children, from the rudimentary attempts of two year olds to construct a meaningful "landscape of action" in their stories to the insights of older children as they grasp the "landscape of consciousness" reflected in the thoughts, feelings, and motivations of different characters (Bruner, 1990; Nelson, 2003). For their own part, social psychologists have studied the construction of autobiographical accounts, and emphasized the means by which we subtly position ourselves as characters of moral worth in the stories we tell to others (Wortham, 2001). And finally, neuropsychologists and brain scientists are beginning to map the widely distributed neural structures that subserve autobiographical memory and narrative reasoning, processes that are surprisingly difficult to disrupt even in the presence of significant brain lesions and disorders (Demasio, 1994; Rubin & Greenberg, 2003). The result is a burgeoning interdisciplinary interest in narrative, as scholars seek out the relations between phenomenological, psychological, neurobiological, and even literary analyses of narrative and consciousness without privileging or diminishing the value of any of these approaches (Flanagan, 1992).

Viewed in a broad sense, this characteristically human orientation toward the formulation of experience in narrative terms can be viewed as having three dimensions: personal, interpersonal, and broadly social or cultural. At a *personal* level, people spontaneously segment their experience into identifiable episodes, organizing these to construct stories with intelligible plots, populated by characters with explicit or implicit motives and intentions, enriched by vivid descriptions of relevant settings, exemplifying underlying themes, and targeted toward abstract goals (Neimeyer, 2000). Nowhere is this narrative activity more evident or important than in the formulation of a *self-narrative*, defined as "an overarching cognitive-affective-behavioral structure that organizes the 'micro-narratives' of everyday life into a 'macro-narrative' that consolidates our self-understanding, establishes our characteristic range of emotions and goals, and guides our performance on the stage of the social world" (Neimeyer, 2004a, pp. 53–54). From this perspective, identity can be seen as a narrative achievement, as our sense of self is established through the stories that we tell about ourselves, the stories that relevant others tell about us, and the stories we enact in their presence. Importantly, it is this very self-narrative that is profoundly shaken by "seismic" life events, instigating the processes of revision, repair, or replacement of basic thematic assumptions and goals emphasized by Tedeschi and Calhoun, a topic to which I will return in some detail in the following text.

At a second, more *interpersonal* level, narration serves vital social and individual functions. In a conversational medium, stories can be told to instruct, entertain, impress, implore, test, admonish, invite, or distance the listener, and occasionally several of these intentions can be compressed into a single telling (Neimeyer, 1995). In the context of greatest relevance to Tedeschi and Calhoun, the recounting of traumatic life narratives to others solicits validation of one's experience and provision of social support, both of which can facilitate healing and growth. Indeed, a good deal of psychological research demonstrates the importance of confiding or "account making" in integrating and transcending difficult life experiences (Harvey, 1996; Rynearson, 2001). It is worth emphasizing, however, that not all disclosures of personal tragedy will be met with sympathetic, concerned, and helpful responses. In the literature on grief, for example, it is clear that many losses are "disenfranchised" (Doka, 2002), in the sense that they are met with "empathic failure" on the part of intimate and nonintimate others in the family and broader community (Neimeyer & Jordan, 2002). Characteristically, the less normative and socially sanctioned the loss (as in the death of a developmentally delayed child or an extramarital partner, or bereavement through stigmatizing causes, such as an overdose of recreational drugs or AIDS), the more unlikely it is that sharing the narrative of one's loss with others will secure the sort of validation and support that fosters integration of and growth from the experience. It is also worth bearing in mind that interpersonal narration is a highly interactive activity, as friends, family, and other social actors variously support, extend, or contest one another's stories regarding the loss, whether through death, divorce, or other forms of relationship dissolution (Nadeau, 1997). Closer attention to the processes entailed in this social construction of meaning could therefore clarify some of the pathways through which PTG is facilitated or impeded at an interpersonal level.

Finally, narrative processes that take place at broadly *social* levels can establish a context for posttraumatic stress or growth not only for individuals living within a society, but also in some sense for the society as a whole. For example, the "historical generation" of Americans who came of age during the twin hardships of the Great Depression and World War II developed a sense of civic responsibility and social interdependence that characterized their political and social behavior throughout their adult lives (Rogler, 2003). Importantly, it was not simply the events that shaped this modal outcome, but rather the terms in which the significance of these events was consolidated in the plot structure, themes, and morals of countless "heroic" narratives of the 1930s and 1940s, whether presented in presidential "fireside chats," films, newsreel coverage of world events, or the popular literature of the period. More generally, the "culture tales" (Howard, 1991) and mythic stories of societies both ancient and modern provide a trove of narrative resources that members of cultures draw upon to find meaning and direction at times of adversity. Conversely, such narratives or discourses of cultural identity can also have more pernicious consequences, being used or explicitly crafted to reinforce oppressive, racist, imperialist, or militaristic actions that can engender traumatic events rather than contribute to their transcendence. Qualitative research on the bereavement narratives of African Americans, for example, documents the pervasive role of racist discourses that limited the lives of the deceased, often adding a heroic dimension to survivors' postloss constructions of their loved one's identity, as they struggled against great odds to live fully (Rosenblatt & Wallace, 2005).

FORMS OF NARRATIVE DISRUPTION

The robustness with which narrative activity structures our psychological, interpersonal, and social lives suggests that it can serve as a powerful resource in integrating and attributing meaning to troubling life transitions. Indeed, recent evidence suggests that human beings are surprisingly resilient even in the face of extremely stressful life events, with upward to half of bereaved persons, for example, showing only modest and transitory symptomatology in the weeks and months following their loss (Bonanno, Wortman, & Nesse, 2004). Such demonstrably healthy profiles of postloss adaptation are consonant with the view that resilient survivors are able to *assimilate* loss into their existing self-narratives in a way that it does not radically undermine the central themes of their life stories and, indeed, may even affirm them. However, when such assimilation is not possible, survivors may find themselves struggling to *accommodate* their self-narratives to integrate the enormity of their loss, in addition to promote adaptation to their changed lives in its aftermath. As argued elsewhere, such a conception can serve as a valuable heuristic frame for interpreting the multiple pathways by which people negotiate the terrain of bereavement (Neimeyer, 2005).

Clearly, the "effort after meaning" through the construction of narratives can be fraught with problems in addition to prospects, although it is often the case that the very ways in which personal, interpersonal, or broadly social narration fails suggests the avenues along which posttraumatic narrative repair and growth will occur. In this section I will summarize and extend a germinal taxonomy of narrative disruptions I have begun to develop elsewhere (Neimeyer, 2000, 2004b) and consider how each form challenges the adequacy of the self-narrative and, by implication, can set in motion the affective, cognitive, and social processes that enlarge and deepen the survivor's identity.

Disorganized Narratives

Perhaps the starkest form of narrative disruption is the substantial, and sometimes pervasive disorganization of the survivor's self-narrative following exposure to a traumatic event. Being a witness to or a survivor of horrific violence, torture, assault, combat, natural catastrophes, or life-threatening accidents can immerse the traumatized individual in a stream of intense and compelling experience that floods the brain with neurotransmitters, "stamping in" vivid sensory images of the event—the sight of blood, the smell of flames, the sound of screams—that can be psychologically welded together with the corresponding emotions of terror, despair, or helplessness (van der Kolk & van der Hart, 1991). Even less direct exposure to the event, as through vivid depictions or eyewitness accounts of personally relevant trauma or loss, can evoke similar responses. Moreover, because these undigested "emotion schemas" (Greenberg, Elliot, & Rice, 1993) operate at the level of the amygdala, a deep-brain structure that in trauma can be functionally stratified from neocortical processing of the event, such memory fragments can persist for months, years, or even decades, intruding periodically into awareness without being integrated into conscious, declarative memory. Construed in narrative terms, trauma memories can therefore be viewed as "prenarrative," falling outside of volitional memory processes, presenting the survivor with a set of tormenting and "unmetabolized" images and experiences that are radically inconsistent with the plot structure of his or her previous life narrative (Neimeyer & Stewart, 1998). Nor is the disorganization of the survivor's self-narrative limited to the disruption of its coherence by the ruminative struggle with radically contradictory images and emotions, as the trauma or loss can also invalidate the thematic assumptions on the basis of which the person has lived (Janoff-Bulman & Berg, 1998; Neimeyer et al., 2002).

An example of narrative disorganization is provided by the case of Sara, a woman in her thirties who sought psychotherapeutic help following the death of her brother David in the terrorist destruction of the World Trade Center on September 11, 2001. That fateful morning, as she was helping her children prepare for school, she received an unanticipated long distance telephone call from New York, from a brother whose panicked voice she scarcely recognized. Feeling a surge of confusion and alarm, she followed his urgent instructions to turn on the television and tell him what was happening in the very office building in which he had reported for work scarcely an hour before. The images and commentary that confronted her when she did so sent a wave of terror through her, as she saw flames and smoke billow from the tower only several floors above that in which David stood, and as she heard background screams and explosions on the cell phone on which he was speaking. For the next 22 minutes Sara coached her brother down the narrow, smoke-filled staircases toward light and safety, providing what encouragement and interpretation she could as she continued to watch the television coverage through eyes filled with tears. She remained on the phone when the horror reached a new level of intensity, and she watched the images of the collapsing structure, just as her brother and his officemates had reached the 11th floor. At that very moment she heard a roar in the receiver and the phone went dead, and Sara knew with a stab of anguish and helplessness that she had just watched and heard the murder of her brother, along with untold thousands of others in the decimated tower.

For months following the attack, Sara was flooded with imagery of the burning collapsing buildings, compounded by intrusive memories of thousands of New York grieving their dead or missing loved ones. In both daytime ruminations and nighttime dreams, she found herself replaying what the last half hour of David's life must have been like, picturing him struggling down the stairwells, covering his mouth with a handkerchief as protection from the smoke, tripping over the abandoned high-heeled shoes of fleeing female executives, and helping a disoriented coworker down the crowded staircase. Obsessively she tried to piece together the fragments she could recall of their conversation and coordinate these with additional sensory details of David's death that she could only imagine or reconstruct from media reports. Harder still than this anguishing effort to organize a meaningful account of the plot structure of what had happened was her struggle with the massive invalidation of the thematic structure on which her worldview had been premised, which had presumed optimistically that the world was relatively safe, that life was predictable, that the universe was just, and that people could be trusted. Now, faced with the horrendous and sudden murder of thousands, she felt the entire supportive structure of her self-narrative collapse along with the building in which her brother had worked, and in which she had watched him die.

In Sara's case, the horrific disorganization of her life narrative triggered a complicated grief reaction (Prigerson & Jacobs, 2001), understood as a decimation of her world of meaning precipitated by the tragic way in which her brother had died (Neimeyer, Prigerson, & Davies, 2002). But, it also set in motion processes of narrative revision, both pursued instinctively and intentionally as a function of therapy, which attempted to assemble a coherent account of the traumatic imagery and then consider the significance of the trauma story for the larger narrative of her life. Ultimately this led Sara toward a more complex, if ambivalent worldview, one that acknowledged the reality of death, the preciousness of life, and the twin conditions of human vulnerability and resilience. Similar increases in narrative complexity, in addition to the fostering of existential awareness, appreciation, and personal growth emphasized by Tedeschi and Calhoun, seem to result from the struggle to integrate and transcend the traumatic disorganization of life narratives in the wake of profound and destabilizing loss (Neimeyer, 2001b).

Dissociated Narratives (2)

Although less striking than the disorganized narratives described in the preceding text, which are most closely associated with the work on PTG, two other forms of narrative disruption deserve at least brief description for their relevance to adjustment following trauma and loss. The first of these is dissociated narratives, silent stories that resist acknowledgement in the public sphere, and often even in the private world of their primary protagonist. "Dissociation" in this context therefore implies both a breach of sociality, a rupture in the interpersonal sphere of account making, in addition to a dissociative blocking or compartmentalizing of awareness in a classical psychodynamic sense. In most instances of dissociated narratives, each implies the other, as the attempt to prevent a traumatic or painfully incongruent private event or story from finding expression in critical relationships requires and reinforces a harsh and vigilant form of self-monitoring and segregation of threatening private memories and images, and vice versa. A general illustration of this is provided by a woman widowed by her husband's suicide, who attempted to convince herself and others that the death arose from accidental causes. In this instance, the silent story ensured that even well-intentioned efforts at support on the part of relevant others will result in a kind of empathic failure, as critical aspects of the plot structure of the traumatic idden, unintegrated, and without social validation and support)02). A second example is that of a history of marital infidelity, in story of one spouse's past affair could radically threaten not only sumed thematic structure of their marital narrative, but perhaps the relationship. In such cases, the transgressing partner may find intimacy with the spouse, in both subtle and unsubtle ways, to of self-disclosure that could lead to open acknowledgement of the threatening extramarital relationship. Ironically, if the relevant relationships can survive disclosure of the dissociated narrative, the result can be a movement toward genuine openness, congruence, and emotional responsiveness both within the self and between the self and others. In this sense, overcoming the personal and relational ruptures associated with dissociated narratives can provide a powerful engine for both personal growth and deeper, more meaningful relationships, as Tedeschi and Calhoun emphasize.

Dominant Narratives

A final form of narrative disruption that deserves brief comment is that of dominant narratives (White & Epston, 1990)—socially, politically, or culturally enforced accounts of who an individual or member of a group is and, by implication, who he or she is not. Dominant narratives, therefore, marginalize more fragile, "preferred" accounts of self, at the same time that they steal the "authorship" of the individual's life narrative. In one sense they represent the antithesis of disorganized narratives, which confront the trauma survivor with a fragmented, incoherent sense of both self and world. In contrast, dominant narratives are, if anything, far *too* cohesive, organizing the person's sense of self under a single hegemonic label or description. When the dominant narrative is negative and preemptive (as when someone contending with serious illness or trauma comes to view him- or herself as "nothing but" a cancer patient or posttraumatic stress disorder [PTSD] case), then the dominant narrative can "colonize" the person's public identity and private self-concept, producing "real effects" on the way in which the person relates to self and others (Foucault, 1970). To the extent that the person can "externalize" the dominant narrative and see it as a problem-saturated story separate from the self, he or she is better able to resist it and reclaim the sense of new possibilities in life that Tedeschi and Calhoun have identified in several studies.

Although I have distinguished each of these patterns of narrative disruption for the sake of clarity, in many cases they overlap, with a single traumatic event precipitating disruptions of two or more kinds. For example, a violent instance of date rape can produce powerful invalidation of a presumed relational narrative, flooding the survivor with disorganizing and highly emotionally charged sights, sounds, smells, and sensations associated with the assault. Subsequently, the story might be held in a silent, dissociated fashion, contributing to a posture of emotional blunting and relational remoteness. Finally, indiscriminate disclosure of the assault can result in a dominant narrative of the survivor as a "rape victim," which in some social contexts might invite embarrassed avoidance or even attributions of blame. Moving through and beyond these multiple levels of personal and social disruption in such cases can be especially daunting, although the impressive gains made by many sexual assault survivors in safe contexts that permit them to tell their stories provides evidence that it is indeed possible (Alexander, Neimeyer, Follette, Moore, & Harter, 1989). Ultimately, then, PTG could entail seeking new coherence in a disorganizing life experience, finding ways to acknowledge and validate one's own suffering and that of others, and resisting the imposition of oppressive postloss identities that constrict one's self-narrative. When the resultant growth is largely an elaboration of the survivor's resilient preloss self-narrative, identity change might be considered evolutionary, but when adaptation requires a radical reordering of life priorities and values and the development of major new capacities and roles, the change can indeed be revolutionary.

IMPLICATIONS OF A NARRATIVE MODEL

Having underscored the centrality of narrative in human life and its frequent disruption in the wake of trauma and loss, I will turn to the use of narrative methods in both studying PTG in research contexts, and fostering its development in clinical settings. Because space constraints preclude fuller discussion of these procedures, I will refer the interested reader to other sources for further details on many of these methods (e.g., Neimeyer, 1993; Neimeyer & Mahoney, 1995; Neimeyer & Raskin, 2000).

Research

Investigators working from a constructivist/narrative base have devised many procedures for studying both structural and process features of people's self-narratives in general, and their meaning constructions regarding traumatic events in particular. One such method involves contemporary adaptations of repertory grid technique (Fransella, Bell, & Bannister, 2004), a procedure for eliciting a person's system of personal constructs for attributing meaning to events. As applied to traumatic narratives, "biographical grids" have been used to help the survivor articulate fundamental life themes (e.g., times I was helpless vs. times I was in control) through a systematic process of comparing and contrasting critical life episodes, of which the trauma is only one. Subsequently, the survivor rates each life episode (e.g., ages 9–12, when I played soccer; when I was bullied in high school; the death of my son in my 30s) on each theme (e.g., times I felt in control vs. times I felt out of control), producing a matrix of ratings that can be analyzed to suggest the level of differentiation or integration of the traumatic experience with other "chapters" in the person's life narrative, in addition to a depiction of the thematic integrity of his or her story (Neimeyer & Stewart, 1998). Such measures have been used to study the degree to which survivors of combat or mass murder are able to integrate such experiences into the structure of their construct systems, a factor shown to predict their current and future levels of posttraumatic adaptation (Sewell, 1996, 1997; Sewell et al., 1996).

A related procedure with strong potential for application to studies of PTG is the Self-Confrontation Method (SCM) (Hermans, 2002), which encourages the respondent to reflect on defining moments in his or her life story, rating them to yield descriptions of different life episodes or "valuations." For example, the respondent might begin by identifying a small set of influential life events that were important in shaping her sense of self (e.g., When I was 11, I felt lost and alone after my parent's divorce and our move to another city; Last year I married a man who really loves me). Such descriptions might actually be considered micronarratives in their own right, and the SCM could be viewed as an invitation for the respondent to integrate them into an overarching macronarrative of his or her life. This involves subsequently rating each of the valuations on affect terms (e.g., strength, intimacy, disappointment, worry), which vary in terms of their positivity and negativity, in addition to orientation toward self or others. The resulting profile, once analyzed, helps locate the individual within a plot of basic life themes, such as those of "unity and love," "unfulfilled longing," or "powerlessness and isolation." Extensions of the SCM, therefore, show promise in helping analyze and map progressive or regressive shifts in the self-narrative following trauma and loss, both for adults (van Geel, De Mey, Thissen-Pennings, & Bendermacher, 2000) and children (Dale & Wagner, 2003).

Complementing these structural measures are other qualitative and quantitative methods for assessing process features of a person's narrative activity. One of these is the Narrative Process Coding System (NPCS) (Angus, Levitt & Hardke, 1999), which provides guidelines for segmenting and coding written or spoken narratives (e.g., personal journals or the content of psychotherapy interviews) into micronarratives that are *external* (focusing on objective "reportage" of observable events), *internal* (elaborating personal feelings and reactions to the events), or *reflexive* (seeking meaning through interpretation and conceptualization of the story). For example, an application of the NPCS to the narrative of the bereaved father mentioned previously in this chapter would clarify his reliance primarily upon a reflexive voice punctuated by occasional internal processing of his son's suicide, with relatively little external description. Preliminary evidence suggests that shifting from one narrative perspective to another (e.g., constructing a coherent external account of a traumatic loss, followed by a detailed exploration of one's emotional response and the search for some larger sense of how it fits with one's life story) can facilitate the integration of the experience and promote better adaptation (Neimeyer & Anderson, 2002).

Alternative reliable coding systems can permit researchers to determine whether the protagonist views him- or herself as an "origin" or "pawn" of fate after a traumatic event (Gottschalk, Lolas, & Viney, 1986), or to identify the dominant themes in an individual's self-narrative (e.g., existential, moral, emotional, relational) and how they evolve over time or therapy (Feixas, Geldschlager, & Neimeyer, 2002). Finally, constructivists have devised detailed text-analytic methods for thoroughly analyzing shifts in narrative form over time, providing extensive "maps" of a storyteller's changing relation to the self and world (Villegas, 2002). These and related procedures could be useful in fostering research on PTG by operationalizing narrative concepts in empirical terms. As such, they can provide a meaningful extension of the carefully validated procedures for measuring such growth described elsewhere in this book, in addition to other scales for assessing the collapse of meaning in the wake of loss (Prigerson & Jacobs, 2001).

Clinical Methods

Among the most promising of narrative contributions to work on PTG is the trove of creative therapeutic procedures devised for fostering its development. Perhaps the best researched of these involves the use of therapeutic journals in helping people find meaning and even positive emotion in the act of writing deeply and consistently about the most painful episodes in their lives, leading to clear health and mental health benefits in numerous well-controlled studies (Pennebaker, 1997). Extending this strategy, several specific narrative methods (e.g., biographical techniques, metaphoric stories, life chapters exercises) have been devised to promote meaning reconstruction following bereavement, each of which can be used as a self-help method or in the context of professional grief therapy (Neimeyer, in press). For example, the *loss characterization* encourages survivors to describe themselves in the wake of their loss, but to do so as if they were the principle characters in a novel, play, or movie. Significantly, they are requested to write as if from the third-person standpoint of an intimate and sympathetic observer to help them step outside their current distress and view their self-narrative from a broader perspective. Although the writing and informal discussion of the resulting accounts can be therapeutic in themselves, a further analysis of the documents using a set of hermeneutic guid can enrich both assessment of postloss complications and sources of resilience, as il trated by Neimeyer, Keesee, and Fortner (2000). Thus, the literal use of narrative strategie through writing and reflecting on traumatic experiences might be more thoroughly and creatively developed to promote integration and transcendence of tragic transitions.

Oral narrative methods also hold promise in clinical settings. For example, emotionally discrepant episodes in a client's self-narrative can be "replayed" through slow-motion recall and renarration, focusing the "camera" of therapeutic attention on particularly painful details, or "panning out" to the larger life pattern in which the problematic event was embedded. Clinical applications suggest that use of this "movieola" method (Guidano, 1991, 1995) can help close the gap between experience and explanation, assisting clients in finding a thread of meaning and self-continuity in the aftermath of narrative disorganization. Other meaning-making interventions, in which bereaved people are invited to articulate the preverbal significance of their loss through the use of metaphor, and to creatively "dialogue" with their distress are illustrated in transcripts and videotapes of constructivist therapy (Neimeyer, 2001c, 2004c).

Carefully crafted group therapy methods for "retelling violent death" also hold promise for survivors of suicide and homicide, inviting controlled outcome evaluations (Rynearson, 2001). Clinical trials of broadly analogous group therapy methods for assisting incest survivors to share and process their stories of abuse have met with favorable outcomes (Alexander et al., 1989), demonstrating that giving voice to silent, dissociated narratives in safe environments that promote attribution of new meaning can prove helpful in fostering posttraumatic adaptation. Moreover, recent extensions of psychodrama, such as therapeutic enactment (Westwood, Keats, & Winensky, 2003), suggest that group settings that permit a healing performance of not only the original loss, but also more adaptive means of responding to it, can powerfully mobilize a client's ability to transcend trauma. Neimeyer and Arvay (2004) provide a full discussion of this work and a detailed illustration of its use in the case of a young man working to transform abusive experiences in relation to his father using intensive therapeutic enactment procedures.

Finally, a well-developed body of work in narrative therapy has special relevance for identifying and resisting dominant narratives. By first encouraging clients to label and externalize the problem (e.g., depression, despair, self-hatred) as something *external* to the self, therapists can help clients to identify its "real effects" on them and others they care about (White & Epston, 1990). Clients are then in a better position to recognize and reinforce actions and attitudes that challenge the hegemony of a problem-saturated story of their identity, which can be elaborated through a host of creative narrative methods (e.g., letter writing, documentation of special achievements, seeking an appropriate audience for the performance of a preferred self-narrative). A hallmark of such interventions is their use of "curious questions" to promote client processing of new themes and plot developments in their life story (Monk, Winslade, Crocket, & Epston, 1997) and to consolidate preferred self-narratives that could provide a bulwark against relapse (Dilollo, Neimeyer, & Manning, 2002). In this fashion narrative methods are congruent with contemporary educational theories, which view learning as anchored in concrete experience, processed through reflective observation, yielding higher order abstract conceptualizations, and giving rise to active experimentation, which produces more concrete experience, and so on (Kolb, 1984). Narrative theories and techniques therefore seem well positioned to help explicate and engender the processes of PTG to which Tedeschi and Calhoun invite further attention.

ed to take up the challenge posed by the editors, who encouraged
ieoretical and empirical research traditions to explore the subtler
enomenon whose existence is already well documented. In doing
est that narrative is more than just a *post hoc* accounting for
...uergo in response to life disruption—though it also serves that
vital, meaning attribution function. In addition, I have argued that self-narratives are the
very substance that is disrupted by trauma and loss, and that public and private narration
of tragedy and transition is heavily implicated in posttraumatic resilience, repair, and
transcendence. I hope that others who share a fascination with the growth often engendered
by great suffering will find in a narrative framework a set of conceptual and practical tools
with which to understand, study, and foster this life-enhancing process.

REFERENCES

Alexander, P. C., Neimeyer, R. A., Follette, V. M., Moore, M. K., & Harter, S. (1989). A comparison of group treatments of women sexually abused as children. *Journal of Consulting and Clinical Psychology, 57,* 479–483.

Angus, L., Levitt, H., & Hardke, K. (1999). Narrative processes and psychotherapeutic change. *Journal of Clinical Psychology, 55,* 1255–1270.

Barsalou, L. W. (1988). The content and organization of autobiographical memories. In U. Neisser & E. Winograd (Eds.), *Remembering reconsidered* (pp. 193–243). Cambridge: Cambridge University Press.

Bonanno, G. A., Wortman, C. B., & Nesse, R. M. (2004). Prospective patterns of resilience and maladjustment during widowhood. *Psychology and Aging, 19,* 260–271.

Bruner, J. (1990). *Acts of meaning.* Cambridge, MA: Harvard University Press.

Dale, M. A., & Wagner, W. G. (2003). Sandplay: An investigation into a child's meaning system via the Self Confrontation Method for Children (SCMC). *Journal of Constructivist Psychology, 16,* 17–36.

Demasio, A. R. (1994). *Descartes' error: Emotion, reason and the human brain.* New York: Putnam.

DiLollo, A., Neimeyer, R. A., & Manning, W. H. (2002). A personal construct psychology view of relapse: Indications for a narrative therapy component to stuttering treatment. *Journal of Fluency Disorders, 27,* 19–42.

Doka, K. (Ed.) (2002). *Disenfranchised grief.* Champaign, IL: Research Press.

Feixas, G., Geldschlager, H., & Neimeyer, R. A. (2002). Content analysis of personal constructs. *Journal of Constructivist Psychology, 15,* 1–19.

Flanagan, O. J. (1992). *Consciousness reconsidered.* Cambridge, MA: MIT Press.

Foucault, M. (1970). *The order of things.* New York: Pantheon.

Fransella, F., Bell, R., & Bannister, D. (2004). *A manual for repertory grid technique* (2nd ed.). West Sussex: Wiley.

Gottschalk, L. A., Lolas, F., & Viney, L. L. (1986). *Content analysis of verbal behavior in clinical medicine.* Heidelberg, Germany: Springer Verlag.

Greenberg, L., Elliott, R., & Rice, L. (1993). *Facilitating emotional change.* New York: Guilford.

Guidano, V. (1995). Self-observation in constructivist psychotherapy. In R. A. Neimeyer & M. J. Mahoney (Eds.), *Constructivism in psychotherapy* (pp. 155–168). Washington, DC: American Psychological Association.

Guidano, V. F. (1991). *The self in process.* New York: Guilford.

Harvey, J. H. (1996). *Embracing their memory.* Needham Heights, MA: Allyn & Bacon.

Hermans, H. (2002). The person as motivated storyteller. In R. A. Neimeyer & G. J. Neimeyer (Eds.), *Advances in personal construct psychology* (pp. 3–38). New York: Praeger.

Howard, G. S. (1991). Culture tales: A narrative approach to thinking, cross-cultural psychology, and psychotherapy. *American Psychologist, 46,* 187–197.

Janoff-Bulman, R., & Berg, M. (1998). Disillusionment and the creation of values. In J. H. Harvey (Ed.), *Perspectives on loss* (pp. 35–47). Philadelphia: Brunner/Mazel.

Kolb, D. A. (1984). *Experiential learning*. Englewood Cliffs, NJ: Prentice Hall.

Mandler, J. (1984). *Scripts, stories, and scenes*. Hillsdale, NJ: Lawrence Erlbaum Associates.

Monk, G., Winslade, J., Crocket, K., & Epston, D. (Eds.) (1997). *Narrative therapy in practice*. San Francisco: Jossey Bass.

Nadeau, J. (1997). *Families making sense of death*. Newbury Park, CA: Sage.

Neimeyer, G. J. (Ed.) (1993). *Constructivist assessment*. Thousand Oaks, CA: Sage

Neimeyer, R. A. (1995). Client-generated narratives in psychotherapy. In R.A. Neimeyer & M. J. Mahoney (Eds.), *Constructivism in psychotherapy* (pp. 231–246). Washington, DC: American Psychological Association.

Neimeyer, R. A. (2000). Narrative disruptions in the construction of self. In R. A. Neimeyer & J. D. Raskin (Eds.), *Constructions of disorder* (pp. 207–241). Washington, DC: American Psychological Association.

Neimeyer, R. A. (2001a). *Meaning reconstruction and the experience of loss*. Washington, DC: American Psychological Association.

Neimeyer, R. A. (2001b). Reauthoring life narratives: Grief therapy as meaning reconstruction. *Israel Journal of Psychiatry, 38*, 171–183.

Neimeyer, R. A. (2001c). The language of loss: Grief therapy as a process of meaning reconstruction. In R. A. Neimeyer (Ed.), *Meaning reconstruction and the experience of loss* (pp. 261–292). Washington, DC: American Psychological Association.

Neimeyer, R. A. (2004a). Fostering posttraumatic growth: A narrative elaboration. *Psychological Inquiry, 15*, 53–59.

Neimeyer, R. A. (2004b). Performing the self: Therapeutic enactment and the narrative integration of traumatic loss. In H. Hermans & G. Dimaggio (Eds.), *The dialogical self in psychotherapy* (pp. 173–189). New York: Brunner Routledge.

Neimeyer, R. A. (2004c). *Constructivist psychotherapy* (videotape/DVD). Washington, DC: American Psychological Association.

Neimeyer, R. A. (2005). Widowhood, grief and the quest for meaning: A narrative perspective on resilience. In D. Carr, R. M. Nesse, & C. B. Wortman (Eds.), *Late life widowhood in the United States*. New York: Springer.

Neimeyer, R. A. (in press). *Lessons of loss: A guide to coping* (2nd ed.). New York: Routledge.

Neimeyer, R. A., & Anderson, A. (2002). Meaning reconstruction theory. In N. Thompson (Ed.), *Loss and grief: A guide for human service practitioners* (pp. 45–64). New York: Palgrave.

Neimeyer, R. A., & Arvay, M. J. (2004). Performing the self: Therapeutic enactment and the narrative integration of traumatic loss. In H. Hermans & G. Dimaggio (Eds.), *The dialogical self in psychotherapy* (pp. 173–189). New York: Brunner Routledge.

Neimeyer, R. A., Botella, L., Herrero, O., Pacheco, M., Figueras, S., & Werner-Wildner, L A. (2002). The meaning of your absence: Traumatic loss and narrative reconstruction. In J. Kauffman (Ed.), *Loss of the assumptive world* (pp. 31–47). New York: Brunner Routledge.

Neimeyer, R. A., & Jordan, J. R. (2002). Disenfranchisement as empathic failure: Grief therapy and the co-construction of meaning. In K. Doka (Ed.), *Disenfranchised grief*, pp. 95–117. Champaign, IL: Research Press.

Neimeyer, R. A., Keesee, N. J., & Fortner, B. V. (2000). Loss and meaning reconstruction: Propositions and procedures. In R. Malkinson, S. Rubin, & E. Witztum, (Eds.), *Traumatic and non-traumatic loss and bereavement* (pp. 197–230). Madison, CT: Psychosocial Press.

Neimeyer, R. A., & Levitt, H. (2001). Coping and coherence: A narrative perspective. In D. Snyder (Ed.), *Stress and coping* (pp. 47–67). New York: Oxford.

Neimeyer, R. A., & Mahoney, M. J. (Eds.). (1995). *Constructivism in psychotherapy*. Washington, DC: American Psychological Association.

Neimeyer, R. A., Prigerson, H., & Davies, B. (2002). Mourning and meaning. *American Behavioral Scientist, 47*, 235–251.

Neimeyer, R. A., & Raskin, J. D. (Eds.). (2000). *Constructions of disorder*. Washington, DC: American Psychological Association.

Neimeyer, R. A., & Stewart, A. E. (1998). Trauma, healing, and the narrative emplotment of loss. In C. Franklin & P. A. Nurius (Eds.), *Constructivism in practice* (pp. 165–183). Milwaukee, WI: Families International Press.

Nelson, K. (2003). Narrative and the emergence of a consciousness of self. In G. D. Fireman, T. E. McVay, & O. J. Flanagan (Eds.), *Narrative and consciousness* (pp. 17–36). New York: Oxford.

Pennebaker, J. W. (1997). Writing about emotional experiences as a therapeutic process. *Psychological Science, 8*, 162–169.

Prigerson, H. G., & Jacobs, S. C. (2001). Diagnostic criteria for traumatic grief. In M. S. Stroebe, R. O. Hansson, W. Stroebe, & H. Schut (Eds.), *Handbook of bereavement research* (pp. 614–646). Washington, DC: American Psychological Association.

Rogler, L. H. (2003). Historical generations and psychology. *American Psychologist, 57*, (pp. 1013–1023).

Rosenblatt, P., & Wallace, B. (2005). *African-American grief*. New York: Brunner Routledge.

Rubin, D. C., & Greenberg, D. L. (2003). The role of narrative in recollection: A view from cognitive psychology and neuropsychology. In G. D. Fireman, T. E. McVay, & O. J. Flanagan (Eds.), *Narrative and consciousness* (pp. 53–85). New York: Oxford.

Rynearson, T. (2001). *Retelling violent death*. New York: Brunner Routledge.

Sewell, K. (1996). Constructional risk factors for a post-traumatic stress response following a mass murder. *Journal of Constructivist Psychology, 9*, 97–108.

Sewell, K. W. (1997). Posttraumatic stress: Towards a constructivist model of psychotherapy. In G. J. Neimeyer & R. A. Neimeyer (Eds.), *Advances in personal construct psychology* (Vol. 4, pp. 207–235). Greenwich, CT: JAI Press.

Sewell, K. W., Cromwell, R. L., Farrell-Higgins, J., Palmer, R., Ohlde, C., & Patterson, T. W. (1996). Hierarchical elaboration in the conceptual structure of Vietnam combat veterans. *Journal of Constructivist Psychology, 9*, 79–96.

Tedeschi, R. G., & Calhoun, L. G. (2004). Posttraumatic growth: Conceptual foundations and empirical evidence. *Psychological Inquiry, 15*, 1–18.

van der Kolk, B., & van der Hart, O. (1991). The intrusive past. *American Imago, 48*, 425–454.

van Geel, R., De Mey, H., Thissen-Pennings, M., & Bendermacher, N. (2000). Picturing valuations in affect space: Comparison of two methods of ordination in Hermans' Self Confrontation Method. *Journal of Constructivist Psychology, 13*, 27–45.

Villegas, M. (2002). Textual analysis of therapeutic discourse. In R. A. Neimeyer & G. J. Neimeyer (Eds.), *Advances in personal construct psychology* (pp. 113–159). New York: Praeger.

Westwood, M. J., Keats, P. A., Wilensky, P. (2003). Therapeutic enactment: Integrating the individual and group counselling models for change. *Journal for Specialists in Group Work, 28*, 122–138.

White, M., & Epston, D. (1990). *Narrative means to therapeutic ends*. New York: Norton.

Wortham, S. (2001). *Narratives in action*. New York: Teachers College.

5

SCHEMA-CHANGE PERSPECTIVES ON POSTTRAUMATIC GROWTH

RONNIE JANOFF-BULMAN
UNIVERSITY OF MASSACHUSETTS, AMHERST

The burgeoning literature on posttraumatic growth (PTG) might lead some to conclude that researchers have lost sight of the devastating impact of traumatic events in people's lives (see, e.g., Wortman, 2004). Surely survivors' pain and losses are all too evident to be ignored or discounted. Rather, in recognizing the depth and pervasiveness of victims' suffering, researchers have been all the more powerfully struck by the coexistence of a very different set of responses, a cluster of reactions that seem positive rather than negative, expansive rather than constrictive, indicative of growth and development rather than regression and decline. Against a backdrop of trauma, growth is not only unexpected and thus inherently interesting, but speaks to the multifaceted, inventive course of human coping and adaptation.

The reversible figure in psychology (see, e.g., Long & Toppino, 2004) provides a useful metaphor for survivors' reactions to their traumatic experiences. As would be expected, in the aftermath of their victimization survivors perceive the traumatic event as singularly negative, just as we might interpret a reversible figure in terms of one set of visual stimuli, such as an old woman or a vase in some classic cases. Yet over time, and it may be a very long time, survivors often begin to perceive their victimization in a new way, as a touchstone for the creation of value and positive appraisals in their lives. The very same traumatic event becomes the basis for a new perspective, just as the very same stimulus lines become the basis for a new perceptual image, be it the young woman or two faces. Both ways of viewing the trauma are available to the survivor, just as both reversible images are available to the viewer. The earlier, initial perception gives way over time to an alternative, but the alternative does not replace the previous image. Even when the trauma

...ived as a basis for growth, its painful negative representation is nevertheless ever-...ent, ready to dominate the survivor's psychological world. Yet, the more positive view, ...ot even accessible early on, becomes increasingly available to the survivor over time and, as with reversible figures, may pervade the perceptual field. The images are fundamentally linked, based on the same outlines, just as the survivor's pain and growth posttrauma are inextricably connected, tied to the same catastrophic events.

It is important to recognize just how common such positive perceptions, or rather accounts of personal growth, are posttrauma. Reviews of empirical studies suggest that between 75% and 90% of survivors report benefits (see, e.g., Davis, 2001; Tedeschi, Park, & Calhoun, 1998; Updegraff & Taylor, 2000), and although intense anxiety and post-traumatic stress are extremely common in the immediate aftermath of extreme negative events, the incidence of debilitating chronic posttraumatic stress disorder (PTSD) is rela-tively low, affecting approximately 5% to 15% of victimized populations (see, e.g., Ehlers, Mayou, & Bryant, 1998; Hanson, Kilpatrick, Freedy, & Saunders, 1995; Keane, Litz, & Blake, 1990; Resnick, Kilpatrick, Dansky, Saunders, & Best, 1993; Sutker, Davis, Uddo, & Ditta, 1995). Again, these numbers do not negate or neutralize the anguish and agony of traumatic life events and the extreme psychological challenges they present. They do speak to the rich and remarkable resources, creativity, and success of the human animal in its efforts to adapt, cope, and survive.

What is posttraumatic growth? The literature on the aftermath of traumatic events doc-uments an array of positive changes and benefits reported by survivors of diverse events, including disease, bereavement, accidents, combat, rapes, and assaults (see, e.g,, Bower, Kemeny, Taylor, & Fahey, 1998; Burt & Katz, 1987; Collins, Taylor, & Skokan, 1990; Edmonds & Hooker, 1992; Elder & Clipp, 1989; Frazier, Conlon, & Glaser, 2001; Joseph, Williams, & Yule, 1993; McMillen, Smith, & Fisher, 1997; Park, Cohen, & Murch, 1996; Tedeschi & Calhoun, 1995; Tedeschi, et al., 1998; Thompson, 1985; Veronen & Kilpatrick, 1983), but it would be inaccurate to assume that all of these represent instances of growth per se. Beneficial changes in external circumstances may influence and engender growth, but are not themselves instances of positive development. Financial help or more car-ing and compassionate responses from others are such benefits. Growth involves internal changes—transformations within the person—rather than external changes in circum-stance. In considering growth, we naturally think about physical increases in size. When considering growth in the context of traumatic life events, we are instead interested in psy-chological "increases," expansions and developments in survivors' cognitive-emotional understandings of themselves and their world.

In considering the nature of PTG, the literature on victimization and trauma typically describes a cluster of responses rather than a single set of positive reactions (for overviews see Calhoun & Tedeschi, 1999, 2001; Tedeschi & Calhoun, 1995, 2004). These indices of growth are well represented by the five discrete factors of Tedeschi and Calhoun's (1996) Posttraumatic Growth Inventory (PTGI): new possibilities, relating to others, personal strength, spiritual change, and appreciation of life. Generally, these positive changes are discussed together and are essentially considered a single type of response, one that is reflective or indicative of growth posttrauma. Surely, they are evidence of growth and positive transformation, but they do not necessarily reflect a single process or path. Rather, these growth-related outcomes may represent disparate psychological processes, each of which reflects a unique way of understanding PTG.

This chapter will discuss three models of PTG, each representing a different process and perspective on survivors' positive transformations. One process—strength through suffering—involves self-discovery and new self-perceptions produced over the course

Trauma

of coping and adaptation. A second route to change—existential re-e
straightforward, but far more interesting, and involves reflective appr
ation of value triggered by perceptions of human fragility in the after
tion. And finally, psychological preparedness is in many ways a by-pr
route, but focuses on changes in the survivor's assumptive world th
complexity and structural growth. All three types of psychological transformation can be
understood in terms of the impact of traumatic events on fundamental assumptions, or
in other words, in terms of schema changes in the content and architecture of our inner
worlds.

TRAUMA, FUNDAMENTAL ASSUMPTIONS, AND SCHEMA CHANGE

To fully appreciate and comprehend PTG, it seems essential to consider the nature of
trauma. When is a negative event traumatic? What makes an adverse experience a trauma?
The term seems to connote something extreme in the nature of the event—an experience
that is *very* negative or adverse. And surely the greater the loss one experiences, the more
likely the experience is to be traumatic. Yet, I would argue that it is not the recognizable,
readily apparent external losses—of one's health, home, community, or a loved one—that
define an experience as traumatic, but rather the internal disorganization and disintegration
that follows from our psychological unpreparedness (Epstein, 1991; Horowitz, 1976, 1979;
Janoff-Bulman, 1985, 1989, 1992; Parkes, 1971, 1975). Traumas are shocks to our inner
worlds.

One way to understand this inner world—and in turn its lack of preparedness—is in
terms of a set of fundamental assumptions (Janoff-Bulman, 1992) that constitute our model
of the world and ourselves. These are the theories, built from our own experiences, that we
use to construct plans, perceive people and events, forecast the future, and generally provide
a cognitive-emotional guide for effectively planning and acting in our world. Variously
labeled assumptive worlds, working models, structures of meaning, and theories of reality
(see, respectively, Bowlby, 1969; Epstein, 1991; Marris, 1974; and Parkes, 1971, 1975),
these assumptions are learned and confirmed by years of experience and make our lives
continuously intelligible.

In recent years, the areas of cognitive psychology and social cognition have popularized
the notion of "schemas," "which act as coherent concepts or naive theories that render the
world manageable. A schema is a cognitive structure containing the attributes of a concept
or type of stimulus and the relationships among the attributes" (Fiske, 2004, p. 143). These
are working and workable structures that we use to organize our experiences and anticipate
outcomes. They come in various forms, from stereotypes to stories (Fiske, 2004), but in
all cases they are structures that provide us with expectations, for new information is
understood by reference to old, familiar schemas.

Our fundamental assumptions are our most general, abstract schemas. The very bedrock
of our conceptual system is the domain of these assumptions, which represent our deepest
and broadest understandings of ourselves and our world. The earliest building blocks of
these fundamental assumptions are no doubt first laid in our early preverbal interactions
(see, e.g., Stern, 1985), as we begin to construct working models of our world based on
caregivers' responsiveness and dependability (see, e.g., Bowlby, 1969; Fairbairn, 1952;
Winnecott, 1965) and, over time, these schemas become increasingly general, compact,
resilient, and resistant to change (see Fiske, 2004). By adulthood, they typically go un-
questioned and unchallenged, yet provide us with our most basic expectations about our
outcomes and interactions in the world.

So, what are our fundamental assumptions? What schemas lie at the bedrock of our cognitive-emotional systems? Arguably, it is unlikely we have direct access to these deeply embedded assumptions; a plethora of recent research in social cognition, such as that on implicit prejudice, demonstrates our common lack of awareness of broad schema content (see, e.g., Greenwald & Banaji, 1995; Greenwald et al., 2002), and the depth and abstract nature of our fundamental assumptions suggests these might be particularly difficult to access directly. The powerful responses of survivors themselves—which I have heard time and again over the course of 30 years—provide the greatest insights into the content of these assumptions. The phrase "I never thought it could happen to me" was echoed again and again. It is as if the potent negative experiences served to unearth and objectify survivors' fundamental assumptions, making explicit what was otherwise implicit. Emotionally, the predominant response of these victims of extreme negative events was terror and intense anxiety. These survivors typically experienced real losses and many experienced depression, as might be expected, but terror was the more powerful response in the aftermath of the victimization. Intense anxiety and a dramatic sense of unpreparedness were crucial keys to understanding trauma.

It appears that at the core of our inner world are fundamental assumptions that provide us with a sense of safety and security. At the deepest levels of our psyche, we believe that we are protected from misfortune. This is not derived from some sense of magical protection, but more likely a set of assumptions about meaning, benevolence, and self-worth that together operate to yield a sense of relative invulnerability (Janoff-Bulman, 1985, 1989, 1992). We assume the world is meaningful, in the sense of person-outcome contingencies. That is, we take it for granted that by doing the right things, engaging in appropriately cautious behaviors, and being decent people, we can prevent misfortune. We minimize the possibility of random outcomes and maximize our control over outcomes by relying on culturally constructed theories of person-outcome contingency, and in the West these are theories of behavioral control and justice (see, e.g., Lerner, 1980). We know bad things happen, but we don't expect them to happen to us. By being the right kind of people who do the right kind of things, we maintain an illusion of safety and security—of relative invulnerability—and believe we can ward off disaster and tragedy.

Of course, common reactions to such assertions are readers' contentions that this doesn't apply to them—they know they're vulnerable, that bad things can happen to them, and so forth. Yet we now know from the considerable work on dual process models in psychology that what we maintain at the conscious, rational level may differ distinctly from what we believe at the more implicit, nonconscious level of processing (for a general overview of this work, see Chaiken & Trope, 1999). Epstein's (1998) cognitive-experiential theory is particularly instructive in this regard. He claims there are two types of knowing—experiential and rational—and these can be quite different, as illustrated by the person who rationally knows flying is very safe, but nevertheless fears flying. Similarly, we may rationally know the world isn't safe, and therefore we aren't either, but in our guts—at the experiential level of our existence—we maintain a fundamental belief in our own safety and invulnerability.

The potency of these assumptions is not only evident in the responses of victims, but in the reactions of nonvictims to the plight of victims as well. Years of research on victim blaming and derogation demonstrate this all-too-common reaction of nonvictims (e.g., Bennett & Dunkel-Schetter, 1992; Cann, Calhoun, & Selby, 1979; Carli & Leonard, 1989; Foley & Pigott, 2000). We seem to engage in a kind of knee-jerk attempt to blame victims, to find some behavior they should or shouldn't have engaged in, something they should or shouldn't have done. Thus, we look for alcohol use or speeding when we hear of a serious auto accident, and in this way we support our beliefs in the contingency between people and their outcomes. How else can we make sense of tragic occurrences? We don't want to know of the innocent victim paralyzed when a car jumped the highway's center median and struck her car or the man hit by a stray bullet on a city street. We manifest and maintain our assumptions about meaningfulness—and in turn our own safety—by blaming others for their misfortune.

Our fundamental assumptions, which afford us a comforting sense of security, are typically reinforced over the years, and essentially represent relatively simple, overgeneralized expectations. As our broadest, most abstract schemas, they are least subject to direct feedback and are essentially conservative. By providing the lens through which we process and interpret new information, our preexisting schemas, or assumptions, maximize the possibility of self-verification; information that doesn't fit can be ignored, forgotten, underestimated in significance, or massaged so as to be assimilated. Protected at the core of our inner world, our fundamental assumptions provide us with the confidence, trust, and positive motivation to go on each day.

It is not that change does not occur in our schemas, but rather that it occurs at the level of our narrower, concrete, specific assumptions. These latter beliefs are most sensitive to feedback gleaned from actions and interactions in the world (e.g., performance on a test or on a sports field might affect one's specific view of competence in that area, or repeatedly unfriendly responses by another person are apt to affect one's beliefs about that individual). Just as small, incremental changes are made in scientific theories through the daily accumulation of knowledge that occurs in "normal science" (Kuhn, 1962), we experience changes in our narrow, concrete schemas using a process of action and feedback. These narrower schemas change. But, our fundamental assumptions are more akin to scientific paradigms (Kuhn, 1962)—the overriding beliefs that color and shape how we act and view the world. Just as in science, these grandest theories—science's most abstract, generalized conceptions—are rarely seriously challenged by the day-to-day exceptions and anomalies, so too our fundamental assumptions typically remain unchallenged as well. Yet there are times in our lives—as in science—when the data of experience are too overwhelming to be ignored, when the anomalies are too powerful to reinterpret. These are regarded as periods of intense crisis in science (Kuhn, 1962), periods associated with scientific revolutions and shifting paradigms. In day-to-day human existence, these are periods of intense crisis, when we must address the inadequacy of our broadest theories and deepest assumptions. These are times of trauma.

Traumatic life events shatter our sense of safety and security, our complacency in a world where tragedy and misfortune do occur to good, careful people. It is not that our behaviors are irrelevant; precautions can minimize our risk of accident or criminal victimization, but they will not reduce the probability to zero. Life is risky, and bad things happen to good, careful people. Psychologically we're dramatically unprepared, and survivors are shocked to discover the naivete of their now-shattered assumptions and the utter sense of danger and insecurity that embraces them. Traumatic life events deal victims a double dose of anxiety—one associated with the recognition that the world is arbitrary and dangerous, and another with the recognition that their inner world is wholly inadequate. For the trauma victim, the outer world is now malevolent and threatening, and the inner world is disintegrated and seemingly useless. Psychologically the consequence is anxiety writ large—terror. Trauma is about confronting the terror of our fragile existence, a task for which we are dramatically unprepared psychologically. It is not primarily about actual intense losses in the external world, although these losses typically precipitate the trauma, but rather about profound psychological losses—of illusions associated with

ʾity, of an effective, coherent inner world; of a comfortable and comforting

ِgiy, recent work in psychology on terror management theory (for overviews Greenberg, Solomon, & Pyszczynski, 1997; Pyszczynski, Greenberg, & Solomon, 1999; Solomon, Greenberg, & Pyszczynski, 1991) has familiarized us with people's strong defensive reactions in the face of reminders of our mortality and vulnerability. These threats lead us to cling to cultural ideologies and practices, to old, comfortable patterns rather than new creative paths. They may lead us to affirm or exaggerate the meaningfulness of our lives (Davis & McKearney, 2003). Yet, traumatic events do not present mild or moderate threats to our assumptive worlds that can be easily neutralized through self-esteem pursuits or renewed faith in cultural worldviews. Rather, they are intense threats that shatter our sense of safety and security. Ordinary defenses are powerless in the face of such an overwhelming onslaught, and the terror of our vulnerability is paramount.

COPING AND POSTTRAUMATIC GROWTH: STRENGTH THROUGH SUFFERING

The coping task confronting the trauma victim is nothing short of overwhelming. It requires not only going through the motions of daily life in a world that now appears alien and threatening, but over time reconstructing a viable yet comfortable inner world (Janoff-Bulman, 1992; Tedeschi & Calhoun, 2004). The rebuilt assumptions must acknowledge the reality of the victim's traumatic experience, yet provide a basis for living a life that is not wholly defined by anxiety and vulnerability. Some survivors are unable to rebuild a more comfortable set of assumptions and struggle with chronic posttraumatic stress (see, e.g., Ehlers et al., 1998; Hanson et al., 1995; Keane et al., 1990; Resnick et al., 1993; Sutker et al., 1995). Yet for most survivors, the immediate terror, which involves blanket perceptions of randomness, uncontrollability, meaninglessness, malevolence, and threat, gives way over time to a less-absolutist, more nuanced set of assumptions. The road to reconstruction and successful coping is a painful, difficult one that provides survivors with a basis for recognizing new strengths and possibilities.

The survivor's cognitive-emotional coping task is to rebuild a viable assumptive world (Janoff-Bulman, 1992; Tedeschi & Calhoun, 2004). This is a task of mammoth proportions, framed by two possible extremes. One is the recovery of pretrauma assumptions, such that there is essentially no change in the fundamental assumptions. Although no doubt very emotionally compelling, given the security and safety associated with one's earlier fundamental schemas, they nevertheless now seem wholly inaccurate and invalid, like naïve illusions. The other extreme is to fully embrace the new negative assumptions implied by the traumatic experience, such that malevolence, meaninglessness, and self-doubt thoroughly pervade the survivor's assumptive world. These assumptions now appear accurate and valid, but are also emotionally uncomfortable and intensely threatening as a basis for day-to-day living. The task for the survivor is to rebuild a viable assumptive world that is both valid and comfortable.

In the immediate aftermath of trauma, the survivor's tendency is to overgeneralize from his or her experience and embrace the negative assumptions implied by the experience. Survivors seem to temporarily substitute threatening assumptions for the previously comfortable ones, and consequently feel intensely anxious in a dangerous world, unprotected from misfortune. Now their world seems fully defined by the traumatic victimization. A key to successful coping and adjustment involves moving from such overgeneralized negative assumptions to a more complex assumptive world, one that can account for their victimization, but nevertheless provides a more positive view of the self and the world.

They struggle with attempts to construct an inner world that is once again comfortable and comforting, yet can account for their experience.

Humans are motivated to survive and adapt, and survivors over time confront the frightening data of their experience and rebuild their inner worlds. Some form of emotional regulation aids in the process, as survivors increasingly move toward approach rather than avoidance processes in incorporating the new data. Although chronic PTSD is relatively uncommon in the long-term aftermath of traumatic events, in the immediate aftermath many survivors experience subclinical stress reactions or short-lived PTSD (Bonanno, 2004), with symptoms of emotional numbing and intrusive thoughts. These symptoms reflect an essentially healthy organism trying to come to grips with an overwhelming threat to the assumptive world (Horowitz, 1976, 1979; Janoff-Bulman, 1992). In the face of intense fear and anxiety, emotional numbing kicks in and allows survivors to minimize the feelings of terror induced by the trauma. They can avoid being utterly overwhelmed by partially shutting out the emotionally laden data of their experience. Yet, the intrusive thoughts that also define PTSD preclude the possibility of complete neglect and denial of the threatening data of experience. Despite the terror associated with the trauma, the experience must be acknowledged and worked on (Horowitz, 1976, 1979), even if in small doses initially—approached rather than avoided, and nonvolitionally if need be (as in intrusive reexperiencing of the event). The traumatic data is confronted in limited doses.

As time passes, the survivor is constantly taking in new data from daily living, information that often belies the threatening nature of the world implied by the traumatic event; small outcomes may appear controllable, people may be supportive. And over time—and it may be weeks, months, or even years for some—there is a movement from nonvolitional confrontation with the traumatic experience to volitional confrontations, from avoidance to approach. The automatic work of numbing and intrusive thoughts abates, and the survivor intentionally and willingly confronts the traumatic experience. As with the automatic processes, such volitional cognitive processing is also in the service of adaptive schema change and is likely to facilitate successful coping (Tedeschi & Calhoun, 2004). Thus, research has demonstrated that rumination and deliberate, repetitive cognitive processing of the traumatic event are associated with PTG (Bower et al., 1998; Calhoun, Cann, Tedeschi, & McMillan, 2000; Tedeschi, Calhoun, & Cooper, 2000). This coping process is long, arduous, and painful, but eventually, for most survivors, the trauma is successfully incorporated into the assumptive world, in that the experience is represented and acknowledged, but does not wholly define the inner world.

In the face of their profound coping challenges, trauma survivors often discover new personal strengths and possibilities. One route to PTG is this process of strengthening and self-discovery, triggered by the survivor's struggles. This route to growth is neither specific to trauma nor unfamiliar. The assumption is that pain, suffering, and struggle are valuable because they both strengthen us and teach us about our own potential. This is the message that is implicit in the redemptive value of suffering so central to many religions and evident in common cultural lore. This attitude is reflected in "What doesn't kill us makes us stronger" and "No pain, no gain." In other words, we develop in the process of facing a difficult challenge, and in turn we become aware of our greater competence and strength.

Two factors in Tedeschi and Calhoun's (1996) PTGI capture this type of PTG: personal strength and new possibilities. The former involves indices of greater self-reliance, fortitude, and self-respect. Survivors report that they now know they can handle difficulties and also are stronger than they had thought. They recognize the coping challenges they confronted and overcame. A common refrain is some variant of "I never thought I had it in me." As one rape victim told me, "I feel much stronger now. . . Part of that rape was to dominate and humiliate me, and he didn't succeed at that. I came through with my dignity—I got through those months of hell." In the aftermath of traumatic victimization, survivors recognize that they have gone through agony and are stronger for it. In the course of their challenges and sufferings, they also learn about new possibilities in their own lives. They recognize new paths, develop new interests, and believe they're more likely to change things that need changing.

Newly recognized coping skills and resources can become the basis for new choices in the way survivors live their lives. For some, new possibilities are created by constraints on former lifestyles. I recall a high school athlete paralyzed in an accident telling me excitedly of the pleasures he derived from reading and intellectual pursuits, activities he hadn't experienced because of his earlier passion for sports. For many survivors, new possibilities follow from a newfound sense of confidence and courage derived from hard-won coping successes. Again, there is nothing unusual about this process of growth through suffering. It is probably associated with all sorts of adversity and difficulties, and not simply trauma. Greater strength and self-confidence are likely self-perceptions when one has been challenged and rises to the occasion. Yet, the psychological and often practical problems posed by traumatic victimization are enormous, and therefore those who adjust over time are perhaps particularly apt to perceive a more competent, stronger self. Although some researchers have begun to question whether these new self-views reflect actual changes in psychological strength and desirable attributes (see, e.g., Maercker & Zoellner, 2004; McFarland & Alvaro, 2000), it is nevertheless the case that perceptions of greater personal strength and confidence can engender positive changes in survivors' willingness to approach new challenges and make changes in their lives.

The greater self-respect and confidence reported by survivors in the aftermath of traumatic events are hard-won and justifiable, but are probably all the stronger because the likelihood of successful coping is apt to be underestimated. Work by Gilbert & Wilson (Gilbert, Pinel, & Wislon, 1998; Wilson, Wheatley, Meyers, Gilbert, & Axsom, 2000) on affective forecasting suggests that people generally believe adverse events will affect us more negatively over time than they actually do. These authors point to the great successes of our emotional immune systems and maintain that people do far better than they expect because they are stronger and more capable than they think. In addition, as affective forecasters, we focus specifically on the negative event and fail to adequately take into account the more positive impact of other activities and experiences in ongoing daily life. Consequently, our affective predictions are erroneous in estimating how likely we are to adjust well and cope with misfortune; we underpredict success. We assume people will do worse than they do, and this no doubt applies to survivors themselves—except in their case it is ironically based on "retrospective" forecasting, which would presumably parallel typical (prospective) forecasting (see Wilson, Meyers, & Gilbert, 2003). By expecting to have done much worse, survivors are able to further amplify perceptions of their own competence. In the course of coping they not only develop new strengths, but recognize strengths that were there all along, but were never previously tested. Trauma provides a dramatic test of human coping abilities.

FROM MEANINGLESSNESS TO MEANING: EXISTENTIAL REEVALUATION

The path to growth involving self-perceptions of strength through suffering is based on survivors' recognition of the extensive coping resources required in the adjustment process posttrauma. Survivors must deal not only with practical issues around evident physical

and/or interpersonal losses, but with intense challenges to their assum
their psychological sense of coherence. Looking beyond severe chall
changes in the assumptive world, we are likely to stumble upon a sec
This type of growth involves reactions that appear more unexpected and ....,
of the anguish and pain of traumatic experiences. These are survivors' reports of great
appreciation of life, as represented in statements, such as "the simple joys of life are
everywhere and boundless" and "everything is a gift," expressed respectively by survivors
of multiple cancers and an air crash (Tedeschi & Calhoun, 2004).

The remaining three (of five) factors in Tedeshi and Calhoun's (1996) PTGI—
appreciation of life, relating to others, and spiritual growth–are instances of this type
of PTG. All stem from a newfound recognition of the preciousness of human existence.
Although often reported in general terms (PTGI factor: appreciation of life), this "gift" of
living is often discussed in terms of appreciation of and increased sensitivity to particular
life domains, especially close relationships (PTGI factor: relating to others) and the spiritual realm (PTGI factor: spiritual growth). There is a sense of joy in these expressions that
surely seems to belie the postvictimization responses of terror and anxiety. If outcomes are
random or uncontrollable and we are not protected from tragedy and misfortune, why such
pleasurable reactions? Instead we might expect that survivors' confrontation with human
vulnerability and fragility would fuel disheartening appraisals of the inconsequentiality
of life, human insignificance, and the futility of living.

Yet, I believe it is this very recognition of the meaninglessness of existence that feeds
the creation of a new sense of meaning and value. To understand this process, we must
distinguish between two types of meaning (Janoff-Bulman & Frantz, 1997; also see Davis,
Nolen-Hoeksema, & Larson, 1998): meaning as comprehensibility and meaning as significance. In the immediate aftermath of traumatic victimization, survivors are concerned with
questions of comprehensibility. That is, they struggle to make sense of the catastrophic
event. Yet it is through wrestling with these questions of comprehensibility that survivors
over time turn to a different kind of meaning—questions of value and significance in their
own lives (see, e.g., Janoff-Bulman & Frantz, 1997; Janoff-Bulman & Yopyk, 2004).

The terror and intense anxiety experienced in the aftermath of traumatic events stem
from the incomprehensible nature of the victimizations. These events don't make sense,
in that their selective incidence cannot be accounted for; that is, they do not fit our theories of social causation, which involve assumptions about behavioral control and justice.
Survivors struggle to find a meaningful person-outcome contingency, a satisfying answer
to "Why me?" Instead, they are left with views of the world that reflect meaninglessness;
randomness and uncontrollability seem to define the distribution of human outcomes.
Human fragility and vulnerability to misfortune cannot be ignored. Survivors incorporate
these new realizations into their assumptive worlds, but over the course of successful
coping, these threatening assumptions increasingly cease to wholly define the survivor's
inner world. Rather, they become integrated into a set of assumptions that are now less
absolutist and presumably more complex. They do not disappear, but are a part of a larger
assumptive world that increasingly recognizes that the world is benevolent—but not always, and the world is comprehensible—but not always. The possibility of misfortune is
now an integrated component of the survivor's assumptive world, but does not overwhelm
the cognitive-emotional system.

As survivors make their peace with a less secure existence, they begin to report heart-
ening appraisals of their life and its significance. In a world that is not wholly comprehensible, controllable, or predictable, survivors realize that living can no longer be taken for
granted. In the face of ever-possible loss and annihilation, human life takes on new value.

_s philosopher Irving Singer (1996) writes of ontological anxiety, "Once our hopeless questioning has reverberated in us, we may intuit the mystery and wonder in everything being what it is. The source of our anxiety will not have changed but our attention will now be focused on the mere fact of existence rather than the obscure possibility of non-existence" (p. 80). Similarly, the survivor's existential anxiety remains, but it prompts a realization of the preciousness of life. Existence is essentially taken off automatic.

Survivors' greater appreciation reflects a process of reevaluation. *Appreciation* refers to an appraisal of increased worth; as in economics, when an object or good appreciates, it increases in value. Typically, we do not value the ordinary, but rather the extraordinary; to appreciate something is to construe it as special (see Janoff-Bulman, 2000). For the trauma survivor, living is no longer taken for granted. Psychologically, its specialness and significance derive largely from a recognition of "potential unavailability." We come to value that which we know we may lose. Such appraisals are no doubt related to a sort of scarcity heuristic, by which we accord greater value to objects and opportunities that are less available. Scarce resources typically cost more (Lynn, 1992), and lay notions of economic value reflect the belief that experiences and objects should be valued to the extent that they are unavailable (Brock; 1968; also see Cialdini, 1993, for a discussion of retailers' "limited number tactic" to increase sales). Of relevance, too, is research indicating that value-related appraisals are strongly influenced by perceptions of possible future loss, or potential unavailability. Kahneman and Tversky's (1979, 2000) work on prospect theory has demonstrated that there are distinct functions for gains versus losses. Not only is the function concave for gains and convex for losses, but it is also steeper for losses than gains. Consequently, when making decisions under uncertainty we are risk-averse; we are more motivated by the possibility of losing something than the possibility of gaining something of equal value. And that which we believe we might lose we value all the more.

Survivors are thus shaken from the complacency that often defines daily routines and instead become exquisitely sensitive to living. They consider what is important, reprioritize what is important, and make conscious choices about how to live their newly valued lives. The focus of their attention shifts from a concern with the meaning *of* life to meaning *in* life (Janoff-Bulman & Frantz, 1997; Janoff-Bulman & Yopyk, 2004). Survivors know they don't have control over some major life outcomes, such as traumatic life events, but they also realize they *do* have control over the choices they make in how to live their lives. They become *committed* to living. Life's value, appreciated through the painful realization that it is essentially fleeting and fragile, becomes the basis for creating newfound significance through goals and choices. Survivors choose activities they deem worthy of their time and effort. Research on "personal projects" has found that the types of activities people in the general population regard as most meaningful are interpersonal and spiritual projects involving the goal of intimacy or connection, and altruistic activities, such as community projects, that are engaged in for the sake of others (Little, 1998). In the aftermath of traumatic life events, as survivors make effortful choices about their commitments, perhaps not surprisingly they too place special emphasis on these valued domains—friends, family, and community, as well as spiritual endeavors. Personality psychologists who have studied people's self-articulated commitments maintain that these activities not only provide structure and sources of identity, but a sense of meaning and purpose (Cantor, 1990; Emmons, 1989; Klinger, 1977; Little, 1983; Pervin, 1989). And thus trauma survivors create their own value.

From the perspective of history and philosophy, the trauma survivor's concern with personal meaning in the face of the meaninglessness of the world has interesting parallels in existentialism. With roots in 19th century romanticism, and its revolt against science and reason, existentialism emerged largely in response to the trauma of World War II. Existentialists recognized no rational basis for our lives and acknowledged that feelings of dread and apprehension are a justifiable and essential element of human experience. Barrett (1962) characterized the movement thusly: "Alienation and estrangement; a sense of the basic fragility and contingency of human life; the impotence of reason confronted with the depths of existence; the threat of Nothingness. And the solitary and unsheltered condition of the individual before this threat... A single atmosphere pervades all like a chilly wind: the radical feeling of human finitude" (p. 36). One could be describing the terror of trauma survivors.

Yet, in the face of this dread, existentialism does not advocate a withdrawal from life or an attitude of passive acceptance. Rather, it argues for human choice and self-determination. At the same time that it recognizes human weakness, it also acknowledges human power (Barrett, 1962). We are to passionately embrace life and create our own meaningful existence through choices and commitments. In the absence of any ultimate justification for our choices, we are what we make ourselves (Sartre, 1957, 1966). This is the powerful lesson learned by trauma survivors.

POSTTRAUMATIC GROWTH REFLECTED IN PSYCHOLOGICAL PREPAREDNESS

Implicit in the growth derived from the survivor's existential reevaluation is a recognition of the schema change that underlies these positive reappraisals of life. Fundamental assumptions now acknowledge the sometimes arbitrary, uncontrollable nature of the universe. The ever-present possibility of loss is psychologically encoded. Obviously we do not have pictures of survivors' new psychic structures and can only speculate about what they might look like. Presumably, over time, for most survivors, the assumptive world is not wholly defined by malevolence and meaninglessness, for this would suggest a chronic state of despair and embitterment. Rather, these are likely to be integrated into a larger, overall more positive framework, such that the world is perceived as generally controllable, predictable, and good, although not always. In other words, survivors' assumptive worlds are apt to become more structurally complex, essentially less simplistic and absolutist. Just as our schematic structures representing stereotypes become more complex through processes of subgrouping and subtyping (see, e.g., Fiske, 2002; Maurer, Park, & Rothbart, 1995; Park, Ryan, & Judd, 1992; Weber & Crocker, 1983) so too our broadest schemas can become more complex by encapsulating substructures related to the tragic traumatic event.

A striking by-product of this process of schema change is the state of psychological preparedness it may engender. Trauma is a case of massive expectancy disconfirmation. Nonvictims' fundamental assumptions make no allowance for such dramatic human vulnerability. Such allowance is made posttrauma, and at the deepest levels of their psyches survivors are aware that misfortune is ever possible. Yet, a crucial by-product of this new realization is a reduced risk of psychological breakdown, disintegration, and terror in the face of future tragedy. This is a different type of PTG, in that it is not captured by the positive changes reported by survivors, which are themselves reflected in the five factors of Tedeschi and Calhoun's (1996) PTGI and represented in the two models of PTG discussed above. Rather, psychological preparedness refers to a psychological state and its structural underpinnings. Most simply, in the course of successful coping, assumptive worlds change so as to better prepare the survivor for subsequent tragedies and thereby minimize the likelihood of future psychological traumatization.

Calhoun's (2004; Tedeschi, Park, & Calhoun, 1998) description of the
:s in the aftermath of an earthquake provides a useful metaphor for under-
nt elements of this preparedness perspective on PTG. In the aftermath of
ent, physical structures are typically rebuilt so as to withstand such shocks
ommunity uses the experience to build more resistant structures. Simi-
larly, in the aftermath of trauma, survivors rebuild their assumptive worlds so as to be more
resistant to future psychological seismic shocks. A "more resistant" assumptive world is
likely to one whose schematic structure has grown in complexity and differentiation. It
would be a less rigid, more multidimensional set of assumptions.

The benefits associated with this type of PTG have some parallels in various inoculation
models in medicine and psychology. Thus, in medicine, vaccinations often involve exposure to a disease so as to ward off future occurrences, and Meichenbaum's (1985) stress
inoculation model involves exposure to moderate stress as a protection against subsequent
stressors. In the area of attitudes, McGuire's (1964; McGuire & Papageorgis, 1961) classic
work on inoculation theory demonstrated that mild persuasive attacks strengthened the
attitudes in question and protected against subsequent influence attempts. Interestingly,
McGuire argued that beliefs such as cultural truisms, which are widely shared in society
and rarely if ever questioned or disputed, would be most vulnerable to persuasion because
people have little experience defending them. McGuire maintained that exposure to a mild
attack would foster subsequent resistance to persuasion by motivating defense building
and providing people with practice counterarguing the attack.

There are limits to these analogies, in that in all cases greater resistance is produced by
exposure to a weaker or moderate form of the stressor. This is certainly not the case with
trauma. It is worth noting, in contrast to McGuire's (1964; McGuire & Papageorgis, 1961)
work, that recent research on attitudes and persuasion has demonstrated that attitude
certainty—and subsequent resistance to persuasion—increases only when the attack is
believed to be strong (Tormala & Petty, 2002). Similarly, it may be actual traumas—
attacks that break down our defenses—that are most apt to establish subsequent resistance.
As in the case of physical illness, once a person has had a particular disease, it is often
physically encoded in the form of antibodies, which act essentially to establish immunity
against future instances of the disease. The person's immune system is now somewhat
more complex, for there is a physical "memory" and recognition of the disease. Similarly,
in the case of trauma, the extreme negative experience is now psychologically encoded
in the assumptive world of the survivor, who is thereby granted some level of immunity
against subsequent traumatization.

The experience recently relayed to me by a remarkable survivor is indicative of this
psychological preparedness, for she recounted how an earlier trauma had steeled her
against a traumatic response to a subsequent extreme event. Now in her mid-40s, this
survivor told me that her husband had died of a brain tumor when they were both in their
30s, and she had been devastated. She felt incredibly anxious, depressed, and vulnerable,
but nevertheless went through the motions of daily life, trying her best to care for her
two small children. Then another catastrophe struck—her house was burned to the ground
and virtually all of her physical possessions were destroyed. She told me how she was
minimally affected, psychologically, by the fire, and her friends and relatives were shocked
by her calmness and strength. Yet, she said, she had learned about what's important in life
after her husband's death, and she and her two children had survived the fire. She knew
bad things happened, but she also knew how to appreciate the good things.

Several studies provide support for this immunity effect (see, e.g., Aldwin, Sutton, &
Lachman, 1996; Burgess & Holmstron, 1978; Elder & Cripp, 1989; Shanan & Shahar,

1983), although such findings are far from universal (see, e.g., Murdock, & Walsh, 1992), and good empirical tests are limited to c are considerable problems of measurement and interpretation in It is not as if people are going to be happy or utterly unfazed by ɛ which typically involve real pain and devastating losses. And tra revictimized are likely to be reminded once again of the uncon nature of the world. In other words, they will be reminded of hi fragility and are surely not apt to report positive feelings of well-be _...........ს, they should not experience the double dose of anxiety associated with an initial trauma. That is, although they will be anxious about the threatening world and human mortality, they should not experience the terror associated with massive expectancy disconfirmation and a disintegrated, inadequate inner world.

Actually, the protective effect of an earlier trauma might be most apt to manifest itself in terms of speed of recovery (i.e., return to positive functioning in relationships, work, etc.) and suggests the importance of longitudinal research. Time is a crucial, yet understudied variable in trauma research. Thus, the first-time trauma survivor who looks worse in the immediate aftermath may well be the person who looks best soon thereafter. In fact this would be an expected pattern of the trauma disconfirmation effect. Those with the most positive, benign assumptive worlds are apt to fall hardest and experience the greatest difficulties immediately after the traumatic event. Yet, the very factors that contributed to the initial construction of these positive self- and worldviews (e.g., supportive others, ego resources) are apt to contribute to the reconstruction process. Interestingly, individuals who begin with negative views of the world and themselves are less apt to experience the terror of trauma, but will also look less psychologically adjusted over time.

This also raises an important distinction to be drawn between initial traumatization in adulthood versus childhood. Childhood versus adult victimizations are quite different when considered in terms of assumptive worlds, and are apt to have different impacts on subsequent traumas. My own work has focused solely on victimizations in adulthood. People's fundamental assumptions are essentially in place by early adulthood (see, e.g., Bowlby, 1969); most, although certainly not all, arrive at adulthood with generally positive assumptive worlds, which are thereby disconfirmed by traumatic experiences. The adult trauma survivor therefore struggles to once again establish—or reestablish—a comfortable, yet viable inner world. In contrast, extreme negative events during childhood have the added burden of contributing to the creation of long-term assumptive worlds and therefore are more apt to be reflected in the fundamental assumptions these children bring to adulthood. Children who have experienced a history of abuse and/or neglect, for example, are apt to carry negative assumptions into adulthood. They may be less likely to experience the terror of traumatic victimization, but subsequent negative events in adulthood will reinforce their already negative views, which are likely to be manifested in greater depression, hopelessness, and decreased well-being in general. And as if this distinction between initial trauma in adulthood versus childhood were not enough to render the empirical enterprise difficult enough, for those children who dissociated their early intensely negative experiences, subsequent victimization in adulthood may serve to break down the victim's defensive structures and in this case create even greater terror and anxiety. All this is to suggest that we need to know much more about our respondents—and much more about them over time—than we typically do in our empirical research (and I am certainly guilty here). I believe, however, that with an eye toward different emotional reactions in addition to changes over time, we will find support for the psychological protection afforded by successfully coping with an initial traumatic experience in adulthood.

L LEGACY OF TRAUMA

iously, a focus on growth is not meant to suggest that over time only benefits can be accrued from traumatic experiences. That there are benefits and true evidence of psychological growth is story enough, given the pain and agony that so readily characterize the survivor's plight. It is important to realize that the benefits associated with trauma are inextricably tied to the pain and losses. This may in part account for the failure to find a consistent relationship between the benefits reported by survivors posttrauma and indices of well-being and decreased psychological stress. Although most studies have found the expected positive relationship, some have found no relationship (for a review of this research, see Park, 1998). Interestingly, the same can be said of wisdom (Baltes & Staudinger, 2000), an attribute most of us would regard as unquestionably positive and valuable. In empirical research, no systematic relationship has been found between wisdom and measures of well-being or mental health (Maercker & Zollner, 2004). Wisdom, like much PTG, may involve a larger perspective, one that includes recognition of both the good and the bad, the positive and the negative in life.

Gains and losses are like opposite sides of the same coin, or reversible figures. As survivors' conceptual structures grow less rigid and more complex, both figures are evident and available, and the very same contours of experience can be the basis for anxiety or appreciation, dread or self-confidence, sorrow or joy. They are apt to feel greater anxiety when they focus on the negative image, whether because of some contextual cue, recent experience, or personal reflection; and they are apt to experience greater appreciation of life and their own strengths when they focus on the positive image. Yet the attention to one does not belie the existence of the other.

Increasingly over time, trauma and its associated negative assumptions about vulnerability and loss function as a touchstone against which to compare the ongoing stream of life's activities. The traumatic experience shifts from an event that is assimilated and overwhelms the cognitive-emotional system to one that serves as a contrast against which to compare other aspects of one's life. Recent work on social comparison demonstrates that the very same target stimulus can be the basis for assimilation or contrast effects, such that we may use the same negative target to feel worse (assimilation) or better (contrast) about ourselves (see, e.g., Markman & McMullen, 2003; Mussweiler, 2003; Stapel & Koomen, 2001; Wanke, Bless, & Igou, 2001). While the former defines our early responses to trauma, contrast becomes psychologically available with time and increasing differentiation in our inner worlds. (For more on the contrast effect, also see, e.g., Brickman, Coates, & Janoff-Bulman, 1978, on adaptation level theory; Helson, 1964; Kahneman & Miller, 1986 on norm theory; Kahneman & Tversky, 1982, and Taylor & Schneider, 1989, on simulation processes; and Kahneman & Tversky, 1973, on anchoring and adjustment processes.)

A uniformly positive assumptive world, as is apt to exist previctimization and predisillusionment, is not particularly likely to foster a life of value and appreciation. Rather, we are apt to take for granted life and its routine, daily pleasures. As Thornton Wilder (1975) made evident in his classic *Our Town*, we "move about in a cloud of ignorance. . . .To spend and waste time as though you had a million years" (pp. 139–140). Uniformly negative assumptions, too, are surely not conducive to the creation of value and appreciation in our lives. Interestingly, work by Brickman (1987) on commitment makes a compelling case for the necessity of both a positive and negative element in the creation of value. Similarly, Singer (1996) also claims that we create meaning by undergoing a dialectic between the positive and negative, doubt and motivation.

These are the survivor's veritable reversible figures—the losses and gains, disillusionments and strengths. Their palpable awareness of vulnerability and loss coupled with their rebuilt, generally positive assumptive world creates the climate for meaning, value, and commitment. Anxiety and doubt remain, but now function so as to focus the survivor's attention on the wonder of life and personal strengths rather than the terror of annihilation, the amazing fact of existence rather than nonexistence. In the end, all three posttraumatic growth processes—strength through suffering, existential re-evaluation, and psychological preparedness—are inextricably tied to the shattered sense of invulnerability and the reconstructed assumptions that define the psychological world of survivors.

REFERENCES

Aldwin, C. M., Sutton, K. J., & Lachman, M. (1996). The development of coping resources in adulthood. *Journal of Personality, 64*, 837–871.

Baltes, P. B., & Staudinger, U. M. (2000). Wisdom: A meta-heuristic to orchestrate mind and virtue towards excellence. *American Psychologist, 55*, 122–136.

Barrett, W. (1962). *Irrational man: A study in existential philosophy.* Garden City, NY: Doubleday.

Bennett, H. Y., & Dunkel-Schetter, C. (1992). Negative social reactions to victims: An overview of responses and their determinants. In L. Montada, S. Fillip, & M. J. Lerner (Eds.), *Life crises and experiences of loss in adulthood* (pp. 497–518). Hillsdale, NJ: Lawrence Erlbaum Associates.

Bonanno, G. A. (2004). Loss, trauma, and human resilience: Have we underestimated the human capacity to thrive after extremely aversive events? *American Psychologist, 59*, 20–28.

Bower, J. E., Kemeny, M. E., Taylor, S. E., & Fahey, J. L. (1998). Cognitive processing, discovery of meaning, CD 4 decline, and AIDS-related mortality among bereaved HIV- seropositive men. *Journal of Consulting and Clinical Psychology, 66*, 979–986.

Bowlby, J. (1969). *Attachment and loss, Vol. I: Attachment.* London: Hogarth.

Brickman, P. (1987). *Commitment, conflict, and caring.* Englewood Cliffs, NJ: Prentice-Hall.

Brickman, P., Coates, D., & Janoff-Bulman, R. (1978). Lottery winners and accident victims: Is happiness relative? *Journal of Personality and Social Psychology, 36*, 917–927.

Brock, T. C. (1968). Implications of commodity theory for value change. In A. G. Greenwald, T. C. Brock, & T. M. Ostrom (Eds.), *Psychological foundations of attitudes* (pp. 243–75). New York: Academic Press.

Burgess, A. W., & Holmstrom, L. L. (1978). Recovery from rape and prior life stress. *Research in Nursing and Health, 1*, 165–74.

Burt, M. R., & Katz, B. L. (1987). Dimensions of recovery from rape: Focus on growth outcomes. *Journal of Interpersonal Violence, 2*, 57–81.

Calhoun, L. G., & Tedeschi, R. G. (1999). *Facilitating posttraumatic growth: A clinician's guide.* Mahwah, NJ: Lawrence Erlbaum Associates.

Calhoun, L. G., & Tedeschi, R. G. (2001). Posttraumatic growth: The positive lessons of loss. In R. A. Neimeyer (Ed.), *Meaning reconstruction and the experience of loss* (pp. 157–172). Washington, DC: American Psychological Association. .

Calhoun, L. G., Cann, A., Tedeschi, R. G., & McMillan, J. (2000). A correlational test of the relationship between posttraumatic growth, religion, and cognitive processing. *Journal of Traumatic Stress, 13*, 521–527.

Cann, A., Calhoun, L., & Selby, L. (1979). Attributing responsibility to the victim of rape: Influence of information regarding past sexual experiences. *Human Relations, 32*, 57–67.

Cantor, N. (1990). From thought to behavior: "Having" and "doing" in the study of personality and cognition. *American Psychologist, 45*, 735–750.

Carli, L. L., & Leonard, J. B. (1989). The effect of hindsight on victims derogation. *Journal of Social and Clinical Psychology, 8*, 331–343.

Chaiken, S., & Trope, Y. (Eds.). (1999). *Dual-process models in social psychology.* New York: Guilford.

Cialdini, R. B. (1993). *Influence: Science and practice.* New York: Harper Collins.

Collins, R. L., Taylor, S. E., & Skokan, L. A. (1990). A better world or a shattered vision: Changes in life perspective following victimization. *Social Cognition, 8*, 263–285.

Davis, C. G. (2001). The tormented and the transformed: Understanding responses to loss and trauma. In R. A. Neimeyer (Ed.), *Meaning reconstruction and the experience of loss* (pp. 137–155). Washington, DC: American Psychological Association.

Davis, C. G., & McKearney, J. M. (2003). How do people grow from their experience with trauma or loss? *Journal of Social and Clinical Psychology, 22*, 477–492.

Davis, C. G., Nolen-Hoeksema, S., & Larson, J. (1998). Making sense of loss and benefiting from the experience: Two construals of meaning. *Journal of Personality and Social Psychology, 75*, 561–574.

Edmonds, S., & Hooker, K. (1992). Perceived changes in life meaning following bereavement. *Omega, 25*, 307–318.

Ehlers, A., Mayou, R. A., & Bryant, B. (1998). Psychological predictors of chronic posttraumatic stress disorder after motor vehicle accidents. *Journal of Abnormal Psychology, 107*, 508–519.

Elder, G. H., & Clipp, E. C. (1989). Combat experience and emotional health: Impairment and resilience in later life. *Journal of Personality, 57*, 311–322.

Emmons, R. A. (1989). The personal striving approach to personality. In L. Pervin (Ed.), *Goal concepts in personality and social psychology* (pp. 87–126). Hillsdale, NJ: Lawrence Erlbaum Associates.

Epstein, S. (1991). The self-concept, the traumatic neurosis, and the structure of personality. In D. Ozer, J. M. Healy, Jr., & A. Stewart (Eds.) *Perspectives on personality* (Vol. 3). London: Jessica Kingsley.

Epstein, S. (1998). Cognitive-experiential self-theory. In D. F. Barone, M. Hersen, & V. B. Van Hasselt (Eds.) *Advanced personality* (pp. 35–47). New York: Plenum.

Fairbairn, W. R. D. (1952). *An object-relations theory of personality*. New York: Basic Books.

Fiske, S. T., (2002). Stereotyping, prejudice, and discrimination. In D. T. Gilbert, S. T. Fiske, & G. Lindzey (Eds.), The handbook of social psychology (Vol. 2, pp. 357–414). New York: McGraw-Hill.

Fiske, S. T. (2004). *Social beings: A core motives approach to social psychology*. New York: Wiley.

Foley, L. A., & Pigott, M. A. (2000). Belief in a just world and jury decisions in a civil rape trial. *Journal of Applied Social Psychology, 30*, 935–951.

Frazier, P., Conlon, A., & Glaser, T. (2001). Positive and negative life changes following sexual assault. *Journal of Consulting and Clinical Psychology, 69*, 1048–1055.

Gilbert, D. T., Pinel, E., & Wilson, T. D. (1998). Immune neglect: A source of durability bias in affective forecasting. *Journal of Personality and Social Psychology, 75*, 617–638.

Greenberg, J., Solomon, S., & Pyszczynski, T. (1997). Terror management theory of self-esteem and cultural worldviews: Empirical assessments and conceptual refinements. In M. Zanna (Ed.), *Advances in experimental social psychology* (Vol. 29, pp. 61–139). San Diego, CA: Academic Press.

Greenwald, A. G., & Banaji, M. R. (1995). Implicit social cognition: Attitudes, self-esteem, and stereotypes. *Psychological Review, 102*, 4–27.

Greenwald, A. G., Banaji, M. R., Rudman, L. A., Farnham, S. D., Nosek, B. A., & Mellott, D. S. (2002). A unified theory of implicit attitudes, stereotypes, self-esteem, and self-concept. *Psychological Review, 109*, 3–25.

Hanson, R. F., Kilpatrick, D. G., Freedy, J. R., & Saunders, B. E. (1995). Los Angeles County after the 1992 civil disturbance: Degree of exposure and impact on mental health. *Journal of Consulting and Clinical Psychology, 63*, 987–996.

Helson, H. (1964). *Adaptation level theory: An experimental and systematic approach to behavior*. New York: Harper.

Horowitz, M. J. (1976). *Stress response syndromes*. New York: Aronson.

Horowitz, M.J. (1979). Psychological response to serious life events. In V. Hamilton & D. M. Warburton (Eds.), *Human stress and cognition* (pp. 235–263). New York: Wiley.

Janoff-Bulman, R. (1985). The aftermath of victimization: Rebuilding shattered assumptions. In C. Figley (Ed.), *Trauma and its wake: The study and treatment of post-traumatic stress disorder*. New York: Brunner/Mazel.

Janoff-Bulman, R. (1989). Assumptive worlds and the stress of traumatic events: Applications of the schema construct. *Social Cognition, 7*, 113–136.

Janoff-Bulman, R. (1992). *Shattered assumptions: Towards a new psychology of trauma*. New York: Free Press.

Janoff-Bulman, R. (2000). The other side of trauma: Towards a psychology of appreciation. In J. H. Harvey & E. D. Miller (Eds.), *Loss and trauma: General and close relationship perspectives* (pp. 29–44). Philadelphia: Brunner-Routledge.

Janoff-Bulman, R., & Frantz, C. M. (1997). The impact of trauma on meaning: From meaningless world to meaningful life. In M. Power & C. Brewin (Eds.), *The transformation of meaning in psychological therapies* (pp. 91–106). London: Wiley.

Janoff-Bulman, R., & Yopyk, D. J. (2004). Random outcomes and valued commitments: Existential dilemmas and the paradox of meaning. In J. Greenberg, S. L. Koole, & T. Pyszczynski (Eds.), *Handbook of experimental existential psychology*. New York: Guilford.

Joseph, S., Williams, R., & Yule, W. (1993). Changes in outlook following disaster: The preliminary development of a measure to assess positive and negative change. *Journal of Traumatic Stress, 6*, 271–279.

Kahneman, D., & Miller, D. T. (1986). Norm theory: Comparing reality to its alternatives. *Psychological Review, 93*, 136–153.

Kahneman, D., & Tversky, A. (1973). On the psychology of prediction. *Psychological Review, 80*, 237–251.

Kahneman, D., & Tversky, A. (1979). Prospect theory: An analysis of decision under risk. *Econometrica, 47*, 263–291.

Kahneman, D., & Tversky, A. (1982). The stimulation heuristic. In D. Kahneman, P. Slovic, & A. Tversky (Eds.), *Judgment under uncertainty: Heuristics and biases*. New York: Cambridge University Press.

Kahneman, D., & Tversky, A., Eds. (2000). *Choices, values, and frames*. New York: Cambridge University Press.

Keane, T. M., Litz, B. T., & Blake, D. D. (1990). Post-traumatic stress disorder in adulthood. In M. Hersen & C. G. Last (Eds.), *Handbook of child and adult psychopathology: A longtitudinal perspective*. New York: Pergamon.

Klinger, E. (1977). *Meaning and void: Inner experience and the incentives in peoples lives*. Minneapolis: University of Minnesota Press.

Kuhn, T. S. (1962). *The structure of scientific revolutions*. Chicago: University of Chicago Press.

Lerner, M. J. (1980). *The belief in a just world*. New York: Plenum.

Little, B. R. (1983). Personal projects: A rationale and method for investigation. *Environment and Behavior, 15*, 273–309.

Long, G. M., & Toppino, T. C. (2004). Enduring interest in perceptual ambiguity: Alternating views of reversible figures. *Psychological Bulletin, 130*, 748–768.

Lynn, M. (1992). Scarcity's enhancement of desirability: The role of naive economic theories. *Basic and Applied Social Psychology, 13*, 67–78.

Maercker, A., & Zollner, T. (2004). The Janus face of self-perceived growth: Toward a two- component model of posttraumatic growth. *Psychological Inquiry, 15*, 41–48.

Markman, K. D., & McMullen, M. N. (2003). A reflection and evaluation model of comparative thinking. *Personality and Social Psychology Review, 7*, 244–267.

Marris, P. (1974). *Loss and change*. Garden City, New York: Anchor/Doubleday.

Maurer, K. l., Park, B., & Rothbart, M. (1995). Subtyping versus subgrouping processes in stereotype representation. *Journal of Personality and Social Psychology, 69*, 812–824.

McFarland, C., & Alvaro, C. (2000). The impact of motivation on temporal comparisons: Coping with traumatic events by perceiving personal growth. *Journal of Personality and Social Psychology, 79*, 327–343.

McGuire, W. J. (1964). Inducing resistance to persuasion: Some contemporary approaches. In L. Berkowitz (Ed.), *Advances in experimental social psychology* (Vol. 1, pp. 191–229). New York: Academic Press.

McGuire, W. J., & Papageorgis, D. (1961). The relative efficacy of various types of prior belief-defense in producing immunity against persuasion. *Journal of Abnormal and Social Psychology, 62*, 327–337.

McMillen, C., Smith, E. M., & Fisher, R. H. (1997). Perceived benefit and mental health after three types of disaster. *Journal of Consulting and Clinical Psychology, 65*, 733–739.

Meichenbaum, D. (1985). *Stress inoculation training*. New York: Pergamon.

Mussweiler, T. (2003). Comparison processes in social judgment: Mechanisms and consequences. *Psychological Review, 110*, 472–489.

Park, B., Ryan, C. S., & Judd, C. M. (1992). Role of meaningful subgroups in explaining differences in perceived variability for in-groups and out-groups. *Journal of Personality and Social Psychology, 63*, 553–567.

Park, C. L. (1998). Implications of posttraumatic growth for individuals. In R. G. Tedeschi, C. L. Park, & L. G. Calhoun (Eds.), *Posttraumatic growth: Positive change in the aftermath of crisis* (pp. 153–177). Mahwah, NJ: Lawrence Erlbaum Associates.

Park, C. L., Cohen, L. H., & Murch, R. (1996). Assessment and prediction of stress-realted growth. *Journal of Personality, 64*, 71–105.

Parkes, C. M. (1971). Psych-social transitions: A field of study. *Social Science and Medicine, 5*, 101–115.

Parkes, C. M. (1975). What becomes of redundant world models? A contribution to the study of daptation to change. *British Journal of Medical Psychology, 48*, 131–137.

Pervin, L. A. (1989). *Goal concepts in personality and social psychology*. Hillsdale, NJ: Lawrence Erlbaum Associates.

Pyszczynski, T., Greenberg, J., & Solomon, S. (1999). A dual-process model of defense against conscious and unconscious death-related thoughts: An extension of terror management theory. *Psychological Review, 106*, 835–845.

Resnick, H. S., Kilpatrick, D. G., Dansky, B. S., Saunders, B. E., & Best, C. L. (1993). Prevalence of civilian trauma and posttraumatic stress disorder in a representative national sample of women. *Journal of Consulting and Clinical Psychology, 61*, 984–991.

Rothbaum, B. O., Foa, E. B., Riggs, D., Murdock, T., & Walsh, W. (1992). A prospective examination of post-traumatic stress disorder in rape victims. *Journal of Traumatic Stress, 5*, 455–475.

Sartre, J. P. (1957). *Existentialism and human emotions*. New York: Philosophical Library.

Sartre, J. P. (1966). *Being and nothingness: A phenomenological study of ontology*. New York: Washington Square Press.

Shanan, J., & Shahar, O. (1983). Cognitive and personality functioning of Jewish Holocaust survivors during the midlife transition (46–65) in Israel. *Archiv fur die Gesamte Psychologie, 135*, 275–294.

Singer, I. (1996). *The creation of value*. Baltimore: The Johns Hopkins University Press.

Solomon, S., Greenberg, J., & Pyszczynski, T. (1991). A terror management theory of social behavior: The psychological functions of self-esteem and cultural worldviews. In M. P. Zanna (Ed.), *Advances in experimental social psychology* (Vol. 24, pp. 91–159). San Diego, CA: Academic Press.

Stapel, D. A., & Koomen, W. (2001). I, we, and the effects of others on me: How self-construal level moderates social comparison effects. *Journal of Personality and Social Psychology, 80*, 766–781.

Stern, D. N. (1985). *The interpersonal world of the infant: A view from psychoanalysis and development al psychology*. New York: Basic Books.

Sutker, P. B., Davis, J. M., Uddo, M., & Ditta, S. R. (1995). War zone stress, personal resources, and PTSD in Persian Gulf War returnees. *Journal of Abnormal Psychology, 104*, 444–452.

Taylor, S. E., & Schneider, S. K. (1989). Coping and the simulation of events. *Social Cognition, 7*, 176–196.

Tedeschi, R. G., & Calhoun, L. G. (1995). *Trauma and transformation: Growing in the aftermath of suffering*. Thousand Oaks, CA; Sage.

Tedeschi. R. G., & Calhoun, L. G. (1996). The posttraumatic growth inventory: Measuring the positive legacy of trauma. *Journal of Traumatic Stress, 9*, 455–471.

Tedeschi, R. G., & Calhoun, L. G. (2004). Posttraumatic growth: Conceptual foundations and empirical evidence. *Psychological Inquiry, 15*, 1–18.

Tedeschi, R. G., Calhoun, L. G., & Cooper, L. (2000). *Rumination and posttraumatic growth in older adults*. Paper presented at the meeting of the American Psychological Association, Washington, DC.

Tedeschi, R. G., Park, C., L., & Calhoun, L. G. (1998). *Posttraumatic growth: Changes in the aftermath of crisis*. Mahwah, NJ: Lawrence Erlbaum Associates.

Thompson, S. C. (1985). Finding positive meaning in a stressful event and coping. *Basic and Applied Social Psychology, 6*, 279–295.

Tormala, Z. L., & Petty, R. E. (2002). What doesn't kill me makes me stronger: The effects of resisting persuasion on attitude certainty. *Journal of Personality and Social Psychology, 83*, 1298–1313.

Updegraff, J. A., & Taylor, S. E. (2000). From vulnerability to growth: Positive and negative effects of stressful events. In J. H. Harvey & E. D. Miller (Eds.), *Loss and trauma: General and close relationship perspectives* (pp. 3–28). Philadelphia: Brunner-Routledge.

Veronen, L. J., & Kilpatrick, D. G. (1983). Rape: A precursor of change. In E. J. Callahan & K. McCluskey (Eds.), *Life span developmental psychology: Non-normative events* (pp. 167–191). San Diego, CA: Academic Press.

Wanke, M., Bless, H., & Igou, E. R. (2001). Next to a star: Paling, shining, or both? Turning interexemplar contrast into interexemplar assimilation. *Personality and Social Psychology Bulletin, 27*, 14–29.

Weber, R., & Crocker, J. (1983). Cognitive processes in the revision of stereotypic beliefs. *Journal of Personality and Social Psychology, 45*, 961–977.

Wilder, T. (1975). *Our town.* New York: Avon Books.

Wilson, T.D., Meyers, J., & Gilbert, D. T. (2003). "How happy was I, anyway?" A retrospective impact bias. *Social Cognition, 21*, 421–446.

Wilson, T., Wheatley, T., Meyers, J., Gilbert, D. T., & Axsom, D. (2000). Focalism: A source of durability in affective forecasting. *Journal of Personality and Social Psychology, 78*, 821–836.

Winnecott, D. W. (1965). *The maturational process and facilitating environment.* New York: International Universities Press.

Wortman, C. B. (2004). Posttraumatic growth: Progress and problems. *Psychological Inquiry, 15*, 81–90.

6

Posttraumatic Growth and Other Outcomes of Major Loss in the Context of Complex Family Lives

John H. Harvey and Katherine Barnett
University of Iowa

Stephanie Rupe
Columbia University

TRAUMA GROWTH: A SPECTRUM OF OUTCOMES

This chapter will describe our view of the diversity of outcomes associated with major losses and traumas. We will focus on how loss and trauma do not usually occur in isolation, but rather in the context of complex family lives. Survivors and family members view losses through the prisms of these webs of relationships and events. In making our case about how such contexts are connected to loss and trauma outcomes, we will present stories from an ongoing project designed to bring together narratives of young persons of who have lost parents to death and a completed project that concerned children of divorce (Harvey & Fine, 2004). We also wish to emphasize how growth after trauma or major loss may be extraordinarily gradual and halting in nature.

What is trauma growth? It is change in a beneficial direction for the survivor or persons closely related to the survivor. One of the themes of this chapter is that from the perspective of persons who suffer major loss, such change may be difficult to specify. Certainly, changes are everywhere for such persons. But positive, accommodating changes may come about in excruciatingly halting and gradual ways. The stories we will report attest to this sense of very gradual progress, if progress at all.

When we began work on the ideas behind this chapter, the senior author heard of the death of a dear friend and mentor who made gigantic contributions to the field of psychology and to the study of subtopics, such as close relationships, group processes, and social influence. During his last year of life, this man knew he was in a very difficult struggle to live, battling colon cancer. His friends and close others watched as he suffered and battled valiantly. His loss is relevant to the present topic, which concerns people's experience of growth in the wake of major loss events. This man's struggle probably could not be construed as involving growth. It was the end battle in a long life, containing many illustrious successes and some major losses as well. Loved ones' reactions to his death may not be readily construed as involving growth either. We will celebrate his life and role in our lives. Most of us, however, cherished the great moments of our times together and accepted his death; acceptance was made easier because of the pain and withering effects of colon cancer.

We believe that this opening example is reflective of the wide spectrum of outcomes associated with loss and traumatic events. Viewing outcomes as along a positive–negative continuum may be less tenable for some loss events than it is for other loss events. For some of these events, it may be enough to simply say that "it's done," without placing a valence on the outcome for survivors.

Posttraumatic growth (PTG), as so well articulated and studied by Tedeschi and Calhoun (1995; Tedeschi, Park, & Calhoun, 1998), is an invaluable concept for work on trauma and loss. These scholar-practitioners have created and pioneered this concept. Their work is imbued with the wisdom deriving from a careful examination of loss in the experience of their respondents and clients. The concept of PTG indeed is a major advance and fits well within the purview of what is called *positive psychology* (Snyder & Lopez, 2001). Our analysis focuses on outcomes of loss and trauma that do not add to the loss spiral of events (Hobfoll, 1988), but that are not necessarily positive in nature either. There other types of outcomes that also are not woeful, but that do not constitute "growth" in any clear sense of the term.

Remembrance and dedication to a cause associated with loss and trauma are frequent outcomes for persons close to those who have died. The first story from the parent loss project tells about the experience of a young movie producer who is in the process of developing a documentary to describe the gruesome killing of his mother and others by three would be robbers whose robbery turned fatal for the victims. This person, now 33, was only six when he was a witness to this horrendous loss. As is true for all of the stories presented in this chapter, his story is presented with his consent. Names of persons mentioned in the story have been changed to protect their confidentiality.

Jack's Story

> *I can remember the day very clearly now. Not that I, at any time, couldn't remember it, I simply never wanted to.*
>
> *It was a warm day in March when we arrived at the Wilson house back in 1977. Dusk was approaching and the sun had begun its descent over the woods which lay behind the house. We thought nothing of the unfamiliar blue van which was parked in the driveway. My mother and friend Luke Wilson entered the house. I was left inside the car to play by myself.*
>
> *I was six years old then.*

So I sat there, and I sat there, until finally a man who I had never seen before emerged from the house. He wore old, dirty clothes and some sort of a snow cap. This perplexed me because it certainly wasn't cold outside.

The man bent down next to the car and I heard some sort of a hissing. I finally realized he was letting the air from the tires. The car began to sink below me. My naïve mind tried to come up with some sort of an explanation. Was he working on the car? Was he a friend of the Wilsons?

The hissing stopped and the car door swung open. I quickly focused my attention towards him. He, in turn, eyed me carefully, then snatched my mother's purse up from the driver's seat.

"Hey kid, your mother wants you."

He said it matter-of-factly. So not really thinking much of it, I made my way out of the car and began to follow him toward the house.

The March winds felt pleasant to me, warm and sweet smelling. I wasn't really frightened, just curious to find out when we could go home and who, exactly, was this man.

We approached the house. The twilight colors of the sky gave the Wilsons' home a sinister silhouette. It was a contemporary set way back on an old blueberry farm. I had spent much of my life nearby, but had since moved from a small ranch house about a quarter of a mile away. This place had been a playground to me.

The door opened. I immediately sensed danger. The house was a wreck, chairs were overturned, drawers were dumped, the floor was a sea of odds and ends. I could hear crying. It was coming from upstairs and sounded to be a little girl, possibly my sister. I then knew that something was seriously wrong. What I didn't know was exactly how horrible the situation really was.

I was allowed no more than a few seconds to survey the huge mess. Once the door squeaked shut, the man promptly grabbed my arm and began to pull me up the stairs. This alarmed me—strangers weren't supposed to touch me this way.

We reached the top of the stairs, and it became obvious to me that it was my four-year-old sister Mary and her young friend Nina crying. Luke, a boy of about my age, tried to calm the little girls down. I next noticed my mother and Sheila Wilson, Luke's mother, sitting in the corner. Two men I hadn't seen before stood over them. My mother looked at me and said nervously, "Jack, just relax." Wanting to reassure me, she tried to mask the fact that she was terrified.

She attempted to talk to the men, saying things like, "What are you going to do with us?" In response, one of the men shoved her and told her to shut up. I was even more confused at this point. Suddenly, I could hold my tongue no longer. I began asking questions. "Who are you?" I burst out. "Why are you here? Mom, what's going on?"

On of the men casually got up and walked over to where I was sitting. He pressed a large gun against my nose and burned five words into my memory that would never leave me.

"Shut the fuck up, kid."

My mother was murdered that day, shot in the head, shot in the back, along with Sheila Wilson. The children were all locked in an adjoining bedroom during the shooting. I was the first to enter the room when it was all over and the van had pulled away. I stood there for a few moments trying to figure out what to do. Then the other children came in. Luke lifted his mother's arm; it dropped lifelessly to the floor.

I ran, out of the room, out of the house, and across the field. My destination: the house where I had once lived. It was just through the woods.

The people living there didn't take me seriously at first, but they were convinced something was awry when the other children soon arrived. Even at that age I could understand why they didn't believe me. What I was telling them was nearly unthinkable.

Samuel Thomas, Willie Jackson, and James Hutton were captured the following day. They had actually tried to return the rented van they used to rob the house. The three went to trial the following year. My father did his best and was successful in keeping us from the courtroom and all of its pain. In the end, Thomas and Jackson, the actual gunmen, received two consecutive life sentences, while James Hutton, who waited in the van for the majority of the time, received one. It is believed that the men had simply come into the neighborhood to rob a house. Some people, however, do speculate otherwise.

So I continued to grow up, the next two years under a woman who was extremely cold and insensitive. This woman did her best to destroy all traces of my mother's presence; old photographs and gifts from my mother began to disappear. It was as if she was trying to pretend my mother has simply never existed. My father, being very vulnerable at the time, made a mistake in marrying the woman. He realized what he had done in the following years and rectified the problem by getting a divorce.

I went through a series of changes concerned how I felt about the crime. My initial reaction upon learning she was dead was to plan some sort of experiment that might bring her back. I thought that was feasible at the age of eight or nine. Then, at around ten, my thoughts and perspective shifted completely.

I wanted them dead, at all costs. I didn't care if I went to jail or not. I began making and buying weapons to protect myself. I wasn't ever going to let anything like this happen again: I would be prepared. The crime wasn't something I thought about all that often. I only acted upon its effects on me. For instance, I became very paranoid that I might lose my father, that he might go away someday and never return. So I did my best to stay with him as often as I could. I was a bitter kid who would've been happy to crawl into a hole with my family and stayed there for eternity. At least we'd all be safe.

In another few year, after numerous housekeepers and babysitters, my father finally found his new wife. I was wary now of becoming very close to a mother type. But in time, without being pressed, I happily adjusted. My sister, who was still quite young, had an easier time of it. My father remains happily married to this day.

Time went by and my father received a job offer he couldn't refuse so my family moved to Florida. There my life changed completely. I became part of a totally different lifestyle. My paranoia nearly ceased. There simply wasn't a place for it. I knew, however, that my time was limited there, college was on the way. The following summer I moved to New York City to attend The School of Visual Arts in hopes of a career in film.

Moving was a huge shock, from the slow, safe state of Florida to the big, brooding city of New York. I was nervous again, watching my back all the time. This brought on memories. I began to think back again, wondering what I didn't know about the events surrounding the crime. I also started to have an odd series of dreams concerning my mother. Once more, my perspective changed again.

I began doing research, going through New York Times *microfilm and copying any information I could find. It remains a painful yet fascinating process as I continue to dig and uncover more facts that had remained hidden from me. So much was locked away from my eyes as a child.*

So, after years of thinking, I have decided to make a documentary. I want to explore my past and examine this crime. I want to find out how it shaped me, changed me. This is a long, painful journey that I have just begun. I don't know what I am going to find when I go back to South Salem. I am prepared for anything and willing to deal with whatever personal horror this might rekindle. I have talked with many of the people who dealt with the crime in one form or another. Everyone has been extremely helpful and most have agreed to be interviewed. I have also gotten in touch with the prison which holds the three murderers. The state does grant interviews in certain cases and I would be greatly interested in meeting the inmates on camera.

With the commercial and critical success of such films as The Thin Blue Line *and* Roger and Me, *documentaries have become quite popular with the moviegoing public in recent years. I want to delve into my uncertain past and come to grips with my central obsession: What exactly does a crime like this do to a family, to real individuals? How does it forever alter the state of their hearts, their minds? I want my audience peering over my shoulder as I try to unravel the facts to reveal whatever truth they may hold.*

I look forward to meeting Willie Jackson, Samuel Thomas, and James Hutton.

Comment

The foregoing narrative reveals many emotions, including possibly the desire for retribution, that may accompany long-term adaptation to such a loss. Does the tinge of revenge make sense in the argument that Jack's story reflects growth? Yes, the horrors experienced by that young boy cannot be readily forgotten or rationalized. His energy as a producer no doubt derives in some large measure from the zeal he feels about honoring his mother, but also from anger at what these three men did to many lives that day.

In the next section, we will describe another common outcome of major loss, a pileup of losses. Sometimes, just survival is a challenge in such circumstances. A sign sold in a sign shop said, "Get up in the morning, survive, go to bed." Those are formidable tasks for people experiencing a pileup of losses.

Movement or "Just Keep on Going"

The late actor Rod Steiger's motto on his California license plate was "Just Keep on Going." Steiger used this saying to symbolize his own life: from having little family support and being on the streets as a teenager to survival using his experience in the U.S. Navy as a foundation to great success later in life as an actor.

"Just keep on going" is another type of outcome that is common and relatively positive. It probably is not growth as much as it is movement—not giving up, not wallowing in despair, not becoming abjectly depressed. It is, plainly put, surviving—like the sign said. In fact, it may be conceived best as a neutral outcome, which is the most that many people can muster under their load of loss and bereavement.

Movement, then, can be seen as being akin to resilience, which Tedeschi and Calhoun (2003) describe as the "ability to go on with life after hardship and adversity" (p.10). They point out that PTG is different from this concept in that, unlike resiliency, it involves a qualitative change in functioning. However, we believe that "movement" after a loss or traumatic event would also require a qualitative change in functioning. To attempt to live life exactly as it had been before such a pivotal event would not only be an attempt at something impossible, it would most likely be counterproductive as well. To "just keep on going," it is necessary to recognize what has happened, realize that there is no return to life as it was once known, and adjust daily functioning accordingly. This adjustment would not necessarily be positive in nature, but a qualitative change nonetheless.

Mary's story is an extraordinary example of how just creeping along can be all that is possible and in the long-run quite adaptive. This 27-year-old woman experienced a decade of huge losses—losses that even the most resilient person would find daunting to survival. After a decade, though, she feels renewal, a sense of mission, and hope.

Mary's Story

My world was already upside down when my mother died. She passed away on Halloween of 1995 from breast cancer. I yelled at her the night before and never got a chance to say good bye, or more importantly, I'm sorry.

I don't remember a lot during the time my mom was sick. I was sick myself, but not with cancer or anything else physical. I had lost my boyfriend in a drowning accident 16 months before my mom died, and I handled it not well at all. I was only 17 when my mom was diagnosed with cancer and a few months later, Karl drowned. I remember going to the hospital with my dad to see his body, and no matter how hard I shook him, and how loud I screamed at him, he wouldn't wake up. The image of him lying on that gurney frequents my dreams. I remember not being able to shut his eyes or mouth and that he had something stuck in his teeth. All I could think of was how could he leave me? How could he leave me when he knows I'm not doing well dealing with my mom and the thought of her possibly dying. I was torn between being devastated and angry as hell.

I lost my hold on reality after that. I tried very seriously to kill myself about a month after he died. I took as many Tylenol as I could, along with whatever else was in the medicine closet. I washed it down with straight whiskey. I remember going to my friends' house, Andy and Jason. Somehow between those two and my friend I came with, Ryan, they knew I did something to hurt myself. I was told it took all three of them to wrestle me into a car to go to an ER. I woke up hearing my mom crying and asking the nurse why I would do something like that. She also said that she bargained with God, but He didn't listen. I never understood that until after she died, and I pleaded with God to take me instead and give my brother (who was 20) and sister (who was only eight) their mom back. He didn't listen to me either.

That was the only serious suicide attempt I made, but that's not to say I didn't end up back in the ER from time to time with self-inflicted injuries. I just didn't care about anything or anyone anymore. I remember that she was so weak and so tired when I graduated from high school, and that's the last picture I have of her and I together. She died 5 months later. I wasn't capable at that time to recognize what was going on. I couldn't get out of my own head long enough to see what was going on around me. She died without us really talking about it.

Her funeral was devastating. She had taught kindergarten before she got sick and all of her students sang at the service and most of them were not only crying, but wailing. That was the hardest thing for me to hear. After the service, we were downstairs for the reception, and I was sitting next to some family member that I can't recall and I looked over to see my brother surrounded by friends. I had no one. My friends didn't know what to do with me after Karl died because I was always so depressed or cutting on myself or drinking or having meaningless sex because it took the pain away sometimes for a few minutes, but usually only seconds. They didn't know what to do so they left me. I was in college, living in the dorm, and basically friendless. I didn't make one single friend my freshman year. Sitting in that church basement, watching my brother and all of his friends, made me realize how unbelievably lonely I was and now even my mom was gone. I felt like death was the only way out, but somehow, I never seriously tried to kill myself again. I stuck with it. Where I found the strength, I don't know. I think that I was just crazy enough so that everyday life passed by me without much notice. That's the only way possible.

I thought that mom dying after Karl died would be the worst things that would happen to me in this lifetime. Unfortunately, things got much worse before they even started to look like they may get better.

I moved home to live with my dad and sister after my freshman year in college. Our house used to be so filled with life; it was the place that all of our friends gathered at because our parents were so cool. Now, it was empty and bleak. My dad didn't change much in the house except give things away to family that wanted tangible memories of mom. Dad never dealt well with mom. Whereas I couldn't stop grieving, and couldn't move on, I don't think he ever grieved and moved on immediately.

He started dating a woman, Carolyn, in July of 1996. He met her because of me. She had hired me for my current job, and after I got into a bad car accident and could no longer work there, dad went to collect my things. They met, he asked her out, and two weeks later, she was moving in, and I was kicked out. I was recovering from surgery where I had bone fused into my neck from my hip to stabilize two cracked vertebrae. My dad paid me $1,000 to leave quietly. Carolyn hated me immediately. She had no choice about Kella; she was only eight, but she could hate me. My brother was too far away (he lived 2 hours from home) to be a threat to her, so I got the brunt of her wrath. My dad chose Carolyn over me, and that was harder to deal with than my mom dying. My mom never had a choice about abandoning us. My dad did. He abandoned me when everyone else had done the same thing, willful or not. He left me to fend for myself when I couldn't think about anything other than wanting to die.

My dad and I had always been close. The few years that Carolyn was around were the epitome of hell. She got rid of mom's stuff, took over our house, then had my dad sell the house because it had too many of my mom's memories in it, and build her a dream house out in the country. Dad did it. We lost everything while she took everything she could. The one thing that makes me the saddest is that Carolyn found a letter that mom had written before she died about how it felt to know she's dying and what we all meant to her. Carolyn threw it away. She didn't want my dad to be reminded of my mother so she threw it away.

During this time, I met a man who made me feel faith in God again, and made me feel hope for my eternal soul. I had no self-esteem at this point. I felt like everyone just took what they could for me, and I was too weak and empty to fight back. Kirk was no different. He said he was a "Christian," but would call me a whore daily and tell me I'm going to hell if I didn't end friendships with people of lesser faith, or if I listened to music or read books that he deemed un-godly. He made me throw away any memories of previous boyfriends, including Karl. That's the one thing that makes me the most ashamed. I threw away memories of Karl that could have been given back to his family simply because I was led to believe that I would go to hell and never see my dead mother again if I didn't. He manipulated me and emotionally abused me every single day that we were together. I finally found the courage to get out a year and a half later, but the damage had been done. Now, not only had everyone I loved and cared for abandoned me, I now felt I was unworthy for God's love and was most certainly going to hell.

Things did start looking up from there. Dad and Carolyn got a divorce back in 2000, and things started getting a little more civilized and normal between us. Although I was happy to be a part of their lives again (they never cut me out completely, but she made it known I was less than welcome and he never did anything to make me feel differently), I was so absolutely angry at my dad for letting this happen to me and to our entire family. However, I wasn't at a strong enough point in my life at that time where I could tell him that. I suffered in silence and pretended that everything was okay if not completely fine.

I've always felt that my brother and my sister handled this all way better than I ever was able to. I always felt like I was the biggest failure because I still was so depressed and minor things were such a set back for me. Meanwhile, my brother finished his master's, married his long-term girlfriend, who also had her master's, and had a appearance-wise wonderful life. He managed to do well, and there I was struggling to hold onto sanity. That sounds overly dramatic, but I had moments where there was no logic or sane thinking in anything I did. I couldn't keep my head above water longer than a few minutes, and my brother and sister seemed fine. I felt like I didn't deserve any happiness or even the right to live because I had made such a mess of everything. But, at the same time, I felt surges of pride because I was still alive and I was still fighting, despite everything that had kept me pushed down.

When my brother got married, it was so achingly sad that mom wasn't there. The minister said something about mom being with them, watching, and my brother broke down, and wasn't able to say his vows for a minute or so. I think most of our family did the same (except, of course, we weren't trying to say any vows!). I missed my mom so much and wished she could have spent that day with us, especially my brother and his new wife.

Those are the things that I wish for the most. I wish I could see her again, and tell her how sorry I am that I was too self-involved to spend much time with her before she died. I want her to meet my boyfriend, the man I know I'm going to marry. He is the first person to make me happy in years. I am angry that she can't meet him, and that he will never know her laugh or see her face. Sure, he's seen her in pictures, but that is in no way even close to the same. I wish she could see my sister now that she's 16. I wish that she could come to my wedding, and be there for my brother and sister-in-law's new baby due in January 2003. I guess on some level, I think she will be there for all of that because it's very possible she can be a spectator of earth from wherever she is right now. I just wish she could have a backstage pass so we could meet once again.

One thing that my mother's death (along with every other loss) taught was to not take people for granted. It made me aware of just how short time can be with someone. Nobody is guaranteed a certain number of hours here on earth, and that is the hardest. Since 1995, I have been terrified of people I love dying. Every time the phone rings, especially late at night, I think that someone must have died. It's so morbid, but I can't help it.

I started therapy again about 8 months ago, and it's the first time that I've really worked on the issues that, at times, still consume me. I am working on my fear of abandonment and death. My dad and I finally addressed what happened after mom died. I wrote him an extremely difficult, long and detailed letter describing my anger, fears, and my sadness. It felt wonderful, as well as completely emotionally draining. Neither my dad nor I handle feelings well. He dismisses them as soon as they announce their presence, and I extend an unlimited welcome to them and analyze them to death. There is one thing we, as well as a large part of my extended family, have in common: We hide our true emotions, and avoid subjects that will bring them out. I'm not sure if this started before or after my try to make the most out of life, and I know everyone says that, but I know it is one of the most challenging things I'm working on right now. How can we ever move past this grief and anger if we don't ever address it?

Now, I am overly aware that tomorrow may not come. I grieve for my mother every day and have nightmares and dreams about her weekly. I would give anything to see her once more, but I am slightly comforted by the fact that I am on my way to becoming mentally healthy once again, and that I do have the strength to wait until it's my time. I was never able to say that before. I wanted to die every single day of my life. Now, I thank God for my life, and try to remember not to take anything for granted. It's not guaranteed to be there in the morning.

Comment

The foregoing narrative highlights the complexity of family and close relationships, which often is enhanced in the context of major loss. Mary's story clearly is one of traumatic growth, but only after great pain. It reflects the difficulty of making progress when hit by a cascade of major losses within a short time frame. Furthermore, dealing with loss becomes a secondary loss in and of itself because of the psychological and physical toil incurred in the process (Hobfoll, 1988). We also would suggest that, as is true for all of us, Mary's journey in dealing with these losses will continue throughout her life. Indeed, growth may make many stutter steps and be always a task in progress.

Psychological Growth in Major Loss

We view trauma as a specific type of loss event (Harvey, 2002; Harvey & Miller, 1998). Figley (1993) has defined trauma as an injury that may be physical or psychological and that involves such features as suddenness and lack of anticipation; violence, mutilation, and destruction; randomness; and lack of preventability. Multiple deaths may be a part of traumatic experience. Traumatic stress does not necessarily lead to posttraumatic stress disorder (PTSD) (Herman, 1992). Major loss experiences also may include nontraumatic events, such as the deterioration of physical or psychological health or the breakdown of a close relationship. What is important to note is that psychological growth may occur for other forms of major loss that technically speaking are not representative of traumatic events.

A good example is the marvelous contribution of Morrie Schwartz. Schwartz had been a Brandeis University sociology professor who in his final year of battling Amyotrophic Lateral Sclerosis (ALS or Lou Gehrig Disease) was interviewed in the mid-1990s by Ted Koppel for his program "Nightline." Millions of people watched a set of interviews over six months as a feisty professor gave sage advice on "lessons of living" (as opposed to what on the surface might seem to be "lessons of dying"). Morrie's sayings and perspective on life were collected by one of his former students Mitch Albom (1997) in the best-selling book *Tuesdays with Morrie*. Although dealing with ALS may not be the same as dealing with most types of trauma, Schwartz reflected well what Tedeschi and Calhoun refer to as PTG. Schwartz taught us many lessons during those sessions on "Nightline."

One riveting lesson pertained to the nature and duration of grief. In one segment, Schwartz read a letter from young children in a school in Pennsylvania who had lost parents, and who had written to Schwartz after he initially appeared on the program. Schwartz began to cry as he read his response to them. He told them of losing his own mother when he was eight—over 70 years ago. Ted Koppel then marveled at Schwartz's pain at this "ancient" loss when Schwartz seemed to be facing his own imminent death with equanimity. Schwartz said that when he grieves, he often grieves for a multitude of losses, including ancient but devastating ones, such as the loss of a parent when one is a young child. Schwartz argued that sometimes when we grieve, we may be grieving for all manner of losses in the world, whether or not they are personal in nature. Could there be a greater lesson of what to take away from a sage old professor showing his most shining moments in his last moments of life? We think not. We think this example epitomizes a type of psychological growth in loss that is similar to, but not the same as, traumatic growth.

As another example of growth associated with nontraumatic loss, Tom, age 22, whose parents divorced, describes how with great effort he has progressed in dealing with the losses associated with this divorce.

Tom's Story

> *Looking back on my childhood I cannot recall a time in which my parents were happy together. What I do recall though are explosive arguments between my father and mother that usually had to be broken up by my older brother, while I locked myself in my room trying to block out the reality of what was happening outside my door. Being young (in elementary school) I*

believed everything would subside and my parents would find away to make their marriage work, not realizing that both of my parents were suffocating in the relationship and desperately seeking ways in which to end the 18-year marriage.

I was 10 years old when my father came to me and informed me that my parents were getting a divorce and that he would be moving out of our house for good. I was very upset because of course I thought this meant he was leaving town forever to never be seen or heard from again. But he soon reassured me that he would only be moving several miles away (in order to keep his job) and that this final separation would be better for the whole family. Initially he was right. The house was more calm and I no longer had to come home to a war zone. I began to feel relieved that my parents were divorced because they were both happier and both were excited to get on with their new single lives. But the more my parents began to reinvent themselves as single people in the community, the more I began to realize one of my fathers' final warnings before he left, "Brent, you are the man of the house now. Housework, lawn work, and taking care of your mother, you are going to have be responsible and learn how to take care of yourself."

I was now in sixth grade, my brother was beginning his first year at another university some three hours away, and both my parents began to date and continue to work fulltime. This left me at home the majority of the time by myself, cooking meals, cleaning, and maintaining the house. The duties that my father took care of were now put onto my shoulders and at the time I felt that I was losing out on the fun of being a regular junior high student. All of this time caring for the house and home needs resulted in me distancing myself from my peers, who I felt did not suffer the hardships that I did. On the weekends while my friends were skiing or playing football I had to remain home and help my mother and do odd jobs around the house. Throughout junior high I felt that I had lost the opportunity to be young and free. I did not see these new responsibilities as life lessons, but as repercussions from my parents' divorce.

Now at age 22, I realize how beneficial those years of quick maturity and early independence have been in the development of my character. I have found meaning in my parents' divorce, that is it allowed me to become an independent and responsible young man early in my life. It taught me that loved ones will be there for you, but you must look out for yourself and not always rely on other to accommodate your needs. I have a stronger sense of independence and have learned how to take care of myself and my responsibilities. A lot of people my age could not honestly say that they could take care of themselves. So even though I lost a parent through divorce I gained a character and a strong personality that will be with me forever.

Comment

Tom's story shows growth deriving from the divorce in his family. He shows one of the many outcomes young people experience when their parents divorce (Harvey & Fine, 2004). His apparent resultant maturity, poise, and articulateness reflect the positive end of the continuum, with many other young people showing signs of great distress and negative outcomes for years into the future. His story also implies that what parents do to make their divorces understandable and civil (Ahrons, 1994) can help young people grow in positive ways during this difficult experience.

Other Needed Additions to the Analysis of Posttraumatic Growth

A pileup of losses. While Tedeschi and Calhoun's (1995, 2003) reviews and analyses are quite comprehensive, there are other key ideas that need to be considered in understanding whether people can readily experience growth in the aftermath of major loss and trauma. As already suggested, an idea that needs elaboration concerns the frequent experience of a pileup of major losses. Mary's story is very representative. It is somewhat unusual for such a young person to experience so much loss. Many people in mid-life and beyond, and sometimes before, find their lives overwhelmed by a pileup of major losses, occurring at approximately the same time. These losses may include the deaths of close others, divorce or dissolution of close relationships, economic difficulties, and the loss of health (Viorst, 1986). Finding psychological growth in the midst of these full plates of issues is a daunting task.

As the present authors were preparing part of this chapter, one of our student colleagues told us of her mother's sudden death due to a heart attack. This 22-year-old woman is not a typical student. She is a survivor of the 1990s Bosnian War. She witnessed death and destruction, including such losses in her family. She and some members of her family immigrated to the United States after the war. Thus, when her mother died, she still was dealing with many loss issues deriving from spending formative years in a battle zone filled with instances of brutal, genocide-like activity.

This young woman not only must grieve multiple losses now, more importantly, she must help her 13-year-old brother and 17-year-old sister cope with these losses and cope with issues of living as well. This load is daunting even for other, experienced persons. It could be overwhelming for a relatively young person. We can report that this woman is holding on fairly well. She is completing her college degree with a high grade-point average and making plans for going on to graduate school someday.

But the task at hand involves many elements, from the practical to the psychological. She has had to be the leader of her family in dealing with funeral and end-of-life legal issues. She has to be especially vigilant to help her brother cope. He is hurt and angry about his mother's death. He needs to talk and figure out how he is going to move forward in his life. He greatly needs the support of his sisters in this process.

Posttraumatic growth may be delayed or impossible in the context of a pileup of major losses. It may come sparingly, or after the individual has begun to make some headway in working through the losses and their consequences. As Tedeschi and Calhoun ably contend, PTG comes about through cognitive-emotional work. How can we process unrelenting losses, especially when we have to work in the role of caretaker of close others? In time, we may get back to our own grief and its unresolved aspects. But another likely course is that many of us die before we have been able to deal with the losses and hurts that a long life may bring.

A pileup of losses may also have the capacity to disrupt PTG already underway. Another one of our student colleagues recently relayed to us the story of the deaths of her mother and brother in a car accident and the resulting impact of this on her life. This young woman, after much therapy and rumination in an attempt to make sense of the tragic event, started to experience what may be construed as the beginning stages of PTG. She started to express her feelings of what had happened through poetry and, as she became aware that there were others who were able to relate to her pain, realized the value of confiding.

Shortly after this initial progress, however, the young woman's father decided to re-marry. Our colleague felt excluded by her father's decision, as well as deeply hurt at the fact that he was able to move on so quickly after her mother's death. The young woman had also recently started college, and her feelings toward her father's remarriage were compounded by the insecurity she felt at being on her own for the first time in her life. Feeling overwhelmed, the young woman stopped writing poetry to express herself and, feeling that there was no longer anyone she could trust, she stopped confiding in people.

Eventually, her grief and pain overtook her, and she attempted suicide, seeing it as the only way out. It seemed that any earlier signs of PTG had disappeared.

Fortunately, our colleague's suicide was not successful. With time and the support of others, she has gotten her life back on track and appears once again to be exhibiting signs of PTG. In fact, she has recently launched a support group for those who have experienced a traumatic event and feel that they have lacked the opportunity to express themselves. However, her story is evidence of the powerful impact a pileup of losses can have on PTG and coping in general.

The story of Stephanie, age 22 (going on 40, as she suggests), is another example of how PTG may occur, but only after an extended period. Her story also reinforces the complex family dynamic theme of our chapter. A new family reality has been constituted for her and her loved ones. It is a family that has many new contours as compared to the family that existed before the loss.

Stephanie's Story

Three years ago, I never would have imagined this day would come. A day that I can honestly say I am happy and thankful for my life.

April 13, 2001, one of my best friends died. I was absolutely devastated by her death, and could not understand how God could take such a young person. Without my dad by my side, I never would have made it through the first days following her death. Dad listened when I called sobbing about the injustice of life. He physically held me up when it was time to view Sarah's body. What was I to do when six days later my dad was killed in a motorcycle accident? Who was I to call? Who was to support me when it came time to view his body?

The answer was and is no one. I have had to grow up from a girl of 19 to a woman of 40 in just three years. All 700 people who attended my dad's funeral seemed to disappear after the event and we were all left floundering alone. Instead of pulling together in the face of disaster, my family withdrew into ourselves. My mom, after spending a few months utterly alone, began to date again. At this time, my sisters, then 14 and 16, felt like they had lost both parents. My dad was gone and my mom essentially was too. My sisters began to live as they wanted without the direct supervision of any adults.

Fast-forward to the present, and it has been three years since we lost our dad. Our family has undergone so many changes that it is difficult to remember how we used to be . . . normal and happy. My mom has been dating another man for two years and she pretty much lives with him. She spends about four evenings a month at home. Though he is a nice man, it is still so hard for my sisters and me to accept another man into our lives. My sister, who was 16 at the time, is now 19 and has a 15-month-old daughter and a two-month-old daughter of her own. She has gone from a carefree youth to a full-time single mother. My sister who was 14 at the time is now 17 and she still lives on her own. The only person she has had to count on was her boyfriend, and they have just broken up. Adolescents need tremendous support throughout this stage of their lives. My sister has had to endure a huge life change during a time when living is hard enough. Her outlook on life is ". . . that's just how it is. I'm used to being alone."

Though I cry for my loss, my heart truly breaks to see how my sisters have needlessly suffered. If only my dad had survived, they could still be just girls rather than girls leading grown up lives. It is not fair that we have all lost the lives we knew and were comfortable with, and we have been thrust into this new life no one would ever choose.

For the three years since these deaths, I have often wondered how I would make it. Worrying about the future was never an option because my days were broken up by hours, minutes, and even seconds that felt like an eternity. I remember days spent counting the cracks in my bedroom walls because I could not convince myself to get out of bed. I have gone through such lows that suicide has felt like the only viable option, but I struggled on so I would not hurt my family any more.

Thankfully, I feel like I have finally ridden through most of the lows on the grief roller coaster. I have been able to learn from my loss and also to turn this knowledge into power. My goal in life is to support others through losses in their lives. I have spent countless hours researching loss and grief to be prepared to speak with university professors and students and high school teachers and students. I am also facilitating a grief support group for my peers who have lost a parent.

Looking back, I know I would do absolutely anything possible to have my dad back but I cannot. What I can do, though, is grow from this experience and use it help others grow too.

Comment

Stephanie's story shows that growth following traumatic loss may occur as a slow process. In talking with Stephanie, she confided that for months she felt as though she would never rise out of depression and would never be able to embrace life again. Yet she has persevered and now is using her experiences with loss as a positive step toward understanding others with similar losses.

She also demonstrates that loss does not happen only to the individual, but within the context of the family. It is difficult for some to grieve while the welfare of surviving family members is of utmost concern; however, for true growth one must also focus on the self.

Hence, when there is a pileup of major losses, the person is faced with the need for movement when movement is excruciating to achieve. Just going from one point to the next may be enough—and constitute a type of outcome that we as analysts and practitioners should greatly respect. It does represent psychological health, as much as psychological health can be represented in the situation.

Stories and confiding in coping with loss and trauma. We applaud Tedeschi's and Calhoun's (1995, 2003) emphasis on the role of narratives in PTG and coping in general. As should be clear from our emphasis on storytelling in this chapter, it is our position (e.g., Harvey, 1996; Harvey, Weber, & Orbuch, 1990) that people often deal with major stresses best by developing an account (or story or narrative, as these terms appear to have similar meaning), that describes the event and experience and provides interpretive comment and maybe even raw emotional expression ("Oh my God, I could not believe it happened"). They then communicate parts of their account to close others, whose support of the storytelling act seems essential for this communication to be helpful in moving the account maker toward a sense of control over the experience, versus a sense that the experience is controlling the account maker (Weiss, 1975). In our work, consistent with Tedeschi and Calhoun's argument, we too have found that people seem to cope better with stressors as they emphasize account making and confiding that includes conscious rumination (Martin & Tesser, 1996). Such rumination is conscious, instrumental, and seems natural. How else could it be that all this cognitive and emotional work not be associated with rumination, or worrying, to a degree?

Our own work suggests that close others' reactions to disclosures and confiding are absolutely critical in influencing how successful the account maker will be in dealing with the loss experience. Close others sometimes react with hostility, incredulity, dismissal, and the like. Unfortunately, some of the greatest pain people experience in trying to confide comes from close others and family members. These reactions may set back the account maker's efforts and success in coping. This type of outcome was shown in research with sexual assault and incest survivors (Harvey, Orbuch, Chwalisz, & Garwood, 1991; Orbuch, Harvey, Davis, & Merbach, 1994). Incest survivors, in particular, sometimes tried to confide about their losses but were met with outcries from family members, telling them that such disclosures if made public would ruin the family. The outcome of this reaction was devastating to the confiding person. Even well-meaning confidants may also produce negative outcomes for the account maker with such misguided platitudes as, "You should be happy, he's in a better place now," or "I know just how you feel," inadvertently invalidating the confiding person's feelings. Additionally, a person's need for certain types of social support may change throughout the coping process. Therefore, the type of support beneficial to the confiding person at one time may not be the same at another, and may, in fact, be less than beneficial (Barnes, 1996).

We believe that much value would derive from studying in more precise detail the social communicative experience associated with confiding about one's losses. What are optimal reactions by confidants? How do confiders recover from dismissive reactions? Are there major gender differences in how confidants react? Depending on the type of loss and type of relationship between the confider and confidant, does confiding need to be gradually done and then continued over an extended period?

Account making and confiding can be dual in nature. While they are instrumental in achieving progress in growth, at the same time they can be a frightening prospect for the account maker in the already painful aftermath of loss and traumatic events. At times, reviewing distressing memories and facing the possibility of unfavorable reactions from others can make avoiding the issue seem like a tempting option. The story of this 23-year-old woman shows her own struggle with the storytelling process after the loss of her father.

Katie's Story

When my father was diagnosed with cancer for the second time, he had already been through so much for a man of only 54 years. He survived a previous diagnosis of throat cancer and grueling radiation therapy, and he successfully recovered from a completely unexpected heart attack and angioplasty. After watching him triumph over such life-threatening adversity, I began to think of him as a real-life Superman, virtually invincible. I thought the worst was over. I was wrong.

In the months before his second diagnosis, Dad was wheezing a lot and getting increasingly short of breath. What we had hoped was asthma turned out to be something much more deadly. We were shocked to learn that a tumor the size of a golf ball had grown, undetected, in between his trachea and esophagus, right above the sternum. It was blocking his air supply—if left alone, he would have suffocated to death. Dad's chances, we learned, were not good. The tumor was malignant, and due to its unusual location, inoperable. Radiation was risky because there was extensive tissue damage from his first encounter with cancer; chemotherapy would serve only as a palliative measure. Faced with few alternatives, but not ready to give up, he enrolled as a participant of a university hospital clinical trial for esophageal cancer patients.

Over the course of Dad's illness, I watched my parents go through sheer hell. Life evolved into a routine of hospitals and I.V. tubes. For three months, every other week, they drove six hours to the university where the clinical trial was being held and stayed in a cramped hospital room, while Dad received chemo and radiation, along with an experimental drug.

As the treatment took effect, he lost the ability to swallow and had to be fed through a gastric tube. He lost weight rapidly, and he looked like a skeleton—he was 6'2" and weighed only 150 pounds. He could not enjoy the comfort of his own bed; he coughed too much when he was prostrate and had to spend all of his time sitting upright in our living room chair, even to sleep. Perhaps one of the most upsetting developments of all was the trachea tube that was installed to allow him to breathe. It was sufficiently large to prevent air from passing through his vocal cords, literally rendering him speechless. He was not able to use his voice for the rest of his life.

Through all of this, Mom remained my father's vigilant caretaker, a daunting and never-ending task. She became his voice when he could not speak for himself, lip-reading and translating his gestures so that other people could understand what he had to say. She measured and administered his many medications several times a day. It was impossible for her to leave him alone for long periods of time, especially towards the end of his illness; there was always the chance that something could go wrong in her absence. Dad was almost completely dependent on her; she was physically and emotionally exhausted.

In my opinion, I did not experience the full horror that my parents did. I was away at college for the majority of this time, although I did come home nearly every weekend. When I was home, I helped take care of Dad as much as I could, but I still felt like I wasn't pulling my weight. I dreaded going back to school; I always felt like I was abandoning my parents. They had to live with Dad's illness and its ramifications 24 hours a day, seven days a week. Why should I have been the one to be able to escape it? I wanted to stay and relieve Mom of some of her burden. I wanted to be with Dad—I didn't really know how much longer he had left. Every time I left home, there was no certainty that he would be there when I came back, and that scared me. But as much as I wanted to, and as guilty as I felt, I did not drop out of school. I knew that if I did, my father would feel responsible for interrupting my education. He was a selfless man, always putting Mom and me before himself, and to know that I gave up school for him would have devastated him. I did not want to put him through that.

Months after Dad's treatment was completed, he took a turn for the worse. His cancer was gone, but in its place was a gaping hole in the wall between his trachea and esophagus— thanks to the radiation. His trachea was swelling shut, forcing him to breathe through an air passage roughly the size of a cocktail straw; he had panic attacks because he couldn't get enough air. Hospice workers and a hospital bed became a fixture in our living room. I knew that he could go at any time, but I did not want to admit that to myself. I kept clinging to the hope that something miraculous would come along and save him.

The miracle never came. Dad died on March 26th, 2003, a little over a year after he was diagnosed. He'd had a stroke. He'd been on the way to the hospital where they were going to attempt an experimental surgery to close the hole in between his esophagus and trachea. He would have had less than a 1% chance of surviving it. When Mom and I arrived at the hospital, we were told that he would die in the next few hours. We sat in the hospital room with him and each held his hand as we watched the time span between each breath gradually increase. I whispered in his ear how much I loved him, how I could never have asked for a better father, and how I would do everything I could to make him proud. I hope he heard me. My worst fear came to life when, about seven hours after we arrived at the hospital, my father took his last breath. My daddy was gone.

It has now been a little over a year since Dad died. I don't think I've grieved enough. I still feel very much the way I did right after he died: numb. While Dad was sick, I didn't allow myself to show how upset I was about what was happening, especially not in front of my parents. I didn't want to add to their burden and make them more upset than they already were; I wanted to be strong, a shoulder for them to cry on. Consequently, I became quite adept at squashing down my emotions and maintaining a stoic demeanor around other people. When he died, I did not cry much at all. Even now, I don't let myself cry much, and if I do, it's almost always in private. A year ago, I didn't want to let myself fall apart, because I didn't know if I would be able to put myself back together again. I still feel that way.

When I'm not numb (which is most of the time), I'm angry. I am outraged that this happened to such a kind and wonderful man when there are so many malicious and horrible people who still have the privilege of living. I am furious that I have been cheated out of time with my father; there are so many things that he won't be able to experience with me—my wedding, the birth of my children. I am angry with myself for not being there more for him and, illogical as it is, for not being able to do anything to stop what was happening to him. Sometimes I feel like a pressure cooker about to explode—I just don't show it. Most people who know me, even those I am closest to, have no idea how angry I am.

I very rarely talk about Dad's death to others. What I have written here is the most I have ever said about it at one time, and it was extremely difficult for me. In part, I suppose my reticence stems from the fact I am afraid that if I do talk about it in depth, all of the feelings I have been repressing will come rushing out, and I don't want to feel all the pain that I know is lurking there. Mostly, however, it is because I am afraid of the reactions of others. I know most people don't want to hear about death, and I know what a struggle it is to find the right thing to say to someone who's lost a loved one. I don't want to cause anyone's discomfort, and I really don't want to watch it. It makes me feel like I should be ashamed for even bringing up the topic, and that's the last thing I need. On a recent first date, the man I was with asked about my parents. I told him that my father had died not long ago. This was his response, verbatim: "Oh, I've never had anyone tell me that before. Let's change the subject." He was not kidding. Needless to say, in that moment, the first date became the last date. I am aware that this was an atypical response, but it is reactions like this that make me reluctant to even mention my father's death unless it is necessary.

I do have someone I can talk with about Dad: Mom. She never tries to change the subject and will always listen, no matter what I have to say. However, although I will discuss Dad as a person with her, I don't usually bring up his actual death, because life has been especially difficult for Mom in the past few years, and I don't want to upset her any more than I have to. I realize that I'm being irrational; I know she would be more than willing to talk about Dad's death, and in fact, she is worried that I don't talk more about what happened. I know I need to, as well. As a result of this, I have recently joined a grief support group for those who have lost a parent. I think it will be beneficial for me to talk about Dad's death to someone my age who on some level, will understand; I will know that I am not alone. Perhaps that is one of the biggest reasons I have been holding back—I am searching for empathy, not sympathy.

Although I do not often reveal my true emotions or discuss Dad's death, he is constantly on my mind. I review everything about him: his voice, the way he smelled, the warmth of his hugs, his silly sense of humor. I rehash all of the experiences I have had with him. I even let myself think about his illness and death—in snapshot images. I will not let myself forget him . . . any of him. I will not let others forget him, either. During the year Dad was unable to speak, he communicated by writing in notebooks that he carried around with him wherever he went. Mom and I saved the notebooks and have been reading through them—they are documentation of what an inspiration he was. He was so courageous; he never gave up, not even when the odds were against him. During his illness, he maintained a sense of humor and optimism that were truly aweinspiring. We are currently planning to write a book about our experience based on his notebooks and our memories. We want others to know what an amazing man he was, perhaps even learn by his example. He was Superman, after all; he just wasn't invincible.

Comment

Katie's narrative demonstrates the importance of account making and confiding in moving toward growth after a loss experience. Her reluctance to share the story of her father's death with others for fear of becoming overwhelmed with emotion and the negative reactions of others is indicative of the sense of control she feels the experience has over her (Weiss, 1975). The numbness she exhibits is a direct reflection of this, as is the gradual nature of her journey toward growth. Nonetheless, growth is evident, particularly in the plans to write a book about the family's experience. The complexity of family lives and its influence on loss outcomes is once again germane here. This is shown through Katie's concern for her mother's well-being as well as through their collaboration effort.

CONCLUSIONS

In this chapter, we have suggested that PTG is a vital concept in the literature of loss and trauma. Similarly, a recognition of other types of outcome that are not negative is needed. These other types of outcome may be construed as neutral in valence, or "relatively positive" given the limitations for constructive growth that exist in many situations of major loss. We also have stressed the complex lives into which loss comes. The stories presented reveal how these lives shape and qualify perceptions of and reactions to major loss.

We have noted a distinction between traumatic events and other types of major loss, such as a slow, debilitating decline in health. For the latter types of loss, psychological growth may be seen, as in the marvelous example of Morrie Schwartz in his lessons of living. For loss and trauma, whether or not PTG is seen, movement—as exemplified in expressions such as "just keep on going"—is essential for survival. To paraphrase Hemingway, a great truth and irony of life is that we may grow stronger at the broken places.

REFERENCES

Ahrons, C. (1994). *The good divorce*. New York: HarperCollins.

Albom, M. (1997). *Tuesdays with Morrie*. New York: Doubleday.

Barnes, M. K. (1996). A case study approach to support needs following the death of a loved one. *Journal of Personal and Interpersonal Loss, 1*, 275–298.

Figley, C. R. (1993). Forward. In J. Wilson & B. Raphael (Eds.), *International handbook of trauma stress syndromes* (pp. xvii–xx). New York: Plenum.

Harvey, J. H. (1996). *Embracing their memory: Loss and the social psychology of story-telling*. Needham Heights, MA: Allyn & Bacon.

Harvey, J. H. (2002). *Perspectives on loss and trauma: Assaults on the self*. Thousand Oaks, CA: Sage.

Harvey, J. H., & Fine, M. A. (2004). *Children of divorce: Stories of loss and growth*. Mahwah, NJ: Lawrence Erlbaum Associates.

Harvey, J. H., & Miller, E. (1998). Toward a psychology of loss. *Psychological Science, 9*, 429–434.

Harvey, J. H., Orbuch, T. L., Chwalisz, K., & Garwood, G. (1991). Coping with sexual assault: The roles of account-making and confiding. *Journal of Traumatic Stress, 4*, 515–531.

Harvey, J. H., Weber, A. L., & Orbuch, T. L. (1990). *Interpersonal accounts: A social psychological perspective*. Oxford: Basil Blackwell.

Herman, J. (1992). *Trauma and recovery*. New York: Basic Books.

Hobfoll, S. E. (1988). *The ecology of stress*. New York: Hemisphere.

Hobfoll, S. E. (1989). Conservation of resources: A new attempt at conceptualizing stress. *American Psychologist, 44*, 513–524.

Martin, L. L., & Tesser, A. (1996). Clarifying our thoughts. In R. S. Wyer (Ed.), *Ruminative thought: Advances in social cognition*, (Vol. 9, pp. 189–209). Mahwah, NJ: Lawrence Erlbaum Associates.

Orbuch, T. L., Harvey, J. H., Davis, S. H., & Merbach, N. (1994). Account-making and confiding as acts of meaning in response to sexual assault. *Journal of Family Violence, 9,* 249–264.

Snyder, C. R., & Lopez, S. (2001). (Eds.) *Handbook of positive psychology.* New York: Oxford University Press.

Tedeschi, R. G., & Calhoun, L. G. (1995). *Trauma and transformation: Growing in the aftermath of suffering.* Thousand Oaks, CA: Sage.

Tedeschi, R. G., & Calhoun, L. G. (2003). Postraumatic growth: A developmental perspective. *Psychological Inquiry, 15,* 1–18.

Tedeschi, R. G., Park, C. L., & Calhoun, L. G. (Eds.). (1998). *Posttraumatic growth: Positive changes in the aftermath of crisis.* Mahwah, NJ: Lawrence Erlbaum Associates.

Viorst, J. (1986). *Necessary losses.* New York: Fawcett.

Weiss, R. S. (1975). *Marital separation.* New York: Basic Books.

PART

II

Posttraumatic Growth in Specific Contexts

7

SPIRITUALITY: A PATHWAY TO POSTTRAUMATIC GROWTH OR DECLINE?

KENNETH I. PARGAMENT, KAVITA M. DESAI,
AND KELLY M. MCCONNELL
BOWLING GREEN STATE UNIVERSITY

INTRODUCTION

While the psychological, social, and physical dimensions of a traumatic experience are well recognized, the spiritual dimension is often overlooked. Yet, spirituality can play a critical role in the way traumas are understood, how they are managed, and how they are ultimately resolved. Spirituality can be potentially helpful or harmful. In this chapter, we will see that spirituality can be a positive resource for posttraumatic growth (PTG) or a source of struggle that may lead to growth or decline. We will consider some of the factors that may determine whether spirituality leads ultimately to growth or decline. Finally, we will conclude by discussing some of the practical implications of this body of theory and research for our efforts to help people coping with major trauma. We begin by discussing the meaning of spirituality and religion and their place in the context of coping with life traumas.

BACKGROUND AND DEFINITIONS

The old saying that there are no atheists in foxholes is an exaggeration. There are people who are nonbelievers before, during, and after they experience major life traumas. Nevertheless, there may be a grain of truth to this old saying, for researchers have identified a link between spirituality and moments of greatest stress. For example, following the September 11 terrorist attacks, 90% of a random sample of Americans reportedly coped by turning to religion (Schuster et al., 2001). Similarly, in a study of people who had been paralyzed as the result of an accident, the most common explanation offered for their situation was "God had a reason" (Bulman & Wortman, 1977).

Despite the evidence of its salience to people facing major life traumas, psychologists, with some exceptions (e.g., Shaw, Joseph, & Linley, 2005), have generally overlooked or oversimplified the roles of religion and spirituality in stressful times. Religion and spirituality have been described as defenses against anxiety, passive forms of coping, or sources of denial of the painful reality (see Pargament & Park, 1995). These stereotypes do not stand up well to empirical scrutiny. Though religion can be a source of comfort and anxiety reduction to many people, it also serves other functions, such as providing meaning in life, a sense of intimacy with others, self-development, and, most importantly, a connection with the sacred. Empirical studies also indicate that religiousness and spirituality are more often linked to active rather than passive forms of coping and are rarely sources of blanket denials of the realities of loss (Pargament & Park, 1995).

In contrast to the stereotypes of religion and spirituality, these phenomena are rich and complex rather than simple and straightforward. *Spirituality* can be defined as a search for the sacred (Pargament & Mahoney, 2002). There are two key terms in this definition: the *sacred* and *search*. The sacred refers to those things that are holy, set apart from ordinary aspects of living, and worthy of veneration and respect. The sacred encompasses not only God, divine beings, or a transcendent reality, but also other aspects of life that take on divine character and significance by virtue of their association with a higher power. The search for the sacred refers to the processes of discovery of the sacred, efforts to conserve or hold on to the sacred once it has been discovered, and attempts to transform the sacred when internal or external pressures insist on change. Although religion can be viewed as a personal as well as a social expression (see Zinnbauer, Pargament, & Scott, 1999), in this chapter we use *religion* to refer to the larger social and institutional context in which the search for the sacred takes place. From our perspective, spirituality always unfolds in a religious context, even if it is a religious context that people may reject. Simple conclusions about the roles of spirituality and religion in peoples' lives are not warranted, given the diversity of sacred "objects," the myriad pathways people can take in their efforts to discover, conserve, and transform the sacred, and the wide range of religious contexts in which spirituality unfolds. It is particularly important to recognize that spirituality can serve both as a resource for coping and as a source of struggle in itself.

SPIRITUALITY AS A RESOURCE FOR COPING WITH TRAUMA

Many people report anecdotally that their spirituality is a source of positive change and growth, even in the face of major life crises, pain, and suffering. One woman facing breast cancer said: "Cancer has, in many ways, been a gift...I have come to a place where I feel peaceful and strong. I have developed an abiding faith that no matter what happens I can cope and it will be alright (all this despite having Stage IV incurable cancer)" (Gall & Cornblatt, 2002, p. 530). A caregiver to parents with Alzheimer's said:

> It is the most rewarding and devastating experience of my life; I would not have given up this period to care for my parents for anything. There has been combativeness, wandering—lots of frustrations. But I'm learning for the first time to take each day at a time. This illness is teaching me to gain strength from the Lord. (Wright, Pratt, & Schmall, 1985, p. 34)

These anecdotal reports are not unusual. Empirical studies have demonstrated that spirituality is significantly tied to measures of PTG. For example, in a study of 174 bereaved HIV/AIDS caregivers involving structural equation modeling, Cadell, Regehr, and Hemsworth (2003) found that a general measure of spirituality was associated with higher levels of PTG. In a series of studies of college students, Park, Cohen, and Murch (1996) developed a measure of stress-related growth and found that measures of intrinsic religious commitment and religious coping were significantly associated with reports of greater growth. Working with people in a hospital awaiting the outcome of cardiac surgery of loved ones, VandeCreek et al. (1999) found that more frequent prayer and higher levels of self-rated religiousness were correlated with reports of more growth as a result of the stressor.

The Critical Ingredients of Spirituality

While these studies point to a significant connection between spirituality and PTG, they do not address what it is about spirituality that may facilitate growth. Additional empirical studies point to three potentially critical "growth-related" spiritual ingredients. First, spirituality may provide people with an important source of support and empowerment in stressful times. One woman described the spiritual strength she derived from God in caring for her mother with dementia: "Sometimes, I think of something mother used to say or do—and, the tears won't stop coming. But you know, I bow my head for a minute—and ask the Lord for the strength to go on. And, girl, I tell you—He just lifts those old burdens from me right away" (Dungee-Anderson & Beckett, 1992, p. 164). Another African American man dealing with HIV/AIDS noted how prayer helped him develop a sense of mastery and control: "My life is enriched. Enriched and empowered. I don't feel helpless anymore . . . I have spiritual resources that can help me achieve [my] ends" (Siegel & Schrimshaw, 2002, p. 95). In addition, measures of spiritual coping that capture perceptions of support from God have been consistently associated with reports of greater PTG (e.g., Hettler & Cohen, 1994; Pargament, Ensing et al., 1990; Pargament, Smith, & Koenig, 1996; Park & Cohen, 1993).

Second, as Tedeschi, Park, and Calhoun (1998) note, life trauma is a "time when meaning may be created and found" (p. 4). Spirituality may play a critical role in the meaning-making process (see Park & Folkman, 1997). For example, one Hindu woman with a disability that left her unable to have children was able to reframe her situation through her religious tradition: "My solace is Vedanta [philosophy of Hinduism]. . .The other day I gained a flash of insight. I suddenly saw myself as having been a wife and a husband hundreds of times, with thousands of children. That is a path I have already traveled, I am on a new one now" (Nosek, 1995, p. 8). Spiritually based forms of meaning-making have been tied to PTG in empirical research. For example, Park and Cohen (1993) studied a group of college students who had suffered the death of a close friend and found that attributions of the death to a purposeful God were correlated with reports of more personal growth. In a five-year prospective investigation that bears at least indirectly on this point, Murphy, Johnson, and Lohan (2003) studied 138 parents of an adolescent or young child who had died as a result of accident, suicide, or homicide. Parents who engaged in more religious coping reported that they were able to find significantly greater meaning five years after their child's violent death.

Third, in response to critical stressors, spirituality may foster life-changing transformations of goals and priorities. Decker (1993) illustrates the potential for this kind of transformation by recounting a vignette from the movie "Gandhi." In the movie, Gandhi meets a Hindu who confesses "I am going to Hell. I murdered two Muslim children after the Muslims murdered my family." Gandhi replies, "You may indeed go to Hell. But there may be a way out. Find two orphaned Hindu children and raise them as Muslims" (Decker,

1993, p. 43). The changes in goals and priorities embodied in spiritual conversion and the performance of good deeds have been associated with PTG. In a study of college students facing major life stressors, Pargament et al. (2000) found that students who scored higher on a measure of religious conversion reported higher levels of stress-related growth. Efforts to perform religious good deeds following life crises have also been correlated with higher levels of PTG (e.g., Park & Cohen, 1993).

It is important to add that growth following trauma may be especially prominent in the spiritual sphere of life. Many people describe feelings of greater closeness to God as the result of critical life events. For example, in one report, "A 14-year-old Maryland boy who was shot and nearly killed by a sniper last fall told a packed courtroom that the terrifying experience 'brought me closer to God,' " (CNN, Wednesday, October 29, 2003). Another 52-year-old African-American man living with HIV/AIDS said, "It [HIV/AIDS] has drawn me more closer, more closer to a God. It has drawn me closer to recognize there's been a force working in my life" (Siegel & Schrimshaw, 2002, p. 97). Consistent with these reports, researchers have found that a significant number of people who have experienced trauma feel they have grown spiritually or become more religious. For instance, Richards, Acree, and Folkman (1999) interviewed 70 bereaved caregivers of male partners who had died of AIDS. Seventy-seven percent reported that their spirituality increased or deepened through their caregiving and bereavement. Higher levels of religious coping with major traumas have also been associated with increased closeness to God, increases in self-rated spirituality, and greater closeness to one's church (Pargament, Ensing et al., 1990; Smith, Pargament, Brant, & Oliver, 2000).

SPIRITUALITY AS A SOURCE OF STRUGGLE WITH TRAUMA

Although traumatic events can lead to spiritual growth, they can also lead to spiritual decline. For example, Falsetti, Resick, and Davis (2003) identified a sample of people with posttraumatic stress disorder (PTSD) through interviews with individuals from the community and mental health treatment sites. They found that 30% of those with PTSD reportedly became less religious after their trauma, while only 20% indicated that they became more religious following the trauma. Similarly, Brenner (1980) surveyed 708 survivors of the Holocaust and found that, of those who reported changes in their beliefs in God during or immediately after the Holocaust, more described a weakening than a strengthening of their faith. How do we account for the loss of spirituality that can accompany critical life events?

Spiritual frameworks of belief, practice, and value are not exempt from the questions that can be raised by crises. Consider, for example, the spiritual turmoil expressed by this 14-year-old adolescent from Nicaragua:

> Many times I wonder how there can be a God—a loving God and where He is ... I don't understand why he lets little children in Third World countries die of starvation or diseases that could have been cured if they would have had the right medicines or doctors. I believe in God and I love Him, but sometimes I just don't see the connection between a loving God and a suffering hurting world. Why doesn't He help us—if He truly loves us? It seems like He just doesn't care. Does He? (Kooistra, 1990, pp. 91–2)

Three Types of Spiritual Struggle

In the midst of crisis, many people struggle with their spirituality. These struggles are a sign of spirituality in tension and in flux. Spiritual struggles can be viewed as efforts to conserve or transform a spirituality that has been threatened or harmed (Pargament, Murray-Swank, Magyar, & Ano, 2005). We can distinguish among three types of spiritual struggles: interpersonal, intrapersonal, and divine. Interpersonal spiritual struggles involve religious tensions and conflicts with family, friends, congregations, and communities. Krause, Chatters, Meltzer, and Morgan (2000) conducted focus groups of older church members and identified several forms of negative interactions within the church, such as gossiping, cliquishness, hypocrisy, and disagreements with church doctrine. Interpersonal spiritual struggles are commonplace. Nielsen (1998), for example, found that 65% of an adult sample reportedly experienced some type of religious conflict, most of which were interpersonal. Failures of presumably "spiritual" or "religious" people may be especially painful because such people are expected to enact their spiritual values. One older woman voices the interpersonal spiritual struggle she experiences with others in her church:

> They get off in a corner and talk about you and you're the one that's there on Sunday working with their children and ironing the priest's vestments and doing all that kind of thing and washing the dishes on Sunday afternoon after church. But they don't have the Christian spirit. (Krause et al., 2000, p. 519)

Intrapersonal spiritual struggles refer to questions, doubts, and uncertainties about spiritual matters. These struggles may focus on questions about one's ultimate purpose in life. They may involve conflicts between desires to gratify human appetites and desires to be virtuous (Exline, 2002). The struggles may center around conflicts about spiritual motivation. Along these lines, Ryan, Rigby, and King (1993) distinguish between a religion that is personally chosen and valued (identification) from a conflictual religion that develops out of social pressure or anxiety and guilt (introjection). Intrapersonal struggles may also focus on religious systems of belief and practice, as we hear in questions one adolescent raises about Christianity: "Is Christianity a big sham, a cult? If an organization were to evolve in society, it would have to excite people emotionally, it would have to be self-perpetuating, it would need a source of income, etc. Christianity fits all of these. How do I know that I haven't been sucked into a giant perpetual motion machine" (Kooistra, 1990, p. 95)? Questions and doubts such as these are not unusual. In a study of a national sample of Presbyterians, only 35% reported that they never had any religious doubts (Krause, Ingersoll-Dayton, Ellison, & Wulff, 1999).

Finally, people can experience struggles with the divine. Traumatic events can pose a threat to views of God as an all-loving, omnipotent being who ensures that good things will happen to good people. In response to crisis, the individual may feel abandoned by God, anger toward God, or feelings of punishment by God. And because they touch on the deepest dimension of life, these struggles may be especially painful. Listen to the bitter words of one victim of incest:

> How could you in all your greatness have abandoned me, a little girl, to the merciless hands of my father? How could you let this happen to me? I demand to know why this happened? Why didn't you protect me? I have been faithful, and for what, to be raped and abused by my own father? I hate and despise you. I regret the first time I ever laid eyes on you; your name is like salt on my tongue. I vomit it from my being. I wish death upon you. You are no more. You are dead. (Flaherty, 1992, p. 101)

Painful as they are, struggles with the divine are not uncommon. For example, in a study of homeless men, 50% reported that their social condition elicited some negative feelings toward God (Smith & Exline, 2002). Similarly, in a study of three groups of medical patients, approximately 20% described moderate to high levels of negative religious coping, defined by feelings of alienation, abandonment, anger, or punishment in relationship to God (Fitchett, Murphy, Gibbons, & Cameron, 2001).

Empirical Links Between Spiritual Struggle and Distress

Empirical studies have shown clear and consistent links between the three types of spiritual struggles and indicators of distress. With respect to interpersonal spiritual struggles, Krause, Ellison, and Wulff (1998) conducted a study of a national sample of clergy, elders, and members of the Presbyterian Church and found that negative church interactions were associated with higher levels of psychological distress. Working with a sample of church members and college students, Pargament, Zinnbauer et al. (1998) also found that higher levels of interpersonal religious conflict and conflicts with the clergy and church dogma were predictive of lower self-esteem, more negative mood, and greater anxiety. In a longitudinal study of medically ill elders, people who reported more interpersonal religious discontent at baseline manifested significant increases in depression over a two-year period (Pargament, Koenig, Tarakeshwar, & Hahn, in press).

Intrapersonal spiritual struggles have also been correlated with more distress. For instance, in a study of Dutch Reformed and Roman Catholic high school students, more religious doubts were associated with greater anxiety and more negative affect (Kooistra & Pargament, 1999). Similarly, religious doubts have been tied to more depression and less positive affect among Presbyterian church leaders and members (Krause, et al., 1999) and less happiness and life satisfaction in a national sample of adults (Ellison, 1991). Religious fears and guilt have also been related to higher risk of suicide in samples of college students and adults seeking outpatient psychotherapy (Exline, Yali, & Sanderson, 2000).

Some of the strongest findings have emerged from studies of struggles with the divine. Ano and Vasconcelles (2005) conducted a meta-analysis of 49 studies of religious coping and reported that divine spiritual struggles were consistently associated with greater psychological maladjustment. Specific indicators of divine struggle (e.g., feeling punished by God, feeling abandoned by God, questioning God's powers, attributing problems to the devil) have been associated with more anxiety and depression among college students (Pargament, Koenig, & Perez, 2000; Pargament, Zinnbauer et al., 1998), more psychological distress among victims of the 1993 Midwest floods (Smith, et al., 2000), more depression among adult psychotherapy outpatients (Exline, Yali, & Lobel, 1999), and more symptoms of PTSD and callousness toward others among members of churches near the Oklahoma City bombing (Pargament, Smith, Koenig, & Perez, 1998).

Two longitudinal studies are particularly noteworthy. In one study of patients in medical rehabilitation, patients who reported more anger at God showed lower levels of independent functioning four months later, even after controlling for other variables including demographic factors, depression, social support, general anger, and level of independent functioning at admission (Fitchett, Rybarczyk, DeMarco, & Nicholas, 1999). In another study of medically ill elderly patients, those who reported more struggles with the divine at baseline experienced significantly greater declines in physical functional status and quality of life, and increases in depression over two years (Pargament, Koenig et al., in press). Moreover, spiritual struggles at baseline resulted in a 22% to 33% increase in risk of dying after controlling for demographic, physical health, and mental health variables (Pargament, Koenig, Tarakeshwar, & Hahn, 2001).

Empirical Links Between Spiritual Struggle and Growth

The strength and consistency of these findings may seem somewhat surprising from a religious perspective. Most of the world's great religious traditions speak of spiritual struggle as a pathway to growth. Moses, Buddha, and Jesus are among the exemplary religious figures who experienced their own periods of spiritual turmoil, only to come through the process strengthened and revitalized. More recently, none other than Mother Teresa described times of spiritual struggle, as we hear in these words: "I am told that God lives in me—and yet the reality of darkness and coldness and emptiness is so great that nothing touches my soul" (*Newsweek*, 2001, p. 23).

In fact, there is evidence of a link between spiritual struggles and PTG. Profitt, Calhoun, Tedeshi, and Cann (2004) studied 30 clergypersons and found that more spiritual struggles, as assessed by a measure of negative religious coping, were associated with higher levels of PTG. Among church members close to the Oklahoma City bombing site, people who reported more spiritual struggle reported not only more symptoms of PTSD, but also more stress-related growth (Pargament, Smith et al., 1998). In a study of college students coping with major life stressors, indicators of struggles with the divine (e.g., greater spiritual discontent, reappraisals of God's powers, demonic appraisals) were associated with higher levels of stress-related growth (Pargament et al., 2000). Magyar, Pargament, and Mahoney (2000) found that college students who perceived violations in their romantic relationships as desecrations (i.e., violations of something sacred) reported higher levels of PTG.

Overall, the empirical literature paints a rich and complex picture of the relationship between spirituality, health, and well-being. Some forms of spirituality have proven to be valuable resources in coping with major life crises. Spiritual struggles, in contrast, have been clearly connected to higher levels of distress. And yet, with a few exceptions (Pargament, Ensing et al., 1990; Pargament, Zinnbauer et al., 1998), spiritual struggles have also been tied to PTG. How do we make sense of these disparate findings?

SPIRITUAL DETERMINANTS OF GROWTH OR DECLINE

What determines whether spirituality becomes a resource in coping or a source of struggle? What determines ultimately whether spirituality leads to PTG or decline? Although these questions have not received much direct empirical attention, indirect evidence points to three potentially important factors: characteristics of the trauma, coping resources, and the individual's religious orienting system.

Characteristics of the Trauma

Research indicates that event severity is related to growth (e.g. Aldwin, Sutton, & Lachman, 1996; Brennan, 2002; Tedeschi & Calhoun, 1996). In the development and initial validation of the Posttraumatic Growth Inventory (PTGI), Tedeschi and Calhoun (1996) found that undergraduate students reporting a traumatic event experienced a "great" degree of PTG, whereas students who did not report a traumatic event experienced "small" to "moderate" degrees of growth (p. 467). Similarly, Park, Cohen, and Murch (1996) reported that the initial stressfulness of an event was a significant predictor of more stress-related growth. Moreover, Brennan (2002) studied an adult sample and found that individuals who had experienced higher levels of adversity reported greater psychosocial development as measured by an Inventory of Psychosocial Balance. Interestingly, the type of negative life event experienced does not seem to impact growth (e.g., Aldwin et al., 1996; Park et al., 1996). Instead, event severity appears to be the key component related to growth.

These findings seem to support the sports adage, "No pain, no gain." How do we explain this seemingly counterintuitive relationship? Perhaps, the shattering of an individual's worldview creates more room for growth (Janoff-Bulman, 1992). Similarly, spiritual struggles that challenge the person's most basic assumptions about life may create more opportunities for fundamental spiritual transformation. Consistent with this interpretation, empirical studies have shown that the relationship between measures of religiousness/spirituality and health and well-being is moderated by the stressfulness of the situation. Specifically, higher levels of religiousness and spirituality are tied to more positive outcomes as the stressfulness of the situation increases (see Pargament, 1997 for a review).

The chronicity of the trauma may be another factor that determines whether spirituality leads to decline or growth. Spiritual struggles may be time-limited for many people. For example, Exline (2002) found that among those who experienced some anger toward God after a negative event, 80% indicated that their anger had decreased over time. But for others, spiritual struggles may be more chronic, increasing the risk for trouble. Relevant to this point is the longitudinal study of medically ill elderly patients by Pargament, Koenig, Tarakeshwar, and Hahn (2004). Based on interviews at baseline and at two-year follow-up, participants in the study were classified into four groups: transitory strugglers (those experiencing spiritual struggles only at baseline), acute strugglers (those experiencing spiritual struggles only at follow-up), chronic strugglers (those experiencing spiritual struggles at baseline and at follow-up), and nonstrugglers (those not experiencing spiritual struggles at baseline or follow-up). Among the four groups, only the chronic spiritual struggles experienced significant declines in physical and mental health over the two-year period of the study. The researchers note that this subgroup of medically ill patients appeared to "get stuck" in their struggles. They experienced their struggles as "less resolvable."

In this vein, Exline (2002) notes that the religious road is littered with "stumbling blocks," such as interpersonal strains, strains in the relationship with God, and internal strains between vice and virtue. When they fall over a stumbling block, people have two options, to stay down or to get up and keep moving down the road. Those who overcome their stumbling blocks may not only restore their faith, but enhance it as well.

Coping Resources

Coping resources may also determine whether an individual encounters a spiritual struggle and grows or declines as a result of the struggle. In response to crisis, people can draw on a variety of internal and external resources. The individual's personal coping style and system of social support represent two potentially significant internal and external resources, respectively. Although researchers have not yet identified coping methods that decrease the likelihood or impact of spiritual struggles, several coping methods have been tied to higher levels of personal growth. These include secular coping methods, such as positive reinterpretation, acceptance, instrumental action, and problem focused coping (Park et al., 1996; Park & Cohen, 1993; Aldwin et al., 1996; Carver, 1998) and, as noted in the preceding text, spiritual coping methods including benevolent spiritual reappraisals of negative events, support from God, and spiritual connection. These latter coping methods may be particularly salient to the resolution of spiritual struggles because spiritual struggles are likely to elicit a search for spiritual solutions. For example, one young woman described the spiritual struggles she experienced after she learned that she had been diagnosed HIV positive on her 16th birthday: "[I] blamed God [for the illness,] had so much anger and hatred towards myself...towards God, [and felt like] I must be nothing [to God]." Ultimately, however, she turned to God for support and now attributes her ability to live with her disease to her ongoing relationship with the divine: "If I didn't have this relationship with God, I'd probably be in jail or dead" (K. M. Desai, personal communication, April 4, 2004).

One empirical study illustrates the potential value of another spiritual coping resource—confession. Working with a sample of college students, Murray-Swank (2003) compared the effects of spiritual confession to secular confession and a control condition. In the spiritual condition, participants wrote a letter to God asking for forgiveness for something they had done wrong. In the nonspiritual confession condition, participants simply wrote an essay about something they had done wrong. The results were interesting and complex. In comparison to the other two conditions, spiritual confession was associated with greater reports of spiritual growth immediately after writing the letter to God and two weeks later. However, spiritual confession was also linked with higher levels of guilt in comparison to the nonspiritual confession condition. It is interesting to note that the impact of spiritual confession on positive affect was moderated by the participants' images of God, such that those who perceived God in loving terms experienced increases in positive affect from baseline to the two-week follow-up, and those with less loving images of God showed a decrease in positive affect.

Yet, another coping resource, social support, may also influence the likelihood of a spiritual struggle and the resolution of a spiritual struggle when it occurs. Researchers have not examined relationships among social support, spiritual struggle, and growth and decline following a major stressor. However, social support has been associated with physical health and psychological benefits in a number of contexts. For instance, in a study of HIV-positive asymptomatic men, a one-point increase in cumulative average social support satisfaction was associated with a 62% decrease in the risk of developing AIDS (Leserman et al., 2000). In their study of undergraduates coping with stressful life events, Park et al. (1996) found that people who perceived greater availability of social support and satisfaction with social support reported significantly greater stress-related growth six months later. Based on these results, the researchers concluded that, "individuals confronting stressful circumstances may be more likely to experience stress-related growth...if they possess relatively strong social resources..." (Park, 1998, p. 270). Spousal support has also proven to be a significant factor affecting outcomes of stressful events. For instance, among cardiac patients, the long-term emotional support provided by the marital relationship significantly predicts recovery and quality of life (e.g., Kulik & Mahler, 1993; Waltz & Badura, 1988).

Support from religious sources may take on greater importance in response to spiritual struggles. Again, there is no direct evidence relevant to this issue. However, empirical studies have shown that support from clergy and congregation members plays a key role in the lives of many people, particularly those who are more religiously involved (Chalfant et al., 1990; Ellison & George, 1994; Taylor & Chatters, 1988). Moreover, people can gain support from various scriptures. For example, following the loss of his home, his flocks, and his family, Job of the Bible wrestles with profound spiritual questions. Although the advice of his friends only makes matters worse, ultimately, he receives the blessings of the Lord: "So the Lord blessed the latter end of Job more than his beginning" (Job 41:12). Christians can also turn to the New Testament for spiritual support when their spirits are troubled: "Come unto me, all ye that labour and are heavy laden, and I will give you rest.

Take my yoke upon you, and learn of me; for I am meek and lowly in heart: and ye shall find rest unto your souls. For my yoke is easy, and my burden is light" (Matthew 12:28-30). Empirical studies have also shown clear connections between religious support and positive outcomes to stressful life events (e.g., Carey, 1974; Pargament, Ensing et al., 1990).

Receiving support from religious groups may be particularly problematic for those facing spiritual struggles. The experience of spiritual struggles may elicit feelings of shame and guilt among many people. Smith and Exline (2002) illustrated this point in their study of African American men in homeless shelters. They found that 46% felt it was not acceptable to have negative feelings toward God. The guilt and shame associated with spiritual struggles may deter individuals from expressing their feelings to others for fear of condemnation or reproach. Members of religious groups may be especially feared.

In fact, religious groups vary in the degree to which they encourage and support the expression of feelings (Pargament, Silverman, Johnson, Echemendia, & Snyder, 1983). Some religious communities may view spiritual struggles as signs of a weak faith and, as a result, condemn those who voice spiritual questions and doubts. For example, one mother expressed her condemnation of spiritual struggles in a letter she wrote to the university where her daughter was a student. The letter was written in response to the university's recent introduction of evolution into the curriculum. "If her [daughter's] faith is shattered or shaken, I'd rather see her dead" (Nesson, 2001). Whether spiritual struggles lead to religious support or religious condemnation may be critical to their ultimate resolution.

Spiritual Orienting System

The probability of experiencing a spiritual struggle and its outcome may also be determined by the religious orienting system of the individual. An orienting system is "a general way of viewing and dealing with the world . . . a frame of reference, a blueprint of oneself and the world that is used to anticipate and come to terms with life's events" (Pargament, 1997, p. 99). This orienting system consists of habits, values, relationships, beliefs, and personality. An orienting system contains both helpful and unhelpful attributes, resources, and burdens, respectively. Resources may include material objects, such as money and transportation, physical and psychological characteristics, such as health and competence, and spiritual attributes, such as a close relationship with God. Burdens include attributes such as financial debt, personality problems, and dysfunctional beliefs about the self and others.

Spirituality is one aspect of the general orienting system. The spiritual orienting system contributes to the individual's framework for understanding and dealing with the world. People with stronger spiritual orienting systems are better equipped to deal with a wider range of stressful life experiences. What contributes to the strength of a spiritual orienting system? Four factors are relevant—the degree to which the spiritual system is well-integrated, flexible, differentiated, and benevolent (see Pargament, 1997 for extended review).

Spiritual integration refers to the extent to which spiritual beliefs, practices, and experiences are organized into a coherent whole. We can conceptualize spiritual integration within several domains: integration of spirituality in daily life, integration of spiritual beliefs and practices, and integration of spiritual motivation and practices. Empirical studies suggest that higher levels of spiritual integration are tied to higher levels of physical and emotional well-being. For example, one study compared four groups of church members: frequent attenders with high religious commitment, infrequent attenders with low religious commitment, infrequent attenders with high religious commitment, and frequent attenders with low religious commitment (Pargament, Steele, & Tyler, 1979). Among the four groups, the less-committed frequent attenders appeared to be the least well integrated and this group reported significantly lower self-esteem, less trust in others, less personal control, and less active coping skills than the other groups. Other studies have shown that individuals whose spirituality grows out of extrinsic motivations (e.g., security, status, sociability) report higher levels of psychological distress than those who are intrinsically motivated by faith (e.g., Bergin, Masters, & Richards, 1987; Genia, 1996). These findings suggest that spiritual orienting systems characterized by greater integration have important psychological benefits. Extrapolating from this literature, we might predict that people with higher levels of spiritual integration may come to terms more successfully with spiritual struggles.

The flexibility of an individual's spiritual orienting system may also influence the ability of that system to deal with stressful events. Flexibility involves the ability to change spiritual beliefs, behaviors, attitudes, and coping strategies in response to changes in the environment (Weinborn, 1999). A few studies have shown that, among religiously committed people, spiritual flexibility is associated with fewer physical symptoms, greater well-being, and better life adjustment (McIntosh & Spilka, 1990; McIntosh, Inglehart, & Pacini, 1990). Spiritual flexibility in the face of spiritual struggles may hold similar advantages.

Spiritual differentiation is defined by a "tolerance of complexity, avoidance of simplification, openness to new ideas and information, and the ability to synthesize and incorporate disparate ideas" in the spiritual realm (Weinborn, 1999, p. 29). People with more differentiated spiritual orientations are less likely to "get stuck" in potentially inappropriate solutions to problem. Rather they are capable of generating a variety of solutions to problems. Although there is little if any research on spiritual differentiation, William James (1902) spoke to the importance of this dimension. He noted that, even though "healthy-minded" religious people (i.e., those who see life in purely positive terms) are able to minimize and even deny the problems of pain and suffering in the world, their undifferentiated religious perspective leaves them vulnerable to problems when they encounter the darker side of life. Ultimately, he wrote, healthy-minded religion is incomplete "because the evil facts which it refuses positively to account for are a genuine portion of reality; and they may after all be the best key to life's significance, and possibly the only openers of our eyes to the deepest levels of truth" (p. 160). A differentiated spiritual orientation may also be a key to determining whether spiritual struggles lead to growth or decline.

Finally, the strength of a spiritual orienting system may be defined in part by its degree of benevolence. Among theistically oriented people, it is important to consider the degree to which God is viewed and related to in benevolent ways. Drawing on parental attachment theory, Kirkpatrick and Shaver (1992) identified three styles of attachment to God: secure, avoidant, and anxious/ambivalent attachment. Secure attachment to God is characterized by feelings of warmth, support, and protection. Individuals with a secure attachment to God feel that God responds to them but allows them to make their own mistakes. Individuals with an avoidant attachment to God see God as impersonal, distant, and uninterested in their problems. They often feel that God does not care about or like them. For individuals with an anxious/ambivalent attachment to God, God appears inconsistent, sometimes exhibiting love and care and sometimes seeming distant and uninterested. Secure attachment, the more benevolent spiritual style, has been associated with greater psychosocial competence, life satisfaction, and religious well-being (Weinborn, 1999). In contrast, the less benevolent styles have less favorable implications. An avoidant attachment to God has been correlated with lower levels of competence, life satisfaction, and religious well-being (Weinborn, 1999). In a community sample, avoidant and anxious/ambivalent attachments to God have been associated with more anxiety and depression, poorer physical health, and lower life satisfaction than secure attachments (Kirkpatrick & Shaver, 1992). Therefore, research suggests that benevolence in the form of a secure attachment to God may help people deal more successfully with stressful experiences. Secure attachments to God may also facilitate the resolution of spiritual struggles. In contrast to those who see God as distant and disinterested, people who feel that God is supporting and protecting them during their struggle may be more likely to grow through their struggles.

In this section, we have suggested a number of factors that may shape the likelihood of spiritual struggles and their ultimate outcome. Whether spiritual struggles lead to growth or decline may well depend on the characteristics of the trauma, the coping style of the individual, and the strength of the individual's spiritual orienting system. However, further research is needed to shed greater light on these important questions.

PRACTICAL IMPLICATIONS AND CONCLUSIONS

The empirical literature points to a clear conclusion: spirituality is part and parcel of the human response to trauma and its resolution. Research indicates that spirituality can facilitate or impede PTG. What determines whether spirituality is a force for growth or decline is less clear. As scientific study in this field advances, we should learn more about the rich and complex ways spirituality shapes the process of coping. Nevertheless, in spite of the questions that remain, practitioners have begun to develop and evaluate interventions that address spiritual struggles and draw upon spiritual resources (see Pargament, Murray-Swank, et al., 2005).

Some of the work in this area attempts to help people deal with specific types of spiritual struggle. For example, Zornow (2001), a pastor, developed a program to help people address their feelings of abandonment, anger, and isolation in their relationships with God. Entitled "Crying Out to God" and based on the psalms of lament, the program encourages people to restore their connection with God by voicing all of their emotions to the divine. Zornow explains: "This spirituality of crying out to God takes seriously the spiritual struggles of the sufferer and their prayer life. Its goal is to encounter God in the midst of fear, pain, distress, and turmoil" (p. 2). The lamentation process involves five steps: the address, the complaint, petitioning, vow to praise, and waiting. Although it has not been evaluated systematically, Zornow's program may help to normalize and support expressions of negative emotion to the divine among people who may be experiencing considerable shame and guilt over their feelings.

Dubow, Pargament, Boxer, and Tarakeshwar (2000) created a program that focuses more on intrapersonal struggles. This program was designed to help Jewish adolescents draw on Jewish values as resources in dealing with their internal questions and conflicts. "Mi Atah" (Hebrew for Who are You?) is a 12-week program in which adolescents are encouraged to integrate the values of learning, honesty, forgiveness, and Tikkun Olam (being a good person and repairing the world) as they cope with the major psychological, social, and spiritual stressors of adolescence. Initial empirical findings indicated that the participants in this program experienced significant increases in Jewish identity and were more likely to integrate Jewish values and resources in the problem-solving process.

With respect to interpersonal spiritual struggles, Kehoe (1998) has led Spiritual Beliefs and Values groups for people diagnosed with schizophrenia, bi-polar disorder, and major depression. Noting that people with serious mental illness often experience a lack of love and acceptance from their religious communities, Kehoe created spiritually supportive group contexts. In these unstructured, interdenominational groups, participants can raise their religious and spiritual concerns and struggles in a more caring milieu. Even though she has not systematically evaluated the groups, Kehoe believes the groups provide an all-too-rare forum for people with serious mental illness to voice and resolve their spiritual concerns.

Other interventions address a wider range of spiritual struggles and resources. For example, Cole and Pargament (1999) compared the effectiveness of a spiritually focused group therapy ("Re-creating Your Life") to a cognitive-behavioral group therapy for adults coping with cancer. Both interventions addressed four existential themes that were relevant to this population: control, meaning, identity, and relationships. In the spiritually focused group, participants were encouraged to draw on their relationship with whatever they defined as transcendent to achieve the therapeutic goals. The results of the study showed that participants in the spiritually focused group maintained their level of mental health before and after treatment, while those in the secular cognitive-behavioral treatment group deteriorated in their mental health.

Murray-Swank (2003) developed and evaluated an eight-session, individual, manual-ized, psycho-spiritual intervention for female survivors of sexual abuse. Recognizing that sexual abuse can impact spirituality in a variety of ways, her program ("Solace for the Soul") addressed several topics: the survivor's image of God, feelings of divine abandon-ment and anger toward God, ways to restore a spiritual connection, letting go of shame, restoring a healthy connection to the body, and facilitating more sexual wholeness. Four of the five clients in the treatment program demonstrated significant reductions in psycho-logical distress over the intervention and at follow-up.

Burke and Cullen (1995) created a group intervention for women struggling with sev-eral spiritually related issues, including post-abortion guilt and spiritual isolation. Tailored to Christians, the program makes use of ritual, spiritual imagery, group discussion, prayer, and "Living Scripture" to facilitate spiritual healing following an abortion. Through Liv-ing Scripture, participants imagine themselves as characters in different Biblical stories. For instance, one story attempts to promote spiritual intimacy. Participants are asked to visualize themselves as the woman at the well in Samaria (John 4: 4-30):

> You are the woman carrying the water jug up to the well. You're feeling burdened. The weight of the earthen jug presses down on your shoulders. Your back and neck ache under the pressure . . . Jesus looks deep into your eyes. He tells you about your life, where you've come from, who you've been with, what you're like. Jesus knows everything about you. (pp. 63–64)

Interventions that build upon spiritual resources and address spiritual struggles are still in their very early stages of development. Only a few of these programs have been formally evaluated and, although the results are promising, additional studies are needed to determine the efficacy of these treatments.

Finally, moving beyond a focus on psychological treatment, it is important to consider how people might be better equipped to anticipate spiritual struggles and draw on their spiritual resources before they encounter serious problems. Religious education may be particularly valuable in this respect. Unfortunately, religious education often ends at the onset of adolescence, just the age when boys and girls could begin to comprehend the deeper meanings of their faith, human complexity and inconsistency, and the paradoxes of life. As a result of this premature end to education, many people move into adulthood carrying only child-like, concrete religious solutions to the major problems they are likely to encounter. Through improvements in religious education, children and adolescents could be taught how to understand and cope with major problems in their lives in ways that are consistent with their religious traditions. Adults too could profit from programs that focus on spiritual resources for dealing with pain and suffering, the nature of spiritual doubt, and interpersonal conflict. Spiritual educators and leaders could provide an important service to their larger community by acknowledging spiritual struggles, and normalizing these struggles as a commonplace and potentially valuable dimension of spiritual experience. By strengthening spiritual resources, recognizing the reality of spiritual struggles, and assisting people in the process of resolving these struggles, practitioners may be able to help people grow rather than decline through encounters with trauma.

REFERENCES

Aldwin, C. M., Sutton, K. J., & Lachman M. (1996). The development of coping resources in adulthood. *Journal of Personality, 6,* 837–871.

Ano, G. G., & Vasconcelles, E. B. (2005). Religious coping and psychological adjustment to stress: A meta-analysis. *Journal of Clinical Psychology, 61,* 461–480.

Bergin, A. E., Masters, K. S., & Richards, P. S. (1987). Religiousness and mental health reconsidered: A study of an intrinsically religious sample. *Journal of Counseling Psychology, 35,* 197–204.

Brennan, M. (2002). Spirituality and psychosocial development in middle-age and older adults with vision loss. *Journal of Adult Development, 9,* 31–46.

Brenner, R. R. (1980). *The faith and doubt of holocaust survivors.* New York: Free Press.

Bulman, R. J., & Wortman, C. B. (1977). Attributions of blame and coping in the "real world": Severe victims react to their lot. *Journal of Personality and Social Psychology, 35,* 351–363.

Burke, T. K., & Cullen, B. (1995). *Rachel's vineyard: A psychological and spiritual journey of post-abortion healing.* New York: Alba House.

Cadell, S., Regehr, C., & Hemsworth, D. (2003). Factors contributing to posttraumatic growth: A proposed structural equation model. *American Journal of Orthopsychiatry, 73,* 279–287.

Carey, R. G. (1974). Emotional adjustment in terminal patients: A quantitative approach. *Journal of Counseling Psychology, 21,* 433–439.

Carver, C. (1998). Resilience and thriving: Issues, models, and linkages. *Journal of Social Issues, 54,* 245–266.

Chalfant, H. P., Heller, P. L., Roberts, A., Briones, D., Aquirre-Hochbaum, S., & Farr, W. (1990). The clergy as a resource for those encountering psychological distress. *Review of Religious Research, 31,* 306–313.

CNN, Wednesday, October 29, 2003.

Cole, B., & Pargament, K. I. (1999). Re-creating your life: A spiritual/psychotherapeutic intervention for people diagnosed with cancer. *Psycho-oncology, 8,* 395–407.

Decker, L.R. (1993). The role of trauma in spiritual development. *Journal of Humanistic Psychology, 33,* 33–46.

Dubow, E. F., Pargament, K. I., Boxer, P., & Tarakeshwar, N. (2000). Initial investigation of Jewish early adolescents' ethnic identity, stress, and coping. *Journal of Early Adolescence, 20,* 418–441.

Dungee-Anderson, D., & Beckett, J. O. (1992). Alzheimer's disease in African-American and white families: A clinical analysis. *Smith College Studies in Social Work, 62,* 155–168.

Ellison, C. G. (1991). Religious involvement and subjective well-being. *Journal of Health and Social Behavior, 32,* 80–89.

Ellison, C. G., & George, L. K. (1994). Religious involvement, social ties, and social support in a southeastern community. *Journal for the Scientific Study of Religion, 33,* 46–61.

Exline, J. J. (2002). Stumbling blocks on the religious road: Fractured relationships, nagging vices, and the inner struggle to believe. *Psychological Inquiry, 13,* 182–9.

Exline, J. J. (2005). Religious and spiritual struggles. In R. F. Paloutzian & C. L. Park (Eds.), *Handbook of the psychology of religion and spirituality.* New York: Guilford.

Exline, J. J., Yali, A. M., & Lobel, M. (1999). When God disappoints: Difficulty forgiving God and its role in negative emotion. *Journal of Health Psychology, 4,* 365–379.

Exline, J. J., Yali, A. M., & Sanderson, W. C. (2000). Guilt, discord, and alienation: The role of religious strain in depression and suicidality. *Journal of Clinical Psychology, 56,* 1481–1496.

Falsetti, S. A., Resick, P. A., & Davis, J. L. (2003). Changes in religious beliefs following trauma. *Journal of Traumatic Stress, 16,* 391–98.

Fitchett, G., Murphy, P., Gibbons, J. L., & Cameron, J. (2001, October). *Spiritual risk: Prevalence and correlates in three patient groups.* Paper presented at the annual meeting of the Society for the Scientific Study of Religion, Columbus, Ohio.

Fitchett, G., Rybarczyk, B. D., DeMarco, G. A., & Nicholas, J. J. (1999). The role of religion in medical rehabilitation outcomes: A longitudinal study. *Rehabilitation Psychology, 44,* 1–22.

Flaherty, S. M. (1993). *Women, why do you weep?: Spirituality for survivors of childhood sexual abuse.* New York: Paulist Press.

Gall, T. L., & Cornblat, M. W. (2002). Breast cancer survivors give voice: A qualitative analysis of spiritual factors in long-term adjustment. *Psycho-oncology, 11,* 524–35.

Genia, V. (1996). I, E, quest, fundamentalism as predictors of psychological and spiritual well-being. *Journal for the Scientific Study of Religion, 35,* 56–64.

Hettler, T. R., & Cohen, L. H. (1994) *Religious coping strategies as predictors of stress-related growth in adult Protestant churchgoers.* Unpublished manuscript.

James, W. (1902). *The varieties of religious experience: A study in human nature.* New York: Modern Library.

Janoff-Bulman, R. (1992). *Shattered assumptions: Towards a new psychology of trauma.* New York: Free Press.

Kehoe, N. C. (1998). Religious-issues group therapy. *New Directions for Mental Health Services, 80,* 45–55.

Kirkpatrick, L. A., & Shaver, H. (1992). An attachment-theoretical approach to the psychology of religion. *International Journal for the Psychology of Religion, 2,* 336–51.

Kooistra, W. P. (1990). The process of religious doubting in adolescents raised in religious environments. Unpublished doctoral dissertation, Bowling Green State University.

Kooistra, W. P., & Pargament, K. I. (1999). Predictors of religious doubting among Roman Catholic and Dutch Reformed high school students. *Journal of Psychology and Theology, 27,* 33–42.

Krause, N., Chatters, L. M., Meltzer, T., & Morgan, D. L. (2000). Negative interaction in the church: Insight from focus groups with older adults. *Review of Religious Research, 41,* 510–33.

Krause, N., Ellison, C. G., & Wulff, K. M. (1998). Church-based support, negative interaction, and psychological well-being: Findings from a national sample of Presbyterians. *Journal for the Scientific Study of Religion, 37,* 725–41.

Krause, N., Ingersoll-Dayton, B., Ellison, C. G., & Wulff, K. M. (1999). Aging, religious doubt, and psychological well-being. *The Gerontologist, 39,* 525–33.

Kulik, J. A., & Mahler, H. I. (1993). Emotional support as a moderator of adjustment and compliance after coronary artery bypass surgery: A longitudinal study. *Journal of Behavioral Medicine, 16,* 45–63.

Leserman, J., Petitto, J. M., Golden, R. N., Gaynes, B. N., Gu, H., Perkins, D. O., et al. (2000). Impact of stressful life events, depression, social support, coping, and cortisol of progression to AIDS. *American Journal of Psychiatry, 157,* 1221–8.

Magyar, G. M., Pargament, K. I., & Mahoney, A. (2000, August). *Violating the sacred: A study of desecration among college students.* Paper presented at the annual meeting of the American Psychological Association, Washington DC.

McIntosh, D., Ingelhart, M., & Pacini, R. (1990). *Flexible and central religious belief systems and adjustment to college.* Paper presented at the meeting of the Midwestern Psychological Association, Chicago.

McIntosh, D., & Spilka, B. (1990). Religion and physical health: The role of personal faith and control. In M. Lynn & D. Moberg (Eds.), *Research in the social scientific study of religion* (Vol. 2, pp. 167–194). Greenwich, CT: JAI Press

Murphy, S. A., Johnson, L. C., & Lohan, J. (2003). Finding meaning in a child's violent death: A five-year prospective analysis of parents' personal narratives and empirical data. *Death Studies, 27,* 381–404.

Murray-Swank, A. (2003). *Exploring spiritual confession: A theoretical synthesis and experimental study.* Unpublished doctoral dissertation, Bowling Green State University.

Murray-Swank, N. (2003). *Solace for the soul: An evaluation of a psycho-spiritual intervention for female survivors of sexual abuse.* Unpublished doctoral dissertation, Bowling Green State University.

Nesson, L. (Narrator). (2001). *What about God?* [Television series]. Boston: WGBH Video.

Newsweek. Perspectives, September 17, 2001, p. 23.

Nielsen, M. E. (1998). An assessment of religious conflicts and their resolutions. *Journal for the Scientific Study of Religion, 37,* 181–90.

Nosek, M. A. (1995). *The defining light of Vedanta: Personal reflections on spirituality and disability.* Unpublished manuscript.

Pargament, K. I. (1997). *The psychology of religion and coping: Theory, research, and Practice.* New York, NY: Guilford Press.

Pargament, K. I., Ensing, D. S., Falgout, K., Olsen, H., Reilly, B., & Van Haitsma, K. et al. (1990). God help me (I): Religious coping efforts as predictors of the outcomes to significant negative life events. *American Journal of Community Psychology, 18,* 793–822.

Pargament, K. I., Koenig, H. G., & Perez, L. (2000). The many methods of religious coping: Initial development and validation of the RCOPE. *Journal of Clinical Psychology, 56,* 193–207.

Pargament, K. I., Koenig, H. G., Tarakeshwar, N., & Hahn, J. (2001). Religious struggle as a predictor of mortality among medically ill elderly patients: A two-year longitudinal study. *Archives of Internal Medicine, 161,* 1881–5.

Pargament, K. I., Koenig, H. G., Tarakeshwar, N., & Hahn, J. (2004). Religious coping methods as predictors of psychological, physical, and spiritual outcomes among medically ill elderly patients: A two-year longitudinal study. *Journal of Health Psychology, 9,* 713–730.

Pargament, K. I., & Mahoney, A. (2002). Spirituality: The discovery and conservation of the sacred. In C. R. Snyder & S. J. Lopez (Eds.), *Handbook of positive psychology* (pp. 646–59). New York: Oxford University Press.

Pargament, K. I., Murray-Swank, N., Magyar, G. M., & Ano, G. (2005). Spiritual struggle: A phenomenon of interest to psychology and religion. In W. Miller & H. Delaney (Eds.), *Religion and human nature.* Washington, DC: APA Press.

Pargament, K. I., & Park, C. L. (1995). Merely a defense? The variety of religious means and ends. *Journal of Social Issues, 51,* 13–32.

Pargament, K. I., Silverman, W., Johnson, S., Echemendia, R., & Snyder, S. (1983). The psychosocial climate of religious coping. *American Journal of Community Psychology, 11,* 351–81.

Pargament, K. I., Smith, B. W., Koenig, H. G., & Perez, L. (1998). Patterns of positive and negative religious coping with major life stressors. *Journal for the Scientific Study of Religion, 37,* 710–24.

Pargament, K., Steele, R., & Tyler, F. B. (1979). Religious participation, religious motivation, and individual psychological competence. *Journal for the Scientific Study of Religion, 18,* 412–19.

Pargament, K. I., Zinnbauer, B. J., Scott, A. B., Butter, E. M., Zerowin, J., & Stanik, P. (1998). Red flags and religious coping: Identifying some religious warning signs among people in crisis. *Journal of Clinical Psychology, 54,* 77–89.

Park, C. L. (1998). Stress-related growth and thriving through coping: The roles of personality and cognitive processes. *Journal of Social Issues, 54,* 267–77.

Park, C. L., & Cohen, L. H. (1993). Religious and nonreligious coping with the death of a friend. *Cognitive Therapy and Research, 17,* 561–77.

Park, C. L, Cohen, L. H., & Herb, L. (1990). Intrinsic religiousness and religious coping as life stress moderators for Catholics versus Protestants. *Journal of Personality and Social Psychology, 59,* 562–74.

Park, C. L., Cohen, L. H., & Murch, L. R. (1996). Assessment and prediction of stress-related growth. *Journal of Personality, 64,* 71–105.

Park, C. L., & Folkman, S. (1997). Meaning in the context of stress and coping. *Review of General Psychology, 1,* 115–44.

Proffitt, D. H., Calhoun, L. G., Tedeschi, R. G., & Cann, A. (2003). *Clergy and crisis: Correlates of posttraumatic growth and well-being.* Unpublished manuscript.

Richards, T. A., Acree, M., & Folkman, S. (1999). Spiritual aspects of loss among partners of men with AIDS: Postbereavement follow-up. *Death Studies, 23,* 105–27.

Ryan, R. M., Rigby, S., & King, K. (1993). Two types of religious internalization and their relations to religious orientation and mental health. *Journal of Personality and Social Psychology, 65,* 586–96.

Saucer, P. R. (1991). Evangelical renewal therapy: A proposal for integration of religious values into psychotherapy. *Psychological Reports, 69*, 1099–1106.

Schuster, M. A., Stein, B. D., Jaycox, L. H., Collins, R. L., Marshall, G. N., Elliott, M. N. et al. (2001). A national survey of stress reactions after the September 11, 2001, terrorist attacks. *New England Journal of Medicine, 345*, 1507–1512.

Shaw, R., Joseph, J., & Linley, P. A. (2005). Religion spirituality, and posttraumatic growth: A systematic review. *Mental Health, Religion, and Culture, 8*, 1–12.

Siegel, K., & Schrimshaw, E.W. (2002). The perceived benefits of religious and spiritual coping among older adults living with HIV/AIDS. *Journal for the Scientific Study of Religion, 41*, 91–102.

Smith, B. W, Pargament, K. I., Brant, C., & Oliver, J. M. (2000). Noah revisited: Religious coping by church members and the impact of the 1993 midwest flood. *Journal of Community Psychology, 28*, 169–186.

Smith, C., & Exline, J. J. (August, 2002). *Effects of homelessness on a person's perceived relationship with God*. Paper presented at the annual meeting of the American Psychological Association, Chicago.

Taylor, R. J., & Chatters, L. M. (1988). Church members as a source of informal social support. *Review of Religious Research, 30*, 193–203.

Tedeschi, R.G., & Calhoun, L.G. (1996). The posttraumatic growth inventory: Measuring the positive legacy of trauma. *Journal of Traumatic Stress, 9*, 455–471.

Tedeschi, R. G., Park, C. L., & Calhoun, L. G. (1998). Posttraumatic growth: Conceptual issues. In R. G. Tedeschi, C. L. Park, & L. G. Calhoun (Eds.), *Posttraumatic growth: Positive changes in the aftermath of crisis* (pp. 1–22). Mahwa, NJ: Lawrence Erlbaum Associates.

VandeCreek, L., Pargament, K. I., Belavich, T., Cowell, B., & Friedel, L. (1999). The unique benefits of religious support during cardiac bypass surgery. *Journal of Pastoral Care, 53*, 19–29.

Waltz, M., & Badura, B. (1988). Subjective health, intimacy, and perceived self-efficacy after heart attack: Predicting life quality five years afterwards. *Social Indicators Research, 20*, 303–332.

Weinborn, M. (1999). *A theoretical approach to the religion-mental health connection: Initial exploration of a religious orienting system*. Unpublished doctoral dissertation, Bowling Green State University.

Wright, S., Pratt, C., & Schmall, V. (1985). Spiritual support for caregivers of dementia patients. *Journal of Religion and Health, 24*, 31–38.

Zinnbauer, B.J., Pargament, K.I., & Scott, A.B. (1999). The emerging meanings of religiousness and spirituality: Problems and prospects. *Journal of Personality, 67*, 889–919.

Zornow, G. B. (2001). Crying out to God: Uncovering prayer in the midst of suffering. Unpublished manuscript.

CHAPTER

8

POSTTRAUMATIC GROWTH AFTER CANCER

ANNETTE L. STANTON, JULIENNE E. BOWER, AND CARISSA A. LOW
UNIVERSITY OF CALIFORNIA, LOS ANGELES

> There really are positive things that come out of bad situations. Every day I look at life so much differently. I have encountered many new people because of my cancer, and they have been such positive influences in my life. My life has been so richly blessed.
> —Research participant diagnosed with breast cancer

Receiving a cancer diagnosis can be a frightening and unexpected event that challenges an individual's core assumptions about the world and one's sense of meaning, mastery, and self-esteem (Janoff-Bulman, 1992; Taylor, 1983). Although medical advances have bolstered survival rates for many cancers, cancer remains a life-threatening illness characterized by fear and uncertainty about the future and accompanied by intrusive medical procedures and aversive treatment, pain and fatigue, changes in social roles and relationships, and other disruptions. As a result, behavioral scientists historically have focused on the potential for negative psychosocial sequelae. Indeed, some cancer patients experience clinical levels of distress and dysfunction, including anxiety, depression, and posttraumatic stress disorder (PSTD) (Cordova et al., 1995; Derogatis et al., 1983; Moyer & Salovey, 1996). However, research suggests that severe affective disturbance is relatively rare and generally not enduring, as most patients resume normal mood and functioning within the year after medical treatment completion (e.g., Andersen, Anderson, & deProsse, 1989). Furthermore, some cancer patients report profound positive changes in themselves, their relationships, and other life domains after cancer.

In this chapter, we review the literature examining posttraumatic growth (PTG) and associated constructs in individuals with cancer. To do so, we conducted a search of the PsycLit and Medline databases for articles published in the years 1960 through June of

2004, pairing the term *cancer* with *benefit finding, posttraumatic gr* *change*. We also examined the reference lists of articles generated from ditional relevant citations, in addition to contacting researchers who recei on the topic for relevant papers.

We included studies that involved assessment of individuals with a and allowed the possibility of reporting positive consequences or changes arising from the cancer experience. Studies that assessed perceived life changes since cancer diagnosis, without any indication through self-report or independent ratings of the positive valence of these changes, were not included. To be included, the manuscript had to report extraction of quantitative data regarding benefit finding or growth. Thus, qualitative studies that focused on a description of themes in PTG without any quantitative analysis were excluded. Also excluded were studies that assessed positive attributes or moods that were not tied specifically to the cancer experience (e.g., measures of general well-being). We also excluded studies that merged items assessing perceived positive cancer-related changes with items that assessed negative life consequences (e.g., "I feel that cancer is something I will never recover from," "I feel that cancer has changed my life permanently so that it will never be as good again," Fife, 1995; Fife, Kennedy, & Robinson, 1994) or other constructs (e.g., causal search, "I have found myself thinking about why I got cancer," Dirksen, 1995; general life meaning, "I feel that my life is meaningful right now," Thompson & Pitts, 1993). Combining items indicating perceptions of positive change with items assessing other constructs would muddy the interpretation of relations between the resulting total score and other variables. Finally, we did not review studies that assessed the intentional use of benefit finding as a coping strategy, as assessed along with other strategies for coping with the cancer experience (e.g., "I look for something good in what is happening" in the positive reinterpretation and growth subscale of the COPE, a measure of coping responses, Carver, Scheier, & Weintraub, 1989). Coping through active attempts at positive reappraisal or benefit reminding (Affleck & Tennen, 1996) is related to, but distinct from, other measures of PTG (Tennen & Affleck, 1999; Sears, Stanton, & Danoff-Burg, 2003; Thornton, Perez, & Meyerowitz, 2005), and an examination of that construct is beyond the scope of this chapter.

Researchers have used a number of terms to describe individuals' reports of benefits in the face of adversity (see Tedeschi & Calhoun, 2004). In this chapter, we use the term *posttraumatic growth* (*PTG*) and *benefit finding* interchangeably. Just like Tedeschi and Calhoun (2004), we are concerned with experiences that "represent significant challenges to the adaptive resources of the individual" (p. 1). Cordova, Cunningham, Carlson, and Andrykowski (2001), in their sample of 70 breast cancer patients, reported that 61% both perceived breast cancer as a threat of death/serious injury/physical integrity and reported responding with intense fear or helplessness, suggesting that the experience constitutes a traumatic stressor for some women. Although not all women perceive the experience of breast cancer as traumatic, our research and applied experience lead us to believe that cancer at least presents a significant adaptive challenge. The definition provided by Tedeschi and Calhoun (2004) of PTG as "positive psychological change experienced as a result of the struggle with highly challenging life circumstances" (p. 1) also is compatible with the approach to the construct we take in this chapter.

The goals of our review were to: (a) characterize the methods and measures used in extant research; (b) describe the current knowledge base with regard to correlates of benefit finding in individuals with cancer; (c) specify how these findings can inform theories of benefit finding and PTG more generally; and (d) identify limitations of the literature to promote future research and theory development. We begin this chapter with rief discussion of the early literature on benefit finding in individuals with cancer and consideration of prevalence and nature of perceived benefit, and we go on to address each of the foregoing goals.

PREVALENCE AND NATURE OF FINDING BENEFIT IN THE CANCER EXPERIENCE

In the past quarter century, empirical attention has been directed to reports of individuals' growth and transformation in the aftermath of cancer. Early research relied primarily on qualitative reports, such as patient interviews and responses to open-ended queries (e.g., Cella & Tross, 1986; Taylor, Lichtman, & Wood, 1984). In the past decade, the development of standardized, psychometrically validated self-report scales of growth has allowed proliferative quantitative work to be conducted. These instruments, including the Posttraumatic Growth Inventory (PTGI) (Tedeschi & Calhoun, 1996), the Cancer Patient Behavior Scale (Ross, Stockdale, & Jacobs, 1978), and the Benefit-Finding Scale (BFS) (Tomich & Helgeson, 2004), ask patients the extent to which various positive changes were experienced as a result of their cancer experience.

This burgeoning literature testifies to the prevalence of positive life changes and personal growth following a cancer diagnosis. For example, Taylor (1983) found that 53% of women with breast cancer reported positive changes in their lives since diagnosis. More recently, Sears and colleagues (2003) found that 83% of breast cancer patients reported finding some benefit in their experience. These positive changes have been reported by the majority of patients with other cancers, including lung and colorectal cancers (O'Connor, Wicker, & Germino, 1990), testis cancer (Rieker et al., 1989), melanoma (Dirksen, 1995), and prostate cancer (Gritz, Wellisch, Siau, & Wang, 1990). Most adolescent and adult survivors of childhood cancers also report that they derived benefits from their experiences, with prevalence estimates ranging from 60% (Fritz & Williams, 1988) to 95% (Wasserman, Thompson, Wilimas, & Fairclough, 1987). Overall, it seems that most individuals perceive that they have grown or benefited in some way from their experiences with cancer.

What positive changes are likely to result from a diagnosis of cancer? From their observations of individuals undergoing a range of traumatic events, Tedeschi and Calhoun (1996) identified five domains of PTG: enhanced interpersonal relationships, greater appreciation for life, sense of increased personal strength, greater spirituality, and valued change in life priorities or goals. Changes in each of these domains have been reported by cancer patients. More than a quarter of cancer patients report strengthened relationships with family and friends, including a greater sense of closeness and connectedness, increased awareness of one's importance to significant others, greater compassion, and improved marital quality (Cordova et al., 2001; Fromm, Andrykowski, & Hunt, 1996; Gritz et al., 1990; Klauer, Ferring, & Filipp, 1998; Sears et al., 2003). Both Petrie and colleagues (Petrie, Buick, Weinman, & Booth, 1999) and Sears et al. (2003) found enhanced relationships to be the most commonly cited category of benefit in their samples of cancer patients responding to an open-ended question regarding perceived positive consequences of the cancer experience, with 33% and 46% of the samples, respectively, reporting this benefit.

Another commonly reported positive change is increased appreciation for life. For example, Cella and Tross (1986) reported that 85% of Hodgkin's disease survivors felt they had become more appreciative of life. Other cancer patient samples have reported gaining a new life perspective, attitude, or outlook, such as "learning to take life more easily and enjoy it more" (Fromm et al., 1996; O'Connor et al., 1990; Taylor et al., 1984; Wasserman et al., 1987). This revised outlook on life also is reflected in reports of valued changes in priorities or life goals, an experience endorsed by 79% of mixed cancer patients (Collins, Taylor, & Skokan, 1990) and by 67.5% of bone marrow transplant survivors (Curbow, Somerfield, Baker, Wingard, & Legron, 1993). Enhanced spirituality is also commonly reported (Cordova et al., 2001; O'Connor et al., 1990; Wasserman et al., 1987), as are improvements in one's perceived psychological resources, skills, and personal attributes (Fritz & Williams, 1988; Fromm et al., 1996; Halttunen, Hietvanen, Jallinoja, & Lonnqvist, 1992; Kennedy, Tellegen, Kennedy, & Havernick, 1976). A category of benefit not identified by Tedeschi and Calhoun (1996), but spontaneously offered by individuals with cancer, is in the health domain (Sears et al., 2003). Women with breast cancer, for example, describe making positive changes in health-related behaviors and engaging in more careful cancer surveillance as benefits of their experience. Thus, individuals with cancer appear to experience positive changes and personal growth in various life domains, including the five identified by Tedeschi and Calhoun in addition to some that may be specific to cancer or other medical stressors.

BENEFIT FINDING IN INDIVIDUALS WITH CANCER: METHODS AND MEASURES

Table 8.1 summarizes the methods of the 29 independent studies, as well as seven substudies based on those samples, located through our review. These data support several observations. First, most studies of PTG in cancer patients are cross-sectional in design, with only a handful of longitudinal studies that allow for greater causal inference. Second, with regard to sample characteristics, most had study samples of fewer than 100 participants, although several had larger samples. Fourteen independent studies included only female participants, 12 included both women and men, and three included only men. On average, samples spanned a large adult age distribution, although no study targeted primarily older adults (> 65 years), which represents the largest proportion of individuals with cancer (Office of Cancer Survivorship, 2004). Ethnic minorities represented less than 15% of the samples, with notable exceptions (Antoni et al., 2001; Bower et al., 2005; Giedzinska, Meyerowitz, Ganz, & Rowland, 2004; Katz, Flasher, Cacciapaglia, & Nelson, 2001; Oh et al., 2004; Urcuyo, Boyers, Carver, & Antoni, 2005; Widows, Jacobsen, Booth-Jones, & Fields, 2005). Most of the cross-sectional studies included participants with mixed cancer types, but all except two of the longitudinal studies were conducted with female breast cancer patients. Time since cancer diagnosis, cancer stage, and point in the medical treatment trajectory at study recruitment were quite variable across investigations.

Measures used to assess benefit finding varied rather markedly across studies. Both interview and questionnaire measures were used. In general, interview questions either asked respondents whether cancer and its treatment had altered their lives and then requested specification (e.g., Carpenter, Brockopp, & Andrykowski, 1999) or asked explicitly about positive and negative consequences of the cancer experience (e.g., Fromm et al., 1996). Questionnaire items typically asked participants to rate the extent to which their experience with cancer had carried presumably positive effects in various life domains.

Standardized scales permit comparison across cancer patient samples in addition to other populations. The most frequently used standardized questionnaire was the PTGI, which was administered in nine independent studies. Descriptive statistics on the PTGI for these studies are presented in Table 8.2. Developed by Tedeschi and Calhoun (1996), the PTGI is a 21-item measure consisting of the five-factor analytically derived subscales shown in the table. In completing the items, respondents refer either to a self-nominated "crisis" or a researcher-specified stressor. The response scale ranges from 0 (I did NOT experience this change as a result of my crisis [or stressor specified]) to 5 (I experienced

TABLE 8.1

Posttraumatic Growth and the Cancer Literature: Study Methods

CROSS-SECTIONAL STUDIES

				Subjects					
	N	% Female	Mean Age (years)	% Minority	Type of Cancer	Active tx	Time Since dx/tx	Stage/Illness Severity	Measures
Andrykowski, Brady, & Hunt, 1993	133*	45	35.1	NR	Mixed (BMT)	Some	$M = 23.4$ months postdx	NR	Cancer Patient Behavior Scale (e.g., rate current status relative to status prior to cancer dx re: "Love for spouse/partner"; "Outlook on life")
Andrykowski et al., 1996	80*	100	53.9	9	Breast	N	$M = 28.2$ months postdx	56% I, 36% II, 8% IIIA	Cancer Patient Behavior Scale
Carpenter et al., 1999	60*	100	53.7	5	Breast	N	$M = 30.8$ months postdx	78% IIA or less	Interview questions ("Have you or your feelings about yourself changed since your breast cancer diagnosis? How have you or your feelings about yourself changed since your breast cancer diagnosis?")
Cella & Tross, 1986	60*	0	31.1	5	Hodgkin's	N	Recent (6–24 months) and distant (30–140 months) posttx	Stratified by early (I – IIIA) vs. late stage	Interview questions (regarding increased appreciation of life, etc.)
Collins et al., 1990	55	55	54	NR	Mixed	20%	$M = 3.2$ years postdx or recurrence	65% probable cure; 35% poorer prognosis	Interview questions (e.g., "In what ways, if any, has having had cancer changed your priorities or altered your daily activities?")

Study	N								
Cordova et al., 2001	70*	100	54.7	10	Breast	N	$M = 23.6$ months posttx	8% 0, 46% I, 34% II, 11.5%III	PTGI
Curbow et al., 1993	135	39.3	30.6	8.9	Mixed (BMT)	NR	$M = 47$ months post-BMT	NR	Personal Changes Scale (measure of positive and negative change in the domains of activities, relationships, physical, and existential)
Daiter, Larson, Weddington, & Ultmann 1988	32	38	28	NR	Leukemia & lymphoma	Y	3–7 months postdx	28% favorable prognosis, 72% less favorable	Interview of patient and significant others + interviewer ratings (e.g., greater family commitment, self-awareness)
Fromm et al., 1996	90	42	38.8	NR	Mixed (BMT)	N	$M = 49.5$ months post-BMT	NR	Phone interview re: positive/negative effects (e.g., family life, outlook on life)
Giedzinska et al., 2004[1]	621	100	55.2	62	Breast	N	$M = 2.9$ years postdx	0, I, II	Meaning Questionnaire (e.g., "Surviving breast cancer has changed my outlook on life")
Ho et al., 2004	188	83	49.3	Chinese	Mixed	N	> 5 years "disease free"	NR	PTGI (Chinese version)
Katz et al., 2001[2]	56	87	53	27	Mixed	NR	$M = 9$ years postdx	NR	Mohr's Benefit-finding Scale (e.g., "Cancer has made me appreciate life more")
Klauer et al., 1998	100	42	53	NR	Mixed	NR	1 to > 5 years postdx	Mixed (18% remote metastases)	Questionnaire assessing degree and nature of change in 17 domains (e.g., marital life, physical appearance)
Kurtz et al., 1995	191	100	60.6	7.3	Mixed	N	>5 years postdx	NR	Questionnaire: Health habits (e.g., "Since my cancer treatment, I exercise more frequently") and philosophical/spiritual view (e.g., "Since having had cancer I have a greater appreciation for everyday life")

(Continued)

TABLE 8.1
(Continued)

CROSS-SECTIONAL STUDIES

				Subjects				
	N	% Female	Mean Age (years)	% Minority	Type of Cancer	Active tx	Time Since dx/tx	Stage/Illness Severity	Measures
Lechner et al., 2003, in press	83	71	62.5	9.6	Mixed	36%	M = 38.8 months postdx	34% 0–I, 28% II, 20% III, 18% IV	PTGI
Oh et al., 2004	108	100	59.5	19	Breast	NR	> 5 years postdx (except recurrent)	0, I, II, recurrent	PTGI, Meaning Scale
Petrie et al., 1999	52	100	54	8	Breast	NR	3 months postradiation	NR	Questionnaire item: "What positive effects do you feel may have occurred in your life due to your cancer?"
Rieker et al., 1985	74	0	30.0 median	NR	Testis	N	Median = 3.9 years posttx	NR	Cancer Patient Behavior Scale; also items about changes in social supports and relationships (strengthened, strained, or no effect)

Study	N	%	Age		Cancer		Time since diagnosis	Stage	Measure
Salmon et al., 1996	200	42	NR	7	Mixed	Y	Median = 12 months postdx	NR-incurable	Life Evaluation Questionnaire (e.g., "I appreciate things more than I did")
Taylor et al., 1984	78	100	53 (median)	NR	Breast	NR	Median = 25.5 months postsurgery	38% I, 45% II, 18% III–IV	Interview questions regarding specific life changes since cancer
Tomich & Helgeson, 2002[3]	164*	100	54.4	5.5	Breast	N	M = 5.5 years postdx	30% I, 65% II, 5% III	Personal Growth and Acceptance adapted from Behr's Positive Contributions Scale and 1-item benefit finding question
Urcuyo et al., 2005	230	100	53.45	37	Breast	31%	3, 6, or 12 months postsurgery	62% 0–I, 38% II	BFS
Weiss, 2002	41	100	52.9	NR	Breast	N	M = 38 months postdx	73% 0–I, 20% II, 7% NR	PTGI
Weiss, 2004	72	100	54.2	NR	Breast	N	M = 38.7 months postdx	68% 0–I, 21% II, 11% NR	PTGI

(Continued)

TABLE 8.1
(*Continued*)

LONGITUDINAL STUDIES

	N	% Female	Mean Age (years)	% Minority	Type of Cancer	Active tx	Time Since dx/tx[5]	Stage/Illness Severity	Measures
Antoni et al., 2001[4] (4–8 wks postsurgery, postintervention, 3 mo f/u 9 mo f/u)	100	100	50.23	26	Breast	Some	8 weeks postsurgery	58% 0–I, 41% II	BFS (e.g., "Having had breast cancer has . . . led me to be more accepting of things; brought my family closer together")
Cruess et al., 2000	34	100	45.7	32	Breast	Some	8 weeks postsurgery	50% I, 50% II	BFS
McGregor et al., 2004	29	100	47.5	24	Breast	Some	8 weeks postsurgery	55% I, 45% II	BFS
Bower et al., 2005 (1–5 years postdx, 5–10 years postdx)	763	100	55.6	16.3	Breast	N	$M = 3.4$ years postdx	Stage 0–II	Meaning Scale
Carver & Antoni, 2004[6] (3–12 months postsurgery, 4–7 year f/u)	96	100	59.14	33	Breast	NR	3–12 months postsurgery	65% 0–I, 35% II	BFS
Manne et al., 2004 (4.5 months postdx, 9 mo & 18 mo f/u)	162	100	49	9	Breast	97% at baseline	$M = 4.5$ months postdx	3% DCIS, 34% I, 37% II, 27% IIIA	PTGI

Study									
Schulz & Mohamed, 2004 (1 mo, 6 mo, & 12 mo postsurgery)	105	39	62	NR	Mixed	45%	1 mo postsurgery	NR	BFS (German version)
Sears et al., 2003, (28 wks postdx, 3 mo & 12 mo f/u)	92	100	51.57	13	Breast	N	$M = 28$ weeks postdx	I or II	PTGI and interview: "Have there been any benefits that have resulted from your experience with breast cancer?"
Thornton et al., 2005 (Presurgery, 1 year postsurgery)	82	0	61.27	10	Prostate	N	presurgery	82% early stage; 17% locally advanced	PTGI
Tomich & Helgeson, 2004 (4 months postdx, 3 mo & 9 mo f/u)	364	100	48.3	7	Breast	Y at baseline	$M = 4$ months postdx	25% I, 69% II, 6% III	BFS
Widows et al., 2005 (Pre-bone marrow transplant [BMT], $M = 2$ years postBMT)	72	74%	47.62	15	Mixed	Y at baseline	NR	Risk of disease recurrence/progression: 39% low; 39% intermediate; 22% high	PTGI

Note. Dotted line between citations indicates overlapping sample (see also table footnotes 1, 3, 6). * = Cancer sample; compared to noncancer comparison sample; dx = diagnosis; tx = medical treatment; DCIS = ductal carcinoma in situ; Y = yes; N = no; NR = not reported.

[1] Subsample of Bower et al. (2005).

[2] Sample included 56 cancer patients and 31 lupus patients. Descriptive statistics are for the combined groups.

[3] Subsample of Tomich & Helgeson (2004).

[4] Found that cognitive-behavioral stress management (intervention) participants reported increased benefit finding relative to an attention control group, particularly among participants low in optimism.

[5] At initial assessment.

[6] Subsample of Urcuyo et al. (2005).

TABLE 8.2
Posttraumatic Growth and Cancer Literature: Mean PTGI Scores Among Cancer Samples

Scale (Maximum score)	Breast Cancer[1] (n = 70)		Healthy Controls[1] (n = 70)		Mixed Cancers[2,3] (n = 83)		Breast Cancer[4] (n = 41)		Breast Cancer[5] (n = 58)	
	M	SD	M	SD	M	SD	M	SD	M	SD
Total (105)	64.1	24.8	56.3	26.3	54.2	27.2	60.2	18.8	58.4	25.8
Relating to others (35)	21.7	9.1	18.1	9.8	19.4	9.6	19.8	7.7	21.1	8.7
New possibilities (25)	13.1	6.4	12.4	6.8	9.9	6.7	11.1	6.1	10.5	6.8
Personal strength (20)	12.5	5.3	11.6	5.7	11.5	6.1	12.3	5.4	11.0	5.7
Spiritual change (10)	6.3	3.4	5.2	3.5	4.5	3.9	4.3	2.8	5.3	3.7
Appreciation of life (15)	10.6	4.2	9.1	3.9	9.0	5.0	11.0	3.8	10.5	4.0

Scale (Maximum score)	Prostate Cancer[6] (n = 82)		Mixed Cancers[7] (n = 188)		Breast Cancer Recurrence[8] (n = 54)		Breast Cancer Disease-Free[8] (n = 53)	
	M	SD	M	SD	M	SD	M	SD
Total (105)	46.6	25.6	NR	NR	47.8	27.1	42.9	29.0
Relating to others (35)	17.8	9.3	23.3	4.5	NR	NR	NR	NR
New possibilities (25)	7.7	6.5	17.0	4.0	NR	NR	NR	NR
Personal strength (20)	9.1	5.7	13.5	2.9	NR	NR	NR	NR
Spiritual change (10)	3.9	3.2	5.9	2.4	NR	NR	NR	NR
Appreciation of life (15)	8.1	4.3	10.2	2.5	NR	NR	NR	NR

Scale (Maximum score)	Breast Cancer[9] (n = 162)						Mixed Cancers[10] (n = 72)	
	Time 1		Time 2		Time 3			
	M	SD	M	SD	M	SD	M	SD
Total (105)	49.0	25.7	52.8	25.5	55.7	24.0	64.67	21.3
Relating to others (35)	19.0	9.9	19.5	9.1	20.3	8.6	NR	NR
New possibilities (25)	7.9	6.2	9.4	6.6	9.7	6.1	NR	NR
Personal strength (20)	9.0	5.8	10.0	5.5	10.6	5.0	NR	NR
Spiritual change (10)	4.3	3.7	4.1	3.8	4.6	3.7	NR	NR
Appreciation of life (15)	9.1	4.5	9.6	4.2	10.3	3.8	NR	NR

[1] Cordova et al., 2001.
[2] We thank Dr. Lechner for recalculating these descriptive statistics to conform to the 0 to 5 response scale.
[3] Lechner et al., 2003.
[4] Weiss, 2002.
[5] Sears et al., 2003.
[6] Thornton et al., 2005.
[7] Ho et al., 2004.
[8] Oh et al., 2004.
[9] Manne et al., 2004.
[10] Widows et al., 2005.

As shown in the table, mean total PTGI scores evidenced rather broad variability across samples, ranging from approximately 43 in a disease-free sample of breast cancer survivors a minimum of five years after diagnosis (Oh et al., 2004) to 64.67 in a sample who had undergone bone marrow transplant for cancer an average of two years earlier (Widows et al., 2005). On average, these scores correspond to participants reporting a small to moderate degree of perceived change as a result of the cancer experience. Because several studies in the general literature have used a 1 to 6 response scale (e.g., Calhoun, Cann, Tedeschi, & McMillan, 2000) or another modification rather than the 0 to 5 scale used in the studies of cancer patients, it is difficult to compare data from cancer patients to other samples. In two studies with undergraduate samples using the 0 to 5 format, Tedeschi and Calhoun (1996) reported PTGI scores in undergraduates selected for their report of a significant negative life event experienced within the past five years (Study 1) or at least one major trauma of great severity in the previous year (Study 3). In those samples, means for young women were 75 and 82, and means for young men were 68 and 70, respectively. These means are considerably higher than those reported in the samples of cancer patients.

In the only study that used a comparison group and the PTGI, Cordova et al. (2001) asked a sample of age- and education-matched women with no cancer history to complete the PTGI to refer to the extent of change experienced on each item since the cancer diagnosis of their matched counterpart with breast cancer (e.g., in the last two years). In a multivariate analysis of the PTGI subscales, women diagnosed with cancer reported significantly higher levels of PTG than did the comparison sample. Specifically, they reported significantly more growth with regard to relating to others, spirituality, and appreciation of life, but not in new possibilities or personal strength.

Although our goal is not to provide a critical review of the PTGI as assessment device, a few observations are warranted. The PTGI does not tap the domain of health-related benefits reported by samples of cancer patients (Sears et al., 2003) and even more frequently by other medical samples (Affleck, Tennen, Croog, & Levine, 1987; Petrie et al., 1999; Siegel & Schrimshaw, 2000) and as such may not capture the range of positive changes that medical samples endorse. The PTGI subscales are highly intercorrelated (e.g., Thornton et al., 2005), suggesting a tendency of individuals to identify benefit in adverse circumstances similarly across multiple life domains. Furthermore, the total PTGI score is highly correlated with other scales to assess benefit finding used in studies of cancer patients. Specifically, the correlation of the PTGI with the BFS was 0.80 at baseline in the Antoni et al. (2001) sample (Lechner, personal communication, July 6, 2004), and it was 0.71 with the Meaning Scale in Bower et al. (2005). These high correlations allow some confidence in the comparability of findings in studies that use different questionnaire measures of PTG.

CORRELATES OF BENEFIT FINDING

Although positive posttraumatic changes are reported by the majority of cancer patients, they are not universal. What attributes distinguish patients who experience and report these positive changes from those who do not? Since the advent of quantitative scales assessing PTG, numerous researchers have examined the correlates and predictors of PTG. As displayed in Table 8.3, these factors fall into several categories, which we address in turn: sociodemographic variables, characteristics of the stressor, personality attributes, social context variables, coping processes, and indicators of psychological or physical health. The list of variables in Table 8.3 examined in relation to PTG is not exhaustive, but does capture the majority of variables examined thus far. Any relation displayed in the table was significant at $p < .05$. Note that we do not specify in the table the data analytic strategy that yielded the relations. For example, many of the relations are zero-order correlations between the correlate and the index of PTG, whereas others represent these relations controlling for various other predictors in multiple regression equations. In the case that a relation between PTG and another variable was reported in multiple studies from the same sample (i.e., Antoni et al., 2001; Bower et al., 2005; Carver & Antoni, 2004; Cruess et al., 2000; Giedzinska et al., 2004; Lechner et al., 2003; Lechner, Antoni & Zakowski, in press; McGregor et al., 2004; Urcuyo et al., 2005), the relation is listed only once in the table for the larger sample. An exception is research conducted by Tomich and Helgeson, who have published two studies on a cohort of breast cancer survivors assessed in the year following cancer diagnosis (Tomich & Helgeson, 2004) and again at five years after diagnosis (Tomich & Helgeson, 2002). Although these studies focus on the same sample, the assessments were conducted at two distinct time points in the cancer trajectory. Thus, for those correlates that are time-dependent (e.g., measures of psychological adjustment), we list relations for both reports; for correlates that are not time dependent (e.g., ethnicity), we list relations only for the larger sample (Tomich & Helgeson, 2004).

Sociodemographic Correlates of Posttraumatic Growth

Socioeconomic status. Socioeconomic status (SES) was operationalized in the reviewed studies as level of income, education, or a composite index of income, education, and employment status. As shown in Table 8.3, of the 19 studies that examined the relation of SES to PTG, 8 found a significant association whereas the others yielded nonsignificant results. Among the significant studies, four yielded a positive association between SES and PTG, such that women of higher income (Bower et al., 2005; Carpenter et al., 1999; Cordova et al., 2001) or education level (Sears et al., 2003) reported more positive changes related to cancer. These associations were relatively modest ($r = .27 - .30$). In contrast, three studies showed a negative association between SES and PTG, with correlation coefficients ranging from $r = -.21$ to $-.37$. It should be noted that the relation between SES and PTG was not consistent within each study but was instead dependent on the measure of SES and growth. For example, Sears et al. (2003) found an association between education and an interview measure of benefit finding, but no association between education and scores on the PTGI, and Widows et al. (2005) reported a significant negative relation of the PTGI with education, but a nonsignificant relation with income.

To explain these divergent findings, we examined differences in methodology across reports. One difference between the studies citing significant versus nonsignificant results was the type of cancer patients assessed. The majority of studies yielding nonsignificant results were conducted with patients with mixed cancer diagnoses, whereas all but one study (Widows et al., 2005) yielding significant results were conducted with breast cancer patients. On the other hand, we were not able to identify any clear differences between the studies citing positive versus negative results in terms of participant age, income, education, and disease stage, or sample size and assessment method. The studies did differ somewhat in the timing of assessment. Two of the four studies that found a negative association between SES and PTG assessed participants within a year of diagnosis, when many were still undergoing treatment, whereas the four studies that found a positive association between SES and PTG focused primarily on women who had completed treatment.

TABLE 8.3
Posttraumatic Growth and the Cancer Literature: Correlates of PTG

Variable	Relationship	Citations
Sociodemographic factors		
SES (income & education)	PTG—Higher SES	Bower et al., 2005; Carpenter et al., 1999; Cordova et al., 2001; Sears et al., 2003 (BF)
	PTG—Lower SES	Tomich & Helgeson, 2004; Urcuyo et al., 2005; Weiss, 2004; Widows et al., 2005 (education)
	NS	Andrykowski et al., 1993; Collins et al., 1990; Cruess et al., 2000; Curbow et al., 1993; Fromm et al., 1996; Katz et al., 2001; Kurtz et al., 1995; Lechner et al., 2003; Manne et al., 2004; Petrie et al., 1999; Sears et al., 2003 (PTGI); Thornton et al., 2005; Widows et al., 2005 (income)
Ethnicity	PTG—Minority status	Bower et al., 2005; Tomich & Helgeson, 2004; Urcuyo et al., 2005
	NS	Carpenter et al., 1999; Cruess et al., 2000; Lechner et al., 2003; Manne et al., 2004; Sears et al., 2003; Thornton et al., 2005; Widows et al., 2005
Age	PTG–Younger patients	Bower et al., 2005; Carpenter et al., 1999; Klauer et al., 1998; Lechner et al., 2003; Manne et al., 2004; Salmon et al., 1996; Widows et al., 2005
	PTG—Midlife (40–79 years old)	Kurtz et al., 1995
	NS	Andrykowski et al., 1993; Collins et al., 1990; Cordova et al., 2001; Cruess et al., 2000; Katz et al., 2001; Petrie et al., 1999; Schulz & Mohamed, 2004; Sears et al., 2003; Thornton et al., 2005; Tomich & Helgeson, 2004; Urcuyo et al., 2005; Weiss, 2004
Gender	NS	Collins et al., 1990; Fromm et al., 1996; Ho et al., 2004; Klauer et al., 1998; Lechner et al., 2003; Salmon et al., 1996; Schulz & Mohamed, 2004; Widows et al., 2005
Stressor characteristics		
Perceived cancer stressfulness	PTG—Greater perceived threat	Bower et al., 2005; Cordova et al., 2001 (perceived life threat); Lechner et al., 2003; Sears et al., 2003; Thornton et al., 2005; Widows et al., 2005 (e.g., concern for life)
	NS	Antoni et al., 2001; Cordova et al., 2001 (IES); Manne et al., 2004; Weiss, 2004; Widows et al., 2005 (e.g., post-traumatic symptoms)

(Continued)

TABLE 8.3
(Continued)

Variable	Relationship	Citations
Disease severity	PTG—Stage II (vs. Stage I or IV)	Lechner et al., 2003
	PTG—More severe disease	Andrykowksi et al., 1996; Daiter et al., 1988; Fromm et al., 1996; Tomich & Helgeson, 2004; Oh et al., 2004 (Meaning Scale); Urcuyo et al., 2005
	PTG—Better prognosis	Collins et al., 1990
	NS	Andrykowski et al., 1993; Carpenter et al., 1999; Cordova et al., 2001; Cruess et al., 2000; Kurtz et al., 1995; Manne et al., 2004; Oh et al., 2004 (PTGI); Petrie et al., 1999; Thornton et al., 2005; Weiss, 2004; Widows et al., 2005
Time since diagnosis/treatment	PTG–More time since diagnosis	Cordova et al., 2001; Klauer et al., 1998; Manne et al., 2004; Sears et al., 2003
	PTG—Less time since diagnosis	Fromm et al., 1996; Weiss, 2004
	NS	Andrykowski et al., 1993; Andrykowski et al., 1996; Carpenter et al., 1999; Curbow et al., 1993; Kurtz et al., 1995; Lechner et al., 2003; Urcuyo et al., 2005; Widows et al., 2005
Type of surgery	NS	Andrykowski et al., 1996; Carpenter et al., 1999; Cruess et al., 2000; Giedzinska et al., 2004; Manne et al., 2004; Sears et al., 2003; Thornton et al., 2005; Tomich & Helgeson, 2004; Urcuyo et al., 2005; Weiss, 2004
Receipt of chemotherapy, radiation, or tamoxifen/raloxifene	PTG–Treatment receipt	Bower et al., 2005 (chemotherapy); Urcuyo et al., 2005 (tamoxifen)
	NS	Andrykowski et al., 1996; Carpenter et al., 1999; Cordova et al., 2001; Cruess et al., 2000; Manne et al., 2004; Sears et al., 2003; Tomich & Helgeson, 2004; Urcuyo et al., 2005; Weiss, 2004
Personality traits		
Optimism	PTG—More optimistic	Antoni et al., 2001; Curbow et al., 1993; Sears et al., 2003 (BF); Urucyo et al., 2005
	NS	Sears et al., 2003 (PTGI)
Neuroticism	NS	Lechner et al., 2003
Self-efficacy/esteem	PTG—Higher self-efficacy/esteem	Carpenter et al., 1999; Schulz & Mohamed, 2004
	NS	Fromm et al., 1996 (self-esteem)
Threat sensitivity	NS	Urcuyo et al., 2005

TABLE 8.3
(Continued)

Variable	Relationship	Citations
Incentive sensitivity	PTG—Reward responsiveness	Urcuyo et al., 2005
Social context		
Marital status	Married—PTG	Carpenter et al., 1999
	NS	Cruess et al., 2000; Fromm et al., 1996; Katz et al., 2001; Lechner et al., 2003; Schulz & Mohamed, 2004; Sears et al., 2003; Thornton et al., 2005; Tomich & Helgeson, 2004; Urcuyo et al., 2005; Widows et al., 2005
Social support	PTG—More social support	Lechner et al., in press; Schulz & Mohamed, 2004
	NS	Cordova et al., 2001; Sears et al., 2003; Weiss, 2004; Widows et al., 2005
Marital support	PTG—More marital support	Weiss, 2004[1]
Prior talking about cancer	PTG—More prior talking	Cordova et al., 2001
Contact with a PTG model	PTG—Contact with a person who experienced PTG	Weiss, 2004
Coping processes		
Approach-oriented coping		
Active coping	PTG—More active coping	Urcuyo et al., 2005
	NS	Thornton et al., 2005
Problem-focused coping	PTG—More problem-focused coping	Collins et al., 1990; Sears et al., 2003[2]; Widows et al., 2005
Planning	NS	Thornton et al., 2005; Urcuyo et al., 2005
Logical analysis	NS	Widows et al., 2005
Positive reappraisal coping	PTG—More positive reappraisal	Collins et al., 1990; Sears et al., 2003; Thornton et al., 2005; Urcuyo et al., 2005; Widows et al., 2005
	NS	Manne et al., 2004
Acceptance coping	PTG—More acceptance coping	Schulz & Mohamed, 2004; Urcuyo et al., 2005
	NS	Thornton et al., 2005
Seeking social support	PTG—More seeking support	Sears et al., 2003[2]; Thornton et al., 2005
	NS	Urcuyo et al., 2005; Widows et al., 2005
Contemplate reason for cancer	PTG—More contemplate reason	Manne et al., 2004[3]
Emotional approach coping	PTG—More emotional approach	Antoni et al., 2001 (expression/processing); Thornton et al., 2005 (venting)

(Continued)

TABLE 8.3

(Continued)

Variable	Relationship	Citations
	NS	Urcuyo et al., 2005 (venting); Manne et al., 2004 (emotional processing); Widows et al., 2005 (emotional discharge)
	Time × emotional expression interaction on PTG	Manne et al., 2004
Avoidance coping		
Denial/behavioral disengagement	NS	Thornton et al., 2005; Urcuyo et al., 2005; Widows et al., 2005
Escape/avoidance	PTG—More escape/avoidance	Collins et al., 1990
Acceptance/ resignation	NS	Widows et al., 2005
Distancing	NS	Collins et al., 1990
Distraction/seek alternative rewards	PTG—More distraction/seek alternative rewards	Thornton et al., 2005; Widows et al., 2005
	NS	Urcuyo et al., 2005
Substance use	PTG—Less substance use	Urcuyo et al., 2005
	NS	Thornton et al., 2005
Other coping		
Humor	NS	Thornton et al., 2005; Urcuyo et al., 2005
Religious coping	PTG—More religious coping	Thornton et al., 2005; Urcuyo et al., 2005
Self-blame	PTG—Blame self for cancer	Thornton et al., 2005
Psychological adjustment		
Psychological distress	PTG—Less distress	Ho et al., 2004; Katz et al., 2001; Taylor et al., 1984; Urcuyo et al., 2005
	PTG—More distress	Thornton et al., 2005 (longitudinal analyses); Tomich & Helgeson, 2004 (for those with more severe disease)
	NS	Antoni et al., 2001; Bower et al., 2005; Cordova et al., 2001; Curbow et al., 1993; Fromm et al., 1996; Sears et al., 2003; Schulz & Mohamed, 2004; Thornton et al., 2005 (cross-sectional analyses); Tomich & Helgeson, 2002; Widows et al., 2005[4]
Psychological well-being	PTG—More well-being	Carpenter et al., 1999; Curbow et al., 1993; Urcuyo et al., 2005
	NS	Cordova et al., 2001
Positive affect	PTG—More positive mood	Bower et al., 2005; Carver & Antoni, 2004; Katz et al., 2001; Sears et al., 2003 (PTGI); Tomich & Helgeson, 2002 (1-item benefit-finding)

TABLE 8.3
(Continued)

Variable	Relationship	Citations
	NS	Fromm et al., 1996; Sears et al., 2003 (BF); Thornton et al., 2005; Tomich & Helgeson, 2002 (Acceptance & Personal Growth); Tomich & Helgeson, 2004
Quality of life	PTG—Worse quality of life	Tomich & Helgeson, 2004 (for those with more severe disease)
	PTG—Better quality of life	Tomich & Helgeson, 2002 (1-item benefit-finding)
	PTG—Less impaired sexual functioning	Rieker et al., 1985
	NS	Bower et al., 2005; Fromm et al., 1996; Manne et al., 2004; Schulz & Mohamed, 2004; Sears et al., 2003; Thornton et al., 2005[5]; Tomich & Helgeson, 2002 (Acceptance & Personal Growth); Urcuyo et al., 2005
Physical health		
Cancer-related medical visits	NS	Sears et al., 2003
Neuroendocrine functioning	PTG—Reduced serum cortisol	Cruess et al., 2000
Immune functioning	PTG—Increased lymphocyte proliferation	McGregor et al., 2004
Pain	PTG—less pain	Katz et al., 2001

Note. When a relation between PTG and another variable was reported in multiple studies from the same sample, the relation is listed only once in the table for the larger sample (see exceptions described in text). IES = Impact of Event Scale. NS = not significant.

[1] But marital depth of commitment and conflict NS.

[2] Reported in text of this chapter using Sears et al. (2003) sample.

[3] But search for meaning and search for cause of cancer NS.

[4] Distress prior to BMT and at follow-up not associated with PTG, but an index of recalled distress (i.e., "—how you were feeling when you completed the psychosocial questionnaires before your BMT") minus pre-BMT distress was associated with greater PTG, as was a greater perceived decrease in distress (i.e., recalled pre-BMT distress minus post-BMT distress).

[5] On 7 of 8 quality-of-life subscales.

What can we conclude from these divergent findings? In the context of breast cancer, results suggest that higher SES may facilitate finding benefit or growth among women who have completed cancer treatment. It is possible that women with greater initial resources, such as higher income, may be better positioned to accrue positive consequences of stressful events (Hobfoll, 1989), or may perceive certain types of events as more threatening, leading to greater perceptions of positive change (e.g., Bower et al., 2005; Cordova et al., 2001; see section on perceived impact of cancer). On the other hand, among breast cancer patients who are undergoing treatment, this enhanced experience of threat may initially lead to decreased PTG. Of note, results from Weiss (2004) are inconsistent with this interpretation, perhaps because participants in this study were all longer term survivors

(> 3 years postdiagnosis) (see also Tomich & Helgeson, 2002). Further, we speculate that the association between SES and PTG is not particularly robust, as indicated by the large number of nonsignificant results.

Ethnicity. Ten studies have assessed the association between ethnicity and PTG. In three of these reports, all conducted with breast cancer patients, minority status was associated with greater PTG. Specifically, African American and Hispanic women reported higher levels of PTG than White women. The association between ethnicity and PTG remained significant in analyses controlling for SES, suggesting an independent effect of minority status (Tomich & Helgeson, 2004). Seven studies yielded nonsignificant associations. These studies had smaller samples and/or a lower percentage of minority participants than the positive reports, which may have limited their ability to find an effect.

Overall, this literature suggests that ethnic minority women diagnosed with breast cancer may be better able to derive meaning or benefit than White women. However, the reasons behind this difference remain obscure. One recurring theme in our examination of the PTG literature is the finding that greater impact of the cancer experience is associated with greater PTG. Ethnic minority women are diagnosed at a younger age and are more likely to be treated with mastectomy and chemotherapy than White women, which may increase the impact of cancer on their lives. The association between ethnicity and PTG may also be related to differences in religiosity/spirituality, as religious coping has been linked to increased benefit finding among cancer patients, and it mediated the relation of minority status with PTG in one study (Urcuyo et al., 2005).

Age. Of the investigations that assessed the relation of participant age with PTG, most ($n = 12$) yielded nonsignificant findings, although seven studies demonstrated significant negative associations, such that younger adults with cancer reported greater PTG than did older adults. For example, Manne et al. (2004) found that younger breast cancer patients had higher PTGI scores shortly after surgery, as well as 9 and 18 months later. Onset of chronic disease is a more normative experience for older adults, whereas a cancer diagnosis necessitates more developmental readjustment for younger adults and is more distressing for them (Klauer et al., 1998; Salmon, Manzi, & Valori, 1996). For example, Salmon et al. (1996) found that adults age 65 and younger reported gaining more life appreciation from their experience with incurable cancer, but also expressed more resentment and preoccupation with the disease than did participants over 65. Manne et al. (2004) also speculated that the younger cohort may be more aware of and motivated to conform to expectations to adopt a positive attitude in the face of cancer than are older patients.

We could detect no systematic explanation for the finding of no significant relation between age and PTG versus an inverse relation (e.g., sample size, age range, cancer-related factors, study design, interview vs. questionnaire assessment). We should also note that, in a sample with a particularly broad age range (22–92 years), Kurtz, Wyatt, and Kurtz (1995) reported that women aged 50 to 79 reported more positive philosophical/spiritual views (e.g., "Since having had cancer I have a greater appreciation for everyday life") than did women under 40 or over 80 years old.

Gender. Some stress researchers have suggested that women are, on average, more emotion focused in their coping strategies and therefore more susceptible than men to distress in addition to discovery of positive meaning (Fife et al., 1994). In the cancer literature, this contention is not supported, as eight investigations examining gender differences in reports of PTG have revealed no differences in the degree of growth described by male and female patients. This null finding is consistent across eight samples encompassing a broad range of diagnoses, age, nationalities, and stage of disease. Though all but two studies investigating gender differences in PTG are cross-sectional rather than longitudinal, no gender differences have been discerned for patients at any point in the cancer trajectory, ranging from one month postsurgery to more than five years postdiagnosis. The lack of gender differences is also consistent across methods of assessment, including standardized quantitative measures of PTG as well as more open-ended queries. Thus, the existing literature strongly suggests that male and female cancer patients do not differ in the extent to which PTG is experienced. However, this research has not adequately explored the possibility that although the degree of positive change is similar across male and female patients, the nature of these changes may differ systematically by gender.

Stressor Characteristics as Correlates of Posttraumatic Growth

Perceived stressfulness of cancer. Of studies assessing the relationship between perceived threat and PTG, four revealed a significant positive relationship, one study demonstrated a significant relation between PTG and perceived life threat, but a nonsignificant relation with cancer-related intrusive thoughts (Cordova et al., 2001), another investigation (Widows et al., 2005) yielded a significant relation between PTG and higher threat appraisals of some aspects of the bone marrow transplant (BMT) experience (i.e., concern for life, emotional distress), but not other threat variables (e.g., hopelessness, posttraumatic symptoms), and three reported nonsignificant relations. Operationalization of perceived threat varied across studies, including likelihood estimates regarding death from cancer (Lechner et al., 2003), Likert-type ratings of stressfulness (Sears et al., 2003; Weiss, 2004), the Impact of Event Scale (Manne et al., 2004), and questions aimed at determining whether the cancer experience met DSM-IV criteria for a PTSD stressor (i.e., experience of threat of death or injury plus intense fear or helplessness; Cordova et al., 2001; Weiss, 2004; Widows et al., 2005). In the studies that tested the association between objective and subjective threat, perceived threat was correlated with clinical indices of disease severity, but the relationship between subjective stressfulness and PTG appears to remain even when stage of disease is controlled (Lechner et al., 2003).

In general, the positive relationship between perceived threat and PTG appears to be fairly robust. Nonsignificant correlations were more likely to be reported in studies using the Impact of Event Scale (Antoni et al., 2001; Cordova et al., 2001; Horowitz, Wilner, & Alvarez, 1979; Manne et al., 2004; cf. Thornton et al., 2005), which may be a less direct indicator of cancer-related threat than measures used in other studies. In another study that did not reveal a relation between perceived stressfulness of cancer and PTG (Weiss, 2004), ratings of perceived stressfulness neared the ceiling ($M = 6.44/7$) and fell into a restricted range, which may have rendered ratings of threat less meaningful in that sample.

Severity of disease. Disease severity was operationalized in several ways across studies, including cancer stage (i.e., a medical index based on tumor size, extent of spread to the lymph nodes, and extent of spread to other parts of the body [metastasis], with higher stage indicating more severe disease; e.g., Andrykowski et al., 1996) or its components (e.g., tumor size, Petrie et al., 1999), global rating by an oncologist (e.g., Collins et al., 1990), or another composite index (e.g, Fromm et al., 1996). As shown in Table 8.3, the studies most frequently revealed no significant relation of disease severity and PTG, but several demonstrated that individuals who had more severe disease were more likely to report finding benefit in their experience than those whose cancer prognosis was less grave.

We could detect no other systematic differences between the two groups of studies (e.g., sample size, range of disease stages, study design, interview vs. questionnaire assessment of PTG, type of cancer, participant sex). The only finding in the opposite direction (i.e., less severe disease related to greater PTG) was that of Collins et al. (1990), but that study differed from the others in several ways, including its indicator of disease severity (i.e., two prognosis groups, stable disease vs. active disease, based on an oncologist's rating of prognosis) and statistical approach (i.e., interaction of prognosis × valence of change [positive or negative, as coded by raters] × domain of change on number of changes reported by participants). The specific finding for changes coded as positive was that individuals with more favorable prognoses reported more positive changes in future plans than did those with negative prognoses.

In one of the few studies that included patients with advanced cancer and the only study that reported testing a quadratic relation between disease severity and PTG, an interesting curvilinear relation between disease stage and PTG was reported by Lechner et al. (2003). In that study, cancer patients with Stage II disease reported significantly greater PTG than did those with Stage I or Stage IV disease (Stage III patients did not differ significantly from the other groups). The lowest level of PTG was reported by individuals with the most severe disease (Stage IV), followed by those with the least severe disease (Stage 0-I). Notably, most individuals who receive a Stage IV diagnosis are experiencing recurrence and spread of an initial, primary cancer, often several years later.

How do we interpret these findings regarding the relation of cancer severity with PTG? When significant relations did emerge, more serious cancers were most likely to be associated with greater PTG. However, findings were not without exception, the significant relations obtained between cancer severity and PTG often were not of large magnitude, and these relations were not always obtained across domains of PTG in single studies. For example, Andrykowski et al. (1996) reported that higher cancer stage was related to reported benefits with regard to love felt for the spouse ($r = .36$, $p < .01$), but no significant relations with other benefits (e.g., self-respect). Notwithstanding those caveats, cancers diagnosed at more advanced stages certainly carry a higher likelihood of mortality, and usually are accompanied by more prolonged and invasive medical treatments than are cancers with more favorable prognoses. Consistent with theories regarding PTG (Tedeschi & Calhoun, 2004; Janoff-Bulman & Berger, 2000), the experience of more advanced cancer, and its attendant mortality threat and life disruption, is likely to provoke the search for meaning and associated opportunity to find benefit in one's experience to a greater extent than does the diagnosis of very early stage disease.

The Lechner et al. (2003) data suggest a limiting condition, however. The experience of very advanced disease, particularly after a previous diagnosis of cancer in an earlier stage, might prompt such high life threat that one cognitively shuts down any search for meaning and benefit or might carry such unambiguous consequence that no generation of benefit is initiated (Lechner et al., 2003). It also is possible that an initial cancer diagnosis catalyzes benefit finding and that cancer recurrence, and its associated grave prognosis, brings no added value. As one of our research participants stated shortly after a diagnosis of metastatic disease, "I learned so much about life and myself from my first diagnosis, but enough already! I don't need this cancer to teach me anything else." Clearly, additional study is needed of the full range of disease severity in its relation to PTG, including a potentially nonlinear relation. Moreover, rather than cancer stage per se, the more powerful predictor of PTG might be the degree of life disruption or mortality salience perceived by the individual with cancer, a possibility that requires empirical attention.

Time Since diagnosis/treatment.   Studies that have examined the relationship between the amount of time elapsed since onset of the stressor and assessment of PTG are divided in evidencing a positive relation, a negative relation, and a nonsignificant relation between those variables. Conceptually, a positive correlation is expected, as more time to process the meaning and impact of an experience, such as cancer, should be associated with the discovery of more benefit and positive life changes. This positive relationship ($r = .24 - .36$) was found in four studies, three of which assessed PTG using the PTGI and included samples of stage 0-III breast cancer patients. Notably, one of the studies finding a positive relationship was longitudinal (Manne et al., 2004), revealing a consistent and significant increase in PTGI scores over 18 months among women with breast cancer.

Seven cross-sectional studies and one longitudinal study found no significant correlation between time since diagnosis/treatment and PTG, and two studies demonstrated a significant correlation in the opposite direction. There did not appear to be large systematic differences between these studies and those citing a significant positive relationship, except that the samples in studies revealing a significant negative relation were on average more than three years postdiagnosis of their cancer, as compared with a diagnosis duration of less than two years in three of the four studies yielding a positive relation. As such, the relationship between PTG and time since diagnosis may be stronger in the one or two years following diagnosis and treatment than after several years of survivorship. Indeed, a participant in the first author's research lamented that she was beginning to lose "the edge," explaining that, more than two years after her cancer diagnosis, she found herself living more on "automatic pilot," losing the sense of immediacy and appreciation for the present moment that her diagnosis had catalyzed. More longitudinal research is necessary to clarify the temporal course of PTG.

Cancer treatment variables.   The research is consistent in its finding that PTG is not associated significantly with factors pertaining to cancer treatments, including receipt of adjuvant therapies (e.g., chemotherapy, radiation, tamoxifen/raloxifene) and type of surgery, although an association of chemotherapy receipt and PTG emerged in the largest sample included in this review (Bower et al., 2005). Of note, chemotherapy was not a significant predictor of PTG in multivariate analyses conducted in that sample. Although theoretically, one might speculate that receipt of more aversive treatments that produce greater life disruption (e.g., chemotherapy) might set the stage for greater PTG, the extant studies provide minimal evidence that such is the case.

Personality Attributes as Correlates of Posttraumatic Growth

Some researchers have suggested that PTG may have dispositional underpinnings, such as optimism, hope, and extraversion (Affleck & Tennen, 1996; Tedeschi & Calhoun, 1996). Within the cancer literature, most studies ($n = 4$) report a modest positive correlation (.19–.24) between PTG and measures of optimism, although one study found no significant relationship of optimism with the PTGI. Thus, extant data suggest that the ability to find positive changes in the aftermath of a specific stressful event (PTG) and a generalized expectancy for positive outcomes (optimism) are distinct but correlated constructs. Furthermore, patients low in optimism may benefit more from cognitive-behavioral psychosocial interventions (Antoni et al., 2001).

Other personality attributes that have been examined in the context of PTG include neuroticism, self-efficacy and self-esteem, and threat and incentive sensitivity. This research is quite limited, with only a handful of studies to date exploring the links between PTG and each of these traits. Nevertheless, preliminary findings suggest that positive personal resources facilitate PTG. Specifically, neuroticism and threat sensitivity are not significantly associated with PTG, whereas self-efficacy/esteem and incentive sensitivity (behavioral approach system sensitivity/dispositional approach) represent personal resources that do seem to be significantly and positively associated with PTG.

Aspects of the Social Context as Correlates of Posttraumatic Growth

Among cancer patients, simply being married does not appear to promote PTG. Global indices of social support quantity or satisfaction also are not consistently related to PTG, such that two relevant investigations revealed a relation between social support indices and PTG, but four other studies did not. However, preliminary evidence suggests that more specific features of a patient's social context may be predictive of PTG. For example, Cordova and colleagues' study of breast cancer patients (2001) found that while PTG and social support satisfaction were not related, the extent to which participants had talked about their cancer with others was significantly associated with PTG. Similarly, Weiss (2004) found that although general social support was not related to PTG, marital support and contact with a role model who had experienced PTG provided a social climate facilitative of PTG. Further, actively seeking support as a coping strategy for dealing with the cancer experience may be associated with PTG (see section on coping processes).

Coping Processes as Correlates of Posttraumatic Growth

The relations of coping processes to PTG were assessed in eight studies, and most assessed multiple coping strategies. In Table 8.3, we have organized the coping processes into those directed toward approaching versus avoiding the stressor, a fundamental distinction in coping research (e.g., Stanton & Franz, 1999; Tobin, Holroyd, Reynolds, & Wigal, 1989). With few exceptions (e.g., distraction/seeking alternative rewards), scales assessing coping strategies directed toward avoiding thoughts and feelings about cancer were not associated significantly with PTG. When significant relations emerged, they were more often positive associations of PTG with approach-oriented strategies, such as problem-focused coping processes and active acceptance. Coping through positive reappraisal of the cancer experience also was associated with PTG in five studies. (The sixth study [Manne et al., 2004] did not find a significant relation of positive reappraisal coping with PTG, but involved assessment of coping with a self-selected stressor rather than with cancer specifically). Spiritual coping was associated with PTG in two studies.

Four of the studies investigating coping strategies were longitudinal, allowing for greater causal inference. Manne et al. (2004) found a significant interaction of time of assessment with coping through emotional expression in her study of breast cancer patients. Specifically, women who used more emotional expression evidenced a trend toward increasing PTG over time ($p < .06$), whereas women low in emotionally expressive coping evidenced no change in PTG. In Schulz and Mohamed (2004), acceptance was associated in a zero-order correlation with later benefit finding, but it did not predict benefit finding when other variables were included in the model. In both Sears et al. (2003) and Widows et al. (2005), coping through positive reappraisal of the cancer experience shortly after medical treatment completion predicted higher PTG at least one year later (but note that PTG was not assessed at baseline). In Sears et al. (2003), we had tested only the predictive utility of coping through positive reinterpretation and not other coping strategies. In an analysis conducted specifically for this chapter, we found that problem-focused coping (i.e., a combination of active coping and planning subscales of the COPE) and seeking social support (i.e., a combination of instrumental and emotional support-seeking subscales) shortly after treatment completion also were unique predictors of the PTGI. Controlling for time since diagnosis and cancer-specific stress, high problem-focused coping ($n = 58$; partial $r = .40$, $p < .005$) and social support seeking ($n = 58$; partial $r = .37$, $p < .005$) at study initiation were associated with greater PTG one year later. Problem-focused coping prior to BMT also predicted PTG an average of two years later in Widows et al. (2005). Taken together, the extant cross-sectional and longitudinal findings suggest that coping oriented toward engagement with the stressor may facilitate PTG, whereas avoidant coping has little influence in this regard.

Also relevant to this conclusion are two studies (Ho, Chan, & Ho, 2004; Lechner et al., in press) that used a version of the Mental Adjustment to Cancer Scale (MAC) (Watson, Greer, & Bliss, 1988; Watson et al., 1989), a scale that has been conceptualized as measuring cancer-related adjustment or coping styles. These were not included in the table because several MAC items appear to measure emotional and cognitive reactions to cancer (e.g., "I suffer great anxiety about it," "I've had a good life, what's left is a bonus") rather than intentional coping attempts, as assessed in the included studies. In those two cross-sectional studies, MAC fighting spirit (e.g., "I see my illness as a challenge") was associated positively with the PTGI scales, and MAC helplessness/hopelessness (e.g., "I feel that life is hopeless") was negatively associated with the PTGI (note that selected MAC fighting spirit and fatalism items were combined and MAC helplessness/hopelessness and anxious preoccupation items were combined in Ho et al., 2004). Lechner et al. (in press) also found that fighting spirit and helplessness/hopelessness mediated the relationship between perceived social support and PTG.

Psychological Adjustment as a Correlate of Posttraumatic Growth

There has been considerable interest in the association between PTG and psychological adjustment. Studies have examined the relation between PTG and measures of psychological distress/negative affect (e.g., Profile of Mood States [POMS]), positive affect (e.g., Positive and Negative Affect Scale – positive [PANAS]), psychological well-being (e.g., Ryff well-being scales, Ladder of Life, positive life quality), in addition to measures of quality of life and adjustment to illness. We consider results in each of these domains.

Psychological distress. Of the 15 studies that examined the association between PTG and psychological distress, the majority ($n = 9$) found no significant relation, four found a negative association (higher PTG associated with lower distress), and one found a positive association (higher PTG associated with increased distress). In addition, one study demonstrated a nonsignificant cross-sectional association between PTG and distress, but a positive longitudinal association between distress at presurgery and PTG one year later (Thornton et al., 2005). We were not able to detect systematic differences between these studies in type of cancer, time since diagnosis, or measures used to assess PTG and distress. However, three of the cross-sectional studies reporting a negative association between PTG and distress did have some unique characteristics. The study by Ho et al. (2004) was conducted with Chinese cancer survivors who were selected based on a social worker's evaluation of their functional status (i.e., only patients judged as "highly functioning" were invited to participate), and the study by Katz et al. (2001) was conducted with a mixed sample of cancer patients and lupus patients who were recruited from support groups. Taylor et al. (1984) used a composite measure of psychological adjustment that included physician and interviewer ratings of adjustment to illness and an index of well-being in addition to the POMS. In contrast, the cross-sectional studies with non-significant findings recruited more general samples of cancer patients (e.g., all patients who underwent a particular type of treatment at the study site) and used specific measures of psychological distress. Thus, it is possible that characteristics of the study population, selection criteria, and/or the measure of psychological distress may have influenced study results.

Longitudinal studies provide a stronger test of the association between PTG and psychological distress. Interestingly, results from the six longitudinal studies that have examined this association mirror the mixed findings from the cross-sectional reports. Four of these studies were conducted with breast cancer patients, and four assessed PTG within one year of cancer diagnosis. Sears et al. (2003) found that interview reports of benefit finding after treatment completion were not associated with POMS distress measures 3 and 12 months later. In a study of breast cancer survivors, Bower et al. (2005) found that reports of positive meaning at 1-5 years postdiagnosis did not predict CES-D negative affect scores at 5 to 10 years postdiagnosis. In contrast, Carver and Antoni (2004) found that scores on a 17-item BFS at 3-, 6-, or 12-months postsurgery were associated with reduced distress and CES-D scores at a 4–7 year follow-up. Because the 3-, 6-, and 12- month assessment points were pooled in this study, it is unclear whether the positive effects of benefit finding were accrued to women who found benefit at 3 months postsurgery, in addition to those who found benefit 6 or 12 months postsurgery. Of note, this study is a subsample of Urcuyo et al. (2005) and thus is not included in the table. A similar association between PTG and reduced distress was also observed in cross-sectional analyses conducted in the larger sample.

Two longitudinal studies have shown a positive association between PTG and psychological distress. Tomich and Helgeson (2004) reported that scores on a 20-item BFS completed at 4 months postdiagnosis (when all women were undergoing chemotherapy) were associated with increased negative affect 3 and 9 months later. This effect was evident primarily among the women who had more advanced disease. Of note, Carver and Antoni (2004) found no evidence that disease stage moderated the association between benefit finding and distress in their sample. The other positive finding was cited by Thornton et al. (2005) in a study of prostate cancer patients. In this report, negative affect was examined as a predictor of PTG. Results showed that presurgery negative affect predicted higher PTGI scores one year later. However, cross-sectional analyses conducted at the one-year follow-up yielded a nonsignificant association between PTG and negative affect.

Finally, one longitudinal study (Widows et al., 2005) revealed nonsignificant associations of distress prior to BMT and distress an average of two years later with PTG. Participants also were asked at follow-up to estimate their distress prior to BMT, and an index of recalled distress (i.e., "how you were feeling when you completed the psychosocial questionnaires before your BMT") minus pre-BMT distress was associated with greater PTG, as was a greater perceived decrease in distress (i.e., recalled pre-BMT distress minus post-BMT distress).

What can we conclude from these mixed findings? Overall, the evidence that PTG is associated with reduced distress in cancer patients is relatively weak. The majority of reports have yielded nonsignificant findings, and interpretation of the negative results is complicated by biased samples and composite measures of adjustment. Results from the longitudinal studies suggest that any effects of PTG may be dependent on the time of assessment. Benefit finding during treatment may have detrimental effects, particularly for patients with more advanced disease (Tomich & Helgeson, 2004). Identifying benefits at this early stage may represent a form of avoidance, perhaps circumventing more adaptive coping efforts. Benefit finding in the weeks after treatment completion has little short-term impact on distress (Sears et al., 2003), but may have more beneficial effects over the long term (Carver & Antoni, 2004). Thus, the question of when PTG is adaptive, and for whom, is a critical question for future research.

Positive affect.   Seven studies have examined the association between PTG and positive affect. Three found a positive relationship, with higher PTG associated with more positive affect, and three yielded nonsignificant results. One study found a positive cross-sectional association between the PTGI and positive affect, but a nonsignificant longitudinal association between interview reports of benefit finding and positive affect (Sears et al., 2003). The samples were roughly similar in time since diagnosis, active treatment, and measures used to assess PTG and positive affect.

Focusing first on the cross-sectional reports, Tomich and Helgeson (2002) found that a one-item perceived benefits measure (though not personal growth or acceptance) was positively correlated with scores on the PANAS-positive in a sample of breast cancer survivors, and Sears et al. (2003) found a positive association between the PTGI and scores on the POMS-Vigor subscale in breast cancer patients one year post-treatment. However, Thornton et al. (2005) found that scores on the PTGI were not correlated with the PANAS-positive among men treated for prostate cancer one year earlier. Similarly, Fromm et al. (1996) found that survivors of BMT who reported more positive changes as a result of their cancer experience did not score significantly higher on the PANAS-positive scale. Of note, the correlation between these measures was positive ($r = .20$), but not significant at the alpha level of $p < .01$ set by the study authors.

In a longitudinal study, Bower et al. (2005) found that women who reported positive changes in outlook and priorities in the first 5 years after breast cancer diagnosis reported increased levels of positive affect at 5 to 10 years postdiagnosis, controlling for positive affect at the initial assessment. Carver and Antoni (2004) examined reports of benefit finding in the year after breast cancer diagnosis, and found that women who reported greater benefits also reported higher levels of positive affect 4 to 7 years later. However, initial levels of positive affect were not assessed in this report. In contrast, Tomich and Helgeson (2004) found no evidence that breast cancer patients who reported finding benefits during treatment with chemotherapy showed increased positive affect 3 and 9 months later. Similarly, Sears et al. (2003) found that interview reports of benefit finding in the weeks after treatment completion did not predict changes in POMS-Vigor at 3- and 12-month follow-ups.

Overall, results from these studies indicate that PTG is not associated with reductions in positive affect, and may in fact lead to enhanced positive affect over the long term. However, these effects may not be evident in the first year after diagnosis.

Psychological well-being.   A handful of studies ($n = 4$) have examined the association between PTG and measures of psychological well-being, including the Ryff well-being scales, the Ladder of Life (a measure of life satisfaction), and a perceived life quality scale (a measure of one's day-to-day experience of interest, challenge, and fulfillment in life). Three of these reports found a positive cross-sectional relationship between PTG and measures of well-being, although there was no evidence that PTG predicted increases in well-being in a 4 to 7 year follow-up in one of these samples (Carver & Antoni,

2004). Nonsignificant results were seen in one study, which found no association between scores on the PTGI and the Ryff personal growth, purpose in life, and self-acceptance scales in a sample of breast cancer survivors (Cordova et al., 2001). The reason for these nonsignificant findings is unclear, particularly because the Ryff scales are conceptually similar to PTG and were positively correlated with interview reports of growth in a similar sample of breast cancer survivors assessed by Carpenter et al. (1999). Overall, these results offer preliminary evidence for an association between PTG and psychological well-being, although the extent to which PTG promotes long-term well-being requires further investigation.

   Quality of life. Investigators have used a variety of measures to probe the association between PTG and quality of life in cancer patients. These include the Psychological Adjustment to Illness Scale (PAIS), Functional Living Index—Cancer (FLIC), Sickness Impact Profile (SIP), Functional Assessment of Cancer Therapy (FACT), the Cancer Rehabilitation Evaluation System (CARES), and the SF-36. These measures assess patients' functioning across a range of domains (i.e., physical, emotional, social, and sexual) and the degree to which their functioning has been influenced by the cancer experience. Of the 10 studies that have examined quality of life measures, 7 have yielded nonsignificant findings, 2 found a positive association, and 1 found a negative association. Focusing first on the positive findings, Rieker, Ebril, and Garnick (1985) reported that survivors of testicular cancer who reported positive changes had less impairment in sexual functioning, the primary area of dysfunction in this patient group. Tomich and Helgeson (2002) found that reports of finding benefit (one-item scale) were associated with higher scores on the physical health component scale of the SF-36 in a sample of breast cancer survivors, although the correlation was somewhat modest ($r = .17$) and perceptions of personal growth and acceptance were not associated significantly with quality of life. However, in a longitudinal study of breast cancer patients undergoing treatment, Tomich and Helgeson (2004) found that benefit finding (20-item BFS) was associated with *lower* scores on the mental health component scale of the SF-36 for women with more severe disease. These results are consistent with the results for psychological distress presented in the preceding text. Overall, there is little evidence that PTG is associated with general measures of quality of life. Benefit finding early in the course of cancer diagnosis and treatment may lead to impairments in mental health, as discussed in the section on psychological distress. However, PTG appears to have little relation to patients' overall adjustment to illness and their physical, mental, and social functioning.

Posttraumatic Growth and Physical Health

Only a handful of studies have examined the association between PTG and measures of physical health. Of note, we distinguish here between measures of physical functioning included on quality of life instruments (reviewed in the preceding text) and more objective measures of physical and physiological functioning. In research conducted with women undergoing treatment for breast cancer, Antoni and colleagues have shown that PTG is associated with reductions in serum cortisol (Cruess et al., 2000) and with increases in lymphocyte proliferation (McGregor et al., 2004). Posttraumatic growth has also been associated with decreases in pain in a mixed sample of cancer and lupus patients (Katz et al., 2001). On the other hand, neither benefit finding nor PTGI scores were associated with cancer-related medical visits in a study conducted with women who had completed breast cancer treatment (Sears et al., 2003). Overall, these preliminary findings suggest that PTG may be associated with alterations in certain measures of physiologic function. This appears to be a promising area for future research.

IMPLICATIONS OF FINDINGS FROM THE CANCER LITERATURE FOR THEORIES OF BENEFIT FINDING

The foregoing findings from the cancer literature bear on current models for understanding the process of PTG. We contend that the findings provide the most compelling and consistent evidence for two facilitative conditions for PTG: substantial perceived impact of the stressor and intentional engagement with the stressor. As we will illustrate with two current theories of PTG, these two themes are prominent in extant conceptualizations. We also will comment on how the literature informs our understanding of the adaptive outcomes (e.g., psychological and physical health) of PTG.

Illustrative Theories of the Potential for Growth Through Adversity

Two prominent conceptualizations of the potential for positive change in the aftermath of trauma are those of Janoff-Bulman (1992, 2004; Janoff-Bulman & Berger, 1998; Janoff-Bulman & Frantz, 1997) and Tedeschi and Calhoun (1995, 1996, 2004; Calhoun & Tedeschi, 1999, 2001). The authors of both frameworks are careful to point out that traumatic events carry the potential for both decidedly negative and positive long-term consequences and that, by and large, the events are not viewed as desirable by those who experience them. Indeed, life disruption is a prerequisite for PTG in these models. According to Janoff-Bulman and Frantz (1997), the stressor must be sufficiently disruptive to core beliefs (i.e., meaningfulness of the world, benevolence of others, self-worthiness) to prompt a search for meaning. A search for *meaning as comprehensibility* (i.e., an attempt to determine whether and how an event makes sense) often catalyzes a newfound recognition of personal vulnerability and randomness. This in turn paves the way for attempts to create meaning in life "by generating significance through appraisals of value and worth" (Janoff-Bulman & Berger, 2000, p. 33), termed *meaning as significance* (Janoff-Bulman & Frantz, 1997).

Janoff-Bulman and Berger (2000) contend that if the reality of death is prompted by the trauma, then an enhanced appreciation for what it means to be alive can ensue: "That which we may lose suddenly is perceived as valuable" (p. 35). If benevolence and self-worth are questioned, then others' reactions can assume special significance and potentially promote greater appreciation for intimate relationships. Self-appreciation also can increase as individuals discover their own competencies in surmounting adversity. Thus, the search for meaning as significance can lead one to find benefits in the traumatic experience, perhaps particularly to the extent that it carries life threat.

Tedeschi and Calhoun (2004) also view life disruption as a necessary condition for PTG, stating "it is important that the events are challenging enough to the assumptive world to set in motion the cognitive processing necessary for growth" (pp. 7–8). In addition, they argue that stressor-induced distress and cognitive processing are prerequisites to PTG and go on to describe particular qualities of cognitive processing that set the stage for PTG. These include a transition from automatic and intrusive images to deliberate and recurrent consideration of the meaning of the event for one's goals and central life schemas. Tedeschi and Calhoun (2004) also suggest that the intrapersonal context (e.g., personality attributes including extraversion and openness to experience) and the interpersonal environment have a substantial impact on the ultimate adaptiveness of cognitive processing.

Perceived Impact of the Stressor

Central to both theoretical models of PTG summarized in the preceding text is the idea that stressful events must challenge fundamental assumptions about oneself and the world to initiate growth. If one's preexisting schemas and routines are not touched by a stressor, there is no need for adjustment and reevaluation and no opportunity for change. In particular, threat of mortality may be a potent stimulus for growth as one faces the possibility of a shortened lifespan and is forced to consider the shape and direction of one's life. Diagnosis with cancer involves an inherent threat to mortality, which may explain the prevalence of PTG in cancer populations. However, there is considerable variability in subjective appraisals of the cancer experience and the degree to which it impacts one's life; if the theories are correct, these factors should be closely linked with reports of PTG.

Overall, the extant literature strongly supports the assertion that greater disruption and threat are associated with greater PTG in cancer patients. Most compelling here is the positive association between perceived stressfulness of cancer and PTG, which has been observed in both cross-sectional and longitudinal reports. Negative affect at presurgery, which may serve as a marker of cancer-related disruption, has also been shown to predict increased PTG, consistent with predictions of Tedeschi and Calhoun. These results indicate that individuals who experience more stress or threat as a result of the cancer diagnosis also report more growth.

The literature also suggests that factors that increase the impact or threat of the cancer experience are associated with PTG. For example, there is evidence that greater disease severity is associated with greater PTG, although this association is not as strong or reliable as the association between stressfulness and growth and may not apply to patients with very advanced disease. In addition, evidence suggests that younger patients, who experience more threat and disruption related to cancer, report more PTG. It is conceivable that perceived threat may also mediate the association between PTG and other demographic characteristics, such as socioeconomic status and ethnicity. For example, higher income has been associated with greater cancer-related threat and vulnerability (e.g., Bower et al., 2005; Cordova et al., 2001), which may account for the relation between higher income and greater PTG found in selected reports. The role of perceived impact as a mediating variable requires empirical evaluation in future research.

Although these findings are compelling, it may be premature to conclude that greater threat is always associated with greater growth. There may be circumstances in which the threat is too great and overwhelms the possibility for positive change. For example, threat may not be associated with growth in the first days and weeks after cancer diagnosis, when individuals are struggling to cope with the reality of the cancer and make decisions about treatment. In addition, growth may be less likely to occur among individuals with very advanced disease, particularly those coping with severe pain and other side effects of disease and treatment. Finally, that greater threat predicts growth does not imply that a shattering of core beliefs is a necessary element of threat. In the case of individuals with cancer, perhaps mortality salience is the most central dimension of threat (Wortman, 2004).

Intentional Engagement with the Stressor

Both Tedeschi and Calhoun (2004), in their focus on the importance of self-disclosure, deliberate cognitive processing of the stressor, and affective engagement, and Janoff-Bulman

(2004), in her emphasis on the centrality of wrestling with the meaning of the event, appear to view intentional engagement with the stressor as a prerequisite to PTG, which in itself is an active process. As Janoff-Bulman (2004) stated, "In recognizing life's worth, survivors become actively engaged through new choices and commitments that create renewed meaning in their lives. In essence, they have moved from concerns about the meaning of life to the creation of meaning in life" (p. 33).

Our review's findings with regard to personality and coping correlates of PTG support the significant role of volitional engagement in facilitating PTG. Both dispositional approach-oriented tendencies (e.g., incentive sensitivity) and approach-oriented coping processes, such as problem solving, emotional expression, and seeking social support, are predictors of PTG, as are active attempts to find benefit as a coping process. Although fewer studies are available, it also appears that active self-disclosure regarding the cancer experience (Cordova et al., 2001) may promote PTG. On the other hand, dispositional tendencies (e.g., threat sensitivity) and stressor-specific coping processes directed toward avoidance consistently have yielded nonsignificant relations with PTG.

Posttraumatic Growth and Adjustment

The outcomes of PTG—that is, the effect of PTG on psychological and physical health—are not considered in any substantive way in either of the theoretical models summarized in the preceding text. Notably, neither of the models predicts that growth will lead to reductions in psychological distress. Instead, Tedeschi and Calhoun state that "some degree of psychological upset or distress is necessary not only to set the process of growth in motion, but also some enduring upset may accompany the enhancement and maintenance of posttraumatic growth" (Tedeschi & Calhoun, 2004, p. 13). This is consistent with Janoff-Bulman, who predicts that "anxiety and loss associated with the known possibility of loss remain, but now function so as to focus our attention on the amazing fact of existence rather than nonexistence, the wonder of life rather than the absolute terror of annihilation" (Janoff-Bulman & Berger, 1998, p. 43). Both models do refer to positive psychological states that may accompany growth; for example, Tedeschi and Calhoun indicate that PTG may facilitate the development of general wisdom about life, while Janoff-Bulman suggests that survivors may experience a heightened sense of commitment and purpose in their lives and feel that they are engaged in more meaningful and fulfilling activities.

To some extent, the literature supports the hypothesis that growth is not associated with reductions in psychological distress in cancer populations, as the majority of studies examining this association have yielded nonsignificant results. Of note, nonsignificant results have been observed even in large-scale, longitudinal studies, suggesting that limitations in research design do not account for the failure to find significant effects. However, the findings are mixed, suggesting that there may be circumstances in which growth leads to decreased (Carver & Antoni, 2004) or possibly increased (Tomich & Helgeson, 2004) emotional distress.

There is more consistent evidence that PTG is associated with modest increases in positive affect and possibly other aspects of psychological well-being. Although the higher level cognitive and motivational states described in the theoretical models have rarely been examined in empirical reports, one study did reveal that breast cancer patients who reported finding more benefits following cancer also experienced a higher level of interest, challenge, and fulfillment in their everyday life (Urcuyo et al., 2005).

Limitations and Future Directions of Research on Posttraumatic Growth and Cancer

In the past decade, researchers have made considerable progress in understanding PTG, and the notion that being diagnosed with cancer or confronting other adversities can catalyze positive personal change is gaining wide acceptance. However, much work remains to be done to clarify the construct of PTG, its adaptive significance, and the basic processes underlying reports of growth. To this end, several limitations of current research and future directions for research are recommended.

Methods and measurement. A foremost limitation is the lack of longitudinal and experimental studies in this area, which seriously constrains causal inference regarding determinants and consequences of PTG. Carefully designed longitudinal and daily process studies could illuminate the contributors to and outcomes of PTG, and experimental studies are needed to evaluate the validity of PTG measures and basic processes underlying the phenomenon.

Issues in measuring PTG also demand attention. At least in the cancer literature, the standardized scales to assess PTG (i.e., BFS and PTGI) appear highly correlated, suggesting that they are measuring similar underlying constructs. However, the association between these scales and other methods for assessing benefit finding (e.g., open-ended interview questions) requires additional study. Most PTG measures used in the cancer literature do not measure negative change, which may lead participants to over-report growth and restricts our characterization of the life changes that cancer may catalyze. Regardless of whether a single scale or separate scales ultimately are determined to be more useful in assessing perceptions of positive and negative change, it is conceptually important to examine these perceptions in tandem, as they commonly co-occur (e.g., Klauer et al., 1998). Indeed, failure to consider negative consequences of the cancer experience may obscure our ability to detect unique effects of PTG. For example, Bower et al. (2005) found a stronger association between meaning and positive mood in analyses controlling for cancer-related vulnerability. In our focus on PTG, we must not neglect the negative impact of the cancer experience on people's lives.

In addition, although assessed dimensions of PTG often are strongly correlated, aggregated measures of PTG may complicate the exploration of predictors and outcomes of growth, as positive changes across different domains (e.g., strengthened interpersonal relationships, increased spirituality) may have distinct determinants and adaptive significance (Janoff-Bulman, 2004; McMillen, 2004). Future research to sharpen the conceptualization of PTG would benefit from multimethod approaches, employing self-report scales, open-ended interview questions, informant reports, and behavioral observations.

Conceptualization of posttraumatic growth. Conceptually, the existing research has not adequately addressed the question of what reports of PTG signify, whether on standardized questionnaires or open-ended interviews (Park, 2004; Tennen & Affleck, 2002). Some investigators have hypothesized that reports of growth are indicative of denial or avoidance, or that they reflect the natural propensity to see oneself as on an upward trajectory. Reports of growth in the aftermath of trauma in part may represent self-protective positive illusions, serving to restore a damaged sense of self-esteem or mastery.

Indeed, both with regard to cancer and other experiences, research has demonstrated that perceptions of growth are achieved in part by derogating one's premorbid attributes (Andrykowski, Brady, & Hunt, 1993; McFarland & Alvaro, 2000; Widows et al., 2005).

However, several lines of evidence suggest that reports of PTG are not solely illusory. First, research investigating peer or partner reports of growth has revealed significant relations between informant reports and self-reports, lending confidence to the assumption that at least some self-reports of growth are accompanied by observable behavior change (e.g., Park, Cohen, & Murch, 1996; Weiss, 2002). Of course, some of the areas in which growth is reported are more private and less likely to be detected by external raters (e.g., changes in self-perceptions, life perspective). Second, though the perception of personal improvement over time may be a natural human tendency, studies comparing cancer patients to matched controls revealed that, although healthy adults also report positive psychosocial change over time, they do so to a lesser extent and more globally (i.e., reporting less differentiated changes) than cancer patients (Andrykowski et al., 1993; Cordova et al., 2001; Tomich & Helgeson, 2002). Third, our review of the literature suggests that PTG is unrelated to dispositional and situation-specific indicators of avoidance in individuals with cancer. Further, an important longitudinal study (Manne et al., 2004) found that PTG increased over time in cancer patients (see also Frazier, Conlon, & Glaser, 2001, for a longitudinal study of sexual assault survivors). These findings are counterintuitive if PTG is merely a defensive process.

Clearly, more work is needed to determine the meaning of reports of PTG. It is possible that these reports serve multiple and distinct motivational functions, perhaps serving self-protective aims for some individuals under particular conditions and reflecting meaningful positive change in other cases. One viable explanation for the variable and often nonsignificant relations of benefit finding and psychological adjustment is that the relationship is moderated by individual difference or other variables. For example, evidence suggest that reports of benefit finding might serve a more avoidant and self-protective function for individuals with low personal resources (e.g., low optimism or self-efficacy) and might indicate more tangible positive change for those with more substantial resources, with distinct adaptive consequences (Rini et al., 2004; Stanton, Danoff-Burg, & Huggins, 2002; Stanton & Low, 2004). The motivational functions of reported PTG also might differ across time, from diagnosis to long-term survivorship. To this end, work aimed at systematically investigating the temporal trajectory of PTG also will contribute to our understanding of this phenomenon, its long-term stability, and how it unfolds over time, in addition to whether PTG has different predictors or functions at different time points in the cancer experience.

Predictors of posttraumatic growth. With regard to understanding the conditions that facilitate and impede PTG, our review of the literature points to important roles for perceived impact of the stressor (i.e., high threat) and intentional engagement as facilitators of PTG. Whether these two constructs hold up as determinants of PTG in additional samples of individuals diagnosed with cancer and those experiencing other stressors awaits additional longitudinal and experimental test. Further, it is easy to imagine conditions under which high impact and intentional engagement would produce maladaptive outcomes, necessitating specification of the central qualities of threat and engagement that facilitate versus inhibit PTG. Perhaps threat facilitates PTG to the extent that one also perceives pathways for reducing the threat, for example. The experience of PTG likely is dependent on specific cognitive and affective engagement processes that require further study (e.g., reflection vs. brooding, Nolen-Hoeksema & Davis, 2004; see also Segerstrom, Stanton, Alden, & Shortridge, 2003; Trapnell & Campbell, 1999; Watkins & Teasdale, 2004). Contextual factors also deserve greater attention, including qualities of the social and larger cultural environments (Armeli, Gunthert, & Cohen, 2001; McMillen, 2004; Wortman, 2004). Research in PTG in couples undergoing stressful circumstances (e.g., Manne et al., 2004; Thornton et al., 2005; Weiss, 2004) is one step toward this goal.

The roles of positive emotions and positive events in facilitating PTG, in addition to their reciprocal relations, also have received minimal attention. Positive emotions might facilitate PTG through mechanisms including broadening cognitive repertoires, for example (see Frederickson, 2001; Frederickson, Tugade, Waugh, & Larkin, 2003). And the experience of concomitant positive events while one is undergoing treatment for cancer might influence the development of PTG (see Zautra, Affleck, Tennen, Reich, & Davis, in press, for a discussion of the importance of positive events and affect in daily life). Clearly, the conditions that set the stage for or impede PTG require further specification.

Posttraumatic growth and adjustment. Perhaps the most notable finding that emerges from the cancer literature regarding the relation of PTG and psychological and physical health is the lack of association between PTG and measures of psychological adjustment; even those studies that yielded positive findings typically cited a relatively weak association between PTG and the outcome of interest. It appears that PTG may have a fairly limited effect on psychological adjustment among cancer patients, perhaps because perceptions of growth exist alongside an increased awareness of one's vulnerability and fragility. However, only a handful of longitudinal studies have examined the association between PTG and adjustment, several of which were not initially designed to test the effects of PTG on psychological outcomes (e.g., Bower et al., 2005; Carver & Antoni, 2004; Sears et al., 2003). Given that notable longitudinal studies of individuals confronting other stressors do document a positive relationship between PTG and adjustment (e.g., Davis, Nolen-Hoeksema, & Larson, 1998; McMillen, Smith, & Fisher, 1997), the lack of consistent association in cancer patient samples warrants further longitudinal investigation. The existing literature also does not inform the question of whether growth may lead to improvements in other aspects of psychological functioning not captured in measures of distress. This possibility merits increased attention in future research, as does increased concentration on the intersection of PTG and physical health parameters and the mechanisms through with PTG may influence physiological functioning (Bower & Segerstrom, 2004).

Posttraumatic growth and clinical interventions. A clearer understanding of the determinants of PTG could inform the development of psychosocial interventions by targeting key predictive factors and providing a supportive social context for growth. There is suggestive evidence that cognitive-behavioral interventions can increase benefit finding in cancer patients (Antoni et al., 2001) and that promoting the consideration of benefits in women diagnosed with breast cancer can produce salutary effects (Stanton et al., 2002). However, neither of these interventions attempted specifically to shape the content of women's perceptions of benefits. As recommended previously (Stanton, Tennen, Affleck, & Mendola, 1992; Tennen & Affleck, 1999), we urge caution in "prescribing" PTG by encouraging cancer patients to think positively or look at the bright side, or even by implying that most people with cancer find benefit in their experience, which ultimately could carry iatrogenic consequences. Sensitive consideration of issues of timing of interventions and framing of questions regarding the experience of benefit in adversity is crucial, and associated research can aid in guiding such intervention.

CONCLUSION

In conclusion, there is much more to learn about the positive changes that may follow cancer. Though the empirical literature on this construct is flourishing, much of the existing research is conceptually and methodologically limited. Longitudinal, multimethod research could provide insight into the predictors and temporal course of PTG; the emotional, cognitive, and motivational processes implicated in growth; and the psychosocial and physiological outcomes of PTG. Despite the work that remains to be done, the recent proliferation of empirical and theoretical attention to PTG represents an important shift from focusing exclusively on the negative consequences of coping with cancer toward conceptualizing cancer as a life transition with the potential to elicit growth in addition to hardship. The research gleaned from this approach yields a more complete and balanced portrait of cancer patients' psychosocial experience and health.

REFERENCES

Affleck, G., & Tennen, H. (1996). Constructing benefits from adversity: Adaptational significance and dispositional underpinnings. *Journal of Personality, 64*, 899–922.

Affleck, G., Tennen, H., Croog, S., & Levine, S. (1987). Causal attribution, perceived benefits, and morbidity following a heart attack: An eight-year study. *Journal of Consulting and Clinical Psychology, 55*, 29–35.

Andersen, B. L., Anderson, B., & deProsse, C. (1989). Controlled prospective longitudinal study of women with cancer: II. Psychological outcomes. *Journal of Consulting and Clinical Psychology, 57*, 692–697.

Andrykowski, M. A., Brady, M. J., & Hunt, J. W. (1993). Positive psychosocial adjustment in potential bone marrow transplant recipients: Cancer as a psychosocial transition. *Psycho-oncology, 2*, 261–276.

Andrykowski, M. A., Curran, S. L., Studts, J. L., Cunningham, L., Carpenter, J. S., McGrath, et al. (1996). Psychosocial adjustment and quality of life in women with breast cancer and benign breast problems: A controlled comparison. *Journal of Clinical Epidemiology, 49*, 827–834.

Antoni, M. H., Lehman, J. M., Kilbourn, K. M., Boyes, A. E., Culver, J. L., Alferi, S. M., et al. (2001). Cognitive-behavioral stress-management intervention decreases the prevalence of depression and enhances benefit-finding among women under treatment for early-stage breast cancer. *Health Psychology, 20*, 20–32.

Armeli, S., Gunthert, K. C., & Cohen, L. H. (2001). Stressor appraisals, coping, and post-event outcomes: The dimensionality and antecedents of stress-related growth. *Journal of Social and Clinical Psychology, 20*, 366–395.

Bower, J. E., Meyerowitz, B. E., Desmond, K. A., Bernaards, C. A., Rowland, J. H., & Ganz, P. A. (2005). Perceptions of positive meaning and vulnerability following breast cancer: Predictors and outcomes among long-term breast cancer survivors. *Annals of Behavioral Medicine. 29*, 236–245.

Bower, J. E., & Segerstrom, S. C. (2004). Stress management, finding benefit, and immune function: Positive mechanisms for intervention effects on physiology. *Journal of Psychosomatic Research, 56*, 9–11.

Calhoun, L. G., Cann, R., Tedeschi, R. G., & McMillan, J. (2000). A correlational test of the relationship between posttraumatic growth, religion, and cognitive processing. *Journal of Traumatic Stress, 13*, 521–527.

Calhoun, L. G. & Tedeschi, R. G. (1999). *Facilitating posttraumatic growth: A clinician's guide.* Mahwah, NJ: Lawrence Erlbaum Associates.

Calhoun, L. G. & Tedeschi, R. G. (2001). Posttraumatic growth: The positive lessons of loss. In R. A. Neimeyer (Ed.), *Meaning reconstruction and the experience of loss* (pp. 157–172). Washington, DC: American Psychological Association.

Carpenter, J. S., Brockopp, D. Y., & Andrykowski, M. A. (1999). Self-transformation as a factor in the self-esteem and well-being of breast cancer survivors. *Journal of Advanced Nursing, 29*, 1402–1411.

Carver, C. S., & Antoni, M. H. (2004). Finding benefit in breast cancer during the year after diagnosis predicts better adjustment 5 to 8 years after diagnosis. *Health Psychology, 23*, 595–598.

Carver, C. S., Scheier, M. F., & Weintraub, J. K. (1989). Assessing coping strategies: A theoretically-based approach. *Journal of Personality and Social Psychology, 56*, 267–283.

Cella, D. F., & Tross, S. (1986). Psychological adjustment to survival from Hodgkin's disease. *Journal of Consulting and Clinical Psychology, 54*, 616–622.

Collins, R. L., Taylor, S. E., & Skokan, L. A. (1990). A better world or a shattered vision? Changes in perspectives following victimization. *Social Cognition, 8*, 263–285.

Cordova, M. J., Andrykowski, M. A., Kenady, D. E., McGrath, P. C., Sloan, D. A., & Redd, W. H. (1995). Frequency and correlates of posttraumatic-stress-disorder-like symptoms after treatment for breast cancer. *Journal of Consulting and Clinical Psychology, 63*, 981–986.

Cordova, M. J., Cunningham, L. L. C., Carlson, C. R., & Andrykowski, M. A. (2001). Posttraumatic growth following breast cancer: A controlled comparison study. *Health Psychology, 20*, 176–185.

Cruess, D. G., Antoni, M. H., McGregor, B. A., Kilbourn, K. M., Boyers, A. E., Alferi, S. M., et al. (2000). Cognitive-behavioral stress management reduces serum cortisol by enhancing benefit finding among women being treated for early stage breast cancer. *Psychosomatic Medicine, 62*, 304–308.

Curbow, B., Somerfield, M. R., Baker, F., Wingard, J. R., & Legro, M. W. (1993). Personal changes, dispositional optimism, and psychological adjustment to bone marrow transplantation. *Journal of Behavioral Medicine, 16*, 423–443.

Daiter, S., Larson, R. A., Weddington, W. W., & Ultmann, J. E. (1988). Psychosocial symptomatology, personal growth, and development among young adult patients following the diagnosis of leukemia or lymphoma. *Journal of Clinical Oncology, 6*, 613–617.

Davis, C. G., Nolen-Hoeksema, S., & Larson, J. (1998). Making sense of loss and benefiting from the experience: Two construals of meaning. *Journal of Personality and Social Psychology, 75*, 561–574.

Derogatis, L. R., Morrow, G. R., Fetting, J., Penman, D., Piasetsky, S., Schmale, A., et al. (1983). The prevalence of psychiatric disorders among cancer patients. *Journal of the American Medical Association, 249*, 751–757.

Dirksen, S. R. (1995). Search for meaning in long-term cancer survivors. *Journal of Advanced Nursing, 21*, 628–633.

Fife, B. L. (1995). The measurement of meaning in illness. *Social Science and Medicine, 40*, 1021–1028.

Fife, B. L., Kennedy, V. N., & Robinson, L. (1994). Gender and adjustment to cancer: Clinical implications. *Journal of Psychosocial Oncology, 12*, 1–21.

Frazier, P., Conlon, A., & Glaser, T. (2001). Positive and negative life changes following sexual assault. *Journal of Consulting and Clinical Psychology, 69*, 1048–1055.

Frederickson, B. L. (2001). The role of positive emotions in positive psychology: The broaden-and-build theory of positive emotions. *American Psychologist, 56*, 218–226.

Frederickson, B. L., Tugade, M. M., Waugh, C. E., & Larkin, G. R. (2003). What good are positive emotions in crises? A prospective study of resilience and emotions following the terrorist attacks on the United States on September 11th, 2001. *Journal of Personality and Social Psychology, 84*, 365–376.

Fritz, G. K., & Williams, J. R. (1988). Issues of adolescent development for survivors of childhood cancer. *Journal of the American Academy of Child and Adolescent Psychiatry, 27*, 712–715.

Fromm, K., Andrykowski, M. A., & Hunt, J. (1996). Positive and negative psychosocial sequelae of bone marrow transplantation: Implications for quality of life assessment. *Journal of Behavioral Medicine, 19*, 221–240.

Giedzinska, A. S., Meyerowitz, B. E., Ganz, P. A., & Rowland, J. H. (2004). Health-related quality of life in a multiethnic sample of breast cancer survivors. *Annals of Behavioral Medicine, 28*, 39–51.

Gritz, E. R., Wellisch, D. K., Siau, J., & Wang, H. J. (1990). Long-term effects of testicular cancer on marital relationships. *Psychosomatics, 31*, 301–312.

Halttunen, A., Hietvanen, P., Jallinoja, P., & Lonnqvist, J. (1992). Getting free of breast cancer: An eight-year perspective of the relapse-free patients. *Acta Oncologica, 31*, 307–310.

Ho, S. M., Chan, C. L. W., & Ho, R. T. H. (2004). Posttraumatic growth in Chinese cancer survivors. *Psycho-oncology, 13*, 377–389.

Hobfoll, S. E. (1989). Conservation of resources: A new attempt at conceptualizing stress. *American Psychologist, 44*, 513–524.

Horowitz, M. J., Wilner, N., & Alvarez, W. (1979). The Impact of Event Scale: A measure of subjective stress. *Psychosomatic Medicine, 41*, 209–218.

Janoff-Bulman, R. (1992). *Shattered assumptions: Towards a new psychology of trauma.* New York: Free Press.

Janoff-Bulman, R. (2004). Posttraumatic growth: Three explanatory models. *Psychological Inquiry, 15*, 30–34.

Janoff-Bulman, R., & Berg, M. (1998). Disillusionment and the creation of value: From traumatic losses to existential gains. In J. H. Harvey (Ed.), *Perspectives on loss: A sourcebook* (pp. 35–47). Philadelphia: Brunner/Mazel.

Janoff-Bulman, R., & Berger, A. (2000). The other side of trauma: Towards a psychology of appreciation. In J. H. Harvey & E. D. Miller (Eds.), *Loss and trauma: General and close relationship perspectives* (pp. 29–44). Philadelphia: Brunner/Mazel.

Janoff-Bulman, R., & Frantz, C.M. (1997). The impact of trauma on meaning: From meaningless world to meaningful life. In M. Power & C. R. Brewin (Eds.), *The transformation of meaning in psychological therapies* (pp. 91–106). New York: Wiley.

Katz, R. C., Flasher, L., Cacciapaglia, H., & Nelson, S. (2001). The psychosocial impact of cancer and lupus: A cross-validational study that extends the generality of "benefit-finding" in patients with chronic disease. *Journal of Behavioral Medicine, 24,* 561–571.

Kennedy, B. J., Tellegen, A., Kennedy, S., & Havernick, N. (1976). Psychological response of patients cured of advanced cancer. *Cancer, 38,* 2184–2191.

Klauer, T., Ferring, D., & Filipp, S. (1998). "Still stable after all this...?": Temporal comparisons in coping with severe and chronic disease. *International Journal of Behavioral Development, 22,* 339–355.

Kurtz, M. E., Wyatt, G., & Kurtz, J. C. (1995). Psychological and sexual well-being, philosophical/spiritual views, and health habits of long-term cancer survivors. *Health Care for Women International, 16,* 253–262.

Lechner, S. C., Antoni, M. H., & Zakowski, S. G. (in press). Coping mediates the relationship between social support and finding benefit in the experience of cancer. *Psycho-oncology.*

Lechner, S. C., Zakowski, S. G., Antoni, M. H., Greenhawt, M., Block, K., & Block, P. (2003). Do sociodemographic and disease-related variables influence benefit-finding in cancer patients? *Psycho-oncology, 12,* 491–499.

Manne, S., Ostroff, J., Winkel, G., Goldstein, L., Fox, K., & Grana, G. (2004). Posttraumatic growth after breast cancer: Patient, partner, and couple perspectives. *Psychosomatic Medicine, 66,* 442–454.

McFarland, C., & Alvaro, C. (2000). The impact of motivation on temporal comparisons: Coping with traumatic events by perceiving personal growth. *Journal of Personality and Social Psychology, 79,* 327–343.

McGregor, B. A., Antoni, M. H., Boyers, A., Alferi, S. M., Blomberg, B. B., & Carver, C. S. (2004). Cognitive-behavioral stress management increases benefit finding and immune function among women with early-stage breast cancer. *Journal of Psychosomatic Research, 56,* 1–8.

McMillen, J. C. (2004). Posttraumatic growth: What's it all about? *Psychological Inquiry, 15,* 48–52.

McMillen, J. C., Smith, E. M., & Fisher, R. H. (1997). Perceived benefit and mental health after three types of disaster. *Journal of Consulting and Clinical Psychology, 65,* 733–739.

Moyer, A., & Salovey, P. (1996). Psychosocial sequelae of breast cancer and its treatment. *Annals of Behavioral Medicine, 18,* 110–125.

Nolen-Hoeksema, S., & Davis, C. G. (2004). Theoretical and methodological issues in the assessment and interpretation of posttraumatic growth. *Psychological Inquiry, 15,* 60–64.

O'Connor, A. P., Wicker, C. A., & Germino, B. B. (1990). Understanding the cancer patient's search for meaning. *Cancer Nursing, 13,* 167–175.

Office of Cancer Survivorship. (2004). http://www.cdc.gov/mmwr/preview/mmwrhtml/mm5324a3.htm.

Oh, S., Heflin, L., Meyerowitz, B. E., Desmond, K. A., Rowland, J. H., & Ganz, P. A. (2004). Quality of life of breast cancer survivors after a recurrence: A follow-up study. *Breast Cancer Research and Treatment, 87,* 45–57.

Park, C. L. (2004). The notion of growth following stressful life experiences: Problems and prospects. *Psychological Inquiry, 15,* 69–76.

Park, C. L., Cohen, L., & Murch, R. (1996). Assessment and prediction of stress-related growth. *Journal of Personality, 64,* 71–105.

Petrie, K. J., Buick, D. L., Weinman, J., & Booth, R. J. (1999). Positive effects of illness reported by myocardial infarction and breast cancer patients. *Journal of Psychosomatic Research, 47,* 537–543.

Rieker, P. P., Edbril, S. D., & Garnick, M. B. (1985). Curative testis cancer therapy: Psychosocial sequelae. *Journal of Clinical Oncology, 3,* 1117–1126.

Rieker, P. P., Fitzgerald, E. M., Kalish, L. A., Richie, J. P., Lederman, G. S., Edbril, S. D., et al. (1989). Psychosocial factors, curative therapies, and behavioral outcomes: A comparison of testis cancer survivors and a control group of healthy men. *Cancer, 64,* 2399–2407.

Rini, C., Manne, S., DuHamel, K., Austin, J., Ostroff, J., Boulad, F., et al. (2004). Mothers' perceptions of benefit following pediatric stem cell transplantation: A longitudinal investigation of the roles of optimism, medical risk, and sociodemographic resources. *Annals of Behavioral Medicine, 28*, 132–143.

Ross, R. D., Stockdale, F. E., & Jacobs, C. (1978). Cancer Patient Behavior Scale: Scores of cancer patients and healthy adults. *Proceedings of the American Association for Cancer Research, 19*, 348.

Salmon, P., Manzi, F., & Valori, R. M. (1996). Measuring the meaning of life for patients with incurable cancer: The Life Evaluation Questionnaire (LEQ). *European Journal of Cancer, 32A*, 755–760.

Schulz, U., & Mohamed, N. E. (2004). Turning the tide: Benefit finding after cancer surgery. *Social Science and Medicine, 59*, 653–662.

Sears, S. R., Stanton, A. L., & Danoff-Burg, S. (2003). The yellow brick road and the emerald city: Benefit-finding, positive reappraisal coping, and posttraumatic growth in women with early-stage breast cancer. *Health Psychology, 22*, 487–497.

Segerstrom, S. C., Stanton, A. L., Alden, L. E., & Shortridge, B. E. (2003). A multidimensional structure for repetitive thought: What's on your mind, and how, and how much? *Journal of Personality and Social Psychology, 85*, 909–921.

Siegel, K., & Schrimshaw, E. W. (2000). Perceiving benefits in adversity: Stress-related growth in women living with HIV/AIDS. *Social Science and Medicine, 51*, 1543–1554.

Stanton, A. L., Danoff-Burg, S., & Huggins, M. E. (2002). The first year after breast cancer diagnosis: Hope and coping strategies as predictors of adjustment. *Psycho-oncology, 11*, 93–102.

Stanton, A. L., Danoff-Burg, S., Sworowski, L. A., Collins, C. A., Branstetter, A., Rodriguez-Hanley, A., et al. (2002). Randomized, controlled trial of written emotional expression and benefit finding in breast cancer patients. *Journal of Clinical Oncology, 20*, 4160–4168.

Stanton, A. L., & Franz, R. (1999). Focusing on emotion: An adaptive coping strategy? In C. R. Snyder (Ed.), *Coping: The psychology of what works* (pp. 90–118). New York: Oxford University Press.

Stanton, A. L., & Low, C. A. (2004). Toward understanding posttraumatic growth: Commentary on Tedeschi and Calhoun. *Psychological Inquiry, 15*, 76–80.

Stanton, A. L., Tennen, H., Affleck, G., & Mendola, R. (1992). Coping and adjustment to infertility. *Journal of Social and Clinical Psychology, 11*, 1–13.

Taylor, S. E. (1983). Adjustment to threatening events: A theory of cognitive adaptation. *American Psychologist, 38*, 1161–1173.

Taylor, S. E., Lichtman, R. R., & Wood, J. V. (1984). Attributions, beliefs about control, and adjustment to breast cancer. *Journal of Personality and Social Psychology, 46*, 489–502.

Tedeschi, R. G., & Calhoun, L. G. (1995). *Trauma and transformation: Growing in the aftermath of suffering.* Thousand Oaks, CA: Sage.

Tedeschi, R. G., & Calhoun, L. G. (1996). The posttraumatic growth inventory: Measuring the positive legacy of trauma. *Journal of Traumatic Stress, 9*, 455–471.

Tedeschi, R. G., & Calhoun, L. G. (2004). Posttraumatic growth: Conceptual foundations and empirical evidence. *Psychological Inquiry, 15*, 1–18.

Tennen, H., & Affleck, G. (1999). Finding benefits in adversity. In C. R. Snyder (Ed.), *Coping: The psychology of what works* (pp. 279–304). New York: Oxford University Press.

Tennen, H., & Affleck, G. (2002). Benefit-finding and benefit-reminding. In C. R. Snyder & S. J. Lopez (Eds.), *Handbook of positive psychology* (pp. 584–597). New York: Oxford University Press.

Thompson, S. C., & Pitts, J. (1993). Factors relating to a person's ability to find meaning after a diagnosis of cancer. *Journal of Psychosocial Oncology, 11*, 1–21.

Thornton, A. A., Perez, M. A., & Meyerowitz, B. E. (2005). Posttraumatic growth in prostate cancer patients and their partners. Unpublished data.

Tobin, D. L., Holroyd, K. A., Reynolds, R. V., & Wigal, J. K. (1989). The hierarchical factor structure of the Coping Strategies Inventory. *Cognitive Therapy and Research, 13*, 343–361.

Tomich, P. L., & Helgeson, V. S. (2002). Five years later: A cross-sectional comparison of breast cancer survivors with healthy women. *Psycho-oncology, 11*, 154–169.

Tomich, P. L., & Helgeson, V. S. (2004). Is finding something good in the bad always good? Benefit finding among women with breast cancer. *Health Psychology, 23*, 16–23.

Trapnell, P. D., & Campbell, J. D. (1999). Private self-consciousness and the five-factor model of personality: Distinguishing rumination from reflection. *Journal of Personality and Social Psychology, 76*, 284–304.

Urcuyo, K. R., Boyers, A. E., Carver, C. S., & Antoni, M. H. (2005). Finding benefit in breast cancer: Relations with personality, coping, and concurrent well-being. *Psychology and Health, 20,* 175–192.

Wasserman, A. L., Thompson, E. I., Wilimas, J. A., & Fairclough, D. L. (1987). The psychological status of childhood/adolescent Hodgkin's disease. *American Journal of Diseases in Children, 141,* 626–631.

Watkins, E., & Teasdale, J. D. (2004). Adaptive and maladaptive self-focus in depression. *Journal of Affective Disorders, 82,* 1–8.

Watson, M., Greer, S., & Bliss, J. (1989). *Mental adjustment to cancer (MAC) scale: Users' manual.* Surrey, UK: CRC Psychological Medicine Research Group.

Watson, M., Greer, S., Young, J., Inayat, Q., Burgess, C., & Robertson, B. (1988). Development of a questionnaire measure of adjustment to cancer: The MAC scale. *Psychological Medicine, 18,* 203–219.

Weiss, T. (2002). Posttraumatic growth in women with breast cancer and their husbands: An intersubjective validation study. *Journal of Psychosocial Oncology, 20,* 65–80.

Weiss, T. (2004). Correlates of posttraumatic growth in married breast cancer survivors. *Journal of Social and Clinical Psychology, 23,* 733–746.

Widows, M. R., Jacobsen, P. B., Booth-Jones, M., & Fields, K. K. (2005). Predictors of posttraumatic growth following bone marrow transplantation for cancer. *Health Psychology, 24,* 266–273.

Wortman, C. B. (2004). Posttraumatic growth: Progress and problems. *Psychological Inquiry, 15,* 81–90.

Zautra, A. J., Affleck, G. G., Tennen, H., Reich, J. W., & Davis, M. C. (in press). Dynamic approaches to emotions and stress in everyday life: Bolger and Zuckerman reloaded with positive as well as negative affects. *Journal of Personality.*

9

Bereavement and Posttraumatic Growth

Hansjörg Znoj

Institut für Psychologie

Universität Bern

I have changed a lot since he died. For the first time I learned to accept help from others. . . . And I think that I became more open—as for myself I know better what I really want from life, what I am afraid of and also who I am. And I stay myself even in company with others. . . . And yes, I think I can really be proud of myself that I have managed everything so well. All these things have prevented me from going crazy: I had to be a mother for my children and I had to worry about all these financial things, otherwise we would be broke by now. . . . And sometimes I think of myself as a lucky person, being a single mother, even when everything has also a tragic aspect.

—Transcript, woman in her 30s, 14 months following the death of her spouse. Taken from the San Francisco Study on spousal bereavement

INTRODUCTION

Although the death of a close person is a devastating experience, sometimes people report a growing sense of themselves as becoming a better, more human, and more able persons. Only recently research has begun to systematically evaluate the positive aspects of the aftermath of trauma and only recently we have instruments to evaluate such personal growth (Park, Cohen, & Murch, 1997; Tedeschi & Calhoun, 1996). But even when people report positive changes, most people would—if they had the chance to change – choose a different course of things, especially when they had suffered human losses. Therefore, posttraumatic growth (PTG) will remain complicated, even "Janus" faced (Maercker & Zoellner, 2004), meaning that there are both adaptive and maladaptive aspects involved. In addition, it is unclear whether perceived PTG must be considered as a coping strategy or as a result of a coping process. There is an ongoing discussion whether PTG has to be evaluated as an outcome or a coping strategy (e.g., Schaefer & Moos, 1992; Wurf and Hazel, 1991). The mentioned instruments suggest that PTG can be measured as an outcome but it may more strongly be related to coping as in making meaning or in accepting what cannot be changed. It has been argued that PTG is the result of coming to terms with adverse or conflicting cognitions and emotions. A better understanding of this process is still necessary.

Calhoun and Tedeschi (1998) emphasize that by rethinking the event over and over (rumination) people manage to cope with the emotional impact and start having new perspectives. They even may develop a completely new frame of reference or world view incorporating the traumatic event and, therefore, become a more fully developed person. However, according to Linville (1987), these changes do not come cheap: For being capable to integrate nonnormative events, the self has to adapt to a more complex representation of the world and the "old" feeling of security may vanish forever. Linville reported that in the sequence of life-threatening crises, not only will people get stronger in the sense of a cognitively buffered self, they become more resistant to depression. On the other hand, their mood may become lower and more moderate (Janoff-Bulman, 1989). Linville explained this paradoxical effect through the mechanism of a lower self-esteem while representing a more complex world. A child represents the world in a simple way, but the sense of self is undisturbed and when a child wants something, it is not hampered by a self-consciousness of representing the world as one often frustrating one's needs. However, during the process of growing up, many frustrations have to be integrated, the needs have to be negotiated and, as a consequence, the sense of oneself becomes less narcissistic and more adapted to the environment's demands. On the other hand, there is evidence that people high in narcissism are more resistant to stress (Bonanno, 2004), although this might be only the case as long as the environment fits into the represented world. Those high in self-esteem would then be better protected from depression and they may be better able to rebuild their cognitive system without loosing a positive outlook. Taken together, the changes following the aftermath of a serious life-event suggest a nonlinearity of different possible outcomes that depend on many, up to now only rudimentarily understood variables.

EMOTION REGULATION

In focusing on emotion regulation, Znoj and coworkers (Znoj & Grawe, 2000; Znoj & Keller, 2002) found that bereaved parents and spouses reported better ability to cope with distressing emotions than controls. The effect was even more impressive considering that many bereaved parents and spouses still suffered from intense and often severely distressing emotions triggered by their grief. By excluding participants who showed high signs of distress, the effects were even stronger. Calhoun, Cann, Tedeschi, and McMillan (2000) have suggested that personal growth can be positively associated with symptoms. The ability to cope better with upsetting feelings may be directly related to the intensity of emotional feelings. The process of habituation offers a quite simple explanation. The pangs of various emotions, the often unbearable pain characterizing grief and the process of mourning may lead to a depression-like state where emotions are felt less. But it could also be the other way round: Toward a more tolerant and less controlling attitude for emotional states in general. As life with its daily chores and activities goes on, people might get used to their emotional states and could learn tolerating emotionally ambiguous situations better than without the experience of loss. We were not able to test this model specifically, but it is plausible and parsimonious. But the question remains: Is there more to PTG than just adaptation?

EMOTION REGULATION—THE PHYSIOLOGICAL ARGUMENT

Why should the experience of overwhelming emotions trigger a learning process? It is unclear as to how and where such learning occurs. Physiological data suggest that the prefrontal cortex might be of importance for handling and modulating emotional response. To integrate the massive emotional pangs following a loss, the cortical control for emotion regulation could be stimulated and the capacity for emotion regulation enhanced. The work of Le Doux (1996) shows that such processes may occur. The consequences of an enhanced emotion regulation could be manifold. Situations that formerly have been avoided lose their fearful impact. The emotional quality might be the same, but by considering the emotional impact of the loss the anxiety seems manageable.

In line with this explanation is the repeated finding that so-called sensation seekers (Zuckerman, 1978) cope better following traumatizing events. In an investigation on Israeli war veterans, Neria, Solomon, Ginzburg, and Dekel (2000) found that high-sensation seekers suffered from lower levels of war-related intrusion and avoidance tendencies and posttraumatic stress disorder (PTSD) symptoms than low-sensation seekers. In an earlier study, high-sensation seekers were found to be better adjusted following the stresses of captivity. Low-sensation seeking ex-prisoners of war reported more PTSD symptoms, more severe psychiatric symptomatology, and more intense intrusive and avoidance tendencies. They differed also on subjective assessment of suffering in prison, ways of coping with prison, and emotional states during captivity (Neria, Solomon, Ginzburg, & Ohry, 1996). These studies suggest that sensation seeking is an important stress-buffering personal resource. Although high sensation seekers may put themselves in danger more often through activities, such as mountain climbing, motorcycle riding and the like, this finding should not be dismissed as an artifact or a lack of fear response of these persons. The challenging situations these individuals have to conquer may increase their ability to cope not only with the situations, but also with the anxiety involved. Sensation seeking can, therefore, be seen as a risky emotion-regulation strategy to cope with adverse emotions.

Problems in Coping for the Bereaved

The experience of loss may shake or even shatter one's assumptions (Janoff-Bulman, 1992, see also this book); the loss may feel unjust and cruel. Grief has the potential to test one's limits and sometimes, the outcome of grief can be devastating (e.g., Horowitz, Siegel, Holen, & Bonanno, 1997; Jacobs, 1999; Raphael, 1983). To come to terms with the emotions triggered by the loss is challenging. All kind of experiences and coping efforts are asked for. Sometimes, unhealthy behaviors become prominent, as the statement of one widower in the San Francisco bereavement study exemplifies: "I used to live in the future. No more of that. So that's one of the first things I did was drink all those Merlots and everything. I figured they'd aged long enough." As Aldwin, Sutton, and Lachman (1996) stated in their deviation-amplification model, the coping repertoire and coping resources following a critical life event are used more often. Depending on the quality of the repertoire, resources can be depleted and, therefore, the vulnerability for psychological problems is enhanced; more coping efforts, however, may lead to more experiences of self-efficacy (Bandura, 1977) and better self-esteem. I would like to argue that sometimes help from others has the paradoxical effect of hampering the process of personal growth. In our own investigation of bereaved parents we found some evidence that indeed this may be the case. Bereaved parents who indicated that their friends and relatives have retreated from them scored higher on the stress-related growth scale (Plaschy, 1999). However, this finding must be contrasted with the significant association between PTG and having new friends. Help from others might only hinder the personal development following the death of one's child, when supporting persons are sometimes blind to the special needs that bereaved parents have.

THE EXPERIENCES OF THE BEREAVED

Let us turn to the various positive (or negative) effects the experience of loss can have on the self. The claims of statements concerning PTG are impressive and can be apparent in various areas of permanent change. However, the changes can also take a negative turn. The following taxonomy was developed in San Francisco together with Nigel Field (Znoj & Field, 1996) in an attempt to develop an observer tool for PTG. As we were not only interested in positive changes, we looked for indicators of change following the experience of loss of the life partner. We ended up with three categories: transformation, meaning, and manageability.

A first area of a changed outlook is the recognition of some kind of transformation. These changes in self are not be always consciously available, but they may occur in settings that can be observed. Significant change is reflected in statements regarding changes in values, goals, beliefs about self, and one's relation to others and the world. These changes may be positive or negative. They are reflected behaviorally in changes in work, social, or family life—such as changes in investment of time dedicated to these activities (e.g., spending more time with children), reordering of priorities (e.g., spending less time at work to have more free time with friends), or new commitments (e.g., beginning a new intimate relationship or shift in profession). The following statements illustrate such changes:

"Things have changed in the sense that my outlook on life has changed dramatically."

"I'm more tolerant of people, I'm more sympathetic toward the disadvantaged."

"In a more positive way I've become more independent, but my independence that has been developing for a long time and now I'm thrust into it that there's no one to rely on."

"I'm probably more concerned about the present and less about the future than I used to be."

"The biggest thing that I had learned through that whole experience from him being ill and dying is the fact that you can't really count on things."

"I always expected my wife to be there forever and now she's gone."

"I've become more bitter about life since the loss." item "I was in an unhappy relationship; I must say I feel better being single."

Successful adaptation to a stressful life events entails not only appraising it as something one is capable of enduring, but as an opportunity for psychological development. Meaning can be shown across different domains including affiliation/intimacy, achievement/competence, autonomy, and self-actualization.

Growth themes identified by Schaefer and Moos (1992) provide clues as to whether transformation is meaningful. Striving for meaning may encompass emergence of new meaning or the exercise of preexisting meaning systems for assimilating the loss, such as religious faith. It involves appraisal of the event in a way that upholds or promotes one's values, goals, and ideals. For example:

> "I got involved with very people-oriented things like public service which I felt more focused on in terms of enjoyment."

> "I tend to be more idealistic in terms of benefiting disadvantaged groups with my talents and experience."

> "I recognized that being able to receive people's love is also a gift to them and that you know it just deepens your relationship with people."

> "I'm more honest and open about who I am and trying to say more what I want and what I'm afraid of and who I am to people that I meet or people that I'm in a relationship with."

> "And probably in a lot of ways I have a stronger sense of what I really want and what I really need to happen in my life to be happy or to feel complete or fulfilled with what I am doing." item "I've developed a stronger liking for myself and don't have to try to be okay in someone else's eyes in order to feel good about myself."

Manageability addresses the extent to which the person experiences him or herself as able to successfully work through the loss. The event is seen as a challenge while fully recognizing the pain of the loss. Perceiving oneself as competent and as having the resources to confront the death and related problems are part of manageability. Also, being able to maintain a sense of self-esteem as opposed to avoiding reminders of the event and/or appraising him or herself as unable to cope would be included in manageability. For example:

> "And so if I want to be a decent human being I have to get about that and continue with my life. It is scary and I hope I can do it, but I feel I can because I have a positive attitude towards doing it."

> "Since deceased passed away it has been really hard but there hasn't been anything I couldn't handle."

> "Yesterday I had to appear in court over a situation that had developed in my store. I wouldn't have done that a year and a half ago. Deceased would have taken care of it but I did alright and I'll come out okay."

> "I've had to be both a father and a mother to my children since my spouse died and I think my children are doing well."

Other authors have stated different approaches to personal growth. Tedeschi and Calhoun (1996) formulated three main categories: changes in self-perception, changes in interpersonal relationships, and a changed philosophy of life. The preceding reports, however, were found repeatedly in statements of bereaved persons. In terms of adaptivity, it is not always clear whether the changed outlook will enhance health or long-term survival. Sometimes, the change in perspective takes even a negative turn, such as in the saying:" I've become more bitter about life since the loss." Clearly, we would not label this statement as a sign of personal growth. Other accounts refer to the capacity to overcome serious life events. It is a capacity that people have not been aware of until after the blow. The capacity has obviously existed already; the growing recognition of this capacity could have the psychological effect to feel more complete as a person, to experience a more complex self. In fact, it will be difficult to distinguish resilience—the capacity to withstand challenging life events—from this aspect of personal growth.

RESILIENCE AND PERSONAL GROWTH

To grow, something must be either incomplete or damaged. It may be important to realize that personal growth and resilience are not the same. Following Dienstbier (1989), Meichenbaum (1985), and others, physical and psychological toughness is gained by adverse experiences. However, stress inoculation only works when there is enough capacity to cope with stressors. Coping can be trained and there is mounting evidence that specific training enhances the capacity to cope with various stressors, such as test anxiety, performance anxiety, or social phobia (Meichenbaum & Deffenbacher, 1988). It is debateable whether such an effect may occur without counseling. Life events are still today seen as unfavorable to psychological in addition to physical health. The current report of the Surgeon General on mental health states: "Stressful life events, even for those at the peak of mental health, erode quality of life and place people at risk for symptoms and signs of mental disorders." In fact, life events are seen as strong predictors of ill-being, labeled in terms such as *vulnerability-stress-model* where adverse life events trigger a hidden proneness for physical and mental disease (e.g., Holmes & Rahe, 1967; Lazarus & Folkman, 1984). Even in the mounting literature on personal growth it is clear that adverse life events produce vulnerability. In fact, personal growth is positively associated with indicators of stress, such as intrusions or hypervigilance and other psychological symptoms (Calhoun, Carr, Tedeschi, & McMillan, 2000; Maercker & Schützwohl, 1998; Park et al., 1997). The term *vulnerability* contradicts *resistance*: One would expect that resilient people are not affected by life events. In fact, this seems to be the case. Bonanno (2004) argues that resilient people are not affected following interpersonal loss or potential traumatic events. He further argues that resilient people maintain a stable (emotional) equilibrium and maintain a healthy level of psychological and physical functioning. He even goes one step further and claims that most people are in fact resilient to loss and trauma. And he might be right in stating that most people do in fact cope perfectly well with human losses of all kind. Meta-analytical studies on intervention for bereavement show little to no effect (Allumbaugh & Hoyt, 1999). On the contrary, psychological interventions may even harm an ongoing self-healing process at least for people in a normal bereavement. Additional data come from early interventions studies on trauma, such as debriefing (Mayou, Ehlers, & Hobbs, 2000). Although, in most cases, life events are adequately coped with, a minority of people are not resilient and may severely be affected by the loss or trauma. Here, I want to focus on an even more vexing finding: That many people are indeed traumatized, do indeed suffer from psychological problems, and still report that in many ways they have profited from the blow they had to suffer. What leads to PTG may be the need or necessity to change in some respect or transform as a human being. James (1936), in his important remarks on religious experiences states that crises are predictors of such personal transformations. In James' view, religious experience can be regarded as a cognitive schema or a state of mind. This schema works like a mysterious filter that turns bad into good or evil into blessings. It may evolve following extreme life events. He writes:

> In this state of mind, what we most dreaded has become the habitation of our safety, and the hour of our moral death has turned into our spiritual birthday. The time for tension in our soul is over, and that of happy relaxation, of calm deep breathing, of an eternal present, with

no discordant future to be anxious about, has arrived. Fear is not held in abeyance as it is by mere morality, it is positively expunged and washed away. (W. James, lecture 2, 1902)

Spirituality has the power to overcome insurmountable obstacles that a more critical mind and "down to earth" stance would recognize as too gigantic a task. Human history is full of examples where heroes and saints overcome single-handedly formidable enemies. For instance, the famous Joan d'Arc was reported to win an already lost battle against the British emperor. I don't want to go into too much detail—it is hard to tell facts from myths in theses cases. The important point here is that spiritual power—in more psychological terms the belief in supernatural powers—overcomes the most disturbing realities.

Following the death of a beloved child, many parents see themselves as mutilated and severely harmed. Still, they do not suffer for themselves, but see a promising life cut short. In many cases, spirituality may help to locate the dead child in heaven although grief remains. Obviously, should growth be experienced it must be different from the growth reported following severe bodily damage, such as spinal cord injury. Growth following bereavement—especially parental bereavement—is probably different both in process and outcome.

PERSONAL GROWTH MAY BE ILLUSORY

The benefice of positive illusions has been demonstrated by many investigators, but most prominently by Taylor and coworkers (e.g., Taylor & Brown, 1988). They showed that most healthy individuals lean toward the bright side of life. Most people are biased in their own judgments in favor of themselves, they perceive themselves as better lovers, car drivers, or healthier than average, in fact, most healthy adults are positively biased in their self-perceptions. Unrealistic optimism seems to be a good predictor of health: Following Scheier und Carver (1985), unrealistic optimism makes people feel better, it is associated with positive relationships and higher motivation. In addition, unrealistic optimism is associated with successful coping and better recovery from health-related stressors (Scheier et al., 1989). However, this perspective has gained widespread criticism (e.g., Colvin & Block 1994). Do positive illusions foster mental health? An examination of the Taylor and Brown (1988) formulation suggests that positive illusions are only beneficial when there is enough realism left enabling the individual to adapt to a specific environment. This truism may help to investigate personal growth more realistically. What we should not expect is that people who report personal growth are completely well and psychologically healthy. Znoj (1999) proposed a model of PTG where reported personal growth was dependent on psychological impact: Following this model, personal growth is both a coping strategy and an outcome following a major life event. It is related to symptoms, because following a life event, usually people get distressed and more symptomatic. But it is a nonlinear relation. Highly distressed participants should experience a low level of personal growth, and people who had experienced high distress following the event, but do not continue to do so, should report high levels of personal growth. On the other hand, people who had experienced a major life event without suffering from symptoms should report no stress-related growth. This was the case with spinal cord injured persons and, to a lower degree, also with bereaved parents. A cluster analysis with the bereaved parents of the Bern study on parental bereavement (Znoj & Keller, 2002) confirmed the earlier reported findings with spinal cord injured patients. Table 1.1 summarizes the results. The data show that the participants of the high depression group (the cluster center in this group was 21 on the Beck Depression Inventory [BDI]) did not report personal growth. But

TABLE 9.1

Three-cluster solution of depression and PTG. The three groups show a curvilinear relationship
of PTG in relation to level of depression

Cluster Centers (z-Values)	Cluster 1 High Symptom Level, Low Personal Growth	Cluster 2 Moderately Low Symptom Level, High Personal Growth	Cluster 3 Low Symptom Level, Low Personal Growth
Depression	1.82	−0.23	−0.36
Personal Growth	−0.45	0.85	−0.87
N	23	80	67

Note.   Total $N = 170$ (missing $= 6$).

low symptoms are not indicative of PTG either. There are obviously many nondepressed
parents who do not claim such a personal development. This finding is in line with the
resilience hypothesis (Bonanno, 2004). Persons who were not affected by the loss to a
"pathological" degree may continue life without further changes, even when they are badly
hurt. But what predicts personal growth in bereaved parents? A systematic approach using
hierarchical regression analysis revealed that the affective quality in the remaining family,
being able to find new friends, a rather strong sense of coherence, especially being able to
find meaning in adverse situations and stress related intrusions were predictors of personal
growth. Together, these variables explained 20% of the variance of PTG measured with
the Stress-Related Personal Growth scale (SRGS) (Park et al., 1997) in the mentioned
Bernese study of bereavement.

THE POWER OF ILLUSIONS

Illusions can be extremely powerful and they can be extremely dangerous. Joan of Arc was
burnt to death when she was 19 years old, condemned as a "relapsed heretic." People who
believed their own reality more than the realities of society always lived in danger. At the
same time, society needed them; in ancient history we hear from the Delphic Oracle where
for more than 1,000 years emperors and peasants alike asked for advice from people who
were in trance-like states. Many healers and magicians used drugs, narcotics, or extreme
sleeping or eating habits to force themselves into these trance-like states were they looked
for a higher, less materialistic reality. It is hard to tell whether a healing ceremony just let
the self-healing occur or whether the spirituality was the healing power.

There are enough empirical findings to suggest that turning to religion may enhance
health (e.g., Koenig, 1998). For Frankl (1997), a survivor of the Holocaust, finding meaning
is the ultimate challenge in life. In his words, meaning is experiencing by responding to the
demands of the situation at hand, discovering and committing oneself to one's own unique
task in life, and by allowing oneself to experience or trust in an ultimate meaning—which
one may or may not call God.

A religious belief may help to order life, but it may also hinder new experiences and
challenges and that respect may even become maladaptive. Without doubt, the comfort of
religion can be the discomfort of the out-group and nonbelievers, especially in fundamental
societies. The powers of the mind, however, are not limited to the religious or spiritual
experience. In a recent review, Rey (2004) gives many examples how the mind operates on
the physical chemistry of our bodies (see also Kiecolt-Glaser & Glaser, 1987). Being able
to turn the mind into a self-enhancing, more hopeful state of mind wherein we experience

more control (or self-efficacy) in our lives, we should stay healthier and psychologically stronger. Of course, other variables may be necessary to make this change of state of mind happen—for instance social support would be very important, not only because of the instrumental help of others, but because we as "social animals" need the emotional support and the social reinforcement to not feel depressed (see also Lewinsohn, 1974). As Lazarus stated: "It is not the situation we fear but the appraisal we make out of the situation" (Lazarus, 1991). The state of mind is a powerful "shaper" of our environment. Depending on it, we perceive others and ourselves and act toward others according to our state of mind (Horowitz, 1987). Psychologically, PTG can be regarded to be a stable state of mind, transforming disturbing past events into a milder light of hope. In Lewins' (1935) words, we perceive the world as a field of forces: In a state of hunger, possible foods and food occasions come into attention. The world is a continuing construct of our experiences, needs, and the encounter with the environments' demands. When in need for meaning, after the impact of a devastating event, we might—as a coping strategy—perceive the world (its parts and contingencies) in being meaningful or not. As the warrior in Lewins' (1917) "Kriegslandschaften" (landscapes of war) we might perceive more clearly what makes sense in terms of survival and what does not. To satisfy the desperate need to construct a beneficial world we even might go so far as to construct our world into one that consists of meaningful events, even when—objectively seen—this is not the case.

Personal growth could be the expression of the necessity to adapt to a hard to integrate experience. Posttraumatic growth must not necessarily be adaptive in the sense of an optimal fit into a sociobiological environment and PTG must not necessarily be adaptive in terms of well-being or emotional stability.

RUMINATION, PSYCHOLOGICAL HEALTH, AND PERSONAL GROWTH

In the Bernese study, having low symptoms and experiencing low PTG predicted the lowest level of stress-related intrusions, the difference was highly significant against the high symptomatic group ($p < .001$, multiple comparisons, Bonferroni corrected). The high PTG group reported lower levels of stress-related intrusions than the high symptom group ($p < .001$) but there was a trend to have more intrusions than the low symptoms, low PTG group ($p < .10$). The finding is in line with the Calhoun and Tedeschi (1998) theory that rumination in the sense of rethinking and building a new frame of reference is a necessary condition for PTG. On the basis of these findings one may conclude that PTG is not necessarily a good predictor of health and well-being. Indeed, correlations with health indicators, such as depressive mood, did not reveal any statistically significant relationship for the bereaved parents. This brings us to the next question: What (if any) function has the experience of personal growth for the human being? Several allusions put PTG close to religious or spiritual experience. Our cognitive abilities not only enhance our sense of orientation, but it may give us a "virtual" life as in imagination. We may live a fantastic life outside of our daily routines. Many people use the fantasies of others, such as in romantic stories, to escape from daily routine; others daydream instead of actually doing something in the real world. The power of spirituality may not be the same as escapist fantasies—it may even enhance ourselves to manage challenges that otherwise would remain beyond possibilities. The example of Joan of Arc—a then 13-year-old girl with religious visions—was clearly not foreseen by any military and realistic forces and yet, she managed to convince people to stand up against a massive enemy—the British troupes that had invaded France in a cruel civil war. And, the French won this battle with Joan and were able to regain their homeland.

EMPIRICAL INVESTIGATIONS

A Model of Personal Growth Following the Death of a Child

There are several important questions concerning the relationship between PTG, the experience of grief symptoms, social support, and resiliency or a capacity to cope with the complex situation. The introductory remarks highlighted the difficulties involved. Structural equation modeling allows us to "test" even complex hypotheses and, by alternating different models, fit indices may help to decide which model fits the empirical data best. Here, I will present two alternative models—the first developed by Hogan and Schmidt (2002), the other resulted from the theoretical reflections that PTG is not directly related to psychological symptoms, but positively related to personal resources (and social support). Additionally we tested the resilience model, leaving PTG out of the equation. The resilience to personal growth model not only has resilience as a necessary additional variable, but differs from the Hogan and Schmidt (2002) model in the direction of some of the paths, indicating a different cause of influence. Figures 9.1 and 9.2 illustrate the similarities and differences of the two PTG models.

Hogan und Schmidt (2002) postulated a model of growth in bereavement, where grief symptoms were predictors of posttraumatic stress symptoms (intrusion and avoidance)—the stress response syndrome axis. The second important path involves social support being modulated by avoidance. Both social support and grief predicted PTG. Hogan and Schmidt (2002) operationalized symptoms of grief with feelings of despair and detachment. In their model, the experience of grief related negatively and social support related positively to PTG.

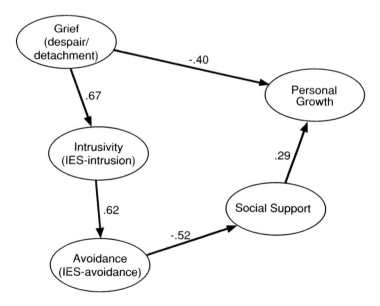

FIGURE 9.1. Grief in the Hogan and Schmidt (2002) model of "grief to personal growth model" includes two main components: (a) the "stress syndrome axis" with intrusion and avoidance being the consequences of grief symptoms and (b) the "resolved grief axis" where social support plays a major role. In the figure, the numbers represent the standardized weights as given in the original report. Grief to Personal Growth Model (Hogan & Schmidt, 2002).

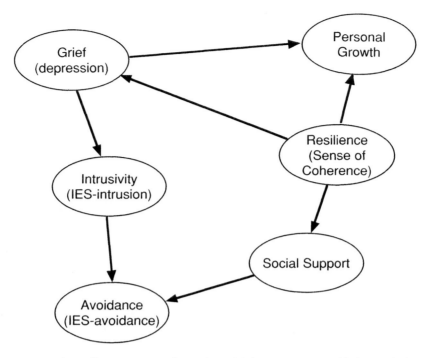

FIGURE 9.2.   In the resilience to personal growth model the important variable for psychological growth is resilience. In contrast to the Hogan and Schmidt (2002) model, the paths from and to social support and grief have inverted directions. Resilience to Personal Growth Model (Znoj, Kruit, & Wüthrich, 2004).

The authors concluded that their finding contradicted the traditional grief theory position where grief work is the antidote to grief and, hence, resolving grief is necessary "returning to normal." The main argument for their position was that "returning to normal" is impossible following the death of a child. Instead, people have to go beyond their former state of being and turn grief into personal growth. This "Grief to Personal Growth Model" contradicts the traditional views of grief in a highly important perspective, namely that a return to the "former self" is not possible. It does not, however, contradict the pain of grief, and it does not contradict the necessity to detach oneself of the deceived person. The process of detachment often leads also to detachment of intimate others, to interpersonal and personal crises. Grief, therefore, will not be "resolved," but transformed. The shattered personal life provides the opportunity to make a transition toward personal growth. Empirically, two pathways have been found: the first represented a direct, but inverse relationship between grief symptoms and personal growth. It was concluded by the authors that this inverse relationship—because this was a cross-sectional design—signified that grief and personal growth does not exist simultaneously. The second pathway leads from grief symptoms to intrusive thoughts and feelings and consequently to avoidance of reminders (Horowitz, 1976). A negative pathway leads to social support, indicating that people in an avoidant state of mind rejected emotional in addition to instrumental support from others. For supporting friends or family the bereaved are a challenge to support because of the avoidant, even hostile manner they are acting toward others. One may conclude that complicate grief may be a grief "stuck" in the process of intrusion and avoidance, as suggested by the stress response syndrome theory (Horowitz, 1976). A positive relation was found between social support and personal growth, indicating that social support is an important variable for personal growth, perhaps especially so for people in distress.

As this proposed Hogan and Schmidt model also fits into a recent theory of coping with bereavement (Stroebe & Schut, 1999), we used this approach to test the proposed pathways with the data of the Bern study of parental bereavement. In fact, the Hogan and Schmidt (2002) study resembled in many ways the Bernese study: Participants were parents who lost a child. In contrast to the Bernese study, the children were (a) mainly male gender and (b) were young adolescents whose cause of death was mainly accidental. A further difference was that the parents in the Hogan and Schmidt (2002) study reported having no notice that their child would die. Mean time since death was comparable (about 4 years).

Method

The complete data of $N = 169$ bereaved parents (male 55, female 114), mean age was 42 years, time since child loss averaged 5 years and mean age of the dead child was around 3 years (0 to 48 years). The cause of death varied, 47% died either from chronic or acute disease; accident (15%) and suicide (14%); newborn or early deliverance (17%); and sudden infant death (7%) were the other causes. As measures we used symptom scales, a measure of social support, the sense of coherence as a measure of resilience, and stress-related growth. The BDI was developed by Beck (1978). We used a German translation (Hautzinger, 1995). The IES (Horowitz, Wilner & Alvarez, 1979) was used in its revised German translation (Maercker & Schützwohl, 1998); social support was measured with singular questions about persons who helped to cope with the event and developed by the author. The Sense of Coherence (Antonovsky, 1987; Noack, Bachmann, Oliveri, Kopp, & Udris, 1993), and a German translation of the SRGS (Park et al., 1997) were given to the participants and in this study served as the database for our modeling approach.

Results

In a first step, we tried to fit our data into the original Hogan and Schmidt (2002) model. Unfortunately, the fit indices showed only poor values (comparative fit index [CFI] was .75, root mean square error of approximation [RMSEA] = .11), indicating that the model did not fit the data of the bereaved parents of the Bernese study well. Although many characteristics of the two studies were similar or differed only slightly—in the Miami sample most respondents were female and reported the loss of a son—it could be that the different measures used in the two studies also may have caused the misfit. One reason might be that PTG as defined by Hogan, Greenfield, and Schmidt (2001) was more clearly related to the experience of grief because it was developed as one instrument. We used the Park et al. (1997) questionnaire, which is a stand-alone instrument directed to measure a universal feeling of personal growth.

In our model (Znoj et al., 2004), PTG is mediated by resiliency and a global sense of coherence. Following Antonovsky (1979) a sense of coherence (SOC) is a global coping capacity acquired within the first 30 years of life. The sense of coherence is shaped by experience and grounded in the overall belief that life is meaningful, comprehensible, and manageable. We used the SOC as the source variable for PTG, assuming that PTG is the consequence of a well-built capacity to cope with adverse life events. The "resilience to PTG model" clearly is different from the "grief to PTG model." Here, resiliency—the capacity to cope with serious life events—not only influences personal growth, but moderates grief symptoms and social support.

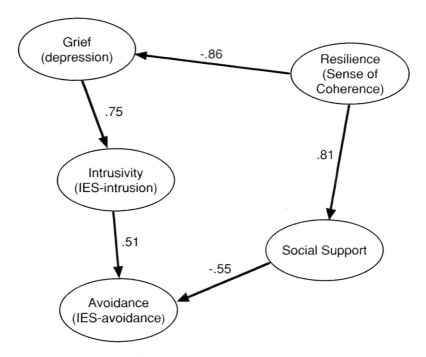

FIGURE 9.3.   The final model of the bereavement process fitted to the data of the Bernese study on parental bereavement. The numbers indicate the standardized weights. For simplification, the observed variables are left out. The fit indices are CFI = .934 and RMSEA = .067, N = 169. Resource Model of Grief (Znoj et al., 2004).

In the Bern sample, the "resilience to PTG model" showed acceptable fit indices (CFI = .87, RMSEA = .08). In contrast to the Hogan and Schmidt model, PTG was practically independent from grief-related symptoms. The only path leading to PTG came from personal resources as measured with the sense of coherence. However, the weight of the path from personal resources to PTG was relatively small (standardized β = .17). Personal resources were highly related to social support, and social support was, as in the Hogan and Schmidt model, inversely related to avoidance. Thus, the stress response syndrome model was replicated, but we were not able to replicate Hogan and Schmidt's (2002) "grief to PTG theory." Interestingly, when PTG was left out as an outcome, the fit indices got better. Figure 9.3 depicts the final model with its relative β-weights on the paths between the latent variables. This model had good fit indices (CFI = .93, RMSEA = .07) and could be labeled as "resource model of grief."

Discussion of the Replication

Considering the discussion of PTG being a necessary construction, similar to Taylor and Brown's concept of positive illusions (1988), I do not want to dismiss the concept at all. In the Bernese study, the participants might have had difficulties distinguishing between a global sense of coherence and the current state of having experienced PTG. Still, the direction of the path was clearly the inverse of the Hogan and Schmidt (2002) model, indicating that resilience or the capacity to cope with adverse life events influenced the grief reaction and not vice-versa.

In the next section of this chapter I want to discuss predictors of PTG using a different study on parental stress and bereavement. Here, the focus is on coping, especially emotion regulation.

PERSONAL GROWTH—THE RESULT OF ADAPTIVE COPING WITH EMOTIONS

In a recent, still unpublished study I, together with Patricia Lannen and Diana Zwahlen, investigated parents whose children had been in intensive hospital care because of cancer. Unfortunately, not all children survive such a treatment. Medical treatment for children with cancer is highly aggressive and all parents suffer, starting from diagnosis through various stages of healing and falling back to the hopeful end of treatment. As we were mainly interested in the coping process and how we could possibly help these parents cope better with the whole process, we used measures of coping in addition to measures of distress to investigate factors that might be malleable with professional help. Here, I will present the results with the Tedeschi and Calhoun (1996) Posttraumatic Growth Inventory (PTGI).

Method

We used a natural experimental design with parents whose children suffered from cancer and had to undergo severe medical treatment. $N = 125$ completed the battery of standardized questionnaires and open questions, 45% were male, 55% female parents. Twenty-five parents experienced the death of their child; thus 80% of the parents experienced the distress of having a child diagnosed with cancer and its medical and social consequences, but in the end were lucky their child had survived the illness. In terms of gender distribution and other demographic variables there was no difference between the two groups. Mean age was 42.7 years, the male participants being somewhat older than the female participants reflecting the marriage pattern in Switzerland. Mean time since the death of the child was 3.5 years in the bereaved group, time since diagnosis averaged 7.6 years for the bereaved group and 4 years for the group with the surviving children. Response rate was higher for parents whose child survived the treatment (39% vs. 21%). The given reason for not completing the questionnaires was mostly the fear of stirring up negative feelings, keeping feelings private, or, in some cases, the sense that our questions did not match the feelings and experiences of the participants. As standardized instruments we used measures of distress (SCL-90R, Derogatis, 1977), emotion regulation (Znoj & Keller, 2002), coping (COPE, Carver, Scheier, & Weintraub, 1989), resilience (SOC, Antonovsky, 1987), and PTGI (Tedeschi & Calhoun, 1996).

Results for posttraumatic growth

The best predictors for PTG were adaptive emotion regulation, spiritual coping, and denial. In sum, 25% of the variance could be explained by these variables. Denial as a coping strategy related positively to PTG ($\beta = .07$, $p < .05$). As in the Znoj & Keller (2002) study, the parents reported higher levels of adaptive emotion regulation than the general population ($t = 5.11$, $p < .01$) and lower levels of maladaptive emotion regulation (avoidance $t = -4.99$, $p < .01$; distortion $t = -5.61$, $p < .01$). There was no difference between the parents whose child survived the treatment versus the bereaved group on PTG in any of the subscales or the total score. However, the bereaved parents had higher levels of symptoms, especially depression on the symptom checklist ($z = -2.86$, $p < .05$). Additionally, the parents with the surviving children had higher levels of acceptance and

TABLE 9.2

Product–Moment Correlations Between Personal Growth and the Three Subscales of the SOC
(in the bereaved sample the correlations were more pronounced)

Personal Growth	Meaningfulness r	Comprehensibility r	Manageability r
Bereaved parents ($N = 25$)	.42*	.27	.12
Parents whose children survived ($N = 100$)	.24*	.04	−.06

Note. $N = 125$; the group difference between the correlations was calculated using a z-transformation.
* = $p < .05$.

active coping, experienced more hope, had higher levels of religious coping, and generally
had a more positive stance toward life (all significant in the 5% probability range). When
looking at the two groups separately, we found the cohesion between PTG and the sense
of coherence, our measure for resilience, being significantly higher in the bereaved group.
Table 9.2 gives the exact results.

There was also a significant difference between psychological symptoms and the SOC
in the two groups: Parents whose children survived did not indicate any cohesion between
the two measures ($r = −.15$, $p > .10$). In the bereaved sample, the correlation between
symptoms and SOC was $r = −.62$, $p < .01$. The same pattern was repeated with coping
and emotion regulation, indicating some kind of interaction between the two groups: PTG
and coping.

Interaction effects

Two-way multivariate analyses were performed to assess the mentioned interaction effect
between group affiliation, level of PTG (total score, dichotomized), and three variables
of coping, namely maladaptive emotion regulation, venting of emotion, and acceptance.
We used emotion-focused coping because of the results from earlier studies indicating
emotion regulation as being a key concept of the experience of PTG (Znoj & Grawe,
2000; Znoj & Keller, 2002). In the former studies we repeatedly found that people who
experienced disruptive life events reported better ability to cope with their own emotions
following this experience: They reported to react calmer and with more clarity in stressful
situations without much effort. When confronted with extreme challenges where there
is no possibility to change the situation, the emotional system may be overwhelmed and
psychological symptoms could be the result of it (e.g., Hayes, Wilson, Gifford, Follette,
& Strohsal, 1996; Kring & Bachorowsky, 1999; Van der Kolk et al., 1996). Adaptive ways
of emotion regulation could be a necessary, relatively immediate response to foster not
only psychological health, but even a sense of mastery and personal growth (Horowitz,
Znoj, & Stinson, 1996). In the presented study, the bereaved parents confronted this taxing
experience to a much higher degree than parents whose child survived. Bereaved parents
reported significant ($p < .01$) changes in their lives and organization (Lannen-Meier &
Zwahlen, 2004). We can take this as a further hint that these parents were more stressed
and had fewer alternatives to cope with, the importance of the emotion-focused coping
being more important than for the other group of parents.

For emotion regulation, this hypothesis could be confirmed only for maladaptive
ways of emotion regulation. For avoidance ($F(1,118) = 4.14$, $p < .05$) and for distortion ($F(1,118) = 7.06$, $p < .05$), there was a clear negative relationship with PTG in the

bereaved group. Parents who reported high scores in avoiding situations linked with negative emotions and distorted thoughts and perceptions to protect themselves from negative feelings had lower levels of PTG.

For venting of emotion, an often as maladaptive labeled coping strategy, the results were replicated ($F(1,118) = 4.92, p < .05$). Accepting showed an inversed relationship ($F(1,118) = 7.38, p < .05$), but again it was only the bereaved group where this coping strategy influenced PTG. Figure 9.4 depicts these interactions more clearly.

GENERAL DISCUSSION

In many ways, people who managed to cope with a devastating life event, experience themselves as being stronger psychologically, even when realizing the sad fact that their lives have turned into a more miserable state. Others, such as medical personal, notice these changes. In our investigations we asked nurses what they thought the important variables for PTG were. These people repeatedly told us that the letting go of parents helped them the most. To accept the illness and even the death are the necessary condition for such a development to occur. But they also mentioned the capacity to focus on new situations, a positive stance, a changed and more pronounced appreciation of life, and new communication patterns. The nurses and medical persons also mentioned "good" parents and very difficult ones. The difficult parents occupy a lot of resources—time and energy. These parents do not accept the situation as it is, they ask for too many services, and they direct their frustration toward those who desperately try to help. In addition, tensions between the parents often are "projected" toward others. The medical system may require passive and cooperative parents (Barbarin & Chesler, 1986), but the difficulties of the "bad" parents may be caused by their inability to cope emotionally with the fact that their child's life is endangered. Again, these observations stress the importance of an adaptive way of emotion regulation. Resilient parents seem to have fewer difficulties to find support from others, to cope with difficult states and feelings, and to find meaning in even desperate situations. Problematic interactional behavior may be an important cause that people do not get the help and support they need. In their research on resilient children, Radke-Yarrow and Sherman (1990) stated that children who survived in bad conditions had in many cases extraordinary capacities to connect to people and commit foreigners to help them in important domains.

Tedeschi and Calhoun (1995) quoted a man with a spinal cord injury, saying that the injury was the best thing to happen in his life. Obviously, this man had envisioned a life course leading into disaster; the accident seemed to stop this course and to give him a new chance. Sometimes, an interruption of the expected course of life is needed to come to terms with real important questions and "to wake up." But, and this is my main point, to achieve personal growth, the ground must have been laid before. The role of coping, especially with focus on emotions, cannot be overestimated in our discussion. To have personal resources, such as the ability to find support from others, to be open minded, to be forgiving and hopeful is important, even necessary conditions for PTG to occur. In our own investigations, we repeatedly found that PTG could not be predicted well. The explained variance being only in the range of 25%. Usually, in social sciences, assuming one has chosen the "right" predictor variables, the amount of explained variance is much higher. The possible nonlinearity of PTG could be better explained with a bifurcational model. The deviation-amplification model of Aldwin, Sutton, and Lachman (1996) illustrates this model in psychological terms. In three studies, the authors found evidence that individuals who were able to perceive advantages from the low points of life were more

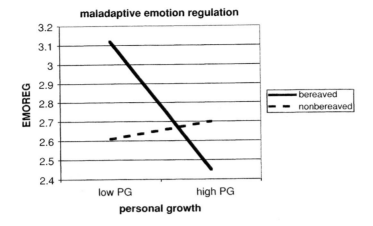

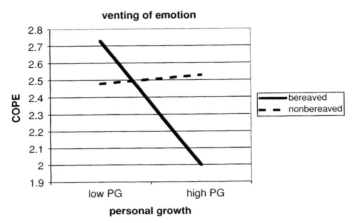

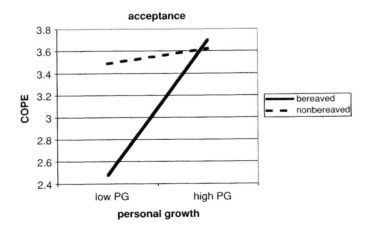

FIGURE 9.4.   This figure depicts the interaction effect between the two parent groups—the bereaved parents and the parents whose children survived. The dependent variable is psychological growth and the moderating variable is coping in three different perspectives. The first two perspectives involve maladaptive emotion-focused coping (avoidance and distortion in the EMOREG and venting of emotion in the COPE). The third perspective is acceptance. These coping strategies have a significant effect on psychological growth only for the bereaved parents.

likely to report long-term effects. They stressed the role of coping in saying that coping strategies differentially predicted positive or negative outcomes. Such a bifurcation or "spiraling" is typical for developmental processes (Carver & Scheier, 1998; Kegan, 1982; Waddington, 1974). In critical life events the sensitivities to react to circumstances are extremely elevated and—depending on resources and coping traits—a developmental process may occur. This process is triggered by inconsistencies in one's representation of the self and between the perceived world. Znoj and Grawe (2000) stated that such inconsistencies can provoke psychological symptoms. More adaptively, inconsistencies can be reduced through personal development. For a negative development, low initial levels of resources lead to further depletion as in Hobfoll's (1989) conservation of resources model. High levels of initial resources then may lead to gain further resources that increase resilience to future stress. In our reanalysis of the Bernese bereaved study, we found support for the resource model. In contrast to Hogan and Schmidt (2002), we were not able to find evidence that grief caused PTG in a direct way. Hogan and Schmidt (2002) stated that grief is not "resolved" to the former state of being, but necessarily must lead to a different state of being where the loss is integrated and changes accepted. Although I agree with this view, resolved grief must not be the same as PTG. Following Wortman and Cohen Silver (2001) it is a "myth" or wishful thinking that grief leads to complete restitution in well-being or the loss to a meaningful event. In the Hogan and Schmidt (2002) model, grief is negatively related to PTG, suggesting that for PTG to occur, grief must be resolved. The parents in the Bernese study, however, often stated that they still feel shaken, reported symptoms, and, at the same time, said that they have, in some almost unexplainable way, found that their lives have become more meaningful, that their outlook has changed, and that in many ways they take things differently. But, and this is my strongest point, these changes are not always adaptive. And there were other people who told us that they were not able to see anything good come out of their experience and felt bitter about the loss. But they reported no symptoms and had resolved their personal grief to a degree that they functioned well.

In our model, the role of resilience and coping is central for PTG. More importantly, our model allows PTG to be nonlinearly related to grief and symptoms of distress. As already said in the introduction, PTG may be illusionary to a certain degree. But these illusions are powerful and life enhancing. In our darkest times, the experience of personal growth may turn out as the beginning of a spiritual birthday that may, or may not, turn into a total different outlook of how we perceive the world.

REFERENCES

Aldwin, C. M., Sutton, K. J., & Lachman, M. (1996). The development of coping resources in adulthood. *Journal of Personality, 64*(4), 837–871.

Allumbaugh, D. L., & Hoyt, W. (1999). Effectiveness of grief therapy: A meta-analysis. *Journal of Counseling Psychology, 46*(3), 370–380.

Antonovsky, A. (1979). *Health, Stress, and Coping.* San Francisco: Jossey-Bass.

Antonovsky, A. (1987). *Unraveling the mystery of health.* San Francisco: Jossey-Bass.

Bandura, A. (1977). Self-efficacy: Toward a unifying theory of behavior change, *84*, 191–215.

Barbarin, O. A., & Chesler, M. (1986). The medical context of parental coping with childhood cancer. *American Journal of Community Psychology, 14*, 221–235.

Beck, A., T. (1978). *Depression inventory.* Philadelphia: Center for Cognitive Therapy.

Bonanno, G. A. (2004). Loss, trauma, and human resilience. Have we underestimated the human capacity to thrive after extremely aversive events? *American Psychologist, 59*(1), 20–28.

Calhoun, L. G., Cann, A., Tedeschi, R. G., & McMillan, J. (2000). A correlational test of the relationship between posttraumatic growth, religion, and cognitive processing. *Journal of Traumatic Stress, 13*(3), 521–527.

Calhoun, L. G., & Tedeschi, R. G. (1998). Posttraumatic growth: Future directions. In R. G. Tedeschi, C. L. Park, & L. G. Calhoun (Eds.), *Posttraumatic growth: Positive change in the aftermath of crisis.* Mahwah, NJ: Lawrence Erlbaum Associates.

Carver, C. S., & Scheier, M. F. (1998). *On the self-regulation of behavior.* Mahwah, NJ: Lawrence Erlbaum Associates.

Carver, C. S., Scheier, M. F., & Weintraub, J. K. (1989). Assessing coping strategies: A theoretically based approach. *Journal of Personality and Social Psychology, 56*(2), 267–283.

Colvin, C. R., & Block, J. (1994). Do positive illusions foster mental health? An examination of the Taylor and Brown formulation. *Psychological Bulletin, 116*(1), 3–20.

Derogatis, C. R. (1977). *SCL-90, Administration, Scoring, and Procedures. Manual 1 for the R(evised) version and other instruments of the Psychopathology Rating Scale Series.* Baltimore: John Hopkins University School of Medicine.

Dienstbier, R. A. (1989). Arousal and physiological toughness: Implications for mental and physical health. *Psychological Review, 96*(1), 84–100.

Frankl, V. E. (1972). *Der Wille zum Sinn (The will to find meaning).* Bern: Huber.

Ginzburg, K., Solomon, Z., Neria, Y., & Ohry, A. (1996, June). *Coping with war captivity: The role of sensation seeking.* Paper presented at the Second World Conference of the International Society for Traumatic Stress Studies, Jerusalem, Israel.

Hautzinger, M., Bailer, M., Worall, H., & Keller, F. (1995). *Beck-Depressions-Inventar (BDI) Handbuch* (2nd ed.). Bern: Hans Huber.

Hayes, S. C., Wilson, K. G., Gifford, E. V., Follette, V. M., & Strohsal, K. (1996). Experiential avoidance and behavioral disorders: A functional dimensional approach to diagnosis and treatment. *Journal of Consulting and Clinical Psychology, 64*(6), 1152–1168.

Hobfoll, S. E. (1989). Conservation of resources: A new attempt at conceptualizing stress. *The American Psychologist, 44*, 513–524.

Hogan, N. S., Greenfield, D. B., & Schmidt, L. A. (2001). Development and validation of the Hogan Grief Reaction Checklist. *Death Studies, 25*(1), 1–32.

Hogan, N. S., & Schmidt, L. A. (2002). Testing the grief to personal growth model using structural equation modeling. *Death Studies, 26*, 615–634.

Holmes, T. H., & Rahe, R. H. (1967). The social readjustment rating scale. *Journal of Psychosomatic Research, 11*, 213–218.

Horowitz, M. (1976). *Stress response syndromes.* New York: Jason Aronson.

Horowitz, M. J. (1987). *States of mind: Configurational analysis of individual psychology.* New York: Plenum.

Horowitz, M. J., Siegel, B., Holen, A., & Bonanno, G. A. (1997). Diagnostic criteria for complicated grief disorder. *American Journal of Psychiatry, 154*(7), 904–910.

Horowitz, M. J., Wilner, N., & Alvarez, W. (1979). Impact of event scale: A measure of subjective stress. *Psychosomatic Medicine, 41*, 209–218.

Horowitz, M. J., Znoj, H. J., & Stinson, C. H. (1996). Defensive Control Processes: Use of Theory in Research, Formulation, and Therapy of Stress Response Syndroms. In M. Zeidner & N. Endler (Eds.), *Handbook of Coping: Theory, Research, Applications.* New York: Wiley.

Jacobs, S. (1999). *Traumatic grief. Diagnosis, treatment, and prevention.* Philadelphia: London: Brunner/Mazel.

James, W. (1936). *The varieties of religious experience.* New York: Modern Library.

Janoff-Bulman, R. (1989). Assumptive worlds and the stress of traumatic events: Applications of the schema construct [Special issue]. Stress, coping, and social cognition. *Social Cognition, 7*(2), 113–136.

Janoff-Bulman, R. (1992). *Shattered assumptions: Towards a new psychology of trauma.* New York: Free Press.

Kegan, R. (1982). *The evolving self. Problem and process in human development.* Cambridge, MA: Harvard.

Kiecolt-Glaser, J. K., & Glaser, R. (1987). Psychosocial moderators of immune function. *Journal of Behavioral Medicine, 9*(2), 16–20.

Koenig, H. G. (Ed.). (1998). *Handbook of religion and mental health.* San Diego: Academic Press.

Kring, A. M., & Bachorowsky, J.-A. (1999). Emotions and psychopathology. *Cognition and Emotion, 13*(5), 575–599.

Lannen-Meier, P., & Zwahlen, D. (2004). *Psychologische Adaptation und Entwicklung persönlicher Reife von Eltern onkologisch erkrankter Kinder. [Psychological adaptation and development of parents with children with cancer].* Unpublished Lizentiat, University of Bern.

Lazarus, R. S. (1991). *Emotion and adaption.* New York: Oxford University Press.

Lazarus, R. S., & Folkman, S. (1984). *Stress, appraisal, and coping.* New York: Springer.

LeDoux, J. (1996). *The emotional brain.* New York: Simon and Schuster.

Lewin, K. (1917). Kriegslandschaft (landscapes of war). *Zeitschrift für angewandte Psychologie, 12,* 440–447.

Lewinsohn, P. H. (1974). A behavioral approach to depression. In R. J. Friedman & M. M. Katz (Eds.), *The psychology of depression: Contemporary theory and research.* Washington, DC: Winston Wiley.

Linville, P. W. (1987). Self-complexity as a cognitive buffer against stress-related illness and depression. *Journal of Personality and Social Psychology, 52*(4), 663–676.

Maercker, A., & Schützwohl, M. (1998). Erfassung von psychischen Belastungsfolgen: Die impact of event skala—revidierte version (IES-R). *Diagnostica, 44*(3), 130–141.

Maercker, A., & Zoellner, T. (2004). The Janus face of self-perceived growth: Toward a two-component model of posttraumatic growth. *Psychological Inquiry, 15*(1), 41–48.

Mayou, R. A., Ehlers, A., & Hobbs, M. (2000). Psychological debriefing for road traffic accident victims: Three-year follow-up of a randomised controlled trial. *British Journal of Psychiatry, 176,* 589–593.

Meichenbaum, D. (1985). *Stress Inoculation Training: A clinical guidebook.* New York: Pergamon Press.

Meichenbaum, D. H., & Deffenbacher, J. L. (1988). Stress inoculation training. *The Counseling Psychologist, 16,* 69–90.

Neria, Y., Solomon, Z., Ginzburg, K., & Dekel, R. (2000). Sensation seeking, wartime performance and long-term adjustment among Israeli war veterans. *Personality & Individual Differences, 29*(5), 921–932.

Neria, Y., Solomon, Z., Ginzburg, K., & Ohry, A. (1996). The experience of war captivity: The role of sensation-seeking. *Psychologia: Israel Journal of Psychology, 5*(2), 188–198.

Noack, H., Bachmann, N., Oliveri, M., Kopp, H. G., & Udris, I. (1993). Fragebogen zum Kohärenzgefühl (Sense of Coherence Questionnaire). Autorisierte Übersetzung auf der Grundlage von Übersetzungen von B. Strub, W. Fischer-Rosenthal, W. Weiss und J. Sigrist (1991). In R. Calmonte, Y. Nakamura, & H. Noack (Eds.), *Messinstrumente im Härz-As—Projekt: Gesundheitsinterview, Fragebogen und Gesundheitsindikatoren.* Bern: Institut für Sozial-und Präventivmedizin, Abteilung für Gesundheitsforschung.

Park, C. L., Cohen, L., H., & Murch, R., L. (1997). Assessment and prediction of stress-related growth. *Journal of Personality, 64(1),* 71–105.

Plaschy, A. (1999). *Sinnvolle Neuorientierung und persönliches Wachstum nach dem Verlust eines Kindes.* Unpublished Lizentiat, University of Bern.

Radke-Yarrow, M., & Sherman, T. (1990). Hard growing: Children who survive. In J. Rolf, A. S. Masten, et al. (Eds.), *Risk and protecitive factors in the development of psychopathology* (pp. 97–119). New York: Cambridge University Press.

Raphael, B. (1983). *The anatomy of bereavement.* New York: Basic Books.

Rey, O. (2004). How the mind hurts and heals the body. *American Psychologist, 59*(1), 29–40.

Schaefer, J. A., & Moos, R., H. (1992). Life crisis and personal growth. In B. N. Carpenter (Ed.), *Personal coping. Theory, research, and application* (pp. 149–170). Westport, CT: Praeger.

Scheier, M. F., & Carver, C. S. (1985). Optimism, Coping, and Health: Assessment and Implications of Generalized Outcome Expectancies. *Health Psychology, 4*(3), 219–247.

Scheier, M. F., Matthews, K. A., Owens, J., Magovern, G. J. S., Lefebvre, R. C., Abbott, R. A., et al. (1989). Dispositional optimism and recovery from coronary artery bypass surgery: The beneficial effects on physical and psychological well-being. *Journal of Personality and Social Psychology, 57,* 1024–1040.

Stroebe, M. S., & Schut, H. A. (1999). The dual process model of coping with bereavement: Rationale and description. *Death Studies, 23,* 197–224.

Taylor, S. E., & Brown, J. D. (1988). Illusion and well-being: A social psychological perspective on mental health. *Psychological Bulletin, 103*(2), 193–210.

Tedeschi, R. G., & Calhoun, L. G. (1995). *Trauma & transformation: Growing in the aftermath of suffering.* Thousand Oaks, CA: Sage.

Tedeschi, R. G., & Calhoun, L. G. (1996). The posttraumatic growth inventory: Measuring the positive legacy of trauma. *Journal of Posttraumatic Stress, 9*(3), 455–471.

Van der Kolk, B. A., Pelcovitz, D., Roth, S., Mandel, F. S., McFarlane, A., & Herman, J. L. (1996). Dissociation, somatization, and affect dysregulation: The complexity of adaptation to trauma. *American Journal of Psychiatry, 153*(7), 83–93.

Waddington, C. H. (1974). A catastrophe theory of evolution. *Annals of the New York Academy of Sciences, 231*, 32–42.

Wortman, C. B., & Cohen Silver, R. (2001). The myths of coping with loss revisited. In M. S. Strobe, R. O. Hannson, W. Stroebe, & H. Schut (Eds.), *Handbook of bereavemt research* (pp. 405–430). Washington, DC: American Psychological Association.

Wurf, E., & Hazel, M. (1991). Possible selves and the psychology of personal growth. In D. Ozer, J. M. Healy, & A. J. Stewart (Eds.), *Perspectives in Personality. Self and Emotion* (Vol. 3, pp. 39–62). London: Jessica Kingsley.

Znoj, H. J. (1999). Model of Growth: Transformation following loss and physical handicap (APA 107th Annual Convention, August 20–24). *ERIC Reports-Research, 143*, 1–15.

Znoj, H. J., & Field, N. (1996). *Observer rating for posttraumatic growth in bereavement.* Unpublished manuscript, University of California, San Francisco.

Znoj, H. J., & Grawe, K. (2000). The control of unwanted states and psychological health: Consistency safeguards. In A. Grob & P. Walter (Eds.), *Control of human behaviour, mental processes and awareness* (pp. 263–282). New York: Lawrence Erlbaum Associates.

Znoj, H. J., & Keller, D. (2002). Mourning parents: Considering safeguards and their relation to health. *Death Studies, 26*(7), 545–565.

Znoj, H. J., Kruit, & Wüthrich, C. (2004). *The resource model of grief. A structural equation modeling approach.*Unpublished manuscript, University of Bern.

Zuckerman, M. (1978). Sensation seeking. In H. London & J. E. Exner (Eds.), *Dimensions of personality* (pp. 487–560). New York: John Wiley.

10

POSTTRAUMATIC GROWTH AFTER WAR

RITA ROSNER

LUDWIG-MAXIMILIANS-UNIVERSITY, MUNICH

STEVE POWELL

*proMENTE ORGANISATION FOR PSYCHOLOGICAL RESEARCH
AND ACTION, SARAJEVO*

CASE VIGNETTE 1

Almir was 15 when the war started in Bosnia and Herzegovina. At first, like most people, he didn't believe it would last long. Then one day, enemy forces approached his town, burning houses and shooting civilians. He fled with most of the rest of his family and was quite lucky to arrive in Sarajevo unscathed, where they were able to live in a relative's apartment, albeit in very crowded conditions. By now, the city was besieged, food was short, and often there was no heating or power. Collecting water meant standing for hours in lines that were targeted by snipers positioned in the surrounding hills. Then he was drafted to fight in the army and defend the city. He often had to fight on the front line that went right through the city. Although he was not seriously wounded, he saw things that still recur in nightmares and that he never talks about, even to his closest friends.

By the end of the war in November 1995, he had lost quite a number of more distant relatives, but no one in his immediate family. The family home had been completely destroyed and they had lost virtually all their possessions. Nevertheless, he looks back on the war with a great deal of nostalgia and quietly thinks of it as the best time of his life. People had to learn to live from day to day and that made everything they did seem more meaningful. There were parties that went on all night where it seemed that there were no rules and everything was allowed. Sometimes he thinks that he had all those feelings just because he was a teenager, but as he has nothing to compare it with it is hard for him to be sure. He felt, and still feels, intensely close to his comrades in his unit and also to his family, even to aunts and uncles he hadn't liked before. Quite early on in the war, he was impressed by the strength that some of his friends gained from their faith and started to go to the mosque with his father for the first time in his life.

After the war, he worked for a Swedish humanitarian organization for a while, earned very good money, and made some friends among the international community in Sarajevo. Nevertheless, he believes that he has been through things that none of them can understand and from which he has learned many important lessons. That knowledge helps him cope with the frustration of living in a very poor and divided country on the edge of Europe, which sometimes feels almost like a prison. Although he still has occasional nightmares and his heart seems to stop whenever there is an unexpected loud noise, he has learned to live with these things and they seem to him much less important than the different ways he feels that he has benefited.

Every now and then, he meets someone he got to know very well in the war but has not seen for a while. Then it is sometimes very difficult to know what to say. It seems too much effort to get back into that feeling of belonging together, and often they just go their separate ways without talking at all.

Almir's story is quite common, but many others, especially older people and those who were seriously injured or lost close family members, remember primarily pain when they think back to the war. However, even many of these people will mention at least some aspects in which they feel they changed for the better due to the war.

CASE VIGNETTE 2

Nermin was persuaded to come to our treatment center by his employer and wife. The employer, although a good friend, threatens to dismiss him if he doesn't do something about his problem. His wife, whom he loves very much, told him that she really feels that she has come to the end of her tether with him. She does not feel that they can live together any more. Nermin's "problem" is that he gets excessively angry without any reason or warning. He yells at people and gets verbally abusive. Every once in a while he gets into fights, but up until now, he has somehow avoided getting into trouble with the police. But the problem is getting worse and as he is a big, powerfully built man, people around him easily get frightened and start to avoid him. Asked how he feels about his problem he describes feeling keyed up and tense almost all the time. He has frequent nightmares and sleeps only a few hours a night. He feels as if he is going to explode at any time. Triggers for an angry outburst wait for him around every corner. A funny look or a certain tone of voice, just about anything can set him off. Further exploration of his symptoms reveals that besides a very high arousal level, Nermin suffers from intense intrusive symptoms. Although he makes efforts to avoid situations that remind him of his past, this seems like a hopeless task: almost everything from high buildings to news about former Yugoslavia can elicit intrusive symptoms. A quantitative questionnaire-based assessment reveals that Nermin has very high scores on the Posttraumatic Diagnostic Scale (PTDS) and scores more than two standard deviations above average on almost all SCL-90 R subscales; and at the same time has a very high score on the Posttraumatic Growth (PTG) Scale.

Nermin had worked as a private bodyguard before the war and so, as there was a shortage of men with any kind of military training when the war broke out, he was quickly enlisted and remained in the army for almost the whole of the war, spending most of it on the front line. Only about 10% of his original unit were alive at the end of the war. Nermin remembers many terrible events. Those that recur most frequently in his intrusions are those during which he felt without hope of surviving the situation. At the beginning of the war he coped by picturing himself talking with his father after it was all over. He imagined that they would have long conversations and cry about all the terrible things that happened during their lives, and that afterward he would feel consoled, safe, and complete again. Yet after the second year of the war he came to believe that the events he had participated in and witnessed were too terrible even to share with his uncle in fact, too terrible to talk about at all. Yet the fighting went on and Nermin felt more and more like a machine. Shortly before the end of the war he was severely wounded. Luckily he was given a place on one of the flights of an international rescue organization and was flown out to Norway. When he woke up he found himself in a peaceful hospital ward far away from the war. Yet his first thoughts were to get better and to return to the fighting as soon as possible. On his first day out of the hospital, using his crutches, he walked to a nearby café. While he was sitting there a wedding procession went by. The people were noisy and seemed to be very happy. At that moment he realized that he has a choice and that he didn't need to go back to war. The future seemed to get all at once a bit brighter and he decided to start a new life in the here and now. During his convalescence the war in Bosnia and Herzegovina ended, and his guilt feelings about being in a safe place while friends and family were still in danger resided. He fell in love, got married, and found his first truly civilian job. He now feels as if every day is a special present for him and values every single moment in his new life with his wife with whom he feels deeply connected. Although symptoms of intrusion and arousal are present all the time he feels confident that they will become less intense over time. Yet although the positive feelings do not diminish, his arousal level seems to be getting worse. After getting into a fight with someone at work about what he perceived to be a spiteful putdown, he lost his job. His family starts to worry about him. Although he found another job, and continues to feel very much connected with his new surroundings, his problems overall seem to be getting worse.

INTRODUCTION

Nearly everyone who survived the war in Bosnia and Herzegovina experienced traumatic events. Our research, combined with our personal and clinical experience, shows that at least some people have experienced positive changes that they attribute to the wartime. In the short literature review that begins this chapter we will put the preceding case reports from Bosnia and Herzegovina in a wider perspective by attempting to summarize what is known about adversarial growth due to war, especially in civilians. In the second half of the chapter we will present some new results on adversarial growth from our own research in Bosnia and Herzegovina.

It is unclear to what extent the positive changes that many of them report are due to the *specifically traumatic* or *generally adversarial* aspects of the war. As traumatic and adversarial aspects are both conceptually and empirically difficult to separate in the case of war, this question is as yet unanswered and so the more conservative formulation "adversarial growth" is probably more appropriate.

During the last years, PTG or adversarial growth has developed into a widely used and recognized concept. However, reviews of published studies indicate that most are based either on individuals surviving individual traumatic events (type-I events) or suffering from chronic diseases (see Linley and Joseph, 2004). Studies on growth following exposure to a complex series of traumatic and adversarial events and situations, and in particular to war, are comparably rare. In a review of the literature we were able to identify only a few studies dealing with war-affected individuals and adversarial growth (Elder & Clipp, 1989; Fontana & Rosenheck, 1998; Jones, 2002; Krizmanic & Kolesaric, 1996; Maercker, Herrle, & Grimm, 1999; Powell, Rosner, Butollo, Tedeschi, & Calhoun, 2003; Schnurr, Rosenberg & Friedman, 1993; Waysman, Schwarzwald, & Solomon, 2001).

Characteristics of War as a Complex Traumatic and Adversarial Environment

In contrast to individual traumatic events, war exposes people to a combination of multiple events in a persistently unsafe environment. It also differs in a number of aspects for soldiers and civilians. These differences are also confounded with the fact that by far the best studied group of soldiers is the U.S. military, who are probably not typical for the rest of the world's soldiers. At least in the case of U.S. soldiers in recent decades, joining the army is usually a deliberate choice, which indicates that there is some sense of control. Furthermore, U.S. soldiers have always fought abroad, which means that their families are safe and their home environment is comparably stable. A different situation arises for war-affected civilians. For many of them, no point in time existed were they were able to make a deliberate decision about living in a war region or not. Not only are they affected by war, but so are their families and their entire environment.

Displacement and Flight

One can differentiate three groups of war-affected civilians in terms of residence status: those who stay at home and are not displaced, those who are forced to leave their homes, but do not cross a national border (internally displaced persons), and those who are forced to leave their homes and then also leave the country (refugees). While displacement is usually a forced process, flight to a different country usually, though not always, involves some deliberate decision to move further away and implies that the person had some control over his or her flight. Often, the head of the household decides and other family members are taken with them. Whether fleeing across borders increases personal and family safety depends on the circumstances in the host country. Most of the refugees from former Yugoslavia certainly improved their safety by fleeing. But all refugees have to adapt to different cultures and often to learn new languages.

Return

Returning to the old home or to another place in the home country usually means coming back to a region that is still suffering from various war outcomes. Houses are destroyed, civil structures are not working, society has changed radically, and sometimes one is seen as a traitor by members of one's own former community. Moreover, the complex geography of ethnic hatred and distrust often means that one has to return to a new and unfamiliar area or run the risk of being harassed or victimized by the changed population of one's former town or village. And as in the case of former Yugoslavia, usually the original conflict has not been fully resolved and the threat of renewed conflict cannot be excluded.

Variables Associated With Growth in General and Within War-Affected Samples

In their review of positive changes following trauma and adversities in general (not only in war-related studies), Linely and Joseph (2004) name a number of variables that were consistently positively associated with growth: Cognitive appraisal variables, such as problem-focused coping, acceptance and positive reinterpretation, emotion-focused coping, controllability, and cognitive processing. Inconsistent associations have been found for demographic variables, such as age, gender, education, and income, and for psychological distress variables, such as depression, anxiety, and Posttraumatic Stress Disorder (PSTD).

The results of this broad and general review are only partially supported by the results of studies on war-traumatized samples. For individuals surviving war, the following findings can be reported:

Elder and Clipp (1989) selected from two longitudinal studies with men born in the 1920s a sample of 149 war veterans from World War II, Korea, and Vietnam and followed this sample from adolescence to old age. Besides looking at the effect of combat exposure on current stress symptoms and negative effects in general the authors were interested in positive outcomes. They found more positive outcomes in terms of "learning to cope with adversity," "self-discipline," "value life more," and a "clearer sense of direction" in the group of veterans with high combat experience as opposed to those with no or only light combat experience. Men who served in heavy combat became more assertive and resilient up to mid-life when compared to veterans with light or no combat experiences.

In a longitudinal study of college students from adolescence to adulthood who attended college during the Vietnam War, Schnurr et al. (1993) estimated changes in MMPI-scores as a measure of adversarial growth. In a comparison of adjusted change scores between men without combat exposure, with peripheral exposure and those with direct exposure positive changes were only found in the group with peripheral exposure.

For a sample of Vietnam veterans, Fontana and Rosenheck (1998) reported a positive association for the two cognitive appraisal variables "perceived harm" and "perceived threat" and adversarial growth in addition to between education and adversarial growth. Nevertheless, growth was measured with only one open question.

Waysman et al. (2001) assessed 164 Israeli prisoners of war (POWs) and a matched group of 184 veterans of the Yom Kippur war in terms of perceived positive and negative changes in a wide range of areas. They were assessed retrospectively as the difference in these areas between the time before their war experiences and the time of the study. Findings indicated a positive correlation between hardiness and positive changes. The interaction of group (POW vs. non-POW) and hardiness also contributed to positive changes. Although the results were statistically significant, the total amount of variance explained by all variables in the regression equation (age, combat exposure, group, hardiness, group X hardiness) for positive changes was very small (3.8%).

Of those studies dealing with soldiers and combat exposure, three are based on assessments of U.S. soldiers (Elder & Clipp, 1989; Fontana & Rosenheck, 1998; Schnurr et al., 1993) and one is based on Israeli veterans (Waysman et al., 2001). Thus the best studied samples share the scenario of "soldiers going to war" whose families and communities were comparably safe and stable. In none of the studies one of the known questionnaires on growth was used. Rather a idiosyncratic item or scale was used.

Within the studies on civilians, three originate from the region of former Yugoslavia and one from Germany. The three studies on civilians in postwar societies yielded the following results: a qualitative study on adolescents from opposite sides of the conflict (Jones, 2002) looked at search for meaning and its association with psychological well-being. "Search for meaning" in the latter study is related, but not identical to, similarly named concepts measured by some growth scales. Jones was interested particularly in the search for a specific meaning of the conflict rather than in the perception of having found more meaning in life in general. Forty adolescents were selected from a sample of 337 adolescents between 13 to 15 years old. Discussing her results, Jones (2002, p. 1351) states: "Searching for meaning did not appear to be protective. Less well adolescents in both cities were more engaged in searching for meaning. Well adolescents appeared to be more disengaged. Searching for meaning appeared to be associated with sensitivity to the political environment, and feelings of insecurity about the prospect of future war." Within the group of those searching for meaning, local social and political context had a mediating effect. An association between exposure to violence and search for meaning was only found in the group of adolescents living in the predominantly Muslim town of Goražde, while there was no such association in the predominantly Serbian town of Foća/Srbinje. The children in Foća/Srbinje had almost no exposure to the war in contrast to the children of Goražde.

Krismanić and Kolesaric (1996) assessed 657 survivors of the war in Bosnia and Herzegovina and Croatia with an adaptation of the Change in Outlook Questionnaire (Joseph, Williams, & Yule, 1993) called the Positive and Negative Consequences of War questionnaire (PANCOW). The questionnaire comprises 15 positive and 15 negative statements and was given to eight different groups of war-affected subjects: disabled and wounded persons, refugees, widows, army physicians and psychologists, soldiers, nurses without exposure, and citizens and students from Zagreb (who were—as Zagreb was not in the war region—almost not exposed). Participants reported generally higher positive changes than negative changes, with the more war-affected subsamples showing the greatest amount of positive changes. The authors interpret their results to the effect that especially refugees and displaced persons had a strong motivation to stay healthy out of spite for the enemy. Another interpretation of the authors is that some subjects were minimizing their traumatic experiences in an attempt to avoid victim status. As the study was carried out right at the end of the war, the results might also reflect a short-term outcome.

Only one study in the area of war traumatization (Powell, et al., 2003) used one of the established measures of PTG, the *Posttraumatic Growth Inventory* (PTGI) (Tedeschi & Calhoun, 1995, 1996). In this study on former refugees and displaced persons from Bosnia and Herzegovina no differences between men and women were found in terms of their PTGI total scores in addition to the scores in the subscales, while older individuals reported less growth than younger persons. Furthermore, symptoms of posttraumatic stress were not correlated with growth. Overall reported growth was smaller than in other studies.

Maercker, Herrle, and Grimm (1999) used a German adaptation of the PTGI. Their study is unusual in that the time lapse between traumatic exposure and assessment was about 50 years. Study subjects were victims of the Dresden bombing night during which 35,000 people were killed within four hours. Results yielded a positive correlation between PTG and traumatic exposure in addition to internal control beliefs.

In general, the intercultural variance of these published studies is limited. On the other hand, the relative homogeny better allows a comparison between groups. Yet, in this short review of adversarial growth it becomes evident that there is an interesting aspect that has been neglected up to now in the research on PTG that is, daily living conditions, unemployment, bad health, poverty, having a permanent place of residence, or just physical security. Yet, from meta-analyses of predictors of PTSD symptoms (Brewin, Andrews, & Valentine, 2000) we know that living conditions after trauma are comparatively potent predictors of PTSD symptoms.

Based on these findings and derived from our personal observations in Sarajevo in addition to clinical experience in Munich with patients coming from war regions, we hypothesized that there is a minimum of safety and distance that is necessary to facilitate growth. Thus we assumed that refugees who spent at least some time outside the war region would quite simply show more growth than those who did not. As displaced versus refugee status incorporates a range of psychologically relevant aspects, such as physical and economic safety in addition to the ability to leave the region or not, we were interested in whether or not refugee or displaced status would be connected with PTG.

The Postwar Situation in Bosnia and Herzegovina

As more recent wars, such as those in Afghanistan and Iraq, are more present in the media and probably in public consciousness, we would like to remind readers of the outline of the war in Bosnia and Herzegovina to which the persons in our samples were exposed. Bosnia and Herzegovina had approximately 4.3 million inhabitants before the war. During the war between 1992 and the end of 1995, approximately 250,000 people died, the majority of whom were Bosnian Muslims. Approximately 2.2 million of the former residents of Bosnia and Herzegovina were displaced. Of these, approximately 1,200,000 refugees found refuge in about 100 countries all over the world (Gesellschaft für bedrohte Völker). By 2002, an estimated number of 300,000 people had returned to Bosnia and Herzegovina. In the whole of Bosnia and Herzegovina there were about 870,000 internally displaced persons in 2002.

Although the threat of violence has very much diminished, living conditions are still quite difficult especially in rural regions and especially so for those returning to areas in which they do not belong to the dominant ethnicity. Unemployment is still very high and a secure future for the country is far from certain as the prevailing political parties in the constituent areas or "entities" continue to disagree about most of the basic parameters of statehood.

HYPOTHESES

Derived from results on the variables associated with growth in mixed trauma, and based on our review of variables associated with growth in war affected samples, the following hypotheses are put forward:

1. Coping styles and PTG are positively associated.
2. Posttraumatic growth and general distress symptoms and depressive symptoms are not associated.
3. Posttraumatic growth is more strongly correlated with current stressors than with traumatic war events.
4. Being a refugee contributes to PTG both overall and when differences in exposure to traumatic events are taken into account.
5. Better current living conditions, such as employment, income, current accommodation status, or being in a stable relationship, are associated with PTG.

The results presented here are based on the same sample as our earlier report (Powell et al., 2003), but are based on previously unpublished analyses of a wider set of variables (coping, refugee status, and depression).

METHOD

Instruments

To assess the effect of demographic characteristics and current living we collected information on age, sex, education, marital status, flight and displacement, and current living conditions. Family status (single as opposed to married or living in a long-term relationship) in addition to monthly income in the household were also assessed with single questions.

The PTDS (Foa, Cashman, Jaycox, & Perry, 1997) was selected for the assessment of PTSD symptoms. The PTDS has been shown in previous research to be reliable and valid in English (Foa et al., 1997) and in Bosnian (Powell & Rosner, 2005).

Exposure to traumatic and other stressful events was measured with the Checklist of War-Related Events (CWE) (Powell et al. 1998), which is a checklist adapted to the war situation in Sarajevo. Fortynine of the 72 CWE items cover traumatic events, such as "Did you eyewitness a loved one being killed during the war," scored either "more than once," "once," "no," or for certain items simply "yes," "no." These 49 items are grouped into 10 categories. A measure of the total number of all traumatic events experienced in all the categories was established by summing the z-transformed scores on each of the aforementioned event category variables. The range of possible scores is from a minimum of 0 to a maximum of 98. It was necessary to z-transform the category scores prior to further analysis because the standard deviations and both the theoretical and empirical ranges were quite different for each category. Scores for prewar traumatic events, stressful (but not necessarily traumatic) events during and since the war, and current stressful events were formed in a similar way. (A copy of the CWE is available from Powell.)

Postraumatic growth was assessed with the *PTGI* (Tedeschi & Calhoun, 1996). The PTGI explicitly states that the respondents are to answer about changes that occurred "in your life as a result of your crisis." However, as the crisis in the present study could have been as wide as the whole complex situation of war and refuge, each item was adapted to include a reference to changes "since April 1992" or "in comparison with the period before the war." A factor analysis of the Bosnian version using orthogonal rotation resulted in a three-factor solution (for details see Powell et al., 2003) explaining 58% of variance. While the factor structure of the original instrument could not be adequately reproduced, the solution that was found did correspond well to the three broad categories of PTG originally identified by Tedeschi & Calhoun (1995). These factors and therefore the subscales used in this study were "changes in self/positive life attitude," "philosophy of life," and "relating to others."

A Bosnian translation of the *Beck Depression Inventory* (BDI) (1978) was used to assess severity of depression. Although the BDI does not allow a diagnosis in the sense of DSM-IV, a cutoff score of 18 is usually regarded as an indicator for moderate depression. The BDI has been used in more than 2,000 studies worldwide (Richter, Werner, Heerlein, Kraus, & Sauer, 1998) and can be regarded as a suitable measure for depression in refugees (Hollifield et al., 2002).

The Symptom-Checklist-90 revised (SCL-90-R) (Derogatis, 1977) measures psychological distress besides being a widespread measure (Franke & Stäcker, 1995) the SCL-90-R has been used in research on refugee populations (Hollifield et al., 2002). The General Severity Index (GSI) is based on the sum of all items, divided by the number of answered items and describes the level of general psychological distress.

As a measure of coping the Coping Inventory of Stressful Situations (CISS) (Endler & Parker, 1994) was used. The CISS consists of three subscales (task-oriented, emotion-oriented, and avoidance-oriented coping) and assesses general coping styles. The psychometric evaluation of the CISS is good with Cronbach's alpha for the subscales between .77 and .92 and adequate convergent validity (Kälin & Semmer, 1996).

Sample

People targeted for inclusion in the study were selected at random from lists prepared by 16 local councils (*Mjesne Zajednice*) of all those registered with them who could meet the inclusion criteria for either of the two samples. These local councils had previously been selected at random from all the local councils in Sarajevo.

Participants in the study had to be (a) adults between 16 and 65 years old who lived in former Yugoslavia for most of 1980–1991; (b) living at the time of interview (1999) in Sarajevo, but who had lived outside Sarajevo for more than 12 months between 1991 and 1995; (c) not suffering from a psychotic disorder or other serious crisis, and (d) literate enough to answer the questionnaire with some help. Current and former military personnel were not excluded.

The terms *refugee* and *internally displaced person* (in this study the latter are referred to just as *displaced persons*) both refer to those who have been forced or obliged to leave their homes, for example, as a result of war or persecution (see Cohen & Deng, 1998, pp. 15–39). Refugees are those who subsequently cross an international border, in this case that of former Yugoslavia. Accordingly, the first sample consisted of 75 former refugees who had taken refuge in countries outside Former Yugoslavia for more than 12 months between 1991 and 1995. The second consisted of 75 displaced (or former displaced) adults now living in Sarajevo who did not take refuge outside Former Yugoslavia. Many of the former refugees are still not able or willing to return to their prewar accommodation. (These two subsamples are each random selections out of larger subsamples in a more comprehensive study.) The sample of internally displaced persons includes some who were displaced because of war, but have now returned to their prewar accommodation. Both groups had experienced a wide range of war experiences. Although the former refugees in the first sample had spent an average of M = 4.02 years outside former Yugoslavia, most had also experienced severe war stress (M = 17.42 months in a war zone) before they left the country. In most cases, they lost family members that stayed in the area of former Yugoslavia while they were abroad.

Those interested in co-operating with the survey were informed of the aims and conditions of participation, given guarantees of confidentiality, and asked to sign an informed consent form. Interviewers were pairs of final-year and third-year students of psychology. The respondents were paid a small amount of money (equivalent to the rate for 1 hour of work) for their co-operation.

Some data was missing for the PTGI, leaving a total of 136 valid questionnaires. The samples are described in Table 10.1.

Chi-Square Tests reveal that the sample was approximately evenly distributed across sex and age group (Pearson Chi-Square for the whole 136 persons who returned complete PTGI datasample = .918, df = 1, n.s.). A Mann-Whitney U test for the level of education between the groups revealed a significant value of 1767.00 (asymptotic two-sided significance $p < .05$) in the sense that the former refugees were somewhat better educated.

TABLE 10.1
Sample Description

		Returnees Column			Displaced Column			Total Column		
		Count	%	Mean	Count	%	Mean	Count	%	Mean
Sex	Female	39	60.9%		38	52.8%		77	56.6%	
	Male	25	39.1%		34	47.2%		59	43.4%	
	Total	64	100%		72	100%		136	100%	
Family status	Single	23	35.9%		28	38.9%		51	37.5%	
	Married or long-term relationship	41	64.1%		44	61.1%		85	62.5%	
	Total	64	100%		72	100%		136	100%	
Years of education	8	8	12.7%		19	27.1%		27	20.3%	
	11.50	46	73%		47	67.1%		93	69.9%	
	16	9	14.3%		4	5.7%		13	9.8%	
	Total	63	100%		70	100%		133	100%	
Monthly household income in KM	41	11	17.5%		9	12.5%		20	14.8%	
	131	6	9.5%		10	13.9%		16	11.9%	
	215	5	7.9%		11	15.3%		16	11.9%	
	275	5	7.9%		7	9.7%		12	8.9%	
	450	20	31.7%		22	30.6%		42	31.1%	
	800	10	15.9%		6	8.3%		16	11.9%	
	1,200	6	9.5%		7	9.7%		13	9.6%	
	Total	63	100%		72	100%		135	100%	
Religion	Other	6	9.4%		3	4.2%		9	6.6%	
	Islam	53	82.8%		63	87.5%		116	85.3%	
	Catholicism	1	1.6%		3	4.2%		4	2.9%	
	Orthodox	4	6.3%		3	4.2%		7	5.1%	
	Total	64	100%		72	100%		136	100%	
Age				36.83			36.58			36.70

TABLE 10.2
Spearman Correlations between Posttraumatic Growth and Coping

	PTGI-Total Score	Changes in Self	Philosophy of Life	Relating to Others
Task-oriented coping	.269**	.115	.166*	.220**
Emotion-oriented coping	.187*	−.004	.119	.230**
Avoidance-oriented coping	.345**	.161*	.180*	.297**
CISS total	.333**	.112	.181*	.309**
BDI	.043	−.254**	−.019	.261**
SCL-GSI	.126	−.160*	.062	.251**
PTSD-symptoms	.100	−.142	.074	.181*
Traumatic prewar events	.100	−.102	.031	.142
Traumatic war events	.058	−.079	.013	.179*
Other stressors during and since war	.032	−.109	.008	.211**
Current stressors	.112	−.114	.028	.324**

* Correlation is significant at the 0.05 level (1-tailed).
** Correlation is significant at the 0.01 level (1-tailed).

Data Analysis

For all analyses the SPSS software package (SPSS Inc., Versions 10.0.5 and 12.0.2) was employed. As not all the variables are normally distributed, where correlations are reported, these are Spearman's coefficients.

RESULTS

Results for Hypothesis 1

Table 10.2 shows means, standard deviations, and the Spearman's correlations between PTGI scores, PTGI subscales, and CISS total scores and respective subscales.

It seems that, as hypothesized, the constructs represented by the CISS coping subscales and the PTGI subscales are strongly related. The PTGI total score correlates strongly with the CISS total score and with the CISS subscales. In particular, most of the shared variance seems to be due to the PTGI subscale "relating to others."

Results for Hypothesis 2

Table 10.2 reveals the correlations between the PTGI and its respective subscales on the one hand and the GSI as a measure of general psychological distress, the BDI as a measure of depression, and the PTDS-symptom score as a measure of PTSD-symptoms on the other hand.

Results indicate, as hypothesized, no significant correlations between the total score for growth on the one hand and depression, general symptoms, and PTSD symptoms on the other, as measured by the BDI, GSI, and PTDS, respectively. However, it is very striking that the interpretation becomes more complicated when one looks at the individual subscales of the PTGI; while the scale "changes in self" shows low negative correlations, the scale "relating to others" shows moderate positive correlations that are contrary to hypothesis. It is this latter subscale that is largely responsible for the moderate correlation with overall coping behavior as reported in the preceding text, and its the only PTGI subscale to be related to the cumulative total of traumatic war events.

Results for Hypothesis 3

As can be seen in Table 10.2, the PTGI subscale "relating to others" shows within the variables examined in this study the highest correlation to current stressors. However, the total PTGI scale is not related to any of the stressor totals. From this limited data about overall levels of different kinds of exposure, ongoing stressors and current stressors, and growth, it is not possible to conclude whether growth in this sample is specifically posttraumatic or whether it should be more broadly classified as adversarial growth.

Results for Hypotheses 4

According to the assumptions set out in the preceding text, we assumed that those who had a more secure environment during the war, operationalized as a refugee, as opposed to the internally displaced persons, and currently have better living conditions; and they operationalized as being employed and have a higher income and a stable relationship, show more growth than those with a less secure environment. A sequential multiple regression was used to test this hypothesis. For a better understanding the correlation of all variables included in the multiple regression can be found in Table 10.3. To control for the effects of demographic variables and exposure to traumatic and stressful war events, these variables were included in the model in the first step. Variables representing a more secure environment during the war were included in the second step, and in the third and final step, variables representing a secure postwar environment were included. The multiple regressions were calculated for the PTGI-total score as dependent variables and for all PTGI-subscales as dependent variables. Table 10.4 yields the results for the PTGI-total score and the subscale "changes in self."

The effect size for model 3 and the dependent variable PTGI-total score is $f^2 = .14$, which can be considered small (Bortz & Döring, 1995). The standardized coefficient for age is significant in the first model and remains so in all three models. From the other variables, only flight status, that is, having been a either a refugee or internally displaced person, makes a significant contribution to predicting the PTGI total score.

Effect sizes for the subscale "changes in self" are with $f^2 = .39$ in the medium range. Within the models, age again is significant and remains significant in all three models. Introducing flight status (refugee vs. displaced) improves the prediction significantly. Adding current living conditions also improves the prediction significantly. From the variables included in the third model, only the standardized beta for family status yielded significant results. Inspection of the direction of effect reveals that those who were younger, refugees, and in a stable relationship reported more positive changes.

Two similar multiple regressions for the two other PTGI-subscales revealed no significant results. With an adjusted R^2 for "philosophy of life" of $-.004$ for model 1, .005 for model 2, and $-.013$ for model 3, effects vary around 0. For the subscale "relating to others," adjusted R^2 equals .019 for model 1, .013 for model 2, and .016 for model 3. None of the standardized betas in any model showed a significant contribution.

TABLE 10.3
Spearman Correlations of All Variables Included in the Multiple Regressions

	Sex	Traumatic War Events	Sample	Unsure If You Can Stay Living Where You Are Now?	Monthly Household Income KM	Family Status	Changes in Self	Philosophy of Life	Relating to Others	PTGI-Total Score
Age	-.136	.154*	-.009	.113	-.247**	.339**	-.413**	-.156*	.149*	-.224**
Sex		.337**	.082	.150*	-.013	.004	.031	-.033	-.041	.006
Traumatic war events			.237**	.305**	-.157*	.215**	-.079	.013	.179*	.058
Sample				.397**	-.057	-.030	-.216**	-.163*	.054	-.185*
Unsure if you can stay living where you are now?					-.277**	.178*	-.175*	-.061	.135	-.082
Monthly household income KM						-.090	.243**	.068	-.149*	.108
Family status							-.275**	-.010	.142	-.140
Changes in self								.102	.071	.647**
Philosophy of life									.070	.618**
Relating to others										.548**

* Correlation is significant at the 0.05 level (1-tailed).
** Correlation is significant at the 0.01 level (1-tailed).

TABLE 10.4

Prediction of Post-Traumatic/Adversarial Growth on the Basis of Demographic Variables, Flight Status, and Current Living Conditions

Model	Variables	Dependent Variable: Total PTGI					Dependent Variable: Changes in Self				
		B	SE B	β	R^2	adj.R^2	B	SE B	β	R^2	adj.R^2
1					.058	.037*				.152	132**
	Constant	48.577	5.032				1.034	.267			
	Sex	-1.577	3.341	-.044			.037	.180	.018		
	Age	-.329	.118	-.244			-.028	.006	-.381		
	Traumatic war events	.297	.273	.100			-.006	.014	-.036		
2					.107	.080**				.206	.181**
	Constant	85.889	14.864				3.229	.791			
	Sex	-1.560	3.266	-.043			.038	.175	.019		
	Age	-.339	.116	-.251			-.029	.006	-.388		
	Traumatic war events	.467	.275	.157			.004	.014	.026		
	Sample	-8.178	3.074	-.228			-.482	.164	-.241		
3					.116	.067				.282	.241**
	Constant	85.313	15.877				3.133	.815			
	Sex	-1.730	3.310	-.048			.037	.169	.018		
	Age	-.295	.123	-.218			-.022	.006	-.294		
	Traumatic war events	.538	.287	.181			.016	.014	.099		
	Sample	-8.308	3.328	-.231			-.480	.171	-.240		
	Unsure if you can stay	-.032	3.516	-.001			-.081	.179	-.041		
	Living where you are now?										
	Household income	.003	.005	.061			.000	.000	.144		
	Family status	-2.853	3.312	-.077			-.495	.169	-.240		

DISCUSSION

Comparably little has been published on the relationship between coping styles and post-traumatic or adversarial growth after war. Yet, our results support Linley and Joseph's (2004) finding of a positive correlation between all coping styles and adversarial growth. Because significant results emerged mostly for "relating to others" and coping style and because the correlations are of small to medium size we think that the results support the position of Tedeschi et al. (1998, S. 3), that posttraumatic or adversarial growth is more than another coping mechanism. Nevertheless, both constructs have much in common. The somewhat lower correlation between PTGI and coping compared to that found by Maercker and Langner (2001) may be due to the different coping instruments used, but may also be due to lower reported growth overall. In particular, in our study the use of coping strategies overall, regardless of their nature, is associated with growth in terms of increased value given to relationships with others. One plausible explanation is that the use of coping, at least in our sample, implies activating personal relationships that are as a result more highly valued. Possibly this result should be seen against the special background of the war in Bosnia-Herzegovina, in which people one had known well before the war, whether the local shopkeeper or one's own child, ended up fighting on the enemy side. Perhaps the events of the war demonstrated that one cannot simply trust other people and that one must work to maintain good relationships that can then provide a strong feeling of support. Furthermore, the war meant going through intensive, sometimes life-threatening situations together, leading to very strong bonding and feelings of togetherness.

There is a significant positive connection between the interpersonal factor of the PTGI and posttraumatic symptoms, general distress, and depression, indicating that those suffering the most evaluate positive relationships more highly. One possible explanation could be that the subscale "relating to others" covers some aspects of social support in difficult situations, an interpretation that seems quite plausible because current stressors show a stronger connection with this subscale than war-traumatic events of several years ago. The variable "stressors during and since war" consistently takes a middle position. However, the results have to be discussed in a more differentiated way as the factors are not equally associated with depression and general symptoms. The first factor, which measures perceiving positive changes in oneself, is most strongly associated with lower depression and general distress symptoms. As depression in the sense of Beck, Rush, Shaw, and Emery (1979) includes a negative view of oneself, this result is quite consistent with the cognitive theory of depression. Yet, only a longitudinal study would be able to answer the question of whether the perceived changes in the self actually contribute to lower depression or whether being depressed prevents one from undergoing (or perceiving) this kind of positive change.

Because the dose-response relationship between exposure to traumatic events and growth is weak in this sample, the search for factors that encourage posttraumatic or adversarial growth must continue elsewhere. It seems that some aspect of having been a refugee rather than an internally displaced person contributes to growth although this effect is quite small. Interestingly, the more specific variables, such as higher income and having a secure place to live, that might be expected to circumscribe this effect do not contribute to growth in this sample when assessed in relation to present day circumstances, which would suggest that other aspects of being a refugee play a role. As we did not use a measure of control attributions, we can only speculate that leaving the country entirely as compared to remaining inside it shows that the former group of people are willing and able to take more control of a situation even under very difficult circumstances and that this eventually leads to more growth and specifically to a more positive picture of oneself. Another possible explanation can be found in the reports of Bosnian patients in treatment centers in Germany, which point to the possible positive effects of geographical separation. For example, the patient whose story is told at the beginning of this chapter and who was flown out to Western Europe due to a serious injury, reported that after his recovery he realized in a flash how much the war had "sucked him in." He reported that the contrast between war and peace, which came so abruptly for him, made him more sensitive to the value of each moment. Perhaps, the effect of flight status (former refugee vs. internally displaced person) is partly explained by distancing: the opportunity to take a step back and view the events and one's involvement in them from further away.

The first case study, of a young man who was displaced inside the country during the war, seems to suggest that some who were exposed to the horrors of war for its whole duration might feel that they grew as people. For them, war-related growth is, perhaps, strongly tied to a collective view of the world. That kind of shared view can, depending on the political circumstances, easily become superseded in the years after the war ends.

CONCLUSIONS

- Based on a narrative review of studies concerning adversarial growth after war it became clear that there is very little overlap in terms of used measures. This means the results are difficult to compare and for future studies in the field the use of previously published scales is recommended.

- For our study, it can be said in summary that there is indeed some limited empirical evidence for posttraumatic or adversarial growth due to war.

- The aspect of valuing relationships with others seems to be particularly important and is connected to coping styles and to traumatic and stressful events in addition to higher symptom levels. The aspect of perceiving positive changes in oneself is negatively related to symptom level.

- Our results were quite different in terms of subscales. While the subscale "relating to others" is probably confounded with social support, the subscale "changes in self" is probably close to self schemas in cognitive theories. Thus, any study on adversarial growth should give detailed information on results based on different subscales.

- As yet there is no empirical evidence that growth during and after war is specifically due to traumatic events. The more conservative formulation "adversarial growth" should be preferred, at least for the meantime.

ACKNOWLEDGMENTS

The research reported here was conducted in co-operation with the Deutsche Gesellschaft für Technische Zusammenarbeit (GTZ GmbH), which provided half of the funding.

The educational part of the project was supported by the Volkswagen-Stiftung (Volkswagen Foundation), Germany: VW II/ 73301.

Our sincere thanks are due to the many people who were involved in this survey, above all to the citizens of Sarajevo who took the time to answer our sometimes distressing list of questions. Thanks are also due to the staff and students of Sarajevo University, the staff at the four Municipality Centers in Sarajevo, and Ernst Hustädt and Bernd Rowek, GTZ-Advisors in Sarajevo.

REFERENCES

Beck, A. T. (1978). *Depression Inventory.* Philadelphia: Center for Cognitive Therapy.

Beck, A. T., Rush, A. J., Shaw, B. F., & Emery, G. (1979). *Cognitive therapy of depression.* New York: Guilford.

Bortz, J., & Döring, N. (1995). *Forschungsmethoden und Evaluation für Sozialwissenschaftler* [Research methods and evaluation for social scientists]. Berlin: Springer.

Brewin, C. R., Andrews, B., & Valentine, J. D. (2000). Meta-analysis of risk factors for posttraumatic stress disorder in trauma-exposed adults. *Journal of Consulting and Clinical Psychology, 68*(5), 748–766.

Cohen, & Deng (1998). *Masses in flight. The global crisis of internal displacement.* Washington, DC: Brookings Institute.

Derogatis LR. (1977). *SCL-90-R: Administration, scoring and procedures manual for the r (evised) version.* Baltimore: Johns Hopkins University School of Medicine.

Elder, G. H., & Clipp, E. C. (1989). Combat experience and emotional health: Impairment and resilience in later life. *Journal of Personality, 57*, 311–341.

Foa, E. B., Cashman, L., Jaycox, L., & Perry, K. (1997). The validation of a self-report measure of posttraumatic stress disorder: The posttraumatic diagnostic scale. *Psychological Assessment, 9*(4), 445–451.

Fontana, A., & Rosenheck, R. (1998). Psychological benefits and liabilities of traumatic exposure in the war zone. *Journal of Traumatic Stress, 11*, 485–505.

Franke, G., & Stäcker, K. H. (1995). *Reliabilität und Validität der Symptom-Check-Liste (SCL-90-R; Derogatis, 1986) bei Standardreihenfolge versus inhaltshomogener Itemblockbildung.* [Reliability and validity of the Symptom-Check-List (SCL-90-R) with standard order versus blocks of items of similar content]. *Diagnostica, 41*(4), 349–373.

Gesellschaft für bedrohte Völker. (n.d.) retrieved October 1, 2002 from www.gfbv-sa.com.ba/ruckkehg.html.

Hollifield, M., Warner, T.D., Lian, N., Krakow, B., Jenkins, J.H., Kesler, et al. (2002). Measuring trauma and health status in refugees. *JAMA, 288*, 611–621.

Jones, L. (2002). Adolescent understandings of political violence and psychological well-being: A qualitative study form Bosnia Herzegovina. *Social Science and Medicine, 55*, 1351–1371.

Joseph, S., Williams, R., & Yule, W. (1993). Changes in outlook following disaster: The preliminary development of a measure to asses positive and negative responses. *Journal of Traumatic Stress, 6*, 271–279.

Kälin, W., & Semmer, N. (1996, September). *Drei Coping-Fragebögen im Vergleich* [Comparison of three copings questionnaires]. Poster presented at the Annual Conference of Deutsche Gesellschaft für Psychologie, Munich, Germany.

Krizmainic, M., & Kolesaric, V. (1996). A salutogenic model of psychosocial help. *Review of Psychology, 3*(1–2), 69–75.

Linely, P. A., & Joseph, S. (2004). Positive change following trauma and adversity: A review. *Journal of Traumatic Stress, 17*(1), 11–21.

Maercker, A., Herrle, J., & Grimm, I. (1999). *Dresdener Bombennachtsopfer 50 Jahre danach: Eine Untersuchung patho- und salutogenetischer Variablen.* [Dresden bombing night victims 50 years later: an study of patho- and salutogenic variables]. *Zeitschrift für Gerontopsychologie & -psychiatrie, 12*, 157–167.

Powell, S., & Rosner, R. (2005). The Bosnian version of the international self-report measure of posttraumatic stress disorder, the Posttraumatic Stress Diagnostic Scale, is reliable and valid in a variety of different adult samples affected by war. *BMC Psychiatry, 5*, 11. Available at http://biomedcentral.com/1471-244X/5/11.

Powell, S., Rosner, R., Butollo, W., Tedeschi, R. G., & Calloun, L.G. (2003). Posttraumatic growth after war: A study of former refugees and displaced people in Sarajevo. *Journal of Clinical Psychology, 59*, 71–84.

Powell, S., Rosner, R., Krüsmann, M., & Butollo, W. (1998). Checklist of war related experiences (CWE). Unpublished manuscript.

Schnurr, P. P., Rosenberg, S. D., & Friedman, M. J. (1993). Change in MMPI-scores from college to adulthood as a function of military service. *Journal of Abnormal Psychology, 102*, 288–296.

Tedeschi, R. G., & Calhoun, L. G. (1995). *Trauma and Transformation.* Sage.

Tedeschi, R. G., & Calhoun, L. G. (1996). The posttraumatic Growth Inventory. *Journal of Traumatic Stress, 9*, 455–471.

Waysman, M., Schwarzwald, J., & Solomon, Z. (2001). Hardiness. An examination of its relationship with positive and negative long term changes following trauma. *Journal of Traumatic Stress, 14*, 531–548.

11

POSITIVE CHANGES ATTRIBUTED
TO THE CHALLENGE OF HIV/AIDS

JOEL MILAM

UNIVERSITY OF SOUTHERN CALIFORNIA

Living with the human immunodeficiency virus/acquired immunodeficiency syndrome (HIV/AIDS) often has a profound impact on an individual's priorities and outlook on life. Although the psychological sequelae of HIV infection includes depression, anxiety, fear, helplessness, and guilt (Hays, Catania, McKusik, & Coates, 1990; Lawless, Kippax, & Crawford, 1996; Metcalfe, Langstaff, Evans, Paterson, & Reid, 1998; Richardson et al., 2001), there is growing evidence that positive changes attributed to diagnosis and living with HIV/AIDS occur. These positive changes, broadly defined as posttraumatic growth (PTG) for the purposes of this review, may influence the adaptation to this disease, from infection to disease progression/stability and death. The purpose of this chapter is to provide an overview of the gathering research that examines PTG among people affected by HIV/AIDS. This chapter does not cover the theoretical foundations of PTG (see Tedeschi & Calhoun, 2004). I provide a summary of HIV/AIDS and the psychological impact of infection and treatment. I discuss the findings concerning PTG and HIV/AIDS and how it may relate to mental, behavioral, and physical health among this population. Several areas worthy of additional research are highlighted.

BACKGROUND OF HIV/AIDS

HIV, typically spread through sexual intercourse and injection drug use, is characterized by a slow disintegration of an individual's ability to fight infections. That is, the immune system decays until the body surrenders to opportunistic infections. In 2003, nearly 5 million people became newly infected with HIV worldwide and the number of people living with HIV has continued to increase from 35 million in 2001 to 38 million in 2003. In the United States, an estimated 950,000 people are living with HIV .(UNAIDS, 2004). Currently, there is no cure for HIV/AIDS. It is estimated that almost 3 million people were killed by AIDS in 2003 and over 20 million have died since the first cases of AIDS were identified in 1981 .(UNAIDS, 2004). However, science has made great strides over the last two decades and due to the introduction of antiretroviral therapies (ART), many people with HIV/AIDS who have dealt with the prospect of impending death now have the possibility to live much longer lives.

Because HIV is a chronic disease with a plethora of disease-related stressors (treatment decisions, disclosure, stigma, side effects, etc.), many of which are uncontrollable, the psychological aspects of this illness are difficult to outline. Nevertheless, they can be categorized into phases related to disease development (Kalichman, 1995; Ostrow, 1997): diagnostic, asymptomatic, symptomatic, and AIDS.

The diagnostic phase is characterized by shock, disbelief, and fear. Although recent combination drug therapies show promise in turning HIV into a chronic disease, diagnosis is still considered a life and death issue (i.e., a severe traumatic event). Denial or minimization is often used to protect against extreme levels of anxiety. Anger, depression, helplessness, feelings of persecution (e.g., "why me?"), and grief may follow. However, there is usually a gradual acceptance and adjustment that continues throughout the disease course. Disclosure is also a major issue because HIV is heavily stigmatized and diagnosis can often reveal lifestyles (e.g., sexual orientation, drug use) that may not be acceptable to friends/family/colleagues. The asymptomatic phase often depends on the course of the disease. Most people cope very well although others may tortuously wait for the onset of symptoms. Uncertainty is a common theme. Immunologic functioning generally declines over time, however, which eventually leads to HIV-related symptoms. Thus, the symptomatic phase involves more active medical management and important treatment decisions. In addition to dealing with newfound fears of mortality, coping during this phase can become more challenging as additional areas of life are affected (e.g., bodily pain/functioning, side effects). The symptomatic phase can last for years until a condition is developed that meets the criteria for the diagnosis of AIDS. Although persons with AIDS can often live for many years, an AIDS diagnosis is a clearly defined step of disease progression that can emphasize the severity of the illness. If symptoms continue to progress, there may be acceptance of impending death, resignation, fear, and regret.

HIV/AIDS AND POSTTRAUMATIC GROWTH

Despite the many difficulties briefly outlined in the preceding text, there is research documenting positive changes and strengths in people living with HIV/AIDS. Studies indicate that between 59% to 83% of people living with HIV/AIDS report experiencing positive changes since diagnosis (e.g., Milam, 2004; Schwartzberg, 1994; Siegel & Schrimshaw, 2000). Although quantitative work is increasing, the majority of the published work explicitly examining PTG (and related constructs) among HIV-positive populations is qualitative. For example, Schwartzberg (1994) documents how finding meaning (or positive changes) through HIV includes increases in feelings of control, a sense of community belonging or membership, a 'here and now' focus, belief in an afterlife, and altruistic behavior. In some cases, HIV was considered a developmental trigger to discover internal resources that had never been put to the test. For example, some people living with HIV become politically active and involved in community action. In these cases, HIV was a motivating source for a sense of membership or belonging to a wider community (Schwartzberg, 1994). Thus, a construct overlapping with PTG is self-transcendence (Frankl, 1963); reaching beyond oneself to discover/make meaning in one's life. Coward & Lewis (1993) documented nine themes of self-transcendence found among gay men with AIDS: experiencing fear, taking care of oneself, seeking out challenge, creating a legacy, accepting what cannot be changed, connecting with others, letting go, accepting help, and having hope. In general, people with HIV/AIDS who experience self-transcendence perceive their experience as a challenge to fully understand themselves, appreciate relationships with others, and improve their overall quality of life (Coward, 1994, 1995; Mellors, Riley, & Erlen, 1997). Indeed, these are common themes among most of the research examining positive sequelae among people living with HIV/AIDS. For example, (Hall, 1990) studied how men with HIV maintain hope and found that this was done through a belief in the future, having a reason to live, and finding an effective treatment. However, at the time of this study, treatments were less effective relative to the ARTs now available.

Antiretroviral Therapy

The successes of antiretroviral medicines had a significant impact on reducing HIV/AIDS death rates. As these combination therapies were introduced in the mid-to-late 1990s, the treatment responses were so dramatic that in many cases, having reconciled the possibility of near-term death, longer term survival became reality. For some patients this was called the "Lazarus syndrome." This shift led to renegotiating feelings of hope, social roles, interpersonal relations, and overall quality of life; a focus on living (Barroso, 1996; Brashers, Neidig, Cardillo, Dobbs, & Russell, 1999). Thus, the possibility that one's psychological status is influenced by ART use warrants empirical examination and research has shown reductions in psychological distress and depression following the introduction and initiation of ART (Judd et al., 2000; Rabkin et al., 2000). Although ART use has been positively associated with PTG, initiating or discontinuing ART use has not been associated with PTG over time (Milam, 2004). However, more detailed analyses are needed. For example, it is unclear whether PTG is spurred by disease stabilization following ART initiation.

Health Behaviors

There are positive relationships between PTG and various health behaviors, such as lower levels of substance use (Milam, Ritt-Olson, & Unger, 2004). That is, in addition to positive changes in relationships and life priorities, positive changes in health behaviors (diet, exercise, etc.) can also stem from HIV diagnosis (Collins et al., 2001; Milam, 2004; Siegel & Schrimshaw, 2000). It is likely that PTG is associated with health behaviors through supportive others and clearer life goals, although more detailed examinations of these relationships are needed, particularly among diseased populations where health behaviors can play major roles in physical adjustment.

Caregivers

Although caring for a family member/spouse/partner living with HIV/AIDS and subsequent bereavement can involve severe distress, many HIV/AIDS caregivers report that their experiences have positive aspects, including joys, triumphs, and personal growth (Clipp, Adinolfi, Forrest, & Bennett, 1995; Folkman, 1997; Viney, Crooks, Walker, & Henry, 1991). Cadell et al. (Cadell, 2001, 2003; Cadell, Regehr, & Hemsworth, 2003) found a majority (78–82%) of HIV/AIDS caregivers report PTG. In addition, PTG was most likely to occur among individuals who have strong spiritual beliefs, support from family and friends, and high levels of distress. These results suggest that research examining the positive impacts of this disease need to consider the potential salutary effects among the wider social networks of the HIV/AIDS patient (e.g., families). Significant personal changes can occur among the people who make up the social networks of those living with HIV/AIDS and the results suggesting that spiritual beliefs are associated with these changes are not limited to caregivers.

Religiosity/Spirituality

A major route to finding meaning in life is through religion and spirituality and research among healthy populations find religiosity/spirituality to be positively associated with PTG (Park, Cohen, & Murch, 1996a; Tedeschi & Calhoun, 1996). Religious beliefs can aid in the adaptation to disease through enacting positive changes, improving outlook in life, and discovering personal strengths and meaning during difficult times (Dull & Skokan, 1995). Research among HIV/AIDS caregivers and patients find spiritual/religious beliefs/practices be associated with both PTG and psychological adjustment (Kaplan, Marks, & Metens, 1997; Milam, 2004; Siegel & Schrimshaw, 2002). These results support the notion that religiosity/spirituality can predispose one toward PTG by providing a framework, through which a trauma can be appraised, and/or a social network that provides ongoing support.

When Does Posttraumatic Growth Occur?

It is uncertain whether time plays an important role in fostering PTG. Some studies find time elapsed since the occurrence of a trauma to be positively associated with PTG (Cordova, et al., 2001; Park et al., 1996a; Park et al., 1996b), although others do not find this association (Lechner et al., 2003; Tedeschi & Calhoun, 1996). However, among people living with HIV, PTG may occur immediately after diagnosis. In a study excluding recently diagnosed patients ($\leq$ 3 months), PTG had a weak inverse correlation with time since diagnosis (Milam, 2004). Although some studies among cancer patients have found different results (Sears, Stanton, & Dannoff-Burg, 2003), the issue of time since HIV diagnosis and PTG needs further clarification.

Demographics

There is research examining the links between PTG and age, socioeconomic status (SES), and race/ethnicity. Among HIV patients, a significant inverse correlation is found between age and PTG, such that older participants experienced less PTG (Milam, 2004). This is consistent with findings among cancer patients (Andrykowski, et al., 1993; Lechner et al., 2003) and suggests that younger people diagnosed with a life-threatening illness may be more amenable to positive changes. Women generally report more PTG than men (e.g., Park et al., 1996b; Tedeschi & Calhoun, 1996), and this relationship is also seen among persons with HIV/AIDS (Milam, 2004). Because there is some evidence that PTG and SES are positively associated (Cordova et al., 2001), it is generally expected that higher SES would predict greater PTG, as PTG may require personal resources that are not available to lower SES individuals. However, the data among HIV populations is mixed; one study found a positive association with SES (Updegraff, Taylor, Kemeny, & Wyatt, 2002) while another found no such association (Milam, 2004). However, both of these studies largely included low-income participants suggesting that the experience of PTG is not limited solely to high SES individuals. Race and ethnic differences in PTG are unknown as most studies concerning PTG have not focused on this issue. Current reports do not suggest clear ethnic differences. One study among women finds White participants to report more PTG (Updegraff et al., 2002) whereas another among both women and men finds non-White participants to report the most PTG (Milam, 2004). Although these conflicting results may be due to differences in the methods used to quantify PTG, it remains unclear how much influence ethnicity and culture have on the development of PTG.

Dispositions

Because optimism, locus of control, self-efficacy, and sense of coherence have been associated with successful coping and adaptation to disease, they are also hypothesized to be associated with PTG (Tedeschi & Calhoun, 1995). In particular, optimism appears to show promise in promoting PTG, although there are mixed findings (Affleck & Tennen, 1996). Although cross-sectional results show optimism is positively associated with PTG among people living with HIV/AIDS, this relationship has not held up in longitudinal analyses; optimism has failed to predict PTG over time (Milam, 2004). Nevertheless, these results provide evidence that PTG does not simply reflect an underlying optimistic disposition.

Depressive Symptoms

Depressive symptoms among HIV patients are prevalent (Richardson et al., 2001), associated with lower levels of quality of life (Kemppainen, 2001), and may be associated with poor immune functioning (Kiecolt-Glaser & Glaser, 2002) and HIV disease progression (Page-Shafer, Delorenze, Satariano, & Winkelstein, 1996). Although HIV diagnosis is the beginning of a difficult time requiring the ongoing adjustment to many issues, including depressive symptoms, PTG will commonly co-occur with the negative psychological sequelae of a diagnosis of HIV/AIDS. However, PTG is hypothesized to aid in the ongoing adjustment to HIV as indicated by higher levels of mental health indicators. In a longitudinal study, baseline levels of PTG did not significantly predict depression levels over time among HIV patients (Milam, 2004). However, change in PTG was a significant predictor of depressive symptoms over time; those who always experienced PTG or gained PTG from baseline to follow-up had fewer depressive symptoms over time compared to those who never experienced or lost PTG from baseline to follow-up (Fig. 11.1). This is consistent with prospective research examining PTG following the death of a family member or close friend where the inverse relationship between PTG and distress grew stronger over time (Davis, Nolen-Hoeksema, & Larson, 1998). These results suggest that the *process* of PTG, achieving and maintaining positive changes, is associated with lower levels of depressive symptoms/distress over time. However, this relationship is likely reciprocal. That is, among HIV patients, developing and maintaining PTG has a protective effect on the development of depressive symptoms, whereas the presence of depressive symptoms is an impediment to achieving PTG.

Women With HIV

A number of studies have exclusively examined PTG among women living with HIV/AIDS. These studies find PTG to be associated with socioeconomic status (Updegraff

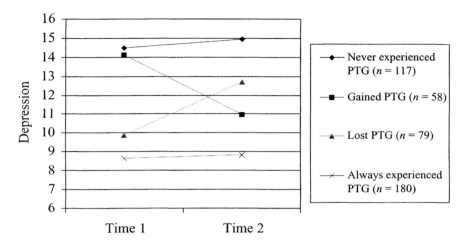

FIGURE 11.1.   Relationship between PTG and depressive symptoms over time. Adapted with permission from *Journal of Applied Social Psychology*, Vol. 24, No. 11, 2353–2376. ©V. H. Winston & Son, Inc., 360 South Ocean Boulevard, Palm Beach, FL 33480. All rights reserved.

et al., 2002) and to include positive changes in health behaviors (Siegel & Schrimshaw, 2000). Feigel (2003) found HIV-positive women with children to report less PTG than those without children. This result suggests that burdens and responsibilities associated with caregiving for children may hamper PTG for HIV-positive mothers.

Posttraumatic Growth and HIV Disease Progression

A major question is whether PTG should be appreciated as a positive outcome by itself, or viewed as a means to some other end. There is promising preliminary data among other populations supporting the possibility of experiencing physical health benefits secondary to experiencing PTG. For example, in a study of heart attack victims, those who found benefits (e.g., change in philosophy of life) after their first attack were less likely to have another attack and had lower levels of morbidity 8 years later (Affleck, Tennen, Croog, & Levine, 1987). Among people whose homes were damaged or destroyed by a fire, focusing on the positive aspects was associated with lower levels of symptom reporting (Thompson, 1985). Another study examined levels of cortisol reactivity among women exposed to a to a lab stress, such as solving a difficult math problem (Epel, McEwen, & Ickovics, 1998). Prolonged elevations of cortisol can break down the body's resources and speed up the disease process. High levels of PTG were associated with lower levels of cortisol reactivity, suggesting that PTG is related to a resilient physiological response toward stress. To explain this finding, the authors suggested that those with high PTG may have coped with the lab stressors more efficiently because they adapt to life stressors (in general) more easily or that they had experienced a form of physiological eustress, a toughening up from their past traumas. PTG may serve as one pathway to improvements in immune functioning. For example, among women with breast cancer, cognitive behavioral stress management has been found to reduce levels of cortisol through the enhancement of benefit finding (Cruess et al., 2000). It remains unclear whether PTG/benefit finding influences these health outcomes indirectly (e.g., through health behaviors).

Because PTG may be an indicator of higher levels of functioning and well-being, it is logical to consider physical benefits that may coincide with PTG among HIV patients. HIV, compared with other diseases, provides a superior model for studying the influence of positive beliefs on health. There are several reasons for this benefit (as noted by Taylor, Kemeny, Reed, Bower, & Gruenewald, 2000). First, individuals with HIV can be identified while asymptomatic allowing for the following of disease course over time. This also allows one to examine possible mediators of the relationship between positive beliefs and the course of the disease. For example, PTG may influence a positive change in health habits, which may subsequently prevent the onset of symptoms. Second, there are known covariates that can be statistically controlled for in analyses to avoid potential confounding. For HIV, these include demographics (e.g., age, SES) in addition to various health behaviors. For example, adherence to ART regimens is particularly important because high levels of adherence are needed for effective treatment and adequate viral suppression (Paterson et al., 2000). Third, HIV has important clinical markers associated with infection. Two important clinical markers include HIV plasma viral load, which is a measure of virus replication in the blood stream (higher numbers indicate a high risk of disease progression) and CD4 T lymphocyte cell count, which is a measure of T-helper cells (low numbers indicate more advanced HIV disease or AIDS). Other clinical markers include symptom appearance and AIDS diagnosis. These markers are particularly important as outcomes because a large amount of variation in HIV disease progression remains unexplained, and some of that variation may be explained by psychological factors (Cole & Kemeny, 1997). Indeed, a number of studies have found salutary relationships between positive psychological factors and HIV disease progression (Milam, Richardson, Marks, Kemper, & McCutchan, 2004; Moskowitz, 2003). Early evidence suggests that PTG may also be one of these factors.

Bower, Kemmy, Taylor, and Faley-Positive (1998) examined 40 HIV-positive men who experienced the loss of a close friend or partner to AIDS and discovered that those participants who found meaning (i.e., a newfound respect for life and a commitment to 'live every day to the fullest') after the death had greater immune system functioning (less rapid declines in CD4 T cell levels) and lower rates of AIDS-related mortality (Bower et al., 1998). Another study among HIV-positive men and women found those with undetectable viral load (< 500) to have significantly higher PTG scores than those with detectable viral loads (Milam, 2004). Although PTG was not associated viral load over time, it was associated with CD4 counts over time, particularly among non-Whites (i.e., there was a significant interaction between ethnicity and PTG in predicting CD4 counts over time). That is, for nonWhite participants, those who experienced PTG had higher CD4 counts over time compared to those who did not experience PTG (Milam, 2005). Importantly, this interaction was not explained by differences in depressive symptons, or health behaviors. These preliminary results provide some promising evidence suggesting that PTG may influence the course of HIV disease and supports new directions in psychoneuroimmunology which explan the effects of positive psychosocial factors on immune functioning and health outcomes.

Intervention Implications

The integration of mental health services and clinical care among HIV patients is needed. Further, health care providers should be educated about the salutary influences of various psychological factors, including the possibility of experiencing PTG, and the potential relationships with disease adaptation. Because it is difficult to enact meaningful changes without a positive outlook, interventions may benefit if they address life perception (positive reframing). For example, Lutgendorf et al. (1998) found a cognitive behavioral stress management intervention to increase positive reframing coping among a group of HIV-positive gay men. Benefits of these types of interventions can include lower levels of depression, positive health behavior change, and the potential slowing of disease progression (Antoni et al., 2001; Antoni et al., 2000). However, positive thinking is not a panacea. That is, any intervention designed to enhance perceptions of positive changes should continue to emphasize traditional health care and a realistic assessment of one's health status. Further, patients should not be chastised for holding negative attitudes.

SUMMARY

In addition to simply going to the doctor and receiving treatment, the healing process can include forms of individual transformation, such as behavioral changes and psychological shifts in perception that change one's sense of identity and priorities in life. These varied reactions toward the traumatic event of HIV diagnosis and subsequent phases of disease progression can influence a patient's psychological, behavioral, and immune responses. Although there are many negative cofactors associated with disease, there are also positive factors and strengths that buffer against mental and physical illness. This review finds ample evidence of PTG, positive changes and perceived benefits, among people living with HIV/AIDS and their caregivers. Further, this evidence is suggestive that experiencing higher levels of PTG is beneficial in the adaptation to HIV/AIDS over time. Because a large amount of variation in HIV disease progression remains unknown and preliminary research finds salutary relationships between PTG and markers of disease course and important health behaviors, the underlying process and secondary benefits of PTG remain a fertile area for future research among this population. Thus, there is strong justification for continuing these and similar efforts as they will not only aid future research examining these processes among other populations, but will also enable health care professionals to better understand the impact of positive beliefs and psychosocial factors on the disease adjustment process.

REFERENCES

Affleck, G., & Tennen, H. (1996). Construing benefits from adversity: Adaptational significance and dispositional underpinnings. *Journal of Personality, 64*(4), 899–922.

Affleck, G., Tennen, H., Croog, S., & Levine, S. (1987). Causal attribution, perceived benefits, and morbidity after a heart attack: An 8-year study. *Journal of Consulting and Clinical Psychology, 55*, 29–35.

Andrykowski, M. A., Brady, M. J., & Hunt, J. W. (1993). Positive psychosocial adjustment in potential bone marrow transplant recipients: Cancer as a psychosocial transition. *Psycho-oncology, 2*, 261–276.

Antoni, M. H., Lehman, J. M., Kilbourn, K. M., Boyers, A. E., Culver, J. L., Alferi, S. M., et al. (2001). Cognitive-behavioral stress management intervention decreases the prevalence of depression and enhances benefit finding among women under treatment for early-stage breast cancer. *Health Psychology, 20*, 20–32.

Antoni, M. H., Wagner, S., Cruess, D. G., Kumar, M., Lutgendorf, S. K., Ironson, G., et al. (2000). Cognitive behavioral stress management reduces distress and 24-hour urinary free cortisol among symptomatic HIV-infected gay men. *Annals of Behavioral Medicine, 22*, 29–37.

Barroso, J. (1996). Focusing on living: Attitudinal approaches of long-term survivors of AIDS. *Issues in Mental Health Nursing, 17*, 395–407.

Bower, J. E., Kemeny, M. E., Taylor, S. E., & Fahey, J. L. (1998). Cognitive processing, discovery of meaning, CD4 decline, and AIDS-related mortality among bereaved HIV-seropositive men. *Journal of Consulting and Clinical Psychology, 66*, 979–986.

Brashers, D. E., Neidig, J. L., Cardillo, L. W., Dobbs, L. K., & Russell, J. A. (1999). "In an important way, I did die": Uncertainty and revival in persons living with HIV or AIDS. *AIDS Care, 11*(2), 201–219.

Cadell, S. (2001). Post-traumatic growth in HIV/AIDS caregivers in Quebec. *Canadian Social Work, 3,* 86–94.

Cadell, S. (2003). Trauma and growth in Canadian carers. *AIDS Care, 15,* 639–648.

Cadell, S., Regehr, C., & Hemsworth, D. (2003). Factors contributing to posttraumatic growth: A proposed structural equation model. *American Journal of Orthopsychiatry, 73,* 279–287.

Clipp, E. C., Adinolfi, A. J., Forrest, L., & LBennett, C. L. (1995). Informal caregivers of persons with AIDS. *Journal of Palliative Care, 11*(2), 10–18.

Cole, S. W., & Kemeny, M. E. (1997). Pyschobiology of HIV infection. *Critical Reviews in Neurobiology, 11*(4), 289–321.

Collins, R. L., Kanouse, D. E., Gifford, A. L., Senterfitt, J. W., Schuster, M. A., McCaffrey, D. F., et al. (2001). Changes in health-promoting behavior following diagnosis with HIV: Prevalence and correlates in a national probability sample. *Health Psychology, 20,* 351–360.

Cordova, M. J., Cunningham, L. L. C., Carlson, C. R., & Andrykowski, M. A. (2001). Posttraumatic growth following breast cancer: A controlled comparison study. *Health Psychology, 20,* 176–185.

Coward, D. D. (1994). Meaning and purpose in the lives of persons with AIDS. *Public Health Nursing, 11,* 331–336.

Coward, D. D. (1995). The lived experience of self-transcendence in women with AIDS. *JOGNN—Journal of Obstetric, Gynecologic, & Neonatal Nursing, 24,* 314–318.

Coward, D. D., & Lewis, F. M. (1993). The lived experience of self-transcendence in gay men with AIDS. *Oncology Nursing Forum, 20*(9), 1363–1368.

Cruess, D. G., Antoni, M. H., McGregor, B. A., Kilbourn, K. M., Boyers, A. E., Alferi, S. M., et al. (2000). Cognitive-behavioral stress management reduces serum cortisol by enhancing benefit finding among women being treated for early stage breast cancer. *Psychosomatic Medicine, 62*(3), 304–308.

Davis, C. G., Nolen-Hoeksema, S., & Larson, J. (1998). Making sense of loss and benefiting from the experience: Two construals of meaning. *Journal of Personality and Social Psychology, 75,* 561–574.

Dull, V. T., & Skokan, L. A. (1995). A cognitive model of religion's influence on health. *Journal of Social Issues, 51,* 49–64.

Epel, E. S., McEwen, B. S., & Ickovics, J. R. (1998). Embodying psychological thriving: Physical thriving in response to stress. *Journal of Social Issues, 54,* 301–322.

Feigel, C. A. (2003). *Stress, coping, and medication adherence among HIV infected mothers.* Unpublished doctoral dissertation, University of Southern California.

Folkman, S. (1997). Positive psychological states and coping with severe stress. *Social Science & Medicine, 45*(8), 1207–1221.

Frankl, V. (1963). *Man's search for meaning: An introduction to logotherapy.* New York: Pocket Books.

Hall, B. (1990). The struggle of the dianosed terminally ill person to maintain hope. *Nursing Science Quarterly, 3,* 177–184.

Hays, R. B., Catania, J., McKusik, L., & Coates, T. J. (1990). Help-seeking for AIDS-related concerns: a comparison of gay men with various HIV diagnoses. *American Journal of Community Psychology, 18,* 743–755.

Judd, F. K., Cocktam, A. M., Komiti, A., Mijch, A. M., Hoy, J., & Bell, R. (2000). Depressive symptoms reduced in individuals with HIV/AIDS treated with highly active antiretroviral therapy: A longitudinal study. *Australian and New Zealand Journal of Psychiatry, 30,* 1015–1021.

Kalichman, S. C. (1995). *Understanding AIDS.* Washington, DC: American Psychological Association.

Kaplan, M., Marks, G., & Metens, S. (1997). Distress and coping among HIV infection: Preliminary finidngs from a multiethnic sample. *American Journal of Orthopsychiatry, 6,* 80–91.

Kemppainen, J. K. (2001). Predictors of quality of life in AIDS patients. *Journal of the Association of Nurses in AIDS Care, 12*(1), 61–70.

Kiecolt-Glaser, J. K., & Glaser, R. (2002). Depression and immune function: Central pathways to morbidity and mortality. *Journal of Psychosomatic Research, 53*(4), 873–876.

Lawless, S., Kippax, S., & Crawford, J. (1996). Dirty, diseased and undeserving: The positioning of HIV positive women. *Social Science & Medicine, 43,* 1371–1377.

Lechner, S. C., Zakowski, S. G., Antoni, M. H., Greenhawt, M., Block, K., & Block, P. (2003). Do sociodemographic and disease-related variables influence benefit-finding in cancer patients? *Psycho-oncology, 12*(5), 491–499.

Lutgendorf, S. K., Antoni, M. H., Ironson, G., Starr, K., Costello, N., Zuckerman, M., et al. (1998). Changes in cognitive coping skills and social support during cognitive behavioral stress managment intervention and distress outcomes in symptomatic human immunodeficiency virus (HIV)-seropositive gay men. *Psychosomatic Medicine, 60*(2), 204–214.

Mellors, M. P., Riley, T. A., & Erlen, J. A. (1997). HIV, self-transcendence, and quality of life. *JANAC, 8*(2), 59–69.

Metcalfe, K. A., Langstaff, J. E., Evans, S. J., Paterson, H. M., & Reid, J. L. (1998). Meeting the needs of women living with HIV. *Public Health Nursing, 15*, 30–34.

Milam, J. E. (2005). *Posttraumatic growth and HIV disease progression*. unpublished manuscript.

Milam, J. E. (2004). Postraumatic growth among HIV/AIDS patients. *Journal of Applied Social Psychology, 34*, 2353–2376.

Milam, J. E., Richardson, J. L., Marks, G., Kemper, C. A., & McCutchan, A. J. (2004). The roles of dispositional optimism and pessimism in HIV disease progression. *Psychology and Health, 19*(2), 167–181.

Milam, J. E., Ritt-Olson, A., & Unger, J. (2004). Posttraumatic growth among adolescents. *Journal of Adolescent Research, 19*(2), 192–204.

Moskowitz, J. T. (2003). Positive affect predicts lower risk of AIDS mortality. *Psychosomatic Medicine, 65*, 620–626.

Ostrow, D. G. (1997). Disease, disease course, and psychiatric manifestations of HIV. In I. D. Yalom (Ed.), *Treating the psychological consequences of HIV* (pp. 33–71). San Francisco: Jossey-Bass.

Page-Shafer, K., Delorenze, G. N., Satariano, W. A., & Winkelstein, W. (1996). Comorbidity and survival in HIV-infected men in the San Francisco Men's Health Survey. *Annals of Epidemiology, 6*, 420–430.

Park, C. L., Cohen, L. H., & Murch, R. L. (1996). Assessment and prediction of stress-related growth. *Journal of Personality, 64*(1), 71–105.

Paterson, D., Swindells, S., Mohr, J., Brester, M., Vergis, R., Squier, C., et al. (2000). Adherence to protease inhibitor therapy and outcomes in patients with HIV infection. *Annals of Internal Medicine, 133*, 21–30.

Rabkin, J. G., Ferrando, S. J., van Gorp, W., Ricppi, R., McElhiney, M., & Sewell, M. (2000). Relationship among apathy, depression, and cognitive impaiment in HIV/AIDS. *Journal of Neuropsychiatry and Clinical Neuroscience, 12*, 451–457.

Richardson, J. L., Barkan, S., Cohen, M., Back, S., FitzGerald, G., Feldman, J., et al. (2001). Experience and covariates of depressive symptoms among a cohort of HIV infected women. *Social Work in Health Care, 32*, 93–111.

Schwartzberg, S. S. (1994). Vitality and growth in HIV-infected gay men. *Social Science and Medicine, 39*, 593–602.

Sears, S. R., Stanton, A. L., & Dannoff-Burg, S. (2003). The yellow brick road and the emerald city: Benefit finding, positive reappraisal coping and posttraumatic growth in women with early stage breast cancer. *Health Psychology, 22*, 487–497.

Siegel, K., & Schrimshaw, E. W. (2000). Perceiving benefits in adversity: stress-related growth in women living with HIV/AIDS. *Social Science and Medicine, 51*, 1543–1554.

Siegel, K., & Schrimshaw, E. W. (2002). The perceived benefits of religious and spiritual coping among older adults living with HIV/AIDS. *Journal for the Scientific Study of Religion, 41*(1), 91–102.

Taylor, S. E., Kemeny, M. E., Reed, G. M., Bower, J. E., & Gruenewald, T. L. (2000). Psychological resources, positive illusions, and health. *American Psychologist, 55*(1), 99–109.

Tedeschi, R. G., & Calhoun, L. G. (1995). *Trauma & transformation: growing in the aftermath of suffering.* Thousand Oaks, CA: Sage..

Tedeschi, R. G., & Calhoun, L. G. (1996). The posttraumatic growth inventory: Measuring the positive legacy of trauma. *Journal of Traumatic Stress, 9*, 455–471.

Tedeschi, R. G., & Calhoun, L. G. (2004). Posttraumatic growth: Conceptual foundations and empirical evidence. *Psychological Inquiry, 15*(1), 1–18.

Thompson, S. C. (1985). Finding positive meaning in a stressful event and coping. *Basic and Applied Social Psychology, 6,* 279–295.

UNAIDS. (2004). *2004: Report on the global AIDS epidemic.* Geneva, Switzerland: Author.

Updegraff, J. A., Taylor, S. E., Kemeny, M. E., & Wyatt, G. E. (2002). Positive and negative effects of HIV infection in women with low socioeconomic resources. *Personality and Social Psychology Bulletin, 28*(3), 382–394.

Viney, L. L., Crooks, L., Walker, B. M., & Henry, R. (1991). Psychological frailness and strength in an AIDS-affected community: A study of seropositive gay men and voluntary caregivers. *American Journal of Community Psychology, 19*(2), 279–287.

12

POSTTRAUMATIC GROWTH IN DISASTER AND EMERGENCY WORK

DOUGLAS PATON
UNIVERSITY OF TASMANIA, LAUNCESTON

On the occasion of every accident that befalls you, remember to turn to yourself and inquire what power you have to turn it to use.

—Epictetus 60–120 A.D.

Since the 1980s, research conducted on the consequences of exposure to traumatic events has witnessed a gradual shift from a focus on their pathogenic nature to a perspective that recognizes the prominent role of positive outcomes in peoples' experiences with adversity. The idea that suffering can lead to personal growth is not new. The quote from Epictetus illustrates that the fundamental idea has been around for some time. Similar historical accounts of the link between suffering and wisdom are discussed elsewhere (Tedeschi & Calhoun, 1995). Recent years have, however, witnessed not just a greater acceptance of this phenomenon, but also the systematic investigation into its causes (Armeli, Gunthert, & Cohen, 2001; Aspinwall & Staudinger, 2003; Tedeschi & Calhoun, 2003). It is this systematic research that affords the opportunity to build understanding of the phenomenon and to apply the lessons learned to assist survivors of trauma.

In a series of studies, Calhoun and Tedeschi (Calhoun, Cann, Tedeschi, & McMillan, 2000; Calhoun & Tedeschi, 1998; Tedeschi & Calhoun, 1995, 1996; Tedeschi, Park, & Calhoun, 1998) reported that, following experience of a traumatic event (e.g., bereavement, chronic illness, human immunodeficiency virus [HIV], cancer, heart attacks, vehicle accidents, rape, sexual abuse, hostage taking), many survivors emerged from their ordeal with a belief that they had benefited from their experience. Irrespective of the specific traumatic event, similar personal transformations were reported. Tedeschi and Calhoun (1995, 1996) encapsulated this outcome in a model that described how the process of struggling with crises provides opportunities for personal growth that would not have been possible without the challenge of the traumatic event. They coined the term *posttraumatic growth* (PTG) (Tedeschi & Calhoun, 1995) to describe this outcome. Tedeschi and Calhoun (2003) define PTG as significant beneficial changes in cognitive and emotional life beyond levels of adaptation, psychological functioning, or life awareness that occur in the aftermath of psychological traumas that challenge previously existing assumptions about self, others, and the future. Its appearance on the traumatic stress landscape has significant implications not only for conceptualising traumatic stress, but also for how traumatic experiences are managed (Tedeschi & Calhoun, 2003). This is particularly so in duty-related populations. To date, the majority of research into PTG has focused on lay populations. While it has not, as yet, attracted the same degree of attention, the literature on duty-related traumatic stress has begun to travel down a similar path.

Given the nature of their role, the careers of protective service (e.g., law enforcement, fire and rescue services), emergency and humanitarion aid (e.g., medial and mental health, Red Cross), and military professionals are regularly punctuated by exposure to emergencies and disasters. To assume that exposure to the adverse events encountered in the course of performing their professional role produces only deficit or pathological outcomes ignores an important reality. Consequently, the validity of the pathological paradigm, which has long dominated research in this area and which fuels the former view, as a basis for conceptualizing duty-related traumatic stress is coming under increasingly critical scrutiny (Stuhlmiller & Dunning, 2000).

Exposure to adverse duties need not always result in negative consequences. A growing body of evidence attests to the fact that such duties can result in positive outcomes (Aldwin, Levenson, & Spiro, 1994; Alexander & Wells, 1991; Anderson, Christenson, & Peterson, 1991; Gist & Woodall, 2000; Hartsough & Myers, 1985; Moran, 1999; Moran & Colless, 1995; North, et al., 2002; Paton, 1994; Paton, Cox, & Andrew, 1989; Paton, Violanti, & Smith, 2003; Raphael, 1986; Tedeschi & Calhoun, 2003). Officers may feel that, despite the horror, they value the traumatic event as a learning and growth experience, and interpret them as rewarding and satisfying. Officers report the knowledge of being able to exercise professional skills to achieve highly meaningful outcomes in a manner rarely possible in routine contexts as a significant positive outcome. They have also reported PTG, a sense of personal and professional development, a greater appreciation for family, life, and colleagues, and an enhanced sense of control over significant adverse events.

Notwithstanding, and despite growing evidence that positives outweigh the negatives, ingrained beliefs regarding an automatic link between traumatic experience and deficit outcomes are difficult to change (Raphael, 2000). Aldwin et al. (1994) discuss several factors that hinder acceptance of positive consequences. These include the predominant focus on measures of pathological symptoms, a failure to accommodate potentially rapid decline in symptoms, and a focus on short- rather than long-term consequences. The availability of instruments such as the Posttraumatic Growth Inventory (PTGI) (Tedeschi & Calhoun, 1996) afford opportunities to challenge beliefs regarding the dominance of the link between trauma and negative outcomes and conduct more balanced analyses of the consequences of traumatic experience.

As a consequence of the dominant focus on lay populations within PTG research, this chapter commences with a brief summary of the key lessons that can be extracted from this literature to inform its relevance for emergency populations. Before commencing with this discussion, an important issue for consideration is the degree to which growth is sustained (Aldwin et al., 1994). This issue is particularly important for emergency pro-fessions. Because their officers will encounter traumatic events repeatedly, organizational commitment to traumatic stress management interventions to promote growth will relate directly to the enduring nature of the benefits that accrue from their implementation.

In their review, Linley and Joseph (2004) note the paucity of longitudinal studies of growth, but state that those that do exist consistently support the conclusion that growth is an enduring phenomenon. The longitudinal studies they reviewed suggest that PTG develops over time, with most occurring between two weeks and two months, with reported levels remaining stable through 6-, 12-, and 36-month periods. Predictors of enduring growth include self-efficacy and positive affect, although the latter has not enjoyed universal support (Linley & Joseph, 2004). Additional issues render the situation with emergency workers more complex. In regard to the latter, questions regarding the sustainability of benefits must be examined in relation to repeated exposure to traumatic events within organizational contexts before a firm conclusion on this issue can be reached. This represents an area where more work is required. In the interim, available evidence confirms the enduring nature of PTG and warrants its systematic study in emergency professions. The next question concerns the degree to which the findings and conceptual frameworks identified in PTG research provide a foundation for its systematic study in emergency populations.

POSTTRAUMATIC GROWTH RESEARCH

Taylor, Wood, and Lichtman's (1983) research on survivors of life-threatening attacks, illness, and natural disasters concluded that not only did the majority of those so exposed overcome the victimizing aspects of the experience, many actually benefited from it. They acknowledge that some people will not readjust successfully. Most, however, do, and they do so substantially on their own. This prompts the need to identify the resources and processes people bring to bear on their experiences to facilitate growth outcomes.

Taylor et al. (1983) concluded that a prominent predictor of growth is finding meaning in the experience. The search for meaning involves not only understanding why the event occurred, but also its implications for life from then on. The role of growth occurring from the integration of experiences in a learning process was also emphasised by McMillen, Zuravin, and Rideout (1995) and Znoj (2000). Posttraumatic growth can also occur from challenges to values and beliefs that arise from vicarious exposure to threatening events (Linley, Joseph, Cooper, Harris, & Myer 2003). From the perspective of emergency professions, the existence of a learning component in the process of PTG is particularly important. It means that once the resources and processes associated with growth are identified, attention can be directed to exploring how these competencies can be developed and sustained (e.g., through training, organizational development). Realizing the benefits of this knowledge can be facilitated by having a conceptual or theoretical framework to guide its application.

The theory of selective evaluation (Taylor et al., 1983) argues that survivors respond to the subjective experience of negative consequences in themselves and others by reframing themselves and their situation in ways that are self-enhancing. This can be achieved using one of several mechanisms of selective evaluation: making social comparisons with less fortunate others (downward comparisons); selectively focusing on attributes that make themselves appear advantaged; creating hypothetical worse worlds; construing benefits from the aversive event; and manufacturing normative standards of adjustment to make their own adjustment appear exceptional. The theory of cognitive adaptation extended this perspective (Taylor, 1983). Positive outcomes following adverse events result when people selectively distort memories of the experience to reduce its negative impact on themselves and the world, or they represent it in as nonthreatening a manner as possible. When negative consequences are inevitable, the person may try to balance them by considering perceived gains from the event, such as finding meaning in the experience, or considering that they are a better person for having withstood the event (Collins, Taylor, & Skokan, 1990).

It is widely held that ruminations and the common symptoms of traumatic experience, intrusion, and avoidance, are associated with both deficit and growth outcomes. They are indicative of the cognitive processing associated with rebuilding schemata thrown into disequilibrium by a traumatic experience (Aldwin et al., 1994; Calhoun & Tedeschi, 1998; Janof-Bulman, 1992; Linley & Joseph, 2004; MacLeod & Paton, 1999; Paton, 1994; Tedeschi & Calhoun, 1995). Schemata describe the cognitive organization of the self and the world in ways that allow a person to render it meaningful, comprehensible, and manageable (e.g., the occurrence of only expected events). Traumatic events call these assumptions into question and necessitate change in schematic content and organization. Cognitive processing and rumination about the event can result in beneficial changes in the understanding of the self and the world, enhance perceived capability to deal with adversity, promote engagement in previously unconsidered or untried activities, and lead to survivors perceiving a sense of growth. Paradoxically, these benefits result from loss or suffering (Tedeschi & Calhoun, 1995). This happens not because of the trauma per se, but rather it is the persons' internal struggle with the event and the changes it has wrought, that is the source of PTG. This struggle takes place internally through the process of rumination (Calhoun & Tedeschi, 1998). They found a relationship between the amount of PTG reported and event-related rumination. The more rumination the participants reported experiencing soon after the event, the greater the degree of PTG reported.

Tedeschi and Calhoun's (1995) model of PTG, and other studies of adversarial growth (e.g., Linley & Joseph, 2004), focus on positive change. However, not everyone triumphs over trauma, and the transformation may also be accompanied by some distress and negative consequences (Tedeschi & Calhoun, 2003). Thus, this more recent expansion in explanatory paradigms does not deny the potential for adverse outcomes to accompany traumatic experience. Rather, it argues for a more comprehensive approach, and one that accommodates both positive and negative dimensions. Importantly, it is also becoming apparent that these outcomes should not be considered in an either/or manner.

Collins et al. (1990) found that while respondents described both positive and negative changes following diagnosis of cancer, overall they reported significantly more positive changes in their lives. Joseph, Williams, and Yule (1993) observed that while many survivors of a passenger ferry disaster remained traumatized three years after the event, most survivors reported strong positive changes in their outlook on life, feeling more experienced about life, and over half rated their life as changed for the better. Some 90% agreed that they no longer took life for granted and that they valued their relationships and no longer took people or things for granted. Overall, positive changes were endorsed more frequently than negative changes. Furthermore, a growing body of empirical evidence from lay and professional populations alike attests to the fact that these dimensions should be regarded as discrete outcomes capable of existing concurrently (Aldwin et al., 1994; Burke & Paton, in preprararion; Frazier et al., 2001; Hart, & Wearing, 1995; Higgins, 1994; Huddleston, Stevens & Paton, in press; Joseph et al., 1993; Linley & Joseph, 2004; Tedeschi & Calhoun, 2003).

THE COEXISTENCE OF POSITIVE AND NEGATIVE OUTCOMES

Frazier et al's. (2001) study of sexual assault victims described how positive changes (e.g., sense of personal strength) coexisted with a new set of negative beliefs (e.g., regarding their safety and the goodness of people). Janoff-Bulman (1989a, 1989b, 1992) concluded that, following traumatic experience, people can reestablish a positive view of the world and themselves while simultaneously recognizing the limitations of their beliefs. Linley et al. (2003) reported that coexisting positive and negative outcomes could result from vicarious exposure to traumatic events.

In a qualitative analysis of the experience of disaster relief workers, Paton et al. (1989) found that positive (e.g., enhanced sense of personal and professional competency and stronger family bonds) and negative (e.g., unfairness and oppression in the treatment of the citizens in third world countries) beliefs were present simultaneously. In a military population, Aldwin et al. (1994) concluded that positive (e.g., increased independence, self-esteem, or coping skills) and negative (e.g., combat anxieties, loss of friends, or death and destruction) outcomes resulted from the same stressor. Data from 1,287 male veterans revealed both positive and negative consequences, but more weight was given to the former, with both increasing linearly with combat experience. Undesirable effects increased, and desirable effects decreased, the relationship between combat exposure and posttraumatic stress disorder (PTSD) (Aldwin et al., 1994).

Growth and deficit outcomes do not lie at opposite ends of a continuum, and should be conceptualized as discrete dimensions (Burke & Paton, in prepraration; Hart & Wearing, 1995; Huddleston et al., in press; Linley & Joseph, 2004) and managed accordingly. Their discrete nature means that managing deficit outcomes will not enhance growth and vice versa. There is a need for research and intervention to address them concurrently. Accommodating the dichotomous nature of traumatic stress outcomes is particularly important for emergency professions. Because they are exposed to potentially traumatic situations repeatedly over the course of their professional careers, traumatic stress risk management will have to facilitate positive outcomes and minimize negative outcomes. Recognition of this need has implications for how the traumatic stress management process is conceptualized. This issue will be discussed in more detail later in this chapter.

Three main trends are evident in these models of positive consequences following traumatic event exposure. Firstly, ecological and psychological variables mediate the relationship between a traumatic experience and positive or negative consequences (Aldwin et al., 1994). Secondly, most people readjust successfully following traumatic event exposure by finding perceived gains from the experience (Taylor et al., 1983). Finally, many people experience enhanced feelings of personal growth and development following traumatic events by finding meaning and understanding from the experience (Janoff-Bulman, 1992; Paton, 1994; Tedeschi & Calhoun, 1995). Of these, those emphasizing schematic change, benefit finding, meaning, and learning provide a foundation for conceptualizing traumatic stress processes in emergency professions (Paton, 1994). From existing empirical and theoretical work, it can be inferred that the PTG construct has considerable relevance for emergency populations.

POSTTRAUMATIC GROWTH AND EMERGENCY PROFESSIONS

Models of occupational and duty-related traumatic stress based on a dynamic-equilibrium conceptualization (e.g., Hart & Cooper, 2001; Paton, 1994) provide a foundation for the analysis of PTG in emergency populations. This approach argues that certain environmental demands, "critical" incidents, can threaten psychological equilibrium by challenging the assumptions and mental models derived from training, operational practices, and experience that guide expectations, behavior, and reactions (Paton, 1994). Disequilibrium represents the period during which previous assumptions have lost their capacity to organize experience in meaningful ways. Therefore, the event that triggers the disequilibrium acts as a catalyst for change. Given the volume of work on lay populations, can it provide a comprehensive account of growth in emergency professionals? Or, to put it another way, should emergency professions be investigated separately?

There are several reasons why the answer to the latter question is "yes." Emergency professionals face exposure to adverse events repeatedly over the course of their professional careers. Assessment of growth must be examined against this background. An important motivational factor for entering an emergency profession is helping people. The importance of this motivational factor is reinforced by the finding that reminding themselves of their helping role is a prominent coping strategy in emergency populations (Miller, 1995). Emergency workers also elect to enter a profession that implicitly increases the likelihood of their exposure to adverse events. Exercising their professional responsibilities and competencies affords the opportunity to interpret their involvement, in some contexts at least, as opportunities to help people (who are faced with significant adversity) in ways that could have salutary and beneficial consequences for them and the communities they have elected to serve. Thus, when responding to an incident, emergency professionals can interpret their experience of both in terms of its adverse qualities and in regard to their role in providing meaningful assistance. This reiterates the importance of accommodating the coexistence of positive and negative outcomes. In addition to understanding the predictors of both outcomes, intervention with emergency professionals requires using this knowledge to manage them in a proactive manner (e.g., through selection, training, organizational change).

Research on PTG in lay populations has focused on person and dispositional variables. While it can be anticipated that they will play a similar role in all people, the possibility of self-selection into professions that involve exposure to traumatic circumstances, may affect the utility of certain variables (e.g., personality) as predictors (Thomson & Solomon, 1991) of growth in emergency professions or reduce their predictive utility relative to, say, interpretive and coping variables and organizational factors.

In contrast to the manner in which lay persons experience traumatic events, emergency workers experience them in the context of their professional and organizational membership. The organizational environment influences patterns of interaction with traumatic events (Aldwin et al., 1994; Alexander & Wells, 1991; Gist & Woodall, 2000; Paton, 1994). Organizational factors are known to affect stress reactions, the meaning of work, and support practices. Variables at this level may exercise a similar influence on PTG.

Emergency and lay populations also differ in the nature of their involvement in a traumatic incident. Emergency profession involvement progresses through a series of stages: mobilization, response, and recovery and reintegration. Each has different implications for the demands officers encounter and the manner in which they interpret them (Paton & Hannan, 2004). In addition to understanding the influence of each stage, the manner in which experiences in each stage interact must also be considered. For example, the cohesion that emerges from a sense of shared fate during an incident can facilitate personal and group growth. However, if routine duties involve working with officers who have not shared this specific experience, growth potential may be replaced with a greater risk of deficit outcomes (MacLeod & Paton, 1999; Paton & Stephens, 1996).

While similarities between lay and professional populations in regard to predictors of PTG exist, significant differences between them necessitates attention being directed to understanding the specific issues faced by professional populations. Identifying the nature of the factors and processes that predict growth provides the foundation for this work (Aldwin et al., 1994; Higgins, 1994; Linley & Jospeh, 2004; Paton et al., 2003). It is to a discussion of these factors, and the context in which they arise, that this chapter now turns. It does so in the context of a risk management paradigm capable of accommodating both positive and negative outcomes.

TRAUMATIC STRESS RISK MANAGEMENT

Managing positive and negative outcomes that can coexist poses conceptual and practical problems for emergency organizations. That is, once they have identified the beliefs, resources, competencies, and processes that result in some traumatic experiences being resolved in a positive manner (e.g., PTG) and some being resolved as deficit outcomes (e.g., learned avoidance of threat situations), emergency organizations need a framework to support the policy and procedures required for comprehensive traumatic stress management. It is proposed here that risk management provides this framework.

The risk management paradigm encapsulates both growth/adaptation and deficit/loss outcomes (Dake, 1992; Hood & Jones, 1996; Paton, Violanti et al., 2003; Paton et al., 2004). According to this paradigm, risk is defined by the interaction between psychological hazards and factors that determine their experience as positive or negative. Hazard analysis identifies the event characteristics, and professional and organizational factors capable of challenging assumptions and creating psychological disequilibrium. By defining event demands as critical experiences that challenge assumptions and thus create a context for change, a priori assumptions regarding assumed automatic links with distress outcomes can be questioned and a more neutral basis for conceptualizing traumatic experiences is created. Rather, the outcome is a product of the interaction between hazards and the growth and vulnerability processes (at individual, group, and environmental levels) brought to bear on or activated in a specific context. Information from these three sources is combined to estimate risk under specific circumstances. The acceptability or otherwise of the ensuing risk estimate informs the development of risk management policies and practices in emergency organizations. While the nature of emergency work precludes preventing exposure to adverse events, choices regarding the consequences of traumatic experience can be made through planning and preparedness interventions designed to reduce vulnerability and enhance potential for growth.

The next stage in the process is identifying the specific resources and processes that contribute to the capacity of individuals, teams, and organizations to confront adversity, organize experience, and reconstruct interpretive schema in ways marked by growth and development. In regard to the nature of growth resources, emergency professions will utilize dispositional and interpretive processes similar to those identified in lay populations. There are, however, others that need to be considered when working with emergency populations (Aldwin et al., 1994; Gist & Woodall, 2000; Linley & Joseph, 2004; Paton, Smith, Violanti, & Eranen, 2000; Paton & Hannan, 2004). In emergency professions, interpretive processes, group/team resources, and organizational factors must also be considered. Analysis of this process commences with a brief introduction to traumatic incident stress hazards—the event characteristics capable of eliciting the loss of equilibrium that provides the foundation for growth.

GROWTH DURING TRAUMATIC INCIDENT RESPONSE

One event characteristic common to lay and professional populations alike is the intensity of the traumatic experience (Linley & Joseph, 2004). In military populations, Aldwin et al. (1994) and Schnurr, Rosenberg, and Friedman (1993) described an inverted-u function for desirable effects. Benefits were stronger at intermediate rather than high or low levels of exposure to combat hazards. However, traumatic events also expose emergency professionals to several psychological hazards capable of challenging operational and professional assumptions (Alexander & Wells, 1991; Davies & Walters, 1998; Gist & Woodall, 2000; Paton, 1994, 1997; Paton & Hannan, 2004).

These can emanate from both event (e.g., physical danger) and professional (e.g., decision making) sources. For example, because they threaten perceived control, events whose cause is attributed to acts of omission (e.g., building collapse from poor workmanship) or commission (e.g., terrorist bombing) are more significant hazards than their natural counterparts (MacLeod & Paton, 1999). Uncertainty regarding threat duration, length of involvement, threat recurrence (e.g., earthquake aftershocks), are factors all capable of challenging operational beliefs and threatening psychological integrity (Paton, 1994, 1997). So, too, is personal danger (e.g., working in unsafe buildings, exposure to toxic chemicals, biological or radiation hazards), managing the scale, complexity, and urgency of demands; making decisions on the basis of incomplete and ambiguous data; and managing contradictory demands.

These hazards are critical in the sense that they can require people and organizations to confront assumptions and so represent a context for personal and organizational change. Whether the new equilibrium state that ensues is characterized by growth or loss is a function of how hazard experience interacts with the resources and processes activated by or brought to bear on the experience. Discussion of these factors commences with personal factors.

Personal Factors

In regard to dispositional factors, personality, attributional style, hardiness, emotional stability, self-awareness, tolerance for ambiguity, self-efficacy, and coping have been implicated (Bartone, 2003; Flin, 1996; Linley & Joseph, 2004; MacLeod & Paton, 1999; Paton, Violanti & Smith, 2003; Shakespeare-Finch, 2002; Tedeschi et al., 1998). In their comprehensive review of individual predictors of PTG, Linley and Joseph (2004) described the following categories of individual factors: cognitive appraisal, social-demographic, personality, coping, and processing. In regard to cognitive appraisal, growth was predicted by perceived threat and controllability. Sociodemographic predictors included being female, older adolescents, income, and education. Factors, such as extraversion, openness to experience, agreeableness, conscientiousness, self-efficacy, hardiness, and optimism were implicated as predictors. Problem-focused and emotion-focused coping predicted growth, as did positive reinterpretation. Their final category, processing, included rumination and the traumatic stress symptoms, avoidance and intrusion.

While research on professional populations has been less extensive, work on the relationship between personality and PTG in emergency professions tends to reiterate their role in lay populations. In the most comprehensive study of personality and coping influences on PTG (using the PTGI), Shakespeare-Finch (2002) demonstrated a role for extraversion, openness to experience, agreeableness, conscientiousness, self-efficacy, optimism, and hope as predictors of PTG in ambulance officers. She also reiterated earlier findings (Tedeschi et al., 1998) regarding the fact that personality factors did not have a direct influence on PTG. Rather, their role is mediated by coping. In regard to coping strategies, Shakespeare-Finch (2002) found that emotional support and expression and positive reframing were the strongest predictors. As with the other dispositional variables examined, the influence of the latter variables is mediated by coping. These relationships

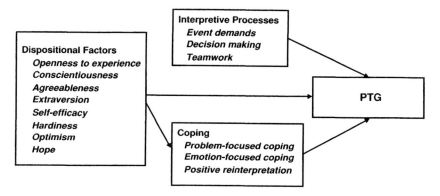

FIGURE 12.1.   A summary of the relationship between person factors and PTG.

are summarised in Figure 12.1. In regard to dispositional predictors of PTG per se, these findings endorse those noted by Linley & Joseph (2004) for lay populations.

Smith and Paton (2002) conducted a prospective study of the relationship between personality and PTG (using the PTGI). This pilot study involved examining whether personality factors, obtained from 68 police officers during their selection, predicted PTG during their subsequent service. Data on PTG was assessed between two and seven years after their recruitment (when the personality data were collected). In this sample, the only significant predictor was extraversion ($r = .38$, $p < .05$). This finding is consistent with Thompson and Solomon's (1991) finding that members of body-recovery teams recorded levels of extraversion that were elevated relative to population norms. A relationship between extraversion and finding benefit from adverse experience has also been noted (Affleck & Tennen, 1996). Age also predicted PTG ($r = .21$, $p < .05$). As point of entry age increased, so did PTG while on active duty. The small sample size and differences in the nature and frequency of traumatic experience suggests caution in the interpretation of these data. It also echoes Linley and Joseph's (2004) call for additional longitudinal work. Longitudinal studies have, to date, provided inconsistent views of the role of dispositional predictors over the longer term (Linley & Joseph, 2004). Once confirmed, knowledge of these relationships can inform selection and monitoring processes (Paton, 1997).

Interpretive Processes

The basic principle of Tedeschi & Calhoun's (Tedeschi & Calhoun, 2003; Tedeschi & Calhoun, 1995) model is that growth occurs when people's schemas develop through interaction with a traumatic event. These schemata render the world of experience meaningful, comprehensible, and manageable. When confronted with a reality that is impossible to assimilate within existing schemata, cognitive processing and rumination about the experience can result in a more profound understanding of the self and the world and enhance capacity to deal with adversity. This occurs less because of the traumatic experience, and more as a consequence of the persons' internal struggle with the event and the changes it has wrought. Thus the source of PTG is this internal struggle involving the process of rumination (Calhoun & Tedeschi, 1998).

Interpretive processes influence outcome in emergency professions. Individuals who find meaning in their work report higher levels of perceived benefits from their work (Britt, Adler, & Bartone, 2001; Paton, 1994). While lacking the benefit of having a systematic way to assess it, qualitative analyses of accounts of the experience of disaster workers (Paton, 1994; Paton et al., 1989) echo the dimensions of PTG. Beneficial consequences were linked to the struggle with experiences and memories, usually over a period of several months. The outcomes of thinking and talking about the experience was reflected in, for example, a stronger sense of individual and professional competence; greater appreciation of family, friends, and colleagues; an enhanced sense of the importance of family and work relationships; increased empathy; and recognizing the importance of living for the day and of appreciating life. The derivation of benefit is linked to the existence of schema capable of facilitating positive interpretation (Paton, 1994).

For example, the scale of disaster impact can limit opportunities for effective action. Vulnerability increases if these limitations are perceived as a failure attributed to personal inadequacy rather than to environmental constraints beyond an individual's control. This process has been labeled *performance guilt* (Raphael, 1986). However, training that develops realistic outcome expectations, an ability to differentiate personal and situational constraints, and interpretive processes that review experiences as learning opportunities that enhance future competence increases the likelihood of positive outcomes (Dunning, 2003; Paton, 1994; Paton & Jackson, 2002). Positive interpretation (e.g., body recovery assists families to begin the grieving process, not a rescue failure) facilitates adaptation (Paton, 1994; Thompson, 1993). These findings suggest a need to develop the capability of operational mental models (essential to response planning and organizing action) to impose the coherence on atypical and complex emergencies (Dunning, 2003; Paton, 1994; Paton & Jackson, 2002) required to facilitate growth.

Paton, Huddlestone, and Stephens (2003) discussed anecdotal accounts illustrating how feelings of personal growth could result from interaction between preemployment traumatic experiences and police training. Female officers who cited sexual assault as their most significant traumatic event prior to employment reported a dramatic decline in Impact of Event Scale (IES) symptoms over this first year of police training and police work. Officers accounted for this decline in terms of their ability to use their training to better understand their experience. That is, training provided a means for imposing meaning on adverse experience.

Strategies designed to develop interpretive schema should address three areas (Inzana, Driskell, Salas, & Johnston, 1996; Paton, 1994; Paton & Jackson, 2002). First, they should cover procedural issues (e.g., events likely to be experienced in the transition from normal to stress conditions and vice versa, event demands). Second, they should cover sensory data—the sights, sounds, smells, and feelings associated with the event. Third, they should include instrumental information (e.g., describing factual information relevant to the upcoming event).

Given the acknowledged importance of schemata capable of rendering challenging or threatening events capable of facilitating growth, it is pertinent to ask whether this mechanism can be applied to the professional response demands capable of challenging assumptions (e.g., decision making). The answer would appear to be "yes." While it remains to be systematically analyzed specifically in relation to PTG outcomes, this section reviews work that supports this approach. It does so with reference to two common sources of professional demand associated with emergency and disaster response, decision making and team work.

Information and Decision Management

For trained personnel, crises enhance alertness and thinking skills (Flin, 1996). However, utilizing this capacity requires a capability to operate in challenging operational environments characterized by both information overload and underload. Situational awareness, a capability to extract or operate on limited cues from a complex or information-sparse context to construct a mental model that allows satisficing decisions to be taken, is a key adaptive capacity (Endsley & Garland, 2000). The decision process used must also be tailored to this circumstance.

Naturalistic decision making, where a person recognizes the type of situation encountered and, from previous experience, selects an appropriate course of action, is highly adaptive in events characterized by substantial time pressure and high risk (Flin, Salas, Strub, & Martin, 1997). Because success in naturalistic decision making is a function of the ability to match current and prior situations, decision effectiveness is enhanced with more options to match. This ability can be developed through experience or simulation. With increasing use of this approach, emergency professionals often engage in more thinking about potential crises and emergencies. This activity can contribute to their developing more sophisticated mental models that facilitate psychological growth and professional development (Flin, 1996).

Team and Interagency Operations

Because emergency response is a team activity, coordination problems and role ambiguity can challenge professional and operational assumptions (Paton, 1994). However, extensive joint planning and activity involving team members, contributes to individual and team development, with exposure to the traumatic event being the catalyst (Paton, et al., 1999; Pollock, Paton, Smith, & Violanti, 2003). Good information sharing is a prominent element of this strategy.

In effective teams, members provide more unprompted information, increasing a capability for proactive response management through better decision making and resource allocation (Entin & Serfaty, 1999). For this to occur effectively, team members must share a "team mental model" that facilitates the provision of goal-related information required by decision makers at critical periods (Cooke, Salas, Cannon-Bowers, & Stout, 2000). As the level of teamwork and planning activity increases, officers develop progressively more sophisticated and more similar mental models of response environments and the roles and tasks performed within them. This, in turn, increases implicit information sharing during high workload periods, enhancing team capacity for adaptive response (Paton & Jackson, 2002; Stout, Cannon-Bowers, Salas, & Milanovich, 1999). The development of these more sophisticated mental models can contribute to growth in team identity and performance capability, particularly when working collectively in complex, threatening environments.

In large-scale disasters, a cohesive interagency team provides the mechanism by which complex and diverse demands are managed (Pollock et al., 2003). However, simply bringing together representatives of agencies likely to have had little contact with one another under normal circumstances increases interagency conflict, results in a blurring of roles and responsibilities, and fuels frustration and feelings of inadequacy and helplessness (Paton, 1994). A capacity for cohesion should thus not be assumed. It can be developed using liaison mechanisms and integrating their respective roles through interagency planning and team development (Flin & Arbuthnot, 2002).

The quality of team development is a function of three factors (Paton et al., 1999). One concerns how participants define interagency team membership. For example, "turf protection" to safeguard an organizations resource base increases vulnerability by reducing willingness to work collaboratively. On the other hand, acceptance of the value of collaboration if complex problems are to be understood and managed can increase a capacity for individual and team development. The second factor concerns patterns of interaction between group members in relation to institutional policies, structures, and culture, and the language and terminology used. The third involves contextual factors, such as understanding of integrated emergency management policies and practices; the status and power accorded to different members; and resource constraints. This introduces the need for organizational change to accompany team development.

At one level, this reflects the level of structural and procedural integration between agencies (Paton et al., 1999). However, it also encompasses participants' understanding of their respective contributions to the same plan and their shared understanding of each member's role in the response. This contributes to their capacity to share a common understanding of evolving events, work toward common goals over time, and, importantly, to anticipate the needs of those with whom they are collaborating (Flin, 1996; Pollock et al., 2003).

The quality of shared understanding and procedural integration thus represents a resource that enhances the capability of the team to develop when dealing with complex, challenging emergencies. It does so by allowing them to utilize their collective expertise (profession, functions, roles), even if dispersed or contributing different perspectives, for problem definition and response coordination. It also helps ensure that they are operating with a shared mental model of the situation that facilitates the effective and efficient allocation and use of scarce resources (Paton & Hannan, 2004).

The development of these interpretive frameworks need not wait for traumatic experiences. Simulation can be used to assist development of realistic performance expectations, increase awareness of stress reactions, and, by facilitating the rehearsal of personal stress response strategies developed in progressively more complex training scenarios, promote stress-related growth (Crego & Spinks, 1997; Paton, 1994; Paton & Jackson, 2002). Support for the potential for simulation to promote PTG comes from work suggesting that it can occur from vicarious challenges to values and beliefs (Linley et al., 2003). In regard to their capacity to stimulate growth, a crucial issue is the inclusion of elements that allow participants to progressively confront operational and professional assumptions (Paton, 1994; Paton & Jackson, 2002; Pollock et al., 2003).

The team issues discussed here are consistent with the concept of organizational coherence discussed by Lissack and Roos (1999) and proposed by Dunning (2003) as a mechanism capable of facilitating adaptation and growth in emergency professions. Lissak and Roos maintain that coherent organizations and people can thrive emotionally, mentally, and physically. A central platform of their thesis is the importance of contemporary organizations focusing on interactions rather than entities. When this philosophy is adopted, coherence enables actions to be grounded in certainty, purpose, identity, context, and future. Similar conclusions can be drawn from work on empowerment and trust (Paton et al., 2003). The preceding discussion outlines components that could be incorporated within a strategy for operationalizing this model in emergency organizations. It remains for future work to identify the specific links between these competencies and PTG. It is also necessary to consider the operation of these competencies within an organizational context.

The Organizational Context

Employee interpretation of traumatic events is influenced by their organizational experience (Gist & Woodall, 2000; Paton et al., 2000). Factors, such as freeing officers from bureaucratic constraints during deployment, rewarding performance in adverse circumstances, and working within a supportive posttrauma environment, can influence the meaning attributed to a traumatic experience. It is becoming increasingly apparent that, in emergency professions, organizational variables represent stronger predictors of posttrauma outcomes than the incidents per se (Dunning, 2003; Gist & Woodall, 2000; Huddleston et al., in press; Paton et al., 2000; Paton et al., 2003; Paton, Violanti et al., 2003). The enduring and influential nature of the context within which traumatic outcomes emerge represents one of the major points of departure between professional and lay populations.

It is also important to distinguish between operational and organizational experiences. Operational (i.e., job critical incident stressor) exposure has, traditionally, been the domi-nant focus of investigation into traumatic stress. Operational issues (experience of which often represents the kind of activity that motivates entering a helping profession in the first place), however, exercise a lesser influence than their organizational counterparts. For example, bureaucratic organizations increase vulnerability through persistent use of estab-lished decision procedures (even when responding to different and urgent crisis demands), internal conflicts regarding responsibility, and a predisposition to protect the organization from criticism or blame (Alexander & Wells, 1991; Gist & Woodall, 2000; Paton, 1997). The adoption of autonomous response systems, a flexible, consultative leadership style, and practices that ensure that role and task assignments reflect incident demands enhance the likelihood of positive outcomes (Gist &Woodall, 2000; Paton, 1994). While these describe the resources required to facilitate a potential for growth, it is also necessary to consider the processes that bind them together to facilitate coherent action. This can be achieved by promoting a climate of trust and empowering officers (Paton, Violanti et al., 2003).

The importance of organizational variables has recently increased as a result of work demonstrating their influence on traumatic stress symptoms and PTG (Huddleston et al., in press; Paton et al., 2003). Figure 12.2 illustrates how traumatic stress exposure, measured using a revised version of the Traumatic Stress Schedule (TSS) (Norris, 1990; Paton, Hud-dlestone et al., 2003), influenced both traumatic stress symptoms (IES) and posttraumatic growth (PTGI). Data were collected from 512 officers at point of entry and again after 12 months (7 months training and 5 months operational duties). During their 5 months

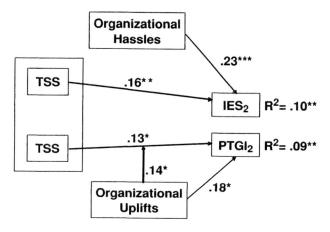

FIGURE 12.2.   The relative contribution of traumatic and organizational experiences to PTG and traumatic stress symptoms. (*$p < 0.05$; **$p < 0.01$; ***$p < 0.001$.)

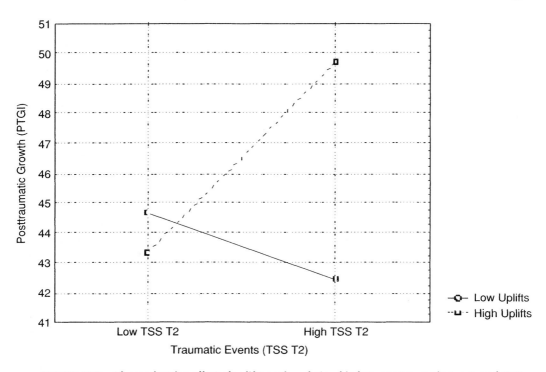

FIGURE 12.3. The moderating effect of uplifts on the relationship between traumatic events and PTG.

of operational duties, 26% of officers experienced no traumatic events, 27% experienced one, and 47% experienced two or more (mean: 1.4 traumatic events). In the course of this experience, these police officers derived feelings of personal growth from their traumatic experience. This was particularly so in regard to the following dimensions of the PTGI scale; relating to others, personal strength, and appreciation of life.

What is particularly interesting is the influence of organizational factors on both symptoms and PTG. Organizational variables were assessed using the Police Daily Hassles and Uplifts Scales (Hart, Wearing, & Heady, 1993, 1994). Traumatic stress symptoms and PTG were influenced by different aspects of organizational experience. That is, organizational hassles (e.g., lack of consultation, poor communication, red tape) had a significant direct effect on traumatic stress symptoms (IES). Organizational hassles did not influence PTGI scores. Organizational uplifts, on the other hand, (e.g., having responsibility, recognition of good work, empowerment) had significant direct and moderating effects on PTG (PTGI), but did not predict IES scores (Fig. 12.2). Impact of event scores and PTG scores were positively correlated ($r = .43$, $p < .01$).

The importance of the relationship between traumatic events and organizational uplifts is further illustrated in Figure 12.3. A moderating effect was observed that indicated that organizational uplifts influenced the relationship between traumatic event exposure and PTG. These data indicated that PTG was positively related to traumatic events if uplifts were high. If uplifts were low, PTG weakened and the relationship between growth and traumatic events was negative. Clearly the existence of a positive organizational climate has a prominent role to play in promoting PTG and should receive considerable attention within the stress management process.

INFLUENCES ON GROWTH DURING REINTEGRATION

Reintegration describes the period of transition from involvement in emergency response roles back into routine operational work. During reintegration, the question becomes one of asking how managing the emotional correlates of an experience, rendering it meaningful, and dealing with the return to work influences growth. Although the thrust of this chapter is toward proactive, primary prevention, postevent support or tertiary interventions will be required for several reasons. They will be required to support officers who experience significant adverse reactions. They also have a role to play in linking accounts of experience with the organizational culture and with organizational development.

Formal Support Intervention

Support practices designed specifically to assist positive resolution and growth are discussed elsewhere (Calhoun & Tedeschi, 1999; Dunning, 2003; Tedeschi & Calhoun, 2003). Dunning (2003) adapted Lissack and Roos (1999) model of coherences to describe ten principles that should underpin any program designed to offer post-event support to officers involved in traumatic events. These involve:

- Using simple guiding principles and rules that are easy to grasp during concrete functioning.
- Respecting the mental models of all concerned and using methods of cognitive interviewing when supervising and investigating a trauma response.
- Understanding that how situations, actions, and events are framed significantly conveys expectation and assessment.
- Combining and recombining information as new knowledge, and combining components in new ways to rehearse potential new situations and desensitize to those experienced.
- Recognizing the multiple roles and the cohesive team ethos of emergency responders.
- Allowing goals to be accomplished in more than one strict, formulaic, mechanistic response and recognizing and encouraging creative and innovative methods while providing a framework of safety catch points to ensure important policies and laws are met.
- Encouraging the telling of stories that allow others the benefit of shared experiences.
- Creating opportunities to enter the field.
- Managers must stay connected with the reality of the "field" and it is imperative after a traumatic event that managers and administrators stay connected to what is happening to workers.
- Identifing and giving credit to individuals who have acted under adverse circumstances.
- Facilitating coherence with words that assist those they are managing (or leading or guiding or influencing) to visualising possibilities that are coherent with the intentions of management. Words of support, encouragement, recognition, and value are especially important in chaotic circumstances.

Support interventions that accommodate these principles will increase the likelihood of officers being able to derive benefit from their experience through a formal support intervention. They should not, however, be regarded as the principle postevent growth strategy in emergency professions. Several studies have demonstrated that they enjoy a lesser influence on recovery than organizational culture and family dynamics (Gist & Woodall, 2000; Huddleston et al., in press; Paton et al., 2000).

Family Issues

Attention to family issues is important both in regard to facilitating their ability to obtain benefits from their relationship with an emergency worker and in regard to their role as a growth resource. Organizational issues (e.g., shift work) are prominent family risk factors (Shakespeare-Finch, Paton, & Violanti, 2003). Practices that enhance the capacity of family members to benefit (e.g., family friendly policies and support groups, including family members in recovery planning) should be included in risk management (Shakespeare-Finch et al., 2003). Given the importance of "relating to others" as a growth outcome, it would be interesting to examine the degree of reciprocity in this outcome between officers and their family members, and if reciprocity occurs, whether similar processes are involved.

The Transition for Traumatic to Routine Work

The period of transition from crisis to routine work and family life poses a unique set of psychological hazards capable of challenging the assumptions of both officers and family members (Paton et al., 1989; Shakespeare-Finch et al., 2003). Vulnerability is not restricted to those who had negative event experiences. Positive response experiences can become a risk factor for adverse outcomes during reintegration. For example, personnel may experience feelings of loss as they leave a period of rewarding professional performance. Readjusting to routine work, reporting pressures, sociolegal issues and catching up with any backlog of work are typical postevent demands. Their implications for reintegration, however, are a function of how they interact with organizational practices and culture.

Deficit outcomes are more likely if officers interpret their hazard experience in an organizational culture that discourages emotional disclosure, focuses on attributing blame to staff, or minimizes the significance of peoples' reactions or feelings (Paton & Stephens, 1996). The likelihood of positive reintegration is heightened if managers work with staff to reconcile the personal impact of the event with the process of returning to work. In a study of the long-term effects of serial exposure to critical incidents among paramedics, Alexander, Klein, and Bowes (2000) concluded that the most important factor regarding recovery for officers exposed to traumatic events is an organizational climate of care (cf. Dunning, 2003). A strategy recommended by them and others (Gersons & Carlier, 2000) involves training senior officers to recognize the symptoms of posttraumatic stress in their officers. Early detection, monitoring, assessment, and treatment involving occupational support teams contribute to the development of an organizational climate of mutual care. Effective management and improved work supervision may permit employees to work comfortably and experience increased feelings of well-being in environments that otherwise would produce high levels of strain (Alexander, Klein, & Bowes, 2000; Best et al., 2000; Greller, Parsons, & Mitchell, 1992).

Managers can assist growth by helping officers appreciate that they performed to the best of their ability and reducing performance guilt by highlighting situational constraints on performance (MacLeod & Paton, 1999). They can also facilitate positive resolution by assisting staff to identify the strengths that helped them deal with the emergency and building on this to plan how future events can be dealt with more effectively. Thus, risk management programs should review the climate of relationships between managers and staff and determine its implications for response and reintegration (Gist & Woodall, 2000; Lissak & Roos, 1999; Paton et al., 2000). Such analyses can inform risk assessment by, for example, identifying response constraints within organizational systems and procedures (e.g., lack of policy and procedures for managing critical incident stress, inadequate reintegration management, lack of a learning culture). This activity can also contribute to the development of an organizational culture that focuses on nurturing strengths.

Interpersonal Support and Cohesion

Several facets of social support have been implicated as predictors of PTG. While a role for social support per se has not been universally endorsed, levels of satisfaction with support have (Linley & Joseph, 2004), particularly in regard to emotional support. These findings are consistent with work on support provision in organizational contexts (Paton & Stephens, 1996; Solomon & Smith, 1994). Solomon and Smith discuss how if demands on a social network for support occur at a time when all members may have support needs—making support provision a highly stressful event in itself—its availability and quality (satisfaction) is diminished. This problem can be managed by providing social support through coworker and peer support groups (Paton, 1997; Williams, 1993). This resource should be developed to ensure its members can manage all the issues (e.g., accommodating others' perspectives, rumination, counterfactual thinking) that characterize the reintegration experience (Gist & Woodall, 2000; MacLeod & Paton, 1999; Paton & Stephens, 1996; Shakespeare-Finch, 2002). Understanding the full role of social relationships as potential growth resources in emergency organizations requires that additional social dynamics are taken into account.

Cohesive teams constitute a natural protective resource and can facilitate the review of experiences in a manner that promotes growth (Higgins, 1994; Park, 1998). However, cohesion can contribute to vulnerability if situational constraints result in a response being perceived as less effective than anticipated. Under these conditions, officers may find it difficult to perceive the positive characteristics in the group necessary to maintain a positive social identity. If this happens, support networks breakdown (Hartsough & Myers, 1985), a negative social identity develops (Paton & Stephens, 1996; Solomon & Smith, 1994), and the likelihood of a deficit outcome increases. Countering this possibility requires team processes that facilitate the realistic interpretation of circumstances, actively differentiate personal and situational response factors, and encourage the interpretation of experience as opportunities to facilitate personal and professional growth (Gist & Woodall, 2000; Lyons, Mickelson, Sullivan, & Coyne, 1998; Park, 1998; Paton & Stephens, 1996).

Lyons et al. (1998) used the term *communal coping* to describe how team activities can contribute to growth. They argue that communal coping requires members' acceptance of shared event-related problems (e.g., regarding situational rather than personal constraints) and discussion on cooperative action to resolve problems. The latter can occur in formal review sessions and in informal day-to-day interactions between team members as they return to work. Acknowledging and building on effective collaboration during the crisis, and working together after the crisis (see preceding section) to develop understanding and better preparedness for future crises, they argue, contributes to personal and team growth.

Organisations, Crises, and Future Risk

During reintegration, crises afford opportunities for organizational change. Evidence described above regarding the relationship between organizational climate and PTG makes attending to this issue a high priority for emergency organizations. However, a capability for change need not always exist and different categories of response can be anticipated.

At one end of the spectrum lies the *non response*. This occurs when bureaucratic inertia, vested political interests, and centralized power and authority conspire to block change and, indeed, sow the seeds of future and more complex crises (Berkes, Colding & Folke, 2003; Mitroff & Anagnos, 2001) that, in turn, will constrain growth potential in officers (Paton & Stephens, 1996). Ignoring signals of potential or actual problems and, therefore, failing to plan for crises increases susceptibility to deficit outcomes at all levels.

A second category is where an organization responds, but lacks the experience to do so effectively. This can occur as a consequence of failing to consider risk from nonroutine events because managerial expectations regarding operating conditions and outcomes become entrenched and insulated from environmental input (Paton, 1994, 1997). This reiterates the importance of managers staying connected to the operational experiences of officers if they are to facilitate coherence (Dunning, 2003). Problems can also occur if organizations have failed to learn from previous crises. The consequent implementation of untried actions, even while recognizing a need for change, can enhance growth or it can increase vulnerability and loss of adaptive capacity (Berkes et al., 2003). That is, the outcome, growth or deficit, is determined more by chance than by sound planning and good judgment.

Consistent with the tenets of PTG at the individual level, Berkes et al. (2003) emphasize that, to increase growth at the organizational level, experience of failure is required. Only when confronting data inconsistent with existing conceptual frameworks can growth be stimulated and new conceptual frames developed. Not only must the organization learn to live with risk, it must develop strategies to learn from any crises and failures that occur. Recognition of the importance of institutional learning leads to a third strategy, one capable of contributing to growth.

According to Berkes et al. (2003), this involves several activities. Firstly, the memory of prior crises and the lessons learned must be incorporated into institutional memory. Secondly, it requires the rehearsal of lessons learned within a paradigm shift based on revised understanding of the precursors of a crisis (e.g., understand risk and its links to threats and opportunities). Finally, these activities lead to the development of new rules and procedures. The effectiveness of this institutional learning approach can be enhanced by creating small-scale, controlled disturbances (e.g., simulations) to facilitate the learning process, challenge complacency, enhance adaptive capacity, and encourage creative decision making (Berkes et al., 2003; Paton, 1994; Paton & Jackson, 2002). The systemic links between people and the organizational environments they inhabit means that organizational capability in this regard is fundamental to facilitating growth potential in emergency personnel.

CONCLUSION

Posttraumatic growth is a reality for emergency professionals. There is considerable over-lap between lay and professional populations in regard to dispositional (e.g., personality, coping) predictors. However, in emergency professionals, growth outcomes are also influenced by the way in which traumatic events interact with interpretive (that render event demands, decision making, and team activities meaningful) and organizational factors.

As with lay populations, growth and deficit outcomes can coexist. Consequently, comprehensive understanding of traumatic stress phenomena in emergency professions requires accommodating both outcomes. The latter can be assimilated into the fabric of organizational policy, planning, and intervention using the risk management paradigm. The latter also affords an opportunity to confront a priori assumptions linking adverse

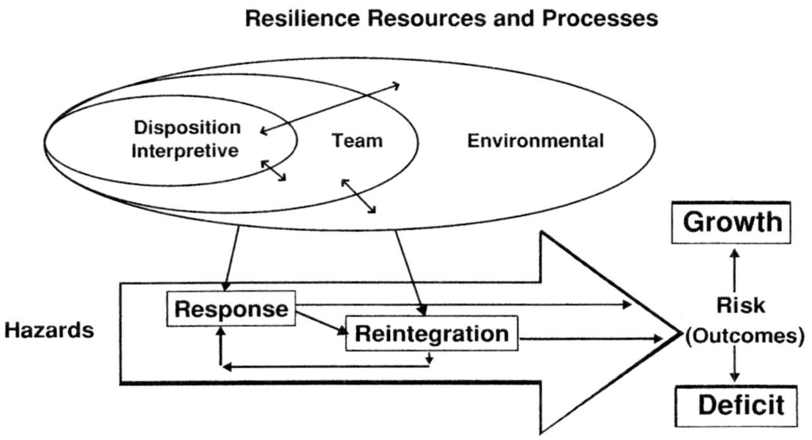

Resilience Resources and Processes

FIGURE 12.4.   A stress risk management framework.

experiences and deficit outcomes. Risk is represented as an interaction between critical event and environmental demands (hazards) capable of challenging schemata or assumptive worlds and creating the state of disequilibrium that is a prerequisite for personal, team, and organizational change. Organizations can make choices regarding the resources and processes brought to bear (e.g., through selection, training, organizational change) on adverse experiences and so influence whether the schematic disequilibrium implicit in traumatic experiences is resolved as PTG or posttraumatic deficits.

While discussed here in terms of their individual contribution, the capacity for growth will be a function of both the effectiveness of resources at person, group, and environmental levels, and the degree to which interaction between them is coherent (Dunning, 2003; Paton et al., 2000). For example, the adaptive capacity of dispositional and interpretive capabilities will be enhanced or constrained by the degree to which team and environmental levels (e.g., organizational culture) empower personnel and harness their capabilities. These relationships are summarized in Figure 12.4. Because traumatic events provide a basis for individual, team, and organizational development, stress risk management should be viewed as an iterative process that encompasses personal and organizational learning.

REFERENCES

Affleck, G., & Tennen, H. (1996). Construing benefits from adversity: Adaptational significance and dispositional underpinnings. *Journal of Personality, 64,* 899–922.

Aldwin, C. M., Levenson, M. R., & Spiro, A., III. (1994). Vulnerability and resilience to combat exposure: Can stress have lifelong effects? *Psychology and Aging, 9,* 34–44.

Alexander, D. A., & Klein, S. (2001). Ambulance personnel and critical incidents. *British Journal of Psychiatry, 178,* 76–81.

Alexander, D. A., Klein, S., & Bowes, L. B. (2000, March 16–19). The long-term effects of serial exposure to 'critical incidents' among paramedics. Paper presented at the *Third World Conference for the International Society for Traumatic Stress Studies,* Melbourne, Australia.

Alexander, D. A., & Wells, A. (1991). Reactions of police officers to body handling after a major disaster: A before and after comparison. *British Journal of Psychiatry, 159,* 517–555.

Andersen, H. S., Christensen, A. K., & Petersen, G. O. (1991). Post-traumatic stress reactions amongst rescue workers after a major rail accident. *Anxiety Research, 4,* 245–251.

Armeli, S., Gunthert, K. C., & Cohen, L. H. (2001). Stressor appraisals, coping, and post-event outcomes: The dimensionality and antecedents of stress-related growth. *Journal of Social and Clinical Psychology, 20,* 366–395.

Aspinwall, L. G., & Staudinger, U. M. (2003). A psychology of human strengths: Some central issues of an emerging field. In L. G. Aspinwall & U. M. Staudinger (Eds.), *A psychology of human strengths: Fundamental questions and future directions for a positive psychology* (pp. 9–22). Washington, DC: American Psychological Association.

Bartone, P. T. (2003). Hardiness as a resiliency resource under high stress conditions. In D. Paton, J. M. Violanti, & L. M. Smith. (Eds.). *Promoting capabilities to manage posttraumatic stress: Perspectives on resilience.* Springfield, IL: Charles C. Thomas.

Berkes, F., Colding, J., & Folke, C. (2003). *Navigating social-ecological systems: Building resilience for complexity and change.* Cambridge: Cambridge University Press.

Best, S. R., Brunet, A., Weiss, D. S., Metzler, T., Rogers, C. E., Rosario, M., et al. (2000, March 16–19). Critical incident exposure and routine work stress in policing: Risk and resilience factors for posttraumatic stress reactions and emotional distress. Paper presented at the *Third World Conference for the International Society for Traumatic Stress Studies,* Melbourne, Australia.

Britt, T. W., Adler, A. B., & Bartone, P. T. (2001) Deriving benefits from stressful events: The role of engagement in meaningful work and hardiness. *Journal of Occupational Health Psychology, 6,* 53–63.

Burke, K. J., & Paton, D. (in press) Well-being in Protective Services Personnel: The Influence of the Organisation. *Work & Stress.*

Calhoun, L. G., Cann, A., Tedeschi, R. G., & McMillan, J. (2000). A correlational test of the relationship between posttraumatic growth, religion, and cognitive processing. *Journal of Traumatic Stress, 13,* 521–527.

Calhoun, L. G., & Tedeschi, R. G. (1998). Beyond recovery from trauma: Implications for clinical practice and research. *Journal of Social Issues, 54,* 357–371.

Calhoun, L. G., & Tedeschi, R. G. (1999). *Facilitating posttraumatic growth: A clinician's guide.* Mahwah, NJ: Lawrence Erlbaum Associates.

Collins, R. L., Taylor, S. E., & Skokan, L. A. (1990). A better world or a shattered vision? Changes in life perspectives following victimization. *Social Cognition, 8,* 263–285.

Cooke, N. J., Salas, E., Cannon-Bowers, J. A., & Stout, R. J. (2000). Measuring team knowledge. *Human Factors, 42,* 151–173.

Crego, J., & Spinks, T. (1997). Critical incident management simulation. In R. Flin, E. Salas, M. Strub, & L. Martin (Eds.), *Decision making under stress.* Aldershot: Ashgate.

Dake, K. (1992). Myths of nature and the public. *Journal of Social Issues, 48,* 21–38.

Davies, H., & Walters, M. (1998). Do all crises have to become disasters? Risk and risk mitigation. *Disaster Prevention and Management, 7,* 396–400.

Dunning C. (2003). Sense of coherence in managing trauma workers. In D. Paton, J. M. Violanti, & L. M. Smith (Eds.) *Promoting capabilities to manage posttraumatic stress: Perspectives on resilience.* Springfield, IL: Charles C. Thomas.

Endsley, M., & Garland, D. (2000). *Situation awareness. Analysis and measurement.* Mahwah, NJ.: Lawrence Erlbaum Associates.

Entin, E. E., & Serfaty, D. (1999). Adaptive team coordination. *Human Factors, 41,* 312–325.

Flin, R. (1996). *Sitting in the hot seat. Leaders and teams for critical incident management.* Chichester: Wiley.

Flin, R., & Arbuthnot, K. (eds.). (2002). *Incident command: Tales from the hot seat.* Aldershot: Ashgate.

Flin, R., Salas, E., Strub, M., & Martin, L. (1997). (Eds.). *Decision making under stress.* Aldershot: Ashgate.

Frazier, P., Conlon, A., & Glaser, T. (2001). Positive and negative life changes following sexual assault. *Journal of Consulting and Clinical Psychology, 69,* 1048–1055.

Gersons, B. P. R., & Carlier, I. (2000). Helping police in coping with trauma: A public health approach. A paper presented to the Third World Conference for the International Society for Traumatic Stress Studies: *The long-term outcomes of trauma in individuals and society,* Melbourne, Australia, March 16–19.

Gist, R., & Woodall, J. (2000). There are no simple solutions to complex problems. In J. M. Violanti, D. Paton, & C. Dunning (Eds.). *Posttraumatic stress intervention: Challenges, issues and perspectives.* Springfield, IL: Charles C. Thomas.

Greller, M. M., Parsons, C. K., & Mitchell, D. R. D. (1992). Additive effects and beyond: Occupational stressors and social buffers in a police organisation. In J. C. Quick, L. R. Murphy, & J. J. Hurrell, Jr. (Eds.), *Stress and well-being at work: Assessments and interventions for occupational mental health* (pp. 33–47). Washington, DC: American Psychological Association.

Hart, P. M., & Cooper, C. L. (2001). Occupational stress: Toward a more integrated framework. In N. Anderson, D. S. Ones, H. K. Sinangil, & C. Viswesvaren (Eds.), *International handbook of work and organizational psychology, vol.2: Organizational psychology*. London: Sage.

Hart, P. M., & Wearing, A. J. (1995). Occupational stress and well-being: A systematic approach to research, policy and practice. In P. Cotton (Ed.), *Psychological health in the workplace*. Carlton: Australian Psychological Society.

Hartsough, D. M., & Myers, D. G. (1985). *Disaster work and mental health: Prevention and control of stress among workers*. Rockville, MD: U.S. Department of Health and Human Services, No. (ADM) 85 - 1422.

Higgins, G. O. (1994). *Resilient adults: Overcoming a cruel past*. San Francisco: Jossey-Bass.

Hood, C., & Jones, D. K. C. (1996). *Accident and design: Contemporary debates in risk management*. London: UCL Press.

Huddleston, L., Stephens, C., & Paton, D. (in press) Traumatic and organisational experiences and the psychological health of New Zealand police recruits. *Work. Psychology, 81*, 429–435.

Inzana, C. M., Driskell, J. E., Salas, E., & Johnston, J. H. (1996) Effects of preparatory information on enhancing performance under stress. *Journal of Applied Psychology, 81*, 429–435.

Janoff-Bulman, R. (1989a). Assumptive worlds and the stress of traumatic events: Applications of the schema construct. *Social Cognition, 7*, 113–136.

Janoff-Bulman, R. (1989b). The benefits of illusions, the threat of disillusionment, and the limitations of inaccuracy. *Journal of Social and Clinical Psychology, 8*, 158–175.

Janoff-Bulman, R. (1992). *Shattered assumptions*. New York: Free Press.

Joseph, S., Williams, R., & Yule, W. (1993). Changes in outlook following disaster: The preliminary development of a measure to assess positive and negative responses. *Journal of Traumatic Stress, 6*, 271–279.

Linley, P. A., & Joseph, S. (2004). Positive change following trauma and adversity: A review. *Journal of Traumatic Stress, 17*, 11–21.

Linley, P. A., Joseph, S., Cooper, R., Harris, S., & Myer, C. (2003). Positive and negative changes following vicarious exposure to the September 11 terrorist attack. *Journal of Traumatic Stress, 16*, 481–485.

Lissack, M., & Roos, J. (1999). *The next common sense: Mastering corporate complexity through Coherence*. Naperville, IL: Nicholas Brealey Publishing.

Lyons, R. F., Mickelson, K. D., Sullivan, M. J. L., & Coyne, J. C. (1998). Coping as a communal process. *Journal of Social and Personal Relationships, 15*, 579–605.

MacLeod, M. D., & Paton, D. (1999). Police officers and violent crime: Social psychological perspectives on impact and recovery. In J. M. Violanti and D. Paton (Eds.), *Police trauma: Psychological aftermath of civilian combat*. Springfield, IL: Charles C. Thomas.

McMillen, C., Zuravin, S., & Rideout, G. (1995). Perceived benefit from child sexual abuse. *Journal of Consulting and Clinical Psychology, 63*, 1037–1043.

Miller, L. (1995). Tough guys: Psychotherapeutic strategies for law enforcement and emergency services personnel. *Psychotherapy, 32*, 592–600.

Mitroff, I. I., & Anagnos, G. (2001). *Managing crises before they happen*. New York: Amacom.

Moran, C. C. (1999). Recruits' prediction of positive reactions in disaster and emergency work. *Disaster Prevention and Management, 8*, 177–183.

Moran, C., & Colless, E. (1995). Positive reactions following emergency and disaster responses. *Disaster Prevention and Management, 4*, 55–61.

Norris, F. H. (1990). Screening for traumatic stress: A scale for use in the general population. *Journal of Applied Social Psychology, 20*, 1704–1718.

North, C. S., Tivis, L., McMillen, C., Pfefferbaum, B., Cox, J., Spitznagal, E. L. et al. (2002). Coping, functioning, and adjustment of rescue workers after the Oklahoma City bombing. *Journal of Traumatic Stress, 15*, 171–175.

Park, C. L. (1998). Stress-related growth and thriving through coping: The roles of personality and cognitive processes. *Journal of Social Issues, 54*, 267–277.

Paton, D. (1994). Disaster relief work: An assessment of training effectiveness. *Journal of Traumatic Stress, 7*, 275 – 288.

Paton, D. (1997). *Dealing with traumatic incidents in the workplace* (3rd ed.). Queensland, Australia: Gull Publishing.

Paton, D., Cox, D., & Andrew, C. (1989). *A preliminary investigation into posttraumatic stress in rescue workers* (Research Reports #1). Aberdeen, Scotland, Robert Gordon University Social Science.

Paton, D., & Flin, R. (1999). Disaster stress: An emergency management perspective. *Disaster Prevention and Management, 8*, 261–267.

Paton, D., & Hannan, G. (2004). Risk factors in emergency response. In D. Paton, J. Violanti, C. Dunning, & L. M. Smith (Eds.), *Managing traumatic stress risk: A proactive approach*. Springfield, IL: Charles C. Thomas.

Paton, D., Huddleston, L., & Stephens, C. (2003, March 31–April 3). The interaction between traumatic stress and organisational demands on police officers traumatic stress and posttraumatic growth. Paper presented at the *10th Annual Conference of the Australasian Society for Traumatic Stress Studies*, Hobart, Tasmania, Australia.

Paton, D., & Jackson, D. (2002). Developing disaster management capability: An assessment centre approach. *Disaster Prevention and Management, 11*, 115–122.

Paton, D., Johnston, D., Houghton, B., Flin, R., Ronan, K., & Scott, B. (1999). Managing natural hazard consequences: Information management and decision making. *Journal of the American Society of Professional Emergency Managers, 6*, 37–48.

Paton, D., Smith, L. M., Violanti, J., & Eranen, L. (2000). Work-related traumatic stress: Risk, vulnerability and resilience. In D. Paton, J. M. Violanti, & Dunning, C. (Eds.), *Posttraumatic stress intervention: Challenges, issues and perspectives* (pp. 187–204). Springfield, IL: Charles C. Thomas.

Paton, D., & Stephens, C. (1996). Training and support for emergency responders. In D. Paton & J. Violanti (Eds.), *Traumatic stress in critical occupations: Recognition, consequences and treatment*. Springfield, IL: Charles C. Thomas.

Paton, D., Violanti, J. M., & Smith, L. M. (2003). *Promoting capabilities to manage posttraumatic stress: Perspectives on resilience*. Springfield, IL: Charles C. Thomas.

Pollock, C., Paton, D., Smith, L., & Violanti, J. (2003). Team resilience. In D. Paton, J. Violanti, & L. Smith (Eds.), *Promoting capabilities to manage posttraumatic stress: Perspectives on resilience*. Springfield, IL: Charles C. Thomas.

Raphael, B. (1986). *When disaster strikes*. London: Hutchinson.

Raphael, B. (2000, March 16–19). Processing trauma: Routes to recovery and growth in disaster, bereavement and injury. Paper presented at the *Third World Conference for the International Society for Traumatic Stress Studies*, Melbourne, Australia.

Schnurr, P. P., Rosenberg, S. D., & Friedman, M. J. (1993). Change in MMPI scores from college to adulthood as a function of military service. *Journal of Abnormal Psychology, 102*, 288–296.

Scotti, J. R., Beach, B. K., Northrop, L. M. E. Rode. C. A., & Forsyth, J. P. (1995). The psychological impact of accidental injury. In J. R. Freedy and S. E. Hobfoll (Eds.), *Traumatic stress: From theory to practice*. New York: Plenum Press.

Shakespeare-Finch, J. E. (2003). *Posttraumatic growth in emergency ambulance personnel: The roles of personality and coping*. Unpublished doctoral dissertation, Queensland University of Technology, Brisbane, Australia.

Shakespeare-Finch, J., Paton, D., & Violanti, J. (2003). The Family: Resilience resource and resilience needs. In D. Paton, J. Violanti, & L. Smith. (Eds.), *Promoting capabilities to manage posttraumatic stress: Perspectives on resilience*. Springfield, IL: Charles C. Thomas.

Smith, C., & Paton, D. (2002). Personality predictors of occupational well-being in police officers. Unpublished research data. Wellington, New Zealand Police.

Solomon, Z., Benbenishty, R., & Mikulincer, M. (1991). The contribution of wartime, pre-war, and post-war factors on self-efficacy: A longitudinal study of combat stress reaction. *Journal of Traumatic Stress, 4*, 345–361.

Solomon, S. D., & Smith, E. S. (1994). Social support and perceived control as moderators of responses to dioxin and flood exposure. In R. J. Ursano, B. G. McCaughey, & C. S. Fullerton (Eds.), *Individual and community responses to trauma and disaster*. Cambridge: Cambridge University Press.

Stout, R. J., Cannon-Bowers, J. A., Salas, E., & Milanovich, D. M. (1999). Planning, shared mental models and coordinated performance: An empirical link is established. *Human Factors, 41*, 61–71.

Stuhlmiller, C., & Dunning, C. (2000). Challenging the mainstream: From pathogenic to salutogenic models of post-trauma intervention. In J. Violanti, D. Paton, & C. Dunning (Eds.), *Posttraumatic stress intervention: Challenges, issues and perspectives.* Springfield, IL: Charles C. Thomas.

Taylor, S. E. (1983). Adjustment to threatening events: A theory of cognitive adaptation. *American Psychologist, 38*, 1161–1173.

Taylor, S. E., Wood, J. V., & Lichtman, R. R. (1983). It could be worse: Selective evaluation as a response to victimization. *Journal of Social Issues, 39*, 19–40.

Tedeschi, R. G., & Calhoun, L. G. (1995). *Trauma & transformation: Growing in the aftermath of suffering.* Thousand Oaks, CA: Sage.

Tedeschi, R. G., & Calhoun, L. G. (1996). The Posttraumatic Growth Inventory: Measuring the positive legacy of trauma. *Journal of Traumatic Stress, 9*, 455–471.

Tedeschi, R. G., & Calhoun, L. G. (2003). Routes to posttraumatic growth through cognitive processing. In D. Paton, J. M. Violanti, & L. M. Smith (Eds.), *Promoting capabilities to manage posttraumatic stress: Perspectives on resilience.* Springfield, IL: Charles C. Thomas.

Tedeschi, R. G., Park, C. L., & Calhoun, L. G. (1998). Posttraumatic growth: Conceptual issues. In R. G. Tedeschi, C. L. Park, & L. G. Calhoun (Eds.), *Posttraumatic growth: Positive change in the aftermath of crisis* (pp. 1–22). Mahwah, NJ: Lawrence Erlbaum Associates.

Tennen, H., & Affleck, G. (1998). Personality and transformation in the face of adversity. In R. Tedeschi., C. Park., & L. Calhoun (Eds.), *Posttraumatic growth: Positive changes in the aftermath of crisis* (pp 65–98). Mahwah, NJ: Lawrence Erlbaum Associates.

Thompson, J. (1993). Psychological impact of body recovery duties. *Journal of the Royal Society of Medicine, 86*, 628–629.

Thompson, J., & Solomon, M. (1991). Body recovery teams at disasters: Trauma or challenge? *Anxiety Research, 4*, 235–244.

Williams, T. (1993). Trauma in the workplace. In J. P. Wilson & B. Raphael (Eds.), *International handbook of traumatic stress syndromes.* New York: Plenum Press.

Znoj, H. J. (2000, March 16–19). Posttraumatic symptoms and experienced growth following spinal cord injury. Paper presented at the *Third World Conference for the International Society for Traumatic Stress Studies,* Melbourne, Australia.

13

GROWING OUT OF ASHES: POSTTRAUMATIC GROWTH AMONG HOLOCAUST CHILD SURVIVORS—IS IT POSSIBLE?

RACHEL LEV-WIESEL AND MARIANNE AMIR

BEN GURION UNIVERSITY, BEER SHEVA

Abraham was 13 years old when the Nazis forced the Jews in Hungary to wear the Yellow Star and prohibited Jewish children from going to school. Abraham's father was taken to a labor camp near the Russian border, never to be seen again. Abraham and his youngest brother had to support the family by trading in the black market in the nearest city—a risky business that endangered their lives. In 1944, they and the rest of the Jewish community were assembled for 3 in a swine house, then were deported to Auschwitz. The brothers were assigned to work in the crematorium, loading and sorting out the dead from their belongings (clothes, shoes, etc.). Abraham saved his brother, who was often ill, by hiding him among the corpses. "The smell of death has been in my nose since then . . . you know how they say, 'From dust you are born, to dust you will return?' You can say that we actually were reborn out of the ashes."

In 1945, the Germans gathered the prisoners for the Death March from Auschwitz to Bergen Belsen. Many prisoners did not survive this journey: the cold, hunger, and immense physical efforts were unbearable for the already exhausted victims. Many fell and died, others were shot by the Germans. Abraham walked behind his brother and decided that they would not give up: "We were determined to survive; we vowed that we would not capitulate until we were the last ones alive." He encouraged his brother by insisting that they both had the will power to sustain themselves. They did survive the march and a few days after they arrived at Bergen Belsen, they were liberated by the British troops.

After they discovered that no one in their family survived the war, they joined a group of Jewish adolescents and illegally immigrated to Palestine where they then fought in

Israel's War of Independence. Three years after the establishment of the State of Israel, Abraham married a Holocaust child survivor who had lost all of her family.

While telling his story, Abraham frequently burst into tears, choked, and sank into deep silence. When referring to the significance and outcome of his own experiences, he said:

"I deeply understand the importance of the State of Israel for the Jews, for me. Israel restored my self-esteem, self pride; Israel gave me back my life. I managed to have a family, children, to provide for them ... I learned to cherish life. Life is fragile: one day you are here, the next you are gone ... you need to appreciate whatever time you are allotted and especially the good times you share with others: every moment should be cherished and valued. I am a strong person: Although I suffer from nightmares and from a chronic disease that prevents me from being able to move freely, I have vitality and can laugh, I enjoy being with my wife and children ... I have done something with my life ... it's like I am happy and sad at the same time, all the time."

Holocaust child survivors comprise a unique group of trauma victims who were exposed to prolonged stress and mass exposure in early childhood, more than 50 years ago. Although it may seem inappropriate to study positive outcomes of such horrific trauma, some survivors have claimed that such a process is possible (Frankl, 1959). Most Holocaust survivors, as other survivors of war such as combat veterans and prisoners of war, did not become totally disabled even though they could not totally erase the trauma from their minds either. Although they managed to lead relatively normal lives, they often suffered recurrent or intrusive distressing recollections, dreams, and intense psychological or physiological reactions when exposed to something that symbolized or reminded them of the trauma.

Several positive factors, such as resilience and adaptation, facilitated the adjustment of Holocaust child survivors. We chose to discuss the concept of PTG which has emerged in the last few years as a powerful explanatory variable. For this purpose, our recent study[1] that examined PTG in Holocaust survivors (Lev-Wiesel & Amir, 2003) will be presented following a literature review of the long-term effects of the Holocaust and the concept of PTG.

THE LONG-TERM EFFECTS OF THE HOLOCAUST

In relation to the impact of the Holocaust traumata, studies focusing on two major issues have been conducted: The first group of studies demonstrated how prolonged traumatic experiences in childhood negatively effected the ability of Holocaust child survivors to maintain cohesive and independent self-identities. The second group of studies, on the other hand, focused on the resilience of Holocaust child survivors and indicated that many of them developed successful careers, stable marriages, and caring families after the war (Krell, 1993). These qualitative and quantitative studies suggest that the level of psychological distress was contingent on the level of survivors' personal resources (sense of potency, self-identity and social support) (Lev-Wiesel & Amir, 2001).

Following the initial clinical observations of the "survivor syndrome" (Niederland, 1964), most researchers who examined Holocaust survivors of concentration and labor camps focused on adult survivors' posttraumatic stress disorder (PTSD) symptoms (Danieli, 1985; Krystal & Niederland, 1968; Yehuda, et al., 1995; Yehuda, Sartorius, Kahana, Southwick, & Giller, 1994). In recent years there has been greater recognition that a wide range of traumatic events were experienced by individuals in the Nazi-controlled

[1]The paper was first published in 2003 in the *Journal of Loss and Trauma*, 8(4), 229–237.

areas, both in concentration camps and while avoiding imprisonment by hiding under false identity in monasteries, orphanages, Christian foster families, woods, or barns (Kestenberg & Brenner, 1986). It has become increasingly clear that the age of the victim at the time of traumatic event exposure is of importance in the long-term consequences. For example, Keilson (1992) who examined the relationship between personality traits and extreme traumatic events experienced by children during the Holocaust, found that child survivors who were younger than 14 years old at the end of the Second World War suffered excessively from neurotic symptoms as opposed to survivors who were older. Others who compared Holocaust survivors in concentration camps to those who were in "hiding" during the Second World War pointed out that the age at the time of trauma and cumulative number of stressful events were associated with increased symptoms of psychogenic amnesia, hypervigilence, and emotional detachment (Yehuda, Schmeidler, Siever, Binder-Brynes, & Elkin, 1997).

There are no exact statistics concerning the number of children who survived the Second World War. After the war, approximately 50,000 settled in Israel, and others immigrated to Canada, the United States, Belgium, and France (Tec, 1993). The Nazi persecution of the Jews and the circumstances of war led to separation of families, physical and psychological suffering, hunger, humiliation, and a constant witnessing of cruelty. The memories of child survivors are usually filled with painful scenes of being separated from their parents, becoming orphaned, being abandoned, feeling cold, experiencing starvation and violence, and being physically unable to move for long periods of time (Kestenberg & Kestenberg, 1988; Krell, 1993; Lee, 1988; Moskovitz & Krell, 1990). Different types of painful memories, those of being separated from warm foster families whom the children had learned to identify with and trust, are common (Valent, 1998).

A number of qualitative studies dealing with PTSD symptoms and adaptation strategies used by child survivors have suggested that most child survivors still suffer from symptoms of the survivor syndrome (Breiner, 1996; Kestenberg & Brenner, 1986; Krell, 1993; Mazor & Mendelson, 1998; Moskovitz & Krell, 1990; Robinson, Rapaport-Bar-Sever, & Rapaport, 1994; Tauber & Van-Der-Hal, 1997). Kestenberg (1992, 1993) claimed that child survivors adopted psychological defenses, such as numbing of affect, splitting, and identification with the aggressor, and frequently suffer from depression, phobias, and distorted self-images. Others emphasize that the most outstanding psychological effects of persecution are the loss of identity and feelings of being worthless (Brenner, 1988; Bunk & Eggers, 1993; Rustow, 1989), accompanied by a lifelong sense of bereavement (Mazor & Mendelsohn, 1998). Bunk and Eggers (1993), Gampel (1992), and Tec (1993) suggested that children are different from adult survivors because they were forced to endure formidable stressors and to function as adults without the benefit of adult coping resources and adaptations. These studies were the first to draw attention to survivors who were children during the Holocaust and to the different long-term effects of experiencing and enduring the Holocaust atrocities in different developmental stages.

Recently, Lev-Wiesel and Amir (2000) examined the impact of the Holocaust setting on the levels of PTSD, psychological symptoms of distress, and quality of life experienced by child survivors. It was found that although there was no difference in the levels of PTSD, survivors who had been sheltered in Catholic institutions suffered less than the other groups (concentration camps, hiding with partisans, and non-Jewish foster families) from this symptom pattern. In addition, survivors who hid in the woods and/or with partisans had lower intrusion scores than the other groups and that this group had higher scores with regard to personal potency, some dimensions of self-identity, and physical quality of life. The preceding study also indicated that those survivors who lived with foster families had significantly higher levels of psychological symptoms of distress and lower physical quality of life than at least one of the other groups.

The Concept of Posttraumatic Growth

Recently, the concept of possible positive outcome of traumatic event has emerged. Posttraumatic growth often refers to positive psychological changes (Yalom & Lieberman, 1991), construing benefits (Calhoun &Tedeschi, 1999), stress-related growth (Park, Cohen, & Murch, 1996), thriving (O'Leary, Alday, & Ickovics, 1998), and resilience (Sigal, 1998). All regard it as both process and outcome in which people not only bounce back from trauma but manage to further develop and grow. Tedeschi, Park, and Calhoun (1998) view PTG as developing out of cognitive process that is initiated to cope with traumatic events that extract an extreme cognitive and emotional toll. According to Janoff-Bulman (1992), traumatic events cause changes through the shattering and rebuilding of assumptive worlds. Traumatic events produce a significant upheaval in the individual's understanding of the world and the prior worldview may become invalidated by the occurrence of loss and tragedy (Calhoun & Tedeschi, 1999). Inherent in traumatic experiences are losses: of loved ones, capabilities, or fundamental ways of understanding life. In the face of such losses, some people manage to establish new psychological constructs that incorporate the possibility of such traumas and better ways to cope with them (Taylor & Brown, 1988). Posttraumatic growth is often seen as the antithesis of PTSD, emphasizing that growth outcomes are reported even in the aftermath of the most traumatic circumstances, and even though distress coexists with the growth (Greenberg, 1995).

A large array of studies have shown that traumatic or stressful life events, such as abuse, violence, or death of a parent have negative cognitive, emotional, and physiological effects on children (Armsworth & Holaday, 1993; Berlinsky & Biller, 1982; Roesler & McKenzie, 1994). Nevertheless, some children show resilience to major stresses such as war, poverty, or family mental illness (Felsman & Vaillant, 1987; Werner & Smith, 1992) and in some cases show enhanced functioning later in life (Anthony, 1987). It was found that protective factors, such as intelligence, easygoing temperament, coping style, and quality of relationship with others (at least one supportive adult), contribute to resilience defined as the ability to recover from a traumatic event (Rutter, 1993; Werner & Smith, 1992). Resilient children, contrary to vulnerable children, often possess characteristics that seem to protect them from developing problems later in life (Valliant, 1993; Wolin & Wolin, 1993). In addition, some children may develop competencies in some areas, such as social relationships or feeling of mastery, yet suffer from symptoms of anxiety or depression (Cowen, Wyman, Work, & Parker, 1990). According to Aldwin and Brustrom (1997), the factors that predict resilience in childhood also contribute to the possibility of continued growth in a sense that some outcomes of stress include increases in coping skills, increases in self-confidence, and changes in perspective.

Coping with Trauma, Personal, and Social Resources

According to stress theory, individuals' personal and social resources are instrumental to their ability to cope with stressful life events (Ben-Sira 1991; Folkman & Lazarus, 1984). While adequate personal resources help individuals to maintain or regain their psychological homeostasis in times of stress, the lack of these resources may lead to difficulty in coping and vulnerability to stress, breakdown, and disease (Folkman & Lazarus, 1984). Evidence indicates that the possession of personal resources, such as self-esteem,

self-efficacy, and social support can predict successful adjustment after being traumatized (Gulliver, et al., 1995). Personal resources can be divided into two types: personality
resources-strengths or traits the individual has at his or her disposal, such as potency (Ben-
Sira, 1993), hardiness (Kobasa, 1979), and a sense of coherence (Antonovsky, 1979); and
social resources, such as social support.

A number of studies have reported evidence for the stress-buffering effects of personality resources (Ben-Sira, 1985, 1991; Lefcourt, et al., 1981; Wheaton, 1985). Others report
that irrespective of the level of stress, personality resources are relatively associated with
psychological well-being (Holahan & Moos, 1986; Kobasa, Maddi, & Kahn, 1982; Nelson
& Cohen, 1983). Among personal resources, potency seems to be a useful concept in studying well-being, especially regarding abusive experiences during childhood, for it reflects
the ability to maintain one's emotional homeostasis in conditions where other resources
lose their effectiveness. It is activated after a previous failure in coping. *Potency* is defined
as an enduring confidence in one's own capabilities, and confidence in and commitment
to one's social environment, perceived as characterized by a basically meaningful order
and by a reliable and just distribution of rewards (Ben-Sira 1993). Empirical evidence
renders inferential support to the stress-buffering and readjustment-promoting function
of potency in society at large and among disabled persons (Ben-Sira, 1985; Lev-Wiesel,
1999; Lev-Wiesel & Shamai, 1998).

Regarding social resources, evidence indicates that social support has a moderating
effect on the adverse consequences of traumatic stress exposure (Ren, Skinner, Lee, &
Kazis, 1999; Wolff, & Ratner, 1999). Yet, different types of social support have varying
beneficial effects on different aspects of health. For example, Ren et al. (1999) found that
social support mediates the deleterious effects of nonmilitary traumatic events, whereas the
adverse consequences of traumatic events in the military were affected by living arrange-
ments. Others found that social support given during war trauma and after war mediates the
long-term negative effects (Paardekooper, de-Jong, & Hermanns, 1999; Solomon, Neria,
& Ram, 1998), and enhances the sense of coherence (Wolff & Ratner, 1999).

In relation to the coping of Holocaust survivors, Orenstein (1999) investigates current
coping styles of Holocaust survivors: optimism that is analogous to acceptance, and map-
ping versus learned helplessness that is analogous to suppression and blame. Then she
examines the relationship between these coping styles and variables, such as the severity
of persecution, age, and presence of social support during the war. According to Orenstein,
those who survived with family members exhibited a more optimistic explanatory style
(the way individuals habitually explain negative events) than those who did not have this
type of social support.

Posttraumatic Growth and Holocaust Survivors

The concept of PTG has not been widely examined in Holocaust survivors, possibly because it seems difficult, even offensive to presume any personal growth outcome of the
Holocaust atrocities. Yet, Sigal (1998) reported that there is irrefutable evidence for resilience among adults who were Holocaust child survivors. Moskovitz (1983) interviewed
twenty-three child survivors, forty years after their experience of being airlifted to a London
therapeutic safe house following World War II, and found that they displayed "an affirmation of life - a stubborn durability" (p. 199). Their adult lives were also distinguished by
social commitment, a high level of spiritual involvement and a staunch desire to maintain
a stable family life. Moskovitz (1983) noted that the adult survivors were characterized by
"endurance, resilience, and great individuality adaptability" (p. 20). Luchterhand (1967)

observed that child survivors demonstrated adaptability and assertiveness and were considered likeable by adults. Others found evidence of the ability to cope with adversity among child Holocaust survivors who were in concentration camps (Sigal & Weinfeld, 1985; Rutter, 1993). Contrary to the preceding, Keilson (1992) in his large-scale follow-up study of Jewish child victims of the Holocaust in the Netherlands, found that the post-Holocaust environment was much more predictive of the adult adjustment of these children than their pre-Holocaust lives. Sigal (1998) concluded that neither pre-Holocaust family history nor postwar care are enough to explain differences in resilience in child survivors.

Posttraumatic Symptoms, Personal Resources, and Posttraumatic Growth in Holocaust Child Survivors

Lev-Wiesel and Amir (2003) investigated the relationship between posttraumatic symptoms, perceived social and personal resources, and PTG among Holocaust child survivors. It was hypothesized that PTSD and PTG coexist in Holocaust child survivors, contingent on their personal and social resources.

METHOD

Participants. Ninety-seven (48% males) nonclinical Holocaust child survivors who were born after 1930 (33% were under the age of five and 67% were younger than 12 when the war had started), average age was 67.90 ($SD = 4.65$), were snow ball recruited in Israel. At the time the data was collected, 71% were married. Seventy-one percent had some education above high school.

Instruments. Participants were administered a self-report questionnaire that included demographic variables, PTSD scale, perceived social support scale, potency scale, and PTG scale.

PTSD-Scale. The 17-item PTSD inventory used in the study was a self-report scale adapted from Horowitz, Wilner, Kaltreider, and Alvarez (1980). This instrument has been used extensively in Israel (e.g., Amir & Sol, 1999). The PTSD-Scale is based on DSM-III-R criteria (American Psychiatric Association, 1987) for the diagnosis of PTSD. The PTSD-Scale measures the intensity of the three primary symptom groups: intrusion, avoidance, and arousal. Following Solomon, Neria, and Ram (1998), the respondent was given one mean score of the 17 items presenting the intensity of posttraumatic symptoms. Cronbach's alpha (α) in this study was .89. In completing the PTSD-Scale, the survivor was asked to specifically relate to Holocaust experiences (even if he or she had experienced additional traumatic life events).

The perceived social support scale (PSS), developed by Procidano and Heller (1983), contains two parts: perceived social support from family members (PSS-Fa) and perceived social support from friends (PSS-Fr), each of which can be used separately. The full scale consists of 40 items (20 items for each part) tapping various expressions of PPS, including instrumental support, affective support, cognitive support, and being the helper. Subjects are asked to choose one of the following three categories: yes, no, or don't know. The PSS measures were internally consistent and appeared to measure valid constructs. The scale has been used extensively in Hebrew (e.g., Lev-Wiesel, 1999). Reliability was .84 for social support from friends and .86 for social support from family (alpha Cronbach).

Potency questionnaire. *Potency* is defined as the level of self-esteem and control that the person has in his or her life, commitment to society (as opposed to alienation), and perception of the society as being a significant and orderly entity (as opposed to anomie). This potency scale, developed by Ben-Sira (1985), has 19 items that measure the following: self-confidence (3 items), control (6 items), social commitment (5 items), and social significance and order (5 items). The items appear in statement form and the respondent is requested to sort them according to five categories that correspond to different levels of agreement with the statement. The measurement has been found to be reliable and valid in a wide range of studies conducted on different populations in Israel (Ben-Sira, 1985, 1991; Lev, 1996). Reliability was .81 alpha Cronbach.

The PTGI was developed by Tedeschi and Calhoun (1996), and is a 21-item scale that measures the degree of reported positive changes experienced in the struggle with major life crises. The scale includes five dimensions that assess the degree to which the individual reports specific positive changes attributed to the struggle with trauma: personal strength, relationships with others, spiritual change, appreciation for life, and new priorities. The inventory has acceptable construct validity, internal consistency (.90), and test-retest reliability over a 2-month interval (.71). Reliability was .94 alpha Cronbach.

RESULTS

Two analyses were performed: First, a correlation analysis between the study variables; second, a multiple regression analysis for the whole sample in which the PTG served as the dependent variable, and the predictors were gender, age, potency, social support, and PTSD variables.

Table 13.1 summarizes the Pearson correlations among the study variables. It also shows the means and standard deviations of the variables. The PTGI total mean score in this study was 43.21 ($SD = 17.32$). Two of the measures emerged as positively associated with PTGI categories in a statistically significant way: social support from friends and arousal, a subcategory of PTSD.

Posttraumatic stress disorder mean score and social support from friends were found to contribute significantly to the level of PTG ($\beta = .43, .21$, respectively), $F(3, 93) = 9.04$, $p < .001$, $R^2 = .20$. Because arousal was found to be positively correlated with all the PTG categories, an additional multiple regression was conducted in which the mean PTSD variable was replaced with arousal. Results indicated that arousal and social support from friends significantly contributed to the level of PTG ($\beta = .31, .20$, respectively), $F(3, 93) = 3.17$, $p < .01$, $R^2 = .37$.

DISCUSSION

The presented study aimed to investigate the relationship between personal resources (potency and perceived social support), PTSD, and PTG among Holocaust child survivors. Illustrations will be added to the discussion of the study findings although they were not part of the original study methodology.

Consistent with previous studies (Amir & Lev-Wiesel, 2001; Lev-Wiesel & Amir, 2000), the findings revealed that the higher the level of the survivors' personal resources, the less they suffered from PTSD symptoms. However, PTG subcategories were found to be positively associated with the subcategory of arousal. One way to explain this unusual relationship is to compare arousal to the biological role of vagal functions, which regulate the energy balance and energy content in the body in a state of hunger to track food (Szekely, 2000). We suggest that arousal, which is one of the symptom clusters of PTSD with symptoms that are similar to fear and anxiety (e.g., lack of concentration

TABLE 13.1

Intercorrelations Among Measures, Means, and Standard Deviations of Variables

	PTSD	Intrusion	Avoidance	Arousal	SSFa	SSFr	Potency	PTG	Relating to Others	New Priorities	Personal Strength	Spiritual Change	Appreciation for Life
PTSD	1.00	.29**	.76**	.39**	−.24*	−.37**	−.32***	.24*	.09	.12	.11	.08	.04
Intrusion			.22*	.49**	.10	.03	−.27**	.15	.14	.23*	.19	.14	.05
Avoidance				.47**	−.26*	−.37**	−.30**	.17	.18	.14	.15	.19	.21*
Arousal					−.06	−.12	−.14	.30**	.29**	.35***	.37***	.26**	.23*
Social support—family (SSFa)						.53**	.21*	.14	.13	.18	.08	−.09	.09
Social support—friends (SSFr)							.35**	.24*	.16	.23*	.05	−.13	.09
Potency								−.01	−.04	.10	.01	−.13	−.06
PTG									.94**	.83**	.89**	.60**	.81**
Relating to others										.75**	.77**	.48**	.76**
New priorities											.66*	.37**	.54**
Personal strength												.53**	.72**
Spiritual change													.50**
Appreciation for life													
Mean & SD total mean score & SD	3.72 (.74)	3.62 (1.85)	3.00 (1.95)	4.51 (1.91)	1.76 (.22)	1.70 (.21)	3.18 (.55)	2.21 (.78) 43.21 (17.32)	2.20 (.84)	2.07 (.84)	2.23 (1.01)	2.06 (.98)	2.61 (1.02)

p < .05, **p* < .01.

and sleeping disruptions), is externalized by these survivors into activity (Hanney & Ko-zlowska, 2002). Possibly, this anxiety is turned into "doing" similar to Bandura's (1982) concept of self-efficacy. This is likely to enhance feelings of mastery and competence - or the sense of growth. However, there might be a negative effect of prolonged arousal. Yehuda, McFarlane, and Shalev (1998) have demonstrated a possible association between increased heart rate and lower cortisol levels immediately after experiencing a traumatic event and later PTSD. These symptoms might have some similarity to arousal symptoms and lead to maladaptive psychological states. Future studies should address this issue.

It should be mentioned that evidence indicates that use of avoidance in coping with stress often predicts depression and vice versa (Feldman, 2002; Felsten, 2002), and that intrusive thoughts are also associated with depression (Courbasson, Endler, & Kocoviski, 2002). However, arousal includes items not directly related to depression (e.g., outbursts of anger and hypervigilence). Therefore, it can be speculated that persons whose PTSD's are expressed mainly by arousal, might experience a form of PTG that does not include elements of depression.

The results also indicated that social support contributes to the level of new possibil-ities. This finding seems to be in line with earlier evidence indicating that social support moderates the negative impact of aversive trauma (Ren et al., 1999). It might be that child survivors who have better social support also have greater PTG. However, the relation-ship between social support and PTG may be reciprocal. It is easier to provide support to survivors whose level of PTG is higher, yet being capable of receiving social support is likely to contribute to one's PTG. Indeed, the literature suggests that children who experi-ence traumas and become resilient adults often demonstrate personal strengths, empathy, intellectual skills, hope, and faith (Gramezy, 1993). Grotberg (1995) claims that children who become resilient adults are often fostered by emotional support, strong role models, and religious affiliation. Miriam was 11 years old when she and her family were deported to Auschwitz from her hometown in Slovakia. As the youngest and most favored of three children, she did not realize where they were going. She remembers their journey in the train and being held by her father who protected her from the suffocating and crowded conditions. She recalls how her father gave her his blessing, telling her that whatever would happen, she must survive and remember how much she was loved. Her parents and siblings were sent to the gas chambers while she was sent to Birkenau. Several older female adolescents adopted her as their younger sister. Miriam said: "They saved my life; I would not have survived without their help and love." After the war she joined a youth organization and later immigrated to Israel illegally, where she graduated high school and married a Holocaust survivor. She kept close contact with those girlfriends who had adopted her during the Holocaust and considered them to be her family. She said "When I am depressed, have nightmares, or become anxious-for example, before Holo-caust Memorial Day-I call my friends. They have been more than sisters or even mothers to me."

The study was limited in several aspects. First, there was no comparison group of survivors of other traumas. Second, based on Lev-Wiesel and Amir's (2000) previous findings indicating differences in the level of psychological distress according to the sur-vival setting, it is possible that the range of Holocaust-related experiences we included was too broad and should be broken down further and examined in relation to its impact. Additionally, it is not known whether this group differs from clinical or other Holocaust survivors. In relation to the level of PTG, Holocaust survivors versus students (Calhoun et al., 2000), it should be noted that the growth of Holocaust survivors lags far behind

FIGURE 13.1. Miriam's drawing of herself during the Holocaust.

the growth of students, more than can be accounted for by the differences in age. Nevertheless, the study findings indicate that PTSD, arousal in particular, and PTG do coexist in the Holocaust child survivor population and this is of great interest to the concept of PTG.

The widely accepted perspective maintains that trauma is transformative in a negative way: that in the aftermath of a traumatic event nothing is ever the same, and that the negative aspects of this change in Holocaust child survivors includes grief, traumatic loss, emotional fragmentation, and psychic devastation (Kestenberg & Brenner, 1986; Krell, 1993; Moskovitz & Krell, 1990; Tauber & Van-Der-Hal, 1997). However, the growing research base that includes personal narratives and clinical lore suggests that trauma also leads to other transformations that are positive and not negative. Transformations that include the reconstruction of meaning, the renewal of faith, trust, hope, and connection, the redefinition of self, self in relation to others, and sense of community (Grossman & Moore, 1995; Harvey, 1996; Tedeschi & Calhoun, 1996; Saakvitne, Tennen, Affleck, 1998; Tedeschi et al., 1998). We would like to offer Tauber and Van-Der-Hal's (1997) concept of compound personality in an attempt to explain the coexistence of psychological symptoms of distress together with vitality, happiness and life satisfaction that we have documented in Holocaust child survivors.

Tauber and Van-Der-Hal assert that these Holocaust child survivors did not employ typical clinical dissociative mechanisms, which is a permanent coping style usually employed

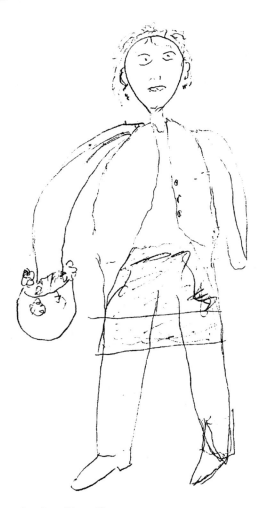

FIGURE 13.2.   Miriam's drawing of herself.

by victims of childhood abuse (Zomer & Zomer, 1997) to escape adverse situations by shutting the self up within one area of the emotional world and escaping into a world of fantasy and daydreams (Cloitre, Scarvalone, & Difede, 1997). Instead, Tauber and Van-Der-Hal assert that Holocaust child survivors grew up in two separate, yet parallel tracks. In the first track, the victimized Holocaust child survivor grew up to be a traumatized Holocaust victim; from a victimized child to a victimized elderly person. This victimized person suffers psychological distress, continuously experiences horrors and fears, exhibits behaviors appropriate for survival during wartime, such as hiding or saving food, avoids getting emotionally involved, and is always ready to escape if necessary. This adult victimized survivor yearns for his or her deceased loved ones, often wishes to join them. However, in the second track the victimized Holocaust child survivor grew up to be a healthy, mature adult who leads a normal life, invests in himself or herself and family, emotionally relates to others, and appreciates life. We found some evidence for this compound personality concept in our clinical work with elderly Holocaust child survivors. We asked survivors to draw two pictures. The instructions were: "Draw yourself at the time of the Holocaust," and, "Draw yourself." In relation to the first instruction, several survivors drew themselves as old Holocaust survivors (see Figure 13.1) ignoring the fact that they were children or adolescents in the Holocaust. In relation to the second instruction, "Draw yourself " survivors drew themselves as senior citizens without any specific symbols of the Holocaust trauma (see Figure 13.2).

We extend this line of thought to propose that PTG is the ability of human beings to turn over a new leaf and resume normal lives, probably the lives that they would have led if the trauma had not occurred. Unlike resilience—a dynamic quality that facilitates people's ability to overcome the challenges of stressful life events (Masten & Coastworth, 1998)—PTG in our view is the ability to make one's life richer and more fulfilling, based on one's deep knowledge and experience prior to, during, and after the traumatic event.

Posttraumatic growth may be viewed metaphorically, as the emergence of new leaves and then entire branches growing on the trunk of a tree that had been brutally severed or destroyed. The tree will never again have the same shape nor will it provide the same shade. Yet the modified shape does not mean the tree will be less beautiful, less vital, or less strong. The core of the tree will remain the same and its roots will continue to feed its branches and leaves, although the angle of the tree is forever altered: the vantage from which the tree absorbs the warm rays of the sun or enjoys the rain will be changed forever. The area where the tree had been cut off will always remain an ugly scar, without leaves or branches; the scarred area will never be restored to its former glory. However, above or below the bare scar may sprout a new treetop, hiding the painful, eternal wound from the world. In this sense, without lessening the impact of the trauma, PTSD may be viewed as posttraumatic disgrowth (meaning dysfunction, barrenness, or distress), whereas PTG may be viewed as natural human strength that represents the very life force in the face of adversity that can compensate for the coexisting posttraumatic distress. Although no exact corresponding idiom exists in English, as Pharoah stated, "the more they are oppressed, the more they multiply and spread," can be applied to the Holocaust.

ACKNOWLEDGMENT

Professor Marianne Amir, a close friend and colleague, was already very sick when Professor Calhoun suggested we join this endeavor. As always, Marianne somehow managed to harness whatever energy she had left to contribute to this study that deals with Holocaust survivors. She and I are both second-generation Holocaust survivors and are, therefore, emotionally involved in this field of research. She was very open about her fears and wishes. Although she knew she would not live long enough to complete all the projects we started together, she made me promise to finish them by myself. I must admit that it was a very difficult task to work alone, without Marianne's incisive and useful comments, in order to fulfill her wishes. In addition, I coped alone with a painful issue that raised personal memories and thoughts. I hope I have not failed her. Following is a brief biographical synopsis about Professor Amir.

Professor Marianne Amir, staff member of Ben-Gurion University's Behavioral Science and Social Work Departments, was born only 53 years ago in Denmark and died of cancer on January 7, 2004. Professor Amir left behind a husband, two sons, numerous friends, students, colleagues and admirers. As a leading researcher (both in Israel and worldwide) in the fields of trauma, posttraumatic disorder, and quality of life, Marianne served as a member of the World Health Organization. Professor Amir contributed in a unique way to understanding the connection between trauma, psychological symptoms of distress, post-traumatic growth, and quality of life among diverse population groups, such as Holocaust survivors, former army soldiers, cancer and fibromyalgia patients, disabled invalids, and casualties of violence. As a researcher, Marianne won research grants from various prestigious foundations. As a lecturer, she was admired by her students for her knowledge, her humor, and the importance she placed on advancing the next generation of researchers, as well as for using her own personal experiences as the basis for a study on how society responds to and copes with terminally ill individuals in their midst. Marianne documented her own coping process with the hope that it would be used by her fellow lecturers as a teaching aid.

REFERENCES

Aldwin, C. M., & Brustrom, J. (1997). Theories of coping with chronic stress: Illustrations from the health psychology and aging literatures. In B. Gotlieb (Ed.), *Coping with chronic stress* (pp. 75–103). New York: Plenum.

American Psychiatric Association, (1987). *Diagnostic and Statistical Manual of Psychiatric Disorders* (3rd ed., rev.). Washington DC: Author.

Amir, M. & Lev-Wiesel, R. (2001). Secondary traumatic stress, psychological distress, sharing of traumatic reminisces and marital quality among spouses of Holocaust child survivors. *Journal of Marital and Family Therapy, 27*(4), 297–308.

Amir, M., & Sol, O. (1999). Psychological impact and prevalence of traumatic events in a student sample in Israel: The effect of multiple traumatic events and physical injury. *Journal of Traumatic Stress, 12*, 139–154.

Anthony, E. J. (1987). Risk, vulnerability and resilience: An overview. In E. J. Anthony & B. J. Cohler (Eds.). *The Invulnerable Child* (pp. 3–48). New York: Giulford.

Antonovsky, A. (1979). *Health, stress and coping*. San Francisco: Jossey Bass.

Armsworth, M. W., & Holaday, M. (1993). The effects of psychological trauma on children and adolescents. *Journal of Counseling & Development, 72*, 49–56.

Bandura, A. (1982). Self-efficacy mechanism in human agency. *American Psychologist, 37*, 122–147.

Ben-Sira, Z. (1985). Potency: A stress buffering link in the coping stress disease relationship. *Social Science and Medicine, 21*, 397–406.

Ben-Sira, Z. (1991). *Regression, stress and readjustment aging: A structured, bio-psychosocial perspective on coping and professional support*. New York: Praeger.

Ben-Sira, Z. (1993). *Zionism at the close of the twentieth century*. Lewiston: The Edwin Mellen Press.

Berlinsky, E. B., & Biller, H. B. (1982). *Parental death and psychological development*. Lexington, MA: D. C. Health.

Breiner, S. J. (1996). Children in and outside the concentration camp. Journal of Psychohistory, *23*, 415–426.

Brenner, I. (1988). Multisensory bridges in response to object loss during the Holocaust. *Psychoanalytic Review, 75*, 573–587.

Bunk, D., & Eggers, C. (1993). Importance of psychodynamic reference factors in psychpathogenesis in persons persecuted by the Nazi regime in childhood. *Fortschritte der Neurologie Psychiatrie, 61*, 38–45.

Calhoun, L. G. & Tedeschi R. G. (1999). *Facilitating posttraumatic growth.*Mahwah, NJ: Lawrence Erlbaum Associates.

Calhoun, L. G., Cann, A., Tedeschi, R. G., & McMillan, J. (2000). A correlational test of the relationship between posttraumatic growth, religion, and cognitive processing. *Journal of Traumatic Stress, 13*(3), 521–527.

Cloitre, M., Scarvalone, P., & Difede, J. (1997). Posttraumatic stress disorder, self- and interpersonal dysfunction among sexually retraumatized women. *Journal of Traumatic Stress, 10*(3), 437–451.

Courbasson, C. M. A., Endler, N. S., & Kocovski, N. L. (2002). Coping and psychological distress for men with substance use disorders. *Current Psychology: Developmental, Learning, Personality, Social, 21*, 35–49.

Cowen, E. L., Wyman, P. A., Work, W. C., & Parker, G. R. (1990). The Rochester Child Resilience project: Overview and summary of first year findings. *Development and Psychopathology, 2*, 193–212.

Danieli, Y. (1985). The treatment and prevention of long-term effects and intergenerational transmission of victimization: A lesson from Holocaust survivors and their children. In C. F. Figley (Ed.), *Trauma and its wake: The study and treatment of post-traumatic stress disorder* (pp. 295–313). New York: Brunner/Mazel.

Feldman, B. N. (2002). The influence of relational factors on men's adjustment to their partners' newly diagnosed breast cancer. *Dissertation Abstracts International Section A: Humanities and Social Sciences, 62*(7-A), 2570.

Felsman, J. K., & Valliant, G. E. (1987). Resilient children as adults: A forty year study. In E. G. Anthony, & B. J. Cohler (Eds.). *The Vulnerable Child*. New York: Guilford.

Felsten, G. (2002). Minor stressors and depressed mood: Reactivity is more strongly correlated than total stress. *Stress and Health: Journal of the International Society for the Investigation of Stress, 18*, 75–81.

Folkman, S., & Lazarus, R. S. (1984). *Stress appraisal and coping*. New York: Springer Pub. Company.

Frankl, V. (1959). *Man's search for meaning*. New York: Washington square Press.

Gampel, Y. (1992). I was a Shoah child. *British Journal of Psychotherapy, 8*, 390–400.

Gramezy, N. (1993). Children in poverty: Resilience despite risk. *Psychiatry, 56*(7), 127–136.

Greenberg, M. A. (1995). Cognitive processing of traumas: The role of intrusive thoughts and reappraisals. *Journal of Applied Social Psychology, 25*, 1262–1296.

Grossman, F. K., & Moore, R. P. (1995). Cognitive processing of traumas: The role of intrusive thoughts and reappraisals. *Journal of Applied Social Psychology, 25*, 1262–1296.

Grotberg, E. H. (1995). *The international resilience project: Research, application and policy*. Paper presented at Symposium International Stress and Violence. Lisbon, Portugal, September 27–30.

Gulliver, S. B., Hughes, J. R., Solomon, L. J., & Dey, A. N. (1995). *Addiction, 90*(6), 767–772.

Hanney, L. & Kozlowska, K. (2002). Healing traumatized children: Creating illustrated storybooks in family therapy. *Family Process, 41*(1), 37–65.

Harvey, M. (1996). An ecological view of psychological trauma and trauma recovery. *Journal of Traumatic Stress, 9*, 3–23.

Holahan, C. J., & Moos, R. H. (1986). Personality, coping and family resources in stress resistance: A longitudinal analysis. *Journal of Personality and Social Psychology, 51*, 389–395.

Horowitz, M., Wilner, N., & Kaltreider, N. (1980). Signs and symptoms of posttraumatic stress disorder. *Archives of General Psychiatry, 37*, 85–92.

Janoff-Bulman, R. (1992). *Shattered assumptions*. New York: The Free Press.

Josepho, S. A., & Plutchik, R. (1994). Stress, coping and suicide risk in psychiatric inpatients. *Suicide Life Threat, 24*, 48–57.

Keilson, H. (1992). *Sequential traumatization in children*. Jerusalem: Magnes Press.

Kestenberg, J. S. (1992). *Children under the Nazi yoke. British Journal of Psychotherapy, 8*, 374–390.

Kestenberg, J. S. (1993). Child victims of persecution and after-effects in later life. *Psyche: Zeitschrift fuer Psychoanalyse und ihre Anwendungen, 47*, 730–742.

Kestenberg, J. S., & Brenner, I. (1986). Children who survived the Holocaust: The role of rules and routines in the development of the superego. *International Journal of Psychoanalysis, 67*, 309–316.

Kestenberg, M., & Kestenberg, J. S. (1988). The sense of belonging and altruism in children who survived the Holocaust. *Psychoanalytic Review, 75*, 533–560.

Kobasa, S. C. (1979). Stressful life events, personality and health: An inquiry into hardiness. *Journal of Personality and Social Psychology, 37*, 1–12.

Kobasa, S. C., Maddi, S. R., & Kahn, S. (1982). Hardiness and health: A prospective study. *Journal of Personality and Social Psychology, 42*, 168–177.

Krell, R. (1993). Child survivors of the Holocaust: strategies of adaptation. *Canadian Journal of Psychiatry, 38*, 384–389.

Lee, B. S. (1988). Holocaust survivors and internal strengths. *Journal of Humanistic Psychology, 28*, 67–96.

Lefcourt, H. M., Miller, R., Ware, E. E., & Sherk, D. (1981). Locus of control as a modifier of the relationship between stressors and moods. *Journal of Personality and Social Psychology, 41*, 457–369.

Lev, R. (1996). *Uncertainty, forced relocation and community role in coping with stress*. Ph.D. dissertation, The Hebrew University: Jerusalem (Hebrew).

Lev-Wiesel, R. (1999). Feelings of adult survivors of child abuse feelings toward their offender-parents. *Child and Adolescents Social Work Journal, 16*(4), 291–304.

Lev-Wiesel, R. & Amir, M. (2000). Posttraumatic Stress Disorder symptoms, psychological distress, personal resources and quality of life in four groups of Holocaust child survivors. *Family Process 39*(4), 445–460.

Lev-Wiesel, R. & Amir, M. (2003). Post-traumatic growth among Holocaust child survivors. *Journal of Loss and Trauma, 8*(4), 229–237.

Lev-Wiesel, R. & Amir, M. (2001). Secondary traumatic stress, psychological distress, sharing of traumatic reminisces and marital quality among spouses of Holocaust child survivors. *Journal of Marital and Family Therapy, 27*(4), 297–308.

Lev-Wiesel, R. & Shamai, M. (1998). Living under the threat of relocation: Spouses' perceptions of the threat and coping resources. *Contemporary Family Therapy, 20*, 107–121.

Masten, A. S., & Coastworth, J. D. (1998). The development of competence in favorable and unfavorable environments. *American Psychologists, 53*(2), 205–220.

Mazor, A., & Mendelson, Y. (1998). Spouse bereavement processes of Holocaust child survivors: Can one differentiate a black frame from a black background? *Contemporary family Therapy: An international Journal, 20*, 79–91.

Moskovitz, S. (1983). *Love despite hate*. New York: H. H. Norton.

Moskovitz, S., & Krell, R. (1990). Child survivors of the Holocaust: Psychological adaptations to survival. *Israel Journal of Psychiatry and Related sciences, 27*, 81–91.

Nelson, D. W., & Cohen, L. H. (1983). Locus of control perceptions and the relationship between life stress and psychological disorder. *American Journal of Community Psychology, 11*, 705–722.

Niederland, W. (1964). Psychiatric disorders among persecution victims. *Journal of Nervous Disorders, 52*, 139–458.

O'Leary, V. E., Alday, C. S., & Ickovics, J. R. (1998). Models of life change and posttraumatic growth. In R. G. Tedeschi, C. L. Park, & L. G. Calhoun (Eds.), *Posttraumatic growth: Positive changes in the aftermath of crisis* (pp. 127–151). Mahwah, NJ: Lawrence Erlbaum Associates.

Orenstein, S. W. (1999). Predictors of explanatory style among Holocaust survivors. *Dissertation Abstracts International: The Sciences and Engineering, 59*(10-B), 5583.

Paardekooper, B., de-Jong, J. T., & Hermanns, J. M. (1999). The psychological impact of war and the refugee situation on South Sudanese children in refugee camps in Northern Uganda: An exploratory study. *Journal of Child Psychology and Psychiatry and Allied Disciplines, 40*(4), 529–536.

Park, C. L., Cohen, L. H., & Murch, R. (1996). Assessment and prediction of stress-related growth. *Journal of Personality, 64*, 71–105.

perceived social support - on abstinent behavior among members of Narcotics Anonymous. *Journal of Social Work Research, 1*(1), 1–9.

Procidano, M. E., & Heller, K. (1983). Measures of Perceived Social Support from Friends and from Family: Three validation studies. *American Journal of Community Psychology, 11*(1), 1–25.

Ren, X. S., Skinner, K., Lee, A., & Kazis, L. (1999). Social support, social selection and self assessed health status: Results from the veterans health study in the United States. *Social Science and Medicine, 48*(12), 1721–1734.

Robinson, S., Rapaport Bar Sever, M., & Rapaport, J. (1994). The present state of people who survived the Holocaust as children. *Acta Psychiatrica Scandinavica, 89*, 242–245.

Roesler, T. A., & McKenzie, N. (1994). Effects of childhood trauma on psychological functioning in adults sexually abused as children. *Journal of Nervous and Mental Disease, 182*, 145–150.

Rutter, M. (1993). Resilience: Some conceptual considerations. *Journal of Adolescent Health, 14*, 626–631.

Saakvite, K. W., Tennen, H., & Affleck, G. (1998). Exploring thriving in the context of clinical trauma theory: Constructivist self development theory. Journal *of Social Issues, 54*(2), 279–300.

Sigal, J. J. (1998). Long-term effects of the Holocaust: Empirical evidence for resilience in the first, second, and third generation. *Psychoanalytic Review, 85*(4), 579–585.

Sigal, J. J., & Wienfeld, M. (1985). Stability of coping style 33 years after prolonged exposure to extreme stress. *Acta Psychiatrica Scandinavica, 71*, 554–566.

Solomon, Z., Neria, Y., & Ram, A. (1998). Mental health professionals' responses to loss and trauma of Holocaust survivors. In J. H. Harvey (Ed), *Perspectives on loss: A sourcebook* (pp. 221–230). Philadelphia, PA: Brunner/Mazel.

Szekely, M. (2000). The vagus nerve in thermoregulation and energy metabolism. *Autonomic Neuroscience Basic and Clinical, 85*(1–3), 26–38.

Tauber, Y., & Van-Der-Hal, E. (1997). Transformation of perception of trauma by child survivors of the Holocaust in group therapy. *Journal of Contemporary Psychotherapy, 27*, 157–171.

Taylor, S., & Brown, J. D. (1988). Illusion and well-being: A social psychological perspective on mental health. *Psychological Bulletin, 103*, 193–210.

Tec, N. (1993). A historical perspective tracing the history of the hidden child experience. In: J. Marks (Ed.), *The hidden children: The secret survivors of the Holocaust* (pp. 273–291). New York: Fawcett Columbia.

Tedeschi, R. G, & Calhoun, L. G. (1996). The posttraumatic Growth Inventory: Measuring the positive legacy of trauma. *Journal of Traumatic Stress, 9*, 455–471.

Tedeschi, R. G., Park, C. L., & Calhoun, L. G. (1998). *Posttraumatic growth: Positive changes in the aftermath of crisis.* Mahwah, NJ: Lawrence.

Valent, P. (1998). Resilience in child survivors of the Holocaust: Toward the concept of resilience. *Psychoanalytic Review, 85*, 517–535.

Valliant, G. (1993). *The Wisdom of the ego.* Cambridge, MA: Harvard University Press.

Werner, E. E., & Smith, R. S. (1992). *Overcoming in the odds.* Ithaca, NY: Cornell University Press.

Wheaton, B. (1985). Models for the stress-buffering functions of coping resources. *Journal of Health and Social Behavior, 26*, 352–364.

Wolff, A. C., & Ratner, P. A. (1999). Stress, social support, and sense of coherence. *Western Journal of Nursing Research, 21*(2), 182–197.

Wolin, S. J., & Wolin, S. (1993). *The resilient self: How survivors of troubled families rise above adversity.* New York: Ullard Books.

Yalom, I. D., & Lieberman, M. A. (1991). Bereavement and heightened existential awareness. *Psychiatry, 54*, 334–345.

Yehuda, R., McFarlane, A. C., & Shalev, A. Y. (1998). Predicting the development of posttraumatic stress disorder from the acute response to a traumatic event. *Biological Psychiatry, 44*, 1305–1313.

Yehuda, R., Kahana, B., Binder-Brynes, K., Southwick, S. M., mason, J. W., & Giller, E. (1995). Low urinary cortisol excretion in Holocaust survivors with posttraumatic stress disorder. *American Journal of Psychiatry, 152*, 982–986.

Yehuda, R., Sartorius, N., Kahana, B., Southwick, S. M., & Giller, E. L. (1994). Depressive features in Holocaust survivors with and without posttraumatic stress disorder. *Journal of Traumatic stress, 7*, 699–704.

Yehuda, R., Schmeidler, J., Siever, L. J., Binder-brynes, K., & Elkin A. (1997). Individual differences in Posttraumatic stress symptom profiles in Holocaust survivors in concentration camps or in hiding. *Journal of Traumatic Stress, 10*, 453–463.

Zomer, E., & Zomer, L. (1997). Dissociative disorder psychodynamic dimensions in art therapy. *Sihot, 11*(3), 183–195 (Hebrew).

14

RESILIENCE AND POSTTRAUMATIC GROWTH IN CHILDREN

RYAN P. KILMER

UNIVERSITY OF NORTH CAROLINA AT CHARLOTTE

Posttraumatic growth (PTG) (i.e., positive change experienced as a result of the struggle with a major loss or trauma) is an emerging area of study and clinical focus that emphasizes the transformative aspects of responding to adversity (Calhoun & Tedeschi, 1999, 2004; Tedeschi & Calhoun, 1996, 2004). Although a significant body of work has identified correlates of PTG and supported Calhoun and Tedeschi's (1998) hypothesized model of the PTG process among adults (e.g., Calhoun & Tedeschi, 2001, 2004, this volume), few studies have examined PTG among nonadults. Early evidence suggests that the growth process occurs, to some degree, among adolescents (Horowitz, Loos, & Putnam, 1997; Milam, Ritt-Olson, & Unger, 2004; Taku, 2005); however, despite the substantial body of work regarding children's responses to stress or trauma (Donaldson, Prinstein, Danovsky, & Spirito, 2000; Grant et al., 2003; Osofsky, 2004a), the PTG construct has been the focus of minimal systematic evaluation among children. Indeed, the current literature appears to include only two studies investigating PTG in children (Cryder, Kilmer, Tedeschi, & Calhoun, in press; Salter & Stallard, 2004), as well as one dissertation (Yaskowich, 2002).

Extending PTG research downward to explore the nature of the growth process in children and enhance understanding of the phenomenon can yield useful information to clinicians and other professionals working with children who have experienced traumatic events. The extant literature on PTG (Cadell, Regehr, & Hemsworth, 2003; Park, 1998; Tedeschi & Calhoun, 2004), and parallel research with children in such areas as risk and resilience, and stress and coping (e.g., Luthar, 2003; Masten & Coatsworth, 1998), can inform and guide research examining the PTG process among youngsters. This chapter seeks to (a) provide a broad overview of the PTG construct, including its distinction from resilience; (b) consider issues in exploring PTG among child populations; (c) summarize key resilience findings and describe a hypothesized model of factors thought to be relevant to PTG in children; (d) detail methods used to assess PTG in children and the limited findings in this area to date; (e) illustrate possibilities for future child PTG research; and (f) discuss implications of this work for clinicians and researchers alike.

POSTTRAUMATIC GROWTH: A BRIEF OVERVIEW OF THE CONSTRUCT

Traumatic events and circumstances can shatter assumptions about one's self and the expected course of one's life (Janoff-Bulman, 1992, this volume), setting in motion attempts to cope and adapt. Importantly, it is this struggle in the aftermath of trauma, not the event or circumstance itself, that appears to yield PTG (Tedeschi & Calhoun, 1995). Although survivors of a variety of traumas tend to report an increased sense of vulnerability and psychological distress (Calhoun & Tedeschi, 1999), reflecting the fact that they have suffered in ways they may not have been able to control or prevent (Janoff-Bulman, 1992), many also report PTG, as manifested by positive changes in several domains (see Calhoun & Tedeschi, 1998, 2004; Tedeschi & Calhoun, 1996, 2004). For instance, an increased sense of personal strength, of one's capacities to survive and prevail, constitutes a common theme among those who have faced major life challenges. Trauma survivors also can discover new perspectives about their relationships, identifying salient characteristics, both positive and negative, in others. For example, many tell of learning who their real friends are or upon whom they can depend. Because of their desire to talk about what has happened during and after trauma, many survivors find themselves developing greater comfort with intimacy. They may become most intimate with others who have suffered through similar circumstances and, therefore, experience a greater sense of compassion for those experiencing life difficulties.

Traumas can raise fundamental existential questions and spur on cognitive engagement with questions about life's purpose and similar issues (Calhoun & Tedeschi, 2004). In response, survivors may report modified priorities and a shift in their perspectives and value systems such that they appreciate and value the "smaller things" in life more. Family, friends, and small pleasures may be viewed as more important than before, perhaps more than other previously valued daily demands and motives. Moreover, many survivors report an increased appreciation for life in general. Similar intrapersonal changes may also be detailed, such that survivors report richer religious, spiritual, and existential lives, with philosophies of life that are more fully developed and satisfying (Tedeschi & Calhoun, 2004).

BEYOND RESILIENCE: THE POSTTRAUMATIC GROWTH PROCESS

Research on child resilience can provide an important backdrop for similar work in PTG. However, although PTG and resilience share substantial conceptual variance, it is important to distinguish the constructs. As Cryder et al. (in press) delineate, whereas resilience typically refers to a dynamic developmental process reflecting positive adaptation, or competence, in the face of challenging life conditions or stress (see, e.g., Luthar, Cicchetti, & Becker, 2000; Masten, 2001), PTG refers to a growth process by which survivors are profoundly affected by the traumatic experience in a way that *transforms*. Put another way, PTG refers to positive changes that go *beyond* effective coping and adjustment in the face of adversity. It involves movement beyond pretrauma levels of adaptation, a qualitative change in functioning across different domains. It bears underscoring that, as Calhoun and Tedeschi note (this volume), although many survivors may recognize some benefit and positive change, they often still report distress and struggle in the trauma's aftermath. Thus, as Cryder and colleagues conclude, many individuals reporting PTG may also report less emotional well-being than those evidencing resilient adaptation.

Posttraumatic growth theorists suggest that this continuing distress and the individual's struggle with his or her new reality contribute importantly to the growth process by facilitating a constructive cognitive processing of trauma, or rumination (Tedeschi & Calhoun, 1995). As one questions the basic assumptions about his or her life and attempts to make sense of and integrate the trauma and its aftermath in a manner consistent with prior worldviews, this productive ruminative process yields schema change, consolidating changed perspectives on self, others, and one's new life and way of living (e.g., Calhoun & Tedeschi, 2004). Contributing further to the PTG process, supportive others may help provide a means to craft narratives about the changes that have occurred and offer perspectives that can be integrated into schema change (Calhoun & Tedeschi, 2004; Neimeyer, 2001).

EXPLORING THE POSTTRAUMATIC GROWTH PROCESS AMONG CHILDREN: ISSUES AND OPPORTUNITIES

Such notions raise potentially relevant concerns about investigating PTG among children. That is, assumptions about the growth process suggest several issues involving the cognitive maturity and "psychological mindedness" (i.e., intrapersonal awareness and insight) of youngsters (Cryder et al., in press). Moreover, the affective quality of the learning and change in PTG may distinguish it from other normative developmental processes and, in considering the potential for PTG among children, it is necessary to address the ways in which children cognitively process traumatic events in a fashion similar to and different from adults. Children respond to trauma in a manner that reflects their developmental level and the tasks and challenges they are attempting to master (Lieberman & Van Horn, 2004), and it appears that reactions vary at different ages and stages because children understand and internalize the experience depending upon their cognitive and emotional capacities (Osofsky, 2004b). Thus, the clear variability in children's cognitive capabilities and 'machinery' across different stages may very well influence their understanding and appraisal of the trauma (e.g., Hasan & Power, 2004), the attributions they make about their circumstance, their repertoire of coping skills and strategies, their ability to marshal resources effectively, and their capacity to attend to and report their internal experiences (Cryder et al., in press). In that vein, Cohen, Hettler, and Pane (1998) discussed the possibility that it might be years before growth on some dimensions manifests in child and youth populations. Similarly, Milam et al. (2004) found a positive relationship between age and PTG among adolescents, positing that a particular level of cognitive maturity is necessary to find meaning or identify salient changes or benefits as a result of trauma and its aftermath.

Given that PTG appears to involve a degree of cognitive sophistication that allows both losses and gains to be recognized, it is unclear whether something akin to PTG is possible for children, or how similar the PTG process in childhood might be to that observed among adults (e.g., Cryder et al., in press). For example, as discussed in the preceding text, one's struggle with his or her new reality is thought to foster a productive rumination process, a critical component of the PTG process that can alter schemas and consolidate changed perspectives in the aftermath of trauma (Tedeschi & Calhoun, 1995). However, if schemas are not clearly set in children or are distinct in nature from those of adults, the notion of schema change as one grapples with traumatic circumstances may be qualitatively different in meaning and scope for children relative to adults.

Indeed, Janoff-Bulman (1992) suggests that a child's assumptive world is more pliable than an adult's, and that his or her basic assumptions and models of oneself, others, and the world may be modified throughout childhood and adolescence as new experiences and outcomes, both positive and negative, become incorporated into these cumulatively-constructed internal representations. Because this less solidified representational world is more capable of accommodating new inputs, some theorists have suggested that it leaves children vulnerable to greater devastation, relative to adults (Janoff-Bulman, 1992).

Many children make basic (developmentally appropriate) assumptions about their worlds—they assume that they will be "kind, protective, safe, consistent, and meaningful" and that their caregivers will be there to provide love, protection, and meaning (Goldman, 2002, p. 194). Exposure to traumatic events or circumstances can create a loss of that assumptive world of safety, protection from harm, and predictability; a loss of trust, meaning, and faith; and a loss of one's known routine and day-to-day experience (Goldman, 2002; Lieberman & Van Horn, 2004). Thus, some authors have noted the great potential for trauma experiences to negatively impact the developing child's representational systems. For instance, Pynoos, Steinberg, and Wraith (1995) state, "the formation of traumatic expectations may represent a breach in the schematic 'averaging,' distorting emotional, cognitive, and moral concepts as well as inner representations of self, object relations, and the social environment" (p. 72). Lieberman and Van Horn (2004) extend this notion, positing that early trauma exposure, whether circumscribed or chronic, can disrupt not only the child's developing sense of self, but also one's emotional regulation and learning through exploration of his or her environment. Supporting this possibility, research suggests that trauma in infancy and early childhood can derail the normative developmental course (Lieberman & Van Horn, 2004; Pynoos, 1990). More specifically, as Bosquet (2004) details, research has demonstrated that children who have experienced trauma may exhibit difficulties in multiple developmental domains, that is, emotional and behavioral symptoms, delays or regressions in developmental skills, and difficulties in cognitive and socioemotional functioning (see, e.g., Cicchetti & Lynch, 1993; Osofsky, 1995).

On the other hand, the fact that a child's assumptive world is less firmly entrenched or embedded than an adult's may also yield greater protection because it is open to potentially adaptive inputs (Janoff-Bulman, 1992). While a number of factors may serve to help buffer the child from the trauma's impact, according to Janoff-Bulman (1992), this protection is largely afforded the child by the emotional investment and interpretive effort of close, caring adults, particularly parents. That is, caregivers can provide an environment in which a child can tussle with, understand, and attempt to incorporate traumatic experiences into their worldview, and such support sources, whether intra- or extrafamilial, can help a child achieve resolution and make meaning of the event. The inputs of others can guide interpretations, reframe, and perhaps even transform the child's sense of the event or condition (Janoff-Bulman, 1992). Such support from important others is thought to foster positive adaptation in trauma's aftermath (see the discussion that follows). In fact, some theorists have suggested that, without positive support sources, a child may be more prone to evidence negative effects of the trauma in the longer term (Janoff-Bulman, 1992).

Research has documented a multitude of negative short- and long-term consequences associated with diverse childhood traumas, from sexual abuse to violence exposure, from surviving a natural disaster to the death of a parent. Nevertheless, this literature has also described the variability in responses across children and even discussed findings akin to PTG, with children reporting perceived benefits following traumatic events or circumstances. As one case in point, work with pediatric cancer survivors (Fritz, Williams, & Amylon, 1988) has suggested that the youngsters experienced a range of positive changes, including heightened sensitivity to others, increased altruism, and modified values. In a more recent study, Salter and Stallard (2004) found that youngsters aged 7 to 18 years reported a changed philosophy of life, improved relationships, and more positive self-perceptions after experiencing road traffic accidents (though the average age of those reporting PTG was 16 years). Other authors have documented instances of children reporting that they feel "stronger" after significant life-altering events, such as the death of a parent (Krementz, 1983). Thus, despite the challenges inherent in studying the PTG process in youngsters, prior research has laid groundwork for examining the construct among children.

DRAWING ON PARALLEL LITERATURES: INFORMING A HYPOTHESIZED MODEL OF POSTTRAUMATIC GROWTH IN CHILDREN

Examining the literatures on stress and coping and, more recently, child risk and resilience can yield fruitful information for investigators working to understand the potential for, and nature of, the PTG process among children, as well as factors that may facilitate growth. More specifically, this research base can shed important light on the factors and processes that may influence children's adjustment in response to trauma. Although chronically stressful processes or conditions (e.g., family discord and violence, growing up in poverty) are thought to have greater risk potential (Cowen, Wyman, Work, & Parker, 1990), researchers have long documented that stress exposure (similar to trauma), whether acute or chronic, predisposes maladjustment in children (e.g., Johnson, 1986). At the same time, and of special relevance in this context, research suggests that children vary considerably in their responses to stress, with some coping and adapting particularly well despite exposure to significant adversity (Cowen, 1994; Wyman, Sandler, Wolchik, & Nelson, 2000).

This notion has guided research in resilience, which has identified child, family, and environmental factors that relate to resilient adaptation and appear to serve a "protective" function under conditions of stress, reducing risk for maladjustment and increasing the likelihood of positive health outcomes (e.g., Werner & Smith, 1992). Despite multiple issues in resilience research, including cross-study differences in construct definitions, target populations, and methodologies, significant common findings have emerged from this body of work (Luthar et al., 2000; Masten, 2001). Indeed, findings have consistently cohered into several clusters of variables, including (a) individual child attributes or competencies, such as positive temperamental or dispositional qualities (e.g., responsiveness, sociability, adaptability to change); good intellectual functioning; self-efficacy; positive self-worth; perceived competence; sound problem-solving skills; an internal locus of control; accurate and realistic attributions of control; and positive future expectations, or a sense of optimism; (b) a warm, supportive family environment, including a sound relationship with a primary caregiver; parenting quality; and a structured, stable, nurturant home; and (c) contextual variables, including links with positive extrafamilial support sources and identification models; effective schools; connections to prosocial organizations; and neighborhood qualities (see, e.g., Luthar et al., 2000; Luthar, 2003; Masten & Coatsworth, 1998; Werner & Smith, 1992; Wyman et al., 2000). Particularly noteworthy here, connections with competent, caring, prosocial adults in the family and community, and positive self-views and self-system functioning are among the most consistently and widely reported of these factors (Luthar et al., 2000; Masten, 2001; Wyman et al., 2000).

In fact, numerous researchers have noted that resilient outcomes are fostered by interplays between characteristics of the child and his or her family context.

Importantly, these potential protective influences stem from multiple levels of the child's context, that is, individual, family, and community. Qualities of the individual child may be antecedents or correlates of resilience to be sure, but resilient adaptation may often be associated with factors external to the child, including aspects of the family (and caregiving environment) and characteristics of the wider social and contextual environments (e.g., Luthar et al., 2000; Werner & Smith, 1992). The resilience findings summarized briefly here are consistent with and reflect elements of multiple developmental theories, viewpoints that must be taken into account in any hypothesized model of child PTG.

Although this chapter will put forth a model of the growth process in children, it is crucial to underscore the need to consider the larger developmental context within which each potential influence may operate; a given factor may prove salutary for children in some contexts, yet be associated with more deleterious outcomes in others. Put another way, although research involving diverse populations of children supports the notion that there are common, core adaptive systems that facilitate positive adaptation, growing evidence also suggests that many protective processes are context specific, that is, different in their effectiveness, according to a child's social context and individual resources and characteristics (see Wyman, 2003 for a discussion of this issue).

That said, in establishing a framework for understanding the growth process in children, it is fruitful to consider the tenets of some basic theoretical approaches, each placing particular weight on the interactions between the child and his or her qualities and the environment. For instance, this notion is core to systems theory, which posits that families are systems characterized by many complex, mutually-influential relationships and interactions (Nichols & Schwartz, 1998). Transactional theories of development also emphasize this idea of bidirectional influence, such that, for example, a child's development (and the caregiver–child relationship) is shaped not only by influence flowing from parent to child, but from child to parent (e.g., Sameroff & Chandler, 1975). Such ideas are captured in Bronfenbrenner's (1977, 1979) ecological approach, which asserts that individual behavior and development are influenced by a variety of factors in one's proximal (e.g., the family milieu, school) and more distal (e.g., cultural values and beliefs, neighborhood qualities) environment, in addition to the interactions and interrelationships between and among the multiple levels of a child's contextual world. At its core, Bronfenbrenner's (1979, p. 3) model defines development as a "lasting change in the way in which a person perceives and deals with his environment," that is, how the person experiences and responds to the setting. Lieberman and Van Horn (2004) note that such a multidimensional approach is crucial to understanding the adjustment of children experiencing trauma, that the child's functioning must be considered within the larger context of that child's relationships and the family's ecological niche (e.g., socioeconomic circumstances, childrearing values), particularly because the child's response is influenced by, for example, the available environmental supports.

Finally, the organizational–developmental model has also been proposed as a framework for understanding children's development and adaptation under conditions of risk and adversity (see, e.g., Egeland, Carlson, & Sroufe, 1993; Waters & Sroufe, 1983; Wyman et al., 1999), and its applications for children experiencing traumatic events or circumstances is clear. According to that model, development is a series of qualitative reorganizations among and within biological and behavioral systems, and provides a lens for viewing growth, integration, and change in cognitive, affective, and social realms (see, e.g., Cicchetti & Schneider-Rosen, 1986). It is a useful way to conceptualize children's adaptation in the face of risk (or trauma) because it views developmental outcomes as resulting from interactions between characteristics of the child and the psychosocial systems that impact his or her caregiving environment and experiences (Sameroff, 1995; Wyman et al., 1999). Adaptation is seen as a process in which a child actively interacts with his or her environment and successfully uses internal and external resources to resolve stage-salient developmental issues (Egeland et al., 1993; Waters & Sroufe, 1983; Wyman et al., 1999). Moreover, adaptation, or competence, at one stage of development, is seen as facilitating successful adaptation at later stages (Cicchetti & Schneider-Rosen, 1986). Hence, early experience critically influences later experience, and resolution of early developmental tasks is thought to have enduring protective value (Cowen, 1999, 2000; Egeland et al., 1993). Thus, adaptation is seen as transactional in this approach, and child and environmental variables may function as either risk or protective factors (Egeland et al., 1993; Sameroff & Chandler, 1975; Wyman et al., 1999). Views about children's adaptation in trauma's aftermath fit well within the organizational–developmental framework because they emphasize interplays between the child's attributes and resources (e.g., temperament), and both characteristics of the family milieu and qualities of the caregiving environment.

Informed by these theoretical frameworks, current research and writings in child trauma, findings of child-oriented research focused on successful coping and adaptation in the face of adversity, and Calhoun and Tedeschi's (1998) model of how PTG may unfold in adults, the next sections adapt and extend the model put forth by Cryder et al. (in press) to illustrate hypothesized linkages involved in the PTG process for children (see Fig. 14.1).

The Child's Pretrauma Beliefs, Characteristics, and Functioning

First, it is important to note that multiple child factors, that is, what the child "brings to the table" in terms of pretrauma mental health and functioning, resources, and belief systems, can mediate aspects of his or her response to a traumatic stressor or circumstance. For instance, consistent with findings from the resilience literature, numerous researchers (e.g., Lieberman & Van Horn, 2004; Pynoos et al., 1995) have noted that the child's temperamental style may play an important role in a child's response to trauma, because his or her dispositional or constitutional characteristics may influence the nature of the response, contribute to attributions made about the events, and impact emotional regulation and social functioning. Similarly, a child's pretrauma mental health (or pre-existing psychopathology) has been identified frequently as an important moderator of trauma response (Bosquet, 2004; Pynoos et al. 1995).

In their model of childhood traumatic stress, Pynoos et al. (1995) note that additional factors, such as the child's developmental level and competencies, self-esteem, history of prior trauma, and ability to make cognitive discriminations, all may influence the degree to which he or she experiences distress and the likelihood of successful adaptation in the face of trauma. Other child factors reflecting cognitive resources and self-system functioning (e.g., self-views, expectations about control) will be discussed in more detail in the sections that follow.

Given the emphasis of PTG models on schema change, the child's pretrauma assumptive world and views about him- or herself, others, and the world, many developmental frameworks would identify the child's internal working model, or representational system, established over cumulative interactions with other persons and his or her world, as a core construct of relevance (see, e.g., Bretherton, 1985; Lynch & Cicchetti, 1998). These working models, impacted greatly by the child's attachment relationships and influenced by the child's affective and cognitive understanding, are thought to inform how the

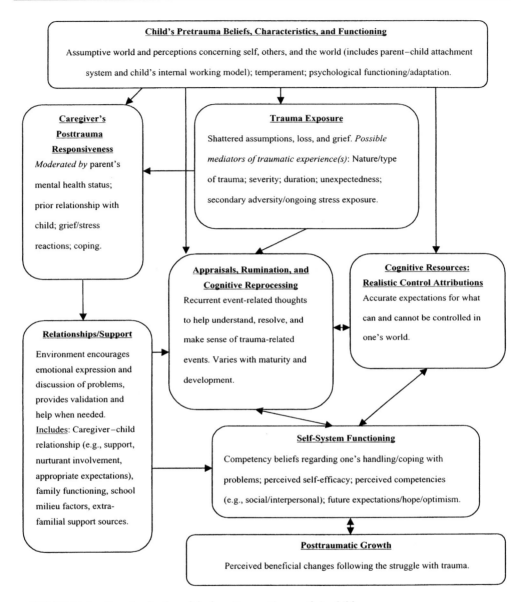

FIGURE 14.1.   Hypothesized model of posttraumatic growth in children.

child engages with or responds to others and the environment and are theorized as useful in making appraisals and guiding behavior in new situations in addition to shaping children's expectations about their futures. As such, they are thought to be critical in considering how a child reacts to and is impacted by trauma.

Trauma Exposure

The nature of the trauma is, of course, a salient factor. The type of trauma, its unexpectedness, the level and duration of exposure, and the existence of traumatic reminders have been noted to serve a potential moderating role in how the child responds to trauma (e.g., Bosquet, 2004; Pynoos et al., 1995). The number and extent of secondary risks or adversities may also be of consequence—for example, disruption to the continuity of daily life routines (e.g., mealtimes, bedtime rituals) that anchor a child's sense of predictability may intensify the immediate effects of a trauma (Lieberman & Van Horn, 2004).

Relationships and Support

As suggested by the brief summary of resilience findings in the preceding text, a child's relational environment is thought to play a rather significant role in his or her adaptation in the face (or aftermath) of stress and trauma. Relationships and intra- and extrafamilial support sources constitute critical factors in a child's ecological context. The next paragraphs consider some of these key factors separately.

Caregivers' posttrauma responsiveness. A substantial body of work suggests that positive parent–child relationships can serve a protective function for children exposed to adversity (see, e.g., Masten & Coatsworth, 1998), and numerous researchers have reported that the response and functioning of parents during and after a stressor or trauma can affect profoundly the child's reactions and behavior (Masten, Best, & Garmezy, 1990). For instance, children's appraisals and interpretations of the circumstances, and their behavioral responses, may be informed by social referencing or observation (e.g., looking to mother to assess the level of danger, imitating a parent's coping style) and, at a more basic level, the trauma may impact caregivers' parenting behaviors and, subsequently, the quality of care and support (emotional and otherwise) they may provide (Masten et al., 1990). This parental responsiveness is posited to moderate children's responses to trauma and, as some researchers have noted, the impact of secondary stressors (Pynoos et al., 1995).

Multiple caregiver-specific factors may be seen as influencing responsiveness, including parental personality and past or current psychopathology, the parent's trauma history, his or her trauma and grief reactions, and the resources available to the caregiver(s) (e.g., social support) (Bosquet, 2004; Pynoos et al., 1995). The trauma experience may disrupt young children's developmentally appropriate expectation that their caregivers serve as safe havens, protecting them from harm, an element of the situation that may stimulate in parents feelings of guilt and self-deprecation and interfere with their ability to help the child in the trauma's aftermath (Lieberman & Van Horn, 2004).

As Osofsky (2004b, p. 4) notes, parenting under "normal" circumstances is complex, a condition further complicated by the difficulties associated with caregiving for a child who has experienced trauma and coping with the event(s) as that child's parent. Regardless, it appears clear that caregivers can help their children by being able to hear their concerns and reassure them. Although many parents may want to minimize the child's feelings and "spare" them the pain because they are "too young" to experience them, it is critical that parents remain available, listen, and follow their child's lead (see, e.g., Osofsky, 2004b). Such efforts can help promote adaptation and recovery in the aftermath of trauma.

The caregiving environment and caregiver–child relationship. Closely tied to parental responsiveness, the overall quality of the caregiving environment and caregiver–child relationship is likely to play a substantial role, influencing the degree to which the caregiver may be attuned to the child's responses and needs, the level of nurturant involvement and support he or she may make available, and the likelihood the child will seek out support and comfort from the caregiver. The impact of the caregiving system has been well documented in child risk and resilience research, as studies have consistently identified emotionally responsive, competent caregiving as a central variable mediating the impact of risk (e.g., Werner & Smith, 1992; Wyman et al., 1999, 2000). As Masten and Coatsworth (1998, p. 213) relate, "caregivers and the attachment relationships that develop between caregivers and children are fundamental to human adaptation and development," and the parent–child relationship is a crucial context for children, both under normative circumstances and under conditions of extreme challenge. Research demonstrates the association between parental warmth and involvement and better outcomes for children who have experienced adversity (Egeland et al., 1993; Masten & Coatsworth, 1998). It appears as though children's early development is highly buffered from the impact of risk by their caregiving system (Masten et al., 1990). One study by Wyman and colleagues (1999) bears specific mention. The investigators found that variables reflecting parenting competence and quality were the most sensitive predictors of resilience in their sample of 7- to 9-year-old highly stressed children. Of particular relevance to child PTG work, variables reflecting warm, close, competent parenting were direct, proximal predictors of resilient classification, and caregivers of children classified as resilient held more nurturant and emotionally responsive parenting attitudes (i.e., more appropriate developmental expectations, clear empathy for children's needs, and more adaptive views of appropriate parent and child roles). Effective and *age appropriate* parenting of children in the aftermath of trauma will facilitate parental attunement and responsiveness to children's needs, critical factors in the child's adjustment posttrauma. Indeed, consistent with the links hypothesized in the PTG model posited here, Yates, Egeland, and Sroufe (2003, p. 254) note that sensitive and emotionally responsive early caregiving relationships can foster the development of children's self-concepts, and that it "is within a framework of available care and positive self-regard that the child develops adaptive emotion regulation patterns, flexible problem-solving skills, and an expectation of success in the face of adversity."

Family relationships: Family cohesion and functioning. Reflecting the need to consider the child's ecology, theories of the growth process in children must take into account the potential impact of the larger family milieu. Dealing with traumatic events or circumstances may overwhelm family resources and contribute to increased caregiver strain, family turmoil, and conflict. Thus, in addition to broader contextual factors that may influence the family (e.g., socioeconomic status), the family's cohesion and functioning warrant attention as factors that may directly impact the child's coping response and adaptation. Research has consistently found that children who follow positive adjustment trajectories grow up in warm, sensitive, cohesive, and communicative family environments (Yates & Masten, 2004) and, of salience to the present model, some studies have suggested that better family relationships and functioning are associated with higher self-concept, social competence, and behavioral control among children at risk (see Moos & Moos, 1994). The section on support that follows further details the hypothesized role of relationships in the current model.

Social support: Intra- and extrafamilial support sources. As noted in the preceding text, the association between sound adjustment in the face of risk and positive adult sources of support (whether in a child's family or his or her broader community) is among the most consistently reported findings in the child-oriented risk and resilience literature (e.g., Masten, 2001; Masten & Coatsworth, 1998; Werner & Smith, 1992; Wyman et al., 2000). Understanding, warm, responsive, and available sources of support—in the home, the school, or the community—are thought to facilitate the PTG process by providing comfort, fostering and even modeling effective coping behaviors, and assisting schema modification by sharing a caring, adult perspective (e.g., Calhoun & Tedeschi, 1998; Israelashvili, 1999). Adult assistance can facilitate the cognitive and emotional reappraisal of the event(s) and provide an empathic legitimization of a child's emotional experience (Pynoos et al., 1995). Thus, children can look to adults to help them understand the meaning of events and the appropriateness of their reactions. Even though difficult emotions may arise in the aftermath of trauma, it is crucial that children do not detect a lack of openness to their distressing feelings—Moody and Moody (1991) report that constraining children's expressions of thoughts and emotions regarding a traumatic event may inhibit the process of assimilating and emotionally resolving their perceptions of the trauma and, in turn, disrupt their ability to find meaning in the experience.

Thus, sound social support sources encourage expression of a child's feelings, provide nonjudgmental validation of event-related thoughts and feelings, and assist with more instrumental aspects of support when needed, roles that are thought to contribute to the constructive rumination process and the development or enhancement of a child's positive self-views and competency beliefs. Research suggests that perceived support enhances children's appraisals that they have resources necessary for coping and, according to a model put forth by Sandler, Miller, Short, and Wolchik (1989), facilitates the coping process because it provides a predictable social environment and enhances control beliefs, increases children's sense of security in their social relationships, and affirms their self-esteem and self-efficacy for dealing with stress. In fact, Yaskowich (2002) suggests that support sources, such as parents, may even directly encourage children to acknowledge positive benefits in the context of stressful situations or circumstances.

Appraisals, Rumination, and Cognitive Reprocessing

In addition to relational factors, conceptual models of resilience and PTG each include components reflecting developing cognitive abilities and important cognitive processes, ranging from actual coping strategies and problem-solving approaches, to appraisals of the stressful or traumatic event, attributions about control, and rumination (see, e.g., Wyman et al., 1999). Traumatic events and circumstances elicit emotional reactions that may be mediated by the types of interpretations and implications an individual links with them. Cognitive appraisals (including cognitive distortions and errors) have been identified as major influences on children's reactions to traumatic events, such as sexual abuse, and attention has been given to their role in the development of psychopathology (Hasan & Power, 2004; Spaccarelli, 1994). However, relatively little is known about appraisal processes and the linkages between children's cognitive appraisals and adjustment in generally healthy children (Hasan & Power, 2004). It does appear clear that a child's subjective appraisals and specific coping strategies vary with maturation, particularly in regard to the degree of reliance on others, such as parents or adult caregivers, siblings, and peers (Pynoos et al., 1995).

A critical (and related) component of hypothesized PTG models, ruminative processing allows the inclusion of some positive appraisals of the traumatic event and subsequent changes, also facilitating schema change to incorporate revised views of one's self and one's world. There is preliminary support for the role of rumination in nonadult samples—research with adolescents (e.g., Martinson & Campos, 1991; Oltjenbruns, 1991) has demonstrated a correlation between positive cognitive appraisals of some aspects of a trauma and positive outcomes, including perceived benefits of the experience. Although younger children may be more limited in their ability to cognitively accommodate the simultaneous existence of positive and negative emotions or attributes in relation to one target event, there is some suggestion that children develop the capacity to understand and express two emotions of different valence (i.e., both positive and negative) to a target between 9 and 13 years of age ($M = 11.34$ years; $SD = 2.12$), with some children evidencing this ability as young as 7.60 years (Harter & Buddin, 1987; see Harter, 1986 for a detailed discussion of this process). With the acknowledgment that children's cognitive capacities may vary widely across individual youngsters—and the recognition that one recent PTG study included children as young as 6 years old (Cryder et al., in press)—these findings suggest a possible lower age limit for the growth process.

Furthermore, Vasey, Crnic, and Carter (1994) found that advances in cognitive development around 7 to 8 years of age may increase the complexity of the "worry" process for children, but it is important to underscore that, in the context of PTG, the focus is on *constructive* rumination, not counterproductive worry about the event or condition at hand. That said, such ruminative thought processes, in which the child frequently returns to thoughts of the trauma and related issues, may initially increase distress for children, perhaps leading them to employ avoidance and denial as coping mechanisms (Gil, 1991; Reyes, Kokotovic, & Cosden, 1996; Terr, 1991). Some authors (Epstein, 1990; Janoff-Bulman, 1992) have framed these approaches positively, suggesting that such avoidance allows for repeated reprocessing of traumatic events over time until the resources needed to gain emotional control of distressing thoughts are developed. An endpoint goal of cognitive reprocessing is "an enhanced age-appropriate understanding of the circumstances and meaning of the traumatic experience(s)" (Pynoos et al., 1995, p. 84). In sum, the ruminative process is thought to help a child better understand, grapple with, and perhaps find meaning in the event, noticing and integrating changes in oneself and one's environment subsequent to the trauma-related events.

This ruminative thinking is hypothesized to be linked to competency beliefs in children. However, preliminary research has not elucidated the specific nature of the relationship (see Cryder et al., in press), though it does appear that the amount of rumination alone is not a significant factor in the development of PTG. Rather, it is possible that the content of the repeated thoughts of the trauma-related events and how an individual engages them— the degree to which the rumination serves to help one understand and learn from his or her responses and emotions, interpret experiences, and focus on meaning, increasing the potential for one to identify a positive aspect of the circumstance—are the factors that carry weight and actively contribute to the growth process (Calhoun & Tedeschi, 1998, 2004; Tedeschi & Calhoun, 1995, 2004).

Cognitive Resources: Realistic Control Attributions

Control attributions are an additional cognitive component in the hypothesized child PTG model, one that can certainly influence how children respond and react following trauma. Having an internal locus of control (LOC) has been linked to perceived benefits and personal growth for adults in the aftermath of threatening circumstances or crisis (Tennen & Affleck, 1998), and early child risk and resilience research typically reported that greater internal control was associated with positive adjustment (e.g., O'Grady & Metz, 1987; Werner & Smith, 1982).

Subsequent research has gone beyond the internal versus external LOC distinction and examined the role of children's realistic control attributions, that is, the accuracy of children's expectations and attributions about what they can and cannot control in their lives (see Wannon, 1990 for a detailed discussion). After all, an internal LOC is *not* adaptive in the face of clearly uncontrollable events. A young child cannot keep an adult he or she cares about from getting drunk or taking drugs, nor his or her parents from fighting or divorcing, and it may take a toll on his or her adjustment in the context of such adversities if the child perceives that he or she had the ability to change the circumstance(s). In contrast, it is appropriate for a youngster to perceive control over his or her relationships with friends (e.g., not initiating conflicts), school performance (e.g., not failing a test if one studies), or getting into trouble at school. In the face of stress or trauma, this notion of realistic control may be more meaningful for children's coping, and selective (or realistic) control attributions—accurate and age-appropriate perceptions about events, outcomes, and problems that are controllable and uncontrollable—may be more adaptive for children than an undifferentiated perception of internal control (Wyman, 2003).

Research involving two high-risk cohorts of urban children tested this notion and supported the view. Among highly stressed 4th, 5th, and 6th graders, children classified as resilient exceeded peers evidencing problems in adjustment on measures of both internal LOC and realistic control (e.g., Cowen et al., 1992). Notably, Wannon (1990) reported that the degree of realistic control predicted multiple positive adjustment indicators (e.g., school engagement, test scores, teacher ratings of children's adjustment) above and beyond the variance accounted for by a more traditional LOC measure (Nowicki & Strickland, 1973). In fact, realistic control total scores were among a cluster of five variables that most sensitively differentiated children exhibiting resilient adaptation from same-age peers exhibiting problems in adjustment (Cowen et al., 1992). A later study with high risk 2nd and 3rd graders also found that children evidencing resilient adaptation reported significantly more accurate control expectations, and this realistic control predicted more positive adaptation (Hoyt-Meyers et al., 1995). As Wyman (2003) noted, importantly, that study demonstrated that many children within this younger cohort (aged 7 to 9 years) had the cognitive capacity to report differentiations regarding the controllability of family and personal problems.

It is hypothesized that realistic control attributions have a bidirectional relationship with other key, cognitive elements of the growth process, such as appraisals and rumination. It appears that the expectations a child has for control and the attributions one makes for life circumstances may impact how that child experiences adversity, regulates affect, and organizes behavior and goals. As one case in point, in Hasan and Power's (2004) community sample, children frequently showed self-blame attributions, but primarily did so in the context of controllable situations (e.g., grades, conflicts with others), rarely exhibiting them in situations that were deemed beyond their control. In such situations, those attributions can be adaptive if they then mobilize the individual to problem solve in the controllable situations (Hasan & Power, 2004). However, some authors have theorized that when circumstances are perceived as uncontrollable, children may utilize more primitive means of emotional regulation and avoidance strategies (Pynoos et al., 1995). Thus, one's expectations about control may also be seen as relating to various aspects of self-system functioning, including one's beliefs about his or her ability to cope with problems and hope for the future.

Self-System Functioning: Perceptions Regarding Competence, Efficacy, and the Future

Indicators of self-system functioning, including positive appraisals and expectations of one's ability to meet daily task demands, cope, and adjust in the face of stress or trauma, one's perceptions of competence across multiple life domains (e.g., interpersonal functioning and acceptance), and one's expectations for his or her future, comprise another core component of the hypothesized PTG process. Expecting a positive impact from such factors is not only consistent with PTG theory, but with the extant child stress and coping literature as well.

In fact, studies examining qualities associated with resilience, or more positive psychosocial functioning during or following negative experiences, have consistently identified aspects of children's self-system functioning as crucial attributes or assets, including perceived competencies, self-esteem or self-worth, sense of efficacy, and future expectations (see, e.g., Luthar et al., 2000; Masten, 2001; Masten & Coatsworth, 1998; Wyman et al., 2000). For instance, children's positive efficacy beliefs, expectations they could achieve desired outcomes for various challenges (e.g., new or difficult situations, problems with people), have generally predicted more positive adjustment in the face of stress (Cowen et al., 1991; Masten & Coatsworth, 1998). Furthermore, in one major resilience study, scores from a measure of self-perceptions/perceived competence were among the most powerful discriminators of children demonstrating stress-resilient versus maladjusted outcomes in two independent cohorts (Cowen et al., 1992; Hoyt-Meyers et al., 1995).

Further underscoring the potential impact of these self-views, Wyman, Kilmer, Cowen, and Lotyczewski (1998) identified child resources predicting resilience under suboptimal caregiving conditions among highly stressed 2nd and 3rd graders. They identified a cluster of child-rated characteristics that distinguished sociodemographically comparable youngsters adjusting well and those exhibiting problems in adjustment, above and beyond the effects of parenting competence. Specifically, after controlling for multiple demographic and parenting variables (e.g., gender; parenting attitudes and behavior; parental education and mental health), three variables were found to account for significant further variance in children's status, including a perceived competence factor that included all subscales of a simplified version of Harter's (1982) Self-Perception Profile for Children, supporting the possibility that child resources may support children's successful adaptation when the caregiving environment is less than ideal.

In their seminal work on resilience, Werner and Smith emphasized that those exhibiting such positive adaptation "worked well, played well, loved well, and *expected* well" (1982, p. 153, italics added), noting that a "central component in the lives of the resilient individuals in this study... appeared to be a confidence that the odds can be surmounted" (1992, p. 207). Such positive beliefs about one's competencies or one's future may influence the degree to which a child perceives an event as threatening or negative, the manner in which he or she responds to a stressful or traumatic event, and the effort he or she sustains in grappling with the traumatic circumstance (see, e.g., Wyman, Cowen, Work, & Kerley, 1993). Positive expectations have been found to be associated with lower anxiety, higher achievement test scores, and better teacher-rated school adjustment (Wyman et al., 1993) and, importantly, seemingly promoted ongoing positive adaptation. For example, positive future expectations reported by children aged 9 to 11 years related to positive self- and teacher-rated adjustment two and a half to three and a half years later, both directly and by moderating the adverse effects of subsequent stress experiences (Wyman et al., 1993). Because these reflections of hope or optimism about the future appear to help children to follow healthy adjustment trajectories, it will be necessary to consider and determine the age at which younger children can reliably consider the notion of the future and how they may change over time (see Wyman, 2003 for further discussion of children's personal mastery beliefs).

Considering the hypothesized model put forth here, it is important to note that (a) research suggests that social support may positively influence these self-views (Aldwin &

Sutton, 1998; see Yaskowich, 2002 for discussion); and (b) these various factors reflecting sound self-system functioning are hypothesized to reflect directly to PTG's manifestation among youngsters, because they not only may affect children's perceptions of traumatic events or circumstances and their ability to deal with them, but also their approach to and persistence in coping (Jerusalem & Mittag, 1995; Wyman et al., 1993). In that vein, some researchers have maintained that efficacy beliefs may influence perceptions or interpretations of stressors, such that those with high self-efficacy may be more likely to perceive positive benefits in negative life events (Jerusalem & Mittag, 1995).

RESEARCHING POSTTRAUMATIC GROWTH IN CHILDREN: METHODS OF ASSESSMENT

Park and Lechner (this volume) consider various issues in the assessment and measurement of PTG. Among children, both qualitative and quantitative methods have been employed to assess the construct. Salter and Stallard (2004) utilized secondary analysis of qualitative data collected through a project that evaluated the efficacy of an intervention to prevent mental health difficulties in children involved in road-traffic accidents. That is, in the course of interviewing participants to assess Posttraumatic Stress Disorder (PTSD) symptomatology, anxiety, and strengths and difficulties, the researchers noted that the participants related numerous experiences and feelings "that were not intentionally assessed by the diagnostic tools being used" (Salter & Stallard, 2004, p. 336). The researchers re-evaluated the interviews with the intention of looking beyond PTSD criteria and used a "framework" approach to qualitative analysis in which they identified, coded, and interpreted relevant themes. This approach suggested that 42% of the 158 young (7 to 18 year-old) participants in their sample reported some element of PTG (e.g., positive change in perception of self, improved relationships), most often a changed philosophy of life. Importantly, the researchers noted that, of the children who evidenced some degree of PTG, 37% also exhibited PTSD, underscoring the notion, reported in the adult literature, that PTG and distress or disorder are not mutually exclusive (Salter & Stallard, 2004).

As a quantitative approach to assessing growth, two independent groups have adapted the most frequently used measure of PTG in adults, the Posttraumatic Growth Inventory (PTGI) (Tedeschi & Calhoun, 1996), for use with children. Yaskowich (2002) utilized a 21-item adaptation of the PTGI, the PTGI-Revised for Children and Adolescents, reworded for children as young as 8 years of age. The adapted scale was validated for use with children and adolescents using a panel of adult judges who evaluated readability and comprehension level and rated the scale on its comparability to the five underlying constructs assessed in the original PTGI (e.g., new possibilities, personal strength, appreciation of life). She then piloted the measure with a group of children as young as 8 years old. This effort led to further revision of the measure, leading to a final scale with a total score alpha of .94. Yaskowich (2002) reported that alphas for the five domains assessed ranged from .68 to .86. Yaskowich also had parents complete the revised child PTGI about their children and found no significant differences between parent and child reports of PTG in the child participants.

In their investigation of PTG in youngsters who experienced a hurricane and the serious flooding in its aftermath, Cryder et al. (in press) also adapted PTGI items to increase their appropriateness for young children, both in terms of content and language. A pool of 29 items was drafted (some items also had multiple variants) and, similar to the approach employed by Yaskowich (2002), evaluated for content consistency and appropriateness and reading level by a panel of three psychologists, a child clinical-community psychologist and the authors of the original PTGI. The final version, deemed the Posttraumatic Growth Inventory for Children (PTGI-C), utilized 21 items and reflected five domains of PTG: new possibilities ("I have new things that I like to do, e.g., hobbies, toys, etc."); relating to others ("I feel closer to other people than I did before"); personal strength ("I learned I can count on myself"); appreciation of life ("I learned that life is important"); and spiritual change ("I understand religious ideas more"). Their sample size was too small for reliable empirical analysis of the scale's principal components or utilization of hypothesized scale or domain scores. However, the alpha for the adapted measure's total score was .89. Additionally, each child rated the severity of the traumatic event (i.e., the Hurricane Floyd flooding) by indicating whether it was "About the worst thing that could happen," "Very bad, but worse things happen to people," "Bad enough to upset me for a while," or "Not too bad."[1] Work to assess the factor structure of these revised scales, develop normative data, and further validate these child PTG measures is clearly warranted.

RESEARCHING POSTTRAUMATIC GROWTH IN CHILDREN: THE "EARLY RETURNS" FROM TESTS OF THE MODEL

Two studies—each with important limitations—bear particular attention because they not only are among the few studies to include child participants in a study of PTG, but they also test components and/or relationships consistent with the PTG model hypothesized here. In one project, a dissertation, Yaskowich (2002) examined whether PTG occurs among children and youth with a variety of types and severities of cancer and assessed the relationship between PTG and multiple disease and demographic variables, as well as constructs thought to be related to PTG (e.g., social support, self-efficacy). The 54 participants were between 8 and 25 years old, with a mean age of 16, and all were at least 2 years post-treatment. The mean age at diagnosis was 8 years, with a range from 4.1 to 16.9 years, and the mean time since treatment was 6.3 years. Study participants and one of their parents completed multiple measures. As one critical limitation, study participants were asked to respond retrospectively to questions about their levels of self-efficacy and social support just prior to their diagnosis. As Yaskowich notes, perceptions of these factors may change over time and may be biased by experience, salient concerns given that the participants were interviewed between 2 and 12 years post-treatment completion. The study's small sample size constituted another important limitation.

Nevertheless, the study yielded some intriguing findings. Results suggest that children with cancer appeared to experience PTG to a similar extent as adults in other samples— 48% of the sample had PTG scores at or above the adult mean scores on the PTGI (Tedeschi & Calhoun, 1996). Higher self-reported PTG scores were positively correlated with the children's ratings of support from their teachers, perceptions of increased diagnosis severity, and awareness of their parents' PTG experience, as well as the presence of both cognitive and physical impairments resulting from the cancer experience and female gender. Consistent with hypotheses, self-efficacy was significantly correlated with social support according to participants' parents' reports, and there was a trend toward that relationship using children's self-reports. However, contrary to expectations, self-efficacy was not a significant predictor of child PTG, though that may more reflect measurement issues tied to the retrospective nature of the scale. Notably, of the social support variables assessed (including parental and peer support), only teacher support related reliably

---

[1]A slightly modified 24-item version of this scale was used in a study involving youth from multiple Romanian orphanages. The scale is available from the author upon request.

to child PTG scores. Given the core role hypothesized for support in the PTG process, Yaskowich concluded that one possible explanation for this finding was that, in light of the traumatic circumstance experienced by her participants (i.e., cancer diagnosis and treatment), they generally were receiving ample parental support and, as such, teacher support may have yielded an added benefit. As Yaskowich notes, the substantial consistency between child and parent reports of PTG supports the validity of the PTG construct (and challenges the notion that PTG may reflect an illusory coping strategy rather than actual change).

Yaskowich also tested hypothesized predictor models of children's PTG. When examining self-efficacy, social support, and parents' PTG as potential predictors, the only significant predictor was social support. In a post hoc analysis, when controlling for the effects of disease and demographic variables, social support did not contribute to the model over and above the effects of those variables. The only significant predictors of children's PTG were female gender (accounting for 13% of the variance in child PTG scores), and the presence of both cognitive and physical impairments resulting from the illness (10% of the variance). Overall, as Yaskowich concludes, study results (a) support the important influence of parent–child interactions in children's adjustment to chronic illness, and (b) underscore the possibility that children can evidence PTG, not only adapting in the aftermath of traumatic events or circumstances, but seemingly transforming them into meaningful and growth-enhancing experiences.

In another study involving children, Cryder et al. (in press) explored the PTG construct among youngsters who experienced a hurricane (Hurricane Floyd) and the subsequent flooding. Using a sample younger than any other studied in PTG work to date, with participant youngsters ranging in age from 6 to 15 years ($M = 9.54$, $SD = 2.64$), the researchers proposed a conceptual model of the growth process in children and investigated potential linkages among PTG and ruminative thinking, social support, and competency beliefs, hypothesizing that that (a) study children would report PTG and (b) those children who experienced frequent event-related ruminations, accompanied by adequate sources of social support, would be more likely to make positive attributions about their competence in coping with stressful events and report greater levels of PTG.

Participants were recruited from three elementary and middle schools in which half of the students were evacuated or displaced from their homes due to the extensive flooding associated with Hurricane Floyd. All study-eligible children had been referred for an intervention for students severely impacted by the flooding. At the time of the study, only 3 of the 46 whose parents provided consent had previously attended the intervention program. Children completed multiple measures approximately 1 year after the hurricane and flooding.

Study findings suggested that there was considerable variability in the youngsters' self-ratings of PTG and results, overall, were consistent with the hypothesized model. Ruminative thinking correlated significantly with competency beliefs ($r = .382$, $p < .01$) but, contrary to expectations, not with social support. As predicted, rumination did not correlate directly with PTG. Moreover, consistent with other PTG theory and research (e.g., Tedeschi & Calhoun, 2004), socially supportive conditions that provided acceptance and understanding of the child's feelings were significantly correlated with competency beliefs ($r = .351$, $p < .05$), and no reliable relationship was detected between social support and PTG. Contrary to the hypothesis, social support was not related to ruminative thinking. In addition to the detected link with both ruminative thinking and social support, competency beliefs correlated significantly with PTG scores ($r = .547$, $p < .01$).

In contrast to prior findings (e.g., Park, Cohen, & Murch, 1996; Tedeschi & Calhoun, 1996), the children's report of the severity of the trauma associated with the flooding was not related to PTG nor the other key constructs assessed. Also contrary to expectations and prior research with adolescents (e.g., Milam et al., 2004), age was not reliably related to responses on most of the measures used for the hypothesized PTG model, correlating only with social support ($r = .326$, $p < .05$). That significant positive correlation may suggest that, as children age, their social networks expand, and they are able to access social support from more sources, including extrafamilial peer and adult relationships.

Although the findings of this study are limited because of the small sample size ($n = 46$); the sample's restricted, voluntary nature (representing 15% of the families contacted); and the cross-sectional and correlational nature of the data, the study also provides intriguing preliminary support for the PTG process in children that is generally consistent with the hypothesized model.

FUTURE DIRECTIONS FOR RESEARCHING POSTTRAUMATIC GROWTH IN CHILDREN

These two downward age extensions of PTG research, and the existing studies involving adolescents (e.g., Horowitz et al., 1997; Milam et al., 2004; Taku, 2005) demonstrate the merit of investigating the construct among nonadults and provide preliminary support for the hypothesized model of the PTG process in the age bands studied. In future studies, investigators will need to further develop the nomological network of variables associated with PTG in children to better understand the phenomenon. As Cryder and colleagues (in press) suggest, several steps are warranted: (a) studying PTG among youngsters experiencing diverse traumatic events (e.g., serious medical concerns, violence exposure, death of a parent or sibling); (b) assessing caregiver, familial, and contextual characteristics (e.g., caregiver–child relationship quality, family cohesion, caregiver resources and mental health); and (c) expanding the range of child measures to include some of the other constructs considered here, such as lifetime stress exposure, realistic control, future expectations, self-perceptions, sense of efficacy, as well as specific perceived competence domains and global child adjustment indicators.

In that vein, one project is exploring responses to trauma, PTG, and correlates of successful adaptation among children and youth in Romanian orphanages (the youngsters were either orphaned or abandoned), an important cross-cultural examination of the phenomenon. Consistent with the preceding recommendations, participant youth have reported about multiple self-system variables (e.g., perceived competence, future expectations, realistic control), and orphanage directors have completed youth adjustment ratings.[2] Another project in development will seek to identify correlates and antecedents of PTG among children in response to struggling with the trauma of a chronic or serious illness diagnosis (e.g., juvenile diabetes). The study will test the hypothesized PTG model with these children and focus on the role of realistic control attributions. Such steps will enhance understanding of PTG in youngsters, elucidating similarities and differences in the PTG process for children and adults.

Furthermore, researchers will need to ascertain if growth is possible in all instances. For example, if the perpetrator of the trauma is one's caregiver, could victimization by a figure looked to for protection, safety, and security be so extreme that PTG may not be possible?

---

[2]Data collection was just recently completed for this work, and analyses are ongoing. Preliminary findings involving a subset of the youth sample suggest that a) some youngsters evidence growth, b) ruminative thinking and positive future expectations relate to PTG, and c) contary to predictions, perceived competencies do not relate reliably to PTG.

That is, some level of trauma appears to be necessary for PTG, and numerous studies have reported positive relationships between the severity of the trauma experienced and the degree of reported growth (Tedeschi & Calhoun, 1996, 2004). However, if the trauma experienced is too intense and devastating to the young child and overly taxes his or her resources, the potential for growth may very well be inhibited.

Additionally, given the trend toward gender differences in PTG, future work can assess if this trend holds among children and attempt to identify the processes at play that may favor females. Yaskowich (2002) raises the possibility of gender-specific coping styles, the tendency for females to rely on relationships, and the suggestion that females may be more likely to process experiences by talking through them, expressing feelings, and ruminating about them, factors that seem to be associated with the growth process.

Similar to the maturation and unfolding of the resilience research base, once the network of variables seemingly related to the PTG process has been identified by early generation child PTG studies, and studies have addressed some of the global, main effect-type questions and issues noted in the preceding text, attention will need to move beyond the identification of factors associated with PTG to the understanding of processes. Early work in resilience identified global variables and factors associated with resilient adaptation, that is, individual characteristics or contextual conditions that seemingly served a protective function. Then, researchers acknowledged the need to conduct projects that would facilitate the move beyond identifying such protective factors to understanding the specific complex processes and pathways that favor healthy developmental trajectories (see, e.g., Cowen, 1994; Masten & Coatsworth, 1998; Masten et al., 1990). Such work, employing longitudinal methodologies (ideally, prospective longitudinal designs), would be a logical developmental progression for child PTG research. Once research has supported and validated a model of the child PTG process, a related strand of investigation could examine the degree to which elements of the model have a differential impact across varying stages of development. For example, it may be the case that, for a young child, responsive caregiving and adult support carry more predictive weight than for an older child, who, in addition to drawing upon familial support, might be able to rely upon the support of peers and more complex cognitive competencies, such as realistic control attributions and positive expectations for the future. Relatedly, research could address whether it is possible, in situations in which the caregiving environment is suboptimal, for child-specific factors and resources and extrafamilial supports to serve a compensatory function and foster PTG.

FUTURE DIRECTIONS: APPLYING THE POSTTRAUMATIC GROWTH CONSTRUCT IN CLINICAL WORK WITH CHILDREN

While it is surely important to underscore and understand the negative impact of traumatic events and circumstances, including loss of the child's familiar assumptive world (Goldman, 2002), acknowledging the possibility of growth and the potential for transformation and positive change in populations experiencing such events can also serve an important function for researchers and clinical professionals. Indeed, as Cryder et al. (in press) describe, in accord with the growing recognition of the insufficiency of mental health's traditional deficit focus or medical model orientation (see Cowen, 1994, 1999; Cowen & Kilmer, 2002; Seligman & Csikszentmihalyi, 2000), many investigators have gone beyond the known negative sequelae of such experiences and increasingly addressed the variability in children's responses to stress and trauma (e.g., the burgeoning child resilience literature). Although the nonadult PTG research base is less well developed, working to better understand the growth process fits well with recent charges to focus upon what "goes right" in development, emphasize positive outcomes, and study strength, virtue, and growth (Cowen, 1994, 1999; Maton, Schellenbach, Leadbeater, & Solarz, 2004; Seligman & Csikszentmihalyi, 2000; Yates & Masten, 2004).

Research supporting the growth process among young people can provide critical information for professionals working with children who have experienced trauma, perhaps serving to guide, inform, or shape elements of their assessments, interventions, and approach. Documenting that PTG occurs in children and identifying factors or conditions associated with effective coping and even perceived benefits or growth among children following a crisis or trauma will assist clinicians in (a) assessing, recognizing, and attending to positive factors, and (b) pursuing means to facilitate the development or enhancement of such factors and foster PTG (see Tedeschi & Kilmer, 2005). Some authors have suggested clinical interventions to help restructure children's cognitive appraisals of the trauma, restrict exposure to trauma-related triggers, and address secondary adversities or grief related to losses associated with the trauma (Kaufman & Henrich, 2000). Such efforts may yield new ways in which to help children make meaning of their experiences. Moreover, given the suggested importance of social support, others (e.g., Yaskowich, 2002) have noted the possible benefits of screening for adequate support, support group interventions (e.g., peer, family), and social skills training to help foster children's experience of support. Such work to help youngsters cope effectively and even grow in trauma's aftermath is consistent with many competence-enhancement and skill-building approaches increasingly utilized in the context of a variety of interventions (Calhoun & Tedeschi, 2000; Paton, Violanti, & Smith, 2003).

CONCLUSION

The PTG phenomenon has been extensively studied in adult populations, but the possibility of this process occurring at earlier developmental stages has not received the same attention, and the factors that may enhance or suppress growth arising from children's struggle with trauma are still largely unknown. Indeed, there is a dearth of research on the PTG process among youngsters. However, although the present literature on PTG in children has clear and significant limitations, it offers reason for optimism regarding the possibilities and potential of more extensive investigations in this important area of child study. The limited research results (e.g., Cryder et al., in press) generally support the relationship posited between cognitive processes (e.g., competency beliefs and rumination) and the PTG process, as well as the hypothesized linkage between social support and competency beliefs. These findings show promise for research in this domain, though further work is needed to better understand these associations and assess their generalizability to other samples. Many questions stand unanswered about the various pathways to growth in child populations. Work toward addressing them can inform more precisely targeted intervention strategies for children who have survived trauma and increase the likelihood that those youngsters perceive substantial benefits as they work to reconcile their circumstances and experience with their sense of their world, themselves, and their new reality.

REFERENCES

Aldwin, C. M., & Sutton, K. J. (1998). A developmental perspective on posttraumatic growth. In R. G. Tedeschi, C. L. Park, & L. G. Calhoun (Eds.), *Posttraumatic growth: Positive change in the aftermath of crisis* (pp. 43–63). Mahwah, NJ: Lawrence Erlbaum Associates.

Bosquet, M. (2004). How research informs clinical work with traumatized young children. In Osofsky, J. D. (Ed.), *Young children and trauma: Intervention and treatment* (pp. 301–325). New York: Guilford Press.

Bretherton, I. (1985). Attachment theory: Retrospect and prospect. In I. Bretherton & E. Waters (Eds.),*Growing points of attachment theory and research. Monographs of the Society for Research in Child Development, 50 (Serial No. 209)*, (pp. 3–35).

Bronfenbrenner, U. (1977). Toward an experimental ecology of human development. *American Psychologist, 32,* 513–531.

Bronfenbrenner, U. (1979). The ecology of human development: Experiments by nature and design. Cambridge, MA: Harvard University Press.

Cadell, S., Regehr, C., & Hemsworth, D. (2003). Factors contributing to posttraumatic growth: A proposed structural equation model. *American Journal of Orthopsychiatry, 73,* 279–287.

Calhoun, L. G., & Tedeschi, R. G. (1998). Posttraumatic growth: Future directions. In R. G. Tedeschi, C. L. Park, & L. G. Calhoun (Eds.), *Posttraumatic growth: Positive change in the aftermath of crisis* (pp. 215–238). Mahwah, NJ: Lawrence Erlbaum Associates.

Calhoun, L. G., & Tedeschi, R.G. (1999). *Facilitating posttraumatic growth: A clinician's guide.* Mahwah, NJ: Lawrence Erlbaum Associates.

Calhoun, L. G., & Tedeschi, R.G. (2000). Early posttraumatic interventions: Facilitating possibilities for growth. In J. M. Volanti, D. Paton, & C. Dunning (Eds.), *Posttraumatic stress intervention: Challenges, issues, and perspectives* (pp. 135–152), Springfield, IL: Charles C. Thomas, Publisher.

Calhoun, L. G., & Tedeschi, R. G. (2001). Posttraumatic growth: The positive lessons of loss. In R. A. Neimeyer (Ed.), *Meaning reconstruction and the experience of loss* (pp. 157–172). Washington, DC: American Psychological Association.

Calhoun, L. G., & Tedeschi, R. G. (2004). The foundations of posttraumatic growth: New considerations. *Psychological Inquiry, 15,* 93–102.

Calhoun, L. G., & Tedeschi, R. G. (this volume). The foundations of posttraumatic growth: An expanded framework. (pp. 1–22). Mahwah, NJ: Lawrence Erlbaum Associates.

Cicchetti, D., & Lynch, M. (1993). Toward an ecological/transactional model of community violence and child maltreatment: Consequences for children's development. *Psychiatry, 56,* 96–118.

Cicchetti, D., & Schneider-Rosen, K. (1986). An organizational approach to childhood depression. In M. Rutter, C. Izard, & P. R. Read (Eds.), *Depression in young people: Developmental and clinical perspectives* (pp. 71–134). New York: Guilford Press.

Cohen, L. H., Hettler, T. R., & Pane, N. (1998). Assessment of posttraumatic growth. In R. G. Tedeschi, C. L. Park & L. G. Calhoun (Eds.), *Posttraumatic growth: Positive change in the aftermath of crisis* (pp. 23–42). Mahwah, NJ: Lawrence Erlbaum Associates.

Cowen, E. L. (1994). The enhancement of psychological wellness: Challenges and opportunities. *American Journal of Community Psychology, 22,* 149–179.

Cowen, E. L. (1999). In sickness and in health: Primary prevention's vows revisited. In D. Cicchetti & S. L. Toth (Eds.), *Rochester Symposium on Developmental Psychopathology, Vol. 9.* (pp. 1–24). Rochester, NY: University of Rochester Press.

Cowen, E. L. (2000). Psychological wellness: Some hopes for the future. In D. Cicchetti, J. Rappaport, I. Sandler, & R. P. Weissberg (Eds.), *The promotion of wellness in children and adolescents* (pp. 477–503). Thousand Oaks, CA: Sage.

Cowen, E. L. & Kilmer, R. P. (2002). 'Positive Psychology': Some plusses and some open issues. *Journal of Community Psychology, 30,* 449–460.

Cowen, E. L., Work, W. C., Hightower, A. D., Wyman, P. A., Parker, G. R., & Lotyczewski, B. S. (1991). Toward the development of a measure of perceived self-efficacy in children. *Journal of Clinical Child Psychology, 20,* 169–178.

Cowen, E. L., Work, W. C., Wyman, P. A., & Parker, G. R. (1990). The Rochester Child Resilience Project (RCRP): Overview and summary of first year findings. *Development and Psychopathology, 2,* 193–212.

Cowen, E. L., Work, W. C., Wyman, P. A., Parker, G. R., Wannon, M., & Gribble, P. A. (1992). Test comparisons among stress-affected, stress-resilient and nonclassified fourth through sixth grade urban children. *Journal of Community Psychology, 20,* 200–214.

Cryder, C. H., Kilmer, R. P., Tedeschi, R. G., & Calhoun, L. G. (in press). An exploratory study of posttraumatic growth in children following a natural disaster. *American Journal of Orthopsychiatry.*

Donaldson, D., Prinstein, M. J., Danovsky, M., & Spirito, A. (2000). Patterns of children's coping with life stress: Implications for clinicians. *American Journal of Orthopsychiatry, 70,* 351–359.

Egeland, B., Carlson, E. A., & Sroufe, L. A. (1993). Resilience as process. *Development and Psychopathology, 5,* 517–528.

Epstein, S. (1990). The self-concept, the traumatic neurosis, and the structure of personality. In D. J. Ozer, J. M. Healy, and A. J. Stewar (Eds.), *Perspectives in personality, Vol. 3.* (pp. 63–98). London: Jessica Kingsley.

Fritz, G. K., Williams, J. R., & Amylon, J. R. (1988). After treatment ends: Psychosocial sequelae in pediatric cancer survivors. *American Journal of Orthopsychiatry, 58,* 552–561.

Gil, E. (1991). *The healing power of play: Working with abused children.* New York: Guilford.

Goldman, L. (2002). The assumptive world of children. In J. Kauffman (Ed.), *Loss of the assumptive world: A theory of traumatic loss* (pp. 193–202). New York: Brunner-Routledge.

Grant, K. E., Compas, B. E., Stuhlmacher, A. F., Thurm, A. E., McMahon, S. D., & Halpert, J. A. (2003). Stressors and child and adolescent psychopathology: Moving from markers to mechanisms of risk. *Psychological Bulletin, 129,* 447–466.

Harter, S. (1982). The Perceived Competence Scale for Children. *Child Development, 53,* 87–97.

Harter, S. (1986). Cognitive-developmental processes in the integration of concepts about emotions and the self. *Social Cognition, 4,* 119–151.

Harter, S., & Buddin, B. J. (1987). Children's understanding of the simultaneity of two emotions: A five stage developmental acquisition sequence. *Developmental Psychology, 23,* 388–399.

Hasan, N., & Power, T. G. (2004). Children's appraisal of major life events. *American Journal of Orthopsychiatry, 74,* 26–32.

Horowitz, L. A., Loos, M. E., & Putnam, F. W. (1997, November). *"Perceived Benefits" of traumatic experiences in adolescent girls.* Paper presented at the Thirteenth Annual Meeting of the International Society for Traumatic Stress Studies, Montreal, Quebec, Canada.

Hoyt-Meyers, L. A., Cowen, E. L., Work, W. C., Wyman, P. A., Magnus, K. B., Fagen, D. B., et al. (1995). Test correlates of resilient outcomes among highly stressed 2nd and 3rd grade urban children. *Journal of Community Psychology, 23,* 326–338.

Israelashvili, M. (1999). Adolescents' help-seeking behaviour in times of community crisis. *International Journal for the Advancement of Counselling, 21,* 87–96.

Janoff-Bulman, R. (1992). *Shattered assumptions.* New York: The Free Press.

Janoff-Bulman, R. (this volume). Schema-change perspectives on posttraumatic growth (pp. 81–99). Mahwah, NJ. Lawrence Erlbaum Associates.

Jerusalem, M., & Mittag, W. (1995). Self-efficacy in stressful life transitions. In A. Bandura (Ed.), *Self-efficacy in changing societies* (pp. 177–201). New York: Cambridge University Press.

Johnson, J. H. (1986). *Life events as stressors in childhood and adolescence.* Newbury Park, CA: Sage.

Kaufman, J., & Henrich, C. (2000). Exposure to violence and early childhood trauma. In C. H. Zeanah (Ed.), *Handbook of infant mental health* (2nd ed., pp. 195–207). New York: Guilford Press.

Krementz, J. (1983). *How it feels when a parent dies.* New York: Knopf.

Lieberman, A. F., & Van Horn, P. (2004). Assessment and treatment of young children exposed to traumatic events. In Osofsky, J. D. (Ed.). *Young children and trauma: Intervention and treatment* (pp. 111–138). New York: Guilford Press.

Luthar, S. S. (Ed.). (2003). *Resilience and vulnerability: Adaptation in the context of childhood adversities.* New York: Cambridge University Press.

Luthar, S. S., Cicchetti, D., & Becker, B. (2000). The construct of resilience: A critical evaluation and guidelines for future work. *Child Development, 71,* 543–562.

Lynch, M., & Cicchetti, D. (1998). Trauma, mental representation, and the organization of memory for mother-referent material. *Development and Psychopathology, 10,* 739–759.

Martinson, I. M., & Campos, R. G. (1991). Adolescent bereavement: Long-term responses to a sibling's death from cancer. *Journal of Adolescent Research, 6,* 54–69.

Masten, A. S. (2001). Ordinary magic: Resilience processes in development. *American Psychologist, 56,* 227–238.

Masten, A. S., Best, K. M., & Garmezy, N. (1990). Resilience and development: Contributions from the study of children who overcome adversity. *Development and Psychopathology, 2,* 425–444.

Masten, A. S., & Coatsworth, J. D. (1998). The development of competence in favorable and unfavorable environments. *American Psychologist, 53,* 205–220.

Maton, K. I., Schellenbach, C. J., Leadbeater, B. J., & Solarz, A. L. (Eds.). (2004) *Investing in children, youth, families, and communities: Strengths-based research and policy.* Washington, DC: American Psychological Association.

Milam, J. E., Ritt-Olson, A., & Unger, J. (2004). Posttraumatic growth among adolescents. *Journal of Adolescent Research, 19,* 192–204.

Moody, R. A., & Moody, C. P. (1991). A family perspective: Helping children acknowledge and express grief following the death of a parent. *Death Studies, 15,* 587–602.

Moos, R. H., & Moos, B. S. (1994). *Family Environment Scale manual* (3rd ed.). Palo Alto, CA: Consulting Psychologists Press.

Neimeyer, R. A. (2001). *Meaning reconstruction and the experience of loss.* Washington, DC: American Psychological Association.

Nichols, M. P., & Schwartz, R. C. (1998). *Family therapy: Concepts and methods* (4th ed.). Boston: Allyn & Bacon.

Nowicki, S., Jr., & Strickland, B. R. (1973). A locus of control scale for children. *Journal of Consulting and Clinical Psychology, 40,* 148–154.

O'Grady, D., & Metz, J. R. (1987). Resilience in children at high risk for psychological disorder. *Journal of Pediatric Psychology, 12,* 3–23.

Oltjenbruns, K. A., (1991). Positive outcomes of adolescents' experience with grief. *Journal of Adolescent Research, 6,* 43–53.

Osofsky, J. D. (1995). The effects of exposure to violence on young children. *American Psychologist, 50,* 782–788.

Osofsky, J. D. (Ed.). (2004a). *Young children and trauma: Intervention and treatment.* New York: Guilford Press.

Osofsky, J. D. (2004b). Different ways of understanding young children and trauma. In J. D. Osofsky (Ed.), *Young children and trauma: Intervention and treatment* (pp. 3–9). New York: Guilford Press.

Park, C. L. (1998). Implications of posttraumatic growth for individuals. In R. G. Tedeschi, C. L. Park & L. G. Calhoun (Eds.), *Posttraumatic growth: Positive changes in the aftermath of crisis* (pp. 153–177). Mahwah, NJ: Lawrence Erlbaum Associates.

Park, C. L., Cohen, L. H., & Murch, R. L. (1996). Assessment and prediction of stress-related growth. *Journal of Personality, 64,* 72–105.

Park, C. L., & Lechner, S. C. (this volume). Measurement issues in assessing growth following stressful life experiences (pp. 47–67). Mahwah, NJ: Lawrence Erlbaum Associates.

Paton, D., Violanti, J. M., & Smith, L. M. (Eds.) (2003). *Promoting capabilities to manage posttraumatic stress.* Springfield, IL: Charles C. Thomas.

Pynoos, R. S. (1990). Posttraumatic stress disorder in children and adolescents. In B. D. Garfinkel, G. A. Carlson, E. B. Weller, & B. F. Weller (Eds.), *Psychiatric disorders in children and adolescents.* Philadelphia: Saunders.

Pynoos, R. S., Steinberg, A. M., & Wraith, R. (1995). A developmental model of childhood traumatic stress. In D. J. Cohen & D. Cicchetti (Eds.), *Developmental psychopathology, Volume 2: Risk, disorder, and adaptation* (pp. 72–95). Oxford: John Wiley & Sons.

Reyes, C. J., Kokotovic, A. M., & Cosden, M. A. (1996). Sexually abused children's perceptions: How they may change treatment focus. *Professional Psychology: Research and Practice, 27,* 588–591.

Salter, E., & Stallard, P. (2004). Posttraumatic growth in child survivors of a road traffic accident. *Journal of Traumatic Stress, 17,* 335–340.

Sameroff, A. J. (1995). General systems, theories and developmental psychopathology. In D. Cicchetti & D. J. Cohen (Eds.), *Developmental psychopathology: Theory and methods, Vol. 1* (pp. 659–695). New York: John Wiley & Sons.

Sameroff, A. J., & Chandler, M. J. (1975). Reproductive risk and the continuum of caretaking casualty. In F. D. Horowitz, M. Hetherington, S. Scarr-Salapatek, & G. Siegel (Eds.), *Review of child development research* (pp. 187–244). Chicago: University of Chicago Press.

Sandler, I., Miller, P., Short, J., & Wolchik, S. (1989). Social support as a protective factor for children in stress. In D. Belle (Ed.), *Children's social networks and social supports* (pp. 277–307). New York: John Wiley & Sons.

Seligman, M. E. P., & Czikszentmihalyi, M. (2000). Positive psychology: An introduction. *American Psychologist, 55,* 5–14.

Spaccarelli, S. (1994). Stress, appraisal, and coping in child sexual abuse: A theoretical and empirical review. *Psychological Bulletin, 116,* 340–362.

Taku, K. (2005). *Sutoresu-taiken wo kikkake to shita seinen no seicho ni kansuru kenkyu [Growth as a result of stress among Japanese adolescents].* Unpublished doctoral dissertation, Nagoya University, Japan.

Tedeschi, R. G., & Calhoun, L. G. (1995). *Trauma and transformation: Growing in the aftermath of suffering.* Thousand Oaks, CA: Sage.

Tedeschi, R. G., & Calhoun, L. G. (1996).The Posttraumatic Growth Inventory: Measuring the positive legacy of trauma. *Journal of Traumatic Stress, 9,* 455–471.

Tedeschi, R. G., & Calhoun, L. G. (2004). Posttraumatic growth: Conceptual foundations and empirical evidence. *Psychological Inquiry, 15,* 1–18.

Tedeschi, R. G., & Kilmer, R. P. (2005). Assessing strengths, resilience, and growth to guide clinical interventions. *Professional Psychology: Research and Practice, 36,* 230–237.

Tennen, H., & Affleck, G. (1998). Personality and transformation in the face of adversity. In R. G. Tedeschi & L. G. Calhoun (Eds.), *Posttraumatic growth: Positive changes in the aftermath of crisis* (pp. 65–98). Mahwah, NJ: Lawrence Erlbaum Associates.

Terr, L. C. (1991). Childhood trauma: An outline and overview. *The American Journal of Psychiatry, 148,* 10–20.

Vasey, M. W., Crnic, K. A., & Carter, W. G. (1994). Worry in childhood: A developmental perspective. *Cognitive Therapy and Research, 18,* 529–549.

Wannon, M. (1990). *Children's control beliefs about controllable and uncontrollable events: Their relationship to stress resilience and psychosocial adjustment.* Unpublished doctoral dissertation, University of Rochester, New York.

Waters, E., & Sroufe, L. A. (1983). Social competence as developmental construct. *Developmental Review, 3,* 79–97.

Werner, E. E., & Smith, R. S. (1982). *Vulnerable but invincible: A study of resilient children.* New York: McGraw-Hill.

Werner, E. E., & Smith, R. S. (1992). *Overcoming the odds: High risk children from birth to adulthood.* Ithaca, NY: Cornell University Press.

Wyman, P. A. (2003). Emerging perspectives on context specificity of children's adaptation and resilience: Evidence from a decade of research with urban children in adversity. In S. S. Luthar (Ed.), *Resilience and vulnerability: Adaptation in the context of childhood adversities* (pp. 293–317). New York: Cambridge University Press.

Wyman, P. A., Cowen, E. L., Work, W. C., Hoyt-Meyers, L. A., Magnus, K. B., & Fagen, D. B. (1999). Developmental and caregiving factors differentiating parents of young stress-affected and stress-resilient urban children: A replication and extension. *Child Development, 70,* 645–659.

Wyman, P. A., Cowen, E. L., Work, W. C., & Kerley, J. H. (1993). The role of children's future expectations in self-system functioning and adjustment to life stress: A prospective study of urban at-risk children. *Development and Psychopathology, 5,* 649–661.

Wyman, P. A., Kilmer, R. P., Cowen, E. L., & Lotyczewski, B. S. (1998, February/March). *Resilience among children experiencing nonoptimal caregiving: Risk and protective effects.* Poster session presented at the Annual Convention of the Eastern Psychological Association, Boston.

Wyman, P. A., Sandler, I., Wolchik, S. A., & Nelson, K. (2000). Resilience as cumulative competence promotion and stress protection: Theory and intervention. In D. Cicchetti, J. Rappaport, I. Sandler, & R.P. Weissberg (Eds.), *The promotion of wellness in children and adolescents* (pp. 133–184). Thousand Oaks, CA: Sage.

Yaskowich, K. M. (2002). *Posttraumatic growth in children and adolescents with cancer.* Unpublished doctoral dissertation, University of Calgary, Calgary, Alberta.

Yates, T. M., Egeland, B., & Sroufe, L.A. (2003). Rethinking resilience: A developmental process perspective. In S. S. Luthar (Ed.), *Resilience and vulnerability: Adaptation in the context of childhood adversities* (pp. 243–266). New York: Cambridge University Press.

Yates, T. M., & Masten, A. S. (2004). Fostering the future: Resilience theory and the practice of positive psychology. In P. A. Linley & S. Joseph (Eds.), *Positive psychology in practice* (pp. 521–539). Hoboken, NJ: Wiley.

Clinical Applications
of Posttraumatic Growth

15

EXPERT COMPANIONS: POSTTRAUMATIC GROWTH IN CLINICAL PRACTICE

RICHARD G. TEDESCHI AND LAWRENCE G. CALHOUN

UNIVERSITY OF NORTH CAROLINA AT CHARLOTTE

In this chapter, we assume that the reader is familiar with the concept of posttraumatic growth (PTG) and we will focus on the application of this concept in clinical work. In earlier discussions of these applications (e.g., Calhoun & Tedeschi, 1999), we have made it clear that we are *not* proposing a new form of treatment, but rather looking for ways to integrate the perspective of PTG into common approaches to therapy for survivors of trauma. We have shown, for example, how therapy for bereaved parents can be enhanced by the inclusion of this growth perspective (Tedeschi & Calhoun, 2004b).

Although empirically validated treatments for posttraumatic stress disorder (PTSD) have primarily included the use of exposure and desensitization, there has recently been an emphasis on other elements. In fact, a recent survey of trauma therapists in the Veterans Affairs (VA) system demonstrated that use of such exposure techniques was rare (Rosen et al., 2004). Psychological treatments have been described that utilize a greater focus on cognitive processing of trauma, and attempts to address issues of meaning and other existential concerns (e.g. Dohrenwend et. al, 2004; Neimeyer, 2001). We believe our approach can fit with any sound intervention, but it may be particularly compatible with cognitive, narrative, and existentially based treatments, given the elements of our model of PTG as described in chapter 1. Our description of therapy takes into account these elements, using them as a guide to inform the clinician about how to focus treatment as the trauma survivor's responses gradually flow through the sequence proposed in the model, from early responses characterized by distress and intrusion to outcomes of PTG, revised narrative, and wisdom.

his process in more detail, we will start with some basic principles
spective. In our first extended discussion of these ideas (Calhoun
we pointed out that we consider ourselves to be *facilitators* of the
than creators of growth or leaders of our clients. More recently,
in our work with bereaved parents, we have written of the clinician as being an *expert
companion* (Tedeschi & Calhoun, 2004b). This term is meant to convey a sense of *humility*
that clinicians, who are indeed well-trained experts, need to have to allow for the kind of
atmosphere that can lead to the personal exploration that is useful in developing a sense
of PTG. Following the example of Shay (1994), in working with Vietnam War veterans,
we have recommended that the clinician adopt the stance that he or she is *open to being
changed* by the trauma survivor's experience, rather than being exclusively intent on doing
the changing (Tedeschi & Calhoun, 1995). This stance requires a good deal of patience,
trust in the capacity for people to cope and recover, and an ability to perceive subtle
indications of future growth. Most of all, this stance reveals respect for trauma survivors'
challenges, and that although they are seeking assistance with these challenges, they have
a harder task than the clinician in living with the psychological repercussions. This stance
also indicates to the survivor that the clinician sees value in the client's experiences as
potential sources of learning, rather than approaching the survivor as merely a collection
of symptoms to be altered.

We also wish to emphasize that our respect for survivors of trauma extends to persons
who do not experience PTG. We recognize that *many people do not experience PTG* and
that such outcomes are not necessarily negative. Some have challenged the wisdom and
usefulness of adopting a stance where PTG is considered to be a part of the picture of
trauma recovery.

> Even without these notions of growth, survivors often suffer at the hands of others who
> expect them to be recovered from their trauma or loss rather quickly. If they show distress,
> they are often regarded as poor copers who are wallowing in their pain. We honor people by
> acknowledging what they are up against following a trauma, not by holding out false hope
> that if they have the right personality characteristics, if they process the event the right way,
> and if they adopt the right coping strategies, they will be able to grow from their experience.
> If outsiders believe that growth is prevalent, this can become a new standard that survivors'
> progress is measured against. Such a standard may lead to negative judgments toward those
> who do not show personal growth, making them feel like coping failures. (Wortman, 2004,
> pp. 88–9)

Certainly there is a danger in developing a culture of "positive psychology" that seeks
to downplay the reality of pain and suffering for survivors of trauma. We would tend to
prefer not to speak of a "positive psychology," a phrase that implies that work that has more
traditionally focused on understanding and assisting persons with emotional suffering and
disorders is somehow "negative." Both positive and negative outcomes are part of the
human experience of trauma, but the study of possible positive aspects has, until recently,
been relatively neglected in psychological research. As researchers and as clinicians, we
have been struck by how most individuals manifest both positive and negative responses to
traumatic events, and that the world is not at all divided into the "growers" and the "coping
failures." As clinicians, we work with people who are sometimes feeling strong and, at
other times, weak. People who feel hopeful and also hopeless. People scarred by trauma

and also remade by it. People who celebrate the change wrought by trauma, people who grudgingly admit to it, people who regret it, and people who show various combinations of these. We have not advocated raising the bar on survivors who have it tough enough already, but in our clinical work, we make clear allowances for experienced benefits to be acknowledged rather than deemed to be mere psychological defenses or illusions.

Taking a PTG perspective on trauma explicitly acknowledges that traumas are "seismic events" that lead to profound challenges that are not easily managed (Calhoun & Tedeschi, 1998). Our model also indicates that continuing distress is likely to be part of the picture for some time, even when PTG is reported. The model also describes a process that probably unfolds gradually, showing that the early phases of the struggle to cope do not define trauma survivors, but are simply a part of a longer term process. Following the process over time can lead to some surprising discoveries in many people, particularly if the survivors are fortunate to find the kind of support that encourages continuing psychological work on the trauma and its aftermath. Often such support is not forthcoming (Wortman, 2004). Our descriptions of appropriate ways of approaching trauma survivors address this possibility. We have pointed out repeatedly that in no way are we suggesting that trauma is, in itself, good (e.g., Calhoun & Tedeschi, 1999, 2004; Tedeschi & Calhoun, 2004a). We focus on the struggle with the trauma as the central determinant of PTG. Although some survivors focus on the event as the turning point, the response in the aftermath of the event is the crucial factor in PTG.

CLINICAL IMPLICATIONS OF THE POSTTRAUMATIC GROWTH MODEL

We will look at the process of PTG from a clinical perspective, and consider how the clinician might respond as an expert companion to facilitate PTG as the process unfolds. This process is, of course, simplified in the model presented. It is in reality somewhat recursive. For example, the cognitive processing set off by the challenges of trauma may lead to many instances of disclosure and attempts to engage social supports. The ability to reduce emotional distress is something that is learned over time, and a trauma survivor may be quite able to accomplish this on some occasions, and struggle greatly on others. Furthermore, different domains of PTG may require different time periods and cognitive processes, so this overall process may be proceeding at varying speeds for these different domains of growth. Each domain of PTG may be gradually built up over time as the processing continues. Posttraumatic growth in clinical work can be a subtle development that must be carefully nurtured. At other times, we have found clients proceeding to create growth outcomes almost automatically, and as clinicians we have felt we have simply been along for the ride. But, no matter the degree to which we have felt that we play a role in facilitating this process, it is clear to us that there is a process involved that includes the elements of the model we have proposed. We will now consider each of these elements and see how they may be addressed by a clinician, and how they fit together in a process that feels natural for a trauma survivor.

The Person Pretrauma

We have discussed how there are characteristics of trauma survivors that existed before the traumatic event that tend to be associated with PTG outcomes. These include certain facets of extraversion, including activity and positive emotions, and openness to experience. We think that, generally, persons who can integrate novelty into their understanding and reactions, and who are familiar with a positive emotional tone in life experiences and blems, are more likely to report PTG. The clinician can assess these reports clients make about life before trauma. Certainly, a question you like before all this happened?" is usually enough to elicit this ⌐ a general way. If further clarification is needed, other questions ...at has been your typical way of responding to problems in life?" or ..as the hardest thing you have had to handle before all this happened? How did you address that?" If additional probing is necessary, the next step might be "Have there been instances where you have sought out new experiences?" It is also important for clinicians to look for the exceptional cases in a person's life when they claim not to have been able to cope well with change or difficulty. "Think of a time when you did manage to get through difficulty." Asking about this implies that the client has managed this at least on certain occasions, and this may be used in the therapy as a basis for a productive approach to the current trauma.

The Challenges of a "Seismic" Event

We have used the metaphor of traumatic events as personal earthquakes (Calhoun & Tedeschi, 1998) that have shaken people to their core beliefs and coping capabilities. Usually, but not always, this event is discussed in some detail in trauma treatments. Recalling that it is not the event, but the adaptation process in its aftermath that is crucial for PTG, the trauma survivor typically indicates the degree to which the event needs to be explored. For example, with bereaved parents, the particular details of the child's death are important in some cases and not in others. If the child died because of the actions of another person—a drunk driver or an incompetent physician—the parent may need to focus a great deal on these elements. We have presented an instance where a parent was driving a car which slid off the road, hit a tree, and killed the child who was reported to have not been wearing a seat belt (Tedeschi & Calhoun, 2004b). This case required a great deal of focus on this parent's responsibility in the death. But most of the discussion in treatment will tend to focus on the changes produced by the seismic event.

When trauma is ongoing, for example in the cases of cancer patients undergoing treatment or even those in remission, there is not a clear "aftermath" of trauma. But, in virtually all cases, there is a clear point at which the trauma enters the person's life and changes it. For the cancer patient it may be at diagnosis or when a cancer that was thought to have been conquered returned. The clients often are able to report the moment when life changed. This is a defining element of a truly traumatic event. Such an event has a profound effect on the life narrative, the story that is being automatically written by each of us to account for and organize the events of our lives into a personal identity. For the trauma survivor, the event in question is often the point in which "I changed."

Perhaps an exception to this idea, that trauma survivors can assign a turning point in their narrative, is the situation of persons traumatized early in life, where it is hard to remember being a different person, or when that different self was so immature that the trauma disrupted the entire developmental process. Here, the clinician may be able to get at the effects of the crisis by asking a question such as "Can you imagine the kind of person you might have become if this hadn't happened to you?" In answering such a question, a survivor of childhood trauma may make surprising discoveries or, more along the lines of our therapy approach, construct "growth" explanations that are useful to them. Here is an example from therapy with a survivor of childhood incest. The growth explanation is embedded in a context of self-blame and self-loathing, but it may at some point be a way to counteract some of these negative elements.

T: Can you imagine the kind of person you might have become if this hadn't happened to you?

C: I don't know. I'm just who I am. And you know I'm bad.

T: I am wondering how much of who you are is the result of what your father did, and how much is a part of you that is separate from all that. Does that make any sense?

C: Yeah, I see what you mean, but it is hard to tell. I know all the others [her multiple personalities] come out of that. I guess they would be all together, or I wouldn't need them so much if it hadn't happened. I guess I'd be more normal. But you know, I wonder if I would be such a caretaker for all the animals if it weren't for that. I just want to protect them. I think I am much more protective—I know what it is like to be scared and hurt.

T: I guess it is hard to say how much that would have been part of your life if you had had a better childhood.

C: I think I feel safe with them too. I trust animals, you know. I know how to relate to them. I think I am sensitive to their feelings, I can sense things, kind of know what they might be thinking, or something. I just know what to do for them, especially if they are scared.

T: So this was kind of honed by your own experience. You became more sensitive and protective.

C: I think so.

T: Some people might have become mean to animals.

C: Yeah, we see that.

T: You are just the opposite.

C: But remember, I'm bad, don't try to tell me I'm good.

T: But your animals certainly benefit from your presence, there is no denying that. You were just saying that you are sensitive to them.

C: Yeah, you're right.

T: Despite what happened, and how bad you feel about it, you are still able to do some good.

This example involves a person who has a history of horrific incest, who has dissociative identity disorder, and is often depressed and has made several suicide attempts. It is hard for her to see herself as a good person after engaging in sexual activities with her father. But she is part of an animal rescue organization and, by her account, has a special sensitivity to these creatures. It is certainly not necessary, or even perhaps advisable, that she attribute her positive qualities to the incest events. What would be important is to see herself as having value in the *aftermath* of all of that.

The clinician who is an *expert companion* in this process facilitates growth by *listening carefully to how the trauma survivor's descriptions of events include ways they showed strength and capability before, during, and after the traumatic experiences*. In the preceding example, the clinician points out that it is the trauma survivor's own idea that she is drawing from, to reach the conclusion about her "goodness," by noting "You were just saying that you are sensitive to them." In this example elements of both *companionship* and *facilitation* of PTG are evident. Listening carefully, the expert companion makes use of these openings in the processing of concepts about the person's self-identity. When working with trauma survivors as expert companions, we follow the advice of Corr (2002): "Appreciate coping not primarily in terms of external evaluations but—more importantly from the standpoint of the individual coper—in terms of how he or she is playing the cards that are available (often poor and difficult ones) in response to major challenges in living" (p. 137).

Trauma brings challenges that involve at least three elements in our model: ability to manage emotional distress, beliefs and goals, and the life narrative. As we have mentioned in the preceding text, the life narrative that can be seen as defining the self is fundamentally altered by events that are traumatic. The "assumptive world," the basic beliefs about oneself, one's place and function in the world, other people, and the future, is shaken or shattered by this psychological earthquake, so that trauma survivors literally do not know what to think about any of these things (Janoff-Bulman, 1992; this volume). Their emotional responses can be extreme due to the loss of essential security. Trauma is breathtaking because it appears that the survivor is faced with "a whole new life" (Price, 1994). As clinicians listen to accounts of trauma and the changes it produces, they will often hear metaphorical descriptions. Meichenbaum (n.d.) has mentioned that trauma survivors become "poets" to try to express the breathtaking ways that trauma has affected them and lists many examples of the metaphors used for hypersensitivity, psychic numbing, intrusive ideation, sense of loss, characteristics of self-identity, past abusive events, and hopes for change. The latter are particularly important to hear for the expert companion who is oriented toward PTG. Trauma survivors sometimes say things, such as "I want to rewrite my own script," and this presents an opportunity to join with the client to utilize the changes and learning in the aftermath of trauma to redefine the self and the future.

It is beyond the scope of this chapter to review all the trauma treatment techniques that can be marshaled to deal with managing emotional distress in the aftermath of trauma. But it is imperative that some success at emotional regulation be accomplished. Great emotional distress is disruptive to a person's ability to think through new plans and develop confidence in their ability to function in the world again. An important part of the process of developing emotional regulation is to clarify for survivors that their emotional reactions are expected in the aftermath of something difficult or threatening. Here the *expertise* of the clinician, assuming the stance of an expert companion, is important. It is somewhat reassuring for most trauma survivors to know that their responses are not "crazy," but that they are the kind of things expected under the circumstances. Using a metaphor to the processes involved in physical injuries and healing is often helpful.

C: I just break down without warning, I can't keep myself together.

T: Break down how?

C: I just start shaking, and my mind starts to spin. I can't figure out what to do.

T: This trauma is still reverberating through you. Unfortunately, this is often what happens to people in these situations.

C: I feel like I'm going to lose it.

T: Having this happen doesn't mean you aren't going to recover from this.

C: But when will it stop?

T: It is hard to say exactly, but we can do some things to help you manage this, and it will get better.

C: So there's hope?

T: Absolutely. It's like if you were physically injured, and your body did something unusual, like bleed, swell, or feel pain, you wouldn't see those things as indicating that your body was necessarily doomed, would you?

C: No.

T: It would be doing what we would expect under the circumstances, and we'd have to help it use its natural healing powers.

C: Like getting the blood to clot.

T: Exactly. That's what we are doing here.

Rumination and Cognitive Processing

A central element in our model of PTG involves rumination or *cognitive processing* of the trauma so that elements of growth can be recognized. This cognitive processing is not merely cognitive, however. We have attempted to emphasize that because strong emotions are part of this process, the understanding of trauma and its aftermath in relation to the self has a quality of knowing that is distinctive. This cognitive processing is a complicated affair that includes experiential learning that leads to constructed reality that is known in a profound way. Here again, metaphorical language is often encountered by clinicians working with trauma survivors as they attempt to make sense of what they have recognized about themselves and their world.

It is important for clinicians to recognize the form of cognitive processing that is likely to be associated with PTG. Nolen-Hoeksema and her colleagues (Treynor, Gonzalez, & Nolen-Hoeksema, 2003) have recently distinguished "brooding rumination" from "reflection rumination" in persons responding to losses. The latter seems to be associated with finding benefits, that is, PTG, while the former is not. An important role for expert companions might be to encourage a form of processing of the stressful event that is akin to reflection. It involves a consideration of how one is reacting to the traumatic events and can include writing these reactions as part of this analysis. Indeed, both Ullrich and Lutgendorf (2002) and Stanton et al. (2002) have shown that this type of writing exercise, based on Pennebaker's work (1997), is related to reports of PTG. Harvey, Barnett, and Overstreet (2004) state that "people seem to cope better with stressors as they emphasize account making and confiding that includes conscious rumination. Such rumination is conscious, instrumental, and seems natural" (p. 28). In our model of PTG, self-disclosure is closely related to this rumination, and *depending on the reactions of the person receiving the disclosures*, can encourage or discourage it and, therefore, critically affect the likelihood of PTG outcomes (Calhoun & Tedeschi, 2004; Harvey et al., 2004; Wortman, 2004). So the expert companion is open to disclosure and encourages a reflective, analytical, conscious, emotionally informed style of cognitive processing of trauma and avoids platitudes or other attempts to reassure that suppress this kind of trauma response. The expert companion must be able to tolerate distress in the survivor, although this kind of processing does not necessarily bring rapid relief. For example, Nolen-Hoeksema and Davis (2004) report that this type of cognitive processing is unrelated to depressive symptoms and related to PTG at 13 months after trauma, but not at 6 months. Stanton & Low (2004) report that with their cancer patients, PTG predicted positive mood at 12 months, though not decreased distress. Therefore, the expert companion must also recognize that positive changes may coexist with distress in trauma survivors.

The goal of our clinical approach is not exclusively the relief of all distress. Why not? Because distress may be related to continuing cognitive processing that can produce better, more meaningful outcomes in the long term that may include PTG, and because PTG can allow some people to manage distress effectively. It is also realistic for many survivors to live with some continuing distress. We have found this to be particularly true of bereaved parents. Similarly, the goal of our clinical work is not necessarily to *produce* PTG (Calhoun & Tedeschi, 1999). We consider ourselves to be *facilitators* of PTG that is created or discovered by persons who are able to process information about themselves in the aftermath of trauma in a relationship with an expert companion. At the same time, the domains of PTG are not the goals and expectations for therapy that we have or that we explicitly agree upon with our clients. Posttraumatic growth represents a possibility that many trauma survivors realize, but we believe it would be difficult, and inappropriate, for most trauma survivors entering therapy to agree on a goal of seeking positive changes in the struggle with trauma. For most bereaved parents, for example, this would be an offensive notion, heard by them as, "so you want me to think that it is a good thing my child died?" Virtually all trauma survivors seek help in *survival*, physically and emotionally, in the aftermath of trauma.

There are exceptions to this however. Upon learning he had prostate cancer, one man composed these lines:

"I want to make this to be a gift
a blessing.
I want this to be an injunction
To live deliberately
And well.
For the rest of my life. (Jordan, 2004. p. 9)

The expert companion to the trauma survivor acknowledges that the first steps in treatment involve establishing a sense of safety in the therapy relationship (Herman, 1992), a step necessary to allow for open disclosure and processing of the traumatic events and their aftermath. The *expert* companion is able to acquaint the trauma survivor with constructive coping with the symptoms of trauma response, the tasks that may need to be accomplished due to the changes produced by trauma, and the reactions of people who are disappointments in terms of support. In working on these problems, the survivor is confronted with the necessity to reevaluate beliefs and goals. In our model of PTG, we divide cognitive processing into early forms that are more automatic and intrusive and later forms that may be more deliberate and associated with changed schemas and narrative. The expert companion helps clients move from the early forms of cognitive processing to the later forms that are more reflective.

Consider this exchange between a therapist and client that is illustrative of the approach that can be taken to guide clients toward reflective cognitive processing.

C: I just keep thinking that she's dead, and that she's in that cold ground out there, and she's cold. When it snowed last week , it really upset me. You must think I'm crazy.

T: Actually, I don't.

C: Well, I wonder about me. I know those are crazy things to think. But that's how I feel.

T: You were always her mother. You always tried to protect her. We can't expect you to stop thinking that way right now.

C: But I'd better stop. It's like I can't think of anything else. And I can't protect her anymore.

T: What is there to protect her from—the cold?

C: It doesn't make sense, does it?

T: I guess these thoughts aren't very useful, to you or to her.

C: No, it's not helping anyone.

T: Maybe when you find yourself thinking such things, you can consider why you are thinking like this, and what it means for your relationship with Julie now.

C: I'm not sure what you mean.

T: Like I was saying before, when you are thinking about Julie being cold, you can think that it's because you are her mother, her protector. Instead of just thinking she's cold, think about how it actually makes sense that you think this.

C: It won't feel so crazy.

T: Right. Also, you might give some thought to your mother–daughter relationship now.

C: That I'm still her mother.

T: How does that feel?

C: OK. I hate to think that I'm not a mother anymore.

T: That's another thought that disturbs you.

C: Yes, I think that a lot.

T: So, you can think about that differently. You are always a mother. I remember that back in World War II, when servicemen died, their mothers were called gold star mothers—they were still mothers, you see.

C: Right. So am I.

T: Yes, and you can think about how to be a mother now.

C: How to be a mother to a dead child.

T: Does that make sense?

C: Well, I start thinking about the pictures I have. Collecting them together.

T: See, now you start thinking about something to *do*, that's better than just going over and over in your mind, "she's cold, I can't protect her anymore, I'm not a mother anymore" and thoughts like that.

C: You know how some people make scholarships and things like that in honor of a loved one? I was just thinking that I wonder if I could do that. It would take some money, but I have some from the insurance, and I have hated that money in a way. I don't want to want it or like it, it's like blood money or something, I know that sounds weird. But I wonder if I could do something for her.

T: That sounds like something worth thinking about.

C: I have no idea about any of that stuff, how it works.

T: Most of us never have to think of such things.

C: Yeah, I'm one of the lucky ones. I get to have a scholarship named after my daughter.

T: Even the good things connected with her are going to be painful now.

C: The pain is always there.

T: But some thoughts just emphasize the pain, like "she's cold, and I'm not a mother." Other ways of thinking may ease it a little? Like about the photos or the scholarship?

C: Its like a combination of pain and something sweet.

T: Like that term *bittersweet*.

C: Exactly. Bittersweet is maybe the best I'm ever going to get.

T: Maybe so.

C: But I don't want to be just bitter.

T: I hope not.

C: So, I'm trying to get more to the bittersweet.

T: And you have some choice in that. Like in your thinking. I can't see how you *can't* think of her.

C: Oh no, I wouldn't want to not think of her.

T: And you can't not think of her, anyway—you're her mother after all.

C: Yes.

T: But maybe you can think in these more useful, bittersweet ways, than the purely painful, bitter ways.

In this exchange, the therapist is an expert companion, in that he does not get too far ahead of this bereaved mother. He stays close by, emotionally and in terms of what she can think about at this point. For example, the therapist in this case, when the client mentioned she had no idea about how to set up a scholarship, thought about saying something about how the mother could get information about creating scholarships and how she could go about researching this. But this would be premature and take the therapist away from the pain that this mother is going through into some intellectual consideration of a supposed solution to this pain. Instead, he stayed close to the tragedy of it—most of us never have to consider such things. It is imperative that clinicians be companions in this way with survivors of trauma, so that they can gently use their expertise to encourage a growth-oriented process. Of course, the therapist here is trying to show the distinction between the intrusive ruminations about the buried daughter being cold and that the client is no longer able to be a mother, and more reflective processing of the situation. This type of thinking is focused on addressing a problem—how do I continue to be a mother now? There is a potential for creativity in the responses. There is the potential for action to be taken, rather than leaving the person to ruminate about something that can not be solved. The client may come to recognize that there is a choice about how to think in this situation, and by thinking in the reflective, essentially creative way she moves on unwittingly toward outcomes that may in time be seen as benefits and experiences that may produce PTG. That is not the goal at the outset. The therapist and client are pursuing ways to ease the pain of this loss. But with expertise in the area of PTG, we know that certain kinds of responses to trauma are likely to lead to more effective coping, that is, reduction in pain, suffering, and trauma symptoms, in addition to setting the stage for PTG.

Much of the cognitive processing engaged in by trauma survivors will involve attempts to comprehend and understand. These attempts to comprehend and understand tend to fall into two broad categories (Calhoun, Selby, & Selby, 1982; Davis, 2001). The first category involves attempts to understand the reasons or causes for the loss—what sequence of events produced the experienced trauma? This attempt to understand causes and sequences of events can also involve the tendency to ruminate about "counterfactuals" (Miller, Turnbull, & McFarland, 1990), that is, the ways in which a traumatic event could have been prevented or "undone." The second category of cognitive processing involves an attempt to make sense of the loss in a more general way that typically involves issues of existential meaning and, for many clients, involves spiritual and religious attempts to find purpose and meaning in what has happened. This second type of cognitive processing involves attempts to reconcile one's worldview with the loss to find a broader existential purpose and meaning in the tragedy that has occurred. This second domain of cognitive processing is one that may provide more fertile ground for the emergence of PTG.

An inability to make sense of an event in terms of how the trauma came about, how it happened, or an unremitting concern with how it could have been prevented can produce a constant state of emotional distress. In the trauma survivor it is often experienced as "being stuck." If this kind of understanding is not achieved within several months of a traumatic event, it may be very difficult to achieve it later (Davis, 2001). In these instances, clinicians who are *expert* companions can be particularly helpful. They can help the client come to some conclusions about why an event occurred and if it could have been prevented. If these more empirical issues, of antecedents and possible causes, are essentially cleared from constant rumination then perhaps it will be easier for a trauma survivor to move toward consideration of the second kind of understanding, of broader questions of purposes and meanings, through a reflective cognitive processing that may lead to PTG. Clinicians can encourage this kind of reflective cognitive processing of the trauma with questions, such as "How has all of this changed you?" or "How does the world look to you now after what you've been going through?"

Here is an illustration of how a clinician might be helpful in moving a survivor beyond the initial process of simply understanding reasons and causes of circumstances by applying the principles of expert companionship. In this situation, a mother is talking about the suicide of her 17-year-old son.

C: I just wish I had gone up to check on him, but it seemed like not that big a deal at the time.

T: Right. It just seemed like a teenager having a temper tantrum.

C: It had happened before.

T: No different this time.

C: But it was different—he hung himself!

T: Of course, but what was leading up to it didn't seem too unusual.

C: I wish I knew what he was thinking. I wish I had talked to him.

T: And you still wish now that you could understand this?

C: Yeah, I guess, but it won't bring him back. But I just can't stop thinking about what he was going through. How did I miss it?

T: It remains a mystery.

C: It does. None of his friends have been able to tell me that he was particularly upset, or anything. I mean there was that thing with his girlfriend. And I know he had had more trouble in school since the accident last year. But I haven't met anyone who thought he was really unhappy or desperate.

T: So, I guess there was no way to anticipate this. No one can even do it in hindsight!

C: That's true. But if just by chance, I had gone upstairs a few minutes earlier, I would have caught him in time.

T: Maybe so. And that is so hard to see.

C: Oh! If only I had just gone up there.

T: Can you see any way that additional thinking about that will help you?

C: What do you mean?

T: I mean, it seems that you have essentially come to a conclusion here. That you couldn't have anticipated such an outcome of this argument, because even in hindsight it doesn't make sense. And that the best you could have done would have been to go upstairs after him a little sooner. That's about it.

C: Like I'll never figure it out more than that.

T: Right. That you have gone as far as you can with trying to understand Charlie, and in imagining what you could have done differently.

C: Well, except I might have had a relationship with him where he felt more free to talk to me about whatever was bothering him.

T: But he did. That's how you knew about his girlfriend even. A lot of teenage boys won't say that stuff to their mothers, you know.

C: Yeah, we were close, at least it seemed like it.

T: Have you found out anything from his friends you didn't know?

C: Nothing major.

T: So you weren't out of the loop with him.

C: I think I was pretty much up on what was going on.

T: What would you tell another mother in this situation?

C: You did the best you could, lady.

T: Hard to say that to yourself.

C: Yeah, there is still that sense I failed him.

T: But when we really examine it, it comes down to "You did the best you could, lady."

C: You know, I guess that's true. I have really grilled myself on this.

T: Maybe it is time to move yourself on to something else.

C: What?

T: Like, what now?

C: Yeah, what now?

T: Life has changed. And maybe you are changing.

C: Yeah, I got to figure out how to live with this. It is the way it is, and nothing's going to change it. I didn't really screw up. I did what I could. Charlie screwed up, I guess, didn't he?

T: He did.

C: So what do I do now?

T: I think thinking about that is potentially more useful, though still hard.

C: What kind of person with a dead kid am I going to be.

T: Yes, you could put it that way.

Although this is just an excerpt from a series of sessions where the clinician was working with this bereaved mother on the causes of her son's death and how it could have been prevented, this was a point where the clinician could gently turn the focus beyond this. Only an expert companion can do this—someone who is very close to the trauma survivor's ways of thinking and feeling about their trauma. Notice that by suggesting the consideration of things in the very general sense of "What now?", the expert companion here speaks in the kind of language likely to be used by a survivor—not the kind of jargon typical of some clinicians. The expert companion also states the obvious in direct terms, "Life has changed." And makes a subtle suggestion that can allow for discussion of PTG at some point in the future: "And maybe you are changing."

It is not possible for us to be formulaic about the clinical maneuvers to make in an approach to trauma treatment that includes the consideration of PTG. There is much in timing and subtle commentary that is involved—but the principle of expert companionship can guide clinicians working with trauma survivors to do the kinds of things that are likely to allow for and support this PTG.

Later on in therapy, clinicians may find that their clients are further along in the process of PTG that we describe in our model. The more deliberate, reflective cognitive processing that involves schema change and development of a new life narrative starts to become more of the conversation. Of course, much of the client's cognitive processing of these elements happens between sessions.

When we developed our measure of PTG (Tedeschi & Calhoun, 1996), we started by interviewing trauma survivors at length to understand their changed perspectives. Statistical analyses yielded five factors of PTG: new possibilities or pathways in life; a greater appreciation for life; improved relationships; a greater sense of personal strength; and spiritual development. These five dimensions clearly capture the core experience of growth that is experienced by persons dealing with any situation. In addition, however, there may be some very specific kinds of changes that are unique to specific difficulties and clinicians should attend to these. For example, cancer survivors may develop healthier eating habits, or prisoners of war may develop a lifelong appreciation for small things from which they were deprived during captivity, for example, ice cream and hotdogs. The clinician should attend to possible changes in all of these areas and encourage discussion of these changes, or the precursors to them.

This process of attending to possible changes in the five broad dimensions of growth that can be applicable for all events, in addition to attending to changes characteristic of only certain kinds of life crises, often requires survivors to engage in dialectical thinking, the consideration of various paradoxes that spring from the basic paradox they may be experiencing, that gains may come from loss. We have discussed extensively how these paradoxes are often better explored metaphorically (Calhoun & Tedeschi, 1999). Using metaphors is helpful to the extent that they occur within the relationship with an expert companion who can use survivor's own metaphorical language or develop metaphors that fit with the survivor's experience. For example, in the book for clinicians entitled *Facilitating Posttraumatic Growth* (Calhoun & Tedeschi, 1999), we highlight clinical work with a professional photographer who experiences PTG in the aftermath of his son's death. A metaphor used to describe his PTG was a picture becoming clear in developing fluid. Expert companions are close enough to survivor's experiences and viewpoints to naturally speak in the terms that resonate with them. We prefer these naturally occurring metaphors to the prepackaged stories and metaphors some clinicians utilize.

These discussions that rely on metaphor are in the service of exploring the paradoxical developments of PTG, which by its nature is essentially paradoxical. The different domains of PTG have their particular paradoxical elements. New pathways in life open up when others are closed off. Personal strength becomes most apparent at times of greatest vulnerability. Improved interpersonal relationships develop when a great deal is asked of them. Life is appreciated most when it is endangered. Spiritual development occurs at a time when the deepest spiritual needs and questions are confronted. Because so much of PTG is rooted in paradox, the clinician that takes the stance of expert companion will need to tolerate the discomfort of survivors' ruminations about these issues. The paradoxical nature of the domains of PTG require this cognitive processing, because these perspectives are not self-evident. The cognitive processing involves emotional aspects of the trauma's aftermath, so that the learning is experienced deeply (Calhoun & Tedeschi, 1998). The knowledge or perspective on life that results comes from both cognitive and affective elements, head and heart, telling the same story. Consider these reflections by a client shortly before his death from lung cancer.

C: I do have my regrets, but at least the cancer gave me enough time to change.

T: So that you could use your hindsight now.

C: Yeah, I got a chance to do things better. I sure had it backwards. My customers were my family.

T: And your family got shortchanged.

C: I have straightened that out, though.

T: And your customers also cared about you. These were not merely business relationships.

C: Right. But still, I wasn't investing my time wisely. I might never have seen how much my family loves me if it weren't for having to deal with this cancer. Boy, have they been troopers. Despite the crap I've given Pam over the years, she stood by me.

T: And she got a better Fred in the bargain.

C: Amazing. In the pain, fear, money problems, and plain nastiness of this disease, we had a better time than ever.

T: Because you were at your best.

C: I was. I do feel good about how I've handled this. Proud of myself, more than I've ever been. I just hope I can keep it together through this part. I'm getting pretty scared at times.

T: So, how are you getting through this part?

C: That's where God comes in. Man, I need Him now. I can feel pretty stupid while feeling proud. How many times do you hear to put God first, family second, then yourself? I had it the wrong way around. Now, it's God and family. I had to live it to get that. I wish it didn't have to come to me like this. Well, I just try to do this part better.

T: This part is important.

C: Yeah, well. It's the only part I got left. It's real important. So I'm focused.

T: Like how focused you were in that game in high school.

C: The championship game.

T: Right.

C: That pales in comparison to the end of this game.

T: I was thinking of the story you told me about getting fired that time.

C: What do you mean?

T: Remember how you messed up that big account?

C: Oh, did I!

T: And how you went to all that trouble and your own expense to straighten it out and they fired you anyway?

C: Yeah, and I was mad at them, and mad at myself, and I couldn't decide who deserved it more.

T: And then the customer hired you!

C: Yeah, I impressed them with my efforts and taking it on the chin, I guess.

T: You kept trying to work it out, even when all seemed lost, and was. That's you, that you do it. You keep going, trying to get it right.

C: That is me. That's what I'm doing.

T: What do you think of that?

C: It might look futile.

T: To others?

C: Sure.

T: To you?

C: You know, I was thinking, 'I couldn't live with myself if I gave up.' That's funny isn't it?

T: That's you, too.

C: Yeah, I've always been funny. You know, I think I'm just more me. More determined, more funny, and more able to put my love in the right places, the right people. More connected to God. I guess this is an OK way to go out.

T: More, rather than less.

In this short excerpt, much is going on. Some domains of PTG are evident: personal strength, improved relationships, spiritual development. At the same time there is regret and fear. The clinician uses some metaphors from the stories the cancer patient had shared earlier to highlight these positive elements. The clinician first refers to the story of the patient's high school championship baseball game, in which he was a reserve who suddenly was called upon to play and played his best game ever, although the team lost. Then he brings up the way the patient had tried to fix a major problem with a sales account, and essentially corrected it only to lose his job. There are parallels here to his current situation, where death is imminent, but he still has choices about how to live out his final days. He is exercising these choices in a way where he is at his best in the end. Some of this is said overtly, but much is left to the metaphors based on his own stories. In this way, expert companionship is evident. The clinician understands the significance of these stories in this man's life, and the clinician and client can reflect on them together, while not needing to discuss the details. They share an understanding of what it all has to do with the current context, and so is a very intimate way of communicating. It is clear what the story of the cancer has come to mean for this patient, but the expert companion does not discuss this in clumsy terms, such as *meaning making*. The reality of PTG can be seen and accepted in this context, when there is this kind of companionship.

NARRATIVE —→ *Research on the Leader*

Traumatic events tend to divide the life story into before and after the event. In working with trauma survivors, expert companions take time to know who the person was before the trauma. By listening to the stories of that time, the clinician stores up material that can be used to construct appropriate metaphors later. The clinician also gets to understand in more personal detail what the trauma has done to the survivor. Knowing the person before and after, positive changes also can become more evident. As both Neimeyer and Meichenbaum discuss in this book, assisting the trauma survivors in reconstructing life narratives in the aftermath of trauma is crucial to integrating it into survivors' lives and

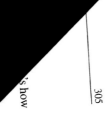

e before and after, the old life and the new, the old self and the
rative is formed in the mind of the trauma survivor. We find
vay of talking, because they have experienced life in terms
new life or new self can be, is often very unclear, however.
from a narrative perspective, is essentially answering this
w they would like to construct their futures, and the expert
vivors can choose to emphasize the PTG. In the following
a couple that is recovering from the extramarital affair of
ne.

Wife: I keep thinking about what he was doing at this time last year. Even though I know he's working to make it right, I keep thinking about what was really going on under my nose.

Husband: It feels like we're going backwards. She's been really testy, and we had a huge fight last week. It's like all these questions are coming back.

T: Remember, this whole process has been full of ups and downs, but you are still much further up than you have ever been, right?

W: I think so. He just needs to be patient. But I'm concerned too with all these thoughts I'm having. I'm not trying to make it hard.

T: I remember we talked earlier about how this time of year has become an unfortunate anniversary of sorts in your marriage. We knew this was going to be hard.

W: I hope we don't go through this every year. I hope that next year we can look back and think, last year we were getting better.

H: I'm afraid she won't do that, and this stuff will just haunt us.

W: Everything just reminds me of this time of year, last year. I mean, I didn't even know it was happening, just that things weren't good. And with Christmas and all, there are so many reminders.

H: Christmas is going to be screwed up for good, I'm afraid.

W: Well, you screwed it up.

H: I know that, there is no denying it. But I wish we could just keep a focus on how much better things have gotten during the past year.

T: Do you want that too, Patty?

W: Of course, but these bad thoughts just have got me right now.

T: And I'll bet you are thinking about January 28, the day it all came out.

W: Oh yes. I think I'll feel like crap that day. It's like I'm building up to that.

T: Although this was actually the turning point.

W: True. That was the day we decided not to break up, too.

T: Perhaps instead of dreading it as the anniversary of the day the affair came to light, you can celebrate it. It can be "Transformation Day" for the two of you, when you began the process that has been producing so much that you now value in your marriage.

W: I like that. We could make it something good.

T: Well, it is good, isn't it, what you've done.

H: I think so. I really feel like a different guy, a different husband.

T: January 28th was the beginning of that. Instead of spending the ne: it, you could be planning for it. Mitch, you might take that day spend it with Patty.

W: I always feel better when he's with me. I don't have as many thoughts.

T: And work together to plan something enjoyable for that day. That will push out the dread and replace it with partnership and positive anticipation. Keep it a private thing between the two of you. A little intimate secret, that only the two of you know the meaning of.

W: I like this a lot. Mitch, will you do this?

H: Absolutely.

In this instance, the clinician has worked with this couple for many months since the extramarital affair was revealed. They have built a great deal of goodwill and trust in this time, although hurt and mistrust persist. For this couple, the process of rebuilding their marriage has been the best of times and the worst of times, a paradox they deeply understand.

This example also demonstrates the potential importance of *positive emotions* in the process of PTG (Stanton & Low, 2004). The months of hard work by this couple on the transformation of their marriage into a relationship better than the one that existed before the affair, has produced positive emotions that allow for PTG and are in turn produced by PTG. This couple understands that these positive emotions have arisen out of suffering and forgiveness. Because of this understanding and their ability to have positive emotions about their situation, they can be open to the suggestion that they can choose January 28th to be "Transformation Day" rather than allow it to be merely a reliving of a dreadful past. Before there was some rebuilding of shattered trust, before there was some forgiveness, before they were able to enjoy each other again, they would not have been able to approach the anniversary of the revelation of the affair in a way that acknowledged a transformative aspect to it. But, with positive emotions available and an experiential understanding of the paradox of how their marriage has improved, they are enthusiastic about reconstructing the meaning of this anniversary and can use this every year to sustain themselves. This choice of meaning will likely further bolster their marriage for years to come by allowing them to experience January 28th and the days leading up to it with more positive emotion. The story of their marriage will include their creative efforts in transforming the meaning of January 28th.

WISDOM

We have previously (Calhoun & Tedeschi, 1998; Tedeschi & Calhoun, 1995) discussed how wisdom (e.g., Baltes & Sautdinger, 2000; Kramer, 1990) is connected with PTG. In our formulation (relying on the extensive work by Paul Baltes and colleagues, e.g., Baltes & Staudinger, 2000) we have focused on how wisdom is a kind of knowing that is experiential and affective, not merely intellectual. Affect appears to be crucial in the development of wisdom, where knowing becomes a synthesis of apprehending and intellectual understanding.

The cognitive processing that is involved in the development of PTG promotes new perspectives in the aftermath of the failure of old worldviews to account for the trauma that has occurred. In these existing worldviews, affect has been involved in the failure and sulting shock, because intellectually, virtually everyone is aware of the possibility of being victimized by trauma—disease, crime, natural disaster, bereavement, betrayal—but people at the affective level feel protected against these possibilities. Hence, we can be fairly comfortable being mortals in a world of potential danger. Trauma demonstrates that this comfort was illusory and our shock is the beginning of an affectively based knowing of truth that had been denied. Wisdom emerges from this.

Trauma survivors who develop wisdom from their experiences tend to be creative thinkers who embrace novelty. Trauma experiences are certainly novel. We have found that openness to experience is a personality dimension associated with PTG (Tedeschi & Calhoun, 1996) and that the facet of openness most closely associated with PTG is openness to feelings—emotional experiences. Wisdom involves a variety of syntheses, so it, like PTG, can appear paradoxical, and so demands complex, dialectical, integrative, creative approaches to emotional and intellectual information. The syntheses include affect and intellectual understanding, but also involve creative thinking that balances order and chaos (Strickland, 1989), active surrendering (Farran, Herth, & Popovich, 1995), chaotic cognition (Finke & Bettle, 1996), integrative complexity (Suedfeld & Bluck, 1993), and similar constructs. We refer the reader to our previous work for additional detail about the links between trauma, emotionally informed cognitive processing, PTG, and wisdom (Calhoun & Tedeschi, 1998).

For our purposes here, we wish to emphasize that the expert companion to the trauma survivor seeks to offer as emotionally safe a journey as possible through the cognitive processing of what had previously been deniable. If the ultimate benefits of coping with this trauma, PTG and wisdom, are to be realized, the survivor must be willing to engage in an extended period of processing. As we stated at the outset, this is why we are not exclusively symptom focused in our trauma treatment, and why management of distress rather than removal of it is involved in our work. Foreclosure on the cognitive processing and other ways of avoiding the trauma and its consequences prevent the survivor from creating, constructing, appreciating the paradoxes, and achieving the syntheses that are found in wisdom. The expert companion can not lead the survivor toward wisdom because this is a creative process. Indeed the expert companion recognizes his or her own limitations and is open to changing, and learning from the survivor. Clinicians who see themselves as expert companions practice this humility with trauma survivors, because it is all that is really possible under difficult circumstances that have no ready answers. So the expert companion encourages the survivor to experiment, both with thinking and with action, because wisdom involves not simply a way of thinking or knowing, but actively turning that into a new way of living.

REFERENCES

Baltes, P. B., & Staudinger, U. M. (2000). Wisdom—A metaheuristic (pragamatic) to orchestrate mind and virtue toward excellence. *American Psychologist, 55,* 122–136.

Calhoun, L. G., Selby, J., & Selby, L. (1982). The psychological aftermath of suicide: An analysis of current evidence. *Clinical Psychology Review, 2,* 409–420.

Calhoun, L. G., & Tedeschi, R. G. (1998). Posttraumatic growth: Future directions. In R. G. Tedeschi, C. L. Park, & L. G. Calhoun (Eds.), *Posttraumatic growth: Positive change in the aftermath of crisis* (pp. 215–238). Mahwah, NJ: Lawrence Erlbaum Associates.

Calhoun, L. G., & Tedeschi, R. G. (1999). *Facilitating posttraumatic growth: A clinician's guide.* Mahwah, NJ: Lawrence Erlbaum Associates.

Calhoun, L. G., & Tedeschi, R. G. (2004). The foundations of posttraumatic growth: New considerations. *Psychological Inquiry, 15,* 93–102.

Corr, C. A. (2002). Coping with challenges to assumptive worlds. In J. Kaufman (Ed.), *Loss of the assumptive world* (pp. 127–138). New York: Brunner-Routledge.

Davis, C. (2001). The tormented and the transformed: Understanding responses to loss and trauma. In Neimeyer, R. A. (Ed), *Meaning reconstruction and the experience of loss* (pp. 137–155). Washington, DC: American Psychological Association.

Dohrenwend, B. P., Neria, Y., Turner, J. B., Turse, N., Marshall, R., Lewis-Fernandez, R., Koenen, K. C. (2004). Positive tertiary appraisals and posttraumatic stress disorder in U.S. male veterans of the war in Vietnam: The roles of positive affirmation, positive reformulation, and defensive denial. *Journal of Consulting and Clinical Psychology, 72,* 417–433.

Farran, C. J., Herth, K. A., & Popovich, J. M. (1995). *Hope and hopelessness: Critical clinical constructs.* Thousand Oaks, CA: Sage.

Finke, R. A., & Bettle, J. (1996). *Chaotic cognition.* Mahwah, NJ: Lawrence Erlbaum Associates.

Harvey, J. H., Barnett, K., & Overstreet, A. (2004). Trauma growth and other outcomes attendant to loss. *Psychological Inquiry, 15,* 26–29.

Herman, J. L. (1992). *Trauma and recovery.* New York: Basic Books.

Janoff-Bulman, R. (1992). *Shattered assumptions.* New York: Free Press.

Jordan, J. R. (2004). Prostate cancer. *The Forum of the Association for Death Education and Counseling, 30*(4), 8–9.

Kramer, D. A. (1990). Conceptualizing wisdom: The primacy of affect-cognition relations. In R. J. Sternberg (Ed.), *Wisdom: Its nature, origins, and development* (pp. 279–313). Cambridge: Cambridge University Press.

Meichenbaum, D. (n.d.). *A clinical handbook/practical therapist manual for assessing and treating adults with post-traumatic stress disorder (PTSD).* Waterloo, Ontario, Canada: Institute Press.

Miller, D. T., Turnbull, W., & McFarland, C. (1990). Counterfactual thinking and social perception: Thinking about what might have been. In M. P. Zanna (Ed.), *Advances in Experimental Social Psychology, Vol. 23* (pp. 305–331). San Diego, CA: Academic Press.

Neimeyer, R. A. (2001). *Meaning reconstruction and the experience of loss.* Washington, DC: American Psychological Association.

Nolen-Hoeksema, S., & Davis, C. (2004). Theoretical and methodological issues in the assessment and interpretation of posttraumatic growth. *Psychological Inquiry, 15,* 60–64.

Pennebaker, J. W. (1997). Writing about emotional experiences as a therapeutic process. *Psychological Science, 8,* 162–169.

Price, R. (1994). *A whole new life.* New York: Antheneum.

Rosen, C. S., Chow, H. C., Finney, J. F., Greenbaum, M. A., Moos, R. H., Sheikh-Javaid, I., et al. (2004). VA practice patterns and practice guidelines for treating posttraumatic stress disorder. *Journal of Traumatic Stress, 17,* 213–222.

Shay, J. (1994). *Achilles in Vietnam: Combat trauma and the undoing of character.* New York: Antheneum.

Stanton, A. L., Danoff-Burg, S., Sworowski, L. A., Collins, C. A., Branstetter, A., Rodriguez-Hanley, A. et al. (2002). Randomized, controlled trial of written emotional expression and benefit finding in breast cancer patients. *Journal of Clinical Oncology, 20,* 4160–4168.

Stanton, A. L., & Low, C. A. (2004). Toward understanding posttraumatic growth: Commentary on Tedeschi and Calhoun. *Psychological Inquiry, 15,* 76–80.

Strickland, B. R. (1989). Internal-external control expectancies: From contingency to creativity. *American Psychologist, 44,* 1–12.

Suedfeld, P., & Bluck, S. (1993). Changes in integrative complexity accompanying significant life events: Historical evidence. *Journal of Personality and Social Psychology, 64,* 124–130.

Tedeschi, R. G., & Calhoun, L. G. (1995). *Trauma and transformation: Growing in the aftermath of suffering.* Thousand Oaks, CA: Sage.

Tedeschi, R. G., & Calhoun, L.G. (1996). The posttraumatic growth inventory: Measuring the positive legacy of trauma. *Journal of Traumatic Stress, 9,* 455–471.

Tedeschi, R. G., & Calhoun, L. G. (2004a). Posttraumatic growth: Conceptual foundations and empirical evidence. *Psychological Inquiry, 15,* 1–18.

Tedeschi, R. G., & Calhoun, L. G. (2004b). *Helping bereaved parents: A clinician's guide.* New York: Brunner Routledge.

Treynor, W., Gonzalez, R., & Nolen-Hoeksema, S. (2003). Rumination reconsidered: A psychometric analysis. *Cognitive Therapy and Research, 27,* 247–259.

Ullrich, P. M., & Lutgendorf, A. K. (2002). Journaling about stressful events: Effects of cognitive processing and emotional expression. *Annals of Behavioral Medicine, 24,* 244–250.

Wortman, C. B. (2004). Posttraumatic growth: Progress and problems. *Psychological Inquiry, 15,* 81–89.

16

THE LINK BETWEEN POSTTRAUMATIC GROWTH AND FORGIVENESS: AN INTUITIVE TRUTH

PAMELA C. FISCHER

OKLAHOMA UNIVERSITY HEALTH SCIENCES CENTER

April 19, 1995 is etched in the memory of Oklahomans and most Americans. It is the day that our assumptions were shattered about the safety of living in the United States, particularly in the "Heartland," as Oklahoma would come to be described. For Oklahomans, the term *disaster* was predominately associated with tornadoes. Most of us who have lived here all of our lives, however, took these in stride. I will never forget the statement I made to my youngest daughter just a few weeks before the bombing of the Murrah Building when she prophetically asked about the possibility of being attacked by other countries or outside forces. "Honey, we are in the middle of the United States. If something were going to happen, it would be on either coast."

When I recall that statement today, I am amazed with my naïveté although I do not believe my view was different than that of most. The bombing in Oklahoma City not only destroyed the Alfred P. Murrah Building, but also a belief system in the predictability and safety of our community and world, and the trustworthiness of other people. For a community founded on the premise that a "man's word is as good as his bond," this was a surreal experience.

Terrorist attacks, such as those in Oklahoma City and the World Trade Center, combine features of a criminal assault, a disaster, and an act of war (Hills, 2002). Miller describes terrorism as the "perfect" traumatic stressor because it combines the elements of malevolent intent, actual or threatened extreme harm, and unending fear of the future (2002, p. 284). Timothy McVeigh accomplished all of that with the use of a homemade bomb to blow up a building filled with innocent people and small children, simply to convey a message of hate toward the government. Healing for individuals and the community is a process still in motion. While survivors have struggled to overcome their injuries and heal their spirits, they have had to contend with the media, the trial of McVeigh, the building of the Memorial, the execution of McVeigh, the terrorist attacks on 9/11, and the recent trial of Terry Nichols, all of which are incremental stressors on this already difficult journey.

Terrorism is a new aspect of American life. Literature on the treatment of its survivors is not as plentiful as research on survivors of other kinds of traumatic events. Not long ago, *traumatic experiences* and *psychological trauma* were terms typically applied to combat veterans and individuals who experienced severe, adverse events in the form of natural disasters or acts of interpersonal violence. These events were considered to be "outside the range of usual human experience" (American Psychiatric Association [APA], 1980).

Unfortunately, traumatic experiences and acts of terrorism are now part of our ordinary existence. In addition to terrorists acts in Oklahoma City, Washington DC, and New York City, the threat of anthrax, the DC snipers, continuous media coverage of the war in Iraq, and the broadcasts of public executions by Al Quada have exposed individuals to events they never dreamed possible. Epidemiological studies indicate that posttraumatic stress disorder (PTSD) is becoming a major health concern worldwide and that work impairment associated with PTSD is similar to the amount of work impairment associated with major depression (Brunello et al., 2001).

The increasing exposure to traumatic events has prompted the development of evidence-based modalities to help individuals decrease the negative impact of traumatic experiences. Correspondingly, there has been an increasing interest in the beneficial aspects of struggling with a traumatic event. Psychological studies have documented that most individuals who experience traumatic events report positive life changes (Linley & Joseph, 2004; Tedeschi & Calhoun, 1995; Tedeschi, Park, & Calhoun, 1998). The experience of growing as a result of suffering is not new. For centuries, individuals have reported an increased appreciation for life after going through adversity. In fact, one premise of existential philosophy is that only when one faces death, can one fully appreciate life. The development of Tedeschi and Calhoun's (1995) model of posttraumatic growth (PTG), however, provided a systematic way of conceptualizing the process of psychological growth that can result from experiencing trauma.

In 1995, I was unaware of the phenomenon of PTG. However, as I treated those affected by the bombing, I became intrigued with the different perspectives offered by clients. I wondered what made a woman in her 60s who was trapped under the rubble for hours and sustained serious injuries to her legs, hobble to my office and conclude that "I'm not scared of anything now," and someone who had minimal exposure to the bombing to remain constantly angry because she was not being compensated enough for the cost of traveling to therapy sessions. What made some individuals, even after coping with serious depression or PTSD, channel their distress into a new mission or purpose in life while others refused to talk about their experiences as if not doing so would make them go away?

Certainly I knew that individuals experience the same situation in very different manners. Cognitive therapy posits that the way we interpret an event determines the way we feel about it. And recovering from trauma is an individual experience. However, it was the difference in an individual's interpretation of the experience and the resulting philosophy or worldview constructed from that interpretation that I found intriguing. The experience of working with survivors also led me to work with veterans suffering from combat trauma in addition to others who had experienced major life crises. I now know that this new positive philosophy or worldview explained by clients was described, among other things, as PTG (Afflect & Tennen, 1996; Tedeschi and Calhoun, 1995).

During the past few years, research findings have provided data on many aspects of successfully coping with trauma and realizing PTG. Personality traits such as persistence, determinism, hardiness (Maddi & Kobasa, 1984), optimism (Carver, Scheier, & Weintraub, 1989; Moos & Schaefer, 1990; O'Leary & Ickovics, 1995), resilience (O'Leary & Ickovics, 1995; O'Leary, 1998; Rutter, 1987), and an internal locus of control (Tedeschi & Calhoun, 1995) may facilitate effective functioning despite stressful circumstances. Behaviors, such as self-disclosure through writing or talking (Pennebaker, 1990), social support (Berkman & Syme, 1994; Coyne & Downey, 1991), and religious coping activities (Aldwin, 1994), can make recovering from the traumatic event easier and promote more positive life adjustment.

It is not yet conclusive exactly how and when growth develops and the relationship between reported positive life changes and psychological functioning. Tedeschi and Calhoun (1995) (Schaefer & Moos, 1998) suggest that PTG is a process that occurs over time. However, there is some evidence that individuals report finding some positive change in as little as one week after the event (Frazier & Burnett, 1994; McMillan, Fisher & Smith, 1997). Likewise, most research indicates a positive correlation between PTG and aspects of healthy psychological functioning (Janoff-Bulman, 2004; Lechner & Antoni, 2004; Nolen-Hokesema & Davis, 2004; Park, 2004; Stanton & Low, 2004); but the meaning of these findings depends on the definition of optimal psychological functioning (Calhoun & Tedeschi, 2004).

In Tedeschi and Calhoun's model (1995, 2004), psychological growth originates from a kind of thinking and perspective that propels individuals to a higher level of functioning than existed before the trauma, (i.e., the acquisition of wisdom). Because of changes in schemas or assumptions about the world, individuals are able to reconstruct their life narratives to include an awareness of the paradoxical quality of life and to understand the "givens" (Sarte, 1956), but to also see the possibilities. Because of the complexity of this growth process and the questions generated by other researchers, Tedeschi and Calhoun's model of posttraumatic stress is still evolving.

This chapter is designed to describe findings from a study with 226 individuals closely affected by the Oklahoma City bombing 7 years after the event (Fischer, 2002) and to provide personal examples of survivors' thoughts and feelings during the recovery process. This chapter will offer some of the major findings relevant to the study of PTG with survivors of a terrorist attack. The responses given by subjects in this study tend to validate Tedeschi and Calhoun's (1995, 2004) premise that cognitive processing is an essential component of building new schemas and acquiring PTG. The data also indicate that PTG and psychological distress can coexist and demonstrate how additional acts of terrorism can trigger significant distress and feelings similar to those experienced in the original trauma. The information derived from this study offers evidence of significant "constructive" PTG (Nolen-Hoeksema, 2004) raises questions about the role of forgiveness in growth outcomes with survivors of a mass terror attack.

THE STUDY

The purpose of the study was to examine the relationship between PTG and forgiveness, and the level of symptomology currently experienced by individuals closely associated with the bombing. Each participant was given the Posttraumatic Growth Inventory (PTGI) (Tedeschi & Calhoun, 1996), the Heartland Forgiveness Scale (Thompson & Snyder, 2000), and a demographics questionnaire assessing symptoms of PTSD, beliefs about the death penalty, and reactions to the execution of Timothy McVeigh. Subjects were grouped by their role in the bombing and categorized as survivor, family member of a survivor, family member of a person who died, rescue worker, mental health professional, emergency medical professional, and volunteer.

MAJOR FINDINGS

Survivors scored significantly higher on PTG than nonsurvivors. Consistent with findings in several other research studies, women scored significantly higher than men on total PTGI scores and on all five factors of the PTGI. Family members reported significantly more PTG than nonfamily members. There was no significant relationship between overall forgiveness and PTG.

AREAS OF REPORTED GROWTH

Calhoun & Tedeschi (1998, 1999) suggest that individuals report PTG in three major domains: changes in relationships with others, change in the sense of self, and changes in the philosophy of life. Others have offered additional domains (McMillen & Fisher, 1998) or slightly different domains of growth (Armeli, Gunthert, & Cohen, 2001; Janoff-Bullman, 2004; McFarland and Alvaro, 2000).

Individuals closely involved in the Oklahoma City bombing experience describe significant PTG. The following comments were responses to the open-ended question "How did the attacks on New York and Washington, DC on 9/11 affect you or change you?" Many of the life lessons learned from surviving the bombing are reaffirmed. Their answers can easily be categorized into the domains outlined by Calhoun and Tedeschi.

Appreciation of Life

A male who worked in rescue efforts wrote: "It solidified my belief that we are here on borrowed time . . . Fear and anguish over your ultimate death is time better spent in celebration and enjoyment with those you love and who love you." A psychologist who worked in emergency mental health at the Oklahoma City post office massacre in 1993 and the Murrah Bombing wrote: "It affirmed what I learned when my own son died in 1979—life is precious and we have to be there for each other." A male rescue worker wrote: "Now I look forward to each day and try to make the most of it. Time with family is more cherished and looked forward to. I don't worry about money problems or situations I cannot control." A female emergency medical care worker wrote: "After the Murray bombing, I feel that the time spent at home and with family and friends is the most important thing. I vowed not to miss any more reunions, birthday parties, etc. And working long hard hours for material things is foolish." A female survivor reported: "I have an increased awareness of temporality and a renewed effort not to put things off, especially pleasurable or family oriented."

Finally, a survivor reported:

> It has caused me to think about my responsibilities as a world citizen in a different way. I have been reminded of my mortality—a poignant reminder to embrace each day and each person in my day with passion and compassion.

New Possibilities

A psychologist involved in emergency mental health treatment in the Oklahoma City bombing reported a change in the direction of her career after 9/11:

> On 9/22/2002, I flew to NYC on AA to participate in the disaster relief efforts. I am currently returning to NYC and DC each month to offer training in disaster relief to mental health and

religious professionals. The work in NYC and DC has been very healing for me—cathartic and also challenging as I listen to many stories and consult with such a diverse group of survivors—I have been changed professionally—I am more patient, tolerant, and so very grateful for life.

However, a disaster mental health professional who was very involved in frontline mental health recovery in the Murrah bombing wrote of her "gut-wrenching" decision not to go to New York, but to make a significant contribution to help those working in the 9/11 disaster in a different way:

> Although it was clear that on-going health issues prevented me from working directly with victims in the frontlines of a disaster, it was a real struggle to face my own limitations. Spiritually I went through a period of questioning God why I had all the experience and training in disaster mental health from the OKC bombing but I could not go where I was needed on 9/11. It took a while for me to find ways of making contributions with which I could live. Finally, avenues opened up which allowed me to provide input from a distance and gave me the satisfaction of feeling like I was helping in some way. Having an opportunity to reach out and pass on the lessons learned added meaning to the tragedy of 4/19/95.

An individual who worked in emergency mental health wrote: "Personally and professionally [it] increased my desire to gain understanding of how terrorism impacts others, particularly children. I was emotionally touched and experienced a strong desire to 'do something' to help." A woman who lost her 4-year-old daughter and her mother-in-law and father-in-law writes: "I had flashbacks about the Murrah Bombing for days after 9/11. However, the 9/11 attacks galvanized my effort to reach out to victims of terrorism. It also renewed my determination to work harder for victim's rights and to work to try to decrease incidents of terrorism in our world."

A male volunteer who worked at the bombing site wrote: "It increased my desire to learn and understand 'why' people resort to violence to affect change."

Personal Strength

A female minister who worked in one of the churches that sustained serious structural damage two blocks away from the Murrah building wrote of the effects of 9/11:

> Initially, I was horrified at the volume of destruction and death, and at the hatred that it exposed. On the other hand, I felt more comfortable than I might have, had I not been through the Murrah experience. I realized in a way I had not before, what my grandparents must have experienced, living through the bombing of London where they lived during WWII.

A fire fighter who worked in rescue wrote: "The attacks on 9/11 reminded me how important my job as a firefighter is and that my brothers in NYC lost their lives doing their jobs and giving service to their fellow man." A father whose adult daughter died in the bombing described his reaction to the 9/11 attacks:

> When I first saw the attacks on TV on that first day, it brought back the nightmares and inability to sleep. But the next day, I started calling the people in NY that I knew to see if they were all right. Then I called my support group to see how they were. Then I called all

the organizations that I knew to see how I could get to NY to help the family members that lost someone.

Increased Spiritual Emphasis

A female survivor who sustained significant injuries wrote: "I find myself much more evangelistic in a sense with my Christian faith. I am very much in favor of more dialogue and humanitarian aid. I have found myself much more interested in things we can learn from peace and justice folks and conflict resolution."

Another survivor wrote of her spiritual faith: "My relationship with God is what I'm most thankful for. With Him all things are possible." Another survivor wrote: "I have experienced an increase emphasis on my family and God. I have placed less importance on work."

Relating to Others

A firefighter wrote: "I was able to work in New York as a volunteer for 2 weeks. The only feeling was for the rescuers and families, and all the families that lost a loved one. I just wanted to help somehow." Other survivors described their immediate reactions:

> I felt so helpless, but spent much of the time that day waiting in line to give blood because it was something that I could do.

> I had a horrific immediate reaction to 9/11. I was thrown back to the day of the OKC bombing and experienced the same body-shaking terror I felt on 4/19/95. I felt like a panic attack was going to overtake me. I couldn't breathe and I started crying. I watched the buildings in NYC fall and felt exactly as I did while sitting in triage on 4/19/1995, that is, this is a nightmare, just a dream, not real; this is a science fiction movie, if I shake my head, I'll wake up. But within 15 minutes of that, I got a hold of myself and knew I had to do something to help. . . . Another survivor came by and we went to give blood. We stood in line for four hours and talked about how terrified those people in the NYC area were, and how awful it was going to be for them for a long, long time. We talked about how we could help NYC people. We decided that we'd be needed by New York more later, like a year from now, when the immediate attention has died down and they are still feeling deeply depressed, and anxious and some will be saying "You should have moved on by now." We can step in and say "No! Your feelings are normal! You don't move on quickly or easily and what you're going through, we understand." If we can help them get better by showing them you can survive, and by letting them talk with us, then our experience will have been worth it. We "owe it back." Many people helped us come back after our event, and now it's up to us to help NYC.

> Personally, I've already flown up once to NYC on my own money and time to be with someone who went through this and is having problems like I did. I wish I had the money and time to fly up there often and speak with people going through all those stages of depression, anger, and still asking "why us?" I wish I could help. Recovering is an individual and often a crushingly lonely journey.

Tedeschi and Calhoun (1995, 2004) suggest that extremely adaptive individuals may learn little that is new by experiencing a traumatic event. There may be a ceiling effect, where little else can be gained in terms of mental health and coping skills beyond a certain point (p. 56). Others may be less distressed by a traumatic event by virtue of having successfully coped with a previous traumatic experience. Because individuals have already reconstructed their assumptive worlds to include "yes it can happen to me" they are more psychologically prepared (Janoff-Bulman, 2004) and better able to withstand the shock of tragedy.

A retired psychologist and a World War II veteran who provided emergency counseling on site, and later worked with many of the victims of the bombing, described his psychological preparedness gained from war experiences:

> The Murrah bombing has diminished significance when compared with 130 consecutive days of combat, including the Huertgen Forrest, Battle of the Bulge, totally destroyed towns, daily fire fights with 25–80% casualties, personal wounds, and killing the enemy.... The growth as a result of WWII has allowed me great stability in the face of current trauma.

Other survivors described this same kind of "protective armor" in responding to the tragedy of 9/11 after going through the Oklahoma City bombing:

> 9/11 did not shake me. After surviving the Murrah bombing, I can handle anything now.

> I was already "changed" by my experience of 4/19/95. The events of 9/11/01 only reaffirmed for me that you never know what life may hold in store. In some ways I have a greater appreciation of life.

> My immediate response was shock, fear, feeling that everything had changed, and great sadness. In some ways, though, having been through the Murrah bombing was helpful in that I was able to be much more empathetic with my friends living in NYC and DC. I had a sense of the depth of feeling experienced on 9/11 and immediately after but also that it would slowly get better.

> Since the bombing I have been so much more aware of my mortality and that of others and the preciousness of every day. As time has passed, I don't want to forget that as there are "should" and "ought" pressures, many aren't all that important in the long term. 9/11 has changed me in terms of more preparedness, as well as reminding me again, life is short and precious.

However, one survivor reported being "hardened" as opposed to prepared as a result of his earlier experiences: "The attacks on 9/11 hardened me even further. I was also a resident of the Khobar Towers in Saudi Arabia. The result of that looked identical to the OKC Bombing. Events seem to be worsening. What is next? Will I be present for that too?" And a woman whose husband died in the bombing found the 9/11 attacks too much to contend with:

> I was going in to work late that morning and watched it unfold on TV. I was shocked and actually felt terror that it would happen again to my work place in the social security building in Birmingham. I could not reach anyone at work for about three hours. We had several bomb threats prior to 9/11/01 and each one left me shaken and unable to concentrate on my job. I opted out of interviewing applicants and retired 11/30/2001.

PSYCHOLOGICAL GROWTH IS NOT INCONSISTENT WITH PSYCHOLOGICAL DISTRESS

Similar to some other studies (e.g., Caddell, Regehr, & Hemworth, 2003; Pargament, Smith, Koenig & Perez, 1998), the findings of this study support Calhoun and Tedeschi's

(1998, 1999, 2004) premise that some degree of continuing distress about a traumatic event may be needed for PTG to occur. Participants who met full criteria for PTSD reported significantly more PTG than those who did not meet the criteria for the diagnosis. The number of women meeting the DSM-IV criteria for posttraumatic stress was significantly higher than males who met the criteria. Females scored significantly higher on all five factors of the PTGI than male subjects. Thus, in this group, PTG and psychological distress seemed to be independent dimensions and the presence of growth was not necessarily reflected in a reduction of psychological pain (Calhoun & Tedeschi, 1998).

One of the most seriously injured survivors suffered 40 broken or crushed bones and underwent 16 surgeries. For several months after the explosion, she was kept in an induced coma by her doctors so she would not remember as much of the pain. She took her first steps 9 months after the bombing. She continues to experience severe pain and symptoms of PTSD. Her responses on the PTGI indicate considerable positive change particularly in appreciating life, feelings of self-reliance, and a significantly stronger religious faith: "Whatever I lost I've gained back triple through my spiritual walk with Jesus. I am so grateful to greet each day" (Pastore, 2000). She works as a volunteer with the Salvation Army Women's Auxiliary helping people in need, such as battered women and alcoholics. She also volunteers one day a week at the Oklahoma State Capitol selling souvenirs.

Another survivor who held a management position was in the bombing and assisted with recovery and relocation efforts for her agency. She returned to work April 20, 1995. One week after the 9/11 attacks she suffered an ocular migraine that resulted in blindness in one eye and she resumed counseling for symptoms of PTSD. However, she reported a significant degree of change in her priorities about what is important in life, an appreciation of the value of her own life and each day, and a new found tendency to change things that need changing and engage in new opportunities.

THE NECESSITY OF REFLECTION AND REEVALUATION

Events are traumatic in that they challenge our basic assumptions about what is meaningful and predictable. When traumas are experienced we are forced to change or re-create schemas to make the world meaningful or manageable again; hence the lay term a *new normal* (Calhoun & Tedeschi, 1998; Janoff-Bulman, this volume) was repeatedly offered by community leaders to explain a new existence postbombing. To make sense of and adapt to the trauma experience and rebuild a new worldview, individuals engage in a process of cognitive processing or rumination.

Unlike the distressing intrusive thought processes that occur for most survivors immediately after the event, this kind of cognitive processing focuses more on repair and accommodation of the assumptive world (Tedeschi & Calhoun, 2004). It is these thought processes that allow one to reconstruct a new view of one's self and the world or realize PTG. Without this reconstructive process, a survivor's experience may remain a silent story, unintegrated, unexpressed, and unsupported by others (Neimeyer, 2004). The survivor is left only with the negative aspects of the trauma without the possibility of potential growth.

The following description summarizes the feelings of a bombing survivor when she received a subpoena to testify in the Terry Nichols trial. This individual resisted talking about surviving the bombing, even in occasional therapy sessions over the years. Her reaction illustrates that the therapist cannot "make" a person engage in the kind of reflection or processing necessary to develop a new world view and find meaning in having experienced the event, even if she feels strongly about the benefits of doing so.

A 33-year-old female who worked in one of the federal agencies was knocked unconscious when the blast occurred. She suffered serious head and eye injuries that caused her to remain in the hospital for several weeks. Because she could not remember the actual event, she maintained that she was not distressed by the bombing and was impatient with those who "complained and brought attention to themselves." While her refusal to be a "victim" as she described it was impressive, her complete denial of any residual effects of the bombing was curious as her injuries necessitated several surgeries and rehabilitation for many years. Her concerns in occasional therapy sessions focused on her unhappiness with her current job and general feelings of boredom with her life. Approximately 9 years after the bombing she came for an appointment because she was angry she had received a subpoena to testify in the Terry Nichols trial. "I told the witness coordinator that she didn't want me to testify because I was not sure what I would do. The courtroom is small and if I saw Terry Nichols sitting right across from me I might just get up and tear him apart—and I could do it too. I'm not about to be in the same room with that man." Her agitation grew as she continued to describe her feelings about the trial and Nichols. Her heightened emotional state was completely incongruent with her previous denial of having any feelings about the bombing. Not surprisingly, she denied any perceptions of positive change in her life as a result of having gone through the bombing experience.

FURTHER EVIDENCE OF THE NECESSITY OF THINKING ABOUT THE TRAUMA

The execution of Timothy McVeigh was a well-publicized event. The U.S. Attorney's office mailed out 1100 letters asking survivors and family members if they would like to personally attend the execution in Terra Haute, Indiana. Those that did not go to Terra Haute were given the opportunity to watch by closed circuit television in Oklahoma City. The impending execution brought out opposing feelings about the death penalty and expectations about what the execution would do for the "healing" process. Many felt they could get on with their lives if "justice" was done and McVeigh was put to death.

One survivor's response to the question about how the events on 9/11 might have affected or changed her wrote that the execution did not give her the relief she anticipated:

> I saw the explosion over and over and it looked somewhat like the Murrah bombing, but on a much larger scale. I was afraid for weeks. I hated going to work. I have a lot of problems with fear. I know how scared they were, my heart cried for them. Sometimes, I just want to get in my car and disappear. Life will never be the same. I do not recommend others watching executions of those guilty.

The study also assessed the feelings experienced at the execution of McVeigh. Participants were asked to select from the following phrases to describe their feelings postexecution of Timothy McVeigh: (a) I experienced a sense of relief, (b) I experienced a sense of closure, (c) I felt justice had been done, (d) I felt anger that he got off too easy, (e) I felt sadness at the loss of another human being, (f) I had no feelings one way or another, and (g) other. Those who responded they "had no feelings one way or another," scored significantly lower on the PTGI than subjects who chose any of the other responses. Because of the extensive media and newspaper coverage of the trial, sentencing, and execution of McVeigh, for an individual closely involved in the bombing to "have no feelings about it one way or another" suggests the possibility of less thinking about or processing of the event. Because cognitive processing may be critical to the process of realizing PTG, it is not surprising that subjects who selected this response indicated significantly lower PTG than those who reported some kind of thought about the event.

FINDINGS ON FORGIVENESS

There was no *significant* relationship between the Heartland Forgiveness Scale and the PTGI for the subjects in the study. However, there were interesting gender differences on the Heartland Forgiveness Inventory responses. Male subjects scored significantly higher than females on the total forgiveness score and two of the three factors: self-forgiveness and situation forgiveness. Subjects with a family member who died in the bombing scored significantly lower on the factors of self-forgiveness and situation forgiveness than non-family members. Subjects who met the criteria for PTSD scored significantly lower than subjects who did not meet the criteria for PTSD on total forgiveness and all three factors of the Heartland Forgiveness Inventory (Self, Other, and Situation Forgiveness).

It is not surprising that family members scored significantly lower on Self-Forgiveness than other subjects. Family members who lose a loved one suddenly have no time to say good-bye and are often left with "unfinished business." They may blame themselves for not being able to prevent the circumstances of their loved one's death. If the death occurred during a time when the relationship was undergoing a stressful period or incident, feelings of guilt and self-blame can be intensified. The significantly lower score on situation forgiveness for family members may reflect unresolved feelings of anger about the government's assumed lack of disclosure of all the facts and/or a belief in one or more of the conspiracy theories that McVeigh did not act alone. It may also reflect a refusal or inability to make peace with the bad situations in life.

The significantly lower score for subjects diagnosed with PTSD on the total score and all three factors of the Heartland Forgiveness Inventory suggests that significant psychological distress may interfere with the process of forgiveness, but does not prevent the realization of positive benefits from going through the experience.

Models of Forgiveness

"To forgive is to set a prisoner free and discover the prisoner was you."—Lewis Smedes

"The weak can never forgive. Forgiveness is the attribute of the strong."—Mahatma Gandhi

Religious leaders and spiritual counselors have long preached the value of forgiveness. The capacity to release bitterness and embrace compassion toward others is a central component of most of the world's spiritual traditions. However, despite its long history in traditional views of optimal human functioning (McCullough & Worthington, 1994), psychology's interest in the concept of forgiveness and its effect on psychological functioning is more recent. Only within the past decade, have social scientists and psychologists begun to empirically study forgiveness as a "key part of psychological healing" (Hope, 1987, p. 240.).

The literature describes several perspectives or models of forgiveness. Scobie and Scobie (1998) group these models under four general headings: (a) health models associated with giving up anger and resentment that result in improved health and well-being; (b) philosophical models concerned with forgiveness as a moral virtue; (c) Christian models based on the premise that individual forgiveness mirrors divine forgiveness; and (d) prosocial models that view forgiveness as a form of altruistic behavior that restores and maintains interpersonal relationships.

Most counseling and psychotherapy models fall under the health model where forgiveness is understood as "letting go" of bitterness toward an offender. The release of negative emotions results in decreased anger, resentment, guilt, and anxiety. When negative feelings are replaced with positive ones toward the offender, such as empathy and humility (McCollough, Sandage & Worthington, 1997) or beneficence and compassion (Enright & The Human Development Study Group, 1991; North, 1987), a change in perspective is possible.

Baumeister, Exline, and Sommer (1999) describe two dimensions of forgiveness: intrapsychic and interpersonal. Intrapsychic involves the emotional and cognitive aspects of forgiveness where interpersonal forgiveness involves social or behavioral aspects. If one engages in interpersonal forgiveness (i.e., verbally expresses the words to the offender) without the presence of intrapsychic forgiveness, then true forgiveness is not achieved. In Haber's (1991) view of forgiveness, the words "I forgive you" are a performance utterance (Austin, 1975), which means it cannot be separated from the behavior it represents (Scobie & Scobie, 1998).

When compassion, benevolence, and love are extended unconditionally toward the offender in spite of the transgressions, forgiveness becomes a moral act (Al-Mabuk, Enright, & Cardis, 1995; Enright & Zell, 1989). Thus forgiveness becomes more than a change in internal feelings; it is a conscious decision to change one's thoughts about and actions towards an offender (Diblasio, 1998, 2000; Sanderson & Linehan, 1999). By doing so, the forgiver is able to begin the process of moving in a new direction, from judgmental to understanding, from resentful to loving, from anxious to relaxed, from conflicted to cooperative (Enright & Fitzgibbons, 2002, p. 24).

ARE THERE PREREQUISITES FOR FORGIVENESS?

Several variables influence whether forgiveness occurs following an offense. Empathy, apology, the severity of the offense, and the relationship between the victim and offender (McCullough, 2000; McCullough et al., 1998) influence forgiveness. Personality traits, early family learning, the self-worth of the victim, (Scobie & Scobie, 1998), and the incomprehensibility of the perpetrator's motives (Baumeister, Stillwell, & Wotman, 1990) influence the victim's capacity to forgive.

Apology is one way of acknowledging the pain and suffering experienced by victims. While there is some evidence that an apology is not associated with forgiveness, (Zechmeister & Romero, 2002), other studies have established that receiving an apology encourages forgiving (Darby & Schlenker, 1982; Enright, Santos, & Al-Mabuk, 1989; McCullough et al., 1998). Forgiveness is more likely if the apology offered "names the offense," communicates the perpetrator's responsibility of wrongdoing, and demonstrates genuine remorse and regret for the harm caused by the act (Tavuchis, 1991). When this occurs, empathy is induced in the victim (Baumeister, Stillwell, & Heatherton, 1995; Gobodo-Madikizela, 2003), which allows the victim to recognize the emotional pain the perpetrator is experiencing as a result of the crime. This identification with the perpetrator occurs "because there is something in the other that is felt to be part of the self and something in the self that is felt to belong to the other" (Gobodo-Madikizela, 2003, p. 127). However, if the apology fails to effectively communicate repentance, genuine remorse, and regret, the result is a "botched apology" (Lazare, 1995), which may create further harm by increasing the victim's anger and bitterness.

Some argue that victim impact statements and truth commissions facilitate the healing process as they give survivors an opportunity to tell their stories, forcing the perpetrator to hear the consequences of the crime. Public testimony before a listening audience allows others to validate the victim's experience, which can be transformative and cathartic (Minow, 1998). Victim impact statements have been a factor in court decisions; however, there is little empirical evidence that public testimony facilitates forgiveness. Kaminer, Stein, Mbanga, and Zungu-Dirwayi (2001) found that giving no testimony, testifying publicly, or testifying privately before the Truth and Reconciliation Commission was not associated with psychiatric status or level of forgiveness in 134 survivors of human rights abuses in South Africa. The only variable associated significantly with forgiveness was gender.

IS THE RESOLUTION OF ANGER NECESSARY FOR FORGIVENESS?

Interventions that promote forgiveness of transgressions are suggested as important components of anger therapies (Digiuseppe & Tafrate, 2001; Enright & Fitzgibbons, 2002; Fitzgibbons, 1986, 1998; Thomas, 2003) in that a good deal of anger occurs from condemning those who have infringed against us. The two most important unforgiving responses, rehearsing past aversive events and harboring grudges, are associated with blame, revenge, hostility, and staying in the role of victim (Kassinove & Tafrate, 2002).

Because traumatic events shatter assumptions about justice and fairness in the world, individuals often experience distrust, betrayal, sadness, and fear. Anger is often a defense for these feelings because it externalizes the responsibility for distress, thereby decreasing the need to confront internal problems (Sipprelle, 1992). When aspects of the traumatic event involve the betrayal of important relationships, the unresolved aspect of the trauma may be centered on this "breach of trust" (Herman, 1992). Chronic feelings of betrayal and injustice can trigger anger episodes that occur immediately or years after the trauma.

An example of feelings of betrayal and unresolved anger is exemplified by a survivor of the Oklahoma City bombing several years after the bombing when he speaks about the government's refusal to pay his medical claims for injuries sustained in the bombing and going back on its promise not to ask the survivors to move into the new federal building: "I have forgiven Timothy McVeigh. I have not forgiven the government for their broken promises." Survivors had initially been promised compensation for their psychological and physical injuries. However, "fighting for benefits" became a way of life for many survivors who were denied payment of certain medical bills or denied worker's compensation. The final insult came when employees of a federal agency were asked to move into the new Federal Building built across the street from the Memorial after being assured they would not have to do so.

Another survivor who worked in that agency echoed similar feelings of betrayal about the location of the new federal building and being asked to move in after the events of 9/11: "It is unforgivable that they [government agency leaders] are so insensitive to us and our needs. It appears that everyone is more concerned about the well-being of the firemen and police in the aftermath of the 9/11 attack than they are to us that endured the Murrah bombing."

Another survivor conveyed feelings of fear, along with anger, about the new federal building:

> The attacks on 9/11 made me more afraid of being another target. Having to move to the new federal building makes me afraid that we will be targeted again by some crazy that has decided he will finish what McVeigh started. I can't believe they would ask us do this after promising us we would not have to move to that location.

For individuals who have been victimized, anger may initially create the psychological distance necessary to feel safe and to preserve a sense of integrity (Davenport, 1991;

Lifton, 1988). However, chronic feelings of anger are associated with higher levels of depression (Enright & Fitzgibbons, 2002), interfere with problem resolution, hinder positive interactions with others, damage interpersonal relationships (Hargrave & Sells, 1997), and may prove to be a burden that prevents victims from fully coming to terms with the trauma and moving on (Gobodo-Madikizela, 2003).

RESOLVING ANGER THROUGH FORGIVENESS

One option for resolving anger resulting from trauma is through forgiveness. Even if divested of its religious significance and moral qualities, forgiveness can be defined as a problem-solving strategy (McCullough & Worthington, 1994) and an adaptive coping skill, (Droll, 1985; Sanderson & Linehan, 1999; Thompson & Snyder, 2000) because it enables a person to release negative cognitions, emotions, and behaviors that are the common sequelae of transgressions. In giving up negative thoughts, emotions, and behaviors, an individual is able to focus on positive strategies to move past the crisis or trauma. There is evidence that forgiveness improves psychological well-being (Al-Mabuk et al., 1995; Coates, 1997; Freedman & Enright, 1996; Hebl & Enright, 1993), improves health (Witvliet, Ludwig, & Vander Lann, 2001), and assists individuals in decreasing anger, anxiety, and grief (Coyle & Enright, 1997). Conversely, people who blame others for their difficult circumstances are likely to have more psychological difficulties than are people who do not (Downey, Silver, & Wortman, 1990; Tennen & Affleck, 1990).

Fitzgibbons (1986, 1998) suggests that the expression of forgiveness may be cognitive, emotional, or spiritual. Cognitive forgiveness occurs when there is conviction and determination to forgive, but there are no feelings of forgiveness, compassion, or love toward the injurer. Others who are deeply hurt simply cannot bring themselves to forgive, despite the desire to do so. In such cases, the individual may express spiritual forgiveness by turning to God and asking for help to forgive. Those that understand and extend compassion toward the offender engage in emotional forgiveness.

Regardless of the expression, forgiveness is a complex task that is often filled with struggles and ambivalence. However, if one could neither forgive nor expect forgiveness from others for all the hurts, wrongs, or disappointments given and received, one would be caught in perpetual punishment, personal despair, social chaos, and war (Sanderson & Linehan, 1999, p. 208).

POSSIBLE EXPLANATIONS FOR THE LACK OF RELATIONSHIP BETWEEN FORGIVENESS AND POSTTRAUMATIC GROWTH

According to Tedeschi and Calhoun's (1995) premise that acquiring PTG propels one to a higher level of functioning posttrauma, factors that promote adaptive coping might be anticipated to facilitate the process of growth. Likewise, unconstructive behaviors, cognitions, and feelings, such as avoidance, pessimism, anger, and lack of forgiveness, would be expected to foster maladaptive coping, decreasing the chance of realizing PTG. Thus the lack of a significant positive association between PTG and forgiveness calls for an exploration of possible explanations.

Forgiveness Means Different Things to Different People

Although *forgiveness* is a word commonly used in conversation, its definition is broad. People think differently about forgiveness and perceive its meaning differently depending on the context. In a study assessing individuals' concepts of forgiveness, Mullet, Girard, and Bakhshi (2004) found strong individual differences in the way people conceptualize forgiveness although parents and their college-age children tended to conceptualize forgiveness similarly.

Forgiveness can be interpreted as condoning, excusing, or justifying an offense. Some believe forgiveness indicates a willingness to reconcile with the offender. Forgiveness is often associated with forgetting: forgive and forget. For those whose family member was killed by the deliberate act of another, forgiveness may be construed as minimizing the significance of the act and, thereby, being disloyal to the memory of the deceased.

Timing of the Study

This study was conducted immediately after the terrorist attacks on September 11, 2001. The protocol for the study was designed and accepted prior to 9/11. However, because the attacks occurred immediately before the distribution of the protocol, an additional open-ended question was added to assess how this event impacted the survivors of the Oklahoma City bombing. In response to the question "How did the attacks on 9/11 affect you or change you?" many of the survivors' responses indicated they experienced severe psychological distress:

> I felt a renewed anxiousness that I have not felt in years. I have once again had to take deliberate actions to protect my emotional well-being (i.e., avoid TV about the bombing, focus on other things).

> Nightmares came back about the OKC bombing. I have cut myself off from friends and only want to be at home all the time. I have again restricted my activities and feel guilty if I have fun.

> I felt as if the bombing had happened all over again. I even went for counseling. I've had to avoid all media coverage of 9/11.

> Since the attacks I have been unable to sleep through the night. I toss and turn like a fish out of water. I have become very nervous. I have begun taking my Paxil once again. I feel so much compassion for the people in NYC and DC. Until you've been through what they have experienced, you cannot possibly know how they feel. Now they know what we survivors have gone through in our lives. You can move on, but the hurt is always lingering in the back of your mind and heart. Nightmares have become a part of my life once again!

> I experienced the same emotions/feelings as I experienced on the day of the bombing. I was fearful, sad, angry, tearful, unable to concentrate, and I immediately wanted to leave the courthouse because of fear for my personal safety. It has increased my need to know where my family members are at all times and my need to be home where I feel safe.

> It took me back to 4/19 and I felt like every thing I experienced that day came back and found me.

> Brought about a flood of the feelings I was dealing with already. I found that what I thought was complete, returned to be dealt with again.

> I watched the TV as the planes flew into the WTC and the Pentagon and broke down completely. It was just like the OKC bombing in that I couldn't take my eyes off the TV—with all the updates, replays, etc. I cried all day and was depressed for days. Memories came back that I had suppressed for years.

Family members of those killed in the bombing had similar reactions. A woman whose sister died described her feelings: "On September 11, 2001, I cried. I felt like I was going through April 19 all over again. The pictures of the destroyed twin towers—ground zero—brought everything back. It has been a very sad time for me."

A man whose 46-year-old wife was killed describes his reaction:

> I was at my desk the morning of September 11 when several coworkers became excited and said "**, come into the conference room." They had the TV on and it was showing the first airplane and the Trade Center. While standing there in numbness, the 2nd plane flew into the 2nd tower. My mind instantly flew back to April the 19th. I felt like my chest was caving in. I spent the whole day with flashbacks for April the 19th. My heart felt like it was breaking in two, not only for the memories but because someone else was fixing to have their world shattered beyond anything they could imagine.

FORGIVENESS AND SURVIVORS OF TRAUMA

Miller describes murder as "the ultimate violation that one individual can inflict on another, a brutal, purposeful assault forced on an unwilling victim" (2002, p. 285). In addition to intense grief for the loss of their loved one, the murder of a family member forces survivors to come face to face with issues of fairness, justice, and assumptions about the very meaning of life. "The especially cruel and purposeful nature of terrorist murder compounds the rage, grief, and despair of the survivors" (Miller, 2002, p. 285). Thus, being the victim of or losing a loved one to a mass terrorist attack complicates and prolongs the task of grief and healing.

Some clinicians who work with victims of trauma claim that the assumption that survivors have to experience forgiveness for the perpetrator is not only unlikely, it may exacerbate feelings of low self-worth or be perceived as minimizing the brutality incurred (McCullough & Worthington, 1994). Some consider forgiveness in the context of sexual trauma unwise (Bass & Davis, 1988) and potentially dangerous (Engle, 1989) because it may indirectly bestow power back on the perpetrator instead of empowering the victim. And forgiving out of a sense of duty or fear of retaliation may increase negative emotions and thoughts about the offense over time (Trainer, 1984).

Herman (1992) warns that some survivors attempt to bypass their outrage altogether through a fantasy of forgiveness that "often becomes a cruel torture because it remains out of reach for most ordinary human beings" (p. 190). Others suggest that a victim's response of hatred and resentment is a necessary prior condition for an expression of forgiveness and that people who show no resentment for the injustices done to them lack self-respect (Taft, 2003).

In writing about the difficulties of forgiving the perpetrators following Apartheid, Gobodo-Madikizela (2003) suggests that many survivors hold on to hatred to distance themselves from pain and avoid acknowledging that the perpetrators are human beings: "Anger and resentment become the only personal 'possessions' that the individual now has in place of the loved one" (p. 97). These emotions stand in the place of what was lost and become an important part of the traumatized person's identity.

To some, letting go of anger and considering the act of forgiveness is embracing evil and perpetuating injustice. For example, the mother of an Israeli woman killed in a terrorist attack by the Popular Front for the Liberation of Palestine tells her daughter's friend who survived the attack that if she forgives the attacker she is encouraging terrorism (Cohen-Gerstel, 2001). Holding on to anger may serve as a barrier to accepting the perpetrator as part of the human race. If we engage the perpetrator as a real person, we will be compromising our morals and lowering entry requirements into the human community (Gobodo-Madikizela, 2003, p. 120).

IS FORGIVENESS POSSIBLE FOR SURVIVORS OF VIOLENT CRIMES?

Despite the potential harm in forgiving perpetrators of violent crimes, there is some evidence that forgiveness decreases negative feelings. Forgiveness therapy for incest survivors has been shown to increase feelings of forgiveness toward the abuser and decrease depression and anxiety (Freedman & Enright, 1996). A study using Enright's Process Model of Forgiveness (Enright & Human Development Study Group, 1991) with adolescent and adult refugees who had experienced war demonstrated a significant correlation between forgiveness and trauma recovery (Peddle, 2001). However, Conner, Davidson, and Lee (2003) found no association between forgiveness and well-being or health status in a sample of 648 survivors of violent trauma.

While some individuals simply cannot or will not forgive the perpetrator, Gobodo-Madikizela (2003) believes that there are internal psychological dynamics that propel us toward forming an empathic connection with another person in pain and draw us into that pain, regardless of who that someone is. She describes this as the "power of human connection" (p. 127) or a moment of humanity.

An example of a "moment of humanity" where forgiveness is granted is exemplified by a woman who lost her 42-year-old husband in the Oklahoma City bombing. A 40-year-old mother of three spent the first year after her husband's murder going to the theater, to concerts, buying tickets to any event she could. She did this in addition to working full time and keeping up a large house on 10 acres (including tending a large garden because her husband had always planted a garden). She coped by spending almost every minute of her time doing something—anything! The second year she ran out of energy and the reality of her husband's death hit her full force. In addition to feelings of intense loss, she found herself consumed with hate for Timothy McVeigh and his attorney, which was quite troubling for her: "I am a Christian and I am not a person who believes that one should feel this kind of hatred towards others. I don't like myself for having this kind of hate—but I cannot seem to let it go."

Like all survivors and family members, she was given an opportunity to fly to Denver, Colorado, to attend the trial for a few days. While she was there she happened to see McVeigh's father sitting alone at the bar in the hotel where she was staying. She commented that "he looked so alone." She spontaneously went over to him and put her hand on his shoulder. "Mr. McVeigh, I want you to know how sorry I am that you have to go through this. I want you to know that I am thinking about you." She did not tell him that her husband had been killed in the bombing or that she was there for the trial. As she later described this experience: "When I put my hand on his shoulder and told him that I was thinking of him I felt the hatred melt away. It was remarkable."

While she did not make a human connection with the man who killed her husband, she did connect with his father because she was able to empathize with his condition. That empathy, extended to his father "in a moment of humanity," allowed her to dissipate her own feelings of hatred toward his son. In writing about her reaction to the 9/11 attacks, she described her heightened emotionality but also the absence of feelings of hate:

> The feelings of sheer disbelief, horror, fear, and anger all came up. I am not sure in what order. I felt sick, physically sick. I have learned never to compare my feelings, as one who has dealt with a purposeful act of murder against someone whom I love, with others who

have been in this same situation. I think more about life as we know it, but I refuse to live in fear. It is impossible for me to understand the thinking of those people responsible for those crashes. How can anyone? But then how can I understand McVeigh? Maybe it's the utter hatred that baffles me. I know about hatred, but I also know how to let it go. He didn't and neither do the people that planned the 9/11 attacks.

CONCLUSION

Living in an era when the threat of violence and terror is real, the concepts of PTG and forgiveness will only grow in importance for those of us in the helping profession. As therapists, our goal is to help individuals who experience purposeful acts of terror or violence not only reduce the distressing emotions that accompany these experiences, but also return to a life of meaning and purpose. The act of forgiveness offers the possibility of a new beginning from the injuries of the past. Posttraumatic growth offers us a way to understand a newfound appreciation for life and psychological strength that may result from coping with past trauma. A therapist's understanding and facilitation of both forgiveness and PTG can offer hope and healing not otherwise available to our clients.

Stories of notable individuals who have forgiven those who have caused them extreme injury are embedded in our culture (e.g., Jesus Christ, Ghandi, Martin Luther King, and Nelson Mandela). Remarkable stories of forgiveness also occur every day. In a recent therapy group, a Vietnam veteran expressed his feelings of forgiveness toward the killers of his daughters. One had been run over by an automobile while she played in the yard at the age of two; the other was raped and murdered and thrown out on a highway at the age of 14: "I had to forgive their killers. I just could not have survived if I had held on to the hate and rage that I initially had. It would have killed me." He also described some new found strengths from having gone through this horrific experience: "I can help others by telling them what I've been through and encouraging them that they can live through tragedy."

Thus, it is clear that some individuals can forgive others for deep injustices and are able to liberate themselves, to some degree, from resentment and bitterness and move forward in life. And when individuals reflect on the experience of having coped with a traumatic event, they can acquire a new way of thinking about and understanding themselves and the world. They are often able to transcend the trauma by finding a new direction in life and give to others in ways they never dreamed possible.

Intuitively, it seems clear that PTG and forgiveness are linked in the journey to make sense of, and heal from, past trauma. However, there is little empirical evidence to support this intuitive "truth."

Perspectives on forgiveness are broad and varied. Theology, philosophy, sociology, and, more recently, psychology, offer theories of forgiveness. However, there are few models of forgiveness that attempt to integrate these different perspectives. Even in the psychology field, there is a continuing debate over how forgiveness should be conceptualized and measured (Enright & Fitzgibbons, 2002; McCullough, 2000), and whether it is a process that takes time to unfold or a change that can be accomplished in a single therapy session (Diblasio, 1998). For subjects in the Oklahoma City bombing study (Fischer, 2002), the level of forgiveness is likely associated with the timing of the study when many subjects were experiencing significant distress triggered by the events of 9/11.

Forgiveness of a crime of violence or terrorism is especially difficult. Attempting to recover from cruel, purposeful acts of violence is an undertaking that appears seemingly impossible to comprehend. The bombing experience in Oklahoma City, for example, did not offer the survivors or victims' families any of the conditions that facilitate forgiveness. The act was random and incomprehensible. McVeigh did not admit his deed or express shame or remorse for his act. To add insult to injury, he described the children who were killed in the Murrah Building as "collateral." He refused to make a final statement and instead released a copy of William Henley's 19th-century poem, *Invictus*, with the words "I am the master of my fate, the captain of my soul."

Unfortunately, McVeigh's refusal to show remorse is not unique. It is not often that victims are given answers as "to why" or witness remorse by the perpetrator. Fortunately, successful coping or the decision to forgive does not depend on contrition from the perpetrator. Both are influenced by personal and cultural factors. To understand the role of forgiveness in growth outcomes, it is essential to consider the influences of the the distal culture and the influences of proximate culture.

The litigious atmosphere of our country impedes the likelihood of expressions of wrongdoing and remorse, at least in the legal system. Lawsuits, the purposes of which are to establish the fault of one party and offer relief to the other (Taft, 2000), have become a common part of our vocabulary. The "we versus them" aspect of our legal system is also demonstrated in our political discourse. Frequently the opposition is demonized and a campaign strategy of dividing the electorate is not only a viable, but also often a successful option. Further, governments that enforce the death penalty prevent the possibility that some perpetrators might eventually acknowledge the damage they have caused and offer remorse to survivors and family members.

Proximate cultural influences may be more important to investigate in assessing PTG (Calhoun & Tedeschi, 2004) and forgiveness. Personal interactions with others, particularly those that have personal significance for the individual, are likely to have a major impact on the way PTG unfolds (Calhoun & Tedeschi, 2004). For example, even when individuals share the same geographic locality, the messages received from family members, coworkers, and friends can vary from empathic listening to sending clear messages that they "do not want to hear it," both of which effect how the survivor construes the traumatic experience. Similarly, conceptualizations about forgiveness are influenced by messages received from proximate, culture-laden systems, such as parenting and child-rearing systems, educational systems, economic systems and the legal system.

Therapists have a unique opportunity to offer a "culture" of forgiveness for clients who seek help dealing with the aftermath of a crisis. However, if they are uncomfortable with the issues of forgiveness and spirituality, the client may be denied the opportunity to explore this possibility. Although interventions to facilitate forgiveness are increasingly being developed, the lack of literature on forgiveness may have more to do with biases that existed in psychology toward concepts associated with spirituality (Diblasio, 2000). One study found that 77% of the therapists studied indicated they try to live their personal lives according to their spiritual beliefs, but only 29% felt that spiritual matters are important for therapy (Bergin & Jensen, 1990). Others indicate they were in favor of discussing forgiveness in therapy, but as a group have not developed techniques and strategies for its clinical use (Diblasio & Benda, 1991).

Calhoun and Tedeschi (2004) suggest that for too long, clinicians may have short-changed trauma survivors by focusing so closely on the reduction of symptoms that they may have inadvertently failed to accompany them as they reorder their lives (p. 98). The same can be said about the possibility of forgiveness and other issues associated with spirituality. In providing the client an opportunity to explore these issues, we may facilitate the reconstruction of a life narrative that includes forgiveness and tolerance, and a greater appreciation of life, increased personal strength, and spirituality.

Individuals can experience PTG without engaging in forgiveness. And some individuals will never forgive. What is undetermined is whether survivors of violence and trauma could acquire more growth if they were able to forgive the perpetrator, or whether they might experience less internal distress or different growth patterns. Could a "more profound understanding of the self and the world" (Tedeschi & Calhoun, 1995, p. 87) also include a greater understanding of our humaneness if trauma survivors were able to forgive? Living in an era when tolerance and understanding of others is crucial, it seems only prudent to embrace all interventions that may help clients overcome bitterness and anger from past injury. To do so might make the connection between PTG and forgiveness more than an intuitive truth.

REFERENCES

Affleck, G., & Tennen, H. (1996). Construing benefits from adversity: Adaptational significance and dispositional underpinnings. *Journal of Personality, 64*, 899–922.

Aldwin, C. M. (1994, August). *The California Coping Inventory.* Paper presented at the annual meeting of the American Psychological Association, Los Angeles.

Al-Mabuk, R. H., Enright, R. D., & Cardis, P. A. (1995). Forgiveness education with parentally love-deprived late adolescents. *Journal of Moral Education, 24*, 427–444.

American Psychiatric Association. (1980). *Diagnostic and statistical manual of mental disorders* (3rd ed.). Washington, DC: Author.

Armeli, S., Gunthert, K. D., & Cohen, L. H. (2001). Stressors, appraisals, coping, and post-event outcomes: The dimensionality and antecedents of stress-related growth. *Journal of Social and Clinical Psychology, 20*, 366–395.

Austin, J. L. (1975). How to do things with words. In J. O. Urmson & M. Sbisa (Eds.), *The William James Lectures delivered at Harvard University in 1955.* Oxford: Clarendon Press.

Bass, E., & Davis, L. (1998). *The courage to heal: A guide for women survivors of child sexual abuse.* New York: Harper & Row.

Baumeister, R. F., Exline, J. J., & Sommer, K. L. (1999). The victim role, grudge theory, and two dimensions of forgiveness. In E. L. Worthington, Jr. (Ed.), *Dimensions of forgiveness. Psychological research and theological perspectives* (pp. 79–104). Philadelphia: Templeton Foundation Press.

Baumeister, R. F., Stillwell, A. M., & Heatherton, T. F. (1995). Personal narratives about guilt: Role in action and interpersonal relationships. *Basic and Applied Social Psychology, 17*, 173–198.

Baumeister, R. F., Stillwell, A., & Wotman, S. R. (1990). Victim and perpetrator accounts of interpersonal conflict: Autobiographical narratives about anger. *Journal of Personality and Social Psychology, 59*, 994–1005.

Bergin, A. E., & Jensen, J. P. (1990). Religiosity of psychotherapists: A national survey, *Psychotherapy, 27*, 3–7.

Berkman, L., & Syme, S. L. (1994). Social networks, host resistance, and mortality: A nine year follow-up study of Alameda County residents. In A. Steptoe, & K. Wardle, (Eds.) *Psychosocial processes and health: A reader* (pp. 43–67) Cambridge: Cambridge University.

Brunello, N., Davidson, J., Deahl, M., Kassler, R. C., Mendlew, J., Racagni, G., et al. (2001). Posttraumatic stress disorder: Diagnosis and epidemiology, comorbidity and social consequences, biology and treatment. *Neuropsychobiology, 43*(3) 150–162.

Cadell, S., Regehr, C., & Hemsworth (2003). Factors contributing to a posttraumatic growth: A proposed structural equation model. *American Journal of Orthopsychiatry, 3*(73), 279–287.

Calhoun, L. G., & Tedeschi, R. G. (1998). Posttraumatic growth: Future directions. In R. G. Tedeschi, C. L. Park, & L. G. Calhoun (Eds.), *Posttraumatic growth: Positive change in the aftermath of crisis* (pp. 215–238). Mahwah, NJ: Lawrence Erlbaum Associates.

Calhoun, L. G., & Tedeschi, R. G. (1999). *Facilitating posttraumatic growth: A clinician's guide.* Mahwah, NJ: Lawrence Erlbaum Associates.

Calhoun, L. G., & Tedeschi, R. G. (2004). Foundations of posttraumatic growth: New considerations. *Psychological Inquiry, 15*(1) 93–102.

Carver, C. S., Scheier, M. F., & Weintraub, J. K. (1989). Assessing coping strategies: A theoretically based approach. *Journal of Personality and Social Psychology, 56*, 267–283.

Coates, D. (1997). The correlations of forgiveness of self, forgiveness of others, and hostility, depression, anxiety, self-esteem, life adaptation, and religiosity among female victims of domestic violence. (Doctoral dissertation California School of Professional Psychology, Fresno, CA) *Dissertation Abstracts International, B, 58*(5-B), 2667.

Cohen-Gerstel, Y. (Writer). (2001). *My Terrorist* [Motion picture]. (Available from Women Make Movies, 462 Broadway, Suite 500, New York, NY 10013)

Conner, K. M., Davidson, J. R., & Lee, L. (2003). Spirituality, resilience, and anger in survivors of violent trauma: A community survey. *Journal of Traumatic Stress, 16*(5), 487–494.

Coyle, C. T., & Enright, R. D. (1997). Forgiveness intervention with post-abortion men. *Journal of Consulting and Clinical Psychology, 65*, 1042–1046.

Coyne, J. C., & Downey, G. (1991). Social factors and psychopathology: Stress, social support, and coping processes. In M. R. Rosenzweig & L. W. Porter (Eds.), *Annual review of psychology, 62*, (pp. 401–425). Palo Alto, CA: Annual Reviews, Inc.

Darby, B. W., & Schlenker, B. R. (1982). Children's reactions to apologies. *Journal of Personality and Social Psychology, 43*, 742–753.

Davenport, D. S. (1991). The functions of anger and forgiveness: Guidelines for psychotherapy with victims. *Psychotherapy: Theory, Research, Practice, Training, 28*(1) 140–141.

DiBlasio, F. A. (1998). Decision-based forgiveness within intergenerational family treatment. *Journal of Family Therapy, 20*, 75–92.

DiBlasio, F. A. (2000). Decision-based forgiveness treatment in cases of marital infidelity. *Psychotherapy: Theory, Research, Practice, 37*(2), 149–158.

DiBlasio, F. A., & Benda, B. B. (1991). Practitioners, religion, and the use of forgiveness in the clinical setting. *Journal of Psychology and Christianity, 10*, 166–172.

Digiuseppe, R., & Tafrate, R. C. (2001). A comprehensive treatment model for anger disorders. *Psychotherapy: Theory, Research, Practice, Training, 38*(3), 262.

Downey, G. Silver, R. C., & Wortman, C. B. (1990) Reconsidering the attribution adjustment relationship following a major negative event: Coping with the loss of a child. *Journal of Personality & Social Psychology 59*(5), 925–940.

Doyle, G. (1999). Forgiveness as an intrapsychic process. *Psychotherapy: Theory, Research, Practice, Training 23*(2), 190–198.

Droll, D. M. (1985). Forgiveness: Theory and research. (Doctoral dissertation, University of Nevada, Reno, 1984). *Dissertation Abstracts International B, 45*(08), 2732.

Engle, B. (1989). *The right to innocence: Healing the trauma of childhood sexual abuse.* Los Angeles: Jeremy P. Tarcher.

Enright, R. D., & Fitzgibbons, R. P. (2002). *Helping clients forgive: An empirical guide for resolving anger and restoring hope.* Washington, DC: American Psychological Association.

Enright, R. D. and the Human Development Study Group. (1991). The moral development of forgiveness. In W. Kurtines & J. Gewirtz (Eds.), *Moral behavior and development* (Vol. 1, pp. 123–152). Hillsdale, NJ: Erlbaum.

Enright, R. D., & Human Development Study Group (1994). Piaget on the moral development of forgiveness. *Human Development, 37*, 63–80.

Enright, R. D., Santos, M. J. O., & Al-Mabuk, R. H. (1989). The adolescent as forgiver. *Journal of Adolescence, 12*, 95–110.

Enright, R. D., & Zell, R. L. (1989). Problems encountered when we forgive one another. *Journal of Psychology & Christianity. 8*(1), 52–60.

Exline, J. J., & Baumeister, R. F. (2000). Expressing forgiveness and repentance. In M. McCullough, K. I. Parament, & C. Thoresen (Eds.), *Forgiveness: Theory, research and practice* (pp. 133–155). New York: Guilford.

Fischer, P. C. (2002, August). Forgiveness, growth and the execution of Timothy McVeigh. In R. G. Tedeschi (Chair), *Posttraumatic growth in the aftermath of terrorism and combat.* Symposium conducted at the annual meeting of the American Psychological Association, Chicago.

Fitzgibbons, R. P. (1986). The cognitive and emotive uses of forgiveness in the treatment of anger. *Psychotherapy: Theory, Research, Practice, Training, 23*(4), 629–633.

Fitzgibbons, R. P. (1998). Anger and the healing power of forgiveness: A psychiatrist's view. In R. Enright & J. North (Eds.), *Exploring forgiveness* (pp. 63–74), Madison: University of Wisconsin Press.

Frazier, P., & Burnett, J. (1994). Immediate coping strategies among rape victims. *Journal of Counseling and Development, 72*, 633–639.

Frazier, P., Conlon, A., & Glaser, T. (2001). Positive and negative life changes following sexual assault. *Journal of Consulting and Clinical Psychology 69*(6), 1048–1055.

Freedman, S. R., & Enright, R. D. (1996). Forgiveness as an intervention goal with incest survivors. *Journal of Consulting and Clinical Psychology, 64*(5), 983–992.

Gobodo-Madikizela, P. (2002). Remorse, forgiveness, and rehumanization: Stories from South Africa. *Journal of Humanistic Psychology, 42*(1), 7–32.

Gobodo-Madikizela, P. (2003). *A human being died that night: A South American woman confronts the legacy of apartheid.* Boston: Houghton Mifflin Co.

Haber, J. G. (1991). *Forgiveness.* Maryland: Rowan & Littlefield Publishers Inc.

Hargrave, T. N., & Sells, J. N. (1997). The development of a forgiveness scale. *Journal of Marital and Family Therapy, 23*(1), 41–62.

Hebl, J. H., & Enright, R. D. (1993). Forgiveness as a psychotherapeutic goal with elderly females. *Psychotherapy, 30*, 658–667.

Herman, J. L. (1992). *Trauma and recovery.* New York: Basic Books.

Hills, A. (2002). Responding to catastrophic terrorism. *Studies in Conflict & Terrorism, 25*, 245–261.

Hope, D. (1987). The healing paradox of forgiveness. *Psychotherapy, 24*, 240.

Janoff-Bulman, R. (2004). Posttraumatic growth: Three explanatory models. *Psychological Inquiry, 15*(1), 30–34.

Kaminer, D., Stein, D. J., Mbanga, I., & Zungu-Dirwayi, N. (2001). The Truth and Reconciliation Commission in South Africa: Relation to psychiatric status and forgiveness among survivors of human rights abuses. *British Journal of Psychiatry, 178*, 373–377.

Kassinove, H., & Tafrate, R. (2002). *Practitioners guidebook to anger management.* Atascadero, CA: Impact Publishers.

Lazare, A. (1995). Go ahead say you're sorry. *Psychology Today*, Jan–Feb, 40.

Lechner, S. C., & Antoni, M. H. (2004). Posttraumatic growth and group-based interventions for persons dealing with cancer: What we have learned so far. *Psychological Inquiry, 15*(1), 35–41.

Lifton, R. (1988). The traumatized self. In J. Wilson, A. Harel, & B. Kahana (Eds.), *Human adaptation to extreme stress: From the Holocaust to Vietnam.* New York: Plenum.

Linley, P. A., & Joseph, S. (2004). Positive change following trauma and adversity: A review. *Journal of Traumatic Stress, 17*(1), 11–21.

Maddi, S. R., & Kobasa, S. C. (1984). *The hard executive: Health under stress.* Homewood, IL: Dow Jones-Irwin.

McCullough, M. E. (2000). Forgiveness as human strength: Theory, measurement, and links to well-being. *Journal of Social and Clinical Psychology, 19*(1), 43–55.

McCullough, M. E., Rachal, K. C., Sandage, S. J., Worthington, E. L., Brown, S. W., Hight, T. L. (1998). Interpersonal forgiving in close relationships II. Theoretical elaboration and measurement. *Journal of Personality and Social Psychology, 75*(6), 1586–1603.

McCullough, M. E., Sandage, S. J., & Worthington, E. L. Jr. (1997). *To forgive is human: How to put your past in the past.* Downers Grove, IL: Intervaristy Press.

McCullough, M. E., & Worthington, E. L. (1994). Encouraging clients to forgive people who have hurt them: Review, critique, and research prospectus. *Journal of Psychology and Theology, 22*(1), 3–20.

McCullough, M. E., Worthington, E. L., & Rachal, K. C. (1997). Interpersonal forgiving in close relationships. *Journal of Personality & Social Psychology, 73*(2), 321–336.

McFarland, C., & Alvaro, C. (2000). The impact of motivation on temporal comparisons: Coping with traumatic events by perceiving personal growth. *Journal of Personality and Social Psychology, 79*(3), 327–343.

McMillan, J. C., & Fisher, R. (1998). The Perceived Benefit Scales: Measuring perceived positive life changes after negative events. *Social Work Research, 22*, 73–187.

McMillan, J. C., Fisher, R., & Smith, E. (1997). Perceived benefit and mental health after three types of disaster. *Journal of Consulting and Clinical Psychology, 65*(5), 733–739.

Miller, L. (2002). Psychological interventions for terroristic trauma: Symptoms, syndromes, and treatment strategies. *Psychotherapy: Theory/Research, Practice, 9*(4), 284.

Minow, M. (1998). *Between vengeance and forgiveness.* Boston: Beacon Press.

Moos, R. H., & Schaefer, J. A. (1990). Coping resources and processes: Current concepts and measures. In H. S. Friedman (Ed.), *Personality and Disease* (pp. 234–257). New York: Wiley.

Mullet, E. Girard, M., & Bakhshi, P. (2004). Conceptualizations for forgiveness. *European Psychologist, 9*(2), 78–86.

Neimeyer, R. A. (2004). Fostering posttraumatic growth: A narrative elaboration. *Psychological Inquiry, 15*(1), 53–59.

Nolen-Hoeksema, S., & Davis, C. G. (2004). Theoretical and methodological issues in the assessment and interpretation of posttraumatic growth. *Psychological Inquiry, 15*(1), 60–64.

North, J. (1987). Wrongdoing and forgiveness. *Philosophy, 62*, 499–508.

O'Leary, V. E. (1998). Strength in the face of adversity: Individual and social thriving. *Journal of Social Issues, 54*, 425–446.

O'Leary, V. E., & Ickovics, J. R. (1995). Resilience and thriving in response to challenge: An opportunity for a paradigm shift in women's health. *Women's Health: Research on Gender, Behavior, and Policy, 1*, 121–142.

Park, C. L. (2004). The notion of growth following stressful life experiences: Problems and prospects. *Psychological Inquiry, 15*(1), 69–76.

Pargament, K. I., Smith, B. W., Koenig, H. G., & Perez, L. (1998). Patterns of positive and negative religious coping with major life stressors. *Journal for the Scientific Study of Religion, 37*, 710–724.

Pastore, P. L. (August 17, 2004). Oklahoma City victim Patty Hall left with daily reminders of the explosion. *Tribune-Star Online.* Retrieved 6/13/04 from http://specials.tribstar.com/mcveigh/june10hall.html.

Peddle, N. A. (2001). Forgiveness in recovery/resiliency from the trauma of war among a selected group of adolescents and adult refugees. (Doctoral dissertation, The Fielding Institute, 2001). *Dissertation Abstracts International B, 62*(5-B), 2252.

Pennebaker, J. W. (1990). *Opening up: The healing power of confiding in others.* New York: Morrow.

Rutter, M. (1987). Psychosocial resilience and protective mechanisms. *American Journal of Orthopsychiatry, 57*, 316–331.

Sanderson, C., & Linehan, M. M. (1999). Acceptance and forgiveness. In W. R. Miller (Ed.), *Integrating spirituality into treatment: Resources for practitioners.* Washington, DC: American Psychological Association.

Sarte, J. P. (1956). *Being and nothingness.* New York: Philosophical Library.

Schaefer, J., & Moos, R. (1998). The context for posttraumatic growth: Life crises, individual and social resources, and coping. In R. Tedeschi, C. Park, & L. Calhoun (Eds.), *Posttraumatic growth: Positive changes in the aftermath of crisis.* Mahwah, NJ: Lawrence Erlbaum Associates.

Scobie, E. D., & Scobie, G. E. (1999). Damaging events: The perceived need for forgiveness. *Journal for the Theory of Social Behaviour, 28*(4), 373–401.

Sipprelle, R. C. (1992). A vet experience: Multievent trauma, delayed treatment type in D. W. Foy (Ed.), *Treating PTSD: Cognitive-behavioral strategies.* New York: Guildford.

Stanton, A. L., & Low, C. A. (2004). Toward understanding posttraumatic growth: Commentary on Tedeschi and Calhoun. *Psychological Inquiry, 15*(1), 76–80.

Taft, L. (2000). Apology subverted: The commodification of apology. *The Yale Law Journal, 109*(5) 1135–1160.

Tavuchis, N. (1991). *Mea Culpa: A sociology of apology and reconciliation.* Stanford, CA: Stanford University Press, p. 21.

Tedeschi, R. G., & Calhoun, L. G. (1995). *Trauma & Transformation: Growing in the Aftermath of Suffering.* Thousand Oaks, CA: Sage.

Tedeschi, R. G., & Calhoun, L. G. (1996). The Posttraumatic Growth Inventory: Measuring the positive legacy of trauma. *Journal of Traumatic Stress, 9*, 455–471.

Tedeschi, R. G., & Calhoun, L. G. (2004). Posttraumatic growth: Conceptual foundations and empirical evidence. *Psychological Inquiry, 15*(1), 1–18.

Tedeschi, R., Park, C., & Calhoun, L. (Eds.). (1998). *Posttraumatic growth: Positive changes in the aftermath of crisis.* Mahwah, NJ: Lawrence Erlbaum Associates.

Tennen, H. & Affleck, G. (1990). Blaming others for threatening events. *Psychological Bulletin. 108(2),* 232.

Thomas, S. P. (2003). Men's anger: A phenomenological exploration of its meaning in a middle-class sample of American men. *Psychology of Men & Masculinity, 4*(2), 163–175.

Thompson, L. Y., & Snyder, C. R. (2000, August). *Forgiveness theory and the development of the Heartland Forgiveness Scale: Freeing oneself from the negative ties that bind.* Poster presented at the 108th annual meeting of the American Psychological Association, Washington, DC.

Trainer, M. (1984). Forgiveness: Intrinsic, role-expected, expedient, in the context of divorce. (Doctoral dissertation, Boston University 1981). *Dissertation Abstracts International B, 45*(04), 1325.

Witvliet, C., Ludwig, T. E., & Vander Laan, K. L. (2001). Granting forgiveness or harboring grudges: Implications for emotion, physiology, and health. *Psychological Science, 12*(2), 117–123.

Zechmeister, J. S., & Romero, C. (2002). Victim and offender accounts of interpersonal conflict: Autobiographical narratives of forgiveness and unforgiveness. *Journal of Personality and Social Psychology, 82*(4), 675–686.

CHAPTER

17

POSTTRAUMATIC GROWTH AND PSYCHOTHERAPY

TANJA ZOELLNER

DRESDEN UNIVERSITY OF TECHNOLOGY

ANDREAS MAERCKER

UNIVERSITY OF ZURICH

GROWTH IN PSYCHOTHERAPY—A NEGLECTED THEME

Posttraumatic or personal growth has supposedly always been taking place within psychotherapy, at least in some patients, but this issue has not been explicitly talked about within scientific discourse or therapeutic reflections on the psychotherapy process. Before talking about growth in psychotherapy, it seems reasonable to give a definition of what might be meant by growth in this context although we might exhaust the reader by reiterations. The term *posttraumatic growth* (PTG) as Tedeschi and Calhoun (1995, 1998) have termed it wants to capture the positive outcomes of people having experienced and coped with an extremely stressful life event (traumatic event). The *growth* term expresses that in people's lives there is something positively new that signifies a kind of surplus compared to precrisis level. Those positive surplus outcomes might include individual development, personal benefits, new life priorities, a deepened sense of meaning, or a deepened sense of connection with others or with a higher power. The expression *growth* stresses that persons have developed beyond their previous level of functioning as a result of coping with the stressful event; they do not only recover from the crisis. The terms PTG or *stress-related growth* further underscore that these positive psychological changes do not happen as part of a developmental process, but as the result of the coping process with a severe outer stressor. In this chapter, we will, by and large, follow Tedeschi and Calhoun's (2004) conceptualization and apply the term PTG to growth processes resulting from coping with crises or other stressful life circumstances, as not all patients seeking therapy have experienced a traumatic event in the narrow sense of the word as used in some diagnostic discussions, such as that found in the current DSM-IV(American Psychiatric Association, 2000). However, one can assume that almost all patients seeking therapy have experienced some kind of crisis or severe stress that have exceed their coping resources. Because we want to avoid making inflated use of the term *trauma*, we will prefer to use the term *stress-related growth* in this discussion of growth and psychotherapy instead of *PTG*.

HISTORY OF GROWTH IN PSYCHOTHERAPY

In mainstream psychotherapy schools, growth of patients has not explicitly been fostered nor has it explicitly been an aim or part of the intervention rationale. Traditionally, the main focus of psychotherapy has been on the "negative" or dark side of the human psyche. Its main mission has been to reduce symptoms and to relieve a somehow defined negative, disturbing state. Patients are usually motivated to seek therapeutic help because they suffer from negative emotions, distressing symptoms, or deficits leading to interpersonal, social, or work-related problems. Therefore, the goal of psychotherapy has been to help patients return to their prior level of functioning or to a somehow defined "normal," more functional state. The goals of psychotherapeutic interventions have been accomplished when the negative states have widely been vanished or when patients have learned techniques on how to deal with certain problems, intruding emotions, or distressing symptoms. In traditional thinking, recovery from a negative state has been the main goal of psychotherapy.

This line of reasoning in regard to the goals of psychotherapy has been especially pronounced by the development of disorder-specific intervention programs or strategies stemming mainly from cognitive-behavioral orientations in the last 20 years. Those programs, by definition, have focused on the treatment of specific symptoms linked to defined disorders. Typically, those programs include the establishment of new skills to compensate deficits, the initiation of interventions (e.g., confrontation) whose goals are to overcome excessive or distressing emotions (e.g., anxiety), and the development of strategies to reduce disturbing negative states (e.g., stress management).

Traditional psychodynamic-oriented psychotherapies have also put their focus on the "negative" side of the psyche. Here, stress-producing inner conflicts have been made the main target of psychotherapeutic interventions and theorizing. Hence, the two dominating schools of psychotherapy, psychoanalysis and cognitive behavioral therapy (CBT), have been guided by a deficit model of the human psyche. In their "Menschenbild," their attitude toward patients and how they conceptualize models of disorders and models of change, they have been lead by a pathogenic perspective. The domination of those two main psychotherapy schools with their "deficit" orientation have long precluded the acknowledgment of positive processes within the psychotherapeutic context. Recent developments of a positive health perspective or a salutary perspective within psychotherapeutic endeavors, do not, however resemble a totally new perspective.

Humanistic and Existential Approaches

In the history of psychotherapy, there are certainly exceptions to those traditional pathogenic-oriented psychotherapy schools. There are examples of quite prominent founders of other therapy schools who have set other emphasizes and have, hence, given more acknowledgment to the human strength to grow.

Carl Rogers

A prominent figure is Carl Rogers who founded the school of "client-centered psychother-apy" as a third psychotherapy school in opposition to traditional psychoanalysis and be-havioral therapy. His theory is grounded in humanistic traditions and proposes the basic goodness of people. Central to his theory is the assumption of a positive, constructive force in everyone to develop oneself to the better and healthier. This force of life is called the "actualizing tendency" and is an built-in motivation that is present in every person to develop its potentials to the fullest extent possible. Rogers regarded this innate need to constantly grow beyond one's current potentials as the single great need or driving motive of human beings. Within this reasoning, mental health is regarded as the normal progression of life if only a person can flourish in an appropriate nurturing environment. Therefore, the main task of psychotherapy is to create such a nourishing environment and support the client's inner growing process. In Roger's conception, personal growth—as he defined it—is seen as a constant natural process in healthy individuals. It is not regarded as something special or exceptional that is initiated by severe stressful events. Personal growth and psychotherapy are connected in as far as persons who seek psychotherapy are assumed to have been blocked in their self-actualization tendency and their natural growth process. Therefore, psychotherapy can help patients to reconnect with this inner force. However, the conception of growth in Rogerian theory is different from the concept of stress-related growth this volume talks about. In contrast to growth as Roger con-ceptualizes it, stress-related growth represents major positive shifts rather than gradual changes occurring within natural development. Therapeutic efforts within client-centered psychotherapy aim at supporting the self-actualization tendency and bringing patients back on track with their inner natural-growth process. In other words, the interventions or therapeutic guidance aim at renewing a former or normal healthy state including con-stant inner growth. They do not aim at growth that goes beyond it. Therefore, Roger's therapy approach—although addressing the growth potential in all human beings—does not explicitly address the issue of posttraumatic or stress-related growth as conceptualized in this book. Due to these different ideas on therapy processes and conceptualizations of growth, considerations on different levels of adaptation, such as recovery versus growth, are not really applicable to Roger's approach.

Victor Frankl

A different example of an effort to acknowledge the human potential for growth stems from Victor Frankl. He is the prominent founder of logotherapy, which represents a spiritually oriented approach to psychotherapy and is also known as the "Third Viennese School of Psychotherapy." Through his work as a psychiatrist and later through his own experience in Nazi concentration camps, he came to discover the importance of finding meaning as a source of strength and growth potential in the face of horrific adversity. With his personal triumph over those traumata he gave testimony to the ideas of logotherapy. A basic assumption of logotherapy is the existence of the "will to meaning" in everyone, which Frankl regarded to be more fundamental than the will to pleasure (according to Freud) or the will to power (according to Adler). It is assumed to be "a basic striving of man to find meaning and purpose" (Frankl, 1969, p. 35). In the ontology of logotherapy, the existence of a spiritual dimension in every person is a basic proposition. Furthermore, logotherapy acknowledges a force within everyone to grow beyond one's former capacities and to self-transcend one's fate. The human spirit is assumed to be an inner resource that refers to the human capacity to tap into the spiritual part of the self and rise above the negative effects of situations, illnesses, or the past.

The main objective of logotherapy is to facilitate the clients' quest for meaning and empower them to live meaningfully and responsibly, regardless of their life circumstances. Frankl (1986) differentiated between two levels of meaning: the present meaning, or the meaning of the moment, and the ultimate meaning or supermeaning. In psychotherapy, he believed it to be more productive to address specific meanings rather than talking about the meaning of life in general. According to Frankl, each moment or situation of life has its own specific meaning that individuals must discover by themselves or with the help of therapy because only individuals can know the right meaning specific to the moment. "According to logotherapy, we can discover this meaning in life in three different ways: (1) by creating a work or doing a deed; (2) by experiencing something or encountering someone; and (3) by the attitude we take towards unavoidable suffering" (Frankl, 1984, p. 133). In logotherapy, patients are encouraged not to focus on what has been lost, but to seek meaning in the future in spite of grief or despair. The foundations of logotherapy rest on three assumptions: (a) Life has meaning under all circumstances; (b) people are motivated by a will to meaning; and (c) humans have free will, within obvious limitations, to find meaning in their lives. In this sense, logotherapy means healing and health through meaning.

Frankl's ideas and the basic tenets of logotherapy have been further developed and elaborated by modern representatives of logotherapy (e.g., Fabry, 1994; Längle, 2000; Lukas, 1986) and have been expanded to family therapy (Lantz, 1993a, b; Lukas, 1991) or have been integrated into cognitive-behavioral approaches (e.g., Wong, 1997).

Although logotherapy deserves credit for making the human spirit and the innate quest for meaning an issue within psychotherapy, controlled trials are still needed to demonstrate the effectiveness of the current practice of logotherapy. Outlining treatment approaches and presenting case studies do not suffice to buffer therapeutic effectiveness in terms of reduced distress and heightened well-being (Schulenberg, 2003).

Originally, logotherapy has not been considered a psychotherapeutic school of its own by Frankl, but has been conceptualized as an additional qualification for psychotherapists trained in one form of traditional psychotherapeutic schools. In this sense, the ideas of logotherapy might represent a useful and important expansion of mainstream psychotherapy approaches, at least in the treatment of some patients who would profit from addressing meaning issues. A contemporary approach of integrating CBT with basic tenets of logotherapy is given by Paul Wong (1999) who has developed the "meaning-centered counseling and therapy" (MCCT).

EXISTENTIAL THERAPIES

Somehow connected to logotherapy, but certainly different from it, are existential therapy approaches (May & Yalom, 2000; Yalom, 1980) that recognize the significance of inner conflicts arising from the confrontations of the individual with the basic tenets of human existence. Existential therapy (Yalom, 1980) addresses fundamental existential problems, such as death, freedom, isolation, and meaninglessness. Themes, such as anxiety about death and uncertainty of purpose, are confronted. Similar to Frankl, Yalom (1980) has written about how meaning can be created through the choices that individuals make in facing tragic or fateful events. This approach—like ideas by Frankl—have been incorporated into group therapies and integrated within cognitive approaches (e.g. Kissane et al., 1997).

Off mainstream, transpersonal therapy approaches directly link psychotherapy and spirituality (e.g., Wilber, Vaughan, Wittine, & Murphy, 1993). In addition to supporting and fostering healthy ego-development, they integrate the spiritual dimension of humans into their treatment approaches grounded on theories of transpersonal psychology (Wilber, 2000). Transpersonal psychology regards itself as largely inclusive of and builds on psychoanalytic, behavioral, experimental, and humanistic psychologies and provides both an extension of and a different perspective from these previous psychologies.

Apart from missing empirical testing of their effectiveness, logotherapy and existential therapy approaches have made an invaluable contribution to the field of psychotherapy by pinpointing a neglected dimension of human functioning. While mainstream psychotherapy schools—especially CBT and behavioral-oriented therapies—have neglected and avoided the whole theme of spirituality, they have identified this omission. Frankl, for example, has made a stand for the importance of this dimension and has made a pledge that themes of spirituality should be integral parts of therapeutic interventions because he was convinced of the basic human need to find meaning. For a long time, themes of religion, God, spirituality, and the like have been subject to suspicion in most mainstream psychotherapy schools. Those issues have been evaluated as irrational, naïve, possibly anxiety-provoking illusions by the scientific-oriented clinical disciplines of psychology and psychotherapy. Religious or spiritual practice has been regarded as an avoidance of personal responsibility and as an escape from the demands of living in the world. The result was that themes linked to a potential spiritual dimension of humans have been denied within most traditional psychotherapies. In the past, possible spiritual needs of human beings and patients have typically not been considered a worthy and important part of the therapeutic process. Certainly, some forms of religiousness have potentially harmful, patronizing, and intimidating effects on the human psyche. Therefore, it is reasonable that therapeutic efforts aim at helping patients to lead an active, self-determined way of life. However, the omission of the spiritual dimension as a whole has denied a possible important dimension of human functioning and healing. This omission may have hindered, to some parts, the recovery process of some patients who would have profited from including a spiritual dimension and address themes of meaning, purpose, life goals, and the like within the psychotherapeutic process. The fact that people spend more money on all sorts of esoteric healers and articles than on professional psychotherapies, illustrates the spiritual vacuum many people feel and their search for fulfillment of spiritual needs.

Personal Growth and Spirituality

Growth and spirituality or existential aspects within psychotherapy are not alike. One can think of stress-related or PTG without any references to a spiritual dimension. However, data on PTG indicate clearly that for many individuals positive changes are identified in this existential or spiritual domain (Tedeschi & Calhoun, 1995). This finding does not come as a surprise because spiritual concerns tend to surface whenever a person faces an existential crisis or a close encounter with death. Furthermore, when giving a closer look at the concept of PTG, the spiritual dimension is a related and connected theme: PTG according to Tedeschi and Calhoun (1995, 1998) includes positive changes in the form of improved sense of inner strength, improved relationships with others, the setting of new life priorities, and a new sense of spirituality or religion. Those dimensions of PTG point to a deepened sense of connection with oneself, the world, other people, or a higher power. These different areas of self-transcendence clearly hint at a spiritual dimension in a broad sense. Also, the omission of both themes in psychotherapeutic contexts, the spiritual or existential dimension, and the potentials for growth, stem from the same source: the dominance of symptom-oriented CBT approaches and the conflict-oriented psychoanalytical therapies. In their deficit orientation, both therapy schools have precluded the view for salutary or positive factors within therapeutic processes. Furthermore orientation of cognitive-behavioral interventions has precluded themes, su spirituality, the soul, God, and the like, that are not easily integrated intc attitude.

The deficit orientation of main schools of psychotherapy and the accompanying omission of important other dimensions of human beings, though correctly criticized, is, however, understandable. Patients usually turn to the help of a psychotherapist when they are in trouble and have problems and conflicts that they can not solve by themselves, or with the informal help of others. The patients' motives are usually also to reduce or eliminate a negative, disturbing state. Very seldom will patients turn to a psychotherapist with the request to grow.

The rediscovery of the salutary perspective in psychology in general and the re-emergence of a positive emphasis in psychology have now opened the doors for a salutary perspective in trauma research and, specifically, for the idea of PTG after traumatic or severe life events. The concept of posttraumatic or stress-related growth indicates that there may be something beyond recovery after a crisis, something new and positive—a kind of positive surplus compared to the precrisis level of functioning. Because most patients come to therapy because they go through some sort of crisis, the issue of growth in psychotherapy is obvious.

Many clinicians know from their experience with patients that some of them talk about major positive changes as a result of their struggle with severe difficulties. Those "positive" results of coping, though often taking place within therapy, have been of anecdotal nature. Until recently, those positive consequences of a therapy-supported coping process have not been targets or outcome measures for evaluating the treatment effectiveness or success of psychotherapy.

THERAPEUTIC INTERVENTIONS AS MECHANISMS OF GROWTH

Although not explicitly acknowledged in most intervention studies and in theorizing on therapeutic-induced changes, one can suppose that some forms of growth are probably part of most therapeutic processes. We do not need to rely solely on the existence of anecdotes and our own clinical experiences to come to this conclusion. When considering the context of psychotherapy and some typical interventions or processes that are typically implemented or supported in many psychotherapies, it will be apparent how many widely used psychotherapeutic techniques might foster posttraumatic or stress-related growth. Several mechanisms and features of psychotherapy in general make growth within therapy quite probable.

Personal growth after a severe life event is more likely when the person has experienced a severe rather than a mild stressor because only a very stressful life event shakes individuals in their foundations causing dramatic psychological imbalances that hold the chance to learn something new. People usually seek therapy when they are in crisis rather than when experiencing mild stressful life situations. They turn to psychotherapeutic help when their coping resources do not suffice to deal with the crisis by themselves. Therefore, life situations of people seeking therapy have—to a high degree of probability—more growth potential than life situations of people not seeking therapy. Also, people in crisis who also seek therapy have more chance to grow than people in comparable crisis situations and with comparable coping resources not seeking therapy or other support.

Whenever there is a crisis that includes some kind of loss, returning to the precrisis level of functioning or becoming the precrisis person again is no longer possible. There are only the alternatives to change for the better or the worse. Usually, psychotherapeutic efforts aim at improving the patient's situation and, thus, raising the chances that there will be changes for the better.

Typical agents in psychotherapy can be assumed to be growth promoting. Therapeutic efforts typically aim at supporting cognitive processing and constructive coping and guide the coping process in a constructive way. Dysfunctional and avoidant strategies that might hinder cognitive-emotional processing of the trauma or the crises are usually prevented in psychotherapy. In other words, mechanisms that might lead to growth are initiated and supported in therapy making growth more likely than without therapeutic help.

According to Tedeschi and Calhoun's conceptual model of PTG (2004), cognitive processing or constructive rumination is one necessary prerequisite for stress-related growth to take place. Cognitive processing is, indeed, often an important, integral part of psychotherapy. Patients are typically encouraged and guided to think thoroughly over a problem, including its distressing elements. Cognitive avoidance is worked against. Instead, patients are guided to confront all aspects of a situation and to consider different aspects and interpretations when evaluating the meaning of a certain situation. To that end, different forms of psychotherapies, with their differing emphases and philosophies, use different strategies. For example, the cognitive-behavioral technique of imaginal exposure of traumatic experiences fosters cognitive and emotional processing, possibly leading to a new evaluation of the meaning of the trauma. In psychodynamic-oriented therapies or schema-oriented therapies, the clarification of motives and personal goals and the knowledge about oneself is underscored. Here again, cognitive processing and constructive rumination are fostered, possibly leading to new or clearer life goals and heightened self-knowledge, including positive changes that might be called *growth*.

Another typical therapeutic technique is cognitive restructuring including positive reinterpretation of a situation. Positive reinterpretation, in turn, can be regarded as a coping mechanisms being involved in the development of PTG.

In psychotherapy, patients are encouraged to be active and learn something new, such as new skills or insights into their own functioning. They make, hopefully, positive experiences while implementing those new learned skills. Therapy-supported experiences, of regained or new mastery by handling situations better than before therapy, make experiences of growth quite likely, especially in the domains of "new possibilities" and "personal strength."

The therapeutic process might possibly include the analyses of motives, self-concept, goals, priorities, current stressors, and the like. Those interventions are usually implemented with the main goal of reducing distress and fostering satisfaction and stabilization. However, as a result, patients may have reorganized their daily activities and set other life priorities more in accordance with their overall life goals. Those changes directly point to growth domains of "new life priorities" or "new possibilities."

Another example of how therapeutic processes may be linked to growth are social relations. In the treatment of some disorders, especially depressive disorders or eating disorders, the strengthening and improvement of the quality of patients' close relationships are regarded as important for the recovery process and the long-term stabilization of patients. Therapeutic efforts to foster the patients' existing relationships or at building new bonds might directly lead to the patient's perception of growth in the relationship dimension. Patients' interpersonal relationships might have improved as a result of therapy.

It is obvious how therapeutic efforts might be linked to growth because the described interventions or therapeutic efforts might lead directly to some positive changes or personal gains in some of the circumscribed growth dimensions. Usually, however, those interventions have not been undertaken with the goal of patients' personal growth, but have been used in the service of other goals linked to the effort to reduce dis... the "positive by-products" of the distress-reducing goals are quite equivalent wi... of growth as described by Tedeschi and Calhoun (1995).

It is usually assumed that stress-related growth or PTG, is an unintentional event, that ... an unintentional result of coping with a severely stressful life event or life situation. Models of PTG are, therefore, model's of unintentional change. It is noteworthy that existing models of intentional change (Hager, 1992; Mahoney, 1982; Nerken, 1993) have placed their models of change within a psychotherapeutic context. Although all authors stress that the models are not confined to this context, the choice to do so illustrates how psychotherapy is assumed to represent a nurturing context in which personal growth is possible.

Recent Developments

In recent years, there have been new developments within the scientific community and by some proponents of modern psychotherapy that address themes, such as religion, spirituality, God, and finding meaning. The life-review therapy developed for older patients directly employs the older people's potential for wisdom and growth by deliberately supporting a critical and rewarding evaluation of their different life phases (Maercker, 2002). In the last two decades, eastern philosophy principles, such as mindfulness or meditation practice, have been integrated into cognitive-behavioral-oriented psychotherapeutic treatments (Hayes, Strosahl, & Wilson, 1999; Kabat-Zinn, 1994; Kabat-Zinn et al., 1998; Teasdale et al., 2002), such as the "dialectical behavior therapy for borderline personality disorder" according to Linehan (1993). Mindfulness—originally developed in Buddhist meditation practice—is a specific attitude of purposeful, nonjudgmental attention paying in the present moment. The emphasis of acceptance, rather than efforts of changing negative experiences, mindfulness practice is associated with experiences of decentering and self-transcendence possibly supporting a growth process. More directly addressing the issue of PTG is a recently developed program for people suffering under posttraumatic stress disorder (PTSD): The brief eclectic psychotherapy by Gersons and coworkers (Gersons, Carlier, Lamberts, & van der Kolk, 2000) that combines cognitive-behavioral interventions with psychodynamically oriented interventions and that has a "meaning" section as an integral part of the psychotherapeutic program.

Other modern psychotherapists who are not confined to mainstream psychotherapy schools have taken the theme of personal growth and the spiritual dimension more as a matter of course. They have naturally incorporated those themes into their therapeutic approaches—not as an additional, extra intervention or program point (like in the Gersons' program). The inclusion of those themes is an integral part of the therapeutic process within the self-understanding of the therapy approaches (e.g., Saakvitne, Tennen, & Affleck, 1998; Schellenbaum, 1988). For example, Saakvitne and colleagues (1998) using clinical trauma theory make explicit how growth is an integral part of insight-oriented therapies that are guided by the self-in-relation-theory: Successful therapy enhances understanding of the self (identity), underlying schemas, beliefs, and the adaptation to trauma (symptoms). In doing so, the approach transforms what has been labeled crazy into a new understanding and widens the patient's choices and freedom.

Likewise, Schellenbaum, a former Jungian psychotherapist, regards growth as integral process within therapy. In his writings, he has described in length how negative, devastating situations can be initiatives for personal growth and transformation and how an existential dimension is ever present (Schellenbaum, 1988, 1994). In this conception, personal growth is inherent and an unavoidable part of a successful therapy process in

ith neurotic states is gradually transformed into more construc-
ating ways pointing to a higher state of functioning. Further-
ideas of western and eastern mystique (e.g., zen-meditation)
ach. For example, stressing the importance of body-based ex-
nitive, emotional, behavioral), he initiates or supports healing
ect experiences of transformation.

To our knowledge, the empirical investigation of personal growth within the context of psychotherapy began within two domains of group treatments: spousal bereavement groups (Yalom & Lieberman, 1991) and breast cancer patients groups (Kissane et al., 1997). Both groups have specific features that deal with the vital confrontation with death and mortality. In spousal bereavement groups, this concerns, in particular, the overcoming (resolution of) the mourning over the loss of the partner and adaptation to the new role as a single person. In the group of breast cancer patients, existential themes center on anxiety about death and uncertainty of purpose.

Initially, research on these group psychotherapies focused on single case reports, quali-tative studies, and narrative presentations about the therapeutic process and therapeutically induced changes in the group participants. Yalom and Lieberman (1991), for instance, pre-sented a case illustration of a female group therapy participant with a high level of personal growth:

> *Mrs. D., a 62-year-old woman, underwent a number of changes after the death of her husband. She felt she first needed to rediscover her own identity—she had been a "we" and had long lost touch with her "I". Hence, she took a pilgrimage back to the country of her birth, searched for the house in which she had been born, spoke to old townspeople and relatives in order to reconstruct her family and her early life. She began a number of new activities—some had been interrupted during her earlier life, some she had long yearned to do: she had braces put on her crooked teeth, took swimming and piano lessons, attended poetry-writing workshops, sold a house she had never liked and designed a new one, and enrolled in the freshman class of a nearby university's intergenerational program.* (Yalom & Lieberman, 1991, p. 340)

In this case report it is not made explicit which changes derived from therapy or were supported by the treatment and which changes developed spontaneously through the pa-tient's psychological resources. This uncertainty is not quite accidental in reports on psychodynamic therapies in which therapists often introduce only minimal interventions. They see their therapeutic role in offering space and create possibilities for clarifying conflicts and in activating resources and potentials of the patient.

By the end of the 1990s, group treatment programs for breast cancer patients have also been developed by cognitive-behavioral-oriented clinicians and have been evaluated in randomized controlled trials (RCT) (e.g., Antoni et al., 2001). After 2000, also Kissani and others (Kissani et al., 2003) published an RCT. In those studies, personal growth or benefit finding served as outcome variables and were, hence, used to estimate the success of interventions for patients with breast cancer. Table 17.1 gives an overview of these studies.

Results of all the studies presented in Table 17.1 show that benefit finding or personal growth frequently increased through treatment. Interestingly, this result appears to be less

TABLE 17.1

Empirical Studies on Personal Growth and Related Variables as Psychotherapy Outcome

Study	Patient Groups	RCT/Sample Sizes	Intervention(s)	General Outcomes	Growth Outcomes
Antoni et al., 2001	Female breast cancer patients (stage I and II)	RCT: yes IC: 100 CC: 53	CBT stress management group intervention 10-week intervention vs. 1-day seminar	IC had no effect on mood disturbance (POMS); Generalized optimism (LOT-R) increased	IC: Benefit finding (BFS) increased; correlations between benefit finding and optimism increased from r = .10 (n.s.) to r = .22 (sign) at follow-up.
Gruess, Antoni et al., 2000 *Subsample of Antoni et al., 2001*	Female breast cancer patients (stage I and II)	RCT: yes IC: 24 CC: 10	CBT stress management group intervention, 10-week intervention vs. waitlist	IC had no effect on mood disturbance (POMS); reduced serum cortisol levels (=indicator of stress resistance)	IC: increased benefit finding; Effect on cortisol was mediated by increases in benefit finding
McGregor, Antoni et al., 2004 *Subsample of Antoni et al., 2001*	Female breast cancer patients (stage I and II)	RCT: yes IC: 18 CC: 11	CBT stress management group intervention, 10-week intervention vs. waitlist	IC had no effect on mood disturbance (POMS); Immune function: Lymphzyte proliferation increased to follow-up	IC: increased benefit finding; Changes in BFS correlated with Lymphocyte proliferation at follow-up (r=.36)
Kissane et al., 2003	Female breast cancer patients (early stages)	RCT: yes IC: 154 CC: 149	IG: 20 sessions cognitive-existential group therapy plus 3 relaxation classes CG: 3 relaxation classes	IG: reduced anxiety, improved family functioning. No effects in Affect Balance Scale	IC: increased personal growth (1-item measure)
Lieberman et al., 2002	Female breast cancer patients (stages I – IV)	RCT: no IC: 67 no CC	Internet delivered electronic support groups (no psycho-therapy). 4 groups met for 1.5 hours weekly for 16 weeks led trained personnel	Reduced depression and reactions to pain; Increase in emotional suppression	IC: increased personal growth (PTGI subscales: New Possibilities and Spirituality)

RCT = randomized controlled trial; IC = intervention condition; CC = control condition; CBT = Cognitive-behavioural therapy; POMS = Profile of Mood States; LOT-R = Life Orientation Test—Revised; BFS = Benefit Finding Scale; PTGI = Post-traumatic Growth Inventory (for description of these instruments see study references).

344

biguous than improvements on distress and mood variables. For those variables, the results are more inconclusive. For instance, the Profile of Mood Scale (POMS) values in the Antoni and colleagues studies (e.g., 2001) did not change through treatment. Neither did the Affect Balance scale (ABS) values in the results reported by Kissane and colleagues (2003). This lack of treatment effect on the distress variables, make the positive, salutary variables from the realm of stress-related growth and benefit finding even more interesting in regard to the potential sensitivity of outcome measures for those kinds of intervention programs. Possibly, in adjuvant psychotherapy programs for lethal illnesses where, by nature, the existential dimension is obvious due to the confrontation with loss, death, life uncertainty, and so forth, finding meaning or personal growth in facing the tragedy is important for psychological adjustment and, therefore, a specifically important goal of those therapeutic interventions.

What kind of therapeutic interventions have been employed to foster personal growth? Antoni and coworkers (Antoni et al., 2001; Gruess et al., 2000; McGregor et al., 2004) did not address this topic directly, but implemented a typical and, as expected, effective CBT stress management program. The group intervention consisted of 10 weekly meetings of approximately 2 hours each. It included both, stress management (e.g., cognitive restructuring, coping skills training, assertiveness, anger management, and social support utilization skills) and relaxation training components (e.g., progressive muscle relaxation, meditation, abdominal breathing, and guided imagery). Group discussions included personal experiences, experiential exercises, role playing, and review of homework exercises emphasizing stress management concepts and relaxation practice. Groups were led by a team of two female therapists. Here, a standard state-of-the-art CBT program showed an increase of benefit finding as a "side effect."

A partly increased PTG as a "side effect" was also evident in the study by Lieberman and colleagues (Lieberman et a., 2003). Based on a psychodynamic approach, central goals of this program were encouraging patients to become empowered and make active choices in their recovery, and, thereby, reducing unwanted aloneness, loss of control, and loss of hope. Group leaders did not impose a set agenda for the sessions. At some times, female participants continued the themes from the previous week, at other times, a pressing problem raised by one participant initiated a general discussion. Group discussions ranged from difficulties in managing the illness, problems with friendships and marriage difficulties to feelings of discrimination and isolation. Groups were led by experienced Trained Wellness Community personnel (TWC, is a U.S. national agency).

In contrast to the studies mentioned, Kissane and colleagues (2003) applied a treatment program that they called a *cognitive-existential approach* because it directly addressed existential themes. The treatment program was again a group format comprising 6 to 8 patients and two therapists who met for 20 weekly sessions, each lasting 90 minutes. Groups typically began with a series of patients' narratives of their experience of illness. Early sessions focused on grief and existential concerns. Cognitive aspects were integrated during the middle phase. Typical themes were cancer as a threat of life and the reality of finitude. Discussions included threat of death, fear of recurrence, living with uncertainty, and the doctor–patient relationship. Principles of existential psychotherapy (Yalom, 1980) were introduced to deal with death anxiety in the recognition that, as a "universal given," it is an inescapable part of human existence. The cognitive position was introduced by employing problem-solving approaches, cognitive reframing to examine and deal with negative thoughts, and anger management. The program added relaxation classes to the end of sessions 10, 11, and 12. In the relaxation classes, women were taught how to use progressive muscle relaxation with guided imagery.

Interestingly, both programs that did not directly address themes of personal growth and programs that did directly address those themes, resulted in higher personal growth at the end of treatment. The studies cited in the preceding text do not yet cover all relevant empirical results in the discussion here of growth and psychotherapy. On the one hand, there exist studies that have personal growth as one goal of therapy without regarding growth as an outcome measure. On the other hand there are studies that investigated personal growth or sense of meaning as mediator variables for the prediction of treatment success.

Growth as Intervention Goal or Mediator of Outcome

Two studies—different in design and target population—made personal growth or benefit finding as one goal of therapy. In a randomized controlled intervention trial for female breast cancer patients, Stanton and others (Stanton et al., 2002) applied a writing assignment with the explicit goal of finding benefits through the cancer experience. Gersons and colleagues (2000) included a substantial topic—"meaning integration"—into their inclusive therapy program for police officers with PTSD. Results are shown in Table 17.2.

In the Stanton et al. study (2002), the intervention was comprised of a writing task over four sessions in which participants were instructed to write about their *positive thoughts and feelings regarding their experience with breast cancer* (benefit-finding condition) or about *their deepest thoughts and feelings regarding their experience with breast cancer* (expressive condition). Results did not show any main effects. However, an interaction effect was evident: Women who were high in avoidance did profit the most from the benefit-finding condition in terms of reduced distress. Women low in avoidance benefited the most from the expressive condition. Results can be interpreted well within the line of thinking of a two-component model of personal growth to be outlined in the following text.

The study by Gersons and others (2000) does not allow conclusions to be drawn on the effects of the therapeutically induced meaning component because the study did not include any outcome measures that covered those variables. However, treatment overall was effective in terms of the usual outcome measures (i.e., reduced distress). The authors describe their work in the domain of meaning or integration as:

> (it) emphasis shifts to issues of meaning and attribution. At this stage, patients begin to realize, often for the first time, that their view of the world and of themselves has irrevocably changed. By exploring and also accepting this *new view*, they gain a new sense of safety and control over their lives. In some cases, similar previous experiences or key figures in their lives are discussed in a focused psychodynamic approach. (Gersons et al., 2000, p. 326, italics added by authors)

In his inclusive and elaborated theoretical model, the Swiss psychotherapy researcher Grawe (2003) postulated that individual approach and avoidance goals, and the congruence/incongruence of those goals, are important mediators for therapy success. Grawes' research group found out that a "belief/sense of meaning" belong to the most important approach goals for the psychotherapy process (Berking, Grosse-Holtforth, & Jacobi, 2003; Grosse-Holtforth & Grawe, 2000). The authors assessed belief/sense of meaning by four items that followed the question format ("please indicate how important the following goals are for you independent from whether or not you have already reached them"): "... to

TABLE 17.2

Empirical Studies on Personal Growth and Related Variables as Intervention Goal and Mediator of Outcome

Patient Groups	RCT/Sample Sizes	Intervention(s)	General Outcomes	Growth Outcomes
Growth, benefit finding or sense of meaning as intervention goal				
Female breast cancer patients (early stages)[1]	RCT: yes IC1: 21 IC2: 21 CC: 18	IC1: written expression about benefit finding IC2: written emotional expression about their deepest thoughts CC: writing about facts of illness and treatment	IC2 decreased stress (POMS) in women low in avoidance Compared with CC at 3 months IC2 had decreased physical symptoms, and IC1 and IC2 had fewer medical appointments for cancer-related morbidity	IC1 decreased stress (POMS) in women high in avoidance;
Police officers with PTSD[2]	RCT: yes IC: 22 CC: 20	Individual "brief eclectic psychotherapy" with phase "meaning and integration" weekly 60-minute sessions over 16 weeks vs. wait list	IC with improvement in PTSD symptoms, work resumption, and in number of comorbid conditions	Not measured
Growth, benefit finding or sense of meaning as mediator of outcome				
Psychotherapy patients (mixed diagnoses)[3]	RCT: no IC : 146 CC : 468	CBT and client-centered (Rogers) therapy	23 types of individual goals in patients reliably measured	Goal "belief/sense of meaning": Patients vs. healthy CC: n.s., women > men (d = .39); elderly > young (d = .36)
Psychotherapy patients (mixed diagnoses)[4]	RCT: no IC: 62 no CC	CBT specific programs for various disorders	Pre-post comparison of goal incongruency decreased over all goals (mean d = .83)	Pre-post comparison of the belief/sense of meaning goal: incongruency decreased (d = .66)

Note. IC = intervention condition; CC = control condition; States.
[1] Stanton et al., 2002.
[2] Gersons et al., 2000.
[3] Grosse-Holtforth & Grawe (2000).
[4] Berking et al., (2003).

experience myself as part of a higher order; . . . to find meaning in my li   348
place in the world; . . . to live my (religious) beliefs."

Table 17.2 (second half) shows that the belief/sense of meaning variab
healthy nontherapy patients as for therapy patients, that it is higher for v
men, and higher for older individuals than for younger ones. Furthermore, re
that this goal was experienced as more congruent after successful treatme... than before
therapy. Future research has to demonstrate whether or not this mediator variable is useful
in investigations on personal growth within the context of psychotherapy.

In sum, the empirical investigation of the relationship between psychotherapy and
personal growth is still in its infancy. So far, research has focused on breast adjuvant
psychotherapy groups for breast cancer patients. It seems desirable for future studies of
psychotherapy with persons dealing with highly challenging events to address the domain
of benefit finding and personal growth.

PROPOSITION OF A TWO-COMPONENT MODEL OF SELF-PERCEIVED GROWTH

In view of a potentially rushed and simple-minded enthusiasm about PTG as the new goal in
psychotherapy or the new outcome measure for evaluating the success of treatment studies,
we want to pledge for a moderate, balanced, and critical view of the phenomenon of stress-
related growth. In spite of the enthusiasm of PTG and its supposedly favorable effects, the
adaptive significance of PTG is still not clear (see Filipp, 1999). The empirical literature
on the relationship between PTG and psychological adjustment outside of therapeutic
contexts gives a mixed and inconclusive picture (Zoellner & Maercker, 2004; see also xy,
this volume). It seems that the relationship is not as straightforward as it may seem at first
sight.

As we have outlined in greater detail elsewhere (Maercker & Zoellner, 2004; Zoellner
& Maercker, 2004), the self-report or self-perception of PTG may have two components
or a "Janus face." We consider a two-component model (the "Janus-Face model") to be
an adequate approach to the phenomenon. The self-perception of stress-related growth
is considered to have a constructive, self-transcending and a self-deceptive, illusory side.
Statements of PTG may, in some cases, be a sign of a coping success and represent
a functional self-transcendence, thriving, or a state beyond the previous level of (dys-)
functioning. Posttraumatic growth in general in those cases, may be considered a positive
outcome as Tedeschi and Calhoun (2004) described it.

However, in other cases, in which the self-perception of PTG is mainly self-deceptive
or illusory, PTG may serve the function of self-conciliation or palliation to buffer the
negative impact of trauma or severe stress. Taylor and coworkers (e.g., Taylor & Armor,
1996; Taylor & Brown, 1994) have written extensively on those illusory cognitions in
the face of threatening information. In their research, they demonstrated that people—
when faced with threatening events—often respond with distorted positive perceptions of
themselves, unrealistic optimistic beliefs, and an exaggerated sense of control. The term
positive illusions captures the essence of this phenomenon, namely the self-deceptive,
illusory side of those self-cognitions. In regard to those robust findings, we argue that
the perception of PTG may, in some cases or to some extent, represent one form of
positive illusion to deal better with trauma-induced distress. The perception of PTG is not
necessarily always a sign of a lasting outcome, but may be a transient coping effort or
strategy. In a similar vein, Affleck and Tennen (1996) have differentiated between benefit
finding (coping outcome) and benefit reminding as a coping strategy.

The Janus-Face model (Maercker & Zoellner, 2004) proposes that the constructive, self-transforming side of PTG is associated with functional adjustment processes (e.g., functional cognitive restructuring), whereas the relationship between adjustment and the illusory side is more complicated. The illusory side of PTG might be a sign of self-conciliation and palliation as a short-term adaptive coping strategy with no long-term effects on adjustment. Or, it might be even linked to dysfunctional coping strategies, such as denial, wishful thinking, or cognitive avoidance. In those cases, the perception of PTG might be detrimental for long-term adjustment because it hinders the cognitive emotional processing of the trauma.

Maercker and coworkers (Maercker, 1998; Maercker, Herrle, & Grimm, 1999; Maercker & Langner, 2001; Zoellner & Maercker, 2004) have provided preliminary evidence for the coexistence of those two components in PTG by pointing to the fact that there is something beyond PTG that is constituted by constructive statements and by illusory statements that may serve as calming down oneself after trauma.

The studies on PTG as an outcome of psychotherapy cited in the preceding text, may—in light of the Janus-Face model—be regarded more critically. The findings by the Antoni and colleagues (2001) may not necessarily be a sign of successful therapy or coping outcome. In those studies, the intervention group usually did not improve on distress variables in the form of reduced distress, but showed increased stress-related growth. These findings possibly point to the perception of growth as an expression of a transient adaptive coping effort. The fact that the perception of growth was mildly positively associated with better physical health status is a remarkable finding. If this association is not due to a third variable, it may point to the significance of benefit-reminding strategies to deal with stress. It is, however, not clear yet as to whether or not the perception of growth has long-term positive effects on health status or whether this is a short-term association. So far, it seems, that the findings provide preliminary support for the view of PTG as an adaptive coping effort to counterbalance the accompanying distress.

The studies that have evaluated PTG as a goal of intervention might also be regarded more critically. The finding by Stanton and others (2002) that women high in avoidance have profited most from the induced finding positives intervention may not be as favorable for long-term psychological adaptation as the authors of the study have regarded it. Possibly, the avoidant coping strategies employed by women high in avoidance have been reinforced by the benefit-finding assignment with a short-term—but possibly not long-lasting—effect on psychological distress. It lies in the nature of avoidant strategies that they have short-term palliative effects, but run the risk of long-term negative effects on adjustment. The detrimental effects of cognitive avoidant and denial strategies for the adaptation to trauma have been extensively researched and demonstrated by Ehlers and coworkers (Dunmore, Clark, & Ehlers, 2001). Posttraumatic growth as a lasting positive coping outcome should be accompanied by the simultaneous recognition and acknowledgment of the whole trauma experience including the negative or painful impact of trauma.

With the critical comments we wanted to propose some caution not to draw too enthusiastic conclusions on the role of growth within psychotherapy in light of the findings of the cited studies. Nevertheless, the outlined studies are important and point to themes and domains of positive psychological functioning that have been neglected by traditional intervention studies. Traditional therapy programs have mainly focused on reducing negative states and have, in their outcome measures, concentrated on the reduction of indices of distress. A general development within empirical endeavors to address the topic of personal growth or other areas of positive psychology and well-being is highly welcomed. The studies cited in the preceding text made important efforts to integrate themes of personal growth into intervention studies. It is desirable for future empirical intervention

studies—also from other domains of psychotherapy—to widen their horizon and emp[...]
indices of positive health in their designs. In doing so, this will be a development to[...]
ward more sophisticated designs and will allow a differential evaluation of those positive
phenomena.

Investigating the Model in a Psychotherapy Trial

As a possible beginning in this direction, guided by the two-component model, we are currently investigating PTG and its predictors within a randomized control trial of traffic accident survivors with PTSD. Traffic accident survivors were randomly assigned to treatment
or waiting list control conditions. The treatment took an average of 10 "double sessions"
of an individually applied, standardized, state-of-the-art CBT program following guidelines developed by Blanchard and Hickling (1997). The program encompassed prolonged
imaginal exposure, cognitive restructuring, traffic related *in vivo* exposure homework, and
progressive muscle relaxation training (Zöllner, Karl, & Maercker, 2004). The therapy
program did not explicitly address personal growth or finding benefits from dealing with
the traumatic accident. When patients mentioned positive changes as a result of coping
with the trauma, the reported benefits were appreciated and attributed as patients' personal successes, but those reported benefits were not purposely promoted. Posttraumatic
growth before, after, and several months posttreatment was measured by the Posttraumatic Growth Inventory (PTGI) (Tedeschi & Calhoun, 1996) and was complemented by
its possible predictors (optimism, openness to experience, and cognitive avoidance).

Preliminary results showed the expected favorable outcome measures in regard to significant and clinically relevant reductions on distress measures (Maercker, Zoellner, Rabe,
& Karl, 2004) and changes in psychophysiological correlates of PTSD (Karl, Rabe, Zoellner, & Maercker, 2004). In regard to PTG, the findings revealed no overall significant
increase in the level of PTG in general for either the therapy group or for the waiting list
control group (Zoellner, Rabe, Karl, & Maercker, 2004). There was, however, a tendency
for an overall increase in both groups with an additional interaction effect with the therapy
group showing a larger increase. Analyses of the subdomains of PTG showed further, more
substantial differences between the intervention and the waiting list control group. A significant interaction effect of time X treatment condition was evident in the PTGI domains
of "new possibilities" and "personal strength," which was caused by substantial increases
in those domains in the therapy group. In regard to the other growth domains (i.e., appreciation of life, religion/spirituality, relationships) there were no systematic differences
between therapy and the control group.

Furthermore, the predictive pattern of the PTGI scores changed over time. At the
beginning of treatment, PTG was best predicted by concurrent intrusion level and openness
to experience. The prediction of PTG by two differing predictors accords to the prediction
of the Janus-Face model that assumes two coexisting components in PTG, a constructive
side (openness), and an illusory, palliative side (distress level). At the end of successful
treatment, however, PTG was predicted only by a constructive factor of openness to
experience and PTSD severity (CAPS score) at the beginning of treatment. The latter
finding suggests that those who suffered to a great degree have simultaneously more
potential to grow from the experience. The change of predictor pattern points to the
procedural nature of the self-perception of PTG and supports propositions of the Janus-
Face model—with growing coping success, the illusory side loses importance over time
and the constructive side gains impact over time.

Individual pre- to posttreatment *changes* in the overall PTGI score were best predicted
by changes in distress level: Gains in overall PTG from pre- to posttest were positively

ction of PTSD severity. In regard to the prediction of the different
uction of PTSD severity was also the best predictor for reported gains
possibilities" and "personal strength." The prediction of the other
TGI was less consistent. For example, gains in the religious domain
ed with concurrent cognitive avoidance.

......; finding was that there seemed to exist a subgroup within the treatment group that had an extremely high PTGI score before treatment and showed a reduction of self-reported growth to a lower, but—compared to the other participants—still
high score at the end of treatment. In this subgroup, the reduction of the extreme growth
score from pre- to post-treatment was associated with reduction of PTSD severity and with
treatment success. From the point of view of the Janus-Face model, one possible explanation for this finding is that the individuals in this subgroup employed the self-perception
of growth as a palliative coping strategy (e.g., benefit reminding) to buffer the existent
distress. With distress reduction, this coping strategy was no longer necessary and the
perception of PTG reduced to a more realistic level at the end of treatment.

Taken together, these preliminary findings indicate that PTG is not a homogenous
construct. The different domains in which PTG is usually reported seem to be differently
associated with adaptive and palliative or, possibly, even maladaptive processes. So far, the
domains "new possibilities" and "personal strength," however, seem to be consistently associated with adaptive processes. Gains in those domains seem to signify coping successes.
Furthermore, there seem to be interindividual differences in the function and significance
of self-perceived PTG and differential changes over the course of the coping process.

From a clinical standpoint, self-transcending or self-transforming dimensions including
growth can be regarded as integral parts of healthy human functioning pointing to "needs
of the soul." At least for a subgroup of patients, the incorporation of those issues seems to
be indicated. Therefore efforts, similar to those outlined in the preceding text, to broaden
the scope of psychotherapies addressing themes of meaning, purpose, spirituality, growth,
and other positive forces are highly needed. Addressing those issues, one always runs
the risk—at least in an academic context—to be downgraded or at least to not be taken
seriously because one talks about "soft" issues that are not easily measured and whose
very existence is challenged. For these reasons, the empirical investigation of growth
and related issues within psychotherapeutic approaches is highly desirable. These matters
should be made the foci of scientific interest, with the inclusion of these kinds of positive
outcome measures, goals of treatment, or mediator variables.

COMING TO PRACTICAL TERMS WITH POSTTRAUMATIC GROWTH IN PSYCHOTHERAPY

Other authors have stressed the need to be open to those issues and incorporate ideas of
growth and related issues into work with clients who have been affected by traumatic
events (Calhoun & Tedeschi, 1998, 1999; Park, 1999). Having said some critical words on
a naïve view of PTG, the following guidelines (cf. Calhoun & Tedeschi, 1999 for a more
extended discussion of these issues) provide clinicians with some ideas for practical use
of how to incorporate those issues into the work with patients.

- Therapists should have an understanding of how the process of working through the impact
of trauma is linked to the potential revision of trauma-affected schemas and challenged
beliefs. Therefore, the coping process of coming to terms with traumatic events is often

associated with the development of a new self-understanding, a new u
the "outer world," and the relationship between the two. Change seems
recovery process, suggesting that growth, or the perception of positive cha
potentially, an integral part of the healing process.

- When patients describe positive changes as the result of their struggle with trauma, clinicians should support, emphasize, and encourage those perceptions. Because positive illusions have been demonstrated to be associated with positive adaptation to trauma and other stressful events, there seems to be no harm for patients when therapists directly address the issue of positive changes, personal growth, or benefits from coping with the traumatic event.

- In doing so, therapists should have a tolerance for obvious false, naïve, unverifiable positive illusions and positive interpretations. Although the accurate perception of reality may be, to some extent, indicated to be a therapy goal in regard to improved coping, perceiving the truth per se seems to be less essential. Many of healthy peoples' perceptions are distorted and biased in a slightly positive way. In psychotherapy, what is helpful and useful for patients is more essential than what is truthful. The decision criteria in regard to tolerating obvious positive illusions held by the patient is whether or not those positive illusions, including personal growth perceptions, support or hinder a constructive, adaptive recovery and healing process.

- Psychotherapy constitutes a good context to explore positive changes in the aftermath of crisis. The simultaneous acknowledgement of patients' suffering and the negative impact of trauma on their lives within the therapy process, enables clients—on the basis of a trustful and intimate therapeutic relationship—to also explore positive changes as result of their coping process. Outside of the therapeutic context, clients may have been given advice by friends to "see the positive" or "concentrate on the good things" when having talked about the negative impact of trauma. That kind of rushed advice is usually not helpful because it is often linked to the denial of suffering and existing negative consequences. It goes without saying that therapists, when fostering growth within psychotherapy, should avoid the fashionable western doctrine to "see the good in bad things" or "to learn from fateful events" that is spread by popular readings.

- This professional avoidance should be accompanied by an open-minded attitude on the part of the therapist that allows patients to find their own specific meanings, interpretations, way of coping, and recovery. Perceptions of growth should be supported and encouraged when they occur or they can be directly addressed by the therapist, but the absence of growth or benefit finding by the patient should not be regarded as a failure. If patients can not see any positives in their struggle with crisis, the issue should be dropped, at least for some time, and therapeutic efforts should continue to reduce distress and encourage a constructive coping process.

- Also, patients' individual differences should be considered when incorporating those issues. The specific clients' belief systems, personality characteristics, and coping styles will predispose them toward particular appraisals and coping responses making the perception or experience of growth more or less likely and more or less important for individual adjustment.

- Addressing issues of growth, benefit finding, meaning construction, and the like need proper timing. In the immediate aftermath of crisis and the first coping stage, it does not seem to be useful to lead clients to focus on positive changes. Before addressing those issues, the most extreme distress needs to be reduced and some coping success need to be existent. As a role of thumb, one could plan to address or be especially alert to those issues during the last third of therapy.

- Whether or not the role of the therapist should be more passive or active in addressing issues of growth depends on the patient's individual character, psychiatric disorders, and the reasons for searching treatment. Different psychiatric disorders and different crisis situations are differently connected to themes of growth or existential issues and call differently to the inclusion of those issues within therapy. In the treatment of particular patient populations, such as trauma survivors, medically ill patients, or bereaved individuals, the inclusion of an existential dimension, and issues of meaning and growth, are probably more important for psychological adaptation and well-being than for some other patient populations. In those cases, therapists should take on a more active role and possibly incorporate explicit elements intended to foster growth from adversity. Other stressful life situations (e.g., having a phobia) call for active and problem-focused coping that aims at changing the situation. In those cases, themes of growth or existential issues are probably less important for successful adaptation.

REFERENCES

Affleck, G., & Tennen, H. (1996). Construing benefits from adversity: Adaptational significance and dispositional underpinnings. *Journal of Personality, 64*, 900–922.

American Psychiatric Association (2000). *Diagnostic and statistical manual of mental disorders—text revision.* Washington, DC: Author.

Antoni, M. H., Lehman, J. M., Kilbourn, K. M., Boyers, A. E., Culver, J. L., Alferi, et al. (2001). Cognitive-behavioral stress management intervention decreases the prevalence of depression and enhances benefit finding among women under treatment for early-stage breast cancer. *Health Psychology, 20*, 20–32.

Berking, M., Grosse-Holtforth, M., & Jacobi, C. (2003). Reduction of incongruence in inpatient psychotherapy. *Clinical Psychology and Psychotherapy, 10*, 86–92.

Blanchard, E., & Hickling, E. (1997). *After the crash: Psychological assessment and treatment of survivors of motor vehicle accidents.* Washington, DC: American Psychological Association.

Calhoun, L. G., & Tedeschi, R. G. (1998). Beyond recovery from trauma: implications for clinical practice. *Journal of Social Issues, 54*, 357–371.

Calhoun, L. G., & Tedeschi, R. G. (1999). *Facilitating posttraumatic growth.* Mahwah, NJ: Lawrence Erlbaum Associates.

Dunmore, E., Clark, D. M., & Ehlers, A. (2001). A prospective investigation of the role of cognitive factors in persistent posttraumatic stress disorder (PTSD) after physical or sexual assault. *Behaviour Research & Therapy, 39*, 1063–1084.

Ehlers, A., & Steil, R. (1995). Maintenance of intrusive memories in posttraumatic stress disorder: A cognitive approach. *Behavioural and Cognitive Psychotherapy, 23*, 217–249.

Fabry, J. (1994). *The pursuit of meaning* (Rev. ed.). Abilene, TX: Institute of Logotherapy Press.

Filipp, S. H. (1999). A three-stage model of coping with loss and trauma. In A. Maercker, M. Schützwohl, & Z. Solomon (Eds.), *Posttraumatic stress disorder: A lifespan developmental perspective* (pp. 43–78). Seattle, WA: Hogrefe & Huber.

Frankl, V. E. (1969). *The will to meaning: Foundations and applications of logotherapy.* New York: The World Publishing Co.

Frankl., V. E. (1984). *Man's search for meaning (revised and updated).* New York: Washington Square Press/Pocket Books.

Frankl., V. E. (1986). *The doctor and the soul: From psychotherapy to logotherapy* (Rev. ed.). New York: Vintage Books.

Gersons, B. P. R., Carlier, I. V. E., Lamberts, R.D., & van der Kolk, B.A. (2000). Randomized clinical trial of brief eclectic psychotherapy for police officers with posttraumatic stress disorder. *Journal of Traumatic Stress, 13*, 333–347.

Grawe, K. (2003). *Psychological therapy.* Seattle: Hogrefe & Huber.

Grosse-Holtforth, M. & Grawe, K. (2000). Fragebogen zur Analyse Motiovationaler Schemata [Questionnaire for the Analysis of Motivational Schemas]. *Zeitschrift für Klinische Psychologie und Psychotherapie, 29,* 170–178.

Gruess, D. G., Antoni, M. H., McGregor, B. A., Kilbourn, K. M., Boyers, A. E., Alferi, S. M., et al. (2000). Cognitive-behavioral stress management reduces serum cortisol by enhancing benefit finding among women being treated for early stage breast cancer. *Psychosomatic Medicine, 62,* 304–308.

Hager, D. L. (1992). Chaos and growth. *Psychotherapy, 29,* 378–384.

Hayes, S. C., Strosahl, K. D., & Wilson, K. G. (1999). *Acceptance and commitment therapy. An experiential approach to behavior change.* New York: Guilford.

Kabat-Zinn, H. J. (1994). *Wherever you f other you are. Mindfulness meditation in everyday life.* New York: Hyperion.

Kabat-Zinn, H. J., Wheeler, E., Light, T., Skillings, A., Scharf, M. J., Cropley, T. G., et al. (1998). Influence of a mindfulness meditation-based stress reduction intervention on rates of skin clearing in patients with moderate to severe psoriasis undergoing phototherapy (UVB) and photocheotherapy (PUVA). *Psychosomatic Medicine, 60,* 625–632.

Karl, A., Rabe, S., Zoellner, T., & Maercker, A. (2004). *Central and peripheral correlates of treatment success in accident-related posttraumatic stress disorder.* Unpublished Manuscript, Dresden University of Technology, Germany.

Kissane, D. W., Bloch, S., Miach, P., Smith, G. C., Seddon, A., & Keks, N. (1997). Cognitive-existential group therapy for patients with primary breast cancer—techniques and themes. *Psycho-oncology, 6,* 25–33.

Kissane, D. W., Bloch, S., Smith, G. C., Miach, P., Clarke, D. M., Ikin, J., et al., (2003). Cognitive-existential group psychotherapy for women with primary breast cancer: A randomized controlled trial. *Psycho-oncology, 12,* 532–546.

Längle, A. (2000). *Sinnvoll leben: Angewandte Existenzanalyse.* Wien, Austria: NP Buchverlag.

Lantz, J. (1993a). Resistance in family logotherapy. *Contemporary Family Therapy, 12,* 405–418.

Lantz, J. (1993b). *Existential family therapy: Using the concepts of Viktor Frankl.* Northvale, NJ: Jason Aronson, Inc.

Lieberman, M.A., Golant, M., Giese-Davis, J., Winzlenberg, A., Benjamin, H., Humphreys, K., et al. (2003). Electronic support groups for breast carcinoma. A clinical trial of effectiveness. *Cancer, 97,* 920–925.

Linehan, M. M. (1993). *Cognitive-behavioral treatment of borderline personality disorder.* New York: Guilford.

Lukas, E. (1986). *Meaning in suffering: Comfort in crisis through logotherapy.* Berkeley, CA: Institute of Logotherapy Press.

Lukas, E. (1991). Meaning-centered family therapy. *The International forum for logotherapy, 14,* 76–74.

Maercker, A. (2002). Life-review technique in the treatment of PTSD in elderly patients: Rationale and three single case studies. *Journal of Clinical Geropsychology, 8,* 239–249.

Maercker, A., Herrle, J., & Grimm, I. (1999). Dresdener Bombennachtsopfer: 50 Jahre danach: Eine Untersuchung patho- und slautogenetischer Variablen. [Dresden bombing night victims 50 years later. A study of patho- and salutogenic variables]. *Zeitschrift für Gerontopsychologie & -psychiatrie, 12,* 157–167.

Maercker, A., & Langner, R. (2001). Persönliche Reifung durch Belastungen und Traumata: Ein Vergleich zweier Fragebogen zur Erfassung selbstwahrgenommener Reifung nach traumatischen Erlebnissen. *Diagnostica, 47,* 153–162.

Maercker, A., & Zoellner, T. (2004). The Janus face of self-perceived growth: Toward a two-component model of posttraumatic growth. *Psychological Inquiry, 15,* 41–48.

Maercker, A., Zoellner, T., Rabe, S., & Karl, A. (2004). A controlled evaluation of cognitive behavioral therapy for posttraumatic stress in motor vehicle accident survivors. Unpublished manuscript, University of Zurich, Switzerland.

Mahoney, M. J. (1982). Psychotherapy and human change process. In J. H. Harvey & M. M. Parks (Eds.), *Psychotherapy research and behavior change* (pp. 77–122). Washington, DC: American Psychological Association.

McGregor, B.A., Antoni, M. H., Boyers, A. E., Alferi, S. M., Blomberg, B. B., & Carver, C. S. (2004). Cognitive-behavioral stress management increases benefit finding and immune function among women with early stage breast cancer. *Journal of Psychosomatic Research, 56,* 1–8.

Nerken, I. R. (1993). Grief and the reflective self: Toward a clearer model of loss resolution and growth. *Death Studies, 17,* 1–26.

Park, C. L. (1999). The roles of meaning and growth in the recovery from posttraumatic stress disorder. In A. Maercker, M. Schützwohl, & Z. Solomon (Eds.), *Posttraumatic stress disorder: A lifespan developmental perspective* (pp. 249–264). Seattle, WA: Hogrefe & Huber.

Rogers, C.R. (1951). *Client-centered therapy: Its current practice, implications, and theory.* Boston: Houghton Mifflin.

Schellenbaum, P. (1988). Die Wunde der Ungeliebten: Blockierung und Verlebendigugn der Liebe. München: Kösel.

Schellenbaum, P., & Nevill, T. (1991). *The wound of the unloved: Releasing the life energy.* Rockport, MA: Element Books.

Schellenbaum, P. (1994). Nimm deine Couch und geh. München: dtv.

Schulenberg, S. E. (2003). Empirical research and logotherapy. *Psychological Reports, 93,* 307–319.

Stanton, A. L., Danoff-Burg, S., Sworowski, L. A., Collins, C. A., Branstetter, A. D., Rodriguet-Hanley, A. et al. (2002). Randomized, controlled trial of written emotional expression and benefit finding in breast cancer patients. *Journal of Clinical Oncology, 20,* 4160–4168.

Taylor, S. E. (1983). Adjustment to threatening events: A theory of cognitive adaptation. *American Psychologist, 38,* 1161–1173.

Taylor, S. E., & Armor, D. A. (1996). Positive illusions and coping with adversity. *Journal of Personality, 64,* 873–898.

Taylor, S. E., & Brown, S. E. (1994). Positive illusions and well-being revisited: Separating fact from fiction. *Psychological Bulletin, 116,* 21–27.

Teasdale, J. D., Moore, R. G., Hayhurst, H., Pope, M., Williams, S., & Segal, Z. V. (2002). Metacognitive awareness and prevention of relapse in depression: Empirical evidence. *Journal of Consulting and Clinical Psychology, 70,* 275–287.

Tedeschi, R. G., & Calhoun, L. G. (1995). *Trauma and transformation—Growing in the aftermath of suffering.* Thousand Oaks, CA: Sage.

Tedeschi, R. G., & Calhoun, L. G. (1996). The Posttraumatic Growth Inventory: Measuring the positive legacy of trauma. *Journal of Traumatic Stress, 9,* 455–471.

Tedeschi, R. G., & Calhoun, L. G. (2004). Posttraumatic growth: Conceptual foundations and empirical evidence. *Psychological Inquiry, 15,* 1–18.

Wilber, K. (2000). *Integral psychology: Conscious, spirit, psychology, therapy.* Boston: Shambhala Publications.

Wilber, K., Vaughan, F., Wittine, B., & Murphy, M. (1993). The quest for wholeness: Transpersonal therapies. In R.Walsh & F. Vaughan (Eds.), *Paths beyond ego: The transpersonal vision* (pp. 156–173). New York: Perigee Books.

Wong, P. T. P. (1997). Meaning-centered counseling: A cognitive-behavioral approach to logotherapy. *The International forum for logotherapy, 20,* 85–94.

Wong, P. T. P. (1999). Towards an integrative model of meaning-centered counseling and therapy. *The International forum for logotherapy, 22,* 47–55.

Yalom, I. D. (1983). *Existential psychotherapy.* New York: Basic Books.

Yalom, I. D., & Lieberman, M. A. (1991). Bereavement and heightened existential awareness. *Psychiatry, 54,* 334–345.

Zoellner, T., Karl, A., & Maercker, A. (in press). Manual zur Kognitiven Verhaltenstherapie von Posttraumatischen Belastungsstörungen bei Verkehrsunfallopfern nach Blanchard & Hickling. Lengerich: Pabst Verlag.

Zoellner, T., & Maercker, A. (2004). *Posttraumatic growth in clinical psychology—a critical review and introduction of a two component model.* Unpublished manuscript, Dresden University of Technology, Germany.

Zoellner, T., Rabe, S., Karl, A., & Maercker, A. (2004). *Changes in predictive pattern of posttraumatic growth in a controlled CBT for traffic related PTSD.* Unpublished manuscript, Dresden University of Technology, Germany.

18

RESILIENCE AND POSTTRAUMATIC GROWTH: A CONSTRUCTIVE NARRATIVE PERSPECTIVE

DONALD MEICHENBAUM
UNIVERSITY OF WATERLOO

PROLOGUE

I have a story to tell and so do the individuals and clients I see who have a history of having been "victimized." Whether the form of trauma exposure is due to intentional human design (e.g., some form of individual or group violence) or due to exposure to natural disasters (e.g., my having recently lived through four hurricanes in Florida over a short period of time), the need to tell "stories" to others, as well as to oneself, about what happened and the implications, is rather pervasive.

As a result, an individual's (or groups') sense of self and the world are established through the "stories" they tell others and themselves. As the adage goes, "Beware of the stories you tell yourself and others for you will be lived by them."

THE MAIN PROPOSAL

The central premise of this chapter is that the nature of the self-narrative (and group narrative) plays a critical role in determining whether individuals and groups manifest chronic persistent distress and posttraumatic stress disorder (PTSD) or whether they will evidence resilience and posttraumatic growth (PTG). In short, a Constructive Narrative Perspective (CNP) of the concepts of resilience and PTG will be offered to explain the marked individual differences that occur in the aftermath of trauma exposure.

The present thesis can be summarized in a simple, straightforward fashion.

TABLE 18.1
A Constructive Narrative Model of Posttraumatic Reactions

1. Human beings are storytellers and account makers, especially following trauma experience.
2. The type of "stories" individuals and groups offer themselves and others act as the "final common pathway," determining the level of distress *versus* degree of resilience.
3. Research indicates the specific features of the "negative" thinking and accompanying behaviors that lead to chronic persistent distress and PTSD.
4. Various individual and group "healing" activities work in large part because of their ability to have individuals and groups engage in the "power of nonnegative thinking."
5. To move from resilience to the point of experiencing PTG, individuals and groups need to engage in such activities as benefit finding, establishing a future orientation, and constructing meaning, and the commensurate accompanying behaviors.

1. While a number of trauma, pretrauma, and posttrauma factors have been found to influence reactions to trauma experience (see Dalgleish, 2004), it is proposed that the narratives that individuals and groups offer act as the "final common pathways" to influence the levels of adjustment and distress.

2. The burgeoning literature on the impact of trauma, especially the role of cognitive and affective processes, has highlighted what individuals have to do and not do, think and not think, to develop persistent distress and PTSD. As summarized in the following text, the key elements of "negative" thinking that contribute to both individuals' and groups' narratives will be examined. Like an ethologist who studies the detailed features and the flow of animal behavior, a "cognitive ethologist" offers a description of the thinking processes of individuals following trauma exposure. One can look upon such a cognitive descriptive account as offering a formula or algorithm on how to increase the likelihood that an individual or a group will develop persistent PTSD and related forms of distress (or what the psychiatric community calls *comorbid disorders*).

3. Individuals and groups may use a variety of means to engage in resilience-building activities and to foster PTG. These activities may range from using spiritual rituals to employing social supports, from using distraction procedures of keeping busy to retelling their stories in the form of artistic expression or commemorative activities. It is proposed that these varied activities "work" or contribute to healing because they reduce the likelihood of individuals and groups engaging in "negative" counterproductive storytelling and accompanying stress-reducing behaviors. It is proposed that a key feature of resilience is the ability to *engage in nonnegative thinking*.

4. Finally, it is proposed that to go beyond the resilient process of adapting well in the face of adversity to the point of experiencing "growth," more is entailed than the power of nonnegative thinking. To experience PTG, individuals and groups have to engage in such activities as benefit finding, establishing a future orientation, and constructing meaning and the commensurate accompanying behaviors (Table 18.1).

THE CHALLENGE

The study of the impact of trauma experience on individuals and groups is a remarkable story of courage and resilience. Several major reviewers have documented the resilience or the "ability to go on with life" after handling adversity (Bloom, 1998; Linley & Joseph,

2002, 2004; McMillen, 1999; Tedeschi & Calhoun, 2004b; Tedeschi, Park & Calhoun, 1988). These authors observe that such resilience reflects the ability to:

1. Show positive adaptation in spite of significant challenging life experiences.
2. "Bend, but not break" or rebound from adversities.
3. Learn to live with ongoing fears and uncertainty.

To document the role of resilience, they highlight that while exposure to traumatic events (Criterion A events according to the Diagnostic Statistical Manual for the diagnosis of PTSD) is quite common (approximately 60% in men and 50% in women), PTSD is quite low in general (approximately 5% in men and 10% in women). Moreover, they observe that up to 75% of people who are confronted with irrevocable loss do *not* show intense distress. Such resilience in the face of unimaginable loss was evident in the aftermath of the terrorist attacks on September 11, as documented by Schuster and Stein (2001) and Sheehy (2003). Nolen-Hoeksema and Davis (2004) observe that following almost any imaginable trauma, approximately 50% of those most directly affected report at least one positive life change or benefit that they link directly to their traumatic experience. But, not all individuals and groups in the aftermath of trauma exposure evidence such "resilience." A sizeable minority (approximately 20% to 25%) will evidence long-term persistent chronic PTSD, even to the point of attempting suicide (see Meichenbaum, in press). Even after treatment, one-third of clients continue to suffer PTSD. The challenging questions are what distinguished those who evidence resilience *versus* those who manifest chronic persistent clinical levels of distress, and what can be done to nurture and foster resilience?

The absence of an answer to the former question of the distinguishing differential processes has *not* inhibited health care providers from offering extensive advice on how to nurture resilience. Consistent with the notion that resilience can indeed be developed, nurtured, and taught, the American Psychological Association (APA) has created a Help Center (www.APAHelpCenter.org or call 1-800-964-2000) to foster resilience in response to terrorism and other stressful events. They have created educational materials for various specialty groups that enumerate "10 Ways to Build Resilience." These guidelines include:

1. Make connections. (They even include a list of places to look for help.)
2. Avoid seeing crisis as insurmountable problems.
3. Accept that change is part of living.
4. Move toward goals, but stay flexible.
5. Take decisive action.
6. Look for opportunities for self-discovery.
7. Nurture a positive view of yourself.
8. Keep things in perspective. Learn from your past.
9. Maintain a hopeful outlook.
10. Take care of yourself.

Like good "storytellers" who use analogies and metaphors to make their points, the authors of the APA educational brochure "The Road to Resilience" encourage their readers to "think of resilience as similar to taking a raft down a river." Such journeys, like life, require plans, flexibility, perseverance, and help from trusted companions.

Why should such analogies and "storytelling" be helpful? A CNP of resilience helps to explicate the reasons why such "storytelling" and the accompanying array of advice giving (that surely is informed and guided by research finding) work.

WHAT IS A CONSTRUCTIVE NARRATIVE PERSPECTIVE?

People are storytellers. They offer accounts that are designed to make sense out of the world and their place in it. They construct narratives that include descriptions of behavioral events and their and other's reactions to those events. As Mair (1990) observed, "We live through stories."

The observation that people are account makers and construct narratives is not new. From the philosophical musings of Immanuel Kant to those of Jean-Paul Sarre, from the psychological writings of Wilhelm Wundt to those of George Kelly, there is a long tradition of the importance of storytelling or the construction of personal meanings. Common to this tradition is the view that individuals do *not* merely respond to events, but they respond to their interpretations of events. This constructivist viewpoint has both an historical and a current tradition. The simplest rendering of the constructive narrative perspective is the Buddhist observation:

> We are what we think. All that we are arises with our thoughts. With our thoughts ["stories"] we make the world (Dhammapada).

In modern form, Howard (1991) observed:

> We are lived by the stories we tell. Beware of the stories you tell yourself (and one might add tell others), for you will surely be lived by them.

Thomas (2003) has characterized such narratives as a form of "inner conversations," in the tradition of the social psychologist George Herbert Mead, who highlighted the manner in which individuals carry on inner conversations with themselves. In this tradition, consider what happens to people's stories when really bad things (traumatic events) are experienced. Several researchers have observed that when such traumatic events occur, the narratives, beliefs, appraisal processes, attributions, and ruminations are each significantly impacted (see Brewin & Holmes, 2003; Dalgleish, 2004; Ehlers & Clark, 2000; Harvey, 2002; Harvey, Weber & Orbuch, 1990; Janoff-Bulman, 1992). Meichenbaum (1997b) has observed that peoples' ordinary language often proves inadequate to capture their posttraumatic experiences. Instead, such victims of trauma often become "poets" of sorts, using metaphors to describe what they have experienced and the accompanying implications they draw about themselves, the world, and the future. Such metaphorical descriptions are *not* mere idle patterns of speech, but they can act as templates that color the ways events are appraised and the coping options that may be considered.

> "I am a prisoner of the past."
>
> "I am soiled goods."
>
> "I am on sentry duty all the time."
>
> "I stuff my feelings."

Consider the ongoing impact of telling themselves and others that they are "prisoners of the past" or that they are "soiled goods." The metaphors that are offered and the language individuals use to fashion their narratives have important implications for how they appraise events and how they cope with the sequelae of trauma exposure.

But it is *not* only the nature of the metaphors that are incorporated into one's narratives, but a variety of other features that contribute to negative counterproductive thinking. Table 18.2, which was gleaned from the literature on cognitive processes in chronic PTSD, highlights the features of the self-narrative that contribute to the persistence of the stress disorder and related clinical problems. These are the characteristics of thinking that lead survivors toward "being stuck" and experiencing higher levels of distress. Beyond the initial shock, disbelief, numbness, sadness, depression, fears, rage, guilt, and the panoply of intense emotions that follow trauma exposure, comes an appreciation that an individual's way of understanding the world and his or her place in it has been "shattered." As Janoff-Bulman (1992) aptly describes, trauma exposure violates one's implicit beliefs and challenges one's assumptions that the world is safe, controllable, and predictable, and that others are benevolent and can be trusted.

An examination of Table 18.2 highlights the features of a narrative that individuals and groups need to offer themselves and others to maintain persistent chronic distress following trauma exposure. The ingredients for the development of chronic PTSD include:

1. Engaging in self-focused cognitions that have a "victim" theme and that undermine ("shatter") core beliefs.

2. Supplementing the "victim" theme of one's narrative with a set of specific cognitive behaviors consisting of remaining hyper-vigilant, ruminating, brooding, engaging in both contra-factual thinking and upward social comparisons, self-blame and blaming others, with the resultant guilt-engendering feelings and thoughts.

3. Viewing the implications of one's reactions to trauma as negative, not only for now but also in the future, while continuing to persistently pine for the past.

4. Searching for "meaning," as evident in continually asking "why" questions, for which there are no satisfactory answers, resulting in the absence of any resolution or closure.

5. Engaging in avoidant and safety behaviors, delaying help-seeking behaviors and failing to share one's trauma experiences with others ("keeping it a secret").

Ehlers and Clark (2000) have highlighted that the failure to share the "trauma story" with supportive others results in the individual's or groups' story being fragmented, disjointed, disconnected from the past, and being poorly elaborated and disorganized. Such traumatic memories are subject to "perceptual priming" with sensory and motor aspects being highlighted in which the worst moments of the trauma stand out. Unshared traumatic stories are usually poorly integrated into existing autobiographical memories. The use of avoidant and safety behaviors to handle the impact of such storytelling may put individuals at risk for further revictimization.

A CONSTRUCTIVE NARRATIVE PERSPECTIVE OF RESILIENCE

The CNP advocates that the way individuals tell themselves and others stories will determine the nature of their future vulnerability, their coping efforts, and the levels of adjustment and resilience that follow exposure to trauma experience. Two important *caveats* need to be highlighted about these propositions. First, this is a dynamic interactive process. How successful an individual's coping efforts prove to be will influence the nature of his or her storytelling that will, in turn, influence resilience-enhancing efforts.

TABLE 18.2

Characteristics of the Narrative Associated With Persistent and Higher Levels of Distress
Following Trauma Exposure

Thinking Pattern	Prototypic Examples
Engage in contra-factual thinking[1]	"If only I had . . . this would not have happened." "Only if . . . ." "I never thought this would happen to me."
Self-blaming and guilt-engendering thinking (blameworthy, ashamed, humiliated, full of regrets)[2]	"I should have . . . ." "I failed to protect her." "I berate myself before others do."
Focus on blaming others[3]	"I have been betrayed." "I won't rest until there is justice."
Espouse culturally based blame attributions[4]	"People will wonder what kind of family we are because we allowed this to happen." "Because I was raped, people will think that (Black, White) women are loose." "They will think I am too weak to cope."
Engage in self-focused thinking[5] (Viewing self as a "victim," mentally defeated and permanently changed)	"I feel trapped." "I have no control over anything." "I am brain dead." "Dead man walking." "My body (reputation) is ruined forever."
Altered beliefs[6] (World is unsafe, future unpredictable, people are untrustworthy)	"No place is safe." "I can't trust my instincts (judgment) any longer." "You can't trust anyone."
Be hyper-vigilant[7] (Perceive ongoing threat and impending doom; distinctions between then and there and here and now are blurred)	"I live in fear." "I am on every day. Danger is everywhere." "I am on the lookout all the time." "I am a walking target." "I can't let the kids out of my sight."
Think negatively about the past, present, and future[8] (Fail to retrieve specific "positive" memories)	"It will never be over." "My life is destroyed." "Time is my enemy."
Ruminate and brood about the past and focus on what has been lost[9] (Continually pine for the past)	"I just wish life would go back to the way it was." "I can't rest until I get even." "I'll never get over it."
Ruminate about "near miss" experiences[10]	"It could have been us." "You know how close we were to being hurt?" "It percolates, over and over. There are reminders everywhere." "My thoughts are like an overcrowded train that jumps from track to track."
Dwell on negative implications of reactions[11]	"If I react like that, it must mean that I am going mad." "This is not normal. I can't control my emotions and this means. . . ."

TABLE 18.2 (*Continued*)

Thinking Pattern	Prototypic Examples
Engage in deliberate avoidant and safety behaviors, even if unwarranted[12] (Cognitive and behavioral avoidance that leads to being "stuck" and disengaging and giving up)	"I can't allow myself to think about it." "I delay seeking help." "I am not worthy of help." "I can't share this with anyone. No one would understand...." "I can't allow myself to have a good time." "If I deprive myself, then...." "I try and keep busy so I don't think about this."
Feel helpless, hopeless, demoralized, and feel victimized by one's thoughts, feelings, circumstances[13]	"These thoughts just keep coming." "I get gripped by my feelings of depression and fear." "I don't think I can stand the pain anymore."
Engage in upward social comparison[14]	"How come she is doing so well and she went through less?" "Others will see that I am a victim." "Why do I have to have problems other people don't have?"
Continually and extensively search for meaning, but fail to find satisfactory resolution[15]	"What did I do to deserve this?" "Why me?" "Why now?" "I lost faith in God."

[1] Davis & Lehman, 1995; Greenberg, 1995
[2] Kubany & Manke, 1995; Lee, Scragg, & Turner, 2001
[3] Janoff-Bulman, & Gunn, 1988
[4] Neville, Heppner, Oh, Spanierman, & Clark, 2004
[5] Ehlers & Clark, 2000
[6] Janoff-Bulman, 1999
[7] Ehlers et al., 2002; Foa, Steketee, & Olasov-Rothbaum, 1989
[8] Nolen-Hoeksema & Davis, 2004; Treyner, Gonzalez, & Nolen-Hoeksema, 2003
[9] Holman & Silver, 1998: Nolen-Hoeksema & Davis, 2004; Wortman & Silver, 1987
[10] Meichenbaum, 1997b
[11] Ehlers et al., 2002
[12] Ehlers & Clark, 2000; Ehlers & Steil, 1995
[13] Meichenbaum, in press
[14] McAdams, Reynolds, Lewis, Patter, & Bowan, 2001   [15] Silver, Boon, & Stones, 1983; Tait & Silver, 1989

A good example of this comes from the treatment literature on exposure-based interventions with rape victims. Foa, Molner, and Cashman (1995) analyzed the narratives of rape victims at the beginning and at the end of successful therapy. The exposure-based treatment involved providing the client with a safe environment to tell and retell her victimization story to "emotionally process" the trauma and reduce the negative affect attached to the memories and residual triggers. In this way, the clients learned to "segment" the trauma story into a beginning, middle, and end, and now also a future. The opportunity to tell and retell such accounts help clients better appreciate what they did to survive and provides them with data that offering such accounts of the "worst moments" of the victimization experiences does *not* result in their "falling apart." Such guided storytelling provides disconfirmatory information and helps clients take back control and experience a sense of mastery.

As the clients began to improve and assimilate and integrate the victimization experiences into the flow of their autobiographical memories, Foa et al. (1995) observed that the nature of the narratives ("stories") they told also changed. The improved clients' narratives evidenced a decrease in unfinished thoughts and repetitions and a greater sense of personal agency. Moreover, such narrative changes correlated with symptom improvement in the form of trauma-related anxiety. Van Minnen, Wessel, Dijkstra, and Roelefs (2002) replicated these findings of narrative changes that accompany symptom reduction. Thus, the changes in adjustment (symptom reduction and reduction of avoidance [safety] behaviors) influenced the changes in the clients' narratives, which in turn, enabled further coping efforts. This, in turn, influenced the nature of the narratives of not only the clients, but also how supportive others can provide a way to craft narratives about the changes that have occurred. As Adler (1997, p. 30) observed: "When we are able to formulate the right story, and it is heard by the right listener, we are apt to deal more effectively with the experience."

Gail Sheehy (2003, p. 32), in her moving account of one town's passage from trauma to hope, following the World Trade Center terrorist attacks observed:

> The best way to build bridges from the land of the dead to the land of the living is to tell and retell the stories of those who are gone; that guarantees a measure of immortality. The key is to shift the emphasis from the way the victim died to the way he or she lived. (Sheehy, 2003, p. 392)

It is proposed that it is *not* only the opportunity to tell one's story, but how one changes the nature of the storytelling over time, that influences the adjustment process.

The *second caveat* when considering the CNP of resilience is the need to recognize the *gradual transformation of the individual's and group's* narratives. Individuals who manifest resilience may continue to evidence *co-concurrent* negative and positive features in their narratives, reflecting both bouts of pining for the past and transforming their mixed emotions into behavioral enactments and "missions" for the future.

With these two caveats concerning a dynamic interactive process and a gradual transformation in mind, we can reconsider why the "10 Ways to Build Resilience" offered by the knowledgeable authors of the APA brochures may work. The suggestions offered fall into the "do" and "not do" categories. Readers are explicitly guided to change their narratives (e.g., avoid seeing the crisis as insurmountable; keep things in perspective; look for opportunities for self-discovery; maintain a hopeful outlook; accept that change is part of living) or to engage in activities that will provide the conditions for changes to one's narrative and accompanying coping efforts (e.g., move toward goals; take decisive action; make corrections; take care of yourself). Each of these suggestions are designed to reduce the likelihood of negative thinking. The "power of such nonnegative thinking" should be distinguished from the limited efficacy and misguided advocacy of "the power of positive thinking," as discussed by Held (2002); Meichenbaum (1997a); Meichenbaum and Fitzpatrick (1993); Taylor (1989); and Wortman (2004). The negative self-punitive elements of one's narratives and the negative elements of social interactions are more strongly related to mental health than are positive elements.

A CONSTRUCTIVE NARRATIVE PERSPECTIVE OF POSTTRAUMATIC GROWTH

The experience of PTG is more than the ability to engage in nonnegative thinking and the coping activities that help to nurture and maintain a constructive narrative. Posttraumatic growth is the experience of *positive change* that occurs as a result of a struggle with

TABLE 18.3

Kinds of Thinking and Behaviors That Lead Survivors Toward "Growth"

Thinking Pattern	Prototypic Examples
Benefit seeking, finding, and reminding—SELF[1]	"I am wiser (stronger) as a result of this experience." "I am better prepared for whatever comes along." "I am less afraid of change." "I never knew I could get along on my own." "I am better now at helping others."
Benefit seeking, finding, and reminding—OTHERS[2]	"This brought us all together." "I learned I am my brother's keeper." "I learned not to immerse myself in other people's pain."
Engage in downward comparison[3]	"I think about others and how it could have been worse." "I recognize that I need to accept help." "My view of what is important in life has changed."
Establish a future orientation[4]	"My view of what is important in life has changed." "I see new possibilities and goals to work on." "I am now able to focus on the fact that it happened and not on how it happened."
Constructing meaning[5]	"We survived and we have a chance to live and we're choosing life." "I am no longer willing to be defined by my victimization." "I survived for a purpose. I accept that responsibility. I owe it to those who perished to tell their stories (honor their memory, share with others, prevent this from happening again)." "I moved from being a victim to becoming a survivor and even a thriver." "I can make a gift of my pain and loss to others." "I now know God."

[1] Affleck & Tennen, 1996; Linley & Joseph, 2002, 2004
[2] McMillen, 2004; McMillen, Zuravin, & Rideout, 1995
[3] Nolen-Hoeksema & Larson, 1999; Monk, Winslade, Crocket, & Epton, 1997
[4] Pals & McAdams, 2004; Tedeschi & Calhoun, 2004b
[5] Frazier, Conlon, & Glasen, 2001; Neimeyer, 2001; Pargament, Koenig, & Perez, 2000; Silver et al., 1983; Tait & Silver, 1989; Wortman, Battle, & Lemkau, 1997

highly challenging life crises. As enumerated in Table 18.3, the kind of thinking and accompanying behaviors that lead toward "growth" include:

1. Seeking, finding, reminding, and constructing benefits for oneself and others.
2. Establishing and maintaining a future orientation with altered priorities.
3. Constructing meaning, a coherent narrative, and engaging in special activities or "missions" that transform loss into something good that will come out of it.

To illustrate resilience and "growth," I will conclude my story with a personal anecdote. Consider the case of Lynn and Michael Aptman whose daughter Melissa was murdered in 1995 during a carjacking. She was about to graduate from Washington University in St. Louis. How does one survive such a devastating tragedy? As Dr. Aptman, a neurologist, (2002, p. 286) observed:

> I have tried not to be too harsh on myself. . . . I have survived by taking life one day at a time. . . . I cherish Melissa's memory even more now. . . . I have great joy in being father to my two surviving children. . . . As a result of Melissa's death I am more sensitive in working with difficult cases in the ICU. . . . Sad as it may sound, I have become a better person as a result of the death of my child. . . . I believe that through prayer and good deeds one can bind up the soul of a loved one as a source of eternal blessing. . . . I find that meditation helps cleanse my soul and allows me to feel closer to Melissa. . . . Every day since Melissa's death I have been the fortunate recipient of acts of kindness. . . . I believe we are defined by how we respond to that kind of pain.

The Aptmans responded to their pain by establishing an institute in Melissa's name to prevent violence and to treat victims of violence (see www.melissainstitute.org). I am privileged and honored to be the Research Director of the Melissa Institute and help a family transform their pain to something good. As it says on Melissa's gravestone, "Her memory lives in each of our hearts. . . . Together we must make a difference."

EPILOGUE

The present analysis of the role that cognitive and affective factors play in the persistence of stress disorders and in the processes of resilience and PTG does *not* preclude the role of other sources of influence. For example, available evidence suggests that exposure to trauma often brings about permanent neurobiological changes that can cause persistent hyper-arousal, resulting in PTSD symptoms, such as difficulty concentrating and sleep problems. Similarly, research has also begun to implicate the neurochemical profile that characterizes resilience (i.e., the neurotransmitters, neuropeptides, and hormones that are known to be altered by exposure to traumatic stressors) (Southwick, Morgan, Vythilingam, Krystal, & Charuey 2003). Perhaps, some day we will be able to identify a neurobiological resilience factor that may be tied to genetic vulnerability (see True et al., 1993). For now, however, the present analysis argues that another important area to search for vulnerability factors is in the area of cognitive processes. The ways in which individuals who have experienced trauma tell "stories" or construct narratives to themselves and to others plays a critical role and is clearly worthy of further investigation.

REFERENCES

Adler, H. M. (1997). The history of the present illness in treatment: Who is listening and why does it matter. *Journal of the American Board of Family Practice, 10*, 28–35.

Affleck, G., & Tennen, H. (1996). Constructing benefits from adversity: Adaptational significance and dispositional underpinnings. *Journal of Personality, 64*, 899–922.

Aptman, M. (2992). Personal history: One is a million? *Neurology, 59*, 784–786.

Bloom, S. (1990). By the crowd they have been broken, by the crowd they shall be healed: The social transformation of traumas. In R. G. Tedeschi, C. L. Park, & L. G. Calhoun (Eds.), *Posttraumatic growth: Positive changes in the aftermath of crisis* (pp. 179–213). Mahwah, NJ: Lawrence Erlbaum Associates.

Brewin, C. R., & Holman, E. A. (2003). Psychological theories of posttraumatic stress disorder. *Clinical Psychology Review, 3*, 339–376.

Dalgleish, T. (2004). Cognitive approaches to posttraumatic stress disorder: The evolution of multirepresentational theorizing. *Psychological Bulletin, 130*, 228–260.

Dalgleish, T. (1999). Counterfactual thinking and coping with traumatic life events. In N. J. Roese & J. M. Olson (Eds.), *What might have been: The social psychology of contrafactual thinking* (pp. 353–374). Mahwah, NJ: Lawrence Erlbaum Associates.

Davis, C. G., & Lehman, D. R. (1995). Counterfactual thinking and coping with traumatic life events. In N. J. Roese & J. M. Olsen (Eds.), *What have been: The social psychology of counterfactual thinking* (pp. 353–374). Mahwah, NJ: Lawrence Erlbaum Associates.

Ehlers, A., & Clark, D. M. (2000). A cognitive model of posttraumatic stress disorder. *Behaviour Research and Therapy, 38*, 319–345.

Ehlers, A., Hackman, A., Steil, R., Clohessy, S., Wenninger, K., & Winter, H. (2002). The nature of intrusive memories after trauma: The warning signal hypothesis. *Behaviour Research and Therapy, 40*, 995–1002.

Ehlers, A., & Steil, R. (1995). Maintenance of intrusive memories in posttraumatic stress disorder: A cognitive approach. *Behavioural and Cognitive Psychotherapy, 23*, 217–249.

Foa, E. B., Molnar, C., & Cashman, L. (1995). Change in rape narratives during exposure therapy for PTSD. *Journal of Traumatic Stress, 8*, 675–690.

Foa, E. B., Steketee, G., & Olasov-Rothbaum, B. (1989). Behavioral/cognitive conceptualization of posttraumatic stress disorder. *Behavior Therapy, 20*, 155–176.

Frazier, P., Conlon, A., & Glaser, T. (2001). Positive and negative life changes following sexual assault. *Journal of Consulting and Clinical Psychology, 69*, 1048–1055.

Greenberg, M. A. (1995). Cognitive processing of traumas: The role of intrusive thoughts and reappraisals. *Journal of Applied Social Psychology, 25*, 1262–1296.

Harvey, J. H. (2002). *Perspectives on loss and trauma: Assaults on the self.* Thousand Oaks, CA: Sage.

Harvey, J. H., Weber, A. L., & Orbuch, T. L. (1990). *Interpersonal accounts: A social psychological perspective.* Oxford: Basel Blackwell.

Held, B. S. (2002). The tyranny of the positive attitude in the U.S.: Observation and speculation. *Journal of Clinical Psychology, 58*, 965–992.

Holman, E. A., & Silver, R. C. (1998). Getting "stuck" in the past: Temporal orientation and coping with trauma. *Journal of Personality and Social Psychology, 74*, 1146–1163.

Howard, G. S. (1991). Cultural tales: A narrative approach to thinking, cross-cultural psychology, and psychotherapy. *American Psychologist, 46*, 187–197.

Janoff, J. B., & Gunn, L. (1988). Coping with disease, crime and accidents: The role of self-blame attributions. In L. Y. Abramson (Ed.), *Social cognitions and clinical psychology: A synthesis.* New York: Guilford.

Janoff-Bulman, R. (1992). *Shattered assumptions: Toward a new psychology of trauma.* New York: Free Press.

Janoff-Bulman, R. (1999). Rebuilding shattered assumptions after traumatic events: Coping processes and outcomes. In C. R. Snyder (Ed.), *Coping: The Psychology of What Works.* New York: Oxford University Press.

Janoff-Bulman, R., & Berger, A. (2002). The other side of trauma: Toward a psychology of appreciation. In J. H. Harvey & E. D. Miller (Eds.), *Loss and trauma: General and close relationship perspectives* (pp. 29–44). Philadelphia: Brunner-Routledge.

Joseph, S., Williams, R., & Yule, W. (1997). *Understanding posttraumatic stress: A psychosocial perspective and its treatment.* Chichester, England: Wiley.

Kubany, E. C., & Manke, F. P. (1995). Cognitive therapy for trauma-related guilt: Conceptual bases and treatment outlines. *Cognitive and Behavioral Practice, 7*, 27–62.

Lee, D. A., Scragg, P., & Turner, S. (2001). The role of shame and guilt in traumatic events: A clinical model of shame-based and guilt-based PTSD. *British Journal of Medical Psychology, 74*, 451–466.

Linley, P. A., & Joseph, S. (2002). Posttraumatic growth. *Counseling and Psychotherapy Journal, 13*, 14–17.

Linley, P. A., & Joseph, S. (2004). Positive change following trauma and adversity: A review. *Journal of Traumatic Stress, 17*, 11–21.

Mair, M. (1990). Telling psychological tales. *International Journal of Construct Psychology, 3*, 121–135.

Martin, L. L., & Tesser, A. (1996). Clarifying our thoughts. In R. S. Wyer (Ed.), *Ruminative thoughts: Advances in social cognition* (Vol. 9, pp. 189–209). Mahwah, NJ: lawrence Erlbaum Associates.

McAdams, D. P., Reynolds, J., Lewis, M., Patten, A. H., & Bowan, P. J. (2001). When bad things turn good and good things turn bad. *Personality and Social Psychology Bulletin, 27*, 474–485.

McMillen, J. C. (1999). Better for it: How people benefit from adversity. *Social Work, 44*, 455–468.

McMillen, J. C. (2004). Posttraumatic growth: What is it all about? *Psychological Inquiry, 15*, 48–52.

McMillen, J. C., Smith, E. M., & Fisher, R. H. (1997). Perceived benefit and mental health after three types of disaster. *Journal of Consulting and Clinical Psychology, 63*, 1037–1043.

McMillen, J. C., Zuravin, S., & Rideout, G. (1995). Perceived benefit from child abuse. *Journal of Consulting and Clinical Psychology, 63*, 1037–1043.

Meichenbaum, D. (1997a). *Cognitive behavior modification An integrative approach.* New York: Plenum Press.

Meichenbaum, D. (1997b). *Treating individuals with posttraumatic stress disorder.* Clearwater, FL: Institute Press.

Meichenbaum, D. (2000). Treating patients with PTSD: A constructive narrative approach. *NC-PTSD Clinical Quarterly, 9*, 55–59.

Meichenbaum D. (in press). Trauma and suicide. In T. Ellis (Ed.), *Cognition and suicide: Theory, research and practice.* Washington, DC: American Psychological Association.

Meichenbaum, D., & Fitzpatrick, D. (1993). A constructive narrative perspective in stress and coping. In L. Goldberger & S. Breznitz (Eds.), *Handbook of stress: Theoretical and clinical aspects.* New York: Free Press.

Monk, G., Winslade, J., Crocket, E., & Epton, D. (Eds.), (1997). *Narrative therapy in practice.* San Francisco: Jossey-Bass.

Neimeyer, R. A. (2001). *Meaning reconstruction and the experience of loss.* Washington, DC: American Psychological Association.

Neville, H. A., Heppner, M. J., Oh, E., Spanierman, L. B., & Clark, M. (2004). General and culturally specific factors influencing Black and White rape survivors' self-esteem. *Psychology of Women Quarterly, 28*, 83–94.

Nolen-Hoeksema, S., & Davis, C. G. (2004). Theoretical and methodological issues in the assessment and interpretation of posttraumatic growth. *Psychological Inquiry, 15*, 60–64.

Nolen-Hoeksema, S., & Larson, J. (1999). *Coping with loss.* Mahwah, NJ: Lawrence Erlbaum Associates.

Pals, J. L., & McAdams, D. P. (2004). The transformed self: A narrative understanding of posttraumatic growth. *Psychological Inquiry, 15*, 65–69.

Pargament, K. I., Koenig, H. G., & Perez, L. M. (2000). The many methods of religious coping: Developmental and initial validation of the RCOPE. *Journal of Clinical Psychology, 56*, 519–543.

Park, C. L. (1998). Stress-related growth and thriving through coping: The roles of personality and cognitive processes. *Journal of Social Issues, 54*, 267–277.

Schuster, M., & Stein, S. (2001). A national survey of stress reactions after the September 11, 2001 terrorist attack. *New England Journal of Medicine, 345*, 1507–1512.

Sheehy G. (2003). *Middletown, America: One town's passage from trauma to hope.* New York: Random House.

Silver, R. C., Boon, S., & Stones, M. H. (1983). Searching for meaning in misfortune. *Journal of Social Issues, 39*, 81–102.

Southwick, S. M., Morgan, C. A., Vythilingam, M., Krystal, J. H., & Charney, D. S. (2003). Emerging neuro-biological factors in stress resilience. *PTSD Research Quarterly, 14*, 1–3.

Tait, R., & Silver, R. C. (1989). Coming to terms with major negative life events. In J. S. Uleman & J. A. Bargh (Eds.), *Unintended thought* (pp. 351–382). New York: Guilford.

Taylor, S. E. (1989). *Positive distortions: Creative self-deception and the healthy mind.* New York: Basic Books.

Taylor, S. E., Kemeny, M. E., Reed, G. M., Bower, J. E., & Gruenewald, T. L. (2000). Psychological resources, positive illusions and health. *American Psychologist, 58*, 99–109.

Tedeschi, R. G. (1999). Violence transformed: Posttraumatic growth in survivors and their societies. *Aggression and Violent Behavior, 4*, 319–341.

Tedeschi, R. G., & Calhoun, L. G. (1996). The posttraumatic growth inventory: Measuring the positive direction of trauma. *Journal of Traumatic Stress, 9*, 455–471.

Tedeschi, R. G., & Calhoun, L. G. (2004a). *Helping the bereaved parent: A clinician's guide.* New York: Brunner-Routledge.

Tedeschi, R. G., & Calhoun, L. G. (2004b). Posttraumatic growth: Conceptual foundations and empirical evidence. *Psychological Inquiry, 15*, 1–18.

Tedeschi, R. G., Park, C. L., & Calhoun, L. G. (Eds.). (1988). *Posttraumatic growth: Positive changes in the aftermath of crisis.* Mahwah, NJ: Lawrence Erlbaum Associates.

Thomas, P. M. (2003). Protection, dissociation and internal roles: Modeling and treating effects of child abuse. *Review of General Psychology, 7*, 364–380.

Thompson, N. (Ed.). (2002). *Loss and grief: A guide for human service practitioners.* New York: Palgrave.

Treynor, W., Gonzalez, R., & Nolen-Hoeksema, S. (2003). Rumination reconsidered: A psychometric analysis. *Cognitive Therapy and Research, 27*, 247–259.

True, W. R., Rice, J., Eisen, S. A., Heath, A. C., Goldberg, L., Lyons, M. J., et al. (1993). A twin study of genetic and environmental contributions to liability for posttraumatic stress symptoms. *Archives of General Psychiatry, 50*, 257–264.

VanMinnen, A., Wessel, I., Dijkstra, T., & Roelefs, K. (2002). Changes on PTSD patients' narratives during prolonged exposure therapy: A replication and extension. *Journal of Traumatic Stress, 15*, 255–258.

Wortman, C. B. (2004). Posttraumatic growth: Progress and problem. *Psychological Inquiry, 15*, 81–90.

Wortman, C. B., Battle, E. S., & Lemkau, J. P. (1997). Coming to terms with sudden traumatic death of a spouse or a child. In R. C., Davis & A. J. Lurigio (Eds.), *Victims of crime* (pp. 108–133). Thousand Oaks, CA: Sage.

Wortman, C. B., & Silver, R. C. (1987). Coping with irrevocable loss. In G. R. Van den Bos & B. K. Bryant (Eds.), *Cataclysms, crisis and catastrophes.* Washington, DC: American Psychological Association.

Wortman, C. B., & Silver, R. C. (2001). The myths of coping with loss revisited. In M. S. Stroebe, R. O. Hannsson, W. Stroebe, & H. Schut (Eds.), *Handbook of bereavement research: Consequences, coping and care* (pp. 405–429). Washington, DC: American Psychological Association.

Author Index

A

Abbot, R. A., 31, 45, 182, 195
Abraido-Lanza, A. F., 58 , 63
Acree, M., 124, 136
Adinolfi, A. J., 216, 222
Adler, A. B., 233, 244
Adler, H. M., 362, 364
Affleck, G., 3, 4, 17, 21, 23, 31, 32, 40, 45, 48, 49,
    59, 60, 61, 62, 63, 64, 66, 67, 139, 149, 159, 168,
    170, 171, 174, 175, 218, 219, 221, 233, 243, 247,
    263, 275, 287, 329, 333, 341, 347, 352, 363,
    364
Ahrons, C., 109, 116
Albom, M., 108, 116
Alday, C. S., 30, 44, 251, 261
Alden, L. E., 169, 174
Aldwin, C. M., 51, 64, 92, 95, 127, 128, 134, 178,
    191, 193, 226, 228, 229, 230, 231, 243, 251, 259,
    277, 283, 313, 329
Alexander, D. A., 226, 230, 232, 237, 240,
    243
Alexander, P. C., 74, 77, 78
Alferi, S. M., 51, 52, 57, 64, 141, 146, 149, 150, 151,
    152, 153, 154, 155, 157,159,163, 164, 167, 170,
    171, 172, 173, 219, 221, 222, 342, 343, 344, 348,
    353
Allumbaugh, D. L., 181, 193
Al-Mabuk, R. H., 321, 323, 329, 330
Alvarez, W., 157, 172, 187, 194, 253
Alvaro, C., 19, 22, 53, 54, 56, 62, 63, 65, 88, 97,
    168, 173, 314, 332
American Cancer Society, 53, 64
American Psychiatric Association, 253, 259, 312,
    329, 335, 352
Amir, M., 7, 248, 249, 250, 253, 254, 256, 259,
    261
Amylon, J. R., 268, 285

Anagnos, G., 242, 245
Andersen, B. L., 138, 171
Andersen, H. S., 226, 243
Anderson, A., 76, 79
Anderson, B., 138, 171
Andrew, C., 226, 246
Andrykowski, M. A., 14, 21, 33, 41, 49, 51, 64, 65,
    139, 140, 141, 142, 151, 152, 157, 158, 168, 169,
    171, 172, 217, 221, 222
Angus, L., 76, 78
Ano, G. G., 125, 126, 134
Anthony, E. J., 28, 40, 251, 259
Antoni, M. H., 51, 52, 57, 61, 64, 65, 141, 146, 149,
    150, 151, 152, 153, 154, 157, 159, 162, 163, 164,
    167, 170, 171, 172, 173, 174, 221, 222, 223, 313,
    331, 342, 343, 344, 348, 352, 353
Antonovsky, A., 30, 31, 40, 187, 189, 193,
    252, 259
Aptman, M., 363, 364
Aquirre-Hochbaum, S., 129, 134
Arbuthnot, K., 235, 244
Armeli, S., 51, 57, 60, 64, 169, 171, 225, 244, 314,
    329
Armor, D. A., 347, 354
Armsworth, M. W., 251, 259
Arvay, M. J., 77, 79
Aspinwall, L. G., 31, 40, 45, 225, 244
Austin, J. L., 321, 329
Axsom, D., 88, 99

B

Bachmann, N., 187, 195
Bachorowsky, J. A., 190, 194
Back, S., 214, 218, 223
Bailer, M., 187, 194
Baker, F., 51, 64, 141, 143, 151, 152, 154, 172

Baker, J. M., 20, 21
Bakhshi, P., 324, 332
Baltes, P. B., 94, 95, 307, 308
Banaji, M. R., 84, 96
Bandura, A., 178, 193, 256, 260
Bannister, D., 75, 78
Bansal, A., 30, 42
Barbarin, O. A., 191, 193
Barkan, S., 214, 218, 223
Barnes, M. K., 113, 116
Barnett, K., 297, 309
Barrett, W., 91, 95
Barroso, J., 216, 221
Barsalou, L. W., 69, 78
Bartone, P. T., 232, 233, 244
Bass, E., 325, 329
Battle, E. S., 363, 367
Bauer, J. J., 50, 64
Baumeister, R. F., 321
Beck, A. T., 181, 187, 213
Becker, B., 25, 43, 265, 285
Beckett, J. O., 123, 134
Behr, S. K., 57, 64, 145
Belavich, T., 123, 137
Belec, R. H., 49, 64
Bell, R., 75, 78, 216, 222
Benda, B. B., 328, 330
Bendermacher, N., 76, 80
Benjamin, H., 344, 353
Bennett, C. L., 216, 222
Bennett, H. Y., 84, 95, 216
Ben-Sira, Z., 251, 252, 254, 260
Berg, M., 72, 79, 172
Bergin, A. E., 131, 134, 328, 329
Berkes, F., 242, 244
Berking, M., 345, 346, 352
Berkman, L., 313, 329
Berlinsky, E. B., 251, 260
Berman, M., 21, 32, 41, 60, 61, 65
Bernaards, C. A., 141, 146, 147, 149, 151, 152, 154,
     155, 159, 162, 163, 166, 168, 171
Bernardy, N. C., 59, 66
Best, C. L., 82, 98
Best, K. M., 272, 286
Best, S. R., 240, 244
Bettle, J., 308, 309
Betz, N. E., 13, 22
Biller, H. B., 251, 260
Binder-Brynes, K., 250, 263
Bishop, M., 33, 45
Blake, D. D., 82, 97
Blanchard, E., 349, 352
Bless, H., 94, 99
Bliss, J., 161, 175
Bloch, S., 337, 342, 343, 344, 353
Block, J., 182, 194
Block, K., 65, 144, 148, 150, 151, 152, 153, 157,
     158, 173, 223
Block, P., 65, 144, 148, 150, 151, 152, 153, 157, 158,
     173, 223
Blomberg, B. B., 146, 150, 155, 164, 173, 344, 353

Bloom, S., 36, 40, 63, 64, 356, 364
Bluck, S., 308, 309
Bonanno, G. A., 25, 26, 28, 30, 36, 40, 71, 78, 87,
     95, 177, 178, 181, 183, 193, 194
Book, A., 34, 42
Boon, S., 361, 366
Booth, R. J., 48, 66, 140, 173
Booth-Jones, M., 141, 175
Bortz, J., 208, 213
Bosquet, M., 267, 270, 272, 284
Botella, L., 72, 79
Boulad, F., 169, 173
Bowan, P. J., 361, 366
Bower, J. E., 9, 49, 64, 82, 87, 95, 141, 146, 147,
     149, 150, 151, 152, 154, 155, 159, 162, 163, 166,
     168, 170, 171, 220, 221, 223, 366
Bowes, L. B., 240, 243
Bowlby, J., 83, 93, 95
Boxer, P., 132, 134
Boyers, A. E., 51, 52, 57, 64, 141, 146, 149, 150,
     151, 152, 153, 154, 155, 157, 159, 164, 170, 172,
     174, 219, 221, 222, 342, 343, 344, 348, 352,
     353
Brady, M. J., 51, 142, 168
Branstetter, A. D., 169, 170, 174, 297, 309, 345, 346,
     348, 354
Brant, C., 124, 137
Brashers, D. E., 216, 222
Breiner, S. J., 250, 260
Brennan, M., 127, 134
Brenner, I., 250, 257, 260, 261
Brenner, R. R., 124, 134
Brester, M., 220, 223
Bretherton, I., 270, 284
Brewin, C. R., 202, 213, 358, 364
Brickman, P., 94, 95
Briones, D., 129, 134
Britt, T. W., 233, 244
Brock, T. C., 90, 95
Brockopp, D. Y., 141, 171
Brofenbrenner, U., 12, 21
Brown, J. D., 182, 188, 195, 251, 262, 347, 354
Brown, S. W., 321, 331
Brunello, N., 312, 329
Bruner, J., 70, 78
Brunet, A., 240, 244
Bruno, M., 26, 43
Brustrom, J., 251, 259
Bryant, B. K., 82, 96
Buddin, B. J., 275, 285
Buick, D. L., 48, 66, 140, 173
Bulman, R. J., 122, 134
Bunk, D., 250, 260
Burgess, A. W., 92, 95
Burgess, C., 161, 175
Burke, K. J., 228, 229, 244
Burke, T. K., 133, 134
Burnett, J., 313, 331
Burt, M. R., 51, 64, 82, 95
Butollo, W., 19, 22, 53, 66, 200, 204, 213
Butter, E. M., 126, 127, , 136, 317

C

Cacciapaglia, H., 141, 173
Cacioppo, J. T., 33, 46
Cadell, S., 7, 16, 21, 123, 134, 216, 222, 264, 284, 329
Calhoun, L. G., 3, 4, 5, 6, 7, 8, 9, 10, 11, 12, 13, 14, 15, 16, 17, 18, 19, 20, 21, 22, 23, 25, 29, 32, 33, 41, 45, 51, 52, 53, 55, 57, 60, 61, 66, 69, 70, 73, 74, 77, 80, 82, 84, 86, 87, 89, 91, 92, 95, 98, 101, 104, 108, 109, 110, 112, 117, 123, 127, 136, 137, 139, 140, 141, 149, 158, 159, 165, 166, 167, 171, 174, 176, 177, 180, 181, 184, 189, 191, 194, 195, 200, 202, 204, 213, 214, 217, 218, 223, 225, 226, 228, 229, 233, 239, 244, 247, 251, 254, 256, 257, 260, 262, 264, 265, 266, 270, 274, 275, 278, 279, 280, 282, 283, 284, 285, 287, 291, 292, 293, 294, 297, 298, 300, 303, 304, 307, 308, 309, 312, 313, 314, 316, 317, 318, 323, 328, 329, 332, 334, 338, 340, 341, 347, 349, 350, 352, 354, 357, 363, 366, 367
Calmonte, R., 187, 195
Cameron, A., 48, 65
Cameron, A. E., 35, 42
Cameron, C. L., 33, 45
Cameron, J., 126, 135
Campbell, J. D., 169, 174
Campos, R. G., 274, 285
Cann, A., 84, 87, 95, 127, 136, 149, 177, 194, 225, 244, 260
Cannon-Bowers, J. A., 235, 244, 247
Cantor, N., 90, 95
Caplan, G., 4, 21
Cardillo, L. W., 216, 222
Cardis, P. A., 321, 329
Carey, R. G., 130, 134
Carli, L. L., 84, 95
Carlier, I. V. E., 240, 244, 341, 352
Carlson, C. R., 14, 21, 33, 41, 64, 139, 172, 222, 269
Carlson, E. A., 269, 285
Carpenter, J. S., 141, 142, 150, 151, 152, 153, 164, 171
Carter, W. G., 275, 287
Carver, C., 128, 134
Carver, C. S., 30, 31, 41, 45, 58, 62, 64, 139, 141, 146, 150, 154, 162, 163, 167, 170, 171, 173, 174, 182, 189, 193, 194, 195, 313, 330, 353
Cashman, L., 204, 213, 361, 365
Cassel, J. B., 28, 44
Catania, J., 214, 222
C'deBaca, J., 61, 66
Cella, D. F., 4, 21, 140, 142, 171
Chaiken, S., 84, 95
Chalfant, H. P., 129, 134
Chamberlain, K., 31, 41
Chan, C. L. W., 19, 22, 58, 65, 161, 172
Chandler, M. J., 269, 270, 287
Charney, D. S., 364, 366
Chatters, L. M., 125, 129, 135, 137
Chesler, M., 191, 193
Chow, H. C., 291, 309

Chung, S., 48, 65
Chwalisz, K., 113, 116
Cialdini, R. B., 90, 95
Cicchetti, D., 25, 27, 41, 43, 265, 267, 269, 270, 284, 285
Clark, D. M., 348, 352, 358, 358, 361, 365
Clark, L. A., 53, 64
Clipp, E. C., 82, 96, 200, 201, 213, 216, 222
Clohessy, S., 361, 365
Cloitre, M., 258, 260
CNN, 124, 134
Coastworth, J. D., 259, 261
Coates, D., 94, 95, 214, 222, 323, 330
Coates, T. J., 214, 222
Coatsworth, J. D., 36, 43, 264, 268, 272, 273, 277, 282, 286
Cocktam, A. M., 216, 222
Cohen Silver, R., 193, 196
Cohen, 205, 213
Cohen, D., 27, 41
Cohen, L. H., 4, 15, 19, 22, 33, 44, 51, 64, 66, 82, 98, 123, 124, 127, 128, 135, 136, 168, 169, 171, 173, 176, 195, 217, 223, 225, 244, 251, 252, 261, 262, 266, 280, 284, 286, 314, 329
Cohen, S., 35, 41
Cohen, M., 214, 218, 220, 223
Cohen-Gerstel, Y., 325, 330
Cohler, B. J., 28, 40
Colding, J., 242, 244
Cole, B., 133, 134
Cole, S. W., 220, 222
Colless, E., 226, 245
Collins, C. A., 33, 45, 170, 174, 297, 309, 345, 348, 354
Collins, R. L., 31, 41, 48, 49, 61, 64, 82, 95, 137, 141, 142, 151, 152, 153, 154, 157, 158, 171, 216, 222, 228, 244
Colon, R. M., 51, 63
Colvin, C. R., 182, 194
Compas, B. E., 264, 285
Concato, J., 30, 42
Conlon, A., 51, 54, 60, 65, 82, 96, 169, 172, 228, 244, 331, 363, 365
Conner, K. M., 326, 330
Conway, M., 62, 66
Cook, C. L., 19, 22, 57, 62, 65
Cook, S. L., 19, 23
Cooke, N. J., 235, 244
Cooper, C. L., 229, 245
Cooper, L., 18, 23, 87, 98
Cooper, M. L., 30, 43, 227, 229, 245
Cooper, R., 227, 245
Cordova, M. J., 14, 21, 33, 41, 55, 57, 64, 138, 139, 140, 141, 143, 148, 149, 150, 151, 152, 153, 154, 155, 157, 160, 164, 166, 167, 169, 171, 172, 217, 222
Cornblat, M. W., 122, 135
Corr, C. A., 295, 309
Cosden, M. A., 275, 286
Costa, P. T., 52, 64
Costello, N., 221, 223, 297

Courbasson, C. M. A., 256, 260
Coward, D. D., 216, 222
Cowell, B., 123, 137
Cowen, E. L., 28, 41, 251, 260, 268, 270, 276, 277,
    282, 283, 284, 285, 287
Cox, D., 234, 240, 246
Cox, J., 226, 245
Coyle, C. T., 323, 330
Coyne, J. C., 35, 41, 241, 245, 313, 330
Cozzarelli, C., 30, 43
Cozzolino, P. J., 16, 21
Crawford, J., 214, 222
Crego, J., 236, 244
Crnic, K. A., 275, 287
Crocker, J., 91, 99
Crocket, K., 77, 79, 363, 266
Crofton, C., 31, 45
Cromwell, R. L., 75, 80
Croog, S., 31, 40, 48, 61, 63, 149, 171, 219, 221
Crooks, L., 216, 224
Cropley, T. G., 341, 353
Crowne, D. P., 52, 64
Cruess, D. G., 146, 150, 151, 152, 153, 155, 164,
    172, 219, 222
Cryder, C. H., 264, 265, 266, 270, 275, 278, 280,
    281, 282, 283, 285
Cullen, B., 133, 134
Culver, J. L., 51, 52, 57, 64, 141, 149, 150, 151, 152,
    153, 154, 157, 159, 170, 171, 221, 342, 343, 344,
    348, 352
Cunningham, L. L. C., 14, 21, 33, 55, 57, 64, 139,
    140, 141, 143, 148, 149, 150, 151, 152, 153, 154,
    155, 157, 160, 164, 166, 167, 169, 172, 217, 222
Curbow, B., 51, 64, 141, 143, 151, 152, 154, 172
Curran, S. L., 49, 140, 142, 152, 157, 158, 171
Cutrona, C. E., 35, 41
Czikszentmihalyi, M., 282, 283, 287

D

Daiter, S., 143, 152, 172
Dake, K., 231, 244
Dakof, G. A., 35, 41
Dale, M. A., 76, 78
Dalgleish, T., 356, 358, 365
Danieli, Y., 249, 260
Danoff-Burg, S., 16, 45, 48, 139, 169, 174, 297, 309,
    345, 346, 348, 354
Danovsky, M., 264, 285
Dansky, B. S., 82, 98
Darby, B. W., 321, 330
Davenport, D. S., 322, 330
Davidson, J. R., 312, 326, 330
Davies, B., 73, 79
Davies, H., 232, 244
Davis, C., 300, 301, 309
Davis, C. G., 10, 22, 31, 36, 41, 44, 57, 66, 82, 86,
    89, 96, 169, 170, 172, 173, 218, 297, 309, 313,
    332, 357, 361, 365, 366
Davis, J. L., 124, 135
Davis, J. M., 82, 98

Davis, L., 325, 329
Davis, M. C., 170, 175
Davis, S. H., 113, 117
Davison, L., 29, 45
De Mey, H., 76, 80
Deahl, M., 312, 329
Deci, E. L., 7, 23
Decker, L. R., 123, 134
Deffenbacher, J. L., 181, 195
Degotardi, P. B., 35, 41
de-Jong, J. T., 252, 262
Dekel, R., 178, 195
Delongis, A., 35, 44
Delorenze, G. N., 218, 223
DeMarco, G. A., 126, 135
Demasio, A. R., 70, 78
Deng, 205, 213
deProsse, C., 138, 171
Derogatis, C. R., 189, 194
Derogatis, L. R., 138, 172, 189, 194, 204, 213
Desmond, K. A., 141, 144, 146, 147, 148, 149, 150,
    151, 152, 154, 155, 159, 162, 163, 166, 168, 170,
    171
Dey, A. N., 252, 260
DiBlasio, F. A., 321, 327, 328, 330
Dienstbier, R. A., 37, 41, 181, 194
Difede, J., 258, 260
Digiuseppe, R., 322, 330
Dijkstra, T., 362, 367
DiLollo, A., 77, 78
Dirksen, S. R., 139, 140, 172
Ditta, S. R., 82, 98
Dobbs, L. K., 216, 222
Doernberger, C. H., 28, 43
Dohrenwend, B. P., 18, 19, 20, 21, 291, 309
Dohrenwend, B. S., 4, 21
Doka, K., 70, 78
Donaldson, D., 264, 285
Downey, G., 313, 323, 330
Driskell, J. E., 234, 245
Droll, D. M., 323, 330
Dubow, E. F., 132, 134
DuHamel, K., 169, 173
Dull, V. T., 217, 222
Dungee-Anderson, D., 123, 134
Dunkel-Schetter, C., 84, 95
Dunmore, E., 348, 352
Dunning, C., 226, 234, 237, 239, 240, 242, 243, 246,
    247

E

Ebersole, P., 51, 64
Echemendia, R., 130, 136
Edbril, S. D., 140, 144, 155, 164, 173
Edmonds, S., 82, 96
Egeland, B., 269, 270, 273, 285, 288
Eggers, C., 250, 260
Ehlers, A., 82, 86, 96, 181, 197, 348, 352, 358,
    359, 361, 365
Eid, J., 38, 42

Eisen, S. A., 364, 367
Elder, G. H., 82, 92, 96, 200, 201, 213
Elkin, A., 250, 263
Ellard, J. H., 35, 41
Elliot, R., 72, 78
Elliott, M. N., 121, 137
Ellison, C. G., 125, 126, 129, 134, 135
Emery, G., 211, 213
Emmons, R. A., 90, 96
Endler, N. S., 190, 205, 256, 260
Endsley, M., 235, 244
Engle, B., 325, 330
Enright, R. D., 321, 322, 323, 326, 327, 329, 330, 331
Ensing, D. S., 123, 124, 127, 130, 136
Entin, E. E., 235, 244
Epel, E. S., 219, 222
Epstein, S., 10, 16, 21, 83, 84, 96, 275, 285
Epston, D., 74, 77, 79, 80
Epton, D., 363, 366
Eranen, L., 231, 246
Erlen, J. A., 216, 223
Evans, G. W., 32, 35, 38, 40, 41, 43
Evans, S. J., 214, 223
Exline, J. J., 125, 126, 128, 130, 135, 137, 321, 329, 330

F

Fabry, J., 337, 352
Fagen, D. B., 269, 270, 273, 274, 276, 277, 285, 287
Fahey, J. L., 49, 64, 82, 87, 95
Fairbairn, W. R. D., 83, 96
Fairclough, D. L., 140, 175
Falgout, K., 123, 124, 127, 130, 136
Falsetti, S. A., 124, 135
Farber, E. W., 30, 41
Farnham, S. D., 84, 96
Farr, W., 129, 134
Farran, C. J., 308, 309
Farrell-Higgins, J., 75, 80
Feigel, C. A., 219, 222
Feixas, G., 76, 78
Feldman, B. N., 256, 260
Feldman, J., 214, 218, 223
Felsman, J. K., 251, 260
Felsten, G., 256, 260
Fenster, J. R., 62, 66
Fernandez-Berrocal, P., 29, 43
Ferrando, S. J., 216, 223
Ferring, D., 140, 173
Fetting, J., 138, 172
Field, N., 179, 196
Fields, K. K., 141, 175
Fife, B. L., 51, 64, 139, 156, 172
Figley, C. R., 108, 116
Figueras, S., 60, 61, 72, 79
Filipp, S., 60, 61, 65, 140, 143, 151, 156, 168, 173, 347, 352
Fine, M. A., 48, 65, 100, 109, 116
Finke, R. A., 308, 309
Finkel, N. J., 4, 21

Finney, J. F., 291, 309
Fischer, P. C., 313, 327, 331
Fisher, R. H., 51, 56, 66, 82, 97, 170, 173, 313, 314, 366
Fiske, S. T., 83, 91, 96
Fiske, V., 35, 41
Fitchett, G., 126, 135
Fitzgerald, 48, 66
Fitzgerald, E. M., 140, 173
Fitzgerald, G., 214, 218, 223
Fitzgibbons, R. P., 321, 322, 323, 327, 330, 331
Fitzpatrick, D., 362, 366
Flaherty, S. M., 125, 135
Flanagan, O. J., 70, 78
Flasher, L., 141, 173
Flin, R., 232, 234, 235, 236, 244, 246
Flores, J., 51, 64
Foa, E. B., 93, 98, 204, 213, 361, 362, 365
Foley, L. A., 84, 96
Folke, C., 242, 244
Folkins, C. H., 29, 41
Folkman, S., 10, 22, 29, 42, 123, 124, 136, 181, 195, 216, 222, 251, 260
Follette, V. M., 74, 78, 190, 194
Fontana, A., 9, 21, 48, 65, 200, 201, 213
Fortner, B. V., 77, 79
Foucault, M., 74, 78
Fox, K., 10, 17, 22, 54, 65, 146, 148, 151, 152, 153, 155, 156, 157, 159, 160, 169, 173
Franke, G., 204, 213
Frankl, V. E., 4, 21, 183, 194, 216, 249, 336, 337, 338, 352
Fransella, F., 75, 78
Frantz, C. M., 89, 90, 97, 165, 173
Franz, R., 160, 174
Frazier, P., 16, 19, 21, 32, 41, 51, 54, 60, 61, 65, 82, 96, 169, 172, 228, 244, 313, 331, 363, 365
Frederickson, B. L., 170, 172
Fredrickson, B. L., 18, 28, 46
Freedman, S. R., 323, 326, 331
Freedy, J. R., 82, 96
Friedel, L., 123, 137
Friedman, M. J., 59, 66, 200, 213, 231, 246
Fritz, G. K., 140, 141, 172, 268, 285
Fromm, K., 49, 65, 140, 141, 143, 151, 152, 153, 154, 155, 157, 163, 172
Fulmer, D., 17, 21

G

Gall, T. L., 122, 135
Gampel, Y., 250, 260
Ganster, D. C., 38, 44
Ganz, P. A., 141, 144, 146, 147, 148, 149, 150, 151, 152, 154, 155, 159, 162, 163, 166, 168, 170, 171, 17, 173
Garland, D., 235, 244
Garling, T., 34, 42
Garmezy, N., 25, 27, 37, 41, 43, 44, 272, 286
Garnick, M. B., 164, 173
Garvill, J., 34, 42

Garwood, G., 113, 116
Gaynes, B. N., 129, 135
Geldschlager, H., 76, 78
Genia, V., 131, 135
George, L. K., 129, 134
Gergen, K. J., 17, 22
Germino, B. B., 140, 173
Gershman, K., 4, 21, 48, 64
Gersons, B. P. R., 240, 244, 341, 345, 346, 352
Gest, S. D., 25, 37, 43, 44
Gibbons, J. L., 126, 135
Gibofsky, A., 35, 44
Giedzinska, A. S., 141, 143, 150, 152, 172
Giese-Davis, J., 344, 353
Gifford, A. L., 216, 222
Gifford, E. V., 190, 194
Gil, E., 275, 285
Gilbert, D. T., 88, 96, 99
Gill, T. M., 30, 42
Giller, E. L., 249, 263
Ginzburg, K., 178, 194, 196
Girard, M., 323, 332
Gist, R., 226, 230, 231, 232, 237, 239, 240, 241, 244
Glaser, R., 183, 194, 218, 222
Glaser, T., 51, 65, 82, 96, 169, 172, 183, 218, 244,
    331, 365
Glueckauf, R. L., 35, 44
Gobodo-Madikizela, P., 321, 323, 325, 326, 331
Golant, M., 344, 353
Goldberger, L., 362, 366
Golden, R. N., 129, 135
Goldman, L., 267, 282, 285
Goldstein, L., 10, 17, 22, 54, 65, 146, 148, 151, 152,
    153, 155, 156, 157, 159, 160, 169, 173
Gonzalez, R., 297, 310, 361, 367
Gordon, E., 35, 45
Goss, R. E., 12, 22
Gottschalk, L. A., 76, 78
Graham, K. Y., 49, 65
Gramezy, N., 256, 260
Gramzow, R. H., 33, 43
Grana, G., 10, 17, 22, 54, 65, 146, 148, 151, 152,
    153, 155, 156, 157, 159, 160, 169, 173
Grant, K. E., 264, 285
Grawe, K., 177, 190, 196, 193, 196, 345, 346, 353
Green, P., 35, 45
Greenbaum, M. A., 291, 309
Greenberg, D. L., 70, 80
Greenberg, J., 86, 96, 98
Greenberg, L., 72, 78
Greenberg, M. A., 26, 41, 43, 251, 260, 361, 365
Greenfield, D. B., 187, 194
Greenhawt, M., 65, 144, 148, 150, 151, 152, 153,
    157, 158, 173, 217, 223
Greenwald, A. G., 84, 96
Greer, S., 161, 175
Greller, M. M., 240, 245
Gribble, P. A., 276, 277, 284
Grimm, I., 200, 202, 213, 348, 353
Gritz, E. R., 140, 172
Grob, A., 177, 190, 193, 196
Grosse-Holtforth, M., 345, 346, 352, 253

Grossman, F. K., 257, 260
Grotberg, E. H., 256, 260
Gruenewald, T. L., 220, 223
Gruess, D. G., 343, 344, 352
Gu, H., 129, 135
Guba, E. G., 17, 22
Guidano, V. F., 77, 78
Guier, C., 51, 63
Gulliver, S. B., 252, 260
Gunn, L., 361, 365
Gunthert, K. C., 51, 64, 169, 171, 225, 244

H

Haber, J. G., 321, 331
Hackman, A., 361, 365
Hager, D. L., 341, 353
Hahn, J., 126, 128, 136
Hall, B., 216, 222
Halpert, J. A., 264, 285
Halttunen, A., 141, 172
Hamera, E. K., 51, 65
Hannan, G., 230, 231, 232, 236, 246
Hanney, L., 256, 260
Hanson, R. F., 82, 86
Hardke, K., 76, 78
Hardy, S. E., 30, 42
Hargrave, T. N., 323, 331
Harlan, D., 10, 21
Harris, S., 227, 245
Harris, S. D., 31, 41
Hart, P. M., 228, 229, 238, 245
Harter, S., 74, 28, 275, 285
Hartig, T., 34, 42
Hartsough, D. M., 226, 241, 245
Harvey, J. H., 70, 78, 100, 108, 109, 112, 113, 116,
    117, 297, 309, 358, 365
Harvey, M., 257, 260
Hasan, N., 266, 274, 276, 285
Hautzinger, M., 187, 194
Havernick, N., 48, 65, 141, 173
Hayes, S. C., 190, 194, 341, 353
Hayhurst, H., 341, 354
Hays, R. B., 214, 222
Hazel, M., 177, 196
Heath, A. C., 364, 367
Heatherton, T. F., 321, 329
Hebl, J. H., 323, 331
Heflin, L., 141, 144, 148, 149, 173
Heim, C., 38, 42
Held, B. S., 362, 365
Helgeson, V. S., 7, 13, 16, 20, 22, 23, 32, 33, 42, 43,
    51, 52, 53, 55, 57, 59, 60, 67, 140, 145, 147, 150,
    151, 152, 153, 154, 155, 156,162, 163, 164, 167,
    169, 174
Heller, K., 35, 42, 253, 262
Heller, P. L., 129, 134
Helson, H., 94, 96
Hemsworth, D., 7, 16, 21, 123, 134, 216, 222, 264,
    284
Henrich, C., 283, 285
Henry, R., 216, 224

Heppner, M. J., 361, 366
Herbert, M., 31, 45
Herman, J. L., 108, 196, 298, 309, 322, 325, 331
Hermanns, J. M., 252, 262
Hermans, H., 69, 75, 78
Herrero, O., 72, 79
Herrle, J., 200, 202, 213, 348, 353
Herth, K. A., 308, 309
Hettler, T. R., 51, 64, 123, 135, 266, 284
Hickling, E., 349, 352
Hietvanen, P., 141, 172
Higgins, G. O., 228, 230, 241, 245
Higgins, P., 31, 45
Hight, T. L., 321, 331
Hightower, A. D., 277, 284
Hills, A., 311, 331
Ho, R. T. H., 19, 22, 58, 59, 65, 143, 148, 151, 154, 161, 172
Ho, S. M. Y., 19, 22, 58, 59, 65
Hobbs, M., 181, 195
Hobfoll, I., 30, 42
Hobfoll, S. E., 30, 42, 101, 107, 116, 155, 172, 193, 194
Hogan, N. S., 185, 186, 187, 188, 193, 194
Holaday, M., 251, 259
Holahan, C. J., 252, 261
Holen, A., 178, 194
Holland, J. C., 39, 42
Hollifield, M., 204, 213
Holman, E. A., 358, 361, 364, 365
Holmes, T. H., 181, 194
Holmstrom, L. L., 92, 95
Holroyd, K. A., 160, 174
Hood, C., 231, 245
Hooker, K., 82, 96
Hope, D., 320, 331
Horowitz, L. A., 264, 281, 285
Horowitz, M. J., 83, 87, 96, 157, 172, 178, 184, 186, 187, 190, 194
Horwitz, R. I., 38, 45
Houghton, B., 228, 229, 230, 232, 235, 236, 240, 241, 246
Howard, G. S., 71, 78, 358, 365
Howard, M. O., 48, 65
Hoy, J., 216, 222
Hoyt, W., 181, 193
Hoyt-Meyers, L. A., 276, 277, 285, 287
Hubbard, J. J., 37, 44
Huddleston, L., 228, 229, 237, 239, 245, 246
Huggins, M. E., 169, 174
Hughes, J. R., 252, 260
Humphreys, K., 344, 353
Hunt, J. W., 49, 51, 64, 140, 142, 168, 171, 221
Hurd, R. C., 36, 42

I

Ickovics, J. R., 4, 22, 30, 44, 219, 222, 251, 261, 313, 332
Igou, E. R., 94, 99
Ikin, J., 343, 344, 353
Inayat, Q., 161, 175

Ingelhart, M., 131, 135
Ingersoll-Dayton, B., 125, 135
Ingram, K. M., 13, 22
Inzana, C. M., 234, 245
Ironson, G., 221, 223, 343, 353
Israelashvili, M., 274, 285
Ituarte, P. H. G., 32, 43

J

Jackson, D. N., 35, 44, 234, 235, 236, 242, 246
Jacobi, C., 345, 352
Jacobs, C., 51, 65, 66, 140, 174
Jacobs, S. C., 73, 76, 80, 178, 194
Jacobsen, P. B., 141, 175
Jallinoja, P., 141, 172
James, S. A., 34, 42
James, W., 131, 135, 181, 182, 194
Janoff, J. B., 361, 365
Janoff-Bulman, R. J., 5, 8, 9, 10, 11, 16, 22, 29, 31, 39, 42, 55, 56, 58, 65, 72, 79, 81, 83, 84, 86, 87, 89, 90, 94, 95, 96, 97, 128, 135, 138, 158, 165, 166, 167, 168, 172, 173, 177, 178, 194, 229, 245, 251, 261, 265, 267, 275, 285, 296, 309, 313, 314, 316, 318, 331, 358, 359, 365
Jaycox, L. H., 121, 137, 204, 213
Jenkins, J. H., 204, 213
Jensen, J. P., 328, 329
Jerusalem, M., 278, 285
Johnsen, B. H., 38, 42
Johnson, J. H., 268, 285
Johnson, L. C., 123, 135
Johnson, P. D., 33, 42
Johnson, S., 130, 136
Johnston, D., 234, 246
Johnston, J. H., 234, 245
Jonathan, B. I., 26, 45
Jones, D. K. C., 231, 245
Jones, L., 200, 201, 202, 213
Jordan, H., 6, 22
Jordan, J. R., 70, 74, 79, 298, 309
Joseph, J., 122, 137
Joseph, S., 9, 10, 15, 18, 22, 51, 53, 56, 65, 82, 97, 200, 201, 202, 211, 213, 227, 228, 229, 231, 232, 241, 245, 312, 331, 356, 363, 365
Judd, C. M., 91, 97
Judd, F. K., 216, 222

K

Kabat-Zinn, H. J., 341, 353
Kahana, B., 249, 263
Kahn, S., 252, 261
Kahneman, D., 90, 94, 97
Kalichman, S. C., 215, 222
Kalish, L. A., 140, 173
Kaltreider, N., 253, 261
Kaminer, D., 322, 331
Kanousc, D. E., 216, 222
Kaniasty, K., 34, 42
Kanouse, D. E., 216, 222
Kaplan, M., 217, 222
Karl, A., 349, 353, 354

Kassinove, H., 322, 331
Kassler, R. C., 312, 329
Katz, B. L., 51, 64, 82, 95
Katz, R. C., 141, 143, 151, 153, 154, 161, 164, 173
Kaufman, J., 283, 285
Kazis, L., 252, 263
Keane, T. M., 82, 86, 97
Keats, P. A., 77, 80
Keesee, N. J., 77, 79
Kegan, R., 193, 194
Kehoe, N. C., 132, 133, 135
Keilson, H., 250, 253, 261
Keks, N., 337, 342, 353
Keller, D. 186, 187, 188, 189, 196
Keller, F., 187, 194
Kemeny, M. E., 48, 49, 45, 53, 63, 82, 95, 97, 217,
    218, 220, 221, 223, 224, 366
Kemper, C. A., 214, 215, 216, 217, 218, 220, 223
Kemppainen, J. K., 218, 222
Kenady, D. E., 138, 171
Kennedy, B. J., 48, 65, 141, 173
Kennedy, S., 48, 65, 141, 173
Kennedy, V. N., 139, 172
Kerley, J. H., 277, 278, 287
Kesler, 204, 213
Kestenberg, J. S., 250, 257, 261
Kestenberg, M., 250, 261
Kiecolt-Glaser, J. K., 33, 46, 183, 194, 218, 221
Kilbourn, K. M., 51, 52, 57, 64, 141, 146, 149, 150,
    151, 152, 153, 154, 155, 157, 159, 164, 170, 171,
    172, 219, 221, 222, 343, 344, 348, 352, 353
Kilmer, R. P., 264, 265, 266, 270, 275, 277, 278,
    280, 281, 282, 283, 284, 285, 287
Kilpatrick, D. G., 82, 96, 98
King, K., 125, 136
King, L. A., 26, 48, 42, 60, 65
Kippax, S., 214, 222
Kirk, S. B., 33, 45
Kirkpatrick, L. A., 131, 132, 135
Kissane, D. W., 337, 332, 343, 344, 353
Klass, D., 12, 22
Klauer, T., 60, 61, 65, 140, 143, 151, 152, 156, 168,
    173
Klein, S., 240, 243
Klibourn, K. M., 51, 52, 57, 64, 141, 149, 150, 151,
    152, 153, 154, 157, 159, 170, 171, 172, 221, 342,
    343, 344, 348, 353
Kliewer, W., 33, 42
Kobasa, S. C., 28, 30, 42, 252, 261, 313, 331
Kocovski, N. L., 256, 260
Koenig, H. G., 126, 128, 136, 183, 194, 317, 332,
    363, 366
Kokotovic, A. M., 275, 286
Kolb, D. A., 77, 79
Kolesaric, V. . 200, 202, 213
Komiti, A., 216, 222
Kooistra, W. P., 124, 125, 126, 135
Koomen, W., 94, 98
Kopp, H. G., 187, 195
Kozlowska, K., 256, 260
Krakow, B., 204, 213

Kramer, D. A., 307, 309
Krause, N., 125, 126, 135
Krell, R., 249, 250, 257, 261
Krementz, J., 268, 285
Kring, A. M., 190, 194
Krizmainic, M., 213 (in Ref only)
Kruit, 186, 187, 188, 196
Krystal, H., 249, 264
Krystal, J. H., 364, 366
Kubany, E. C., 361, 365
Kuhn, T. S., 85, 97
Kulik, J. A., 129, 135
Kumar, M., 221
Kurtz, J. C., 143, 151, 152, 156, 173
Kurtz, M. E., 143, 151, 152, 156, 173

L

Laberg, J. C., 38, 42
Labi, N., 26, 42
Lachman, M., 92, 95, 127, 178, 191, 193
LAF (Lance Armstrong Foundation), 39, 42
Lamberts, R. D., 240, 244, 341, 345, 352
Langner, R., 211, 348, 353
Langstaff, J. E., 214, 223
Lannen-Meier, P., 190, 195
Lantz, J., 337, 353
Lanza, A. F., 35, 42
Larkin, G. R., 18, 22, 170, 172
Larson, J., 31, 41, 89, 96, 170, 172, 218, 222, 363,
    366
Larson, R. A., 152, 172
Lawless, S., 214, 222
Lawson, K. D., 29, 41
Lazare, A., 321, 331
Lazarus, R. S., 10, 22, 25, 29, 41, 42, 45, 181, 184,
    195, 216, 251, 260
Leadbeater, B. J., 283, 286
Lechner, S. C., 4, 19, 20, 47, 53, 61, 65, 144, 148,
    149, 150, 151, 152, 153, 157, 158, 161, 173, 217,
    223, 278, 286, 313, 331
Lederman, G. S., 140, 173
LeDoux, J., 178, 195
Lee, A., 252, 262
Lee, B. S., 250, 261
Lee, D. A., 361, 365
Lee, L., 326, 365
Lefcourt, H. M., 252, 261
Lefebvre, R. C., 31, 45, 82, 182, 195
Leff, J. P., 35, 43
Legro, M. W., 51, 62, 64, 141, 143, 151, 152, 154,
    172
Lehman, D. R., 36, 40, 50, 63, 65, 361, 365
Lehman, J. M., 51, 52, 57, 64, 141, 149, 150, 151,
    152, 153, 154, 157, 159, 170, 171, 221, 342, 343,
    344, 348, 352
Lemkau, J. P., 363, 367
Leonard, J. B., 84, 95
Lepore, S. J., 11, 13, 22, 24, 26, 27, 29, 32, 33, 35,
    37, 38, 40, 41, 42, 43
Lerner, M. J., 84, 97

Leserman, J., 129, 135
Lev, R., 254, 261
Levenson, M. R., 51, 59, 64, 226, 243
Levine, S., 31, 40, 48, 61, 63, 149, 171, 219, 221
Levitt, H., 69, 76, 78, 79
Lev-Wiesel, R., 7, 248, 249, 250, 252, 253, 254, 256, 259, 261
Levy, J. S., 38, 43
Lewin, K., 184, 195
Lewinsohn, P. H., 184, 195
Lewis, F. M., 216, 222
Lewis, M., 361, 366
Lewis, S., 39, 42
Lewis-Fernandez, R., 18, 19, 20, 21, 291, 309
Lian, N., 204, 213
Lichtman, R. R., 49, 67, 140, 174, 227, 247
Lieberman, A. F., 266, 267, 269, 270, 272, 285
Lieberman, M. A., 251, 262, 342, 353, 354
Lifton, R., 322, 331
Light, T., 341, 353
Lincoln, Y. S., 17 , 22
Linehan, M. M., 321, 323, 332, 341, 353
Link, B. G., 32, 43
Linley, P. A., 9, 10, 15, 18, 22, 53, 56, 65, 122, 137, 200, 211, 227, 228, 229, 230, 231, 232, 233, 236, 241, 245, 309, 312, 331, 356, 363, 365
Linville, P. W., 177, 195
Lissack, M., 237, 239, 245
Little, B. R., 90, 97
Litz, B. T., 82, 97
Lobel, M., 126, 134
Lohan, J., 123, 135
Lolas, F., 76, 78
Long, G. M., 81, 97
Long, J., 32, 41, 60, 65
Longman, A. J., 49, 65
Lonnqvist, J., 141, 172
Loos, M. E., 264, 281, 285
Lopez, S. J., 101, 117
Lotyczewski, B. S., 277, 284, 287
Lounsbury, P., 35, 45
Low, C. A., 9, 18, 23, 138, 169, 174, 297, 307, 309, 313, 332
Ludwig, T. E., 323, 333
Lukas, E., 337, 353
Lutgendorf, S. K., 221, 223, 297, 310
Luthar, S. S., 25, 28, 43, 264, 265, 268, 269, 277, 285
Lynch, M., 267, 270, 285
Lynn, M., 90, 97
Lyons, M. J., 364, 367
Lyons, R. F., 241, 245

M

MacLeod, M. D., 228, 230, 232, 240, 241, 245
Maddi, S. R., 252, 261, 313, 331
Maercker, A., 6, 19, 88, 94, 97, 176, 181, 187, 195, 200, 202, 211, 213, 334, 341, 347, 348, 349, 353, 354
Magnus, K. B., 269, 270, 273, 274, 276, 277, 285, 287

Magovern, G. J. S., 31, 182, 195
Magyar, G. M., 125, 127, 135, 136
Mahler, H. I., 129, 135
Mahoney, A., 122, 127, 135
Mahoney, M. J., 341, 353
Mair, M., 358, 365
Majerovitz, S. D., 35, 44
Major, B., 30, 33, 43
Mandel, F. S., 190, 196
Mandler, J., 69, 79
Manke, F. P., 361, 365
Manne, S., 10, 17, 22, 54, 65, 146, 148, 151, 152, 153, 155, 156, 157, 159, 160, 169, 173
Manning, W. H., 77, 78
Manzi, F., 156, 174
Markman, K. D., 94, 97
Marks, G., 220, 222, 223
Marlowe, D., 52, 64
Marris, P., 83, 97
Marshall, G. N., 121, 137
Marshall, R., 18, 19, 20, 21, 29, 291, 309
Martin, L. L., 9, 22, 112, 116, 117, 235, 244, 365
Martinson, I. M., 274, 285
Maslow, A. H., 4, 22
Mason, J. W., 249, 263
Massey, S., 48, 65
Masten, A. S., 25, 27, 29, 32, 34, 36, 37, 41, 43, 44, 259, 261, 264, 265, 268, 272, 273, 277, 282, 283, 286, 288
Masters, K. S., 131, 134
Maton, K. I., 283, 286
Matthews, K. A., 31, 45, 182, 195
Maughan, N., 27, 44
Maurer, K. I., 91, 97
Mayou, R. A., 82, 96, 181, 195
Mazor, A., 250, 261
Mbanga, I., 322, 331
McAdams, D. P., 12, 50, 58, 64, 66, 361, 363, 366
McCaffrey, D. F., 216, 222
McCann, L., 48, 66
McCrae, R. R., 52, 64
McCullough, M. E., 320, 321, 323, 325, 327, 331
McCutchan, A. J., 220, 223
McDaniel, J. S., 30, 41
McElhiney, M., 216, 223
McEwen, B. S., 38, 44, 45, 219, 222
McFarland, C., 19, 22, 53, 54, 56, 62, 63, 65, 88, 97, 168, 173, 300, 309, 314, 332
McFarlane, A. C., 256, 263
McGrath, P. C., 138, 142, 152, 157, 158, 171
McGregor, B. A., 146, 150, 155, 164, 173, 343, 344, 353
McGuire, W. J., 92, 97
McIntosh, D., 131, 135
McKearney, J. M., 86, 96
McKenzie, N., 251, 262
McKusik, L., 214, 222
McMahon, S. D., 264, 285
McMillan, J., 87, 95, 149, 171, 177 , 181, 194, 225, 260, 313, 332
McMillen, C., 66, 82, 97, 226, 227, 245

McMillen, J. C., 19, 22, 48, 49, 51, 56, 57, 58, 59, 62, 65, 66, 168, 169, 170, 173, 314, 357, 363, 366
McMullen, M. N., 94, 97
Meichenbaum, D. H., 48, 66, 92, 97, 181, 195, 296, 305, 309, 355, 357, 358, 361, 362, 366
Mellors, M. P., 216, 223
Mellott, D. S., 84, 96
Meltzer, T., 125, 135
Mendelson, Y., 250, 261
Mendlew, J., 312, 329
Mendola, R., 31, 445, 48, 66, 170, 174
Merbach, N., 113, 117
Metcalfe, K. A., 214, 223
Metens, S., 217, 222
Metz, J. R., 275, 286
Metzler, T., 240, 244
Meyerowitz, B. E., 139, 141, 171, 172, 173, 174
Meyers, J., 88, 99
Meyers, L. S., 16, 21
Miach, P., 337, 342, 343, 344, 353
Mickelson, K. D., 241, 245
Mijch, A. M., 216, 222
Mikulincer, M., 233, 246
Milam, J. E., 19, 22, 214, 215, 216, 217, 218, 220, 223, 264, 266, 281, 286
Miles, H. J., 38, 43
Miller, A. H., 38, 42
Miller, D. T., 94, 97, 300, 309
Miller, E., 108, 116
Miller, L., 230, 245, 311, 325, 332
Miller, P., 274, 287
Miller, R., 252, 261
Miller, W. R., 61, 66
Mindes, E. J., 13, 22
Miner, K. N., 48, 65
Minow, M., 321, 332
Mitchell, D. R. D., 240, 245
Mitroff, I. I., 242, 245
Mittag, W., 278, 285
Mohamed, N. E., 146, 151, 152, 153, 154, 155, 160, 174
Mohr, J., 143, 223
Molnar, C., 361, 362, 365
Monk, G., 77, 79, 363, 366
Moody, C. P., 274, 286
Moody, R. A., 274, 286
Moonen, D. J., 30, 41
Moore, M. K., 74, 78
Moore, R. G., 341, 354
Moore, R. P., 257, 360
Moos, B. S., 273, 286
Moos, R. H., 4, 23, 56, 177, 179, 252, 261, 273, 286, 313, 332
Moran, C. C., 226, 245
Mordkoff, A. M., 29, 45
Morgan, C. A., 364, 366
Morgan, D. L., 125, 135
Morrow, G. R., 138, 172
Mortimore, P., 27, 44
Moskovitz, S., 250, 252, 257, 261
Moskowitz, J. T., 220, 261

Moyer, A., 138, 173
Mullet, E., 323, 332
Murch, L. R., 123, 127, 136
Murch, R. L., 4, 15, 19, 33, 44, 82, 168, 176, 217, 223, 251, 280, 286
Murdock, T., 93, 98
Murphy, D. L., 57, 64
Murphy, M., 337, 354
Murphy, P., 126, 135
Murphy, S. A., 123, 135
Murray-Swank, A., 123, 125, 129, 133, 135
Murray-Swank, N., 135, 136
Mussweiler, T., 94, 97
Myer, C., 227, 245
Myers, D. G., 226, 241, 245

N

Nadeau, J., 71, 79
Neeman, J., 25, 43
Neidig, J. L., 216, 222
Neimeyer, G. J., 75, 79
Neimeyer, R. A., 68, 69, 70, 71, 72, 73, 74, 75, 76, 77, 78, 79, 80, 266, 286, 291, 305, 318, 332, 363, 366
Nelson, D. W., 252, 261
Nelson, K., 70, 80, 268, 287
Nelson, S., 141, 173
Nemeroff, C. B., 38, 42
Neria, Y., 178, 194, 252, 253, 309
Nerken, I. R., 341, 354
Nesse, R. M., 71, 78
Nesson, L., 130, 136
Nevill, T., 341, 354
Neville, H. A., 361, 366
Newport, D. J., 38, 42
Newsweek, 127, 136
Nicholas, J. J., 126, 135
Nichols, M. P., 269, 286
Niederland, W., 249, 261
Nielsen, M. E., 125, 136
Noack, H., 187, 195
Nolen-Hoeksema, S., 10, 26, 31, 36, 41, 44, 57, 66, 89, 96, 169, 170, 172, 173, 218, 222, 297, 309, 310, 313, 332, 357, 361, 363, 366, 367
Nomikos, M. S., 29, 42
Noriega, V., 31, 41
Norris, F. H., 34, 42, 237, 245
North, C. S., 226, 245
North, J., 321, 332
Nosek, B. A., 84, 96
Nosek, M. A., 123, 136
Novaco, R., 48, 66
Nower, L., 48, 65
Nowicki, S., 276, 286

O

O'Brien, T. B., 35, 44
O'Connor, A. P., 140, 141, 173
O'Grady, D., 275, 286

O'Leary, V. E., 4, 22, 30, 44, 251, 261, 313, 332
Office of Cancer Survivorship, 141, 173
Oh, E., 361, 366
Oh, S., 141, 144, 148, 149, 152, 173
Ohlde, C., 75, 80
Ohry, A., 178, 194, 195
Oishi, S., 19, 21
Olasov-Rothbaum, B., 361, 365
Oliver, J. M., 124, 137
Oliveri, M., 187, 195
Olsen, H., 123, 124, 127, 130, 136
Olsson, T., 34, 42
Oltjenbruns, K. A., 274, 286
Opton, E. M., Jr., 29, 41, 42
Orbuch, T. L., 112, 113, 116, 117, 358, 365
Orenstein, S. W., 252, 262
Oskin, D., 33, 42
Osofsky, J. D., 264, 266, 267, 272, 286
Ostroff, J., 22, 65, 173
Ostrow, D. G., 215, 223
Ouellette, S., 48, 65
Ouston, J., 27, 44
Overstreet, A., 297, 309
Owens, J. F., 31, 45, 182

P

Paardekooper, B., 252, 262
Pacheco, M., 72, 79
Pacini, R., 131, 135
Page-Shafer, K., 218, 223
Paivio, S., 9, 19, 23
Palmer, R., 75, 80
Pals, J. L., 12, 22, 50, 58, 66, 363, 366
Pane, N., 51, 64, 266, 284
Papageorgis, D., 92, 97
Pargament, K. I., 121, 122, 123, 124, 125, 126, 127,
    128, 130, 132, 133, 134, 135, 136, 137, 317, 332,
    363, 366
Park, B., 91, 97
Park, C. L., 4, 15, 19, 20, 22, 25, 33, 44, 45, 47, 51,
    53, 54, 55, 57, 62, 64, 66, 82, 92, 94, 98, 101,
    117, 122, 123, 124, 127, 128, 129, 136, 137, 168,
    173, 176, 181, 183, 187, 195, 217, 223, 225, 241,
    245, 247, 251, 262, 264, 278, 280, 286, 312, 313,
    332, 350, 354, 357, 366, 367
Parker, G. R., 205, 251, 260, 268, 284
Parkes, C. M., 16, 22, 83, 98
Parsons, C. K., 240, 245
Pastore, P. L., 318, 332
Paterson, D., 220, 223
Paterson, H. M., 214, 223
Paton, D., 225, 226, 228, 229, 230, 231, 232, 233,
    234, 235, 236, 237, 239, 240, 241, 242, 243, 244,
    245, 246, 283, 286
Patten, A. H., 361, 366
Patterson, T. W., 75, 80
Peddle, N. A., 326, 332
Pelcovitz, D., 190, 196
Peltzer, K., 59, 66
Penman, D.,138, 172

Pennebaker, J. W., 26, 44, 76, 80, 297, 309, 313, 332
Perez, L., 126, 136, 317, 332, 366
Perez, L. M., 363, 366
Perez, M. A., 139, 174
Perkins, D. O., 129, 135
Perry, K., 204, 213
Pervin, L. A., 90, 98
Petitto, J. M., 129, 135
Petrie, K. J., 31, 48, 66, 140, 144, 149, 151, 152,
    157, 173
Petty, R. E., 92, 98
Pfefferbaum, B., 226, 245
Phelan, J., 32, 43
Piasetsky, S., 138, 172
Pierce, C. A., 30, 42
Pigott, M. A., 84, 96
Pinel, E., 88, 96
Pitts, J., 139, 174
Plaschy, A., 179, 195
Polk, L. V., 28, 44
Pollock, C., 235, 236, 246
Poorman, P. B., 48, 66
Pope, M., 341, 354
Popovich, J. M., 308, 309
Powell, S., 19, 22, 53, 57, 59, 66, 197, 200, 202, 203,
    204, 213
Power, T. G., 266, 274, 276, 285
Pozo, C., 31, 41
Pratt, C., 122, 137
Price, R., 296, 309
Price, R. H., 32, 44
Prigerson, H., 73, 76, 79, 80
Prinstein, M. J., 264, 285
Procidano, M. E., 253, 262
Putnam, F. W., 264, 285
Pynoos, R. S., 267, 270, 272, 274, 275, 276, 286
Pyszczynski, T., 86, 96, 98

Q

Quittner, A. L., 35, 44

R

Rabe, S., 349, 353, 354
Rabkin, J. G., 216, 223
Racagni, G., 312, 329
Rachal, K. C., 321, 331
Radke-Yarrow, M., 191, 195
Ragan, J., 29, 43
Rahe, R. H., 181, 194
Ram, A., 252, 253, 262
Ramirez, M., 37, 44
Ramos, N., 29, 43
Rankin, N. O., 29, 42
Rapaport Bar Sever, M., 250, 262
Rapaport, J., 250, 262
Raphael, B., 116, 178, 195, 226, 234, 246
Raskin, J. D., 69, 75, 79
Raspin, C., 60, 65
Ratner, P. A., 252, 262

Redd, W. H., 138, 171
Reed, G. M., 220, 223, 366
Reed, M. J., 25, 29, 32, 34, 36, 44
Reeve, C., 28, 44
Regehr, C., 7, 16, 21, 123, 134, 216, 222, 264, 284, 317, 329
Reich, J. W., 170, 175
Reid, J. L., 214, 223
Reilly, B., 123, 124, 127, 130, 136
Ren, X. S., 252, 256, 262
Resick, P. A., 124, 135
Resnick, H. S., 82, 86, 98
Revenson, T. A., 11, 24, 28, 30, 35, 42, 44, 45
Rey, O., 183, 195
Reyes, C. J., 275, 286
Reynolds, J., 361, 366
Reynolds, R. V., 160, 174
Rice, J., 364, 367
Rice, L., 72, 78
Richards, C., 30, 43
Richards, M., 49, 67
Richards, P. S., 131, 134
Richards, T. A., 124, 136
Richardson, J. L., 214, 218, 220, 223
Richie, J. P., 140, 173
Ricppi, R., 216, 223
Rideout, G., 66, 227, 245, 363, 366
Rieker, P. P., 140, 144, 155, 164, 173
Rigby, S., 125, 136
Riggs, D., 93, 98
Riley, T. A., 216, 223
Rinholm, J., 49, 67
Rini, C. M., 169, 173
Ritt-Olson, A., 216, 223, 264, 286
Roberts, A., 129, 134
Robertson, B., 161, 175
Robinson, D. S., 31, 41
Robinson, L., 139, 172
Robinson, S., 250, 262
Rodriguez, R., 31, 45
Rodriguez-Hanley, A., 170, 174, 297, 309
Roelefs, K., 362, 367
Roesler, T. A., 251, 262
Rogers, C. E., 240, 244
Rogers, C. R., 336, 346, 354
Rogler, L. H., 71, 80
Romero, C., 321, 333
Ronan, K., 228, 230, 232, 235, 236, 240, 241, 246
Roos, J., 237, 239, 240, 245
Rosario, M., 240, 244
Rose, A. J., 13, 23
Rose, G., 35, 45
Rosen, C. S., 291, 309
Rosenberg, S. D., 200, 213, 231, 246
Rosenblatt, P., 71, 80
Rosenheck, R., 9, 21, 48, 65, 200, 201, 213
Rosner, R., 19, 22, 66, 197, 200, 204, 213
Ross, M., 62, 66
Ross, R. D., 51, 65, 66, 140, 174
Roth, S., 190, 196
Rothbart, M., 91, 97
Rothbaum, B. O., 93, 98

Rowe, J. W., 38, 45
Rowland, J. H., 141, 171, 172, 173
Rubin, D. C., 70, 80
Rudman, L. A., 84, 96
Rush, A. J., 211, 213
Russell, D. W., 35, 41
Russell, J. A., 216, 222
Rustow, M. W., 250
Rutter, M., 25, 27, 38, 44, 251, 253, 262, 313, 332
Ryan, C. S., 91, 97
Ryan, R. M., 7, 23, 125, 136
Rybarczyk, B. D., 126, 135
Rynearson, T., 70, 77, 80

S

Saakvitne, K. W., 3, 23, 257, 341
Salas, E., 234, 235, 244, 245, 247
Salmon, P., 145, 151, 156, 174
Salovey, P., 138, 173
Salter, E., 15, 23, 264, 268, 278, 286
Samboceti, J., 16, 21
Sameroff, A. J., 269, 270, 286, 287
Sandage, S. J., 321, 331
Sanderson, C., 321, 323, 332
Sanderson, W. C., 126, 135
Sandler, I., 268, 274, 287
Santos, M. J. O., 321, 330
Sarte, J. P., 313, 332
Sartorius, N., 249, 263
Sartre, J. P., 91, 98
Satariano, W. A., 218, 223
Saunders, B. E., 82, 96, 98
Scarvalone, P., 258, 260
Schaefer, J. A., 4, 23, 56, 66, 177, 179, 195, 313, 332
Schaper, P. E., 30, 41
Scharf, M. J., 341, 353
Schaubroeck, J., 38, 44
Scheier, M. F., 30, 31, 41, 45, 62, 64, 139, 171, 182, 189, 193, 194, 195, 313, 330
Schellenbach, C. J., 283, 286
Schellenbaum, P., 341, 354
Schiaffino, K. M., 35, 44
Schlenker, B. R., 321, 330
Schmale, A., 138, 172
Schmall, V., 122, 137
Schmeidler, J., 250, 263
Schmidt, L. A., 185, 186, 187, 188, 193, 194
Schmitt, M. M., 13, 22
Schneider, M. L., 35, 43
Schneider, S. G., 31, 45
Schneider, S. K., 94, 98
Schneider-Rosen, K., 269, 270, 284
Schnurr, P. P., 59, 66, 200, 201, 213, 231, 246
Schrimshaw, E. W., 48, 53, 66, 123, 124, 137, 149, 174, 215, 216, 217, 219, 223
Schulenberg, S. E., 337, 354
Schulz, U., 146, 151, 152, 153, 154, 155, 160, 174
Schurg, R., 30, 42
Schuster, M. A., 121, 137, 216, 222, 357
Schut, H. A., 187, 195
Schwartz, C. E., 66

Schwartz, J. A., 30, 41
Schwartz, R. C., 286
Schwartzberg, S. S., 48, 66, 215, 223
Schwarzwald, J., 200, 213
Scobie, E. D., 320, 321, 332
Scobie, G. E., 320, 321, 332
Scott, A. B., 122, 136, 137
Scott, B., 228, 232, 235, 236, 240, 241, 246
Scragg, P., 361, 365
Sears, S. R., 16, 23, 48, 50, 52, 63, 66, 139, 140, 141,
    147, 148, 149, 150, 151, 152, 153, 154, 155, 157,
    160, 162, 163, 164, 170, 174, 217, 223
Seddon, A., 342, 337, 353
Seeman, T. E., 38, 45
Segal, Z. V., 341, 354
Segerstrom, S. C., 169, 170, 171, 174
Selby, J., 300, 308
Selby, L., 84, 95, 300, 308
Seligman, M. E. P., 282, 283, 287
Sells, J. N., 323, 331
Seltman, H., 32, 42
Selye, H., 25, 45
Semmer, N., 205, 213
Senterfitt, J. W., 216, 222
Serfaty, D., 235, 244
Sewell, K. W., 75, 80
Sewell, M., 216, 223
Shahar, O., 92, 98
Shakespeare-Finch, J. E., 232, 240, 241, 246
Shalev, A. Y., 256, 263
Shamai, M., 252, 261
Shanan, J., 92, 98
Shaver, H., 131, 132, 135
Shaw, B. F., 211, 213
Shay, J., 292, 309
Sheehy, G., 357, 362, 366
Sheikh, J. I., 14, 23
Sheikh-Javaid, I., 291, 309
Shepel, L. F., 49, 67
Sherk, D., 252, 261
Sherman, T., 191, 195
Shontz, F. C., 51, 65
Short, J., 274, 287
Shortridge, B. E., 169, 174
Siau, J., 140, 172
Siegel, B., 178, 194
Siegel, K., 48, 53, 58, 66, 123, 124, 137, 149, 174,
    215, 216, 217, 219, 223
Siever, L. J., 250, 263
Sigal, J. J., 251, 252, 253, 262
Silver, R. C., 13, 22, 25, 26, 31, 33, 43, 45, 193, 323,
    361, 363, 365, 366, 367
Silverman, W., 130, 136
Simon, W. E., 26, 45
Singer, B. H., 38, 45
Singer, I., 90, 94, 98
Sipprelle, R. C., 322, 332
Skillings, A., 341, 353
Skinner, K., 252, 262
Skokan, L. A., 31, 41, 48, 64, 82, 95, 141, 171, 217,
    222, 228, 244
Sloan, D. A., 138, 171

Smith, B. W., 124, 126, 127, 136, 137, 317, 332
Smith, C., 126, 130, 137, 233, 246
Smith, D. A. F., 35, 41
Smith, E. M., 66, 82, 97, 170, 173, 366
Smith, E. S., 241, 246
Smith, G. C., 353
Smith, L. M., 226, 231, 232, 235, 246, 283, 286
Smith, N. J., 13, 22
Smith, R. S., 27, 28, 30, 36, 46, 251, 262, 268, 269,
    273, 275, 277, 287
Smith, S. G., 19, 23
Smyth, J. M., 26, 43
Snyder, C. R., 101, 117, 313, 323, 333
Snyder, P., 32, 42
Snyder, S., 130, 136
Sol, O., 253, 259
Solarz, A. L., 283, 286
Solomon, L. J., 252, 260
Solomon, M. 230, 233, 247
Solomon, S. D., 86, 241, 246
Solomon, Z., 178, 194, 195, 200, 213, 246, 252, 253,
    262
Somerfield, M. R., 51, 64, 141, 172
Sommer, K. L., 321, 329
Southwick, S. M., 249, 263, 364, 366
Spaccarelli, S., 274, 287
Spanierman, L. B., 361, 366
Speisman, J. C., 29, 45
Spilka, B.,131, 135
Spinks, T., 236, 244
Spirito, A., 264, 285
Spiro, A., 51, 64, 226, 243
Spitznagal, E. L., 226, 245
Squier, C., 220, 223
Sroufe, L. A., 269, 270, 273, 285, 287, 288
Stallard, P., 15, 23, 264, 268, 278, 286
Stanik, P., 127, 126, 136
Stanton, A. L., 9, 16, 18, 23, 30, 33, 45, 48, 66, 139,
    160, 169, 170, 174, 217, 223, 297, 307, 309, 313,
    332, 345, 346, 348, 354
Stapel, D. A., 94, 98
Staples, A. D., 16, 21
Starr, K., 221, 223
Staudinger, U. M., 94, 95, 225, 244, 307, 308
Steele, R., 130, 136
Steger, M., 19, 21, 32, 41, 60, 65
Steil, R., 352, 361, 365
Stein, B. D., 121, 137
Stein, D. J., 322, 331
Stein, S., 357, 366
Steinberg, A. M., 267, 286
Steketee, G., 361, 365
Stephens, C., 230, 234, 240, 241, 245, 246
Stern, D. N., 83, 98
Stewart, A. E., 72, 75, 80
Stillwell, A. M., 321, 329
Stinson, C. H., 190, 194
Stockdale, F. E., 51, 65, 66, 140, 174
Stokols, D., 34, 45
Stones, M. H., 361, 366
Stout, R. J., 235, 244, 247
Strickland, B. R., 276, 286, 308, 309

Stroebe, M. S., 187, 195
Strohsal, K., 190, 194
Strosahl, K. D., 341, 353
Strub, M., 235, 244
Studts, J. L., 142, 152, 157, 158, 171
Stuhlmacher, A. F., 264, 285
Stuhlmiller, C., 226, 247
Suedfeld, P., 308, 309
Sullivan, M. J. L., 241, 245
Suls, J., 35, 45
Summers, J. A., 57, 64
Sutker, P. B., 82, 86, 98
Sutton, K. J., 92, 95, 127, 134, 178, 191, 193, 278, 283
Suzanna, R. O., 26, 45
Swindells, S., 220, 223
Sworowski, L. A., 169, 170, 174, 297, 309, 345, 346, 348, 354
Syme, S. L., 313, 329
Szekely, M., 254, 262

T

Tafrate, R., 322, 330, 331
Tafrate, R. C., 322, 330
Taft, L., 325, 328, 332
Tait, R., 361, 363, 366
Taku, K., 264, 281, 287
Tarakeshwar, N., 126, 128, 132, 134, 136
Tashiro, T., 32, 41, 60, 65
Tauber, Y., 250, 257, 258, 262
Tavuchis, N., 321, 332
Taylor, R. J., 129, 137
Taylor, S., 251, 262
Taylor, S. E., 31, 35, 41, 45, 48, 49, 64, 66, 67, 82, 94, 95, 98, 140, 141, 145, 154, 161, 171, 174, 182, 188, 195, 217, 220, 221, 223, 224, 227, 228, 229, 244, 247, 347, 354, 362, 366
Teasdale, J. D., 169, 175, 341, 354
Tec, N., 250, 262
Tedeschi, R. G., 3, 4, 5, 6, 7, 8, 9, 10, 11, 12, 13, 14, 15, 16, 18, 19, 20, 21, 22, 23, 25, 29, 32, 33, 36, 39, 41, 45, 51, 52, 53, 55, 57, 60, 61, 64, 66, 67, 69, 70, 73, 74, 77, 80, 82, 86, 87, 89, 91, 92, 95, 98, 101, 104, 108, 109, 110, 112, 117, 123, 127, 136, 137, 139, 140, 141, 149, 158, 159, 165, 166, 167, 171, 174, 176, 177, 180, 181, 184, 189, 191, 194, 195, 200, 202, 204, 211, 213, 214, 217, 218, 223, 224, 225, 226, 228, 229, 232, 233, 239, 244, 247, 251, 254, 257, 260, 262, 264, 265, 266, 270, 274, 275, 278, 279, 280, 282, 283, 284, 285, 287, 291, 292, 293, 294, 297, 298, 303, 304, 307, 308, 309, 310, 312, 313, 314, 316, 317, 318, 323, 328, 329, 330, 332, 333, 334, 338, 340, 341, 347, 349, 350, 352, 354, 357, 363, 366, 367
Tellegen, A., 25, 27, 37, 41, 43, 44, 48, 65, 141, 173
Tennen, H., 3, 4, 17, 21, 23, 31, 32, 40, 45, 48, 59, 60, 61, 62, 63, 64, 66, 67, 139, 149, 159, 168, 170, 171, 174, 175, 218, 219, 221, 233, 243, 247, 257, 262, 275, 287, 312, 323, 329, 333, 341, 347, 352, 363, 364

Terr, L. C., 275, 287
Tesser, A., 9, 22, 112, 117, 365
Thayer, J. F., 38, 42
Thissen-Pennings, M., 76, 80
Thomas, P. M., 358, 367
Thomas, S. P., 322, 333
Thompson, E. I., 140, 175
Thompson, J., 233, 234, 247
Thompson, L. Y., 313, 323, 333
Thompson, M., 48, 67
Thompson, S. C., 82, 98, 139, 174, 219, 224
Thornton, A. A., 139, 147, 148, 149, 151, 152, 153, 154, 155, 157, 161, 162, 163, 169, 174
Thurm, A. E., 264, 285
Tivis, L., 226, 245
Tobin, D. L., 160, 174
Tomich, P. L., 7, 16, 20, 23, 51, 52, 53, 55, 57, 59, 60, 67, 140, 145, 147, 150, 151, 152, 153, 154, 155, 156, 162, 163, 164, 167, 169, 174
Toppino, T. C., 81, 97
Tormala, Z. L., 92, 98
Trainer, M., 325, 333
Trapnell, P. D., 169, 174
Treynor, W., 297, 310, 367
Trope, Y., 84, 95
Tross, S., 4, 21, 140, 142, 171
True, W. R., 364, 367
Tugade, M. M., 18, 28, 46, 170, 172
Turnbull, W., 300, 309
Turner, J. B., 18, 19, 20, 21, 291, 309
Turner, S., 361, 365
Turse, N., 18, 19, 20, 21, 291, 309
Tversky, A., 90, 94, 97
Ty, T., 16, 21
Tyler, F. B., 130, 136

U

Uchino, B. N., 33, 46
Uddo, M., 82, 98
Udris, I., 187, 195
Ullrich, P. M., 297, 310
Ulrich, R. S., 34, 46
Ultmann, J. E., 143, 172
UNAIDS, 215, 224
Unger, J., 216, 223, 264, 286
Updegraff, J. A., 48, 53, 67, 82, 98, 217, 218, 224
Urcuyo, K. R., 141, 145, 147, 150, 151, 152, 153, 154, 155, 156, 162, 167, 174
Urrows, S., 31, 45
Ursin, H., 38, 46

V

Valent, P., 250, 262
Valentine, J. D., 202, 213
Valliant, G., 251, 262
Valliant, G. E., 260
Valori, R. M., 156, 174
VandeCreek, L., 123, 137
Van-Der-Hal, E., 250, 257, 258, 262

van der Hart, O., 72, 80
van der Kolk, B. A., 72, 341, 352
van Geel, R., 76, 80
van Gorp, W., 216, 223
Van Haitsma, K., 123, 124, 127, 130, 136
Van Horn, P., 266, 267, 269, 270, 272, 285
Vander Laan, K. L., 323, 333
van Olphen, J., 34, 42
Vasconcelles, E. B., 126, 134
Vasey, M. W., 275, 287
Vaughan, F., 337, 354
Vergis, R., 220, 223
Veronen, L. J., 82, 98
Villegas, M., 76, 80
Viney, L. L., 76, 78, 216, 224
Violanti, J. M., 226, 231, 232, 235, 237, 240, 246, 283, 286
Viorst, J., 7, 23, 110, 117
Vythilingam, M., 364, 366

W

Waddington, C. H., 193, 196
Wagner, D., 38, 42
Wagner, S., 221
Wagner, W. G., 76, 78
Walker, B. M., 216, 224
Wallace, B., 71, 80
Walsh, F., 27, 46
Walsh, W., 93, 98
Walters, M., 232, 244
Waltz, M., 129, 137
Wang, H. J., 140, 172
Wanke, M., 94, 99
Wannon, M., 275, 276, 284, 287
Ware, E. E., 252, 261
Warner, T. D., 204, 213
Wasserman, A. L., 140, 141, 175
Waters, E., 269, 270, 287
Watkins, E., 169, 175
Watson, D., 53, 64
Watson, M., 161, 175
Waugh, C. E., 18, 170, 172
Wayment, H. A., 13, 33, 43
Waysman, M., 200, 201, 213
Wearing, A. J., 228, 229, 238, 245
Weber, A. L., 112, 116, 358, 365
Weber, R., 91, 99
Weddington, W. W., 143, 172
Weinborn, M.,131, 137
Weinman, J., 48, 66, 140, 173
Weintraub, J. K., 62, 64, 139, 171, 189, 194, 313, 330
Weiss, D. S., 240, 244
Weiss, R. S., 112, 116, 117
Weiss, T., 9, 14, 17, 23, 54, 55, 62, 67, 145, 148, 151, 152, 153, 155, 157, 160, 168, 169, 175
Wellisch, D. K., 140, 172
Wells, A., 226, 230, 232, 237, 243
Wenninger, K., 361, 365
Werner, E. E., 27, 28, 30, 36, 46, 204, 251, 262, 268, 269, 273, 275, 277, 287

Werner-Wildner, L. A., 72, 79
Wessel, I., 362, 367
Westwood, M. J., 77, 80
Wheatley, T., 88, 99
Wheaton, B., 252, 262
Wheeler, E., 341, 353
White, M., 74, 77, 80
Wicker, C. A., 140, 173
Widows, M. R., 141, 147, 148, 149, 150, 151, 152, 153, 154, 157, 160, 161, 162, 168, 175
Wienfeld, M., 253, 262
Wigal, J. K., 160, 174
Wilber, K., 337, 338, 354
Wilcox, M. M., 38, 42
Wild, N., 9, 19, 23
Wilder, T., 94, 99
Wilensky, P., 77, 80
Wilimas, J. A., 140, 175
Williams, A. F., 50, 65
Williams, J. R., 140, 141, 172, 268, 285
Williams, R., 51, 65, 82, 97, 202, 213, 228, 245, 365
Williams, S., 341, 354
Williams, T., 241, 247
Wilner, N., 157, 172, 187, 194, 253, 261
Wilson, K. G., 190, 194, 341, 353
Wilson, T. D., 88, 96, 99
Wingard, J. R., 51, 64, 141, 172
Winkel, G., 10, 17, 22, 54, 65, 146, 148, 151, 152, 153, 155, 156, 157, 159, 160, 169, 173
Winkelstein, W., 218, 223
Winnecott, D. W., 83, 99
Winslade, J., 77, 79, 363, 366
Winter, H., 361, 365
Winzlenberg, A., 344, 353
Wittine, B., 337, 354
Witvliet, C., 323, 333
Wolchik, S. A., 268, 287
Wolff, A. C., 252, 262
Wolin, S., 251, 262
Wolin, S. J., 251, 262
Wong, P. T. P., 337, 354
Wood, J. V., 49, 67, 140, 174, 227, 247
Woodall, J., 226, 230, 231, 232, 237, 239, 240, 241, 244
Worall, H., 187, 194
Work, W. C., 28, 41, 251, 260, 268, 277, 284, 285, 287
Wortham, S., 70, 80
Worthington Jr., E. L., 320, 321, 323, 325, 329
Wortman, C. B., 13, 14, 15, 22, 23, 25, 26, 29, 31, 32, 33, 40, 43, 45, 46, 50, 62, 65, 67, 71, 78, 81, 99, 122, 134, 166, 169, 175, 193, 196, 292, 293, 297, 310, 323, 330, 361, 362, 363, 367
Wotman, S. R., 321, 329
Wraith, R., 267, 286
Wright, S., 122, 137
Wulff, K. M., 125, 126, 135
Wurf, E., 177, 196
Wyatt, G. E., 48, 67, 156, 217, 224
Wyman, P. A., 251, 260, 268, 269, 270, 273, 274, 276, 277, 278, 284, 285, 287

Y

Yali, A. M., 126, 134, 135
Yalom, I. D., 4, 251, 262, 337, 342, 344, 354
Yaskowich, K. M., 264, 274, 278, 279, 280, 282, 283, 288
Yates, T. M., 273, 283, 288
Yehuda, R., 249, 250, 256, 263
Yopyk, D. J., 89, 90, 97
Young, J., 151, 175
Young, S., 30, 42
Yule, W., 51, 65, 82, 97, 202, 213, 228, 245, 365

Z

Zakowski, S. G., 61, 65, 144, 148, 150, 151, 152, 153, 157, 158, 161, 173, 217, 223
Zautra, A. J., 170, 175
Zechmeister, J. S., 321, 333

Zell, R. L., 321, 330
Zemore, R., 49, 67
Zerowin, J., 126, 127, 136
Zigler, E., 28, 43
Zinnbauer, B. J., 122, 126, 127, 136, 137
Znoj, H. J., 6, 19, 176, 177, 179, 182, 186, 187, 188, 189, 190, 193, 194, 196, 227, 247
Zoellner, T., 19, 88, 176, 195, 334, 347, 348, 349, 353, 354
Zollner, T., 94, 97
Zomer, E., 258, 263
Zomer, L., 258, 263
Zornow, G. B., 132, 137
Zubek, J., 30, 43
Zuckerman, M., 178, 196, 221, 223
Zungu-Dirwayi, N., 322, 331
Zuravin, S., 66, 227, 245, 363, 366
Zwahlen, D., 189, 190, 195

Subject Index

accounts, *see* narrative
AIDS/HIV, 48, 58, 123, 124, 129, 214–21; *see also* posttraumatic growth
    intervention implications, 220–21
assumptions, *see* schema

benefit finding, *see also* posttraumatic growth
    correlates in cancer, 140, 149–65
bereavement, 176–93, 342
    coping, 189–93

cancer, 31–3, 48–55, 57, 105, 113–14, 138–75, 189–93, 279–80, 304, 342, 345
clinical work, 75–7, 170, 220–1, 334–50
    case examples, 295–7, 299–302, 304–5
    children, 282–3
    empirical studies, 342–5
    expert companion, 292–3, 295, 297–8
    interventions, 170, 220, 239
    growth model, 293–308
    practical recommendations, 76–7, 132–4, 239–42, 291–305, 350–2
cognitive processing, *see* rumination
combat, *see* war
constructive narrative perspective, 355–64
    definition, 355
    posttraumatic growth 362–4
    resilience, 359–63
counseling, *see* clinical work

disaster work, 225–43
    family issues, 240
    future risk, 241–2
    information and decision management, 234–5
    interpretive processes, 233–4
    organizational variables, 237–8

    team and interagency operations, 235–7
    transition to routine work, 240–1
disclosures, 13–15, 18, 33–4, 49, 74, 112–13, 166–7, 215, 297

emergency work, *see* disaster work
emotion regulation, 177–9, 189–93
    in children, 273
existential
    approaches, 335–7
    themes, *see* spirituality
    therapies, 337–9
    reevaluation, 88–91

forgiveness, 313–29
    anger, 322–9
    violent crimes, 326–7
Frankl, Viktor, 336–7

Health, *see also* posttraumatic growth
    posttraumatic growth, 164–5, 170, 216, 219–20
    resilience-promoting environments, 32–4
    relationship with spirituality, 126–33
HIV, *see* AIDS/HIV
Holocaust, child survivors, 248–59
    posttraumatic growth, 252–3

illusions, 182–4, 347, 351
interventions, *see* clinical work

measurement issues, *see also* posttraumatic growth
    comparison groups, 55
    conceptualization of growth, 168
    cross-sectional, 16
    dimensions of growth, 56–7
    directionality of change, 59–60, 48–50

methods, 48–56, 168
  qualitative approaches, 16–17, 48–50
  quantitative approaches, 19–21, 50–4
  timing, 60–1
  validity, 17, 19–21, 54–5, 61–3
meaning, 6–8, 10, 69–78, 83–91, 227–8
  reconstruction, 69, 76
  in children, 274–6
narrative, 50–1, 104–16, 305–8
  clinical methods, 76–7, 305–7
  constructive narrative perspective, 355–64
  disclosures, 112–13
  disruption, 71–5
  grid technique, 75
  interpersonal level, 70
  model of posttraumatic growth, 8
  NPCS, 76
  personal level, 70
  social level, 71

organizational hassles, 236, 238
organizational uplifts, 236, 238

performance guilt, 234, 240
personal factors, *see* posttraumatic growth
physical health, 33, 39, 126, 129, 132, 164–5, 167,
      169; *see also* posttraumatic growth
  HIV/AIDS, 219
pileup of losses, 104, 109–12
positive emotions, 18, 28, 169, 293, 307
posttraumatic growth
  adjustment, 7, 49, 161–71
  age, 156
  beginnings, 1–2
  bipolar items, 20
  cancer, 138–75
  children, 264–83
    future directions for research, 281–3
  cognitive engagement, *see* rumination
  cognitive processing, *see* rumination
  coping processes, 160–1
  correlates, 139, 149–67
  corroboration of, 54–5
  co-rumination, 13
  cross-sectional, 16
  cultural context, 12–15, 17, 19, 58–9, 70–1
  description, 5–6, 82, 139
  directions for future research, 16–21, 36, 56, 163,
        165–70, 221, 347
  distress, 8, 317–18
  domains, 4–6
  experience of, 4–6
  ethnicity, 156, 217–18, 220
  gender, 156–7, 279–80, 282, 313
  HIV/Aids disease progression, 218–21
  Holocaust survivors, 252–9
  in communities, 63
  illusory, 182–4, 347–9
  interpretive processes, 231–4
  major loss and, 104–12

measurement, 19–21, 47–63; *see also*
      measurement issues
  behavioral measures, 54, 56
  Benefit Finding Scale, 51–2, 140
  benefit finding in cancer, 141–9, 170
  children, 264–79
  Posttraumatic Growth Inventory, 4, 32, 50,
        52, 82, 127, 140, 189, 202, 226, 278–9,
        313, 349
  Stress Related Growth Scale, 15, 51–2, 179
  Validity, 19, 47, 55, 61–5, 254, 280
Methodologies, 16–17, 168–9, 282
model of, 8–15, 297–8, 313, 340
  bereavement, 185–6, 188
  children, 268–78
  two-component, 345, 347–50
mortality salience, 16, 158, 166
negative outcomes, 228–31
narrative, 8, 50–1, 104–16, 305–8; *see also*
      narrative
optimism, 30–2, 62, 159, 182, 218, 232, 252,
      268, 271, 277, 313
personal factors, 8, 159–60, 232–3, 293–4
physical health, 164–5, 170, 216, 219–20
positive emotions, 18, 28, 163, 169, 294, 307
positive response bias *see* self-serving bias
psychological distress, 161–3, 204, 207, 249,
      256, 317–18
psychological preparedness, 8, 11, 55, 58, 83,
      91–4
psychotherapy outcome, 342–9
predictors, 150–70, 183, 185, 189–90, 202, 227,
      230, 232–3, 280, 349
qualitative methodologies, 16–17, 48–50
quantitative methodologies, 19–21, 50–4
rumination, 87, 177, 184, 232–3, 266, 271,
      274–6, 280, 297
socio-cultural context, 8–9, 12–15, 19, 160
socioeconomic status, 49, 150–5, 166, 217–18
strength, 5, 86–8
theories, *see also* model of
perceived impact, 8–9, 165–6
traumatic incident response, 231–8
Posttraumatic Growth Inventory, 4, 32, 50, 52, 82,
      127, 140–50, 156–7, 159, 164, 189, 202,
      207–10, 226, 278–9, 232, 313, 349; *see
      also* post traumatic growth
primary reference group, *see* posttraumatic growth
psychological adjustment, 49, 161–3, 167, 170, 217,
      347
psychological preparedness, 8, 11, 55, 58, 83, 91–3
psychotherapy, *see* clinical implications

Rogers, Carl, 336
realistic control attributions, 271, 275–6, 281–2
reconfiguration, 24–32, 38–40
recovery, 24–32, 38–40, 51, 93, 129, 182, 240, 326,
      340
religion, 121–32
  defined, 122